Making Connections

Reading and Understanding College Textbooks

THIRD EDITION

SHEILA ALLEN
Harford Community College

THOMSON

WADSWORTH

Australia • Canada • Mexico • Singapore • Spain • United Kingdom • United States

Making Connections: Reading and Understanding College Textbooks,
Third Edition
Sheila Allen

Publisher: *Michael Rosenberg*
Acquisitions Editor: *Stephen Dalphin*
Development Editor: *Julie McBurney*
Production Project Manager: *Lianne Ames*
Executive Marketing Manager: *Carrie Brandon*
Senior Print Buyer: *Mary Beth Hennebury*
Compositor: *Carlisle Communications*

Project Manager: *Emily Bush*
Photography Manager: *Sheri Blaney*
Permissions Manager: *Kiely Sexton*
Photo Researcher: *Deborah Nicholls*
Cover Designer: *Design 5 Creatives*
Text Designer: *Carlisle Communications*
Printer: *West Group*

Cover Image: Piet Mondrian 1872–1944, *Broadway Boogie Woogie,*
1942–1943 Oil on Canvas, 50" × 50" © 2004 Mondrian / Holtzman Trust
c/o hcr@hcrinternational.com;
Photo Credit: © Digital Image © The Museum of Modern Art/Licensed by
SCALA/Art Resource, NY

For more information contact Thomson Wadsworth, 25 Thomson Place,
Boston, Massachusetts 02210 USA, or you can visit our Internet site at
http://www.thomson.com

Credits appear on pages 425–426, which constitutes a continuation of the
copyright page.

For permission to use material from this text or product, submit
a request online at http://www.thomsonrights.com

Any additional questions about permissions can be submitted
by email to thomsonrights@thomson.com

ISBN: 1-4130-0241-2

Library of Congress Control Number:
2004109165

I dedicate this third edition to my colleagues who consistently and often courageously seek to create a learning environment that nurtures a commitment to speaking and seeking the truth.

BRIEF CONTENTS

CONTENTS

Unit 3   Comprehension Skills: Understanding Passages and Graphics   29

Chapter 2 Finding Main Ideas   30

Chapter 3 Determining Organizational Patterns   56

Chapter 4 Reading and Interpreting Graphics   69

Chapter 10 Business: Human Resource Management and Motivation 230

PREFACE

The idea for this reading textbook resulted from suggestions made by college students in a reading course. The students wanted a reading course and a textbook that helped them with the other courses they were taking. Some of the students were concurrently taking college-level courses. They wanted to know how to apply reading skills in these courses to make their reading and studying easier.

Making Connections: Reading and Understanding College Textbooks teaches the basic reading skills necessary for college students to read content-area textbooks successfully. However, it also takes students one step beyond learning those skills by giving them practice in applying the skills in four content-area chapters. Students practice reading, understanding, and studying chapters from college textbooks on health, American history, business, and psychology. Then they are tested in those content areas to obtain a realistic evaluation of how they will do in college-level courses. All parts of this textbook work together to provide students with the skills and practice necessary to succeed in college.

ORGANIZATION

This textbook is divided into three parts. Part One teaches the basic reading skills and provides practice exercises from college-level textbooks for each skill. Part Two, containing content-area chapters, provides information about and practice with applying the reading skills. Part Three provides reading selections related to the topics in Part Two for students to practice skills that they would use in their out-of-class reading assignments in college-level courses.

Part One begins with a unit on the student's role as learner. This information is provided so that the student knows what is expected in any college-level course and has some knowledge of how to deal with college-level coursework. Part One then continues with the skills. The first skill—vocabulary—teaches students how to use information provided in the textbook to determine the meanings of words. Comprehension skills, which include main idea, paragraph organization, and graphics, are then covered. Finally, critical thinking skills are presented. This last set of skills includes making inferences, distinguishing between fact and opinion, and interpreting test questions. All practice exercises in Part One are excerpted from the content-area chapters in Part Two, with the exception of some lower-readability practice exercises for main idea and organizational patterns. Additionally, students are taught to summarize and journal prompts in each chapter to help them practice metacognition. New Textbook Link exercises at the end of each skills chapter ask the students to practice the newly learned skills in another textbook they may be using.

Part Two, containing the content-area chapters, is the heart of the textbook. Using all of the skills in Part One, students learn how to take notes, mark and annotate, and outline. Then they are introduced to different methods of studying and preparing for a discipline test. Finally, the students take tests covering each of the content-area chapters and have the opportunity to analyze their tests to determine which study/reading methods worked best for them and what they can do to improve their work. The test questions come from the study guide or test bank of each textbook and hence were written by teachers in the field of study. Changes in this third edition include the following in Part Two: the inclusion of a health textbook chapter on stress, the newest edition chapters of history and business, and pre-, during, and postjournal entry prompts to assist students in understanding and using the notetaking techniques in other disciplines.

Part Three, which presents the journal articles, may be used by the instructor in a variety of ways. Practice with Periodicals exercises and Journal Entry suggestions can be found in each of the skills chapters in Part One to provide added reinforcement. Making Connections sections in the discipline chapters in Part Two refer students to the articles and suggest they read them for background knowledge. Finally, each of the articles in Part Three is followed by questions and can be used to provide students with practice reading for research. New articles in health and history have been included in this edition.

TEACHING SEQUENCE

Instructors may begin a course by teaching the basic reading skills during the first third of the semester. The articles in Part Three may be used at this time to begin skills reinforcement, or an instructor may decide to wait until some or all of the skills have been taught before assigning a selection. Students should have progressed at least through Chapter 2 before a summary of a selection is required. However, the other writing exercises may be assigned anytime during the course.

The second part of the textbook (Part Two) should take the major portion of the semester. Practice and success with each of the study/reading techniques (notetaking, marking and annotating, and outlining) are important to the success of the student in later classes. Individual conferences, to provide feedback to the students on each of the techniques, are recommended. Conferences can be completed during class time when students are completing an assignment or outside the class during a lab time.

Another sequence for teaching the course would be to teach the first three chapters of skills and then move the students to the first discipline chapter where they would apply these skills using the first notetaking method. Discipline chapters are taken from textbooks on other subjects studied in college. After completion of the discipline chapter, students would be directed back to the next two skills chapters before going to the next discipline chapter. Then students would complete the last two skills chapters before working on the third discipline chapter. Finally, students would determine their best method of reading/studying and complete the final discipline chapter.

ACKNOWLEDGMENTS

I would like to thank my colleagues at Harford Community College for their cooperation and support.

I would also like to thank the students who tested various chapters and provided feedback for the textbook, particularly Nicole Amato, Michael Andrews, Inge Besterache, Steven Benton, Marisol Braun, Ashleigh Bryant, Ronnie Candelario, Abby Chrest, Jenn Curry, Scott Cushing, Matt Dinunno, Ryan Estayan, Christine Farley, Christine Kennedy, Kimberly Lauback, Cierra Lucas, Megan MacPherson, Katelyn McKenzie, Laura Moran, and Nicole Norris.

My thanks also go to instructors who have used *Making Connections* with their students and were kind enough to contact me with suggestions or took the time to respond to questionnaires from my publisher. These people include Ulanda Forbess, North Central Texas College; Bernette Henry, Essex Community College; Rosemary Johnsen, Grand Valley State University. Also, thanks to Dr. David Caverly, whom I met at the Mid-Atlantic College Reading Association Conference, and who so kindly gave me permission to adapt his idea of the pre-, during-, and postjournal entries in Part Two.

Thanks to my family—my husband Bob, and my children Dan and Claire—who continue to bear with me as I continue to write. Also, acknowledgment goes to my brothers, Len and Mark Romutis, and my mom Agrafina whom I promised to recognize in this edition.

Finally, thanks go to the staff of Wadsworth, including Steve Dalphin, senior acquisitions editor; Julie McBurney, development editor; and Lianne Ames, production project manager. I would also like to thank Emily Bush and Carlisle Communications for their excellent work on the production of this book.

NOTE TO THE INSTRUCTOR

My reasons for writing this text are twofold. The first is being accountable to the students. The effectiveness of my reading course was being determined by how well students were doing in other courses once they had successfully completed the reading course. Talking to students and instructors and understanding how students best learn, I became aware that many factors other than how well students read determine their success in a course. I also knew that I had to do more than just teach and practice reading skills with the students. Many of them saw my course as something they had to take and pass in order to get into some college-level courses. I wanted them to understand the connection between my course and their future success in college coursework.

That brings me to the second reason for creating this textbook—adapting to the students' needs. My old reading course was skills based. Students learned and practiced skills such as finding the main idea, making inferences, distinguishing fact from opinion, and determining important details; the last unit of the semester was on outlining and notetaking. Each semester I would receive student evaluations exclaiming that they wished that last unit could have come earlier in the semester to help them with other courses they were taking. Even after explaining to subsequent classes that this unit *had* to come at the end because they needed to know the "skills" in order to do the outlining and notetaking, students still didn't understand why they couldn't learn those skills earlier in the course. I decided they were right, and if I had them for only 14 or 15 weeks, I needed to cut down the number of skills that they were learning and spend more time practicing application of those skills.

This textbook is set up in three parts. The first part covers skills; all of the skills have practice exercises using passages from the discipline chapters in Part Two or from textbook chapters in similar topics. I suggest that you spend no more than one class on each of the skills. The most important part of this textbook is Part Two. Students need to apply and practice what they learn after they finish the reading course. I found that students can know all the skills and do well in Part One and still do terribly on the discipline tests in Part Two. It's not just knowing how to find main ideas and important details; it's also knowing what to do with ideas and details once they have found them. Part Two of this text will help students learn how to study/read.

Part Three provides journal articles on different reading levels to give students practice reading those types of material. When students take a course, the textbook is not the only material they will be required to read. They will often be required to find journal articles and report on those. Use these articles as you wish. They may be used to provide background knowledge for the discipline chapters, to help students become interested in the topics, or to help them better understand the discipline chapters. Using paragraphs from the selections, you can have students practice the skills, or you can have them write summaries. Use the Practice with Periodicals exercises in Part One and include discussion of the articles in Making Connections in Part Two. Talk to some of your faculty colleagues and ask them what type of outside reading is required in discipline courses. Have students practice what they will be doing when they exit your course.

It is important for students to experience success in the discipline chapter tests because of the work they have accomplished. It is more important to ensure that they are taking the correct notes, so be sure to spend some time conferring with them to check notes, markings and annotations, and outlines. After each discipline test, have them analyze the test questions and determine why they marked an answer wrong. Students should look for patterns and work on weaknesses as well as build on strengths.

My goal with this textbook is to help students learn how to read a college textbook and know what to do to help themselves be successful in college-level courses.

NOTE TO THE STUDENT

READING JOURNALS: AN ASSIGNMENT

This reading textbook will teach you how to read a college-level textbook successfully and show you what to do with the information you acquire to be successful in a college course. In the first part of the book you will learn various reading skills, and in the second part you will apply and practice those skills on actual textbook chapters. Then you will learn different strategies to help you do well on discipline tests, taken from the actual subject area textbooks studied in college.

In large part, your success as a reader depends on what you think about as you read and your awareness of these thoughts. Being aware of what you think is called *metacognition*. Metacognition is important in all types of reading, whether it be reading for enjoyment or reading for some type of information. Have you ever read part of a book only to look up and ask yourself, "What did I just read?" While reading, have you ever found yourself daydreaming about something that has happened or will happen? This happens to all readers whether they are good or poor readers. The difference is that good readers will be aware of this daydreaming much sooner than poor readers because they are aware of their thoughts.

The best way to increase metacognitive abilities is to practice. The best method of practicing is with a journal. Writing about what you are thinking will make your thoughts visible and allow you to determine how you need to change that thinking. Use the journal prompts in each of the skills chapters in Part One to help you practice metacognition.

Do not write a book report or summary of what you have read. Stop reading and write whenever you realize you are thinking about something other than the words. Think about what goes on in your head as you watch a movie; reading should provoke similar thoughts. Thinking about what someone or something looks like can be one of the thoughts you have. Other thoughts may include why the author used a particular word or phrase, what may happen later in the selection, and how the article or chapter may end. You may also be thinking about what has happened and what is happening. Sometimes you may not understand a word, a sentence, or a paragraph. You may find yourself confused and rereading or reading beyond the confusing material to help you understand. These are the things that you need to record. You can write about facts that are important and about what thoughts they may trigger. When reading about history, you may be visualizing the people or battles. In health, you may be deciding on a particular strategy to use to improve your own health. In business you may be comparing what you read with your own experiences at work. In psychology, you may be thinking about how the personality theories compare to each other, with your own theories, or with your friends' personalities. The important thing is to be aware of what you are thinking.

Don't be afraid to write that you found yourself thinking of something other than the text. The more you think about your thinking, the less you will find your mind wandering to topics other than the text.

Another type of journal will help you understand what you know and can use in other courses. As you begin to learn how to take notes in Part Two of this textbook, write a journal entry that explains what you already know about the form of notetaking. For example, before beginning the American history chapter, write a journal entry on what you know about underscoring. Then after you have completed taking notes on the chapter, write a second journal explaining what you know about underscoring. Finally, use underscoring in your other courses that require reading and then write a journal entry explaining how the technique worked and how you will use it in the future. This type of journal will be a learning log for you to see what you have learned and how you are using it.

Read some of the following journal entries from students like you. Then use the information in this note as well as the journal entry ideas in Chapters 1 through 7 to guide your thinking as you write journals. Remember to always be aware of what is going on in your mind as you read.

Credit to David Caverly, Ph.D., from South Texas University, for the pre-, during, and postjournal entry idea.

JOURNAL WRITTEN **BEFORE** LEARNING ABOUT MARKING AND ANNOTATING

I have always found that marking in a textbook was useful. When marking I look for bold or italized words, because they are usually key words I have to know. Then, I highlight the words and usually write the key term to the side of the highlighting. I also highlight the title of each section in the chapter and turn it into a question. I highlight the answer to the title, because that is probably on the test. I also look names and dates, because they are usually on the test.

JOURNAL WRITTEN WHILE READING A CHAPTER ON THE CIVIL WAR

Journal #8

As I was reading and underscoring this chapter on the Civil War, I remembered one time when my sister, her friend, and I visited a Civil War battlefield. I remember thinking how it was too peaceful and beautiful there for it ever to have been the site of so much chaos and death — so much ugliness. Park rangers told us the soldiers cut down a lot of the trees so enemy soldiers couldn't sneak up on them as easily. The soldiers built battlements down near the Cumberland River. Many of the clearings along the river the day we visited looked like great spots for a picnic. I think wars are bad even if they are fought for a good cause.

JOURNAL WRITTEN **AFTER** INSTRUCTION WITH NOTETAKING IN THIS TEXTBOOK

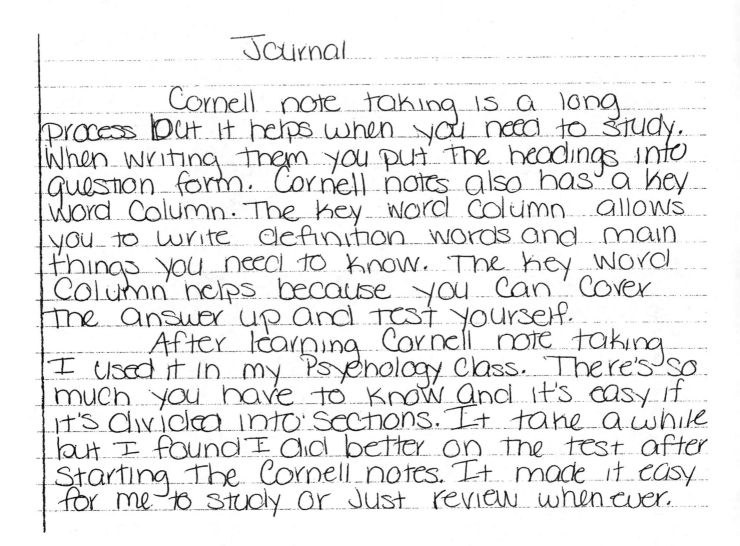

Journal

Cornell note taking is a long process but it helps when you need to study. When writing them you put the headings into question form. Cornell notes also has a key word column. The key word column allows you to write definition words and main things you need to know. The key word column helps because you can cover the answer up and test yourself.

After learning Cornell note taking I used it in my Psychology class. There's so much you have to know and it's easy if it's divided into sections. It take a while but I found I did better on the test after starting the Cornell notes. It made it easy for me to study or just review when ever.

READING SKILLS

Part One presents the reading skills necessary for college students to do well in college-level courses. It begins with some general information that you need to know about your role as a learner and participant in the learning process. You will learn some techniques for self-motivation, practice metacognitive strategies, begin to determine your best learning style, and discover what you can do to better understand a difficult textbook.

The following three units and chapters in this part cover basic vocabulary, comprehension, and critical thinking skills. Each chapter presents a particular skill, provides models to show you how to perform the skill, and then supplies exercises for you to practice that skill. All of the passages used in the exercises are taken from the content-area chapters in Part Two of this book or from related chapters in other discipline or content-area textbooks. The purpose of Part One is to provide you with the basic knowledge of skills necessary for you to do well in the next two parts of this textbook and in other college-level textbooks.

You might compare this progression with learning to drive. Before you can take a car out onto the road, you need to have some basic knowledge about how to drive: you need to know which pedal is used for acceleration or braking and which controls operate the turn signals, windshield wipers, lights, and other parts of the car. You also need to learn about traffic laws—when to yield to another car or when to proceed first through an intersection when two cars stop at the same time. All of this is similar to learning basic reading skills in Part One. View the practice exercises as simulations. If you have taken a driver's education class, you may have had simulations in which you sat behind a steering wheel in front of a screen and practiced driving a simulated course. Part One is similar to being on the road but is not "the real thing."

Before you progress into Part Two, make sure that you understand how to perform the reading skills in Part One. Practicing the vocabulary, comprehension, and interpretive skills in Part One will help you understand the content-area textbook chapters in Part Two. Using these skills in reading and studying college textbooks and other scholarly materials will be the goals of Part Two and Part Three.

1

THE STUDENT'S ROLE AS LEARNER

What you learn in a course and the grade that you earn can be determined largely by just two factors: what you did to learn the material and the time that you spent to learn it. Some courses will require little time and effort, whereas other courses will require that you spend more time using techniques that you might never use again. This unit will help you discover your role as a learner and the factors that you need to know in order to become a better reader and a better college student.

In this unit you will learn to

- Increase your interest and motivation using PQ3R, a study/reading technique
- Develop strategies for dealing with difficult-to-read textbooks
- Think about your thinking while reading a textbook chapter
- Determine your primary learning style
- Schedule your time effectively

MOTIVATION AND PQ3R

Your motivation is determined by your interest in the material you are reading as well as by your background of knowledge in the subject. It is also determined by the grade that you want and by how much you want it. PQ3R is a study/reading technique that will improve not only your motivation but also your ability to learn and remember textbook material. Each of the letters in PQ3R stands for a procedure in a sequence of steps. The basic steps are easy to remember and follow:

done before	⎰ PREVIEW	
reading (preview)	⎱ QUESTION	*done during*
	READ	*reading*
done after	⎰ RECITE	*(monitor)*
reading recall	⎱ REVIEW	

To understand how PQ3R helps you, picture your brain as a closet. If you threw your clothes into the closet every time you came home, when you wanted to wear those clothes again, they would not be fit to wear. First, it would be difficult to find what you wanted to wear;

second, if you did find it, it would probably be all wrinkled from lying in the bottom of the closet. Some of your clothes might also need mending.

Your brain is just like that closet. If, when you read, you just throw the material into your brain with no organization or use of hooks, when you want to get the material out for use on a test, you either will not be able to find it, or it will not be usable. You will remember only part of the information, or else, you will not remember it in context.

If you want to be able to take out that information when you need it, then you must have a clean, organized closet. Hooks need to be set up, and information needs to be placed onto those hooks. Just opening a textbook and reading it is like opening your closet and throwing in clothes. You are just throwing in information. This is acceptable if you are not going to be tested on the information. For example, when you are standing in the checkout line at the grocery store and pick up the *National Enquirer* to read an article, it is fine to just read it and then put back the newspaper. Later, when you talk to your friends, you may remember parts of that article, or you may not. But if you *have to* remember certain information, you have to *do* more with that information. PQ3R provides steps you can follow to help you set up hooks and use those hooks to keep yourself motivated and learning. The following sections describe the five steps:

Preview

- Survey the pages of the chapter before you read the chapter.
- Read all headings, subheadings, graphics, and captions; read introductory and summary material provided by the author.
- Think about what you might already know and what you still need to know about the contents of the chapter.
- Make personal connections to the reading material.
- Determine what organization the author is using so that you will know what information is still to come as well as what information you need to read more closely because you have little or no knowledge about it.
- Use the entire preview process as a brain teaser; it gives you a little information about what you are to learn and should motivate you to question (the next step) and want to continue reading to find out more information.

Question

- As you preview the chapter, look for any questions that the author may have included within and/or at the end of a chapter. Read these questions before beginning to read the chapter and take notes.
- Use the questions to help guide your reading and any notes that you take. Make up your own questions as you read.
- Relate the material to your own life and ask questions of relevance to you. For example, in the business chapter you may wonder if different compensation systems are used where you work. Or, in the health chapter you may review some health statistics and compare your own health to what is described.

Read

- Students may enjoy one of the discipline chapters in Part Two more than the other three because they find the topic more interesting. Other students groan when they hear that they have to take notes on the Civil War or health. If you do not find any of the topics interesting, you need to create interest by determining a way that you can use the information in your own life. Your motivation for reading a textbook chapter is important to your overall learning. You create the amount of interest you have in a subject.

- Continue to ask questions and read for the answers.
- Determine main ideas.
- Make connections to your own life, and think about what you are thinking as you read.

Recite

- Take notes. Taking notes forces you to think about what you are reading. Whether you write some notes or mark and annotate, you are forced to find main ideas and to summarize important information. Use your own words; force yourself to think about your thinking.
- Answer your questions and take notes on the material; as it becomes clearer and you make connections, you'll find yourself becoming more interested in the material. You also narrow down information that you need to study and help ensure a good grade for yourself.

Review

- Find time in your schedule to review as many of your notes as possible as often as possible. The more often you review, the more information you will remember.
- As you review, make connections to new material that you have read. Begin to see the "big picture"—how subsections are related, how chapters are related, and even how other courses might be related.

All of the techniques that you will learn throughout Part Two of this textbook can be placed into one of these five steps. All are performed before you read the chapter, while you read the chapter, or after you read the chapter. All of them can be used to help you motivate yourself and perform better in a course. You may also use these steps in Part One as you learn the skills. Preview each chapter and question what you know or need to know. Then, as you read and work through the exercises, keep notes on what you still need to practice.

Some of the steps overlap. For example, you need to ask questions about what you are going to read before you read, but you also need to continue asking questions as you read. Questions keep you curious about what you are reading and what you still need to read. The "recite" step is the other overlap; this step keeps you on task while you are reading and enables you to determine what you know and what you still need to know after you have read. Many of the activities that you will encounter in the discipline chapters' Recall sections are activities you can complete while you are reading as well as after you have finished reading the chapter. For example, writing a summary of a subsection and/or predicting test questions can be done both while you are reading and after you have completed reading the chapter.

You do not need to use all of the steps with every textbook that you read. One of the mistakes that students make is not to use PQ3R because they think that all of the steps need to be used and that using them takes too much time. Look at PQ3R as the closet organizer. For some courses, you will need a greater amount of organization, so use more of the steps.

TEXTBOOK DIFFICULTY—WHAT TO DO

Some textbooks are more difficult to read than others. The difficulty that you have reading a particular selection is determined by a number of factors.

The *readability* of a text is the reading level at which an author writes. You can use a number of formulas to determine the readability of a textbook, but most focus on two criteria—the length of the words and the length of the sentences. The longer the words and the longer the sentences, the higher the readability of the textbook will be. For example, a 1st-grade reader has sentences like the following: "See the dog run." This sentence contains only 4 words, each word containing 3 letters, and each word of one syllable. Compare this with the following sentence taken from the business text *Contemporary Business:* "These managers must meet their challenges by developing programs and policies that satisfy an increasingly diverse employee population while at the same time monitoring a growing number of employment-related laws that influence how they implement their firms' practices." This sentence contains 38 words ranging from 2 to 12 letters and one to four syllables. The text is written on a 12th-grade level.

Besides readability, other factors determine how difficult a book is to read. These are factors that you can control. The first is background knowledge. The more knowledge that you have on a topic, the easier the passage will be to read. For example, if you were to read an article about Pizza Hut's pizza ingredients and another about the chemical properties of lipids, assuming that you know more about the pizzas, you'd have an easier time reading the Pizza Hut article even if both articles are written at a high readability level. You may not be able to control how much knowledge you have before taking a course, but you can get other books to read and help you get more knowledge as you are taking the course. Looking through a chapter before you read it will also give you some background knowledge and help set up some hooks in your brain.

Another factor is interest; the more interest you have in a topic, the easier it will be to read. This can be closely tied to the last factor, background knowledge, because if you are interested in something, you often have more knowledge about it. However, you can make yourself interested in something in which you have had no previous interest (and therefore little background knowledge). For example, you may not be interested in reading about how personnel are hired and the benefits that they receive, but you can generate interest by looking over a chapter before you read it and making up some questions about it (you will learn this in Part Two of this textbook). You can also generate interest by trying to make some connections to your own life. For example, if you do not already have a job, you probably soon will have one. What steps will you have to follow to get hired? Which benefits do you want? Which do you need? After you begin to answer these questions and make connections to your own life, the material will become easier to read and remember.

Even when the grade level of a textbook is the only factor making it difficult, you can get other books on the same topic at a lower readability level. For example, if you had difficulty reading a science textbook, much of the same information can be found in a middle school textbook covering the same topic. You could get this textbook from a local library. You might also find some articles in journals and magazines that better explain a concept. Use the related journal and magazine articles in Part Three to help you better understand concepts and to create interest in the topics in Part Two.

METACOGNITION

Metacognition, thinking about your thinking, is an extremely important skill when you are study-reading. If you read the section at the beginning of this textbook on reading journals and have written a journal, then you have had some practice with metacognition. As you read through the following chapters, continue to practice being aware of what you are thinking as you read and continue to keep track of this thinking in your journal.

As you are reading a section, you need to think about the author's main idea and important details as well as organizational patterns. You need to think about figurative language that the author is using and inferences that you make. You also need to think about the author's choice of words and style. How is the reading making you feel, and what is it making you think about? Are there any words that you do not know? How are you handling those words? (You'll learn about word parts and context clues in the next section.) You also need to think about what you think will be on a test.

The fact is that your brain can work much faster than you can read. Right now while you are reading these words, you may be thinking about what you will be doing this coming weekend. Your brain gets bored while you are reading; it needs information at a faster pace. Even speed readers need to focus their minds on the material and to think about it as they read. Your job is to think about the "right stuff" while you read. That right stuff is everything you will learn in Part One of this book.

Have you ever read a page or two of something only to stop and say to yourself, "What did I just read?" Well, this happens to everyone because the brain just took off with some other topic that was much more stimulating. However, this will *not* happen to an effective reader after one or two pages. Effective readers will realize that they are not thinking about the chapter much sooner because they are constantly thinking about their thinking. All of the skills in Part One of this book are what you should be thinking about as you read a college textbook chapter. It may seem awkward at first, and there may be large gaps of time during which you forget to think about your thinking. But just get back to it. You may have to reread parts of your text, but keep practicing. In the long run, this will cut down on the time that you need to study. You will find yourself getting better at this with time, and you will find yourself becoming a more effective reader as well as a better student. Part Two will help you with this skill because you will be required to perform various activities while reading. Be aware of what activities work for you; use these activities in other courses that you are taking, and use them with the psychology chapter at the end of Part Two, where you will be employing all of the skills that you have learned to deal with a chapter on your own.

Remember that all of the activities will take extra time to complete. You will get better and faster at them as you practice them with different subjects. The time that you use while you are reading will be saved later when you study for the test.

LEARNING STYLES

Your brain takes in and remembers information visually (through the eyes), auditorially (through the ears), kinesthetically (through touch), and tactilely (through movement). Each of us has one area that works better than the others to help in learning. Think about a time when someone asked you to remember something simple, possibly one or two items to purchase at a store. Did you remember by hearing the person repeat the items? Did you have to see the items written on a list? Did you have to write the list yourself or actually touch the items in order to remember them?

Most people are either visual or auditory and remember information by seeing (the written list) or hearing (the items repeated). A smaller portion of the population uses the sense of movement or touch as the primary source of learning.

You can learn and remember better by using a combination of methods, but you should be aware of your primary method of learning. This will help you learn the material better. For example, if you are an auditory learner, reading your notes aloud into a tape recorder and then listening to those notes will help you remember the material better than will silently rereading those same notes. If you are a kinesthetic learner, drawing or forming some sort of organizer will enable you to remember the material better. For example, in the history chapter, drawing a time line and plotting each of the major events on it will help you remember better than reading or listening about them.

Determining your learning style is important to determining how best to study. If you are not sure about your learning style, your college testing or counseling center will probably have a test that you can take to determine it. Make an appointment to take this test and discover how you learn best. As you continue in this textbook, use the information about your learning style to help you with the skills in Part One. Read the excerpts aloud if you are an auditory learner or draw a visual aid if you are a kinesthetic learner. As you progress through each of the discipline chapters in Part Two, keep in mind that all of the study/reading techniques are there to help you improve your reading and studying. Try all of the techniques and use the ones that make you successful. You will learn to outline, take notes, and annotate as well as learn many other study/reading techniques. When you progress to the psychology chapter where you will be on your own to read and learn the material, knowing your learning style will help you choose the techniques that worked best for you.

SCHEDULING YOUR TIME

The amount of time that you need to spend studying and reading to do well in a course depends on a number of factors: your background of knowledge, textbook difficulty, the grade that you need or want, and so on. Therefore, you need to determine and schedule for each course the amount of time that you will need to be successful in that course. Begin with the 2:1 ratio—2 hours of study time for each hour that you spend in class each week. If you have a three-credit course, your class meets for approximately 3 hours each week, so place 6 hours of study time for that course in your schedule each week. As the semester progresses and you determine that you need more or less time, make adjustments.

Part Two of the textbook will present many activities to help you read and remember the material. Use the 6 hours each week to complete activities like previewing, writing questions, reading, taking notes, and reviewing. Some courses, because of your interest and background knowledge, will take less time and studying. Others will require more time. You will need to determine, *with each course you take,* what is necessary for you to perform well in that course. You will have to decide how much you want to learn and what grade you want. If it is important to get the A, then you will have to spend more time and complete many of the activities. Earning a C will require less time and fewer techniques. The bottom line is that you cannot just read a chapter the way that you read a novel. The techniques will take time, but in the long run you will have extra time before tests, and you will do better on those tests. Having the 6 hours set aside in your weekly schedule will help you avoid running out of time to study as a test date approaches. It will also help you avoid procrastinating. The sooner you begin to read and take notes, the more time you'll have to think about and to review the notes.

Use the grid schedule on page 9 to plan your time for the semester. First, fill in all of your class times and any other times that will not change throughout the semester (for example, work times). Next, fill in activities that are necessary but can be flexible in terms of time (for instance, study time and meal time). Keep in mind your best times for accomplishing activities. If you are a morning person, schedule study time earlier in the day when you are most energetic. Finally, look at your schedule and fill in fun times—times when you will be able to do what you want to do (meet with friends, watch television). Be sure that you include these fun times as well as study times so that you have a balanced schedule.

	Sunday	Monday	Tuesday	Wednesday	Thursday	Friday	Saturday
5 A.M.							
6 A.M.							
7 A.M.							
8 A.M.							
9 A.M.							
10 A.M.							
11 A.M.							
12 noon							
1 P.M.							
2 P.M.							
3 P.M.							
4 P.M.							
5 P.M.							
6 P.M.							
7 P.M.							
8 P.M.							
9 P.M.							
10 P.M.							
11 P.M.							
12 midnight							
1 A.M.							
2 A.M.							
3 A.M.							
4 A.M.							

U N I T

VOCABULARY SKILLS: CONTEXT AND WORD PART CLUES

Reading a college textbook can be difficult because the vocabulary, the terms and words used in a textbook, is difficult. Many terms are unique to specific content areas and need to be understood and memorized. Passages are difficult to read because vocabulary, in general, is on a higher level. Many college textbooks contain a glossary of terms in the back of the book; use this to find content-specific definitions. A dictionary may also be helpful when you cannot understand a passage because of the vocabulary. However, some of the best skills you can learn to help you with vocabulary are discussed in this unit. Knowing how to use context clues (clues that an author includes in a sentence or passage to help you understand the meaning of a word) and word part clues (parts of words that give you clues to their meaning) will help you become a better reader of college textbooks. These two skills keep you focused on and thinking about the passage you are reading. As you progress through Chapter 1, you will find information about how to learn vocabulary unique to a particular content area. The last exercises in the chapter provide you with specific directions to help you remember discipline-specific vocabulary terms. All of the techniques introduced in Part One you will use in Part Two; learning and using them now as you complete the exercises will provide you with some initial practice.

CHAPTER 1

UNDERSTANDING TEXTBOOK VOCABULARY

In this chapter you will learn to

- Recognize six types of context clues through word and punctuation clues
- Determine word meanings from context clues
- Determine word meanings from word part clues
- Learn and practice techniques to help you remember important discipline-specific vocabulary

DETERMINING MEANING FROM CONTEXT CLUES

Context clues are words or phrases an author includes to explain the meaning of a particular word. In discipline textbooks such as those for business and psychology, the author will use context clues to define words specific to that discipline as well as to help you understand and make sense of a passage. Authors often use **boldface** or *italics* to emphasize important vocabulary; these boldfaced and italicized terms are defined with context clues because the author wants to be sure that you understand those terms. In Part Two, you will learn that these important terms need to be included in any type of notes that you take. They are important to understand and to review for an exam.

This chapter will teach you six types of context clues that will help you identify and define important vocabulary terms and to read a textbook. The first three clues listed are those most commonly used by textbook authors to define important vocabulary terms, whereas the last three are used to help you understand the general text.

Definition

The most common type of context clue used in textbooks is the definition clue. The author tells you that a term means something, is something, or is defined as something. Look at the following examples:

> **Employment at will** means that the employment relationship can be started or terminated at any time by either the employee or the employer for any reason.
> **Distress** refers to the negative effects of stress that can deplete or even destroy life energy.

Each of these sentences, taken from different textbooks, defines a term. The authors state that the term is being defined.

Restatement or Synonym

Another type of context clue used almost as frequently as definition is the restatement or synonym clue. A *synonym* is a word or phrase that has nearly the same meaning as another word. To help you identify the meaning of a specific term, authors place the restatement or synonym after the specific term they want to explain and with some type of distinguishing punctuation marks. This punctuation may be parentheses, commas, brackets or dashes.

> People who have an **external locus of control**—those who attribute events to chance or forces beyond themselves—have higher burnout rates than those with an internal locus of control.

If the restatement or synonym ends the sentence and the type of punctuation being used to set off the restatement is the comma, then the final punctuation will be a period.

> Most organizations devote considerable attention to **human resource management,** the function of attracting, developing, and retaining sufficient numbers of qualified employees to perform the activities necessary to accomplish organizational objectives.

The difference between this type of context clue and the definition context clue in that here the authors are not as direct; they do not state that the term is being defined, but the definition is clearly in the sentence.

Example

A third type of context clue is the example. The author provides one or more examples to illustrate a term rather than stating a definition. By itself this type of context clue is not as effective as restatement and definition, so it is used less frequently.

> **Episodic stressors** like monthly bills or quarterly exams cause regular but intermittent elevations in stress levels.

Here the author does not define *episodic stressors,* but lists two examples of episodic stressors to help you conclude that these stressors occur on a regular and predictable basis and "cause regular but intermittent elevations in stress levels."

These three types of context clues just discussed are most commonly used in textbooks in which vocabulary is italicized or boldfaced. Be careful not to stop with one sentence when these terms are presented. At times an author will use an entire paragraph to define or explain a term. You need to include much of the information the author provides in any type of notes that you take. Look at the following example:

> People use the word *stress* in different ways: as an external force that causes a person to become tense or upset, as the internal state of arousal, and as the physical response of the body to various demands. Dr. Hans Selye, a pioneer in studying physiological responses to challenge, defined **stress** as "the nonspecific response of the body to any demand made upon it." In other words, the body reacts to **stressors**—things that upset or excite us—in the same way, regardless of whether they are positive or negative.

If you defined *stress* with only the words in the first sentence above, the sentence in which the word itself appears, your definition would be incomplete. You must also know that stress is a nonspecific response of the body in reaction to stressors, which can be positive or negative.

Three other types of context clues may be used by an author. These are not used as often to explain or to define important vocabulary terms in college textbooks, but they can be used by a reader to understand the general text.

Details or Explanation

Often, when you do not know the specific meaning of a word, you can still understand the meaning of the text. Key details within the writing can provide important clues. Read the following example:

However, recent research shows that letting anger out only makes it worse. "**Cathar-sis** is worse than useless," says psychology professor Brad Bushman of Iowa State University, whose research has shown that letting anger out makes people more ag-gressive, not less. "Many people think of anger as the psychological equivalent of the steam in a pressure cooker that has to be released or it will explode. That's not true. People who react by hitting, kicking, screaming, and swearing aren't dealing with the underlying cause of their anger. They just feel more angry."

What does the word *catharsis* mean? You may have some idea of its meaning, but you can use the context to determine a meaning. The professor states that allowing the anger to escape by kicking and screaming is not good and also states that *catharsis* is useless. Therefore, cathar-sis probably means to allow one's emotions to escape uncontrolled.

Comparison

Another context clue is the comparison. Authors compare a particular term with something that they believe will be familiar to you. Words often used to signal the comparison clue are *similar to, like, comparable to,* and *resembling.*

> Jung argued that the collective unconscious can explain **archetypes,** which are like patterns for the symbols found in a wide variety of different cultures and religions.

You may not know what an archetype is, but you do know that a pattern is the model that is used to create other similar symbols or creations. This helps you understand *archetype.*

Contrast or Antonym

The final type of context clue is the contrast or antonym clue. Writers don't often use this type of clue to help readers understand important vocabulary terms in a textbook, but you should be aware of it for general understanding of a textbook. This context clue will use par-ticular signal words that indicate an opposing idea: *in contrast, however, on the other hand, yet,* and *but.*

> **Altruism** is listed as one of Maslow's qualities of a self-actualized person. How-ever, selfishness is not included in Maslow's hierarchy, and would certainly not be associated with a self-actualized person.

Using the contrast term *however,* you can determine that *altruism* means to not be self-ish. The first sentence states an opposite meaning of the word.

Be aware of one important point when using context clues to increase comprehension. Context clues usually do *not* give an exact definition. The meaning of a term derived from a context clue will seldom be what you would find in a dictionary. However, it is the first method that you should use to help understand a written passage. Stopping to look up a word in the dictionary each time you don't know the meaning pulls you away from the text and interrupts your thoughts about that text. Using context clues, you remain with the text and you continue to think about the ideas on the page.

When you are reading and come to a word with which you are not familiar, you need to use context clues to understand the sentence and ultimately, perhaps, the main point of an en-tire subsection. Many vocabulary words may not be boldfaced or italicized, but these words nonetheless may be important to determining the meaning of the text and to understanding what you are reading.

EXERCISE 1: USING CONTEXT CLUES

Read the following sentences taken from the discipline textbook chapters in the sec-ond part of this book. Some of the sentences contain specific boldfaced vocabulary terms that you would need to know when taking a test in that content area. Other sen-tences contain underlined words that are not important to the content area but that are important for helping you understand the paragraph and the main idea. Determine the type of context clue being used and the meaning of the underlined or boldfaced word or words. Then write the definition on the lines provided.

1. In his <u>hierarchy</u> of needs theory, Maslow proposed that all people have basic needs that they must satisfy before they can consider higher-order needs. According to Maslow, people must satisfy the lower-order needs in the <u>hierarchy</u> before they are motivated to satisfy higher-order needs.

Type of Clue: _____

Definition: _____

_____

2. <u>Recruitment</u> and selection is an expensive process, because a firm incurs costs for advertising job openings, interviewing applicants, and conducting background checks, employment tests, and medical exams.

Type of Clue: _____

Definition: _____

_____

3. **Self-actualization needs** drive people to seek fulfillment, realizing their own potential, fully using their talents and capabilities.

Type of Clue: _____

Definition: _____

_____

4. Often, it resolves the conflict by using **defense mechanisms,** which are mental activities designed to reduce the anxiety resulting from this conflict.

Type of Clue: _____

Definition: _____

_____

5. Flextime is a scheduling system that allows employees to set their own work hours within <u>constraints</u> specified by the firm. For example, an employer may require employees to be at work between the core hours of 10 A.M. and 3 P.M; rather than regular workday hours of 9 A.M. to 5 P.M.

Type of Clue: _____

Definition: _____

_____

6. A **performance appraisal** is an evaluation of an employee's job performance by comparing actual results to desired outcomes.

Type of Clue: _____

Definition: _____

_____

7. Home-based workers are sometimes called teleworkers, or <u>telecommuters,</u> because many "commute" to work via telephones, e-mail, computers, and fax machines.

Type of Clue: _____

Definition: _____

_____

8. He postulated that our bodies constantly strive to maintain a stable and consistent physiological state, called **homeostasis.**

Type of Clue: _____

Definition: _____

_____

9. **Employee benefits** are rewards such as retirement plans, insurance, sick leave, child care and elder care, and tuition reimbursement, provided entirely or in part at the company's expense.

Type of Clue: _____

Definition: _____

_____

10. Physiological needs: These most basic human needs include food, shelter, and clothing.

Type of Clue: _____

Definition: _____

_____

11. [The humanistic approach] relies on subjective experience. It emphasizes that reality lies in a person's own interpretation of the world.

Type of Clue: _____

Definition: _____

_____

12. The research on twins reared together and apart typically reports a measure called **heritability,** which is an estimate of how much of the variation in a characteristic can be traced to differences in heredity, as opposed to differences in environment.

Type of Clue: _____

Definition: _____

_____

13. The failure of General George Pickett's magnificent but futile charge finally broke the back of the Confederate attack—and broke the heart of the Confederate cause.

Type of Clue: _____

Definition: _____

_____

14. **Self-efficacy** is a person's belief in his or her ability to organize and perform the actions required to reach desired goals.

Type of Clue: _____

Definition: _____

_____

15. One consequence is **burnout,** a state of physical, emotional, and mental exhaustion brought on by constant or repeated emotional pressure.

Type of Clue: _____

Definition: _____

_____

16. At election time many Northern soldiers were <u>furloughed</u> home to support Lincoln at the polls.

Type of Clue: _____

Definition: _____

_____

17. A number of functions that were performed previously by company employees may be contracted to other firms whose employees will perform them on a contractual basis in a practice called <u>outsourcing.</u>

Type of Clue: _____

Definition: _____

_____

18. **Theory X** assumes that employees dislike work and whenever possible try to avoid it. So, managers must coerce or control them or threaten punishment to achieve the organization's goals.

Type of Clue: _____

Definition: _____

_____

19. In other words, the body reacts to **stressors**—the things that upset or excite us— in the same way, regardless of whether they are positive or negative.

Type of Clue: _____

Definition: _____

_____

20. The presidential pen did not formally strike the shackles from a single slave. Where Lincoln could presumably free the slaves—that is, in the loyal Border States—he refused to do so, lest he spur disunion. Where he could not—that is, in the Confederate states—he tried to. In short, where he could he would not, and where he would he could not. Thus the Emancipation Proclamation was stronger on proclamation than <u>emancipation.</u>

Type of Clue: _____

Definition: _____

_____

DETERMINING MEANING FROM WORD PARTS

Good readers have a general knowledge of prefixes, suffixes, and root words. This chapter contains lists of common prefixes (word parts added to the beginning of words), root or base words (word parts to which prefixes and suffixes are added), and suffixes (word parts added to the end of words). Take the time to learn these word parts. When you come to a word you don't know, your knowledge of the meanings of these word parts may help you just enough to understand that word and the paragraph in which you find it. You already know many of these word parts because of past experience with them. For example, you are probably familiar with the prefix *dis-* found in the word *dishonest;* you know the word means "not honest," so you can determine that the prefix *dis-* means "not." Good readers will use their knowledge of word parts in combination with context clues to help them decode and understand words.

Do not just memorize the parts and their meanings. A much easier way to remember them is to remember or memorize a word that uses the word part, like the word *dishonest.* Memorize the following word part meanings by using the example word in the third column to help you remember the word part and its meaning. For instance, remembering that *absent* means being away from a certain place at a certain time will help you remember that the prefix *ab-* means "away from." If you are able to think of an example of your own that uses the word part and helps you remember its meaning, write it in the margin.

Prefixes

Prefixes	Meaning	Example
a	without	amoral
ab	away from	absent
ad-	to, toward	advance
ambi-	both	ambidextrous
ante-	before	anteroom
anti-	against	antiabortion
bene-	good	beneficial
bi-	two	bicycle
circum-	around	circumference
co-, con-, com-	with, together	comrade
contra-, counter-	against	contradict
de-	away from	derail
dis-	opposite of	disappear
eu-	good	custress
ex-	out of	expand
extra-	above	extrasensory
homeo-	like, similar	homeostasis
in-, im-, a-, en-, il-, ir-	not	illegal
inter-	between	interchange
intra-	within	intradermal
iso-	equal	isometric
kilo-	thousand	kilogram
macro-	large	macronutrient
mal-, mis-	wrong	malnutrition
mega-	big	megaphone
meta-	change	metabolism
micro-	small	microscope
misa-	hatred	misanthrope
mono-	one	monocle
multi-	many	multicultural
non-	not	nonnegotiable
omni-	all	omnipresent
poly-	many	polygon
post-	after	postgame
pre-	before	preheat

pro-	forward	proactive
quad-	four	quadruple
re-	again	reread
retro-	backward	retroactive
sub-	under	submarine
super-	over, above	superhighway
syn-	together	synonym
trans-	across	transatlantic
tri-	three	tricycle
uni-	one	unicycle

Roots

Root	Meaning	Example
acer, acr	sour	acrid
anthropo	humankind	anthropology
bio	life, living organism, or tissue	biology
cap, cept	receive	reception
ced, cess,	go, move along	proceed
chron	time	chronological
clud	shut	conclude
dem, demo	people	democracy
derm	skin	dermatology
dic, dict	say	dictation
duc, duct	lead	deduct
fac, fact	make	manufacture
fid	faith	fidelity
geo	earth	geography
gest	carry	digest
graph	write	autograph
idea, ideo	idea	ideology
immuno	state of being immune	immunology
later	side	trilateral
log, logue	speak	monologue
morph	form	amorphous
mort	death	mortician
neur, neuro	nerve	neuritis
nil, nul	nothing	nullify
path	feeling	empathy
ped, pod	foot	podiatrist
pel	push	propel
port	carry	portable
psych	mind	psychology
rupt	break	interrupt
sat, satis	enough	satisfy
scope	watch	microscope
scrib	write	prescribe
spect	see, look	spectacle
ten	hold	tenacious
tend	stretch	tendons
ven, vent	come	convention
ver, veri	truth	verify
viv	life	vivacious

Suffixes

Suffixes	Meaning	Example
-able, -ible	able to	responsible
-al	relating to	communal
-archy, -cracy	rule	democracy
-arium, -orium	place for	aquarium
-ation	act of	devastation
-er, -eer, -el, -ist, -or, -ar	person who	teacher
-est	highest degree	happiest
-ful	full of	careful
-gamy	marriage	polygamy
-gon	angle	polygon
-ic, -ics	pertaining to, art of	scientific
-ify, -fy	make	magnify
-ion	act or process	validation
-ish	like	foolish
-ism	doctrine	communism
-itis	inflammation of	appendicitis
-oid	in the form of	tabloid
-ology	study of	mythology
-ous	full of	cancerous
-ship, -tude	quality of	friendship

In addition to the preceding lists, many textbooks contain important vocabulary terms that utilize word parts. Good readers are aware of those word parts and use them to help remember the words.

Read the following sentences from a health textbook; the author gives the meanings of the word parts in parentheses to help you understand the words. Remember these words as well as the particular word parts because they will turn up often later in the text.

Selye coined the term **eustress** for positive stress in our lives (*eu* is a Greek prefix meaning "good").

Another example comes from the psychology chapter in Part Two of this text. A list of defense mechanisms and their meanings is provided. Many of the terms sound alike and the list can be difficult to memorize. Knowing the meaning of the prefix of many of the terms can help you remember the word meanings. For example, you can remember that *regression* means "a return to an earlier life stage" because *re-* means "again," and you can remember the definition as though someone were acting as a child again. Another example would be the term *displacement*. This term means to redirect an emotion toward someone other than the "real" object of emotion. You can remember the meaning by knowing that *dis-* means "the opposite of" and the term means that one directs an emotion toward the opposite of the person to whom they really feel the emotion. One more term in the list is *projection,* which means to attribute your own unacceptable feelings to another person. You can remember that *pro-* means "forward," so *projection* means the movement of your unacceptable feelings forward to someone else.

Knowing word parts will help you with important vocabulary. Identify word parts of new vocabulary and use them to help you remember word meanings.

EXERCISE 2: USING WORD PART CLUES

Use your knowledge and the meanings of word parts on the previous pages to determine the meanings of the underlined words in the following sentences from the content-area texts. Write the meaning of each word on the lines below the sentence.

1. We'll then discuss (Freud's) methods, the stages of <u>psychosexual</u> development, Freud's views on defense mechanisms, and his representation of women.

Definition: _____

_____

2. Where Lincoln could presumably free the slaves—that is, in the loyal Border States—he refused to do so, lest he spur <u>disunion.</u>

Definition: _____

_____

3. The <u>compressed</u> workweek is a scheduling option that allows employees to work the regular number of weekly hours in fewer than the typical five days.

Definition: _____

_____

4. Lincoln's <u>renomination</u> at first encountered surprisingly strong opposition.

Definition: _____

_____

5. Factions within his own party, <u>distrusting</u> his ability or doubting his commitment to abolition, sought to tie his hands or even remove him from office.

Definition: _____

_____

6. Complex carbohydrates are an ideal <u>antistress</u> food because they boost the brain's level of mood-enhancing chemical serotonin.

Definition: _____

_____

7. In the past, <u>posttraumatic</u> stress disorder was viewed as a psychological response to out-of-the-ordinary stressors, such as captivity or combat.

Definition: _____

_____

8. Internet recruiting is a quick, efficient, <u>inexpensive</u> way to reach a large, global pool of job seekers.

Definition: _____

_____

EXERCISE 3: USING CONTEXT AND WORD PART CLUES

Use your knowledge of word parts and context clues to determine the meanings of the underlined words in the following sentences from the content-area texts. Write the meaning of the underlined word or words on the lines below the sentence.

1. London, although not happy, <u>acquiesced</u> in the disagreeable doctrine.

_____

2. <u>Reaffirming</u> his limited war aims, (Lincoln) declared that he had "no purpose, directly or indirectly to interfere with slavery in the states where it exists."

_____

3. Events finally <u>converged</u> toward a critical battle at Antietam Creek, Maryland.

_____

4. Unlike traditional plans, cash balance pensions are <u>portable</u>—workers can transfer them from one company to another when they change jobs—making them potentially more valuable in today's less permanent work arrangements.

_____

5. Others are called <u>specialists,</u> because they focus on individual areas of human resource management such as diversity training or employee benefits.

_____

6. <u>Biofeedback</u> is a method of obtaining feedback, or information, about some physiological activity occurring in the body.

_____

7. Among the <u>nonbiological</u> theories is the cognitive-transactional model of stress, which looks at the relation between stress and health.

_____

8. The scientific field of <u>psychoneuroimmunology</u> has been exploring these intricate interconnections.

_____

9. In contrast, Rogers believed that everyone should be given <u>unconditional positive regard,</u> which is a nonjudgmental and genuine love, without any strings attached.

_____

10. The most common type, tension headache, is caused by <u>involuntary</u> contractions of the scalp, head, and neck muscles.

_____

Practice with Periodicals

Read the article "Is Freud Finished?" in Part Three. In the article, find and list five vocabulary words with which you are unfamiliar. Use context and/or word part clues to write a definition for each word. Check each definition with your instructor or in a dictionary.

Journal Entry

After reading the article "Is Freud Finished?" in Part Three, write a journal entry explaining the following quote: "There's a whole lot more to folks than meets the eye." In your entry, explain what this quote has to do with Freud and if you agree or disagree with it.

Textbook Link

In another textbook you are using, analyze how the author presents vocabulary. Choose at least five vocabulary terms and determine what type of context clues are being used to help you understand them.

REMEMBERING CONTENT-RELATED TERMS

When authors set a term in boldface or italics, it's important to write down that definition in your notes. To go a step further, you should also include an example or illustration in your notes to help you memorize that term. If the term has an acronym (a word formed from the initial letters of words; for example, MASH = *m*obile *a*rmy *s*urgical *u*nit), you need to memorize that acronym as well as the term.

Using Meaningful Examples to Remember Definitions

Read the following paragraph from the psychology textbook chapter on personality. Then note how the word *id* is defined with an example.

> Freud envisioned three basic components to personality: the id, the ego, and the superego. He proposed that humans are born with an **id,** which is immature and illogical. The id consists of basic drives—such as eating and sexual activities—and it provides the energy (or **libido**) for all human behavior. Freud also maintained that the id lacks moral judgment; it cannot distinguish between good and evil. The id is unconscious, a "hidden self" that can influence our everyday actions.

> Definition: *id* = according to Freud, a part of the personality that is immature, cannot tell good from bad; unconscious; consists of basic needs and gives energy to behavior. Example: baby (wants things now/immature).

The definition is taken from the entire paragraph, not just the sentence in which the word *id* is located. Also, the example is an analogy, a comparison that will help you remember the function of the id. The id is compared with a baby because both stand for something that is immature, illogical, and lacking in moral judgment.

The following excerpts are taken from the psychology and business chapters in Part Two of this textbook.

EXERCISE 4: USING MEANINGFUL EXAMPLES TO REMEMBER DEFINITIONS

Write a definition as well as an example to help you remember the boldfaced terms in the following sentences. No example is wrong as long as it has meaning to you and helps you connect the term to some past knowledge or experience that you have.

1. The **ego,** in contrast, supposedly develops because the individual needs some factor that will mediate between the id and reality. For example, Freud argues that the ego helps young children delay their impulses until the situation is appropriate.

Definition: _____

_____

_____

Example: _____

_____

2. So far, we have an irrational id, governed by pleasure, and a cooler, calmer ego. Freud's third personality component is the **superego,** which includes a person's conscience, ideals, and values. Parents and society convey these principles. Because the society in Freud's era often discouraged sexual expression, Freud argued that the superego suppresses sexual impulses.

Definition: _____

_____

_____

Example: _____

_____

3. and 4. A **central trait** is a general characteristic, found to some degree in every person, that shapes much of our behavior. Some central traits could be honesty, cheerfulness, and shyness. A **secondary trait** is a characteristic seen only in certain situations. These must be included to provide a complete picture of human complexity. Some typical secondary traits might be "uncomfortable in large crowds" and "likes to drive sports cars."

Definition: _____

_____

_____

Example: _____

_____

Definition: _____

_____

_____

Example: _____

_____

5. Of the four personality approaches described in this chapter, the trait approach most strongly emphasizes our theme of individual differences. As we discussed in the introduction to this chapter, the trait approach proposes that personality is a combination of specific stable, internal personality characteristics called traits. Thus, a **trait** is a consistent tendency to have certain kinds of beliefs, desires, and behaviors.

Definition: _____

_____

_____

Example: _____

_____

6. **Theory X** assumes that employees dislike work and whenever possible try to avoid it. So, managers must coerce or control them or threaten punishment to achieve the organization's goals. Managers who accept this view feel that the average person prefers to receive direction, wishes to avoid responsibility, has relatively little ambition, and can be motivated only by money and job security. Managers who hold these assumptions are likely to keep their subordinates under close and constant observation, holding out the threat of disciplinary action, and demanding that they adhere closely to company policies and procedures.

Definition: _____

_____

_____

Example: _____

_____

7. One approach sets up **flexible benefit plans,** also called cafeteria plans. Such a benefit system offers employees a range of options from which they can choose, including different types of medical insurance coverage, dental and vision plans, life and disability insurance, and extra vacation days.

(Note: Be sure to place the alternate name, cafeteria plans, in the definition because either term may be used on a test.)

Definition: _____

_____

_____

Example: _____

_____

8. **Employee benefits** are rewards such as retirement plans, insurance, sick leave, child care and elder care, and tuition reimbursement, provided entirely or in part at the company's expense.

Definition: _____

_____

_____

Example: _____

_____

9. **Contingent workers** are employees who work part-time, temporarily, or for the length of time involved in fulfilling a specific contract. Traditionally, contingent workers earned less pay than full-time employees, and did not receive benefits or have access to employer-provided pension plans.

Definition: _____

_____

_____

Example: _____

_____

10. One popular instructional method is **on-the-job training,** which prepares employees for job duties by allowing them to perform the tasks under the guidance of experienced employees.

Definition: _____

_____

_____

Example: _____

_____

Visual Aids as a Memory Tool

Sometimes it is more beneficial to draw a visual aid that represents the material to be understood and memorized. For example, Freud's three basic components of human personality (the id, the ego, and the superego), which you read about at the beginning of this section, can be shown as three concentric circles as illustrated in Figure 1.1.

Figure 1.1 Memory-aiding diagram of Freud's basic components of personality

This visual aid shows the ego between the id and the superego; it helps you "see" the mediating role that the ego plays between the two components. Another example is one that the health textbook author has already drawn for you (see below): the three stages of the General Adaptation Syndrome (GAS) are shown above the vertical line whereas other factors are shown below the line.

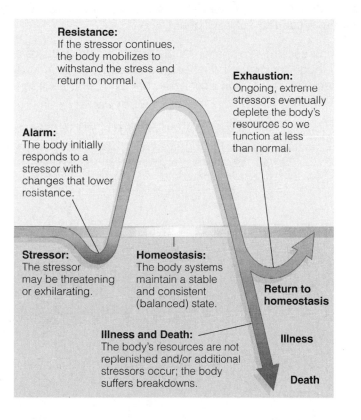

Creating or copying a visual aid forces you to comprehend the material and to draw it in terms that are your own.

EXERCISE 5: USING VISUAL AIDS TO IMPROVE MEMORY

Read the following passages and create a visual aid to help you remember and understand the concepts presented.

1. Let's examine the five levels in Maslow's hierarchy, beginning with the most basic level.

    1. *Physiological needs:* We need food, water, sleep, and sex. Notice that these needs are also those that motivate lower animals.

2. *Safety needs:* These needs include security, protection, and the avoidance of pain.

3. *Belongingness and love needs:* These needs focus on affiliation with other people, affection, and feeling loved; sexual relationships as an expression of affection can also be included in this category.

4. *Esteem needs:* We also need to respect ourselves and to win the esteem of other people. Otherwise we feel discouraged and inferior, according to Maslow, so we will not strive for the highest level of hierarchy.

5. *Self-actualization needs:* A person who has satisfied all the lower need can seek self-actualization, attempting to reach her or his full potential.

2. Each person is motivated to take action designed to satisfy needs. A **need** is simply a felt lack of some useful benefit. It reflects a gap between an individual's actual state and his or her desired state. A **motive** is an inner state that directs a person toward the goal of satisfying a felt need. Once the need—the gap between where a person is now and where he or she wants to be—becomes important enough, it produces tension. The individual is then moved—the root word for motive—to reduce this tension and return to a condition of equilibrium.

3. Bandura has proposed an explanation for the way initial individual differences become even stronger through reciprocal influences. According to the principle of **reciprocal influences,** three factors—personal/cognitive, behavior, and environmental—all influence one another.

(Note: The key to remembering important vocabulary is to make connections to information and facts that you already know. That is why making up examples and drawing pictures and copying illustrations will help you remember new terms. Do whatever you need to do to help you remember.)

3

COMPREHENSION SKILLS: UNDERSTANDING PASSAGES AND GRAPHICS

Determining the main idea of a paragraph, a subsection of a textbook, or even an entire chapter is probably the most important skill that you will need to know in reading college textbooks. Chapter 2 will help you determine the main idea of a paragraph by supplying you with two questions to ask and to answer. You will also learn where authors usually place main idea sentences within a paragraph. You can apply these strategies for determining main ideas to a subsection of a textbook or an entire chapter. This chapter and the next chapter on paragraph types and supporting details will help you determine what main points you need to understand and what details you need to memorize to do well in a course.

Using graphics appropriately also requires the reader to determine a main idea. In the last chapter in this unit, you will learn to apply the same main idea questions to graphics.

CHAPTER 2

FINDING MAIN IDEAS

In this chapter you will learn to

- Find the topic and main idea of a paragraph by asking and answering two questions
- Find a main idea sentence in a paragraph
- Determine an implied main idea
- Determine main ideas of longer selections

DETERMINING STATED MAIN IDEAS

If you have taken or are taking a writing course, you have probably talked about the topic sentence; this is the same thing as the main idea. To determine the main idea, you must understand the topic or what the paragraph is about. For example, if you were writing a paragraph, the first question you would ask yourself is, "What am I going to write about?" If you chose dogs or college or vacations, the one that you chose would be your topic. So the first question to ask after you finish reading a paragraph is,

"What is this paragraph about?"

The answer to this question is the topic of your paragraph. The answer can usually be stated in one to three words.

Determining the topic can be like playing *The $10,000 Pyramid.* If you have ever seen this game show, you know that players are given clues to what belongs in a category and are then to come up with a category name.

Here is an example: If the clues are *red, blue, green, white,* and *purple,* the category name will be "Colors." Here is another: If the clues are *oak, maple, apple, pear,* and *evergreen,* the category name will be "Types of Trees."

The problem is that some categories, like paragraphs, are not that easy. Try this one: The clues are *cars, trucks, school bands, bulls, devils,* and *rhinoceroses.* This one is tougher because it does not follow a pattern in your mind. You know that cars and trucks are in a category called "Vehicles" or "Transportation." Bulls and rhinoceroses are in another category called "Animals." How do school bands and devils fit in? What do they have in common? They all have horns. So the category name is "Things with Horns."

Determine the topic of each of the following:

1. accountant, CPA, Wall Street analyst, store manager

   _____

2. slavery, states rights, Confederacy and Union, secession of states

   _____

3. deep breathing, meditation, laughter, serenity break

   _____

The answers would be (1) jobs for business majors, (2) issues in the Civil War, and (3) methods of reducing stress.

After determining the topic, you need to ask a second question in order to determine the main idea. If you were the author, the next question to ask yourself after choosing the topic would be, "What do I want to write about this topic?" You could write about how to choose a dog as a pet or how colleges can be grouped into categories based on courses of studies offered. As a reader, after you answer the first question, you need to ask this second question,

"What is the author telling me about this topic?"

The answer to this second question should begin with the topic and should be as close to a complete sentence as you can make it. For example, "Colleges can be grouped by the courses offered," or "Dogs are easy pets to choose if you know the right steps."

If you have difficulty with a paragraph, read and think about all the sentences in that paragraph one by one, determine the main point of each of the sentences, and then determine how they all fit together. For example, read this paragraph from the business textbook chapter.

> [1]Businesses access both internal and external sources to find qualified candidates for specific jobs. [2]Policies of hiring from within emphasize internal sources, so that employers consider their own employees first for job openings. [3]Internal recruiting is less expensive than external methods, and it helps to boost employee morale. [4]But if recruiters can find no qualified internal candidate, they must look for people outside the organization. [5]Recruitment from external sources involves advertising in newspapers and trade magazines, placing radio and TV ads, and working through employment agencies, college recruiting and internship offices, retiree job banks, job fairs, and state and private employment agencies.

Look at each sentence individually.

Sentence 1 is about businesses searching internally and externally for new employees.
Sentence 2 is about searching internally.
Sentence 3 is about the benefits of internal searching.
Sentence 4 is about external sources.
Sentence 5 is also about external searching.

Because this paragraph includes details about both internal and external sources, the best main idea sentence is the first sentence because it includes both supporting details. The supporting details would be (1) businesses usually encourage internal hiring and (2) managers look externally if no internal candidates are qualified. The third and fifth sentences are minor details to support the major details about internal and external hiring.

Be careful not to choose a main idea sentence that focuses on only one detail. For example, look at the following paragraph taken from the America history textbook chapter.

> [1]The "military picnic" at Bull Run, though not decisive militarily, had significant psychological and political consequences. [2]Victory was worse than defeat for the South, because it inflated an already dangerous overconfidence. [3]Many of the Southern soldiers promptly deserted, some boastfully to display their trophies, others feeling that the war was now surely over. [4]Southern enlistments fell off sharply, and preparations for a protracted conflict slackened. [5]Defeat was better than victory for the Union, because it dispelled all illusions of a one-punch war and caused the Northerners to buckle down to the staggering task at hand. [6]It also set the stage for a war that would be waged not merely for the cause of Union but also, eventually, for the abolitionist ideal of emancipation.

The topic of the paragraph is the Battle of Bull Run. What is the author telling you about Bull Run? You could not choose the second sentence about the victory hurting the South because this sentence is about the South only. Sentences 3 and 4 are also about the South; they explain how the victory hurt the South. The remainder of the paragraph is about the North and how the defeat was a positive outcome for it. To choose a sentence about either the North or the South would be wrong because the paragraph is about both sides in this battle. The first sentence of the paragraph is the main idea because the author states the psychological and political significance of the battle. The explanation that the defeat was a victory for the North and that the victory was a defeat for the South is true because of how the battle played out in the minds of those involved in the war.

Here's another example for you to consider.

[1]Later in that dreary autumn of 1863, with the graves still fresh, Lincoln journeyed to Gettysburg to dedicate the cemetery. [2]He read a two-minute address, following a two-hour speech by the orator of the day. [3]Lincoln's noble remarks were branded by the London *Times* as "ludicrous" and by Democratic editors as "dishwatery" and "silly." [4]The address attracted relatively little attention at the time, but the president was speaking for the ages.

List the main point of each sentence and then double underline the sentence that includes all of the points.

1._____
2._____
3._____
4._____

Sentence 1 is about Lincoln speaking at Gettysburg.
Sentence 2 is about the length of the speech.
Sentence 3 states negative reactions to the speech.
Sentence 4 states that although the initial reaction to the speech was negative, the remarks were "for the ages."

The topic of the paragraph is Lincoln's speech. You should have double underlined the last sentence as the main idea. The first three sentences are supporting details. Lincoln gave his Gettysburg address, which did not receive positive reviews at the time. This is rephrased in the last sentence with the addition of the fact that the speech was important to later times.

PLACEMENT OF A MAIN IDEA SENTENCE

Authors of textbooks are not trying to hide their main ideas. If an author uses headings or sub-headings in boldface or italics (and almost all textbooks have these) then usually these reference the topic, so the first question—what the section is about—is already answered for you.

Main Ideas in First Sentences

Authors want you to know and understand what they have written. They often write a main idea sentence somewhere in the paragraph for you. The most common place for an author to write a main idea sentence is at the beginning of a paragraph. This means that it's either the first or the second sentence. Authors may place the main idea as the second sentence because they want to use a lead-in sentence to connect to the preceding paragraph and/or to get your interest.

Here's an example of a paragraph with the main idea as the first sentence.

Black fighting men unquestionably had their hearts in the war against slavery that the Civil War had become after Lincoln proclaimed emancipation. Participating in about five hundred engagements, they received twenty-two Congressional Medals of Honor—the highest military award. Their casualties were extremely heavy; more than thirty-eight thousand died, whether from battle, sickness, or reprisals from vengeful masters. Many were put to death as slaves in revolt, for not until 1864 did the South recognize them as prisoners of war. In one notorious case, several black soldiers were massacred after they had formally surrendered at Fort Pillow, Mississippi. Thereafter vengeful black units cried "Remember Fort Pillow" as they swung into battle, and vowed to take no prisoners.

Each of the sentences after the first sentence states an example of how black fighting men had their hearts in the war. They participated in 500 engagements, won 22 medals, suffered heavy casualties, and often were put to death.

Main Ideas in the Final Sentences

If you don't find the main idea at the beginning of a paragraph, sometimes you will find it at the end. Placing it at the end permits the author to summarize the details in the paragraph.

> Fearing defeat, the Republican party executed a clever maneuver. Joining with the War Democrats, it proclaimed itself to be the Union party. <u>Thus the Republican party passed temporarily out of existence.</u>

This first two sentences of this paragraph explain why and how the Republican party temporarily passed out of existence. The main idea is that it did temporarily pass out of existence.

Main Ideas Midparagraph

A main idea sentence may also be found in the middle of a paragraph. The author leads up to the main idea with details and then continues with more details.

> A new slaughter pen was prepared when General Burnside yielded his command to "Fighting Joe" Hooker, an aggressive officer but a headstrong subordinate. <u>At Chancellorsville, Virginia,</u> May 2–4, 1863, Lee daringly divided his numerically inferior force and sent "Stonewall" Jackson to attack the Union flank. The strategy worked. Hooker, temporarily dazed by a near hit from a cannonball, was badly beaten but not crushed. <u>This victory was probably Lee's most brilliant, but it was dearly bought.</u> Jackson was mistakenly shot by his own men in the gathering dusk and died a few days later. "I have lost my right arm," lamented Lee. Southern folklore relates how Jackson outflanked the angels while galloping into heaven.

Part of a second sentence is double underlined because the name of the battle, the topic, is not included in the main idea sentence. Often, when the main idea is in the middle of a paragraph, part of another sentence needs to be underlined. Because authors have already stated the topic, they may use a pronoun to refer to it in the middle of the paragraph.

In the following paragraph, you need to double underline three sentences for the main idea because the author writes of some contrasts. (Note the use of the words *but* and *however.*) Whenever you recognize a contrast term (such as *but, yet, on the other hand, however*) read carefully to determine the points about which the author is writing. Often you will need to double underline those sentences that contain these contrast terms for the main idea.

> The high compensation of U.S. executives has also received attention from CEOs in other companies. <u>The salaries of U.S. top managers compare to those of their counterparts</u> in Brazil, France, Hong Kong, Germany, the United Kingdom, Japan, and Canada. <u>But this similarity masks a huge difference in total compensation,</u> mainly because of long-term incentives such as stock options, which are seldom given in other countries. Firms in Germany and Japan are prohibited by law from giving stock options to executives. <u>However, many foreign firms are finding ways to boost the compensation of their CEOs.</u> The globalization of business and international search for top executive talent are forcing foreign companies to increase their CEO compensation.

The first sentence states the topic of the paragraph—compensation for executives. The paragraph is about how U.S. compensation is both similar to and different from other countries. The major details would be (1) U.S. CEO salaries are similar to CEO salaries in other countries; (2) U.S. CEOs, unlike CEOs of other countries, receive incentives as part of their salaries; and (3) foreign firms are finding ways to increase their compensation.

EXERCISE 6: FINDING STATED MAIN IDEAS I

The following paragraphs have been excerpted from textbook chapters written on the same topics as those found in Part Two of this book; however, the readability is slightly lower because they are not from college textbooks. Use this exercise to practice finding the main idea. Then continue with Exercise 7 and more difficult excerpts from the college textbook chapters in Part Two of this book.

Each of the following paragraphs has a stated main idea. Double underline that main idea.

1. Jim Lewis and Jim Springer were identical twins who were separated at birth and reunited for the first time when they were 39 years old. At their meeting, they both were six feet tall and weighed 180 pounds and were so similar in appearance that strangers could rarely tell them apart. The physical resemblance was to be expected, but when the two men sat down to talk for the first time, they found some rather strange similarities. Both had been married twice, first to women named Linda and then to women named Betty. One had a son named James Alan, the other James Allen. As boys, they both named their dogs Toy. Thirty-nine years after they were separated, they both smoked Salem cigarettes and drank Miller Lite.

—Dean Hamer and Peter Copeland, *Living With Our Genes*

2. Grant offered generous terms. Lee's men would be allowed to return to their homes. Officers could keep their weapons, and soldiers who privately owned horses could keep them for use in their respective livelihoods. Lee agreed to all conditions, and at 3:00 p.m. the two commanders signed the surrender document.

—Ed. Carter Smith, *The Road to Appomattox*

3. Some employers want to see more than resumes and references. An applicant for a newspaper reporting job should bring writing samples. An artist should bring copies of drawings or paintings. A hair stylist should bring a copy of his or her license.

—Stuart Schwartz and Craig Conley, *Interviewing for a Job*

4. When our bodies stay on alert for long periods of time, we can suffer health problems. Research shows that stress hormones make the immune system function less well. This makes us more vulnerable to infectious diseases, such as the flu and colds. Headaches, stomach problems, nervous tension, and heart disease have also been linked to stress.

—Laurie Beckelman, *Stress*

5. It is said that the Chinese word for crisis is written by combining the symbols for the words danger and opportunity. Stress is just that: a danger and an opportunity; a friend and a foe. If you use it well, stress can be a good friend, indeed.

—Donald Oken, M.D., *Stress . . . Our Friend, Our Foe*

6. New black enlistees could not count on having dramatic opportunities to show their courage and ability. Most black troops continued to serve behind the battle lines. When Port Hudson fell to the Yankees in July 1863, for example, the Union had more than six hundred miles of the Mississippi to oversee and protect. Much of this work fell to black soldiers. They manned fortifications along the river, guarded plantations and contraband camps, and arranged for the transportation of supplies and equipment.

—Zak Mettger, *Till Victory Is Won: Black Soldiers in the Civil War*

7. Like all soldiers away from home, black troops relied mainly on letters to keep in touch with their families and friends. But exchanging written correspondence was difficult for former slaves and their wives. Most could not read or write. Only family members lucky enough to have a literate friend or to know a local Union sympathizer could

correspond. Their husbands, sons, and fathers had an easier time. Army chaplains and northern missionaries in the camps were usually willing to read and write letters for soldiers.

—Zak Mettger, *Till Victory Is Won: Black Soldiers in the Civil War*

8. Some caution is good since it prevents us from walking off cliffs or into fires. But when caution controls you too much, you stop growing. Push back your protective mental walls to be more of who you can be. The walls are there to protect you from harm, but unless you expand the space within the walls, you stop living and become like a programmed robot.

—Matthew Ignoffo, Ph.D., *Everything You Need to Know About Self-Confidence*

9. The healing power of human communication is amazing. The ability to communicate with other hostages was one of the things that enabled Terry Waite to survive his long and stressful ordeal of being held hostage in Lebanon from 1987 to 1991. Chained in their separate, solid-walled cells, the hostages could not hear one another's voices, so they could not talk. But they could tap on the walls. And they did, sending messages to each other. That tapping, that crude form of communication, became a lifeline.

—Laurie Beckelman, *Stress*

10. Lincoln also had a wonderful sense of humor on which he relied when the burdens of office became heavy. He especially enjoyed laughing at himself. A political enemy once called the homely-looking Lincoln a two-faced man. Lincoln replied: "Now I leave it to my audience. If I had another face, do you think I would wear this one?"

—James I. Robertson, Jr., *Civil War! America Becomes One Nation*

11. Sherman the soldier was not a likable man. Unkempt hair and beard surrounded a face that was naturally grim and frowning, and there was always a wild expression in his eyes. He disliked newspapermen, whom he accused of being unable to tell the truth. . . . In 1861, when Lincoln issued the first call for 75,000 men to serve for three months, Sherman snorted: "You might as well attempt to put out the flames of a burning house with a squirt gun."

—James I. Robertson, Jr., *Civil War! America Becomes One Nation*

12. Handsome and confident, "Little Mac" proved to be the most skillful army organizer of the Civil War. He personally created the Army of the Potomac, equipped it, trained it, and gave it deep pride and high morale. But McClellan's good points were not enough to balance his weaknesses. Boastful and overly ambitious, he would pose for photographs with one hand inside his coat as Napoleon Bonaparte had done. And he proved to be a field commander who lacked any enthusiasm for battle.

—James I. Robertson, Jr., *Civil War! America Becomes One Nation*

13. Most people in our society have trouble talking about, thinking about, and experiencing anger. If you come to terms with this powerful emotion, however, you'll be discovering a new and exciting source of energy in your life. Learning productive ways of thinking about and expressing anger can help you feel more peaceful and content with yourself while making your relationships with others closer and more satisfying. Best of all, you'll come to know yourself better, and to appreciate yourself as a fascinating human being capable of experiencing a wide range of emotions. This may not always make life easier—but it certainly makes life more interesting!

—Christine Dentemaro and Rachel Kranz, *Straight Talk About Anger*

14. To begin his men's education, McClellan imposed strict new rules in camp. Recruits could no longer wander about Washington as they pleased. In order to leave camp, a soldier had to have a pass granted by his commanding officer. Military police

swarmed through the saloons and gambling houses of the city, arresting all soldiers found away from their posts.

—Delia Ray, *Behind the Blue and Gray: The Soldier's Life in the Civil War*

15. Whenever soldiers from the North and South did manage to hold a serious conversation, they were strangely moved by how much they had in common. They often shared the same backgrounds, the same likes and dislikes, the same fears. Their respect for one another often outweighed their resentments. One Confederate soldier, after a long talk with a Union man, wrote home sadly, "We could have settled the war in 30 minutes had it been left to us."

—Delia Ray, *Behind the Blue and Gray: The Soldier's Life in the Civil War*

16. In both the North and the South, most soldiers fell between the ages of eighteen and twenty-nine. But also scattered among the ranks were hundreds of volunteers who did not meet the minimum age of requirement of eighteen. Some boys were so anxious to enlist that they lied outright about their age. Others felt pangs of guilt about deceiving recruitment officers. To ease their worries, a few clever boys wrote the number eighteen on slips of paper, which they placed inside their shoes. When the officer asked their age, they could cheerfully and truthfully reply, "I'm over eighteen."

—Delia Ray, *Behind the Blue and Gray: The Soldier's Life in the Civil War*

17. People who are looking for work have many things to consider. Every job has advantages and disadvantages. For example, construction jobs might be hard on workers' bodies. Most teachers do not work during summer. But they may have to work extra hours during the school year.

—Stuart Schwartz and Craig Conley, *Finding Work*

18. Traditionally, psychiatrists believed that post-traumatic stress disorder (PTSD) was caused by a single, terrible event. Increasingly, however, mental health professionals have grown to recognize that another category of trauma can also result in symptoms of PTSD. When a patient has a history of continued threat of physical or sexual abuse, or exposure to violence, all of the symptoms of PTSD can also occur. In fact PTSD often results when you believe that the frightening experience was not a single, isolated event but instead could occur again.

—Marvin Rosen, Ph.D., *Understanding Post-Traumatic Stress Disorder*

19. Because of the city's importance, the river roadway to it was strongly defended. Some 75 miles (120 kilometers) below the city, the Mississippi was guarded by two forts: St. Philip on the east bank and Jackson on the west shore. Together, they boasted 126 artillery pieces and 1,200 men. A fleet of warships hovered just upriver of the two.

—Edward F. Dolan, *The American Civil War: A House Divided*

20. In the White House, Lincoln received word of the two great victories. But he looked on Gettysburg as a defeat because of Meade's behavior following the battle. The general, with 23,000 casualties but with an army still far outnumbering Lee's, had not struck at the bedraggled enemy to win what could have been a war-ending victory. Instead, he had rested his troops for a week before moving on Lee's encampment, only to find that the Confederates had departed south and escaped back to Virginia.

—Edward F. Dolan, *The American Civil War: A House Divided*

EXERCISE 7: FINDING STATED MAIN IDEAS II

Double underline the main idea sentence in each of the following paragraphs taken from the college discipline textbook chapters. Be careful because sometimes there is more than one sentence used as the main idea. If you have a difficult time, write out the supporting details on a sheet of paper, and choose the sentence or sentence parts that include the other ideas in the paragraph.

1. Union strategy now turned toward total war. As finally developed, the Northern military plan had six components: first, slowly suffocate the South by blockading its coasts; second, liberate the slaves and hence undermine the very economic foundations of the Old South; third, cut the Confederacy in half by seizing control of the Mississippi River backbone; fourth, chop it to pieces by sending troops through Georgia and Carolinas; fifth, decapitate it by capturing its capital at Richmond; and sixth (this was Ulysses Grant's idea, especially), try everywhere to engage the enemy's main strength and grind it into submission.

2. For example, Mischel and Shoda examined the personality trait of "verbal aggression" in children. One child seemed to be fairly low in verbal aggression on some occasions, for example, but very high on this same trait on other occasions. On the surface, the child's personality appears to be inconsistent. When Mischel and Shoda reexamined the data, however, they found that this child was consistently low in aggression when a peer approached, but consistently very high in aggression when an adult gave a warning. Other children showed different profiles. Most important, if we can specify the external feature of the situation (e.g., "peer approaching" or "adult warning"), then people *can* show remarkable consistency in their personalities.

3. Good nutrition can help soothe a stressed-out stomach. Complex carbohydrates are an ideal antistress food because they boost the brain's level of the mood-enhancing chemical serotonin. Good sources include broccoli, leafy greens, potatoes, corn, cabbage, spinach, whole-grain breads and pastas, muffins, crackers, and cereals. Leafy vegetables, whole grains, nuts, and seeds also are rich in other important nutrients, including magnesium and vitamin C.

4. Relationships between employers and employees changed enormously during the past century. At the beginning of the 20th century, firms hired employees by posting notices at their sites stating that workers were needed and would be hired the following day. Such a notice might list required skills, such as carpentry or welding, or simply list the number of employees the firm required. People looking for work would line up at the employer's shop or factory the next day—a small number in prosperous times and a larger number in less prosperous times. Someone in authority made hiring decisions after reviewing these candidates, often based on arbitrary criteria; sometimes the first people in line were hired, sometimes the healthiest and strongest were hired. After being hired, the new employees were expected to work under a precise set of rules.

5. Other Union thrusts in the West were in the making. In the spring of 1862, a flotilla commanded by David G. Farragut joined with a Northern army to strike the South a staggering blow by seizing New Orleans. With Union gunboats both ascending and descending the Mississippi, the eastern part of the Confederacy was left with a precarious back door. Through this narrowing entrance, between Vicksburg and Port Hudson, flowed herds of vitally needed cattle and other provisions from Louisiana and Texas. The fortress of Vicksburg, located on a hairpin turn of the Mississippi, was the South's sentinel protecting the lifeline to the western sources of supply.

6. While the self-esteem of college freshmen typically falls, students recover their self-confidence in their second year. They become more positive, introspective, and independent and have a stronger sense of their own intellectual ability. It may well be that as students acclimate to college, they experience less stress and therefore view themselves more positively.

7. One can view human resource management in two ways. In a narrow sense, it includes the functions performed by human resource professionals. But in a broader

sense, it involves the entire organization, even when a special staff department assumes those responsibilities or when a firm outsources the functions. Supervisors and general managers also participate in hiring, training, evaluating performance, and motivating employees. Since a company's success depends largely on the commitment and talents of its people, a growing number of firms are measuring and rewarding managers' performance in retaining employees and attracting qualified job candidates.

8. For years therapists encouraged people to "vent" their anger. However, recent research shows that letting anger out only makes it worse. "Catharsis is worse than useless," says psychology professor Brad Bushman of Iowa State University, whose research has shown that letting anger out makes people more aggressive, not less. "Many people think of anger as the psychological equivalent of the steam in a pressure cooker that has to be released or it will explode. That's not true. People who react by hitting, kicking, screaming, and swearing aren't dealing with the underlying cause of their anger. They just feel more angry."

9. The presidential pen did not formally strike the shackles from a single slave. Where Lincoln could presumably free the slaves—that is, in the loyal Border States—he refused to do so, lest he spur disunion. Where he could not—that is, in the Confederate states—he tried to. In short, where he could he would not, and where he would he could not. Thus, the Emancipation Proclamation was stronger on proclamation than emancipation.

10. Yet stress in itself isn't necessarily bad. What matters most is not the stressful situation itself, but an individual's response to it. By learning to anticipate stressful events, to manage day-to-day hassles, and to prevent stress overload, you can find alternatives to running endlessly on a treadmill of alarm, panic, and exhaustion. As you organize your schedule, find ways to release tension, and build up coping skills, you will begin to experience the sense of control and confidence that makes stress a challenge rather than an ordeal.

11. The physical work environment also has changed. Casual dress policies have become widespread. Even such hallowed institutions of Wall Street as Dean Witter, Goldman Sachs, and J. P. Morgan have permitted their employees to leave their dark suits in the closet—or at least hanging on the office door, in case an important client shows up. HBO and Credit Suisse First Boston each have invited Banana Republic to set up shop in their offices temporarily to help employees define—and find—casual clothing.

12. Many current psychologists have abandoned Freud; we will examine some of their criticisms later. However, his ideas still influence many areas of popular culture. Phrases such as "Freudian slip" and "unconscious" are part of our daily vocabulary. High school health textbooks present terms such as "reaction formation" and "repression" as if they were documented facts, rather than theoretical speculations.

Determining Implied Main Ideas

Some paragraphs do not contain a main idea sentence. In these instances, the main idea is implied; you need to determine it yourself. This should not be difficult because even with stated main ideas, you are first determining the main idea in your head. You need to ask the same two questions and to use any headings or subheadings as an aid to help you determine the topic.

A tiny Union ironclad, the *Monitor,* built in about one hundred days, arrived on the scene in the nick of time. For four hours, on March 9, 1862, the little "Yankee cheesebox on a raft" fought the wheezy *Merrimack* to a standstill. Britain and France had already built several powerful ironclads, but the first battle-testing of these new craft heralded the doom of wooden warships. A few months after the

© Thomson Wadsworth

historic battle, the Confederates destroyed the *Merrimack* to keep it from the grasp of advancing Union troops.

After reading the paragraph, you need to answer the first question, "What is this about?" Your answer should be: battling ironclads (ships). "What is the author telling you about these fighting ironclads?" First, the Union built one called the *Monitor,* and on March 9, 1862, it fought off the South's ironclad, the *Merrimack.* Next the author states that France and Britain had ironclads, but that this was the first battle using them, and wooden ships would no longer be used. Finally, the author states that the Confederates destroyed their ironclad to prevent the North from getting it. The implied main idea could thus be stated as follows:

> *The first battle using ironclads, fought on March 9, 1862, saw the North's **Monitor** defeat the South's **Merrimack** and signaled the end of wooden war ships.*

This sentence combines all three ideas. Again, it's like playing *The $10,000 Pyramid.* To take only one supporting detail and determine a main idea leaves out the other supporting details. You must also recognize minor details like France and Britain having built ironclads and the South destroying its ironclad so that the North would not get it. These sentences support the ideas that ironclads were important and that wooden ships would no longer be used.

Try this example yourself:

Employers sometimes terminate employees due to poor job performance, negative attitudes toward work and co-workers, or misconduct such as dishonesty or sexual harassment. Terminating poor performers is necessary, because they lower productivity and employee morale. Co-workers resent employees who receive the same pay and benefits as themselves without contributing fairly to the company's work. But employers need to document reasons for terminating employees carefully. Complaints of wrongful dismissal are often involved in complaints filed by the Equal Employment Opportunity Commission (EEOC). Besides poor performance, reasons for terminating employees include downsizing and outsourcing.

What is the topic of this paragraph?

_____

The answer is termination of employees. What is the author telling you about termination? Write the three important details.

1._____
2._____
3._____

The details would be these: (1) Employers terminate employees for different reasons. (2) It is important that employers terminate poor employees. (The third sentence provides a reason for this point.) (3) Employers should document reasons for termination. (The fifth sentence states a reason for this point and the sixth sentence provides some reasons for termination.)

Now look at the three supporting details and write a main idea incorporating the topic phrase *termination of employees.*

_____

_____

_____

Your answer may not be worded exactly as the following main idea sentence, but it should have the same basic idea:

> *Termination of employees is done by employers for many reasons and should be carefully documented.*

Now try the following exercises. Remember to determine the topic and supporting details first.

EXERCISE 8: DETERMINING IMPLIED MAIN IDEAS I

The following paragraphs have been excerpted from textbook chapters written on the same topics as those found in Part Two of this book; however, the readability is slightly lower because they are not from college textbooks. Use this exercise to practice finding the implied main idea. Then continue with Exercise 9 and more difficult excerpts from the college textbook chapters in Part Two of this book.

Write the implied main idea on the lines provided after each paragraph.

1. Abraham Maslow was an American psychologist. He developed what is called Maslow's hierarchy. A hierarchy shows the order of importance of something. Maslow's hierarchy shows the importance of people's needs. Maslow believed that five needs motivate people in this order: 1) physical, 2) safety, 3) belonging, 4) self-esteem needs, and 5) self-actualization. This hierarchy is much like climbing a ladder or going up steps. To get to the next higher step, you have to stand on the one below it.

—Robert Wandberg, *Making Tough Decisions*

Topic: _____

Main Idea: _____

_____

_____

2. Most Confederate wives had children equal in number to the years they had been married. What meager wages the soldiers sent home were likely to be lost in the mail. Since three out of four Southern families did not own slaves, the women left behind on the farms had to do everything.

—James I. Robertson, Jr., *Civil War! America Becomes One Nation*

Topic: _____

Main Idea: _____

_____

_____

3. The word stress has become a part of our vocabulary. Correctly, we label a large number of events as stressful: a death in the family, undergoing an operation, learning that the company one works for is going out of business, flunking an exam, having a serious illness, being stranded in the mountains by a blizzard. Some are mostly physical. Others are more emotional. Some are sudden short-term crises, while others are more chronic.

—Donald Oken, M.D., *Stress . . . Our Friend, Our Foe*

Topic: _____

Main Idea: _____

_____

_____

4. After the homecoming parades and celebrations were over, black veterans had to find work. Sadly their choices were often limited by discrimination and lack of experience. Most ended up in the same low-paying jobs they had held before the war, as day laborers in the North and field hands in the South. But many others obtained an education and trained for a profession or a skilled trade; others opened small businesses.

—Zak Mettger, *Till Victory Is Won: Black Soldiers in the Civil War*

Topic: _____

Main Idea: _____

_____

_____

5. In April 1861, the Civil War began with cheering crowds, waving flags, and patriotic songs. Both sides expected a short, glorious war. By the beginning of 1864, after thirty-two months of struggle and hundreds of thousands of casualties, the glory was gone but the war remained. The Civil War had become a struggle not just between armies but between entire populations.

—Ed. Carter Smith, *The Road to Appomattox*

Topic: _____

Main Idea: _____

_____

_____

6. Stress can be imposed by external demands, like parental expectations, deadlines, and peer pressure. It can also be generated from within by a teen's own expectations and goals. Regardless of whether the demands are internal or external, when adolescents perceive that the demands exceed the resources they think they have, their nervous systems activate a special response that disrupts normal body functions and produces physical and chemical changes within their bodies. These changes are called the General Adaptation Syndrome and are the body's way of preparing itself to deal with the new demand.

—Joe Anne Adler, *Stress: Just Chill Out!*

Topic: _____

Main Idea: _____

_____

_____

7. In November 1861, Lincoln added to McClellan's duties by naming him commander of all Union forces. But "Little Mac" soon showed a trait that angered Lincoln. He was far too cautious a soldier. A commander must often take risks to win battles, but, fearful of sacrificing his men, McClellan was reluctant to fight unless his army was in perfect order. Consequently, he delayed the Richmond attack throughout the rest of 1861 and the first months of 1862. The delay rankled Lincoln. It gave the South time to train its own men to a fighting pitch.

—Edward F. Dolan, *The American Civil War: A House Divided*

Topic: _____

Main Idea: _____

_____

_____

8. The most typical battle injury was a bullet wound. A soldier's chances of survival pretty much depended on where he was hit: Shots in the chest were almost always fatal. The poet Walt Whitman, a nurse during the war, described conditions in Washington where he served: "There is every kind of wound, in every part of the body. . . . There are twice as many sick as there are wounded. The deaths range from 7 to 10 percent

of those under treatment." Infections posed a constant threat, and during the Civil War, for every soldier killed in battle, almost two died of disease.

—Catherine Clinton, *Scholastic Encyclopedia of the Civil War*

Topic: _____

Main Idea: _____

_____

_____

9. Atlanta was one of the most important railroad junctions in the Confederacy, a crossroads filled with stores, foundries, warehouses, and arsenals. Its capture would strike terror in the hearts of civilians and politicians alike. Union General William T. Sherman made Atlanta his chief objective when he left Chattanooga on May 6. The fierce red-bearded warrior was known affectionately as "Uncle Billy" to his men, but he became one of the most hated figures in the Civil War South. Marching toward Atlanta, Sherman carried out the Union policy of total war.

—Catherine Clinton, *Scholastic Encyclopedia of the Civil War*

Topic: _____

Main Idea: _____

_____

_____

10. Some post-traumatic stress disorder sufferers may be unable to forget what happened. They may constantly feel anxious. They have trouble falling asleep at night. They may find it impossible to concentrate at school. They seem always to be looking over their shoulder, expecting something bad to happen. They may be extremely sensitive, misinterpreting or misunderstanding harmless words or innocent actions. They may be irritable with frequent outbursts of anger. They startle easily. They may feel they are damaged and will never lead a normal life.

—Marvin Rosen, Ph.D., *Understanding Post-Traumatic Stress Disorder*

Topic: _____

Main Idea: _____

_____

_____

EXERCISE 9: DETERMINING IMPLIED MAIN IDEAS II

Each of the following paragraphs is taken from the college discipline textbook chapters in Part Two and has an implied main idea. First write the topic; then write a complete sentence stating the main idea.

1. Notorious among the Copperheads was a sometime congressman from Ohio, Clement L. Vallandigham. This tempestuous character possessed brilliant oratorical gifts and unusual talents for stirring up trouble. A Southern partisan, he publicly demanded an end to the "wicked and cruel" war. The civil courts in Ohio were open, and he should have been tried in them. But he was convicted by a military tribunal in 1863 for treasonable utterances and was then sentenced to prison. Lincoln decided that if Vallandigham liked the Confederates so much, he ought to be banished to their lines. This was done.

Topic: _____

Main Idea: _____

_____

_____

2. One effect of cortisol and the other hormones, for example, is to speed the conversion of proteins and fats into carbohydrates, the body's basic fuel, so we have the energy to fight or flee from a threat. Another effect is to increase appetite and food-seeking behavior. Cortisol can cause excessive central or abdominal fat, which heightens the risk of diseases such as diabetes, high blood pressure, and stroke. Even slender, premenopausal women faced with increased stress and lacking good coping skills are more likely to accumulate excess weight around their waists, thereby increasing their risk of heart disease and other health problems.

Topic: _____

Main Idea: _____

_____

_____

3. In their continuing efforts to remain competitive against domestic and international rivals, a growing number of firms choose to hold down costs by evolving to a leaner organization. A number of functions that were performed previously by company employees may be contracted to other firms whose employees will perform them on a contractual basis in a practice called outsourcing. Outsourcing began on a small scale, with firms contracting out services such as maintenance, cleaning, and delivery. Services commonly outsourced today include housekeeping; architectural design; grounds, building, utility, and furniture maintenance; food service; security; and relocation services. Today, outsourcing has expanded to include outside contracting of many tasks once considered fundamental internal functions.

Topic: _____

Main Idea: _____

_____

_____

4. Off-the-job training involves some form of classroom instruction such as lectures, conferences, audiovisual aids, programmed instruction and special machines to teach employees everything from basic math and language skills to complex, highly skilled tasks. Some firms are replacing classroom training with computer-based training and online training programs. These programs can save an employer money by reducing travel costs and employee time away from work. In addition, computer-based training offers consistent presentations, since the training content won't vary with the quality of the instructor. Audio and visual capabilities help these systems to simulate the work environment better than some classroom training could and employees also benefit from greater control over the learning process. They can learn at their own pace and convenience, and they generally do not have to wait for the company to schedule a class before they can begin adding to their knowledge. Despite these advantages, firms also offer traditional classroom training, because it usually provides more opportunities for employees to interact with the instructor and with one another. Some people learn more readily from human interaction, and some have difficulty disciplining themselves to complete a computer-based learning program on their own.

Topic: _____

Main Idea: _____

_____

_____

5. The most alarming Confederate threat to the blockade came in 1862. Resourceful Southerners raised and reconditioned a former wooden U.S. warship, the *Merrimack,* and plated its sides with old iron railroad rails. Renamed the *Virginia,* this clumsy but powerful monster easily destroyed two wooden ships of the Union navy in the Virginia waters of Chesapeake Bay; it also threatened catastrophe to the entire Yankee blockading fleet. (Actually the homemade ironclad was not a seaworthy craft.)

Topic: _____

Main Idea: _____

_____

_____

6. Companies will continue to focus on reducing costs, including labor costs. For human resource managers, this trend creates a challenge of finding ways to motivate employees to increase their productivity by making the workplace attractive while reducing employment costs. Employee discontent with executive compensation will grow, and workers will demand an increasing portion of firms' profits. Company shareholders and investors will want stronger voices in determining the employment-related policies that influence a firm's economic performance.

Topic: _____

Main Idea: _____

_____

_____

7. The popular press has widely publicized the research on identical twins who have been reared apart. After all, it's fascinating to read about a pair of twins reared in separate homes who behave identically at the beach; both enter the water backwards and avoid water levels above their knees. Some critics suggest that the high degree of similarities between the twin pairs is partly due to a nonrandom sample. Furthermore, we must remember from the discussion of decision making in Chapter 8 that many unusual-looking outcomes can occur by chance alone.

Topic: _____

Main Idea: _____

_____

_____

8. The use of contingent workers, already about one-quarter of the workforce, is expected to grow. Contingent workers are employees who work part-time, temporarily, or for a length of time involved in fulfilling a specific contract. Hiring contingent workers enables companies to maintain the efficiency of a pared-down workforce while being flexible enough to meet new and changing needs. Traditionally, contingent workers often earned less pay than full-time employees and did not receive benefits or have access to employer-provided pension plans. However, among highly skilled workers, contingent work may be a profitable alternative to traditional employment, as these workers negotiate contracts with generous enough pay to cover self-paid benefits.

Topic: _____

Main Idea: _____

_____

_____

9. A prominent object-relations theorist is Nancy Chodorow, who argues that Freud did not pay enough attention to mothers in his theory. Chodorow argues that boys and girls both identify with their mother initially. Infant girls grow up with a feeling of similarity to their mother, which develops into interdependence, or a connection with others in general. Infant boys, in contrast, must learn that they are different from their mothers in order to develop a male identity. As a consequence, the two genders face different potential problems in their relationships. Specifically, females may not develop sufficient independence, and males may not develop close attachments.

Topic: _____

Main Idea: _____

_____

_____

10. A grimly determined Grant, with more than one hundred thousand men, struck for Richmond. He engaged Lee in a series of furious battles in the Wilderness of Virginia, during May and June of 1864, notably in the leaden hurricane of the "Bloody Angle" and "Hell's Half Acre." In this Wilderness Campaign, Grant suffered about fifty thousand casualties, or nearly as many men as Lee had at the start. But Lee lost about as heavily in proportion.

Topic: _____

Main Idea: _____

_____

_____

EXERCISE 10: DETERMINING MIXED STATED AND IMPLIED MAIN IDEAS

Determine the topic and the main idea of each of the following paragraphs. Write the topic on the line provided. If you find a stated main idea, double underline it; if the main idea is implied, write it on the lines provided.

1. You've probably heard that these are the best years of your life, but being a student—full-time or part-time, in your late teens, early twenties, or later in life—can be extremely stressful. You may feel pressure to perform well to qualify for a good job or graduate school. To meet steep tuition payments, you may have to juggle part-time work and coursework. You may feel stressed about choosing a major, getting along with a difficult roommate, passing a particularly hard course, or living up to your parents' and teachers' expectations. If you're an older student, you may have children, housework, and homework to balance. Your days may seem so busy and your life so full that you worry about coming apart at the seams. One thing is for certain: You're not alone.

Topic: _____

Main Idea: _____

_____

_____

2. In his book *A Great Place to Work,* author Robert Levering examined 20 top U.S. firms to discover what made them outstanding employers. He identified three factors, which he calls "the three *R*s." The first *R* is expanding workers' *responsibility* for their jobs. The second involves sharing the *rewards* that the firm generates as fairly as possible. The third *R* calls for ensuring that employees have rights, including some kind of grievance procedure, access to corporate records, and the right to confront those in authority without fearing reprisals.

Topic: _____

Main Idea: _____

_____

_____

3. Cocky George McClellan embodied a curious mixture of virtues and defects. He was a superb organizer and drillmaster, and he injected splendid morale into the Army of the Potomac. Hating to sacrifice his troops, he was idolized by his men who affectionately called him "Little Mac." But he was a perfectionist who seems not to have realized that an army is never ready to the last button and that wars cannot be won without running some risks. He consistently but erroneously believed that the enemy outnumbered his, partly because his intelligence reports from the head of Pinkerton's Detective Agency were unreliable. He was overcautious—Lincoln once accused him of having "the slows"—and he addressed the president in an arrogant tone that a less forgiving person would never have tolerated. Privately the general referred to his chief as a "baboon."

Topic: _____

Main Idea: _____

_____

_____

4. The TAT was designed to bring forth unconscious tendencies that a person may be unwilling or unable to reveal, such as difficulties with one's parents. The test takers presumably project their personality traits onto one or more of the characters in the scene. The people administering and scoring the test must be professionally trained, as you can imagine. Furthermore, the results are often interpreted within a psychodynamic framework. For instance, when a person omits reference to a gun shown in a TAT picture, the examiner may conclude that he or she tends to repress aggressive impulses.

Topic: _____

Main Idea: _____

_____

_____

5. Employer-sponsored benefits and programs for elder care and child care will become increasingly common as employers recognize the need to accommodate aging workers, single parents with children, and two-income families. As a result of improved treatments, some AIDS patients have returned to work. Employers must integrate these workers into their organizations and comply with laws that prohibit discrimination against them.

Topic: _____

Main Idea: _____

_____

_____

6. Employers must also observe various other legal restrictions governing hiring practices. Some firms try to screen out high-risk employees by requiring drug testing for job applicants, particularly in industries where employees are responsible for public safety, such as airlines and other public transportation. Drug testing is controversial, however, due to concerns about privacy. Also, positive test results may not accurately indicate drug use; traces of legal drugs, such as prescribed medications, may chemically resemble traces of illegal substances. Several states have passed laws restricting drug testing by employers.

Topic: _____

Main Idea: _____

_____

_____

7. In a ghastly gamble, on June 3, 1864, Grant ordered a frontal assault on the impregnable position of Cold Harbor. The Union soldiers advanced to almost certain death with papers pinned on their backs bearing their names and addresses. In a few minutes, about seven thousand men were killed or wounded.

Topic: _____

Main Idea: _____

_____

_____

8. Companies downsize for many reasons. The two most common objectives of downsizing are to cut overhead costs and streamline the organizational structure. Some firms report improvements in profits, market share, employee productivity, quality, and customer service after downsizing. Others, however, lose so many valuable, high-performing employees that their ability to compete declines.

Topic: _____

Main Idea: _____

_____

_____

9. As an example of reciprocal influences, consider a young woman who is outgoing and friendly and expects that she will be successful in interpersonal interactions (personal/cognitive). She will therefore be likely to introduce herself to strangers and react positively to them (behavior). Furthermore, someone who is outgoing and friendly is likely to seek out social situations, rather than sitting in her room (environment). The environment, in turn, promotes even more friendly behavior, more self-confidence, and an even greater expectation for success in interpersonal interactions. In contrast, a shy, withdrawn person will dread interpersonal interactions, avoid strangers, and stay away from social situations. This behavior and lack of exposure to new environments will encourage the person to become even more withdrawn and to expect future interactions to be unsuccessful.

Topic: _____

Main Idea: _____

_____

_____

10. Changes in the economic environment will create new sets of human resource needs. With a significant portion of economic growth occurring in countries outside the

U.S. and Europe, programs and practices of American firms will show a growing influence from conditions and cultures of other countries. Employers will need to recruit global managers and employees with international skills and experience. They also will require human resource plans that address the needs of employees in more than one country. Many will work with benefits providers and professional employer organizations that can help with international operations.

Topic: _____

Main Idea: _____

_____

_____

Determining the Main Idea of Longer Selections

One difference between an author's writing in a textbook and the writing that you learn about in a writing class is that authors do not always follow the rules about one main idea in each paragraph. Sometimes there are two or more main ideas in a paragraph and other times the same main idea may continue for two or three paragraphs. If the author has used a heading or subheading in boldface or italics, then the topic will remain the same for all paragraphs under the heading or subheading. What you need to do is keep asking yourself the second question,

"What is the author telling me about this topic?"

Sometimes the answer will be that the author is continuing the same idea, and other times you will realize that the details have changed.

Look at the following paragraph, the first paragraph under the subheading "Structure of Personality" in the psychology chapter. The first sentence of this paragraph is the main idea of the section; it defines the structure of personality. The remainder of the paragraph is about one part of the personality structure, the id.

Freud envisioned <u>three basic components to human personality: the id, the ego, and the superego.</u> He proposed that humans are born with an id, which is immature and illogical. The id consists of the basic drives—such as eating and sexual activities—and it provides the energy (or libido) for all human behavior. Freud also maintained that the id lacks moral judgment; it cannot distinguish between good and evil. The id is unconscious, a "hidden self" that can influence our everyday actions.

The subsequent paragraphs in the section define the other two parts of the personality and then go on to explain how they work together. You need to double underline the first sentence to indicate that it is the main idea of the entire section and not just the main idea of that paragraph. You also need to write an implied main idea sentence for this paragraph:

The id, the unconscious part of the personality, has many negative characteristics.

Look at a longer section titled "The Aftermath of the Nightmare," from the American history textbook. The entire section explains the effects of the Civil War, whereas each paragraph contains its own main idea. Double underline the main idea sentence in each paragraph.

[1]The Civil War took a grisly toll in gore, about as much as all of America's subsequent wars combined. Over 600,000 men died in action or of disease, and in all over a million were killed or seriously wounded. To its lasting hurt, the nation lost the cream of its young manhood and potential leadership. In addition, tens of thousands of babies went unborn because potential fathers were at the front.

[2]Direct monetary costs of the conflict totaled about $15 billion. But this colossal figure does not include continuing expenses, such as pensions and interest on the national debt. The intangible costs—dislocations, disunities,

wasted energies, lowered ethics, blasted lives, bitter memories, and burning hates—cannot be calculated.

[3]The greatest constitutional decision of the century, in a sense, was written in blood and handed down at Appomattox Courthouse, near which Lee surrendered. The extreme states' righters were crushed. The national government, tested in the fiery furnace of war, emerged unbroken. Nullification and secession, those twin nightmares of previous decades, were laid to rest.

[4]Beyond doubt the Civil War—the nightmare of the Republic—was the supreme test of American democracy. It finally answered the question, in the words of Lincoln at Gettysburg, whether a nation dedicated to such principles "can long endure." The preservation of democratic ideals, though not an officially announced war aim, was subconsciously one of the major objectives of the North.

[5]Victory for Union arms also provided inspiration to the champions of democracy and liberalism the world over. The great English Reform Bill of 1867, under which Britain became a true political democracy, was passed two years after the Civil War ended. American democracy had proved itself, and its success was an additional argument used by the disfranchised British masses in securing similar blessings for themselves.

[6]The "Lost Cause" of the South was lost, but few Americans today would argue that the result was not for the best. The shameful cancer of slavery was sliced away by the sword, and African-Americans were at last in a position to claim their rights to life, liberty, and the pursuit of happiness. The nation was again united politically, though for many generations still divided spiritually by the passions of the war. Grave dangers were averted by a Union victory, including the indefinite prolongation of the "peculiar institution," the unleashing of the slave power on weak Caribbean neighbors, and the transformation of the area from Panama to Hudson Bay into an armed camp, with several heavily armed and hostile states constantly snarling and sniping at one another. America still had a long way to go to make the promises of freedom a reality for all its citizens, black and white. But emancipation laid the necessary groundwork, and a united and democratic United States was free to fulfill its destiny as the dominant republic of the hemisphere—and eventually of the world.

The first paragraph is about the loss of men and the first half of the first sentence is the main idea: <u>The Civil War took a grisly toll in gore.</u>

The second paragraph discusses the costs, both monetary and intangible; thus, parts of two sentences need to be underlined to indicate the main idea: <u>Direct monetary costs of the conflict totaled about $15 billion,</u> and <u>The intangible costs</u> . . . <u>cannot be calculated</u>.

Paragraph 3 is about the agreement made at Appomattox and the end of secession and nullification. The last sentence mentions these by name and is therefore the best main idea sentence: <u>Nullification and secession, those twin nightmares of previous decades, were laid to rest.</u>

The fourth paragraph explains how the Civil War tested the American democracy and how democracy won. Again, the first sentence is the main idea: <u>Beyond doubt the Civil War . . . was the supreme test of American democracy.</u>

The fifth paragraph describes the war's effect on the world. The first sentence states the main idea best: <u>Victory for Union arms also provided inspiration to the champions of democracy and liberalism the world over.</u>

The last paragraph argues that the loss for the South was best for many American interests and that the United States was free to fulfill its destiny. The last sentence states this main idea best: <u>But emancipation laid the necessary groundwork, and a united and democratic United States was free to fulfill its destiny as the dominant republic of the hemisphere—and eventually of the world.</u>

Each of the paragraphs has its own main idea, but there is also a main idea for the entire section. Reread each main idea sentence and write a main idea for the entire section.

_____

_____

The main idea is as follows:

> *In the aftermath of the Civil War, the United States had to deal with both good and bad effects.*

Now, let's look at another example from the business textbook chapter. This subsection, "Downsizing," is a little different because the author writes about different aspects of downsizing rather than focusing on one aspect like the effects of the war in the previous example. The first and second paragraphs have implied main ideas. Write those implied main ideas in the margin. Double underline the main idea in the third and fourth paragraphs.

[1]During the 1980s and 1990s, employers terminated millions of employees, including many middle managers, through downsizing. Downsizing is the process of reducing the number of employees within a firm by eliminating jobs. Many downsizing firms have reduced their workforces by offering early retirement plans, voluntary severance programs, and opportunities for internal reassignment to different jobs. Employers who valued their employees helped them to find jobs with other companies and set up job counseling centers.

[2]Companies downsize for many reasons. The two most common objectives of downsizing are to cut overhead costs and streamline the organizational structure. Some firms report improvements in profits, market share, employee productivity, quality, and customer service after downsizing. Others, however, lose so many valuable, high-performing employees that their ability to compete declines. Chevron downsized some years back and ended up losing some of its most experienced managers. For a while, enough talented people remained, but eventually the company had to begin focusing more on developing management expertise. Now the company conducts annual reviews to spot possible human resource shortages before they occur, and it actively encourages retired employees to serve as consultants.

[3]Eliminating jobs through downsizing often has devastating effects on employee morale. Workers who remain after a downsizing worry about job security and become angry when they have to work harder for the same pay. As their feelings of commitment to their jobs wane, many employees may leave the firm voluntarily to seek employment offering greater job security. This situation has contributed to a shift in values away from loyalty to an employer in favor of concern for individual career success.

[4]Recent employee surveys reveal that workers are now more interested in *career security* than in *job security*. Specifically, the typical employee wants opportunities for training to improve the skills needed for the next job. People are willing to work hard at their current jobs, but they also want to share in the success of their companies by receiving pay-for-performance compensation and stock options. For human resource managers, the new employer–employee relationship requires developing continuous training and learning programs for employees.

The main idea of the first paragraph is implied; compare what you wrote in the margin to this main idea:

> *Downsizing is defined as the process of reducing the number of employees within a firm by eliminating jobs, which can be done in a number of ways.*

The second paragraph also has an implied main idea; check your main idea in the margin with the following main idea:

> *Downsizing is done for many reasons and has both advantages and disadvantages.*

The main idea of the third and fourth paragraphs can be found in the first sentence of each paragraph: <u>Eliminating jobs through downsizing often has devastating effects of employee morale. Recent employee surveys reveal that workers are now more interested in career security than in job security.</u> (The second sentence would also be acceptable for this paragraph because it restates the main idea in specific terms.)

The main ideas you have underlined and written become the supporting details of the subsection. Notice that the first three paragraphs all deal with downsizing, but the last paragraph deals with employee needs. Keep this in mind as you write a main idea for the entire subsection titled "Downsizing."

_____

_____

Because the author first discusses downsizing and then completes the section by discussing employee interests, the main idea of the subsection must include both of the topics. The following sentence is a good main idea sentence for this subsection:

Downsizing, the reduction of employees through the reduction of jobs, can be both positive and negative, but meeting employee needs can lessen the negative aspects.

Sometimes an author continues the same main idea in two or more paragraphs. Read the following two paragraphs:

Many firms are using the Internet as a recruiting tool. They may post jobs and accept résumés at their own Web sites, as well as list positions at job banks such as Headhunter.net, HotJobs.com, Monster.com, and America's Job Bank (www. ajb.dni.us), sponsored by the U.S. Department of Labor. Internet recruiting is a quick, efficient, inexpensive way to reach a large, global pool of job seekers. According to employers and career counselors, online recruiting is becoming the prevalent method of finding qualified job candidates.

Cisco Systems, which develops and sells Internet connection technology, relies heavily on electronic recruiting to help the company find thousands of new employees every year. To lure job hunters to the recruiting pages of its own Web site, Cisco posts banner ads on a variety of Web sites. The company targets its efforts by placing ads on job search sites like Monster.com, as well as by directing that ads appear on the screens of people with designated Web addresses, such as those of competitors. Other recruiting efforts, from newspaper advertising to booths at public events, also direct interested people to the Cisco Web site. Once there, job hunters find links to job descriptions, which they can search by title, job type, location, and other relevant factors. Links are even provided to Cisco employees who will share information about working there. Job hunters also can provide information about themselves, which helps the company link them to appropriate jobs. With these resources, Cisco receives over two-thirds of candidates' résumés electronically. Once those résumés arrive at Cisco, the company uses software to screen each one for key words that signal the expertise or backgrounds it needs to match résumés with job openings.

The first sentence of the first paragraph is the main idea for both paragraphs. The first paragraph states that the Internet is being used for recruitment. The second paragraph provides an extended example of this.

As you read a text, determine main ideas of individual paragraphs and sections headed by headings or subheadings. Authors use such headings to indicate that all of the paragraphs under them deal with the same topic. Use the headings or subheadings to help you determine the main ideas.

Writing a Summary of an Article

Writing a summary or summarizing something you have read is an assignment you will be required to complete in many different college classes. If you know how to determine the main idea of paragraphs as well as of a longer selection, then summarizing should be easy.

Follow these steps to summarize an article:

1. Preview the article: look over the length, read the title and any subtitles, look at any graphics and read their captions, and then read the first and last paragraphs.

2. Read the entire article.

3. Read the article a second time. Underscore the stated main ideas of paragraphs or write the implied main ideas in the margins as you read.

4. At the top of a sheet of looseleaf paper, begin your summary by recording the following bibliographic information and using the punctuation indicated in parentheses:

    author(s), last name first (comma) first name (comma)

    title of the article in quotation marks (use a comma before the end marks if no other punctuation is part of the title)

    title of the journal underlined or italicized

    date of the journal in parentheses and followed by a colon

    page(s) on which the article can be found followed by a period

5. Begin your summary with one sentence that summarizes the entire article.

6. Read the first two or three main ideas of the article; then, without looking at those main ideas, rewrite them in paragraph form. Continue until you have finished all of the main ideas. Use the author's name and/or refer to the author when restating the main ideas.

7. Check your draft against the original for accuracy and emphasis. Add transitions so that your summary is coherent and unified.

8. Edit for mechanical and grammatical correctness.

9. Ask someone to read your summary and give you feedback on how well you wrote it.

As an option, you may include bibliographic information in the first sentence of your summary instead of in a heading. If you use this option, the title of the article should be placed within quotation marks; the name of the journal or magazine should be underlined or italicized. Also include the author name, date of the journal or magazine, and page number(s).

SAMPLE SUMMARY: "FOOD FIGHT!"

Following is an article from the June 1999 issue of *American Demographics* titled "Food Fight!" by Heather Chaplin (pp. 64–65). Read the article, then read the summary of the article. Use it as a model for your own summarizing.

Food Fight!

Children of the World, Unite

Tongue Splashers Really Tap into a Kid's Id

by Heather Chaplin

Pancakes with syrup poured in the shape of a smiley face. Spaghetti thrown against the wall and made to stick. Mashed potatoes molded into peaks and valleys. Peas shoveled up the nose. Ever since the first parent crawled out of the slime and plunked down a plate of victuals in front of the first kid, <u>children have played with their food.</u>

Today's kids still mess around at mealtime and still consider the objectively gross extremely cool. Nothing new there. What is new is that savvy <u>manufacturers and marketers are creating delectables that play right back,</u> or at least encourage a sense of play. Take Tongue Splashers. One of four new Popsicles just out from Good Humor-Breyers, the Tongue Splasher is literally a big red mouth of strawberry and lemon ice, complete with dangling tonsil and lolling tongue, atop a Popsicle stick. Embedded in the tongue is a gum ball which releases food dyes that turn one's mouth different colors, or "awesome hues," as Good Humor puts it.

Geez, what's wrong with a good old ice-cream sandwich? Born in an era when change is as much a part of life as rising in time for Saturday morning cartoons, <u>today's kids</u> have different standards of what's a treat. Their <u>taste for the new and exciting has accelerated,</u> and, to keep pace, <u>treats aimed at children are growing more outrageous every year.</u> The key words bandied about—extreme, mega, fun, surprising, interactive—are not ones I immediately associate with something that goes in my mouth. But then, my idea of food fun when I was a kid was letting my ice cream melt into soup and then slurping it up. Cool!

Things are much more complicated now. Last year, <u>6-to-11-year-olds,</u> as the kids market is generally defined, <u>spent $25 billion of their own money and influenced another $187 billion of spending,</u> according to Paul Kurnit, president of Griffin Bacal, a Manhattan-based advertising agency that specializes in marketing to kids and families. Those are big numbers from such little people, especially considering kids spent less than half that five years ago, Kurnit says. The <u>increase is due</u> in part to the country's <u>growing affluence</u> in recent years, <u>but</u> also to a tendency toward bigger <u>allowances,</u> more <u>dual-income families,</u> and <u>greater childhood freedom,</u> generally. Raised by baby boomers and Gen Xers who encourage them to participate in family decisions, and exposed to media from all sides, kids are becoming active and sophisticated consumers at an extremely young age. At the same time, marketers say, their very childishness makes them <u>particularly good targets.</u>

"Carving out a niche for yourself is what childhood is all about," says Johann Wachs, a senior partner and director of planning and research at Ogilvy & Mather and a children's marketing specialist. "Products can help define who you are."

Other marketers agree that <u>kids</u> possess the combination of being "<u>fundamentally insecure and trying to find their place in the world,</u>" according to Kurnit. Translation: they're <u>really into new stuff.</u>

So what do these little <u>consumers want?</u> Well, they wa<u>nt things</u> that seem <u>disgusting to their parents.</u> They want products that will be the <u>subject of school-yard chatter.</u> They want to <u>interact with and be entertained by</u> what they purchase, whether it's a toy, a pair of sneakers, or an ice-cream cone. <u>Good Humor–Breyers' 1999 summer line of Popsicles,</u> which hit the shelves last month, <u>satisfies all of the above.</u> Besides the Tongue Splasher, with its exploding-color gum ball, the ice cream giant has developed the Big Bang, a layering of sweet and sour ice embedded with little popping candies. There's also Micro Pops, made of tiny water ice beads of different flavors that explode when you bite them.

"The products seem right on," says Ogilvy & Mather's Wachs. "If it grosses out Mom, if it empowers me [the kid] by setting me apart from my parents, then it's good." And really, what self-respecting adult is going to buy a Popsicle that turns the teeth funny colors,

DROP ME OFF AT THE STORE

The top five items kids bought with their own money			
	TOTAL 8–17	AGES 8–12	AGES 13–17
Food/drink	25%	28%	21%
Clothes	14%	6%	23%
Audio/visual	9%	6%	12%
Shoes	4%	3%	6%
Toys	3%	5%	—

Source: Roper Starch Worldwide 1995

Figure 2.1

MAKE UP YOUR OWN MIND

Top ten items kids say they can choose without parental permission	1998				1997
	TOTAL 6–17	AGES 6–7	AGES 8–12	AGES 13–17	TOTAL 6–17
Candy or snacks	72%	38%	66%	93%	72%
Soft drinks	70%	30%	63%	93%	72%
Food from fast-food places	64%	30%	54%	98%	64%
Breakfast cereal	56%	36%	49%	71%	NA
Games or toys	53%	29%	48%	70%	45%
Books	50%	22%	42%	71%	51%
Clothes	47%	NA	25%	67%	41%
Athletic shoes or sneakers	47%	NA	26%	67%	41%
CDs/pre-recorded tapes	42%	8%	28%	71%	41%
Magazines	41%	12%	28%	37%	38%

Source: Roper Starch Worldwide 1998

Figure 2.2

explodes, or comes in the shape of a giant tongue? It's a pretty safe bet that Tongue Splashers, Micro Pops, and Big Bangs will be the domain of the 6-to-11 crowd, which already spends the largest percentage of its income on snacks.

"The products say, 'Come play with me,'" notes Kurnit of Griffin Bacal. "They will appeal to kids across the board."

It's good to know kids are still united in their appreciation of a good treat. While we old folks often shy away from products and brands that would identify us with the wrong demographic group—too white, too black, too working class, too upper crust—kids don't pay attention to such things, Kurnit says. They really do bond over the longing for the newest Popsicle. In fact, Popsicles do roughly as well across economic, regional, gender, and ethnic lines, according to Brian Manning, director of marketing at Good Humor–Breyers. This is due partly to the fact they still cost less than 80 cents a pop. But it's also about the idea that kids have a well-developed sense of what is kid stuff, and what is not. And nothing else really matters.

"Kid culture is a culture unto itself," Kurnit says. "It cuts across demographic origins."

I have no doubt that Tongue Splashers will be easily absorbed into the highest realms of kiddie culture. I keep wondering, though, how parents feel about this. There's no way my mother would have condoned Tongue Splashers, unless it was my birthday, or I'd recently fallen off the roof, or lost a limb. Apparently, though, fighting over food is as passé as the anti-consumerist values my mother preached. Parents today, exhausted by their work lives and loathe to waste precious family time arguing, have loosened the reins of control when it comes to food, marketers say.

"Today's parents don't have the time or the energy," Wachs says. "They pick their battles extremely carefully and they decide what is really worth fighting over." Food does not make the short list.

Here is the sample summary:

Chaplin explains that today's kids, like all kids, enjoy playing with food, but unlike kids of yesteryear, today's kids have new standards and more money for companies to attain. Food manufacturers are creating foods that are not only fun but encourage playfulness. Six-to-eleven-year-olds spent $25 billion of their own money in 1998 and influenced the spending of another $187 billion. This increase from previous years comes from growing allowances and more freedom from dual-income families. Consequently, manufacturers see this population as an easy target; they are kids who want to gross out their parents and stand out among their peers. Good Humor–Breyers fulfills these needs with new products that contain popping bubbles or color-changing gumballs. It is a good market because these products attract kids of both genders across economic, regional, and ethnic lines. Kids know what good kid stuff is and parents have loosened controls on food products.

Practice with Periodicals

Practice finding the main ideas and summarizing an article. Read the article "Is Freud Finished?" in Part Three. Then do steps 1 through 9 on page 52 to complete your summary.

Journal Entry

Choose five sentences from "Is Freud Finished?" in Part Three. Write each sentence on a sheet of looseleaf paper and under each sentence write what you were thinking as you read that sentence.

Textbook Link

In another textbook you are using, read through one section under one heading. Determine the main idea of each paragraph in that section. Analyze the writing style: Does the author have one main idea in each paragraph? Is there more than one? Does the author continue the main idea in more than one paragraph?

CHAPTER **3**

DETERMINING ORGANIZATIONAL PATTERNS

In this chapter you will learn to

- Identify six organizational patterns of expository (factual) paragraphs
- Identify transitions or signal words to help you determine the organizational pattern
- Use organizational patterns to help you determine important details

Knowing the organizational patterns of paragraphs will help you find the supporting details you need to know and to study for a content-area test. When you read and take notes from a textbook, you have to be selective. It is impossible to remember everything for a test, so your job as a student is to narrow the information so that you have to remember only a small amount. Knowing the organizational patterns will also help you remember the details.

ORGANIZATIONAL PATTERNS OF EXPOSITORY WRITING

Sometimes in order to understand the main idea of a paragraph, you need to know in what organizational patterns the author is writing. In a writing class, you become familiar with different organizational patterns of paragraphs or essays. Narratives (personal stories) and descriptions are two organizational patterns seldom used in textbooks, with the exception of literature textbooks. Authors of textbooks primarily use expository writing—writing that states facts.

A number of organizational patterns are used in expository writing: example or list, comparison or contrast, cause and effect, definition, steps or time order, and classification. If you can identify the type of expository writing the author is using with the topic, then it becomes easier to determine the main idea and supporting details. For example, if you were reading a cause-and-effect paragraph, the important details would be the causes or effects. If you know the main idea and organizational pattern, then the major details fall into place.

Certain signal words, or *transitions,* will help you decide the organizational pattern the author is using and what kinds of details you have to know. The following sections discuss six organizational patterns listing common signal words or transitions for each, along with a sample paragraph for which important transitions are underlined, and the main idea and supporting details are identified.

Example or List

In this organizational pattern, the author offers examples to clarify or to prove a point. If more than one example is included (a list) the examples are not placed in any specific order. They may be moved around within the paragraph without any change in the meaning. If a transition is used, it is often used to show one extended example. When authors list a number of different examples in one paragraph, they often use no transitions.

Transitions: *for example, for instance, to illustrate this point, to be specific, such as, specifically*

Read the following paragraph, which contains one example introduced by the underlined transitional phrase and another marked by an asterisk.

Increases in protected employees and discrimination lawsuits have elevated the importance of human resource managers in the hiring process. To prevent violations, human resource personnel must train managers involved in interviewing to make them knowledgeable about employment law. For example, the law prohibits asking an applicant any questions relating to marital status, number of children, race, nationality, religion, or age. Interviewers also may not ask questions about applicants' criminal records, mental illness histories, or alcohol-related problems. In addition, human resource managers can help organizations establish systems to promote fair employment practices. *Home Depot was sued by women who claimed they were more often unfairly steered toward lower-paying jobs than were males with similar qualifications. As part of the settlement, Home Depot began using software called the Job Preference Program, which automates the process of ranking candidates for jobs and promotions. Not only does the software provide store managers with lists of candidates based on legitimate criteria, it also creates lists of questions and criteria for evaluating the answers. Besides creating more opportunities for its female employees, Home Depot's software has helped its managers make better employment decisions.

Main Idea: First sentence (Increases in protected employees and discrimination lawsuits have elevated the importance of human resource managers in the hiring process.)

Important Details: The authors provide specific examples of questions that interviewers may not ask of prospective employees. Then, the authors continue the main idea by stating that human resource managers can also assist in establishing fair employment practices. The asterisked example of Home Depot is a specific example of this type of assistance in a workplace. The authors do not introduce this example with a transition, but it is obvious that an example is being used.

The following paragraph is one of multiple examples of different types. The single asterisks indicate the important details or types of benefits and the double asterisks indicate the examples of the important details.

In addition to wages and salaries, firms provide many benefits to employees and their families as part of the compensation they pay. *Employee benefits are rewards **such as retirement plans, insurance, sick leave, child care and elder care, and tuition reimbursement, *provided entirely or in part at the company's expense. *Some benefits are required by law. **Firms are required to make social security contributions and payments to state employment insurance and workers' compensation programs that protect workers in case of job-related injuries and illnesses. **The Family and Medical Leave Act of 1993 requires covered employers to offer up to 12 weeks of unpaid job-protected leave to eligible employees. *Firms voluntarily provide other employee benefits, **such as child care and health insurance, to help them attract and retain employees. Sometimes companies try to change the way benefits, such as pension plans, are structured, which creates controversy.

Main Idea: First sentence (In addition to wages and salaries, firms provide many benefits to employees and their families as part of the compensation they pay.)

Important Details:

1. Employee benefits are rewards provided entirely or in part at the company's expense (for example, retirement plans, insurance, sick leave, child care, elder care, and tuition reimbursement).

2. Some benefits are required by law (such as, social security contributions, payments to state employment insurance and workers' compensation, and up to 12 weeks' leave for certain health conditions).

3. Some benefits are voluntary (for instance, child care and health insurance).

When you read a paragraph that contains many examples of the main idea, it is important to know one or two of the examples for a test.

Comparison or Contrast

In a *contrast* paragraph, the author presents opposing ideas.

> **Transitions:** *but, however, on the contrary, on the other hand, otherwise, rather, while, yet*

A *comparison* paragraph shows both similarities and differences between two topics.

> **Transitions:** *all of the transitions found in the contrast paragraph plus the following—similarly, likewise, by the same token, by comparison*

Some psychodynamic therapists and theorists believe that people can temporarily forget about an especially traumatic event. More specifically, they argue that traumatized individuals may repress these memories. In contrast, cognitive psychology researchers are more likely to argue that the memories are not really repressed, and some people may even create false memories for events that did not really occur.

Main Idea: Psychodynamic therapists and cognitive psychologists have different views on what happens to memories of traumatic events.

Important Details:

1. Psychodynamic therapists and theorists believe that memories of traumatic events are repressed.
2. Cognitive psychologists do not believe in repression and do believe that sometimes people make up traumatic events.

Cause and Effect

This organizational pattern will usually contain either one cause and several effects or one effect and several causes. The effects are the direct results of the causes. For example, read the following paragraph about the Battle of Bull Run. The Battle of Bull Run is the topic, and the author is stating the effects of the battle. The author may also include a separate paragraph about the causes of the battle. Seldom does the author mix both causes and effects in one paragraph. When you read this cause-and-effect paragraph, note that the effects occurred because of the Battle of Bull Run. When you read any cause-and-effect paragraph, determine whether the author is presenting one cause and many effects or one effect and many causes.

> **Transitions:** *because, thus, consequently, as a result, hence, then, therefore*

The "military picnic" at Bull Run, though not decisive militarily, bore significant psychological and political consequences, many of them paradoxical. Victory was worse than defeat for the South, because it inflated an already dangerous overconfidence. Many of the Southern soldiers promptly deserted, some boastfully to display their trophies, others feeling that the war was now surely over. Southern enlistments fell off sharply, and preparations for a protracted conflict slackened. Defeat was better than victory for the Union because it dispelled all illusions of a one-punch war and caused the Northerners to buckle down to the staggering task at hand. It also set the stage for a war that would be waged not merely for the cause of Union but also, eventually, for the abolitionist ideal of emancipation.

Main Idea: First sentence

Important Details: Effects of the Battle of Bull Run

1. Inflated Southern confidence and caused Southern soldiers to desert; impacted enlistment and caused preparations for extended conflict to slacken
2. Helped the North realize that the war would not be an easy one for it and caused it to buckle down
3. Set the stage for the Civil War, not just for union but also eventually for emancipation

Definition

In this organizational pattern, the author defines an important term for the reader. Examples may be given, but the main purpose of the paragraph is to define; each sentence helps the reader understand the term.

Transitions: *in other words, defined,* (**vocabulary term**) *is/are, means*

Flextime <u>is</u> a scheduling system that allows employees to set their own work hours within constraints specified by the firm. An employer may require employees to be at work between the core hours of 10 A.M. and 3 P.M. rather than the regular workday hours of 9 A.M. to 5 P.M. Outside the core hours, employees can choose when to start and end their workdays, opting either to arrive at work early, say at 7 A.M., and leave early, or to arrive later and work later than the standard day. Flextime works well in jobs where employees can work relatively independently but not so well when they must work together in teams, such as in manufacturing, or must provide direct customer services. Flextime is common in European countries; an estimated 40 percent of the Swiss workforce and 25 percent of German workers set flextime schedules. Growing numbers of U.S. firms are offering flextime, and increasing numbers of employees are taking advantage of this benefit.

Main Idea: Flextime is defined.

Important Details:

1. A scheduling system that allows employees to set their own work hours within constraints set by the firm
2. Works well when employees can work independently
3. Common in European countries
4. Growing numbers of U.S. firms are offering flextime

Time Order

This organizational pattern can be used for two purposes. The first involves instances in which the author wants to explain the steps necessary for a particular process. The order of details is extremely important.

Transitions: *first, second, then, next, finally, now, before, after, while, during*

Selye's general adaptation syndrome, which describes the body's response to a stressor—whether threatening or exhilarating—consists of three distinct stages. <u>1</u>. Alarm—When a stressor <u>first</u> occurs, the body responds with changes that temporarily lower resistance. Levels of certain hormones may rise; blood pressure may increase. The body quickly makes internal adjustments to cope with the stressor and return to normal activity. 2. Resistance—If the stressor continues, the body mobilizes its internal resources to try to sustain homeostasis. For example, if a loved one is seriously hurt in an accident, we initially respond intensely and feel great anxiety. <u>During</u> the subsequent stressful period of recuperation, we struggle to carry on as normally as possible, but this requires considerable effort. 3. Exhaustion—if the stress continues long enough, we cannot keep up our normal functioning. Even a small amount of additional stress at this point can cause a breakdown.

Main Idea: The stages in the general adaptation syndrome

Important Details:

1. Alarm—when a stressor occurs, the body's resistance lowers.
2. Resistance—if the stressor continues, the body strives for homeostasis.
3. Exhaustion—if the stress continues, normal functioning discontinues.

The other purpose for writing a time order paragraph is to explain a series of events in the order that the events occurred. Again, the order in which the details occur in the paragraph is important. Transitions may be used, but other time word clues may also be included in the paragraph.

Abraham Maslow (1908–1970) was born in Brooklyn, New York. As a young psychologist, he was initially attracted to behaviorism. However, when his first child was born, Maslow realized that behaviorism could not account for the miracle and mystery of human infancy.

Main Idea: Details of Abraham Maslow's life are given.

Important Details:

1. Maslow was born in New York.
2. He is attracted to behaviorism.
3. When his first child is born, he realizes that behaviorism does not have all the answers.

Classification

This organizational pattern divides a whole into parts or categories. Usually three or more categories are used. Many of the transitions and signal words are the same as those for other organizational patterns, depending on what is being categorized and why the author is categorizing. The categories may be made to show similarities or differences, to show processes, to give examples, to define, or to show causes or effects of each category.

Transitions: Look for specific words that signal categorization: *classify, categorize, sort, group, kinds of, levels, styles, types.*

Many employers balance rewarding workers with maintaining profits by linking more of their pay to superior employee performance. They try to motivate employees to excel by offering some type of incentive compensation in addition to salaries or wages. Most implement several types of incentive compensation programs:

- profit sharing, which awards bonuses based on company profits;
- gain sharing, which awards bonuses based on surpassing predetermined performance goals;
- lump-sum bonuses, which award one-time cash payments based on performance; and
- pay for knowledge, which distributes wage or salary increases as employees learn new job tasks.

Main Idea: Four types of incentive compensation exist.

Important Details:

1. Profit sharing—bonuses based on company profits
2. Gain sharing—bonuses based on surpassing predetermined performance goals

3. Lump-sum bonuses—one-time cash payments based on performance
4. Pay for knowledge—wage or salary increases as employee learns new job tasks

As with main ideas, authors do not always stay with one particular organizational pattern in each paragraph. When the main idea changes, often the organizational pattern changes with it. Read the following paragraph; it contains two main ideas and two organizational patterns.

> [1]Employers must also observe various other legal restrictions governing hiring practices. [2]Some firms try to screen out high-risk employees by requiring drug testing for job applicants, particularly in industries where employees are responsible for public safety, such as airlines and other public transportation. [3]Drug testing is controversial, however, due to concerns about privacy. [4]Also, positive test results may not accurately indicate drug use; traces of legal drugs, such as prescribed medications, may chemically resemble traces of illegal substances. [5]Several states have passed laws restricting drug testing by employers.

This paragraph begins by stating that legal restrictions governing hiring practices exist and then cites an example; however, the third sentence changes the main idea to drug testing being controversial, the fourth sentence states the reasons or causes, and the last sentence states an effect.

As you read the textbook chapters, be aware that sometimes organizational patterns change just as main ideas change within a paragraph. Always ask yourself what the author is telling you about the topic. The answer to this question helps you determine the main idea and the organizational pattern.

EXERCISE 11: DETERMINING ORGANIZATIONAL PATTERNS AND IMPORTANT DETAILS I

For each of the following paragraphs, determine and write the main idea, the organizational pattern, and the supporting details on the lines provided. The excerpts are taken from textbooks covering the same topics as those chapters in Part Two of this book but are slightly easier reading.

1. As May ended, Grant approached Cold Harbor. Although Cold Harbor was just a run-down crossroads tavern, Lee and Grant both realized its importance. It was only eight miles from Richmond; if Grant maneuvered Lee into a decisive fight so close to the Confederate capital, he could destroy the Army of Northern Virginia and link up with Union reinforcements moving inland from the Pamunkey River.

—Ed. Carter Smith, *The Road to Appomattox*

Main Idea: _____

_____

Organizational Pattern: _____

Important Details: _____

_____

_____

_____

2. Of all the injustices experienced by black soldiers during the Civil War none stung more sharply than the issue of unequal pay. Though they did the same work and ran the same risks as white soldiers, black soldiers were paid much less. In 1863, the standard monthly salary for a white enlisted man was thirteen dollars, plus a three-dollar clothing allowance, for a total of sixteen dollars. White noncommissioned officers received up to twenty-one dollars a month, as well as three dollars for clothes.

—Zak Mettger, *Till Victory Is Won: Black Soldiers in the Civil War*

Main Idea: _____

_____

Organizational Pattern: _____

Important Details: _____

_____

_____

_____

3. Besides helping freedmen and women seek justice, black soldiers helped in organizing and building schools and churches for their communities. In the spring of 1866, members of the Third Colored Arkansas Volunteers built a home for orphaned children in Helena, Arkansas. "The amount of work that has been done on the grounds by the Soldiers is immense," reported a company lieutenant. "From an almost unbroken forest, it has been cleared, fenced and a large part of it planted, and four substantial buildings erected suitable for the wants of the children and those who have the care of them."

—Zak Mettger, *Till Victory Is Won: Black Soldiers in the Civil War*

Main Idea: _____

_____

Organizational Pattern: _____

Important Details: _____

_____

_____

_____

4. Abraham Lincoln and Jefferson Davis had much in common. They were fellow Kentuckians, born within one hundred miles of each other. They were only eight months apart in age. Both men were unusually tall and thin. Both read much, thought deeply, and were skilled public speakers. Each was elected president of his nation on the eve of war. Each proved to be a devoted patriot who sincerely loved his country.

—James I. Robertson, Jr., *Civil War! America Becomes One Nation*

Main Idea: _____

_____

Organizational Pattern: _____

Important Details: _____

_____

_____

_____

5. Some employers ask applicants to submit letters of recommendation with their resumes. A letter of recommendation is a letter from a reference. It tells employers why an applicant is a good worker. These letters tell what skills applicants have. Applicants can give copies of these letters to employers.

—Stuart Schwartz and Craig Conley, *Interviewing for a Job*

Main Idea: _____

_____

Organizational Pattern: _____

Important Details: _____

_____

_____

_____

6. Applicants should also think ahead about questions employers may ask during interviews. Employers may ask why applicants want the jobs. They may ask why applicants left their last jobs. Some employers ask about applicants' strengths and weaknesses.

—Stuart Schwartz and Craig Conley, *Interviewing for a Job*

Main Idea: _____

_____

Organizational Pattern: _____

Important Details: _____

_____

_____

_____

7. Stress has been defined as the physical and chemical response of the body to any demand made upon it. That demand includes good things, such as winning a class election, and bad things, such as being picked on by the class bully. The body's mechanical response is the same; the only difference is the intensity of the response and the length of the response. When good things happen to us, like sinking the hoop in an important basketball game or being chosen for the pep squad, the body's reaction is short, complete, and most often not as intense as the body's reaction when facing fearful or bad stress. Whether the stressor (the collective name for any demand) is good or bad, the body's reaction is stress.

—Joe Anne Adler, *Stress: Just Chill Out!*

Main Idea: _____

_____

Organizational Pattern: _____

Important Details: _____

_____

_____

_____

8. Research has shown that people who are optimistic—who understand that bad things can happen and that there is little they can do to prevent them, but that they will be temporary—are healthier and more successful in life. People who are pessimistic—who feel somehow responsible for the bad things that happen to them, and believe that the bad things will continue to happen to them—are more depressed and feel helpless.

—Marvin Rosen, Ph.D., *Understanding Post-Traumatic Stress Disorder*

Main Idea: _____

_____

Organizational Pattern: _____

Important Details: _____

_____

_____

_____

9. Giving up after a few "failures" is like trying to hit a bull's eye the first time. It is unrealistic to expect to be on target immediately. You have to "fail" a number of times to succeed. By "failing," you discover ways that don't work. You go step by step toward the way that does work. This is how you aim for excellence.

—Matthew Ignoffo, Ph.D., *Everything You Need to Know About Self-Confidence*

Main Idea: _____

_____

Organizational Pattern: _____

Important Details: _____

_____

_____

_____

10. How can we tell the difference between needs and goals? Needs are something all people have, even if they are not aware of it. Goals are the way each individual seeks to meet the need. People will likely have different goals to meet the same need. For example, two people may be meeting the need for self-esteem. One may choose to become a professional athlete. The other may study hard to pass the next math quiz. Each person has a different goal, yet each goal builds that person's self-esteem.

—Robert Wandberg, *Making Tough Decisions*

Main Idea: _____

_____

Organizational Pattern: _____

Important Details: _____

_____

_____

_____

EXERCISE 12: DETERMINING ORGANIZATIONAL PATTERNS AND IMPORTANT DETAILS II

For each of the following paragraphs taken from the discipline textbook chapters in Part Two, determine and write the main idea, the organizational pattern, and the supporting details on the lines provided.

1. The campaign was noisy and nasty. The Democrats cried, "Old Abe removed McClellan. We'll now remove Old Abe." They also sang, "Mac Will Win the Union Back." The Union party supporters shouted for "Uncle Abe and Andy" and urged, "Vote as you shoot." Their most effective slogan, growing out of a remark by Lincoln, was "Don't swap horses in the middle of the river."

Main Idea: _____

_____

Paragraph Type: _____

Supporting Details: _____

_____

_____

_____

2. Organizations also help employees improve their performance by providing feedback about their past performance. A performance appraisal is an evaluation of an employee's job performance by comparing actual results with desired outcomes. Based on this evaluation, managers make objective decisions about compensation, promotions, additional training needs, transfers, or firings. Rating employees' performance and communicating perceptions of their strengths and weaknesses are important elements in improving a firm's productivity and profits. Performance appraisals are not confined to business. Government agencies, not-for-profit organizations, and academic institutions also conduct them.

Main Idea: _____

_____

Paragraph Type: _____

Supporting Details: _____

_____

_____

_____

3. Let's examine the five levels in Maslow's hierarchy, beginning with the most basic level:

1. *Physiological needs:* We need food, water, sleep, and sex. Notice that these needs are also those that motivate lower animals.

2. *Safety needs:* These needs include security, protection, and the avoidance of pain.

3. *Belongingness* and love needs: These needs focus on affiliation with other people, affection, and feeling loved; sexual relationships as an expression of affection can also be included in this category.

4. *Esteem needs:* We also need to respect ourselves and to win the esteem of other people. Otherwise we feel discouraged and inferior, according to Maslow, so we will not strive for the highest level of hierarchy.

5. *Self-actualization needs:* A person who has satisfied all the lower needs can seek self-actualization, attempting to reach her or his full potential.

Main Idea: _____

_____

Paragraph Type: _____

Supporting Details: _____

_____

_____

_____

4. The landmark Battle of Antietam was one of the decisive engagements of world history—probably the most decisive of the Civil War. Jefferson Davis was perhaps never again so near victory as on that fateful summer day. The British and French governments were on the verge of diplomatic mediation, a form of interference sure to be angrily resented by the North. An almost certain rebuff by Washington might well have spurred Paris and London into armed collusion with Richmond. But both capitals cooled off when the Union displayed unexpected power at Antietam, and their chill deepened with the passing months.

Main Idea: _____

_____

Paragraph Type: _____

Supporting Details: _____

_____

_____

_____

5. The first signs of stress include muscle tightness, tension headaches, backaches, upset stomach, and sleep disruptions (caused by stress-altered brain-wave activity). Some people feel fatigued, their hearts may race or beat faster than usual at rest, and they may feel tense all the time, easily frustrated and often irritable. Others feel sad; lose their energy, appetite, or sex drive; and develop psychological problems, including depression, anxiety, and panic attacks. Stress can lead to self-destructive behaviors, such as drinking, drug use, and reckless driving. Some people see such acts as offering an escape from the pressure they feel. Unfortunately, they end up adding to their stress load.

Main Idea: _____

_____

Paragraph Type: _____

Supporting Details: _____

_____

_____

_____

6. Human resource managers develop staffing plans based on their organization's competitive strategies. They forecast the number of employees their firm will need and determine the types of skills necessary to implement its plans. Human resource managers are responsible for adjusting their company's workforce to meet the requirements of expanding in new markets, reducing costs (which may require laying off employees), or adapting new technology. They formulate both long-term and short-term plans to provide the right number of qualified employees.

Main Idea: _____

_____

Paragraph Type: _____

Supporting Details: _____

_____

_____

7. Raw Yankee recruits swaggered out of Washington toward Bull Run on July 21, 1861, as if they were headed for a sporting event. Congressmen and spectators trailed along with their lunch baskets to witness the fun. At first the battle went well for the Yankees. But "Stonewall" Jackson's gray-clad warriors stood like a stone wall (here he won his nickname), and Confederate reinforcements arrived unexpectedly. Panic seized the green Union troops, many of whom fled in shameful confusion. The Confederates, themselves too exhausted or disorganized to pursue, feasted on captured lunches.

Main Idea: _____

_____

Paragraph Type: _____

Supporting Details: _____

_____

_____

_____

8. Meditation helps a person reach a state of relaxation, but with the goal of achieving inner peace and harmony. There is no one right way to meditate, and many people have discovered how to meditate on their own, without even knowing what it is they are doing. Among college students, meditation has proven especially effective in increasing relaxation. Most forms of meditation have common elements: sitting quietly for 15 to 20 minutes once or twice a day, concentrating on a word or image, and breathing slowly and rhythmically. If you wish to try meditation, it often helps to have someone guide you through your first sessions. Or try tape recording your own voice (with or without favorite music in the background) and playing it back to yourself, freeing yourself to concentrate on the goal of turning the attention within.

Main Idea: _____

_____

Paragraph Type: _____

Supporting Details: _____

_____

_____

_____

9. The terms *wages* and *salary* are often used interchangeably, but they refer to different types of pay systems. Wages represent compensation based on an hourly pay rate worked or the amount of output produced. Firms pay wages to production employees, maintenance workers, and sometimes retail salespeople. Salaries represent compensation calculated on a weekly, monthly, or annual basis. Office personnel, executives, and professional employees usually receive salaries.

Main Idea: _____

_____

Paragraph Type: _____

Supporting Details: _____

_____

_____

_____

10. Today, off-the-job training frequently involves use of the Internet. The Web provides a convenient means of delivering text, audio, and video training materials to employees wherever they are located. Online training programs also can offer interactive learning, such as simulations in which employees see the results of their decisions.

Main Idea: _____

_____

Paragraph Type: _____

Supporting Details: _____

_____

_____

_____

Practice with Periodicals

Read the article "Alternative and Complementary Modalities for Managing Stress and Anxiety" in Part Three. Choose three different paragraphs, and indicate your choice by copying the first sentence of each on a sheet of paper. Then write the main idea, the organizational pattern, and a list of the major details for each.

Journal Entry

Read "Alternative and Complementary Modalities for Managing Stress and Anxiety" in Part Three. Choose and use one of the alternative therapies for one week; then write a report on how well it relieved your stress. Be sure to give specific examples of how you used the therapy and whether it worked.

Textbook Link

In another textbook you are using, read through one section under one heading. Determine the organizational pattern and important details for each paragraph. Explain why the author uses the specific organizational patterns to give you the information you need to understand.

CHAPTER 4

READING AND INTERPRETING GRAPHICS

In this chapter you will learn to

- Identify and interpret seven types of graphics
- Determine the main idea of a graphic
- Read a graphic and answer questions about it

Many students look at a graphic as something that takes up space and requires that many fewer words to read. Realistically, graphics (pictures) are worth a thousand words. If you take the time to look at, read, and understand all of the graphics and their captions within a chapter before you actually read that chapter, you will end up saving yourself valuable time. This chapter will present information to help you interpret different types of graphics and save you that time.

SEVEN TYPES OF GRAPHICS

In a textbook chapter, graphics may include pictures, illustrations, maps, charts, and graphs. Authors often use graphics to present a large amount of information in a small space. They also use them to present information in a systematic and easy-to-read format. Finally, authors use graphics to aid reader understanding—to help you understand concepts.

Just as when you read a paragraph, you should determine the main idea of a graphic by answering these two questions:

"What is this graphic about?"

"What is the author telling me about the topic in this graphic?"

Now, add one additional question to help you understand the author's purpose for the graphic:

"Why is the author presenting this information in a graphic?"

The answer to the third question will give you an idea of what types of test questions could be derived from a graphic. You may even want to formulate some test questions of your own to prepare for a test. Authors use seven types of graphics along with photographs in their textbooks. Whenever you come upon any graphic or photo, make sure to look at its title and read any caption under or beside it. Do this as you preview or page through the chapter before reading it. These graphics will help set up hooks in your brain so that when you read about that information in the text, you will have some background knowledge. As you read a chapter, stop and make connections to what is presented in the graphics. At times, the same information is discussed in the text, and the graphic presents a systematic method to help you remember it. At other times, the author will not discuss a graphics material in the text, so you need to rely on your interpretation of the graphics.

The following sections describe the seven types of graphics and provide tips to help you interpret each type when you come upon it in your reading. Answer the questions after each subsection and then check your answers.

Illustration

An illustration is a diagram of something (see Figure 4.1). An author will use an illustration to help the reader visualize a concept. Many science textbooks will use illustrations to depict what is being said in the text. Copy them in your notes; often, your brain will remember the illustration more easily than the verbal explanation. Be sure to read the illustration's title and any captions so that you clearly understand what is being shown.

1. Topic: _____
2. Main Idea: _____
   _____
3. Why did the author use an illustration?
   _____
   _____
4. What needs are at the base of the hierarchy?
   _____
5. What needs must one fulfill before needing love?
   _____

Answers

1. The topic is Maslow's hierarchy of needs; this is taken from the title as well as the illustration.
2. The main idea is that Maslow's hierarchy has five levels: physiological, safety, love, esteem, and self-actualization.
3. The author uses this illustration so that the reader can easily see, in graphic form, how the needs build on one another.
4. Physiological needs are at the base.
5. One must fulfill physiological and safety needs first.

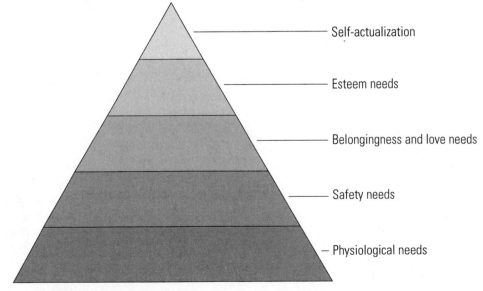

Figure 4.1 Maslow's hierarchy of needs

Table

A table presents information in columns and rows (see Table 4.1). The information is organized and compact. To find specific information, look in the left column and usually the top row for specific titles; then go across and down to find the cell that intersects both the column and the row.

1. Topic: _____

2. Main Idea: _____

   _____

3. Why did the author use this table?

   _____

   _____

4. In the category of independence, what percentage of people do the Japanese men feel are superior to them?

   _____

5. People from which country and gender are most modest about their abilities?

   _____

6. People from which country and gender are most self-serving or least modest about independence?

   _____

Answers

1. The topic is judgments about the percentage of people who are superior to self in specific categories or domains.

2. The main idea is that U.S. men and women have different perceptions about how others are superior to them than do Japanese men and women.

3. The author uses this table to help the reader easily compare perceptions of U.S. men and women to Japanese men and women in categories of ability, independence, and interdependence.

4. Forty-six percent.

5. Japanese women are most modest about abilities. (Note that high numbers indicate modesty.)

6. U.S. men are least modest about their independence. (Note that low numbers indicate self-serving bias.)

Table 4.1 Judgments about the percentage of people who are superior to the self in each specified domain (averaged across all participants in each group)*

Domain	UNITED STATES		JAPAN	
	Men	Women	Men	Women
Abilities	36%	47%	49%	58%
Independence	33%	34%	46%	54%
Interdependence	30%	26%	40%	49%

*High numbers indicate modesty, and low numbers indicate a self-serving bias.
Source: Markus & Kitayama (1991b).

Pie Chart

A pie chart is so named because it looks like a pie that has been cut into slices. Each slice represents part of the whole pie; therefore, you can compare numbers within the pie. For example, in the pie chart shown in Figure 4.2, you can determine that more money is spent on legally required benefits than retirement benefits even though only percentages are given.

1. Topic: _____

2. Main Idea: _____

   _____

3. Why did the author use a pie chart?

   _____

   _____

4. On what benefit is the second highest amount of money spent?

   _____

   _____

5. List two examples of legally required benefits.

   _____

   _____

Answers

1. The topic is types of employer-paid benefits.
2. The main idea is that money spent for employee benefits can be categorized into six areas.
3. The author used a pie chart so that the reader can compare the amounts spent for each area.
4. The second highest amount of money is spent on paid leave (24 percent).
5. Each of the following is a type of legally required benefit: Social Security, Medicare, unemployment insurance, and workers' compensation.

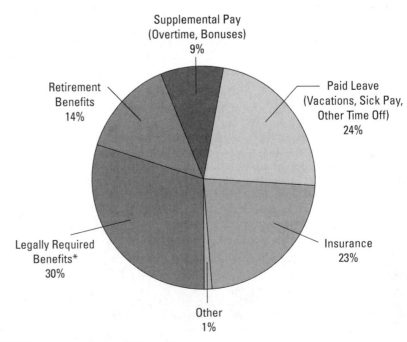

Figure 4.2 Types of employer-paid benefits

Line Graph

A line graph is probably the most common graphic used to show change over time. If time is being used as a means of measure, the bottom horizontal line will show the time, and the vertical line on the left will show some increment that deals with the topic of the graph. Be careful to determine the increments being used on both lines. For example, the graph in Figure 4.3 provides the number of adults using the Internet for business from home *in millions* on the vertical line and the years on the horizontal line. In all graphs, it is important to understand what numbers represent. Finding the main idea of the graph first will help you determine this.

1. Topic: _____

2. Main Idea: _____

   _____

3. Why did the author use this line graph?

   _____

   _____

4. Approximately how many adults were using the Internet for business from home in 1999?

   _____

5. Approximately how many adults were using the Internet for business from home in 2000?

   _____

Answers

1. The topic is the number of adults using the Internet for business at home between 1995 and 2004.

2. The main idea is that the number of adults using the Internet for business at home increased from 1995 to 2004.

3. The author uses the line graph to show the how the numbers of employees using the Internet at home has increased.

4. Twenty-one million adults used the Internet at home for business in 1999. (You must have the million specified.)

5. Between 24 and 25 million adults used the Internet at home for business in 2000.

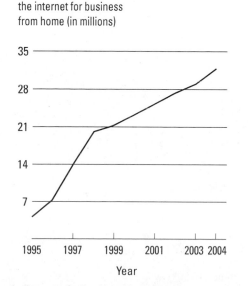

Figure 4.3 Workers using the internet for business from home

Map

A map represents an area or part of it (see Figure 4.4). A map is used by an author to familiarize readers with a specific area and to provide information about that area. If you are not familiar with the particular area, be sure to get a frame of reference; know what countries or bodies of water border the map being shown. You also need to have a good understanding of what the author is showing on the map. Be sure to read all captions and know what any numbers or shadings represent.

1. Topic: _____

2. Main Idea: _____

   _____

3. Why did the author use a map?

   _____

   _____

4. Which states declared the slaves free by state action?

   _____

   _____

5. Which states set the slaves free as a result of the Thirteenth Amendment in 1865?

   _____

Answers

1. The topic is emancipation in the South.
2. The main idea is that emancipation in southern states occurred at different times as a result of different laws.
3. The author probably used a map to help the reader visualize where the states are and to show a pattern for emancipation.
4. The following states freed slaves by state action: Maryland, West Virginia, Tennessee, and Missouri.
5. The states that freed the slaves as a result of the Thirteenth Amendment in 1865 were Kentucky and Delaware.

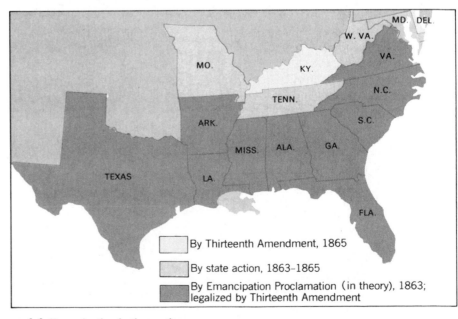

Figure 4.4 Emancipation in the south

Bar Graph

A bar graph can be shown either vertically or horizontally (as is the one in Figure 4.5). The base of the bars usually indicates time, if time is being shown, whereas the sides are another numerical increment. As you did with the line graph, note the increments between numbers and be sure you know what the numbers represent. For example, in the bar graph pictured here, the bars represent percentages, not whole numbers, of respondents.

1. Topic: _____

2. Main Idea: _____
   _____

3. Why did the author use the bar graph?
   _____
   _____

4. What percentage of respondents indicated that affiliation is very or extremely important?
   _____

5. Do more people find affiliation or work content very or extremely important?
   _____
   _____

Answers

1. The topic is the results of rewards of work.
2. The main idea is that employees find different motivators very or extremely important in their work.
3. The author uses a graph to compare the different types of motivation for work.

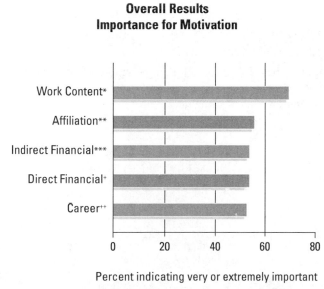

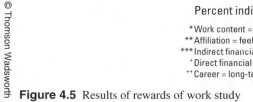

Figure 4.5 Results of rewards of work study

4. Approximately 55 percent of the respondents reported affiliation as very or extremely important.

5. This is not answered on the bar graph. Because no total number of surveyed respondents is given, the answer to this question cannot be stated or implied.

Flow Chart

A flow chart presents written information in steps with arrows used to show the direction of the steps. For some information, the arrows move in only one direction as in Figure 4.6. Other times, the arrows may go in different directions to show how some steps may be repeated or lead to each other. A flow chart may even be circular to show a process that does not begin or end in any one particular place.

1. Topic: _____

2. Main Idea: _____

   _____

3. Why did the author use the bar graph?

   _____

   _____

4. What can influence behavior?

   _____

5. If an employee has a need for belongingness, how can an employer motivate that employee to work harder?

   _____

   _____

Answers

1. The topic is the process of motivation.

2. The main idea is that the process of motivation begins with a need and moves toward need satisfaction.

3. The author uses a flow chart to show the process of how a need is satisfied and how motivation is part of that satisfaction.

4. Needs and motivations influence behavior.

5. If an employee has a need for belongingness, the employer may motivate that employee with team meetings and teamwork. (Other answers that provide social opportunities during work are acceptable.)

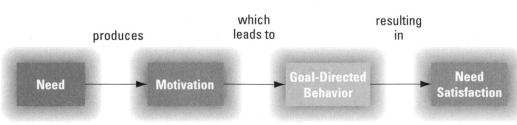

Figure 4.6 The process of motivation

© Thomson Wadsworth

EXERCISE 13: READING AND INTERPRETING GRAPHICS

Read and interpret each graphic to help you answer the questions.

A.

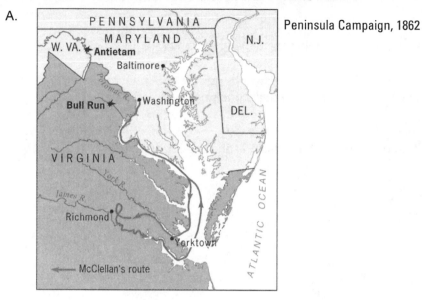

Peninsula Campaign, 1862

1. Topic: _____

2. Main Idea: _____

_____

3. Which river did McClellan come to on his way to Richmond?

_____

4. Which river did McClellan use to depart from Richmond?

_____

B.

Table 4.2 Freud's five stages of psychosexual development

Age	Stage	Description
0–18 months	Oral stage	Stimulation of the mouth produces pleasure; the baby enjoys sucking, chewing, biting.
18–36 months	Anal stage	Stimulation of the anal region produces pleasure; the toddler experiences conflict over toilet training.
3–6 years	Phallic stage	Self-stimulation of the genitals produces pleasure; the child struggles with negative feelings about the same-gender parent.
6–puberty	Latency	Sexual feelings are repressed; the child avoids members of the other gender.
Puberty onward	Genital stage	Adolescent or adult has mature sexual feelings and experiences pleasure from sexual relationships with others.

1. Topic: _____

2. Main Idea: _____

_____

3. During which stage would sex not be important?

_____

4. During which age is the individual concerned with oral pleasure?

_____

     C. Freud's model of the conscious and the unconscious

1. Topic: _____

2. Main Idea: _____

_____

3. Which part of the personality is mostly in the conscious?

_____

4. Why does this model show the id as completely submerged?

_____

     D.

1. Topic: _____

2. Main Idea: _____

_____

3. Why do the arrows in this flow chart move both right and left?

_____

4. How is the Type Z method of control influenced by the American and Japanese methods?

_____

_____

5. Was Type Z decision making influenced by the American or Japanese methods?

_____

American	Type Z	Japanese
Short-Term Employment	Long-Term Employment	Lifetime Employment
Individual Decision Making	Consensual Decision Making	Consensual Decision Making
Individual Responsibility	Individual Responsibility	Collective Responsibility
Rapid Evaluation and Promotion	Slow Evaluation and Promotion	Slow Evaluation and Promotion
Explicit, Formalized Control	Implicit, Informal Control with Explicit, Formalized Measures	Implicit, Informal Control
Specialized Career Path	Moderately Specialized Career Path	Nonspecialized Career Path
Segmented Concern	Holistic Concern, Including Family	Holistic Concern

E.

Table 4.3 Some representative defense mechanisms proposed

Defense Mechanism*	Definition	Example
Repression	Pushing back unacceptable thoughts and feelings into the unconscious.	A rape victim cannot recall the details of the attack.
Regression	Acting in ways characteristic of earlier life stages.	A young adult, anxious on a trip to his parents' home, sits in the corner reading comic books, as he often did in grade school.
Reaction formation	Replacing an anxiety-producing feeling with its exact opposite, typically going overboard.	A man who is anxious about his attraction to gay men begins dating women several times a week.
Displacement	Redirecting an emotion (e.g., anger) toward someone who is less dangerous than the "real" object of that emotion.	A husband, angry at the way his boss treats him, screams at his wife.
Projection	Attributing your own unacceptable thoughts and feelings to another person.	An employee at a store, tempted to steal some merchandise, suspects that another employee is stealing.

*These five defense mechanisms are listed with the New Terms at the end of this chapter.
Sources: Holmes, 1984b; Monte, 1995; Plutchik, 1995.

1. Topic: _____

2. Main Idea: _____

_____

3. Which defense mechanism explains why a student who has been cheating would accuse other students in the class of the same act?

_____

4. Create your own example of displacement.

_____

_____

_____

5. What words accompanying this figure alert you to the fact that the information on this chart is important to know for a test?

_____

_____

F. Student Snapshot: Freshman Stress

1. Topic: _____

2. Main Idea: _____

_____

3. In what year did approximately 18 percent of freshmen say that they felt overwhelmed?

_____

4. Between what long period of years did the percentage of freshman stress continue to go only up on this graph?

_____

Practice with Periodicals

Write a paragraph summary of Table 1 in the article "Self-Esteem and Self-Efficacy of College Students with Disabilities" in Part Three. Read the article to help you understand the graphic.

Reading Journal Entry

As you read the article and analyze Table 1 in "Self-Esteem and Self-Efficacy of College Students with Disabilities" in Part Three, think about your thinking and record the thoughts you have about the table as you interpret it.

Textbook Link

Find two graphics in another textbook you are using, write the main idea, and explain why the author is using each. Determine if the author also explains the information in the text.

CRITICAL THINKING SKILLS: UNDERSTANDING AN AUTHOR'S INTENT

At the college level, you will be required to use higher levels of thinking when reading a textbook and taking a test. Making inferences and differentiating between fact and opinion are important skills to help you interpret the reading material both in a college textbook and on a test. This unit will help you learn those skills necessary to think critically. Understanding the main idea is the first step, but skills beyond this literal step require you to analyze the author's writing and to make predictions about as well as evaluations of the textual material. Unit 4 will help you understand these skills and will introduce those levels of thinking to you.

CHAPTER 5

MAKING INFERENCES

In this chapter you will learn to

- Differentiate between connotative and denotative meanings
- Identify and interpret figurative language
- Make an inference

An *inference* is a conclusion that one draws based on information that one has. To *infer* means to read between the lines, to draw conclusions from what has been put down for you in black and white. It means you have to think about what you have read and sometimes to mix that with some background knowledge or experience that you have had. But you cannot read too much into the material, or you may draw incorrect conclusions that the material does not support. You need to be aware of how words are used. This chapter will give you some guidelines to follow when you have to make an inference.

SKILLS TO USE IN MAKING AN INFERENCE

Distinguishing between Connotation and Denotation

The *denotative* meaning of a word is its dictionary meaning. It is straightforward and factual. The *connotative* meaning of a word has a unique feeling or picture that it evokes. For example, if you read that a beautiful young lady was handed a rose and that a cute young chick was given a daisy, your mind draws two very different pictures. The first has a much more positive connotation, even though both pictures are about a female receiving a flower. Authors use connotative meanings of words to supply information without writing it all out in black and white. For example, read the following sentence from the American history textbook chapter:

> Later in that dreary autumn of 1863, with the graves still fresh, Lincoln journeyed to Gettysburg to dedicate the cemetery.

The words *dreary* and *graves still fresh* give a connotation to this sentence. The author might have stated the sentence in this manner:

> In autumn of 1863, not long after the Battle of Gettysburg, Lincoln journeyed to Gettysburg to dedicate the cemetery.

By using the first sentence rather than the second, the author helps the reader feel the sadness and grief of that time.

Read the following sentences. Change the underlined words first to convey a positive connotation and then to present a negative connotation.

EXAMPLE

He gave the <u>girl</u> a <u>flower.</u>

Positive: He gave the princess a rose.
Negative: He gave the babe a dandelion.

1. The <u>animal</u> was in a <u>shelter.</u>

    Positive:_____

    Negative: _____

2. The <u>dress</u> was made of <u>material.</u>

    Positive:_____

    Negative: _____

3. The <u>bird</u> landed on the <u>house.</u>

    Positive:_____

    Negative: _____

4. <u>John</u> walked from the <u>building</u> to the <u>car.</u>

    Positive:_____

    Negative: _____

Authors of textbooks are not as obvious with connotative language as you may have been with some of the examples you created in the sentences above, but they still use connotative language in their writing. For example, the authors of an American history textbook might have a bias for the North as they write about the Civil War; the words they choose might lead the reader to feel that Southerners were the "bad guys."

Interpreting Figurative Language

Figurative language is the use of an expression to convey a meaning; it is language that cannot be taken literally. The author compares or identifies one thing to or with another that has a connotation or meaning familiar to the reader. For example, a rose has a positive connotation, so to compare your love with a rose identifies your love in a positive way.

Writers use many types of figurative language; some types are used more often by authors of expository textbooks. The following list defines several types of figurative language and gives examples from textbooks.

Personification attributes human characteristics to an animal, an object, or a concept.

EXAMPLE

"War . . . is all hell," admitted Sherman later, and he proved it by his efforts to "make

Georgia howl."

Georgia (a state) cannot yell, but the author has given it this human characteristic to emphasize the terrible destruction that took place.

A **simile** is a comparison of things that are essentially unlike. It is expressed using words or phrases such as *like* or *as*. For example, you might say that a tulip is like a lily. This comparison uses the word *like* but is not considered a simile because the two flowers are essentially alike. However, if you were to say that your love is like a rose, this would be a simile because you use the word *like* and compare two things—your love and a flower—that are essentially not alike.

EXAMPLE

Like a shameful cancer, slavery was sliced away by the sword.

The authors compare slavery with cancer in order to explain how slavery is like a disease that spreads and kills.

A **metaphor** is a comparison that does not use words such as *like* or *as*. The figurative term is substituted for or identified with the literal term.

EXAMPLE

Nullification and secession, those twin nightmares of previous decades, were laid to rest.

The authors do not say that nullification and secession were *like* twin nightmares; they use a direct comparison. This gives the reader a stronger idea of how unsettling they were to the country.

Metonymy is using some significant aspect or detail of an experience to represent the entire experience.

EXAMPLE

The presidential pen did not formally strike the shackles from a single slave.

The presidential pen is associated with the Emancipation Proclamation. Here, the example tells the reader that the writing and issuing of the Emancipation Proclamation did not free a single slave.

Synecdoche is substituting a part of something for the whole or the whole for a part.

EXAMPLE

His numerous critics, condemning him for not having boldly pursued the ever-dangerous Lee, finally got his scalp.

The words *his scalp* (a part of McClellan) are used instead of *McClellan* in this sentence.

Allusion is a comparison with some incident in history, a well-known quotation, geographic location, or current event.

EXAMPLE

As a serious student of warfare who was dubbed "Young Napoleon," McClellan had seen plenty of fighting, first in the Mexican War and then as an observer of the Crimean War in Russia.

"Young Napoleon" is a reference to Napoleon Bonapart, who is considered a military genius.

Interpreting Idioms

Aside from figurative language, authors may also use idioms. An *idiom* is an expression that cannot be understood from the individual meanings of the words of which it is composed. For example, some common idioms that we use are *take a break, hardly scratch the surface, once in a blue moon,* and *keep your eye on the basket.* If you think about each of these statements, none of them literally makes sense; to take a break does not mean to break anything, and basketball players do not literally keep their eyes on the basket. Yet, you know what these idioms mean because you have heard them in context many times. Authors of textbooks also use idioms. For example, in the American history textbook chapter, the authors note that General Lee remarked that he had lost his right arm when "Stonewall" Jackson was killed in battle. If you were not aware that this is an idiom, you might think that General Lee had lost his right arm in battle. However, if you identify it as an idiom and know the meaning, you understand that Jackson was extremely important to Lee (like one's right arm is important to anyone), and that Lee felt that he had lost an important commander.

If you read material containing figurative language or idioms and are not aware that they are being used, the material will not make sense. When this happens, reread the material and look for possible uses of these types of speech. You may even have to ask someone for the particular meaning of an idiom or for an explanation of a comparison. Literature textbooks will contain many more uses of figurative language than other textbooks. Do not be afraid to ask for help if you do not understand.

EXERCISE 14: INTERPRETING FIGURATIVE LANGUAGE

Read the following examples of figurative language used in the American history textbook chapter. Write the literal meaning of each underlined word or words on the line provided.

1. The Northern navy enforced the blockade with <u>high-handed</u> practices.

_____

2. Antietam served as the needed emancipation <u>springboard.</u>

_____

3. A new <u>slaughter pen</u> was prepared when General Burnside yielded his command to "Fighting Joe" Hooker, an aggressive officer but a head-strong subordinate.

_____

4. The twin victories also conclusively <u>tipped the diplomatic scales</u> in favor of the North, as England stopped delivery of the Laird rams to the Confederates and as France killed a deal for the sale of six naval vessels to the Richmond government.

_____

5. After seizing Savannah as a <u>Christmas present</u> for Lincoln, Sherman's army veered north into South Carolina, where the destruction was even more vicious.

_____

6. Political infighting in the North added greatly to Lincoln's <u>cup of woe.</u>

_____

7. The greatest constitutional decision of the century, in a sense, was <u>written in blood</u> and handed down at Appomattox Court House, near which Lee surrendered.

_____

8. Hostile factions whipped up considerable agitation to <u>shelve</u> homely "Old Abe" in favor of his handsome nemesis, Secretary of the Treasury Chase.

_____

9. A soldier of <u>bulldog tenacity,</u> Grant was the man for this meat-grinder type of warfare.

_____

10. A soldier of bulldog tenacity, Grant was the man for this <u>meat-grinder type</u> of warfare.

_____

Making an Inference

In order to answer an inference question, remember that you will not find the information in black and white. If you are asked a question to which you cannot find the answer, assume that you are being asked to infer. Go to the part of the text that refers to the idea in the question.

Reread that section of the text. Look for something that you have read in the passage to back up an answer that you have chosen as you make your inference. Sometimes you need to determine the answer through the process of elimination. In these instances, you will be able to find reasons why some of the answers are not true.

If you are being asked to make an inference, remember that authors will sometimes draw on universal experiences. A *universal experience* is one that many people have had or know about. To understand what an author is implying you may have to use some background experience or knowledge, something that you have previously learned or experienced. For example, you overhear two students talking in the student lounge. Here's the conversation:

Student 1: Did you have a good time Friday night?
Student 2: Yeah, the music was great.
Student 1: Was it crowded?
Student 2: I'll say, but we were pretty close to the stage and could see the group really well.

Here are the facts that you know:

1. Student 2 was out on Friday night.

2. Student 2 heard some great music while she was out.

3. Student 2 was close to a stage and could see a group well.

Because of your individual experience with or knowledge of concerts, here is what you can reasonably infer, and why: Student 2 attended a musical concert. You can infer this because of your experience with or knowledge of concerts; they are usually crowded, and groups play music on a stage. You cannot infer what type of concert it was or where it was even if you know that there was a concert near you. Student 2 does not give enough information to infer those facts. Your background knowledge, together with what you heard, helps you make the inference.

When you read a textbook and need to make inferences, follow these rules:

- Determine the main idea of the selection.
- Carefully reread the section that you think contains the information that you need to make the inference.
- Use your background knowledge to fill in gaps of information.
- Do not infer more than what can be true from the given information.

EXERCISE 15: MAKING INFERENCES

When you need to infer, it is important that you understand the main idea first. In the following exercises, first determine and main idea of each paragraph; then answer the inference questions.

1. When President Lincoln issued his call to the states for seventy-five thousand militiamen on April 15, 1861, he envisioned them serving for only ninety days. Reaffirming his limited war aims, he declared that he had "no purpose, directly or indirectly, to interfere with slavery in the States where it exists." With a swift flourish of federal force, he hoped to show the folly of secession and rapidly return the rebellious states to the Union. But the war was to be neither brief nor limited. When the guns fell silent four years later, hundreds of thousands of soldiers on both sides lay dead, slavery was ended forever, and the nation faced the challenge of reintegrating the defeated but still recalcitrant South into the Union.

Northern newspapers, at first sharing Lincoln's expectation of a quick victory, raised the cry, "On to Richmond!" In this yeasty atmosphere, a Union army of some thirty thousand men drilled near Washington in the summer of 1861. It was ill prepared for battle, but the press and the public clamored for action. Lincoln eventually concluded that an attack on a smaller Confederate force at Bull Run (Manassas Junction), some thirty miles southwest of Washington, might be worth a try. If successful, it would demonstrate the superiority of Union arms. It might even lead to the capture of the

Confederate capital at Richmond, one hundred miles to the south. If Richmond fell, secession would be thoroughly discredited, and the Union could be restored without damage to the economic and social system of the South.

Main Idea of Both Paragraphs: _____

_____

In 1861, what did Lincoln see as the main cause of the Civil War? (Circle the letter of the *best* answer.)

     a. slavery

     b. federal force

     c. secession

     d. militiamen

Why did the authors title this section "Bull Run Ends the 'Ninety-Day War' "?

_____

_____

_____

Why was Bull Run chosen as the battle site? (Circle the letter of the *best* answer.)

     a. It was not far from the Southern capital.

     b. It was occupied by a small Confederate force.

     c. It wasn't far from Washington.

     d. All of the above.

2. Either employer or employee can take the initiative to terminate employment. Employees decide to leave firms to start their own businesses, take jobs with other firms, or retire. Some firms ask employees who leave voluntarily to participate in exit interviews to find out why they decided to leave. These interviews give employers a chance to learn about problems in the workplace, such as unreasonable supervisors or unfair work practices.

Main Idea: _____

_____

Why would an employee leave when he or she really didn't want to leave? (Circle the letter of the *best* answer.)

     a. The employee is retiring.

     b. The employee doesn't feel valued.

     c. The employee is starting his or her own business.

How does an exit interview help the company? (Circle the letter of the *best* answer.)

     a. It gives input on what is wrong with the company.

     b. It imparts information on how to make employees happy.

     c. It gathers information about office morale.

     d. All of the above.

3. Robert E. Lee, having broken the back of McClellan's assault on Richmond, next moved northward. At the Second Battle of Bull Run (August 29–30, 1862), he encountered a Federal force under General John Pope. A handsome, dashing, soldierly figure, Pope boasted that in the western theater of war, from which he had recently come, he had seen only the backs of the enemy. Lee quickly gave him a front view, furiously attacking Pope's troops and inflicting a crushing defeat.

Main Idea: _____

_____

What do the authors mean by writing that Lee had "broken the back of McClellan's assault"?

_____

_____

Where had General Pope fought prior to the Second Battle of Bull Run?

_____

_____

Explain what General Pope meant when he boasted that he had seen only the backs of the enemy.

_____

_____

4. For years therapists encouraged people to "vent" their anger. However, recent research shows that letting anger out only makes it worse. "Catharsis is worse than useless," says psychology professor Brad Bushman of Iowa State University, whose research has shown that letting anger out makes people more aggressive, not less. "Many people think of anger as the psychological equivalent of the steam in a pressure cooker that has to be released or it will explode. That's not true. People who react by hitting, kicking, screaming, and swearing aren't dealing with the underlying cause of their anger. They just feel more angry."

Over time, temper tantrums sabotage physical health as well as psychological equanimity. By churning out stress hormones, chronic anger revs the body into a state of combat readiness, multiplying the risk for stroke and heart attack—even in healthy individuals. In one study by Duke University researchers, young women with "Jerry-Springer type anger," who tended to slam doors, curse, and throw things in fury, had higher cholesterol levels than those who reacted more calmly.

Main Idea: _____

_____

True or False: According to the research in these paragraphs, when you're angry, you should "let it out." Explain your answer.

_____

Chronic anger affects the following: (Circle the letter of the *best* answer.)

     a. physical health

     b. psychological health

     c. both *a* and *b*

     d. none of the above

When you are extremely angry with someone, what should you do?

_____

_____

5. Lee had achieved a brilliant, if bloody, triumph. Yet the ironies of his accomplishment are striking. If McClellan had succeeded in taking Richmond and ending the war in mid-1862, the Union would probably have been restored with minimal disruption to the "peculiar institution." Slavery would have survived, at least for a time. By his successful defense of Richmond and defeat of McClellan, Lee had in effect ensured that the war would endure until slavery was uprooted and the Old South thoroughly destroyed. Lincoln himself, who had earlier professed his unwillingness to tamper with slavery where it already existed, now declared that the rebels "cannot experiment for ten years trying to destroy the government and if they fail still come back into the Union unhurt." He began to draft an emancipation proclamation.

Main Idea: _____

_____

What did Lee's victory ensure? (Circle the letter of the *best* answer.)

       a. a longer war

       b. an end to slavery

       c. the Old South

       d. both *a* and *b*

Why is Lee's victory considered an irony? (An irony is an outcome or result opposite of what is expected.)

_____

_____

_____

6. How was the blockade regarded by the naval powers of the world? Ordinarily, they probably would have defied it, for it was never completely effective and was especially sievelike at the outset. But Britain, the greatest maritime nation, recognized it as binding and warned its shippers that they ignored it at their peril. An explanation is easy. Blockade happened to be the chief offensive weapon of Britain, which was still Mistress of the Seas. Britain plainly did not want to tie its hands in a future war by insisting that Lincoln maintain impossibly high blockading standards.

Main Idea: _____

_____

Identify the two reasons why Britain recognized the blockade. (Circle the letter of the *best* answer.)

       a. The blockade was Britain's chief offensive weapon.

       b. Britain wanted the North to win the war.

       c. Britain hoped to use the blockade in a future war.

       d. Britain did not believe in high standards.

What word do the authors use to give you the picture that the ships could easily get through the blockade?

_____

7. Bloody Antietam was also the long-awaited "victory" that Lincoln needed for launching his Emancipation Proclamation. The abolitionists had long been clamoring for action: Wendell Phillips was denouncing the president as a "first-rate second-rate man." By midsummer of 1862, with the Border States safely in the fold, Lincoln was ready to move. But he believed that to issue such an edict on the heels of a series of military disasters would be folly. It would seem like a confession that the North, unable to conquer the South, was forced to call upon the slaves to murder their masters. Lincoln therefore decided to wait for the outcome of Lee's invasion.

Main Idea: _____

_____

Why was Lincoln waiting for a victory before declaring the Emancipation Proclamation?

_____

_____

_____

What is an abolitionist?

_____

_____

What did Phillips mean by stating that Lincoln was a "first-rate second-rate man"?

_____

_____

8. Pickett's charge has been called the "high tide of the Confederacy." It defined both the northernmost point reached by any significant Southern force and the last real chance for the Confederates to win the war. As the Battle of Gettysburg raged, a Confederate peace delegation was moving under a flag of truce toward the Union lines near Norfolk, Virginia. Jefferson Davis hoped his negotiators would arrive in Washington from the south just as Lee's triumphant army marched on it from Gettysburg to the north. But the victory at Gettysburg belonged to Lincoln, who refused to allow the Confederate peace mission to pass through Union lines. From now on the Southern cause was doomed. Yet the men of Dixie fought on for nearly two years longer, through sweat, blood, and weariness of spirit.

Main Idea: _____

_____

Why was Jefferson Davis sending a delegation to the Union line?

_____

_____

_____

Underline a sentence that states who won the Battle of Gettysburg and explain how you know that from the sentence.

_____

_____

9. A second Freudian method was dream analysis. Freud believed that the unconscious reveals itself through symbols in our dreams. Freud argued that the ego censors our thoughts when we are awake. However, the ego relaxes its control when we sleep, so that the unconscious is more obvious in our dreams. People supposedly try to disguise their own wishes from themselves by constructing symbols. For example, an individual may report a dream about riding on a bull in an amusement-park carousel. This conscious, remembered story line of a dream is called its manifest content. The analyst may interpret the bull as a symbol of the person's father. These underlying, unconscious aspects of the dream (as interpreted by the analyst) are called the latent content.

Main Idea: _____

_____

According to Freud, symbols are constructed in dreams for the following reason: (Circle the letter of the *best* answer.)

      a. People remember the symbols.

      b. Manifest content makes dreams more enjoyable.

      c. People do not want to know the latent content.

      d. The ego relaxes.

True or False: The latent content of a dream includes those aspects of the dream people recall as soon as they awake from the dream. Explain your answer.

_____

_____

You have a dream about selling flowers at the beach. What is the latent content? (Circle the letter of the *best* answer.)

      a. flowers

      b. the beach

      c. both *a* and *b*

      d. none of the above

10. Consider a trait called sensation seeking. People who are high in sensation seeking actively look for adventure, new experiences, and risky situations. In general, the heritability for sensation seeking is estimated to be 58 percent, which is relatively high for personality traits. The research comparing high sensation seekers with low sensation seekers shows that the two groups differ in a variety of brain chemicals, including neurotransmitters, endorphins, and hormones. Recent studies have also focused on DNA analysis, identifying a genetic basis for the novelty-seeking component of sensation seeking. This is the first step toward understanding the specific genetic maps of personality.

Main Idea: _____

_____

A person having the trait called sensation seeking would be most likely to do which of the following? (Circle the letter of the *best* answer.)

      a. work as an engineer

      b. bungi jump

      c. sing in a chorus

      d. play tennis

Which of the following would help prove inheritability? (Circle the letter of the *best* answer.)

    a. DNA analysis

    b. hormone measurement

    c. brain chemical analysis

    d. all of the above

Why is 58 percent considered a high percentage of heritability for a personality trait?

_____

_____

11. Yet much unofficial do-it-yourself liberation did take place. Thousands of jubilant slaves, learning of the proclamation, flocked to the invading Union armies, stripping already rundown plantations of their work force. In this sense the Emancipation Proclamation was heralded by the drumbeat of running feet. But many fugitives would have come anyhow, as they had from the war's outset. Lincoln's immediate goal was not only to liberate the slaves but also to strengthen the moral cause of the Union at home and abroad. This he succeeded in doing. At the same time, Lincoln's proclamation clearly foreshadowed the ultimate doom of slavery. This was legally achieved by action of the individual states and by their ratification of the Thirteenth Amendment in 1865, eight months after the Civil War had ended. The Emancipation Proclamation also fundamentally changed the nature of the war because it effectively removed any chance of a negotiated settlement. Both sides now knew that the war would be a fight to the finish.

Main Idea: _____

_____

The Emancipation Proclamation resulted in which of the following? (Circle the letter of the *best* answer.)

    a. slaves leaving their Southern plantations

    b. the war continuing without a compromise

    c. an eventual end to slavery

    d. all of the above

"The drumbeat of running feet" refers to which of the following? (Circle the letter of the *best* answer.)

    a. Northern soldiers moving south

    b. Southern soldiers chasing slaves

    c. slaves leaving plantations

    d. Lincoln proclaiming the slaves free

To where did many of the Southern slaves go? (Circle the letter of the *best* answer.)

    a. Northern farms

    b. rundown plantations

c. Northern armies

d. the White House

12. Off-the-job training involves some form of classroom instruction such as lectures, conferences, audiovisual aids, programmed instruction, and special machines to teach employees everything from basic math and language skills to difficult, highly skilled tasks. Some firms are replacing classroom training with computer-based and online training programs. These programs can save an employer money by reducing travel costs and employee time away from work. In addition, computer-based training offers consistent presentations, since the training content won't vary with the quality of the instructor. Audio and visual capabilities help these systems to simulate the work environment better than some classroom training could, and employees also benefit from greater control over the learning process. They can learn at their own pace and convenience and they generally do not have to wait for the company to schedule a class before they can begin adding to their knowledge. Despite these advantages, firms also offer traditional classroom training, because it usually provides more opportunities for employees to interact with the instructor and with one another. Some people learn more readily from human interaction, and some have difficulty disciplining themselves to complete a computer-based learning program on their own.

Main Idea: _____

_____

True or False: At lunchtime, an employee works at a computer to complete a lesson in her online course. This is a form of off-the-job training. Explain your answer.

_____

_____

Why does an online course provide consistent teaching? (Circle the letter of the *best* answer.)

a. The same lectures and activities are part of the course each semester.

b. Students may take the course from any location at any time.

c. The instructor may change from one semester to the next.

d. Students are able to e-mail questions to the same instructor.

Which of the following topics could be taught with off-the-job training? (Circle the letter of the *best* answer.)

a. algebra

b. leadership

c. English grammar

d. all of the above

13. Grant's triumph in Tennessee was crucial. It not only riveted Kentucky more securely to the Union but also opened the gateway to the strategically important region of Tennessee, as well as to Georgia and the heart of Dixie. Grant next attempted to exploit his victory by capturing the junction of the main Confederate north-south and east-west railroads in the Mississippi Valley at Corinth, Mississippi. But a Confederate force foiled his plans in a gory battle at Shiloh, just over the Tennessee border from

Corinth, on April 6–7, 1862. Though Grant successfully counterattacked, the impressive Confederate showing at Shiloh confirmed that there would be no quick end to the war in the West.

Main Idea: _____

_____

Why was the Tennessee victory important? (Circle the letters of the *best* answers.)

      a. Shiloh became an easy victory.

      b. The North had greater control of Kentucky.

      c. A gateway to the Mississippi was opened.

      d. The North had better access to Georgia.

Who was the victor at Shiloh? (Circle the letter of the *best* answer.)

      a. The North was the victor.

      b. The South

      c. It was a tie.

      d. Shiloh.

True or False: Grant was able to take the junction of the main Confederate north-south and east-west railroad in the Mississippi Valley. Explain your answer.

_____

_____

14. The Union victory at Vicksburg (July 4, 1863) came the day after the Confederate defeat at Gettysburg. The political significance of these back-to-back military successes was monumental. Reopening the Mississippi helped to quell the Northern peace agitation in the "Butternut" area of the Ohio River valley. Confederate control of the Mississippi had cut off that region's usual trade routes down the Ohio-Mississippi River system to New Orleans, thus adding economic pain to that border section's already shaky support for the "abolition war." The twin victories also conclusively tipped the diplomatic scales in favor of the North, as Britain stopped delivery of the Laird rams to the Confederates and as France killed a deal for the sale of six naval vessels to the Richmond government. By the end of 1863, all Confederate hopes for foreign help were irretrievably lost.

Main Idea: _____

_____

To what countries do the authors refer when they state that the "diplomatic scales" were tipped?

_____

To what two victories do the authors refer when they discuss the back-to-back victories? (Circle the letters of the *best* answers.)

      a. Mississippi

      b. Vicksburg

    c. Gettysburg

    d. Ohio River valley

Why were the two victories so significant to the North? (Circle the letter<u>s</u> of the *best* answers.)

    a. The North gained support from the Ohio River valley area.

    b. An area to the Mississippi was opened.

    c. France decided not to sell ships to the South.

    d. The Richmond government was no longer in power.

15. Research confirms that people with a strong sense of self-efficacy do indeed manage their lives more successfully. In general, these people tend to be more persistent in school, intensifying their efforts when a task is difficult. They also have higher aspirations, as well as more flexible problem-solving strategies. They also have better metacognitive skills; they think about their thinking processes and regulate how they approach tasks. People who are confident about their abilities typically approach new challenges with optimism, and they set high goals for themselves. In contrast, people with low self-efficacy may set inappropriate goals, often leading to depression.

Main Idea: _____

_____

According to the theory of self-efficacy, which factor is most important in doing well on a test? (Circle the letter of the *best* answer.)

    a. studying the night before

    b. balancing play and study all semester

    c. believing one will do well on the test

    d. discussing with the instructor how well one thinks he or she will do

Which of the following will a person with self-efficacy do? (Circle the letter<u>s</u> of the *best* answers.)

    a. Set an attainable goal.

    b. Determine what needs to be done to accomplish a goal.

    c. Believe one can complete all the steps to reach a goal.

    d. Think about what needs to be done during each step of the process to reach the goal.

Which of the following characteristics do people with a strong self-efficacy have? (Circle the letter<u>s</u> of the *best* answers.)

    a. persistence

    b. pessimism

    c. optimism

    d. shyness

Practice with Periodicals

Read the article "Women in Battle in the Civil War" in Part Three. Write a journal entry explaining your views of these women. Make inferences about the character or personality of three of the women mentioned in the article. Include your inferences in your journal.

Journal Entry

Read "Women in Battle in the Civil War" in Part Three. As you read, be aware of any visualizations you are creating. Each time you visualize something, write the sentence from the article that caused that visualization and then immediately following the sentence, write a description of your visualization. Write at least five sentences and descriptions in your journal.

Textbook Link

In another textbook you are using, do one of the following: find a figure of speech and explain why the author uses it; find a paragraph in which the author makes an inference and explain that inference; or find a paragraph in which the author assumes you have some background information to understand the context, and explain what you need to know in order to understand it.

CHAPTER 6

DETERMINING FACTS AND OPINIONS

In this chapter you will learn to

- ▪ Differentiate between facts and opinions
- ▪ Identify support for opinions

DISTINGUISHING FACTS FROM OPINIONS

You often state facts and share opinions with friends. For example, if some of your friends tell you that they saw a great movie last weekend, you know that is their opinion. Your friends will also probably continue to tell you about different parts of the movie (facts) that made it great. Sometimes it is difficult to tell the difference between a fact and an opinion when you read it in a textbook. Many students have a tendency to accept as fact everything that they read in a textbook. This chapter will help you distinguish between facts and opinions in textbooks and enable you to determine when opinions are valid and reliable.

At first, distinguishing between a fact and an opinion seems to be easy, but many students make the mistake of thinking that everything that is true is a fact. A *fact* is something that can be proved true or false. Emphasis is on the word *proved*.

EXAMPLE

The capital of Maryland is Annapolis.

The capital of Pennsylvania is Philadelphia.

Both of the preceding statements are considered facts. The second statement happens to be a false fact because you can prove that the capital of Pennsylvania is not Philadelphia but Harrisburg.

An *opinion* is something that cannot be proved true or false but that can be backed up with facts to give credence to the opinion.

EXAMPLE

Baltimore, Maryland, is a great place to visit.

This statement is an opinion because of the word *great*. Opinions can often be identified by words that cannot be measured. These words imply someone's feeling, view, or belief.

Specific words can signal an opinion: *beautiful, ugly, right, wrong, good, bad, best, worst, wonderful, awful, fast, slow,* and so forth. Other words such as *should* and *must,* and words that indicate that a statement is about the future also signal an opinion.

Many times authors will let you know that they are writing an opinion by stating just that.

EXAMPLE

In my opinion . . . , I think . . . , I believe . . .

Be careful of statements that begin with "It is a fact . . ." This does not necessarily mean that what follows is a fact. For example, consider the statement "It is a fact that the president is doing a good job." This statement is an opinion because the word *good* cannot be measured. It would be factual to say, "The president recently proposed a bill to balance the budget." This fact may be used to support the opinion, but it does not prove the opinion true or false.

Most textbooks are pretty factual, but be aware that authors can be biased. The author took the time to write an entire textbook on a particular topic, so he or she obviously has done a great deal of reading on the subjects and has definite opinions on issues.

Just as important as being able to distinguish fact from opinion in your textbooks is being able to distinguish fact from opinion in readings and research that you do outside your class. When you are asked to use the library, you will need to be able to decide what is fact and what is opinion in journals and books. If you are asked to write an argumentative paper, you will be required to form your own opinion and back it up with facts that you have gathered from different authors. A summary or reaction paper will require you to summarize the facts and opinions in an article that you have read and then state your own opinion, backing it up with facts.

EXERCISE 16: DISTINGUISHING FACTS FROM OPINIONS

Determine whether the following sentences are fact (F) or opinion (O). If the statement is opinion, underline the portion that makes it opinion.

_____ 1. Lee had achieved a brilliant, if bloody, triumph.

_____ 2. The Northern navy enforced the blockade with high-handed practices.

_____ 3. As finally developed, the Northern military plan had six components.

_____ 4. As Lincoln moved to emancipate the slaves, he also took steps to enlist blacks in the armed forces.

_____ 5. A new slaughter pen was prepared when General Burnside yielded his command to "Fighting Joe" Hooker, an aggressive officer but a headstrong subordinate.

_____ 6. Pickett's charge has been called the "high tide of the Confederacy."

_____ 7. The law prohibits the use of polygraph (lie detector) tests in almost all prehiring decisions, as well as in random testing of current employees.

_____ 8. An effective compensation system should attract well-qualified workers, keep them satisfied in their jobs, and inspire them to produce.

_____ 9. A growing number of companies are meeting employee demands for "family-friendly" benefits that help them care for children, aging parents, or other dependents.

_____10. Job enlargement is a job design change that expands an employee's responsibilities by increasing the number and variety of tasks they entail.

_____11. Building the three *R*s into an organization should contribute to employee morale.

_____12. Many large companies award part of employees' compensation in the form of stock options, which reward executives for increases in their firms' stock prices by giving them opportunities to buy stock at preset prices within certain time periods.

SUPPORTING OPINIONS WITH FACTS

Opinions are not bad. Opinions are valid as long as they are backed by facts or evidence. For example, the author of an American history textbook may state that George Washington was one of the greatest leaders of our country. Although many historians as well as Americans might agree, you as a reader must realize that this is an opinion with which another history textbook author or you may disagree. Your job is to look for the facts, which the author should have supplied, that back up that opinion.

For example, read the following paragraph from the business textbook chapter:

> Recruitment and selection is an expensive process, because a firm incurs costs for advertising job openings, interviewing applicants, and conducting background checks, employment tests, and medical exams. A bad hiring decision is even more expensive, though. A hiring mistake costs a firm in efforts to train and motivate a less than optimal employee, as well as potential costs of poor decisions by that employee. Other costs resulting from a bad hiring decision may include lawsuits, unemployment compensation claims, recruiting and training a replacement, and reductions in productivity and employee morale.

This paragraph begins with an opinion in the first part of the first sentence; the word *expensive* expresses an opinion. However, in the remainder of the first sentence, the author states facts to back up this opinion: he lists the steps in the recruiting process that cost money. The second sentence contains another opinion, again because of the word *expensive*. The remainder of the paragraph lists facts to support the opinion.

Here is another example from the American history textbook chapter:

> The most alarming Confederate threat to the blockade came in 1862. Resourceful Southerners raised and reconditioned a former wooden U.S. warship, the *Merrimack,* and plated its sides with old iron railroad rails. Renamed the *Virginia,* this clumsy but powerful monster easily destroyed two wooden ships of the Union navy in the Virginia waters of Chesapeake Bay; it also threatened catastrophe to the entire Yankee blockading fleet. (Actually the homemade ironclad was not a seaworthy craft.)

The first sentence states an opinion; something seen as a threat is an opinion. Many other words in the paragraph are also opinion: *resourceful, clumsy, powerful, monster, easily,* and *threatened.* However, the authors do have facts to support the first sentence: Southerners raised and reconditioned the *Merrimack* and plated its sides with iron railroad ties; this warship destroyed two Union wooden ships.

Sometimes an author states an opinion and supports it with one or more examples. Read the following excerpt from the business textbook chapter:

> One of the most effective external sources is employee referrals, in which employers ask current employees to recommend applicants, rewarding them with bonuses or prizes for new hires. The demand for employees with high-tech skills is so great that some companies are offering generous rewards to employees who refer qualified candidates. Docent, which provides online learning resources, pays $5,000 to any employee whose referral the company hires. Software firm Adobe Systems also pays $5,000 for referrals, and employees with three referrals get an additional $5,000 toward a vacation. Respond.com awarded an employee a Hawaii trip for two for referring an engineer who joined the company.

The first sentence begins with an opinion (it uses the word *effective*) and continues to define "employee referrals." The author then proceeds to support the opinion with examples from three different companies.

Opinions of authors are often as important as facts because tests contain statements of opinion and you must determine whether they are valid based on what you read in the chapter. For example, read this statement taken from a study guide test on the business chapter:

> Motivational factors are not important if the employees are well paid.

The words *not important* are opinion words. To answer the question correctly, the reader must remember facts from several sections of the chapter on motivation and maintenance factors and determine the importance of (an opinion) salary in relation to all other factors stated by the author.

It is important to read and determine facts that support an author's opinions. Think about what you read as you read. Look for words that signal an opinion. Look for facts that validate opinions. Understand an author's opinions and know the facts that support those opinions. As you read, differentiate between what is opinion and what is fact. Be prepared to be tested on both.

EXERCISE 17: IDENTIFYING FACTS THAT SUPPORT OPINIONS

Each of the following excerpts contains an author's opinion. Double underline the opinion statements; then single underline the fact or facts that support that opinion. Briefly discuss whether you believe the author has provided sufficient support for the opinion.

1. Entrepreneurs and small-business owners usually assume most of the responsibility for human resource management. However, a growing number of small firms are outsourcing the function of human resource management to professional employer organizations (PEOs). A PEO is a company that helps small and midsized firms with a wide range of human resource services, including hiring and training employees, administering payroll and benefits programs, handling workers' compensation and unemployment insurance, and maintaining compliance with labor laws. PEOs work in partnership with employers in these key decisions. Because the PEO typically negotiates benefits for all its clients, it can shop for better deals. And by handling a firm's human resource activities, a PEO enables a small firm to focus on production, marketing, and finance, as well as on motivating and leading employees.

_____

_____

2. Employees are increasing their requests for training so they can build skills and knowledge that will prepare them for new job opportunities. Training is also a good investment from the employer's perspective. Untrained employees take six times longer to perform tasks than trained employees, so it is important to help new employees build their skills quickly. In a relatively new industry, such as Internet retailing, companies need to train their employees.

_____

_____

3. One of the simplest, yet most effective, ways to work through stress is by putting your feelings into words that only you will read. The more honest and open you are as you write, the better. According to the research of psychologist James Pennebaker of the University of Texas, Austin, college students who wrote in their journals about traumatic events felt much better afterward than those who wrote about superficial topics. Recording your experiences and feelings on paper or audiotape may help decrease stress and enhance well-being.

_____

_____

4. Cocky George McClellan embodied a curious mixture of virtues and defects. He was a superb organizer and drillmaster, and he injected splendid morale into the Army of the Potomac. Hating to sacrifice his troops, he was idolized by his men, who affectionately called him "Little Mac." But he was a perfectionist who seems not to have realized that an army is never ready to the last button and that wars cannot be won without running some risks. He consistently but erroneously believed that the enemy outnumbered him, partly because his intelligence reports from the head of Pinkerton's Detective Agency were unreliable. He was overcautious—Lincoln once accused him of having "the

slows"—and he addressed the president in an arrogant tone that a less forgiving person would never have tolerated. Privately the general referred to his chief as a "baboon."

5. Blockade-running soon became riskily profitable, as the growing scarcity of Southern goods drove prices skyward. The most successful runners were swift, gray-painted steamers, scores of which were specially built in Scotland. A leading rendezvous was the West Indies port of Nassau, in the British Bahamas, where at one time thirty-five of the speedy ships rode at anchor. The low-lying craft would take on cargoes of arms brought in by tramp steamers from Britain, leave with fraudulent papers for "Halifax" (Canada), and return a few days later with a cargo of cotton. The risks were great, but the profits would mount to 700 percent and more for lucky gamblers. Two successful voyages might well pay for capture on a third. The lush days of blockade-running finally passed as Union squadrons gradually pinched off the leading Southern ports, from New Orleans to Charleston.

6. Ironically, the great mass of Southern slaves did little to help their Northern liberators, white or black. A thousand scattered torches in the hands of a thousand slaves would have brought the Southern soldiers home, and the war would have ended. Through the "grapevine," the blacks learned of Lincoln's Emancipation Proclamation. The bulk of them, whether because of fear, loyalty, lack of leadership, or strict policing, did not cast off their chains. But tens of thousands revolted "with their feet" when they abandoned their plantations upon the approach or arrival of Union armies, with or without emancipation proclamations. About twenty-five thousand joined Sherman's march through Georgia in 1864, and their presence in such numbers created problems of supply and discipline.

7. Lincoln's renomination at first encountered surprisingly strong opposition. Hostile factions whipped up considerable agitation to shelve homely "Old Abe" in favor of the handsome nemesis Secretary of the Treasury Chase. Lincoln was accused of lacking force, of being overready to compromise, of not having won the war, and of having shocked many sensitive souls by his ill-timed and earthy jokes. ("Prince of Jesters," one journal called him.) But the "ditch Lincoln" move collapsed, and he was nominated by the Union party without serious dissent.

8. Freud's theory is biased against women. As we noted earlier, Freud maintained that women have inferior moral judgment, a gender bias that is not supported by the research. He also proposed that women are masochistic, which means that they would derive pleasure from being mistreated. This view does a disservice to women, and it encourages people to think—incorrectly—that women enjoy being battered or raped.

9. Furthermore, traits are more easily expressed in some situations than others. For instance, some situations constrain our behavior, so the traits cannot be easily expressed. At a funeral, the friendly people will not act much different from the unfriendly people. However, at a picnic, individual differences will be strong. Cross-situational consistency will be higher if the situation is familiar, if people receive no instructions about how they should act, and if they are observed for a long time, rather than a brief period.

_____

_____

10. Carl Rogers (1902–1987) was born in Illinois and began his professional career working with troubled children, though he later extended his therapy to adults. Rogers's approach requires the therapist to try to see the world from each client's personal perspective, rather than from the therapist's own framework. Rogers emphasized that each of us interprets the same set of stimuli differently, so there are as many different "real worlds" as there are people on this planet.

_____

_____

Practice with Periodicals

Read the article "Beyond the Suggestion Box" in Part Three. Find and list five facts and five opinions from that article.

Journal Entry

Read the article "Beyond the Suggestion Box" in Part Three. As you read, be aware of those statements with which you strongly agree or disagree. Choose three of those opinion statements and explain why you agree or disagree.

Textbook Link

In another textbook you are using, find and list three opinions and the facts the author uses to support each.

CHAPTER 7

READING AND ANSWERING TEST QUESTIONS

In this chapter you will learn to

- Recognize and answer objective test questions on different levels of thinking
- Recognize and answer essay questions on different levels of thinking
- Prepare for a test
- Use techniques to help you do well on a test
- Review an exam and use information to help you do better on later tests

Some test questions are easy, and some are hard. Why is this? Well, part of the reason may be that you do not study certain facts as well as others. Sometimes you simply study the "wrong stuff." The second part of this textbook will help you with that problem. Being able to determine the main idea, paragraph type, and important details will help you narrow down what to study, and other techniques will help you effectively remember those facts and details. This chapter will help you understand why some test questions are more difficult than others. It will also help you determine what you need to do to answer those more difficult questions correctly.

BLOOM'S LEVELS OF THINKING

Assuming that you know all of the "right stuff," there is another reason why some test questions are difficult: there are different levels of thinking. In 1956, Dr. Benjamin Bloom researched this topic and was the senior author of a book titled *Taxonomy of Educational Objectives: Handbook I, Cognitive Domain*. In this book, Dr. Bloom analyzed the intellectual development of the brain and developed a continuum of skills arranged according to the degree of intellectual activity necessary to perform each skill. Bloom's levels of thinking are arranged chronologically, from those requiring the least amount of intellectual activity to those requiring the greatest amount.

Knowledge level. You are required to remember exactly what you read. Dates and names of important people and places are some facts that you would be asked to remember.

Comprehension level. You need to have information that you have not only memorized but also understand; you can put it into your own words or understand it when stated in different words than the author used.

Application level. You need to know the facts and understand them, but you also need to know when and how to use them. Questions that have a scenario are usually application questions. Math word problems are another example.

Analysis level. You need to be able to break a whole into its parts. This is a higher level of thinking because you must be aware of not only the parts but also the intellectual process that you are using to determine the parts. Questions that ask you to compare or to contrast are analysis questions.

Synthesis level. You need to combine or to unify parts into a new whole. This usually means creating something new from the knowledge or materials on hand. Being asked to predict or propose something is a type of synthesis question.

Evaluation level. You need to evaluate or determine the value of something as well as set the criteria by which to evaluate it. Test questions that require you to agree or disagree or that require a revision are on this level of thinking.

Each level of thinking becomes more difficult because it requires you to be able to use all of the levels that precede it. For example, if you are asked to compare two speeches (analysis level), you need to know what those speeches are about (knowledge level), have an understanding of the meaning of those speeches (comprehension level), and have an idea of how those speeches could be used in different situations (application level).

You may believe that if you memorize material, you will do well on a test. This may have worked on a lower school level because you needed to set up a knowledge base, and memorization is important in that setting. However, college courses require you to use the higher levels of thinking. When you leave the college campus and move out into the workforce, you will be required to do more than answer questions. Most of your work will be at the higher levels of thinking. You'll need to apply the information that you have as well as make decisions, solve problems, and create new ideas. College classes and tests can help prepare you for that experience.

When you read a test question, it is important to determine what you need to know to answer that question. Don't just think about what you have read and memorized. Think about the concepts and ideas you have studied. If you have a good understanding of the topics, you will do better on a test than if you have simply memorized the facts.

OBJECTIVE TEST QUESTIONS

An objective test question is one that has one correct answer. Types of objective test questions include true or false, multiple choice, and matching questions. Take a look at some objective questions, the levels on which they are written, and what you need to do to answer those questions.

Sample Knowledge Question

What Northern general was placed in charge of conquering Georgia?

a. Lee
b. Grant
c. Sherman
d. Meade

If you had read and studied the American history chapter from which this question was taken, you would remember one subsection titled "Sherman Scorches Georgia." This section explains how "Georgia's conquest was entrusted to General William Tecumseh Sherman." The section then goes on to explain how he went through Georgia burning buildings and tearing up railroad rails. This section also includes a map showing Sherman's march through Georgia and the Carolinas.

Sample Comprehension Question

According to Maslow, which of the following meets esteem needs?

a. regular increases in salary
b. pension programs
c. good working conditions
d. performance recognition awards

The section of the business textbook chapter referring to this question states the following:

> *Esteem needs.* People like to receive attention, recognition, and appreciation from others. Employees feel good when they are recognized for good job performance and respected for their contributions.

This paragraph does not mention any of the five answers; however, understanding "esteem needs" (needs to receive attention, recognition, and appreciation from others) would lead you to answer "performance recognition awards"—answer *d.* No other answer deals with a sense of accomplishment. Regular increases in salary could have something to do with recognition, but it would be a better answer if it stated "regular increases in salary due to an accomplishment."

Here's another example of a comprehension level question:

> *True or false:* Most firms prefer to hire people outside the company for new positions in order to bring in new ideas.

The business chapter contains the following information:

> Businesses access both internal and external sources to find qualified candidates for specific jobs. Policies of hiring from within emphasize internal sources, so employers consider their own employees first for job openings. Internal recruiting is less expensive than external methods, and it helps boost employee morale. But if recruiters can find no qualified internal candidate, they must look for people outside the organization.

The author never directly states whether a firm prefers to hire within; however, the author lists the advantages of hiring inside the company and then states that if no qualified candidates are available within, a firm must go outside the organization. Your understanding of this information leads you to answer "false" to this question.

Sample Application Questions

> Armand is talking to his friend Hans about his weekly counseling session with Dr. Gomez. If Armand mentions the following words—*unconscious, childhood,* and *conflict*—then Dr. Gomez is most probably a psychologist who advocates the _____ approach to the explanation of personality.

a. trait
b. humanistic
c. psychodynamic
d. social cognitive

Application questions have you apply your knowledge and comprehension to real-life situations. Nowhere in the psychology chapter will you read about Armand, but the entire chapter is about the four possible answers to this question. The text at the beginning of the section titled "The Psychodynamic Approach" will provide the facts to answer this question.

> The psychodynamic approach emphasizes three central ideas: (1) childhood experiences determine adult personality; (2) unconscious mental processes influence everyday behavior; and (3) unconscious conflict underlies most human behavior.

Your general understanding of Freud and his beliefs would lead you to the same answer: *c.* Read another application question.

> Freddy, a used-car salesman, doesn't care what he tells people—truth or lies—as long as he is able to meet his sales quota each month. Freud would <u>most</u> likely describe Freddy as having a weak

a. id.
b. ego.
c. libido.
d. superego.

First, you need to pay careful attention to the underlined word in this question. Test makers highlight by underlining or italicizing the key words to help you do well on tests. You need to find the one answer that is most likely weak in Freddy. The following passage from the psychology chapter would help you answer this question:

> So far, we have an irrational id, governed by pleasure, and a cooler, calmer ego. Freud's third personality component is the superego, which includes a person's conscience, ideals, and values. Parents and society convey these principles.

With this knowledge and understanding of the superego, you would then choose answer *d* because having a weak superego would mean that one would have a weak conscience, weak ideals, and weak values.

Sample Analysis Questions

Which of the following statements <u>best</u> describes the similarity between the defense mechanisms of displacement and projection?

    a. Both of these defense mechanisms involve redirecting feelings toward another target.
    b. Both of these defense mechanisms involve converting unacceptable impulses into socially desirable behaviors.
    c. Both of these defense mechanisms involve acting in ways characteristic of an early stage of personality development.
    d. Both of these defense mechanisms involve actively repressing anxiety-producing impulses into the preconscious level of consciousness.

To answer the above question, you would need to have a good understanding of the two defense mechanisms, displacement and projection; it would also help if you were able to give an example of each. This information can be found in Table 13.2 in the psychology chapter. The author defines and gives an example of five defense mechanisms. *Displacement* is defined as redirecting an emotion toward someone who is less dangerous than the "real" object of that emotion. The example is of a husband who is angry at the way his boss treats him, so he screams at his wife. The definition of *projection* is attributing one's own unacceptable thoughts and feelings to another person. For example, an employee at a store, tempted to steal some merchandise, suspects that another employee is stealing. Because both defense mechanisms involve someone redirecting or attributing an emotion or feeling to another, the best answer is *a*.

An important point to keep in mind about objective questions like multiple choice and true and false is that if you don't remember the information from the text or your notes, you should try to make intelligent guesses. Use all of the knowledge that you have to narrow down the answers. Here is an application question from the psychology chapter. The discussion that follows the question tells you how you might answer this question if you had no memory of reading about the particular psychologist and his or her theory.

The psychodynamic approach to personality that emphasizes the development of ideas about one's self in relation to significant people in one's life is called

    a. social cognition.
    b. self-efficacy theory.
    c. object relations.
    d. ego development theory.

First, you could probably eliminate the answers *a* and *b* because the terms *social cognition* and *self-efficacy* are not used in the psychodynamic approach section of the chapter. Answers *c* and *d* are both possible answers because they are found in the information about the psychodynamic approach. Next, answer *d* is possible, but ego development refers to oneself, so answer *c* is the best answer because it refers to a relationship with another.

Remember that if you have study-read the chapter and prepared for the test, you may not have all the answers, but you will have many of them. Do not look at a question that you think you do not know and give up. Use every piece of knowledge that you can recall to narrow down your choices to the correct answer. Believe in yourself (that's called *self-efficacy*) and don't be afraid to use the information that you have.

EXERCISE 18: READING AND ANSWERING TEST QUESTIONS

Use the information in the text that precedes each question to help you answer the test questions. Underline the sentence or sentences that lead you to the correct answer.

1. Companies downsize for many reasons. The two most common objectives of downsizing are to cut overhead costs and streamline the organizational structure. Some firms report improvements in profits, market share, employee productivity, quality, and customer service after downsizing. Others, however, lose so many valuable, high-performing employees that their ability to compete declines.

Downsizing can be used to

    a. eliminate layers of management.

    b. reduce costs.

    c. increase efficiency.

    d. increase customer satisfaction.

    e. all of the above

2. North American cultures and many Western European cultures emphasize an individualistic viewpoint. These individualistic cultures (also called independent cultures) maintain that you must assert yourself and appreciate how you are different from other people. In contrast, people in Asia, Africa, Latin America, and many southern European cultures—such as Italy and Greece—have a different perspective. These collectivist cultures (also called interdependent cultures) maintain that you must fit in with other people and live in interdependent relationships with them.

Which of the following statements would be more characteristic of people from collectivist cultures than individualistic cultures?

    a. "I rely on myself most of the time: I rarely rely on others."

    b. "It is important to consult close friends and get their ideas before making a decision."

    c. "It is important that I do my job better than others."

    d. "When another person does better than I do, I get tense and aroused."

3. Freud envisioned three basic components to personality: the id, the ego, and the superego. He proposed that humans are born with an id, which is immature and illogical. The id consists of the basic drives—such as eating and sexual activity—and it provides the energy (or libido) for all human behavior. Freud also maintained that the id lacks moral judgment; it cannot distinguish between good and evil. The id is unconscious, a "hidden self" that can influence our everyday actions.

    The ego, in contrast, supposedly develops because the individual needs some factor that will mediate between the id and reality. For example, Freud argues that the ego helps young children delay their impulses until the situation is appropriate.

    So far, we have an irrational id, governed by pleasure, and a cooler, calmer ego. Freud's third personality component is the superego, which includes a person's conscience, ideals, and values. Parents and society convey these principles.

Ten-year-old Mario spent the whole sermon daydreaming about the new bike he wanted but couldn't have because his savings account was still $20 short. It was his family's turn to clean up the church after the service, and while he was walking between the pews, he found a $20 bill that must have fallen out of the collection plate. His mind was immediately flooded with confusing and disturbing thoughts telling him to do different things. Freud would say his _____ would tell him to take the money and use it to buy the new bike; his _____ would tell him to give the money to the priest immediately before God could have a chance to punish him; and his _____ would tell him to take the money to his father who might reward him for his honesty by lending him the rest of the money he needed to buy his new bike.

    a. id, ego, superego

    b. superego, ego, id

    c. id, superego, ego

    d. ego, id, superego

4. The terms *wages* and *salary* are often used interchangeably, but they refer to different types of pay systems. Wages represent compensation based on an hourly pay rate or the amount of output produced. Firms pay wages to production employees, maintenance workers, and sometimes retail salespeople. Salaries represent compensation calculated on a weekly, monthly, or annual basis. Office personnel, executives, and professional employees usually receive salaries.

Omar, an electrician for Quality Builders, is paid $35 for each hour he works during the day. After 5 P.M. and on weekends, he is paid the overtime rate of one and one-half times the regular hourly rate. Omar is paid a(n)

    a. wage.

    b. bonus.

    c. commission.

    d. employee benefit.

    e. salary.

5.

Humanistic Approach	Trait Approach
Obtained from self-reports from the general population and people in therapy	Obtained from observation of behavior and questionnaire responses from the general population as well as people in therapy
Self-concepts, self-actualizing tendencies	Stable, internal characteristics; some emphasize genetic basis
Optimistic explanation	Neutral explanation
Fairly comprehensive	Not very comprehensive

Compared to the humanistic approach to personality, the trait approach

    a. is more likely to rely on behavioral observations.

    b. is more likely to emphasize situational determinants of behavior.

    c. provides a more comprehensive view of personality.

    d. places greater emphasis on parents' roles in personality formation.

6. Biofeedback training consists of three stages:

    1. Developing increased awareness of a body state or function.

    2. Gaining control over it.

    3. Transferring this control to everyday living without use of the electronic instrument.

All of following are stages of biofeedback training *except:*

    a. developing an increased awareness of a body function.

    b. gaining control over a body function.

    c. controlling the function without the monitoring device.

    d. developing mental pictures to focus your mind.

7. Research confirms that people with a strong sense of self-efficacy do indeed manage their lives more successfully. In general, these people tend to be more persistent in school, intensifying their efforts when a task is difficult. They also have higher aspirations, as well as more flexible problem-solving strategies. They also have better metacognitive skills; they think about their thinking processes and regulate how they approach tasks. People who are confident about their abilities typically approach new challenges with optimism, and they set high goals for themselves. In contrast, people with low self-efficacy may set inappropriate goals, often leading to depression.

Results of social cognitive research in personality support the prediction that if you are a person with high self-efficacy you are

    a. less likely to feel depressed.

    b. more likely to be persistent in school.

    c. more likely to feel optimistic about new challenges.

    d. all of the above.

8. Cocky George McClellan embodied a curious mixture of virtues and defects. He was a superb organizer and drillmaster, and he injected splendid morale into the Army of the Potomac. Hating to sacrifice his troops, he was idolized by his men, who affectionately called him "Little Mac." But he was a perfectionist who seems not to have realized that an army is never ready to the last button and that wars cannot be won without running some risks. He consistently but erroneously believed that the enemy outnumbered him, partly because his intelligence reports from the head of Pinkerton's Detective Agency were unreliable. He was overcautious—Lincoln once accused him of having "the slows"—and he addressed the president in an arrogant tone that a less forgiving person would never have tolerated. Privately the general referred to his chief as a "baboon."

The primary weakness of General George McClellan as a military commander was

    a. his inability to gain the support of his troops.

    b. his tendency to rush into battle with inadequate planning and preparation.

    c. his lack of confidence in his own abilities.

    d. his excessive caution and reluctance to use his troops in battle.

9. Theory X assumes that employees dislike work and whenever possible try to avoid it. So, managers must coerce or control them or threaten punishment to achieve the organization's goals. Managers who accept this view feel that the average person prefers to receive direction, wishes to avoid responsibility, has relatively little ambition, and can be motivated only by money and job security. Managers who hold these assumptions are likely to keep their subordinates under close and constant observation, holding out the threat of disciplinary action, and demanding that they adhere closely to company policies and procedures.

Gloria, a supervisor of data entry clerks, uses a time clock to document the attendance of her employees. Gloria believes that without the monitoring system, the employees' attendance records would decline rapidly. Gloria's assumption about worker behavior is based on

    a. Theory X.

    b. Maslow's hierarchy of needs.

    c. Theory Y.

    d. management by objectives (MBO).

10. But Sherman's hated "Blue Bellies," sixty thousand strong, cut a sixty-mile [97 kilometer] swath of destruction through Georgia. They burned buildings, leaving only the blackened chimneys ("Sherman's Sentinels"). They tore up railroad rails, heated them red-hot, and twisted them into "iron doughnuts" and "Sherman's hairpins." They bayoneted family portraits and ran off with valuable "souvenirs." "War . . . is all hell," admitted Sherman later, and he proved it by his efforts to "make Georgia howl." One of his major purposes was to destroy supplies destined for the Confederate army and to weaken the morale of the men at the front by waging war on their homes.

Sherman's march "from Atlanta to the sea" was especially notable for

    a. its tactical brilliance against Confederate cavalry forces

    b. its effective use of public relations to turn Southern sympathies against the Confederacy.

    c. its brutal use of "total war" tactics of destruction and pillaging against Southern civilian populations.

    d. its impact in inspiring Northern public opinion to turn against slavery

ESSAY QUESTIONS

Synthesis and Evaluation

The highest two levels of thinking, synthesis and evaluation, are rarely tested with the use of objective questions. The reason for this is that there is usually more than one correct answer, so if instructors wish to test these levels of thinking, they usually do so with essay questions.

    Essay questions are similar to objective questions in that they are written on different levels of thinking. However, they are graded differently because there is usually no one correct answer.

Understand the Question: Key Words

Instructors use different terms to begin essay questions, and these terms are extremely important for you to memorize and understand. Many students lose points on an essay exam because they do not answer the question being asked. Following are Bloom's levels of thinking, along with terms used in essay exams and their meanings at each level. You should memorize the meanings of these terms.

Bloom's Taxonomy of Thinking Levels with Key Question Words

Knowledge Level—identification or recall of information
  define—give a clear precise meaning
  recall, record, repeat—state what was written in the text
  name, list—give important points

Comprehension Level—organization and selection of facts and ideas
  restate—state the information in your own words
  describe, discuss—give a detailed explanation
  identify—give the origin, nature, characteristics, and/or classification
  locate—find or place in a certain location
  report—state the results
  tell—give a detailed account
  summarize—state the main points in your own words

Application Level—use of facts, rules, and principles
  translate, interpret—explain the meaning of given facts
  apply—use information
  employ, use—apply information that you have for another purpose
  demonstrate—give evidence to show that something is true
  elaborate, illustrate—give examples to support a statement
  explain why—give reasons for an observation or occurrence

Analysis Level—separation of a whole into its parts
  distinguish—show how one thing is different from others
  analyze—break into parts
  test—determine the properties of a substance
  compare—give similarities and differences
  differentiate, contrast—give differences
  outline, diagram—give the main parts or points
  inspect—study or examine carefully for flaws
  inventory—give a detailed itemized list
  relate—show how one thing has an effect on another
  solve—explain something puzzling
  examine, analyze—study something thoroughly and break it down into its parts

Synthesis Level—combination of ideas to form a new whole
  compose—use knowledge and/or experience, make up the main parts of something new
  propose—present something for consideration
  design—plan something in a systematic way
  formulate—prepare according to a specific formula
  prepare, assemble—fit parts and pieces together
  arrange—plan by distributing things or persons in a particular way
  construct—create by arranging ideas or terms
  organize—put together into an orderly, structured whole
  predict—make an educated guess based on past knowledge and/or experience

Evaluation Level—development of opinions, judgments, or decisions

> *evaluate, appraise*—form a judgment by considering advantages and limitations
>
> *debate*—discuss by offering opposing points
>
> *criticize*—state good and bad points
>
> *judge*—form an opinion after careful consideration of important points
>
> *agree, disagree*—give a positive or negative opinion
>
> *justify*—give supporting information to defend a statement
>
> *estimate*—form an opinion based on past knowledge
>
> *revise*—change or modify to come up with a new version

In the sections that follow, you will find more tips to remember when taking tests.

Answer the Entire Question

Sometimes an instructor will ask you to complete more than one task when answering an essay question:

> List and explain the benefits and drawbacks to the various kinds and sources of new recruits.

To answer this question completely, you have to include many different pieces of information. First, you need to know and list the kinds and sources of new recruits, internal and external. Next, you need to list and give reasons for the benefits of each. Finally, you need to list and give reasons for the drawbacks of each.

Check the Number of Points Awarded for Each Answer

Besides being sure to answer each question, you should also check to see the number of points awarded for the answer. For example, if 8 points are awarded for the correct answer to the preceding question, then you can assume that half of the points are being awarded for benefits and drawbacks of internal recruitment and half are being awarded for the benefits and drawbacks of external recruitment. Be sure to understand how points are awarded. Are you penalized for wrong information? Do you need to list 3 points in order to receive 3 points? Do you need to supply information from the text? class notes? outside reading? Ask these questions *before* you begin an essay exam.

Begin Answers with a Topic Sentence

Begin an answer to an essay question by rewording the question. For example, the answer to the preceding question ("List and explain the benefits and drawbacks to the various kinds and sources of new recruits") would begin with the following statement:

> Two sources of recruitment exist. The benefits of internal recruitment are . . .

The next part of the answer would begin with the following statement:

> The drawbacks or internal recruitment include . . .

You would then follow with sentences about the benefits and drawbacks of external recruitment. Using this procedure will help ensure complete sentences and a more organized answer.

Practice with Periodicals

Read the article "10 Simple Ways to Manage Stress" in Part Three. Write five test questions based on the information in the article. Include only one question on the knowledge level and at least one essay question. Answer your questions.

Journal Entry

As you read the article "10 Simple Ways to Manage Stress" in Part Three, think about what material would be important to remember. Choose three pieces of information, explain why you think they are important, and describe what types of questions you would use to be sure that readers had learned the material.

Textbook Link

After completing a chapter in another textbook you are using, write five questions that you think will be on a test. Do not write more than one "knowledge" question. Then answer your questions.

PREPARING FOR AND TAKING THE TEST

Before the Exam

- **Spend the night before the exam rereading all of your notes.** (You will learn how to take these notes in Part Two.) *Do not* add any new information. Reread your outline and summaries, test yourself with vocabulary cards and predicted test questions you have created, and review any practice tests that you have taken.

- **Arrive a few minutes early for the test.** Arriving late or at the last minute will make you only more anxious. Reread your notes one last time and trust that you will do well. If you have completed some type of notes and many of the study techniques, you should do well.

During the Exam

- **Read all directions carefully.** Budget your time. If you need to answer essay questions, determine how much time you will need for each question.

- **Read the exam twice.** Answer all of the questions that you know the first time that you read through the exam; then go back and answer those questions that you are not sure about or have no idea about. Sometimes a question is answered with information in another question.

- **Take intelligent guesses.**
  - *Use word clues:* Sometimes objective questions contain word clues that help you eliminate a particular answer. For example, a multiple choice question may end with the verb *are,* a verb that indicates a plural answer, and one or two of the choices may be singular; the plural verb would eliminate those answers.
  - *Use logic and narrow down your choices:* On many multiple choice questions, often one choice is obviously not the answer. When you eliminate that possibility, your chances of guessing the correct answer become better. Eliminate any choices that you do not recall reading in the text or hearing in a lecture. If a term is unfamiliar, then it is probably not the answer. Read all parts of true or false statements; if any part is incorrect, the entire statement must be false.
  - *Determine the level of thinking:* If you have no idea about an answer, try to determine the level of thinking of the question. Most of the time, exam questions do not use the same wording that you find in the text. Narrow down where in the text the answer might be found and then base your answer on what you remember reading about the topic.

- **Answer all questions on a test** unless you have been told that you will be penalized for guessing. Whether a test contains objective or essay questions, you receive zero points if you leave a question blank. Taking a guess makes it possible to receive some points.

- **Answer all questions completely.**

- **Relax** if you become nervous. Close your eyes and visualize a peaceful scene or take a few deep breaths to calm yourself. Then continue reading the questions and answering them.

- **Ask your instructor any questions you might have** about any one of the questions. Do not be afraid to ask a question about something that you do not understand.

After the Exam

- **Reward yourself.** No matter how well or poorly you think that you did, you have completed a great deal of work, and you deserve a reward. Treat yourself to a nice meal or just relax and take a break. You can worry about your grade later if you feel the need to worry. When the test is returned, you will then be able to spend some time analyzing what you did right and wrong to avoid repeating the mistakes.

EXAM REVIEW

In Part Two of this book, you will read and study four college-level textbook chapters. After each chapter, you will take a test on the information in the chapter. When your tests are returned, you will analyze the questions to determine why you understood and were able to answer some questions and not others. Using the charts in this section, record reasons for incorrect and correct answers to each of the discipline tests you take. After you have taken two or three tests, review the chart to determine whether you consistently list the same reasons. Use the information to help you study for subsequent tests.

To complete these charts after you have taken and have received the graded chapter tests in Part Two, look first at the questions that are answered incorrectly. Following is a list of reasons why you may have marked the incorrect answer. If you have a reason that is not listed, add it to the list.

1. I took a guess; I had no idea because I couldn't remember this information.
2. I narrowed down the answer to this and another answer and chose the wrong one.
3. I misread the question.
4. I misunderstood the material in the text.
5. I did not study this.
6. _____
7. _____

Place the numbers of the questions that you answered incorrectly in the first column of the chart. Then write the numbers of the reasons why you answered incorrectly in the second column.

Health Test		History Test		American Business Test		Psychology Test	
Incorrect Item No.	Reason	Incorrect Item No.	Reason	Incorrect Item No.	Reason	Incorrect Item No.	Reason

Next, analyze the correct answers on your test. Choose the same number of correct answers as you have incorrect answers. Determine which techniques you used to help you remember and understand the particular information. Here is a list of study techniques that you will have learned and used in the second part of this textbook:

1. notetaking, outlining, or underscoring
2. key word columns
3. summaries
4. vocabulary
5. concept maps
6. practice tests
7. textbook review questions
8. tape-recorded summaries and terms
9. group or partner study
10. _____

After each test is returned to you, place the numbers of the questions that you answered correctly in the first column of the chart. Then place the numbers of the study techniques that you used to learn that information in the second column.

Business Test		Health Test		American History Test		Psychology Test	
Correct Item No.	Reason	Correct Item No.	Reason	Correct Item No.	Reason	Correct Item No.	Reason

APPLYING STUDY/READING TECHNIQUES TO TEXTBOOK CHAPTERS

Part Two contains four chapters excerpted from content-area textbooks: health, American history, business, and psychology. The first three chapters present methods of using the reading skills in Part One to help you study/read these chapters. One study/reading technique—for example, notetaking, marking and annotating, or outlining—is presented with each chapter. A model of each technique, using a section of the excerpted chapter, is given along with an explanation of how to use that technique. Then, using the technique, you are guided through part of the content-area chapter, and finally, you are left to complete the chapter on your own. The fourth chapter excerpt, psychology, is provided as an opportunity for you to choose and use one of the study/reading techniques you have learned and to practice study/reading a chapter entirely on your own.

Recalling the comparison about learning to drive discussed in the Part One introduction, Part Two actually takes you out on the road. You will need to read the excerpted chapters, take some type of notes, and study those notes to prepare for a test in each content area. When you have completed the test for each chapter, you will have a chance to determine how you performed and why, so that the next time out you can do better. But, don't think of this work as like being out on a main highway in rush-hour traffic; that will come once you begin taking college-level courses. Working through Part Two will be more like driving on the weekends when traffic is light and then getting a chance to analyze how you did so that when it is rush hour, you will have already had some experience on the road.

The goal of Part Two, then, is to give you the practice that you need using college-level textbooks. When you exit this course, you will have a knowledge of the reading skills (Part One), a supply of study-reading techniques that you have learned and applied (Part Two), and an understanding of how to read and use periodicals in a course (Part Three). You will be able to use those skills and choose those techniques that work best for you when dealing with other college textbooks and courses.

5

FOUR TEXTBOOK CHAPTERS

This unit contains four excerpted textbook chapters, with study/reading strategies to help you understand the reading material and do well on a test. Each of the first three chapters presents a study/reading technique for you to learn and practice. The last chapter presents you with a choice of study/ reading techniques.

This unit is the heart of this textbook. It provides you with the practice you will need to do well in college-level courses. Learn the techniques, practice the strategies, and become successful at reading college-level textbooks.

CHAPTER 8

HEALTH

In this sample health textbook chapter titled "Personal Stress Management" you will learn to

- Preview the chapter
- Make connections to health
- Take notes in an adapted Cornell notetaking form
- Create and use a key word column
- Study for a health exam by
  - Using the chapter outline to write summaries
  - Making vocabulary cards for each of the important terms
  - Creating a concept map
  - Taking a practice test from the study guide
  - Predicting test questions
  - Recording and listening to your notes
  - Working with a partner or group

The sample health textbook chapter, "Personal Stress Management," can be found immediately following the worksheets. Because you should work with both the worksheets and the health chapter at the same time for many of the activities, pulling out the worksheets will make your work easier. Otherwise, you would need to flip back and forth between these pages and the textbook chapter pages.

PREVIEW

Before you even begin to read a textbook chapter, it is important to get yourself ready to read. This includes mentally and physically preparing yourself to read and understand the information in the chapter. Make sure that you have a comfortable place to study with all of the supplies that you'll need, such as paper, pens, pencils, and a dictionary. Set a goal of how many pages you want to complete, and schedule breaks for yourself. Begin by looking over the chapter and finding something of interest in the material.

Because this chapter is excerpted from a health textbook, you also need to begin to think like a physician. Physicians closely observe people, look for symptoms to illnesses, and prescribe methods of healing the illness. They also research the problems that cause illnesses to prevent further complications. This health chapter will look at the symptoms of stress, causes, and methods of relieving stress. As you read, think about how the chapter might relate to you. Begin to consider any symptoms of stress that you may exhibit, reflect on those experiences that may be causing you stress, and examine the different techniques of stress relief that might be beneficial to you. Throughout your reading and studying of the chapter, continue to think like a physician and question what you read; be sure you differentiate between fact and opinion, and when opinions are given, search for the facts to substantiate them.

Survey the Chapter

Surveying (looking over) the chapter is the first activity that you need to perform. Each textbook is different because authors use different techniques to help get their ideas across to the readers. A textbook chapter may contain a chapter outline, key concepts, lists of important terms, an introductory or concluding summary, important concepts in the margins, added stories to pique your interest, and practice test questions within or at the conclusion of the chapter. All textbook chapters have a title, headings and subheadings (indicated in different ways), and graphics that you should review before reading. Complete the following list of activities to survey this chapter effectively:

1. Read the first page, a scenario about Maria with connections to the topic of stress and what this chapter is all about.

2. Read the "Frequently Asked Questions" and chapter objectives on the second page of the sample chapter. The author provides a page number for the answers to the questions; additionally, each of the questions is addressed in at least one of the objectives.

3. Page through the chapter. Read the main topic headings, defined by the dark outlines, the subheadings, shown in a large boldfaced font, and the minor subheadings, set in smaller font. Think about how each of the subheadings relates to the main topic under which it is written. For example, under "Other Personal Stressors" found about halfway through the chapter, the author uses the following subheadings: "Why Is Everyone so Angry?", "Job Stress," and "Illness and Disability." "Why Is Everyone So Angry?" and "Job Stress" are further broken down into smaller topics ("Getting a Grip" and "Conflict Resolution"; "Workaholism and Burnout," "Who Experiences Burnout?", "Preventing Burnout," and "Desk Rage," respectively). Think about how all of the subtopics relate to the larger topics as well as the chapter topic of stress.

4. As you scan through the pages, focus on the boldfaced vocabulary terms and read the sentences in which they're found. In some textbooks, the author will pull these terms into the margins so that they are more visible.

5. Look at the photographs and graphics; read all captions. These give you an idea of the information that you will be reading. They begin to set up hooks to help you remember the material as you read.

6. Read the various information boxes the author has provided throughout the chapter: "The X & Y Files," "Strategies for Prevention" (all three of these), "Pulse Points," "Strategies for Change," and "Savvy Consumer." Also be sure to complete the "Self-Survey" on page 161. This text will help set up the hooks to enable you to remember the information for a test.

7. Read through and attempt to answer the questions in "Making This Chapter Work for You" at the end of the chapter, and review the "Critical Thinking" questions, "Sites and Bytes" information, "CNN," and the "Key Terms." The questions in the first two sections can act as a guide for your reading. Reading over these questions before you read the chapter will help trigger key points while you read the chapter. You do not need to memorize the questions; your brain will recognize many of the points when you are reading the material. These questions also act as a practice test when you are preparing for a test on the chapter. The "Critical Thinking" questions provide practice with the higher levels of thinking. If you know that you will be taking an essay test, it is important to read these and be able to answer them when you have completed the chapter.

8. Scan the "References" found at the end of the chapter. You may use these if you need more information about any of the topics.

Make Connections

When reading a chapter on health it is especially important to make connections to what you already know because science-related text can be much more difficult to read than other disciplines, such as American history or business. This is because many scientific terms are not familiar words. At times, reading a science textbook can be like reading a foreign language. You can make these connections by determining what you already know about the topics included in science chapters and using that information as the foundation for the new knowledge that you will be learning.

On the lines below, write down what you know about stress. *Do not* write down what you just read as you surveyed the chapter; write about what you may have read or heard previously heard about stress symptoms, terrorism and stress, or any other related topic. Do not worry about being wrong. At this point you are looking for information to build upon and setting up hooks. If you have not already read the two health articles in Part Three, read them now to gain additional knowledge on this topic. Use them to help you add to your information on health.

_____

_____

_____

_____

_____

_____

Writing down information that you already know or about some experience that you have had will help you make a connection with the material that you are about to read. It will help you not only to set up the hooks that you read about in Unit One on PQ3R but also to remember the material more easily.

Discuss the information that you wrote down with a partner or with the class and think about what interest you have in this subject. Is there anything that you like or wish to know about this subject? Other than to understand the material in order to pass the test, why do you wish to read this chapter? What possible influence can this subject have on your life? For example, you might want to know some methods of relieving stress. Think of a question to which you want an answer. This will keep you interested in reading the chapter for your own purpose rather than for the instructor's purpose. Add your questions here.

_____

_____

_____

_____

Writing down what you already know about a topic and then discussing it with someone else will also help you form hooks to organize the new material in your memory and remember it.

Journal Entry

Before you begin the next section, write a journal entry describing what you know about taking notes on loose-leaf paper from a textbook chapter.

MONITOR

Taking Notes

This notetaking method is an adaptation of the Cornell method of taking notes. Before you begin to take notes, whether it is from a textbook or from a lecture, you should prepare your paper by placing the name of the chapter and date in the upper right-hand corner. Then, about 2 inches from the left edge of the paper, draw a vertical line down the side. If you are using loose-leaf paper, your line should be a little to the right of the red margin line. This column that you have created on the left side of the line will be the key word column. After you have completed taking some notes on this chapter, you will learn how to determine key words and use this column. Your paper should look like this:

	Name Date
○	
○	
○	

You will begin to take notes on the first page of the health textbook chapter. Follow these points when writing your notes:

1. Read at least one paragraph before determining the topic, main idea, and important details to put into your notes. Be sure to review all graphics to help you understand and to add information to the material in the text.

2. Write main ideas in complete sentences; added details do not have to be in complete sentences. For instance, you would not have to write examples or reasons in complete sentences.

3. Use telegraphic speech to write your notes. For example, instead of writing "Stress can be acute, episodic, or chronic, depending on what causes the stress," you would write "Stress is acute, episodic, or chronic, depending on cause."

4. Abbreviate words. Be consistent with these abbreviations. You will be rereading the notes 2 or 3 weeks after you write them, and you want to be able to read and understand the abbreviations and symbols at that time.

5. Write the headings and subheadings in your notes. Some of them are already in the form of questions. Change those that are not, into questions. For example, "Stress and the Student" could be changed into the question "How does stress affect students?" Use the question words—*who, what, when, where, why,* and *how*—to turn

headings and subheadings into questions. Write your questions next to the headings and subheadings in the chapter. This gives you information to look for while you are reading. Making up these questions is also a method of performing the "question" step of PQ3R.

6. Check the objectives listed on the second page of the chapter as you read so that you know that you have included all important concepts in your notes.

7. Put all important vocabulary terms in your notes.

8. Leave a space at the end of each subsection and each time that you come to a new subheading. This keeps the page uncluttered and allows you room to add additional information later if you need the space.

Determining the Notes to Write

As you take notes, you need to determine only main ideas and important details. This is done in a number of ways.

1. Use the information that you learned in Part One of this book. Ask the two questions to determine the main idea of each paragraph: "What is this paragraph about?" and "What is the author telling me about this topic?"

2. Think about the organizational pattern of each paragraph; for example, if an entire paragraph is used to define a term, then all that you need in your notes are the definition and term.

3. Remember that not all paragraphs will have one main idea. Some paragraphs will continue the same main idea as the last, and sometimes one paragraph will have more than one idea.

4. Use the headings and subheadings. If they are not already in the form of a question, turn them into questions to help you determine what information is important in a paragraph.

5. Finally, use the questions at the end of the chapter as you read. If you recognize the answer to any of the questions, be sure to place that answer in your notes.

The first page of the sample chapter begins with information about Maria and the stress she experiences. The authors include this for two reasons. First, Maria is a first-year college student, someone to whom you can relate. Second, because you can relate to Maria, the authors use her story to help you relate to the chapter topic, thus setting up hooks to assist you in remembering the information. You have already read this as part of your previewing. Read it again and think about the connections among health, stress, and school and relate these to what you remember from previewing.

Now read the first paragraph under "What Is Stress?" and determine the main idea and important details. Because the heading is in the form of a question, look for the answer to that question as you read this entire section. Each paragraph will give you different details to answer the question. Write your main idea and details here:

_____

_____

Check your notes against those on the following page and then copy them onto your loose-leaf paper to the right side of the margin line that you drew. Your notes should look similar to the following:

	Health
	Date
	What Is Stress?
	Stress has different meanings—external force that causes tense-
	ness in response to internal state of arousal and physical re-
	sponse to demands. Dr. Selye defines stress as nonspecific
	response of body to any demand; reaction to positive and nega-
	tive stressors.
	Stressors = things that upset or excite us

Notice that both *stress* and *stressors* are defined in the notes because they are boldfaced in the paragraph.

Now read the second paragraph and write its main idea and details about the definition of *stress*. This paragraph explains types of stress; be sure to include the different types with examples.

There are three types of stress depending on cause:

	Acute or short-term stress = brief but intense (e.g., pop quiz)
	Episodic = regular intermittent elevations (e.g., monthly bills)
	Chronic = long-lasting or frequent reoccurrences (e.g., learning
	disabilities or daily traffic jams)

Read the third paragraph and write the main idea. Be sure to include the boldfaced terms in your notes.

	We need to balance good stress with bad stress.
	Eustress = positive stress that challenges us to grow and adapt.
	Distress = negative effects of stress

Because the next heading is a major heading, skip two lines and add that heading. Again, the author has already placed the heading in the form of a question; be sure to look for the answer as you read the entire section.

Read the first paragraph and write the main idea and details; include the definitions of boldfaced terms.

_____

_____

	What Causes Stress?
	Best-known theory of stress (by Selye) is the general adaptation
	syndrome (GAS).
	Bodies strive to maintain a balanced state = homeostasis
	Adaptive response = body's method of restoring homeostasis
	when stressors cause response
	Allostasis = body's ability to adapt

The next paragraph explains the GAS process of how the body responds to stressors. Write the main idea and include the three steps of the process in your notes.

_____

_____

_____

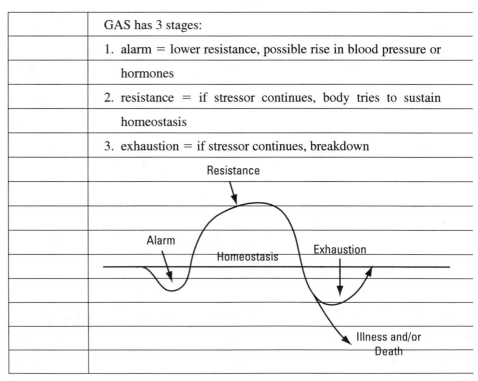

	GAS has 3 stages:
	1. alarm = lower resistance, possible rise in blood pressure or
	hormones
	2. resistance = if stressor continues, body tries to sustain
	homeostasis
	3. exhaustion = if stressor continues, breakdown

The next paragraph is about a different theory. Write the theorist's name and describe the theory in your main idea and details.

_____

_____

	Lazarus's nonbiological theory states that stress and health af-
	fect each other. Stress = a relationship between demands and
	ability to deal with them without negative cost (e.g., speaking in
	front of class may or may not be a stress)

Read the next paragraph and write the main idea and details.

_____

_____

	Stress affects people differently; reactions to stress are affected
	by past experience with stressors—number and frequency along
	with time and setting impact response.

Now read the next paragraph and determine the main idea.

_____

_____

	Levels of ongoing stress affect our ability to handle new stress;
	we all have a breaking point.

In the next paragraph, the author discusses research by two doctors. Write the main idea of the research along with the doctors' names.

_____

_____

	Holmes and Rahe created a scale to evaluate levels of stress,
	measured in life-change units, which estimate a change's impact
	on a person.
	300 units = health problems but actual impact of each stressor
	depends on the individual

The author continues to discuss this research in the last two paragraphs; each has one main idea. Read both paragraphs and determine the main ideas.

_____

_____

	Different groups of people exhibit high or low life-change unit
	totals with college students 2nd highest after addicts.
	You can take steps to move toward stability.

The next heading is a major heading. Skip two lines and add the heading to your notes. This section deals with the hazards of stress to physical health. In this section, the author discusses the general hazards and then focuses on specific parts of the body in the next few subsections. Reading the first paragraph and write the main idea.

_____

_____

	Is Stress Hazardous to Physical Health?
	Stress affects the body's ability to stay well.

The next paragraph has a main idea and important details including the vocabulary term. Determine and write the main idea and details here.

_____

_____

	Stress affects the body's endocrine, or hormone-secreting,
	system.
	Psychoneuroimmunilogy = scientific field studying intercon-
	nections between stress and endocrine system.
	Adrenal glands produce stress hormones; speed up heart rate
	and blood pressure = fight or flight response (muscles tense,
	breathing quickens, digestive and immune systems shut down).

Read the next paragraph in this section and write the main idea and main detail.

_____

_____

| | Stress hormones are water-insoluble and stay in bloodstream a |
| | long time. Cortisol has most important effects on health. |

The next paragraph has one main idea and three effects. Add these to your notes.

_____

_____

	Stress hormones have negative effects.
	Speeds conversion of protein and fat to carbohydrates.
	Leads to excessive central or abdominal fat.
	Leads to risk of diabetes, high blood pressure, or stroke.

Read the next short paragraph and write the main idea with an example or two.

_____

_____

	Stress hormones have emotional negative effects (e.g., long-lasting negative memories or inability to remember).

For the next paragraph, choose two or three examples and make reference to the figure in your notes. (You probably won't have to know all of the physical responses to stress unless your health instructor states that you do; then you would have to add all of the responses.)

_____

_____

	Other problems caused by stress include blood clotting, suppression of immune system, and increase in anxiety levels. See Figure 2-2 in textbook.

Read the next paragraph and write the main idea.

_____

_____

	Research show stress contributes to 80% of all major illnesses.

Read the last paragraph, which has two main ideas. Add both of these to your notes.

_____

_____

	Many symptoms of stress exist: headache, fatigue, sadness.
	Stress can lead to self-destructive behavior.

The next subheading is the first in this subsection. Skip a line and write this subheading; after the subheading, write a question you can form from it. Then read the first paragraph and write a main idea and a detail.

_____

_____

_____

	Stress and the Heart (How does stress affect the heart?)
	Friedman and Rosenman, cardiologists, compared their patients
	to similar individuals with healthy hearts.
	They found two categories—Type A and Type B.

Read the next paragraph and write a short description of each category for your details.

_____

_____

	Type A = hardworking, aggressive, competitive; leads to heart
	disease.
	Type B = more relaxed, not necessarily less successful.

Read the next paragraph, which continues with information about these categories. Write the main idea.

_____

_____

	Degree of danger of being Type A is controversial; chronic hos-
	tility and cynicism are worst behaviors leading to heart attack.

Now read the last paragraph and write the main idea.

_____

_____

	Depression is a mental disorder linked with stress; affects the
	prognosis of individuals with heart attacks.

Skip a line before adding the next subheading and changing it into a question. Then write the main idea of the first paragraph.

_____

_____

	Stress and the Immune System (How does stress affect the immune system?)
	Chemicals triggered by stress suppress the immune system.

Read the next paragraph and write its main idea.

_____

_____

	Traumatic stress can affect immune system for as long as a year;
	even minor stress like exams heightens infections.

The next four paragraphs (through the paragraph beginning with "Stress hormones also may play . . .") are examples of how stress affects the immune system. Read all four and add notes in one sentence about the effects.

_____

_____

	Stress is linked to the common cold, pneumonia, the body's
	ability to heal, and breast cancer.

Now read the next paragraph on how aging compounds stress and write the main idea in your notes.

_____

_____

	Aging compounds the negative impact of stress on health.

The last two paragraphs are about what can help fight the negative effects of stress. Read these last two paragraphs and write a main idea for each.

_____

_____

	Humor and altruism have been shown to fight negative effects
	of stress.
	Writing helps improve health of those suffering from immune
	disorders.

Now skip a line and write the next subheading followed by the subheading turned into a question. Then write the main idea of the first paragraph.

_____

_____

	Stress and the Digestive System (How does stress affect the digestive system?)
	Poor eating habits and stress can cause stomach pain.

Read the second paragraph and write a main idea.

_____

_____

	Stress has been found to contribute to the development of ulcers.

Read the third paragraph and write a main idea with some examples of antistress foods.

_____

_____

	Good nutrition can help a stressed stomach. Complex carbohydrates are great antistress foods (e.g., broccoli, spinach, potatoes).

The last two paragraphs deal with the same main idea, so write that with some examples from each paragraph.

_____

_____

	Simple strategies help avoid stomachaches: drink water, eat fiber-rich foods, don't skip meals, don't overeat, avoid caffeine and sugary snacks.

Finally, skip a line and write the last subheading in this section. Turn it into a question, and then read the first paragraph for a main idea.

_____

_____

_____

	Other Stress Symptoms (What other stress symptoms are there?)
	Stress can affect any organ and increase the risk of accidents.

Read the second paragraph and be sure to define the boldfaced term in your details.

_____

_____

	Headaches are most common stress-related condition.
	Migraines are result of narrowing and widening of blood vessels
	in brain; chemicals leak into nearby tissues and send pain sig-
	nals to the brain.

Read the last paragraph in this section and write the main idea. You will then learn how to use the key word column before continuing to take notes on this chapter.

_____

_____

	Stress affects skin condition.

RECITE

Key Word Column

At this point, you have completed notes for the first one-third of the excerpted health chapter. Now is a good time for review. First, you need to add key words to the key word column. Use key words to indicate topics (stress), boldfaced vocabulary terms, and numbers in lists (stages of GAS). Writing key words forces you to think about what you have written and to condense it into fewer words. The key words become the hooks to help you remember more information.

To write key words, read the first section of notes up to the first blank space. Think of a word or short phrase (a topic) that would summarize those notes. Often it is a word that is repeated in the notes. Write that key word in the key word column next to the notes. Review the following notes and key words after you have completed the key word column for all of your notes.

	What Is Stress?
Stress	Stress has different meanings—external force that causes
	tenseness in response to internal state of arousal and
	physical response to demands. Dr. Selye defines stress as
	nonspecific response of body to any demand; reaction to positive and negative stressors.

Stressors	Stressors = things that upset or excite us
3 types	There are three types of stress depending on cause:
	Acute or short-term stress = brief but intense (e.g., pop quiz)
	Episodic = regular intermittent elevations (e.g., monthly bills)
	Chronic = long-lasting or frequent reoccurrences (e.g., learning disabilities or daily traffic jams)
	We need to balance good stress with bad stress.
Eustress	Eustress = positive stress that challenges us to grow and adapt
Distress	Distress = negative effects of stress
	What Causes Stress?
GAS theory	Best-known theory of stress (by Selye) is the general adaptation syndrome (GAS).
Homeostasis	Bodies strive to maintain a balanced state = homeostasis
Adaptive response	Adaptive response = body's method of restoring homeostasis when stressors cause response
Allostasis	Allostasis = body's ability to adapt
GAS	GAS has 3 stages:
3 stages	1. alarm = lower resistance, possible rise in blood pressure or hormones
	2. resistance = if stressor continues, body tries to sustain homeostasis
	3. exhaustion = if stressor continues, breakdown
Stress/health theory	Lazarus's nonbiological theory states that stress and health affect each other. Stress = a relationship between demands

	and ability to deal with them without negative cost (e.g.,
	speaking in front of class may or may not be a stress)
stress reactions	Stress affects people differently; reactions to stress are
different	affected by past experience with stressors—number
	and frequency along with time and setting impact
	response.
	Levels of ongoing stress affect our ability to handle new
	stress; we all have a breaking point.
stress scale by	Holmes and Rahe created a scale to evaluate levels of
Holmes and Rahe	stress, measured in life-change units, which estimate a
	change's impact on a person.
	300 units = health problems but actual impact of each
	stressor depends on the individual
	Different groups of people exhibit high or low life-change
	unit totals with college students 2nd highest after addicts.
	You can take steps to move toward stability.

Now, you may complete Part I of the study guide practice test on pages 148–149. This test is a good review and will help you determine if you are taking good notes and understanding the information. Check your answers in Appendix A.

Journal Entry

Write a journal explaining what you have learned about using the Cornell system of taking notes.

Continue Notetaking

As you read through the next third of the chapter, write your notes *directly in your notebook* and then compare them to those on the next few pages. Use these notes as a guide; the wording does not need to be exact, but similar.

Skip two lines before writing the next major heading and a question that you create from it. Then add the main idea of the first paragraph to your notes.

	Stress and the Student (What kinds of stress do students have?)
	Being a student can be very stressful.

Write the main idea of the next paragraph with one or two examples of stressors.

	Stress levels of students have been rising, especially in females
	(e.g., test pressure, financial problems, competition).

Read the next paragraph and write a main idea.

	Students bring psychological problems that are brought out by
	stress of campus life.

Read the next two paragraphs together as they deal with the same topic. Each has a different main idea, but they can be combined as one.

	The first year at college is the most stressful, but students re-
	cover self-confidence in the 2nd year.

When you write the main idea of the next paragraph, be sure to include the four ways students react.

	Students react to stress in 4 ways: physiologically, emotionally,
	behaviorally, or cognitively.

Read the next paragraph and write a main idea.

	Social support and time management help students deal with
	stress.

Now read the last paragraph and write that main idea in your notes.

	Colleges are providing more services to help students with
	stress.

Before reading the next section on test stress, return to "The X & Y Files: Men, Women, and Stress" information box found near the beginning of this section. Because a test may contain some questions on this section, you need to take notes on this text also. Skip a line and write the heading; then turn it into a question. Read the section and write one main idea for each paragraph. Check your notes against those that follow.

	The X & Y Files: Men, Women, and Stress (How do men and
	women deal differently with stress?)
	More women than men feel stressed.
	Lifestyle makes a difference; men have more fun.

	Female stress comes from more commitments.
	To deal with stress, women should turn to other women.
	Men have the fight-or-flight response; women tend-and-befriend.
	The gender difference may be from hormones and evolution.

Now turn to the section titled "Test Stress," skip a line, and place that subheading in your notes. Turn it into a question, read the section, and write one main idea for each paragraph.

	Test Stress (How do tests stress a student?)
	Test time brings stress, colds, flu, headaches, and other symptoms.
	Test stress affects students in different ways.
	Students most susceptible are those who don't think they'll do well on tests.
	Test stress can be reduced with relaxation techniques (e.g., meditation, visualization).

Before moving on to the next section, take notes on "Strategies for Prevention" in the information box. Put only the main points in your notes unless you feel you need more of an explanation for any one of the points.

	Defusing Test Stress (How can a student defuse test stress?)
	Plan ahead, be positive, take regular breaks, practice, talk to other students, be satisfied with your best.

Do the same for the information box titled "Pulse Points."

	Top Ten Stress Busters (What are the top 10 stress busters?)
	Strive for balance, get the facts, talk to someone, exercise, express yourself in writing, take care of yourself, set priorities, help others, cultivate hobbies, master a form of relaxation.

Finally, skip a line and place the last subheading of this section in your notes. Turn the subheading into a question and take notes by writing the main ideas and details. The last two paragraphs under this subheading have the same main idea; the author is giving specific examples of different minorities and their stress. You will have only one main idea for these last two paragraphs.

	Minorities and Stress (What types of stress do minority students have?)

	To all students, college may bring culture shock even among
	students of the same race.
	Minority students may feel extra stress.
	Racism has been shown to be a source of stress that can affect
	health.
	However, students have not proven that there is a link between
	stress and ethnicity.
	More research is needed.
	Some common stressors exist among minority students: sensi-
	tivity to social climate and interpersonal tensions with nonmi-
	nority students, but ethnic identity helps buffer the stressors.

The next heading is a major one, so skip two lines before adding it to your notes along with your question created from the heading. Then skip one line and add the next subheading. The short paragraph under the main heading is an introduction and you do not need a main idea for it. In this section, the first two paragraphs have the same main idea and the last two paragraphs have the same main idea, so you'll need to write only two main ideas in your notes. Check yours against those below.

	Other Personal Stressors (What are other personal stressors?)
	Why Is Everyone So Angry?
	Many instances of anger exist today (e.g., driving, sports).
	Evans research points to 3 causes: time, technology, and
	tension.

This next subheading and the following one are not as large as the others the author has used; they both deal with the anger that everyone seems to have. Treat them as regular subheadings, except do not skip lines between them; turn them into questions and determine the main ideas and details under each. The first section has one main idea for each paragraph.

	Getting a Grip (How does one get a grip when angry?)
	We've found that letting anger out makes one more aggressive.
	Chronic anger puts out stress hormones that lead to health risks.
	First, figure out what's really making you mad; stress doesn't
	cause a blowup but can cause overreaction.
	Helmering states anger lasts 3 seconds; the individual keeps it
	going.

Without skipping a line, write the second subheading and turn it into a question. This section has only one main idea with a process. Write the main idea and steps of the process.

	Conflict Resolution (How can I resolve conflict?)
	Learn to deal with the disagreement; focus on the problem, put
	aside biases and focus on what others say. Steps to follow: lis-
	ten, assimilate (keep open to possibilities), and respond calmly.

Before going on to the next subheading, be sure to take some notes on the "Strategies for Change" information box. Skip a line and take notes.

	How to Deal with an Angry Person (How should I deal with an
	angry person?)
	Become an impartial observer, stay calm, refuse to engage, and
	find something to agree with.

Now skip a line and write the next subheading. Each paragraph under this subheading has one main idea. Write each one in your notes.

	Job Stress (What is job stress?)
	People are working more and enjoying it less.
	People's attitudes are the real threats and not the work itself.

Notice that the next four subheadings are smaller and deal with job stress. Do not skip a line before writing the first subheading and a question; then determine the main idea and details of each paragraph. Be sure to add the boldfaced term.

	Workaholism and Burnout (What are workaholism and
	burnout?)
	Workaholic — person who becomes obsessed by work and
	career
	Burnout = consequences of workaholism; state of physical,
	emotional, and mental exhaustion brought on by repeated emo-
	tional pressure; found more in helping professions.
	There are many different signs of burnout (e.g., exhaustion,
	muscle tension, diarrhea).

Add the next subheading without skipping a line. All three paragraphs in this section have one main idea, which is implied. Determine that main idea and add the example details.

	Who Experiences Burnout?
	There are many different variables associated with burnout.
	Examples include the highest burnout between ages 30 and 40,
	unmarried, North American and Asian countries, helping pro-
	fessions, and those with external locus of control.

Without skipping a line, add the next subheading, turn it into a question, and write the main idea of the paragraph.

	Preventing Burnout (How do I prevent burnout?)
	Different factors can prevent burnout but best is learning to cope
	with day-to-day stress.

Again without skipping a line, add the next subheading, turn it into a question, and write one main idea for each paragraph.

	Desk Rage (What is desk rage?)
	Desk rage = name given to job stress that has intensified to a
	dangerous condition.
	Many factors can lead to desk rage (e.g., downsizing, competi-
	tion, long hours).
	Worst conditions include ambiguous job responsibilities and
	fear of speaking what one thinks.
	Ignoring negative emotions can lead to negative effects (e.g.,
	gossip, physical symptoms, withdrawing).

Before going to the next subheading, take notes from the "Strategies for Prevention" information box.

	Defusing Desk Rage (How can someone defuse desk rage?)
	Take care of self, take time to monitor problems, get feedback
	from friends, discuss problems in a nonthreatening way, learn
	from experience, and do immediate damage control.

Now skip a line and write the last subheading in this section. Turn it into a question and write four main ideas, one for each paragraph.

	Illness and Disability (How do illness and disability affect stress?)
	Physical problems can impact emotions.
	Learning disabilities are a common source of stress for college students.
	Learning disabilities may be hard to recognize; characteristics may be inability to engage in a focused activity, extremely distractible, easily frustrated.
	Characteristics indicate someone be tested for a disability.

Now that you have completed notes for the second part of the outline, go back, fill in the key word column, and then take Part II of the practice test on pages 149–150. Again, check your answers in Appendix A.

Continue to take notes on the last third of the chapter. Look over the pages now. Remember to review the information boxes such as "Savvy Consumer" and "Strategies for Prevention." Skip lines when you begin with a new subheading and continue to determine and write main ideas as well as important details and vocabulary terms. Check your notes with your instructor.

REVIEW

Review Your Notes

To prepare yourself to take *the health exam,* you need to use a number of different techniques to help you study. This section will introduce you to various aides and strategies to use in studying. Many of the study techniques can also be used to read more effectively. For example, you will learn about section summaries and vocabulary cards. These techniques can be employed as you read the chapter and used again to study or review the chapter for a test.

You began to study when you first previewed the chapter. You continued to study as you read and took notes by answering the questions formed from the headings and subheadings, addressing the learning goals, and determining main ideas and details with each topic and subtopic. Your notes have helped you narrow down the points that you need to continue to study.

If you were taking Health 101, you would have not only the notes from this chapter to study for a test but also notes from three or four other chapters in the textbook. You would also have lecture notes, old quizzes, assignments, and handouts for your classes. You would need to gather and review all of these materials to prepare for a test.

The health test that you will take in this class will be based on the one textbook chapter only, so the amount of material that you need to study is much less. However, the techniques that you use to study are the same no matter how much material you need to know.

One important adage to remember about studying is that it is not how *long* you study but how *often* you study that determines how well you remember ideas and facts for a test. Schedule your time so that you can study every day for at least 1 week prior to a major test. That way, you will be able to use any or all of the following study techniques.

Methods of Studying

Studying for a major exam involves more than rereading notes. Your outline is a good first step, but you can use many study techniques to improve how well you perform on an exam.

KEY WORD COLUMN

When you have completed taking notes, return to the beginning of the third part of your notes and complete the key word column. Once you have concluded writing all of the key words, use the key word column to help test yourself. Do this by covering up the notes that you have taken, looking only at the key words, and trying to recall what was in the notes. Recite as many of the notes as you remember. Review all of your notes in this manner at least once a week.

SUMMARIES

Write a summary of each heading and subheading in the chapter outline on an index card. Include the main points for each heading in your own words. For example, on the summary card for the second heading, "What Causes Stress?", you would include Selye's general adaptation syndrome process and definitions of the vocabulary terms. You would also include information about Lazarus's theory and Holmes and Rahe's scale to evaluate levels of stress.

VOCABULARY CARDS

The health textbook chapter contains 18 key vocabulary terms. One way to help you memorize the terms is to use index cards. Write the term on one side of the card and the definition on the other side. Refer to the section titled "Remembering Context-Related Terms" in Chapter 1 to help you write effective definitions that will help you remember the terms.

Study the cards by using either side: read the definition and recite the term, or read the term and recite the definition. Keep these cards as well as your summary cards with you. Use spare moments while waiting for a class to begin, sitting in the student lounge or standing in line at the bank to review and study. Remember, it is not how long you study but how often you study that will make you successful.

CONCEPT MAPS

If you recall information better by drawing rather than by writing the words, concept maps will help you. Concept mapping forces you to organize the textbook material and look for relationships between and among subheadings. Use the following guidelines to help you create concept maps:

- When creating concept maps, use the main headings to help you begin the map. Place the main concept (usually a noun from the heading) in a circle or square at the top or in the middle of a piece of paper.
- All concepts should appear only once but may be linked to one or many other concepts.
- Use connecting lines to link concepts.
- Use connecting words like verbs, prepositions, or phrases to show the connection between two concepts. The connecting words along with the paired concepts should create a complete sentence.
- If you have a concept with no connecting lines, try turning the concept into a question (similar to the questions used as headings and subheadings in the health chapter). The answers to the questions become the information that is mapped to the concept.
- There is no correct way to create a concept map. Most of the time, your concept map will not look like someone else's concept map. It is important to be sure that the map is spread out enough on the paper to see relationships and that all writing is legible. Think about the information before you write; plan your map.

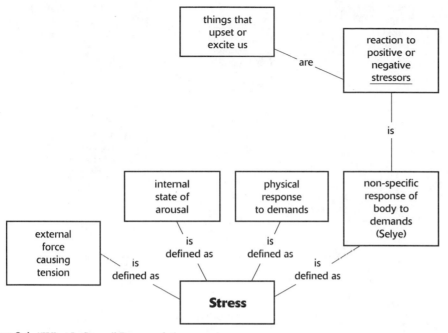

Figure 8.1 "What Is Stress" Paragraph 1 concepts

The example concept maps that follow organize information from the first third of the health chapter—the sections titled "What Is Stress?" and "What Causes Stress?" Begin the concept map by placing "stress" in the middle of the page because both sections focus on the concept of stress.

The first concept map (Figure 8.1) shows information from the first paragraph in the section "What Is Stress?" The second concept map (Figure 8.2) includes information from all three paragraphs in that section. The third and final concept map (Figure 8.3) shows the completed map for the first two sections of the chapter. You will find definitions and information about the GAS process as well as the stress scale by Holmes and Rahe. Take your time and review all of the information about stress. Then try mapping the second and third parts of the chapter on stress.

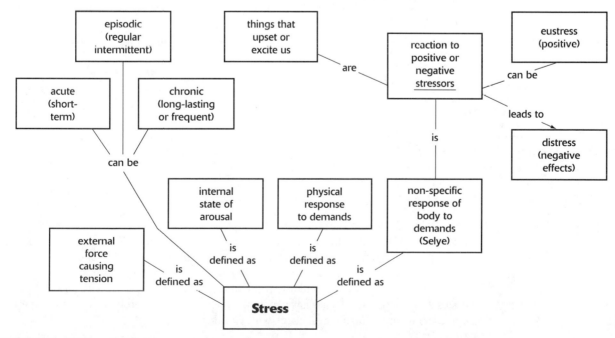

Figure 8.2 "What Is Stress" concepts

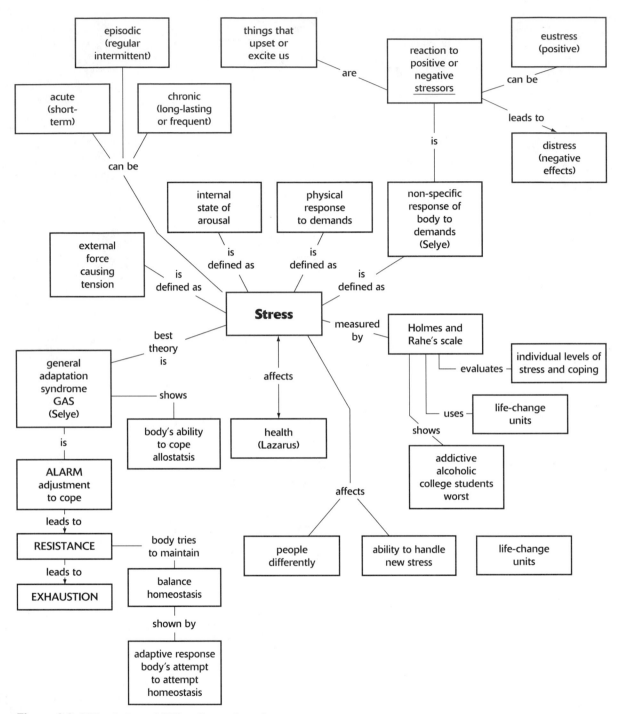

Figure 8.3 "What Is Stress" "What Causes Stress" concepts

PRACTICE TESTS

One of the best methods of preparing for a test is to take practice tests. The health chapter excerpt includes a quiz at the end of the chapter as well as "Critical Thinking" questions. Answer these questions; then check your answers against your notes and the text. You may also want to compare your answers with those of a classmate because the critical thinking questions are written at a higher level of thinking. If possible, form a study group with a few of your classmates and discuss all of your answers to the questions and exercises as well as your notes. If you are not sure of an answer, check with your instructor.

STUDY GUIDE

Many textbooks have a study guide that can be purchased separately in your college bookstore or can be found at the textbook publisher's Web site. If you need extra help, particularly with test questions, this can be a smart method of getting that help. Study guides usually contain a summary of each chapter along with many practice test questions and their answers.

If you do not perform well on tests, a study guide is a perfect practice strategy. Complete and check as many practice test questions as you can. If you cannot purchase a study guide and the publisher's Web site does not have one, you may want to ask your instructor for tests that are no longer used.

As you have completed each section of the notes, you have been completing the parts in the health textbook study guide practice test. You also should have been checking each section with the answer key in Appendix A. Now that you have finished taking notes on the chapter, review your key words for the last third and then take Part III of the practice test. Correct your test after you have completed it, and pay careful attention to the questions that you answered incorrectly. Look up the correct answers in the textbook chapter and determine why you marked them incorrectly.

PREDICTED TEST QUESTIONS

Another method to help you study is to make up or predict test questions for each section of the chapter. This is different than turning subheadings into questions; you need to consider the different levels on which questions can be written and to compose questions on different levels. For example, the following questions could be composed from the information in the first third of the health textbook chapter.

> **Knowledge**—What term is used to mean good stress?
> **Comprehension**—In your own words, explain the general adaptation syndrome.
> **Application**—What physical symptoms of stress do you experience?
> **Analysis**—How is Lazarus's definition of stress different from Selye's definition?
> **Synthesis**—Create a situation in which all three stages of the GAS theory would be achieved.
> **Evaluation**—Is stress worse for the heart or the digestive system? Explain why you chose your answer.

You don't need to ask questions on all levels of thinking for each section. Using the terms listed in Chapter 7, make up one or two questions for each subsection; be sure not to ask only knowledge questions. After you have written the questions, answer each one.

RECORDING AND LISTENING

Because of your learning style, you may remember information better when you hear it rather than see it. Reading your summaries and key terms into a tape recorder and listening to it may help you remember the information better and longer. Use a portable recorder and carry the tape with you; use it whenever you have a few spare moments to review some information.

GROUP OR PARTNER STUDY

Ask others taking the course to study with you. Compare notes, quiz each other with the vocabulary cards, exchange and answer predicted test questions, and review summaries with each other. Discussing the information in the chapter with other students will help clarify it for you by forcing you to put it into your own words. You will also benefit from another individual's interpretation of the material.

PREPARE FOR THE TEST

To help you prepare for the test, review the section in Chapter 7 of this textbook titled "Preparing For and Taking the Test."

REVIEW THE TEST

Complete the exam review charts at the end of Chapter 7 to help you determine what you did right and what you did wrong.

Journal Entry

Try using the Cornell system of taking notes on a chapter from a textbook in another course you are taking, and then write a journal entry explaining whether it was helpful or not and why.

HEALTH STUDY GUIDE PRACTICE TEST

Part I

LEARNING OBJECTIVES

After studying the material in this part of the chapter, you should be able to

- Define *stress* and *stressors* and describe how the body responds to stress according to the general adaptation syndrome theory
- List the physical changes associated with frequent or severe stress and discuss how stress can affect the cardiovascular, immune, and digestive systems

KEY TERMS

You should be able to define these terms.

adaptive response	general adaptation syndrome (GAS)	psychoneuroimmunilogy
allostasis	homeostasis	stress
distress	migraine headache	stressor
eustress		

MULTIPLE CHOICE

Write the letter of the best answer in the blank.

_____ 1. Stressors are

    a. life events.
    b. negative thoughts.
    c. things that upset or excite us.
    d. major life changes.

_____ 2. Positive stress describes

    a. eustress.
    b. distress.
    c. nonspecific stress.
    d. chronic stress.

_____ 3. The body's stable physiological state is called

    a. allostasis.
    b. homeostasis.
    c. stress.
    d. adaptation.

_____ 4. The negative effects of stress refers to

    a. chronic stress.
    b. nonspecific stress.

    c. eustress.

    d. distress.

_____ 5. Type A personality may be a major contributing factor for

    a. cancer.

    b. heart disease.

    c. diabetes.

    d. stroke.

_____ 6. Within Type A personality, which of the following personality traits may be the most harmful?

    a. aggressiveness

    b. determination

    c. pride

    e. hostility

TRUE OR FALSE

Write *T* in the blank if the statement is true, *F* if the statement is false.

_____ 7. The nonspecific response of the body to any demand made upon it defines stress.

_____ 8. The things that upset or excite us are known as life events.

_____ 9. Positive stress in our lives is called eustress.

_____ 10. The body's ability to adapt to consistently changing environments is known as homeostasis.

_____ 11. The biological theory of stress developed by Hans Selye is known as the fight-or-flight response.

_____ 12. Type A personality has been linked to the development of heart disease.

_____ 13. Headaches are one of the most common stress-related conditions.

SHORT ANSWER

    14. Define *homeostasis, allostasis,* and *adaptive response.*

    15. Describe psychoneuroimmunology.

    16. Discuss stress as it relates to heart disease and give the personality type associated with heart disease risk.

Part II

LEARNING OBJECTIVES

After studying the material in this part of the chapter, you should be able to

- Describe some personal causes of stress, especially those experienced by students, and discuss how their effects can be prevented or minimized

KEY TERM

You should be able to define this term.

    burnout

MULTIPLE CHOICE

Write the letter of the *best* answer in the blank.

_____ 1. Nightmares, decreased alertness, and muscular tension are all signs of

    a. burnout.

    b. test stress.

    c. family problems.

    d. job stress.

_____ 2. Having a learning disability is a common source of stress for

    a. high school students.

    b. college students.

    c. middle-age, working adults.

    d. senior citizens.

_____ 3. A workaholic is someone who

    a. uses alcohol before going to work.

    b. becomes obsessed by their work.

    c. is addicted to stress.

    d. strives to be in management.

TRUE OR FALSE

Write *T* in the blank if the statement is true, *F* if the statement is false.

_____ 4. Supervisors are those people who become obsessed by their work and careers.

_____ 5. A state of exhaustion brought on by constant pressure is known as burnout.

Part III

LEARNING OBJECTIVES

After studying the material in this part of the chapter, you should be able to

- Discuss the major social issues that can cause stress
- Identify ways of managing time more efficiently
- Describe some techniques to help manage both short-term and long-term stress
- Explain how stressful events can affect psychological health and describe the factors contributing to posttraumatic growth

KEY TERMS

You should be able to define these terms.

biofeedback	mindfulness	visualization
guided imagery	posttraumatic stress disorder (PTSD)	
meditation	progressive relaxation	

MULTIPLE CHOICE

Write the letter of the *best* answer in the blank.

_____ 1. Which of the following best describes meditation?

    a. maintaining awareness in the present moment

    b. creating mental pictures

    c. sitting quietly, concentrating on a work or image

    d. increasing and decreasing muscle tension

TRUE OR FALSE

Write *T* in the blank if the statement is true, *F* if the statement is false.

_____ 2. Changing the way you interpret events or situations is known as refocusing.

SHORT ANSWER

3. Describe one way of dealing with long-term stress.
4. List and describe five relaxation techniques for managing stress.

CHAPTER 2

Personal Stress Management

Two months into her freshman year, Maria feels as if a tornado has torn through her life. She is living thousands of miles from her family and the friends who share her culture and ethnic background. Her dormmates range from different to downright difficult. Her professors expect her to read and learn more in a week than in an entire month of high school. After blowing her budget decorating her room, she took on a part-time job—only to end up so exhausted that she dozes off in lectures. Stress? Maria considers it a way of life.

Like Maria, you live with stress every day, whether you're studying for exams, meeting people, facing new experiences, or figuring out how to live on a budget. You're not alone. Everyone, regardless of age, gender, race, or income, has to deal with stress—as an individual and as a member of society.

As researchers have demonstrated time and again, stress has profound effects, both immediate and long-term, on our bodies and minds. While stress alone doesn't cause disease, it triggers molecular changes throughout the body that make us more susceptible to many illnesses. Its impact on the mind is no less significant. The burden of chronic stress can undermine ability to cope with day-to-day hassles and can exacerbate psychological problems like depression and anxiety disorders.

Yet stress in itself isn't necessarily bad. What matters most is not the stressful situation itself, but an individual's response to it. By learning to anticipate stressful events, to manage day-to-day hassles, and to prevent stress overload, you can find alternatives to running endlessly on a treadmill of alarm, panic, and exhaustion. As you organize your schedule, find ways to release tension, and build up coping skills, you will begin to experience the sense of control and confidence that makes stress a challenge rather than an ordeal.

After studying the material in this chapter, you should be able to:

- **Define** stress and stressors and **describe** how the body responds to stress according to the general adaptation syndrome theory.

- **List** the physical changes associated with frequent or severe stress and **discuss** how stress can affect the cardiovascular, immune, and digestive systems.

- **Describe** some personal causes of stress, especially those experienced by students, and **discuss** how their effects can be prevented or minimized.

- **Discuss** the major social issues that can cause stress.

- **Identify** ways of managing time more efficiently.

- **Describe** some techniques to help manage both short-term and long-term stress.

- **Explain** how stressful events can affect psychological health and **describe** the factors contributing to posttraumatic growth.

HEALTH

What Is Stress?

People use the word *stress* in different ways: as an external force that causes a person to become tense or upset, as the internal state of arousal, and as the physical response of the body to various demands. Dr. Hans Selye, a pioneer in studying physiological responses to challenge, defined **stress** as "the nonspecific response of the body to any demand made upon it." In other words, the body reacts to **stressors**—the things that upset or excite us—in the same way, regardless of whether they are positive or negative.

Stress can be acute, episodic, or chronic, depending on the nature of the stressors or external events that cause the stress response. Acute or short-term stressors, which can range from a pop quiz to a bomb threat in a crowded stadium, trigger a brief but intense response to a specific incident. Episodic stressors like monthly bills or quarterly exams cause regular but intermittent elevations in stress levels. Chronic stressors include everything from rush-hour traffic to a learning disability to living with an alcoholic parent or spouse.

Not all stressors are negative. Some of life's happiest moments—births, reunions, weddings—are enormously stressful. We weep with the stress of frustration or loss; we weep, too, with the stress of love and joy. Selye coined the term **eustress** for positive stress in our lives (*eu* is a Greek prefix meaning "good"). Eustress challenges us to grow, adapt, and find creative solutions in our lives. **Distress** refers to the negative effects of stress that can deplete or even destroy life energy. Ideally, the level of stress in our lives should be just high enough to motivate us to satisfy our needs and not so high that it interferes with our ability to reach our fullest potential.

What Causes Stress?

Of the many biological theories of stress, the best known may be the **general adaptation syndrome (GAS),** developed by Hans Selye. He postulated that our bodies constantly strive to maintain a stable and consistent physiological state, called **homeostasis.** Stressors, whether in the form of physical illness or a demanding job, disturb this state and trigger a nonspecific physiological response. The body attempts to restore homeostasis by means of an **adaptive response. Allostasis** describes the body's ability to adapt to constantly changing environments.

Selye's general adaptation syndrome, which describes the body's response to a stressor—whether threatening or exhilarating—consists of three distinct stages:

1. *Alarm.* When a stressor first occurs, the body responds with changes that temporarily lower resistance. Levels of certain hormones may rise; blood pressure may increase (see Figure 2-1). The body quickly makes internal adjustments to cope with the stressor and return to normal activity.
2. *Resistance.* If the stressor continues, the body mobilizes its internal resources to try to sustain homeostasis. For example, if a loved one is seriously hurt in an accident, we initially respond intensely and feel great anxiety. During the subsequent stressful period of recuperation, we struggle to carry on as normally as possible, but this requires considerable effort.
3. *Exhaustion.* If the stress continues long enough, we cannot keep up our normal functioning. Even a small amount of additional stress at this point can cause a breakdown.

© CORBIS

▲ An automobile accident is an example of an acute stressor. Getting married is an example of a positive stressor.

© 2000 PhotoDisc

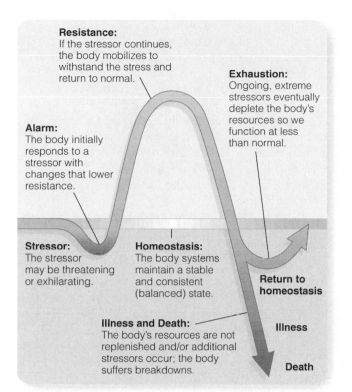

Resistance:
If the stressor continues, the body mobilizes to withstand the stress and return to normal.

Exhaustion:
Ongoing, extreme stressors eventually deplete the body's resources so we function at less than normal.

Alarm:
The body initially responds to a stressor with changes that lower resistance.

Stressor:
The stressor may be threatening or exhilarating.

Homeostasis:
The body systems maintain a stable and consistent (balanced) state.

Return to homeostasis

Illness and Death:
The body's resources are not replenished and/or additional stressors occur; the body suffers breakdowns.

Illness

Death

▲ **Figure 2-1** The three stages of Selye's General Adaptation Syndrome (GAS): alarm, resistance, exhaustion.

Among the nonbiological theories is the cognitive-transactional model of stress, developed by Richard Lazarus, which looks at the relation between stress and health. As he sees it, stress can have a powerful impact on health. Conversely, health can affect a person's resistance or coping ability. Stress, according to Lazarus, is "neither an environmental stimulus, a characteristic of the person, nor a response, but a relationship between demands and the power to deal with them without unreasonable or destructive costs."[1] Thus, an event may be stressful for one person but not for another, or it may seem stressful on one occasion but not on another. For instance, one student may think of speaking in front of the class as extremely stressful, while another relishes the chance to do so—except on days when he's not well-prepared.

At any age, some of us are more vulnerable to life changes and crises than are others. The stress of growing up in families troubled by alcoholism, drug dependence, or physical, sexual, or psychological abuse may have a lifelong impact—particularly if these problems are not recognized and dealt with. Other early experiences, positive and negative, also can affect our attitude toward stress—and our resilience to it. Our general outlook on life, whether we're optimistic or pessimistic, can determine whether we expect the worst and feel stressed or anticipate a challenge and

feel confident. The when, where, what, how, and why of stressors also affect our reactions. The number and frequency of changes in our lives, along with the time and setting in which they occur, have a great impact on how we'll respond.

Our level of ongoing stress affects our ability to respond to a new day's stressors. Each of us has a breaking point for dealing with stress. A series of too-intense pressures or too-rapid changes can push us closer and closer to that point. That's why it's important to anticipate potential stressors and plan how to deal with them.

Stress experts Thomas Holmes, M.D., and Richard Rahe, M.D., devised a scale to evaluate individual levels of stress and potential for coping, based on *life-change units* that estimate each change's impact. The death of a partner or parent ranks high on the list, but even changing apartments is considered a stressor. People who accumulate more than 300 life-change units in a year are more likely to suffer serious health problems. Scores on the scale, however, represent "potential stress"; the actual impact of the life change depends on the individual's response. (See Self-Survey: "Student Stress Scale," on page 47.)

Holmes has evaluated variations in life events among many groups, including college students, medical students, football players, pregnant women, alcoholics, and heroin addicts. Heroin addicts and alcoholics have the highest totals of life-change units, followed by college students. In general, younger people experience more life changes than do older people; factors such as gender, education, and social class also have a strong impact.[2] Marriage seems to promote greater stability and fewer changes.

If you score high on the Student Stress Scale, think about the reasons your life has been in such turmoil. Are there any steps you could take to make your life more stable? Of course, some changes, such as your parents' divorce or a friend's accident, are beyond your control. Even then, you can respond in ways that may protect you from disease.

Is Stress Hazardous to Physical Health?

These days we've grown accustomed to warning labels advising us of the health risks of substances like alcohol and cigarettes. Medical researchers speculate that another component of twenty-first-century living also warrants a warning: stress.[3] In recent years, an every-growing number of studies has implicated stress as a culprit in a range of medical problems. While stress itself may not kill, it clearly undermines our ability to stay well.[4]

Stress triggers complex changes in the body's endocrine, or hormone-secreting, system. The scientific field of **psychoneuroimmunology** has been exploring these intricate interconnections. When you confront a stressor, the adrenal glands, two triangle-shaped glands that sit atop the kidneys, respond by producing stress hormones, including catecholamines, cortisol (hydrocortisone), and epinephrine (adrenaline), that speed up heart rate and blood pressure and prepare the body to deal with the threat. This "fight-or-flight" response prepares you for quick action: Your heart works harder to pump more blood to your legs and arms. Your muscles tense, your breathing quickens, and your brain becomes extra alert. And because they're nonessential in a crisis, your digestive and immune systems practically shut down.

Unlike many other molecules in the body (such as the neurotransmitters that transmit messages in the brain), most stress hormones are water-insoluble, which means that they remain in the bloodstream longer. The effects of neurotransmitters disappear within seconds or milliseconds; stress hormones persist in the blood for hours. Cortisol remains elevated for the longest period and has the most important long-term effects on our health.

One effect of cortisol and the other stress hormones, for example, is to speed the conversion of proteins and fats into carbohydrates, the body's basic fuel, so we have the energy to fight or flee from a threat. Another effect is to increase appetite and food-seeking behavior. Cortisol can cause excessive central or abdominal fat, which heightens the risk of diseases such as diabetes, high blood pressure, and stroke.[5] Even slender, premenopausal women faced with increased stress and lacking good coping skills are more likely to accumulate excess weight around their waists, thereby increasing their risk of heart disease and other health problems.[6]

In the brain, stress hormones linked to powerful emotions may help create long-lasting memories of events such as the Colombine shootings. But very prolonged or severe stress can damage the brain's ability to remember and can actually cause brain cells, or neurons, to atrophy and die.

As Figure 2-2 illustrates, persistent or repeated increases in the stress hormones can be hazardous throughout the body. Catecholamines cause a rise in blood

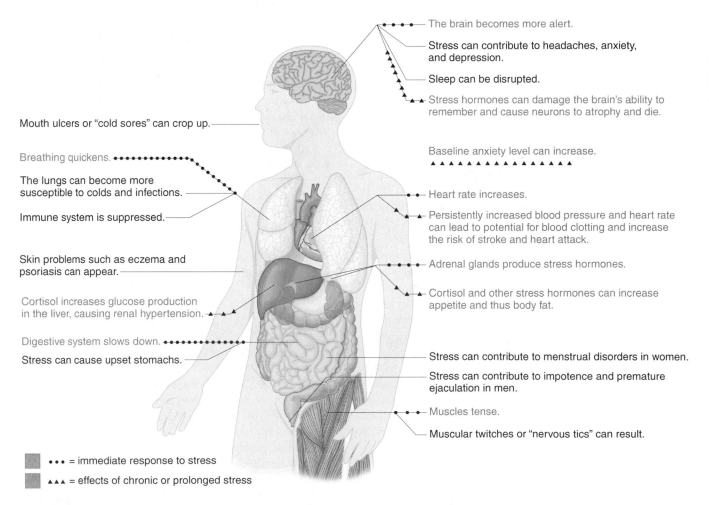

▲ **Figure 2-2** The effects of stress on the body.

pressure and heart rate, make breathing short and shallow, and increase the potential for blood clotting, upping the risk for stroke and heart attack. Cortisol increases glucose production in the liver, causes renal hypertension (which also raises blood pressure), and suppresses the immune system. Chronically elevated stress hormones raise the baseline anxiety level, making it harder to cope with daily annoyances.

Hundreds of studies over the last 20 years have shown that stress contributes to approximately 80 percent of all major illnesses: cardiovascular disease, cancer, endocrine and metabolic disease, skin rashes, ulcers, ulcerative colitis, emotional disorders, musculoskeletal disease, infectious ailments, premenstrual syndrome (PMS), uterine fibroid cysts, and breast cysts. As many as 75 to 90 percent of visits to physicians are related to stress.

The first signs of stress include muscle tightness, tension headaches, backaches, upset stomach, and sleep disruptions (caused by stress-altered brain-wave activity). Some people feel fatigued, their hearts may race or beat faster than usual at rest, and they may feel tense all the time, easily frustrated and often irritable. Others feel sad; lose their energy, appetite, or sex drive; and develop psychological problems, including depression, anxiety, and panic attacks (discussed in Chapter 3). Stress can lead to self-destructive behaviors, such as drinking, drug use, and reckless driving. Some people see such acts as offering an escape from the pressure they feel. Unfortunately, they end up adding to their stress load.

Stress and the Heart

In the 1970s, cardiologists Meyer Friedman, M.D., and Ray Rosenman, M.D., suggested that excess stress could be the most important factor in the development of heart disease. They compared their patients to individuals of the same age with healthy hearts and developed two general categories: Type A and Type B.

Hardworking, aggressive, and competitive, Type A's never have time for all they want to accomplish, even though they usually try to do several tasks at once. Type B's are more relaxed, though not necessarily less ambitious or successful. Type-A behavior has been found to be the major contributing factor in the early development of heart disease.

The degree of danger associated with Type-A behavior remains controversial. According to a 22-year follow-up study of 3,000 middle-aged men by researchers at the University of California, Berkeley, both smoking and high blood pressure proved to be much greater threats than Type-A behavior with respect to heart attack risk. Of all the personality traits linked with Type-A behavior, the one that has emerged as most sinister is chronic hostility or cynicism. People who are always mistrustful, angry, and suspicious are twice as likely to suffer blockages of their coronary arteries.

Depression, a mental disorder often linked with stress, clearly affects the prognosis of individuals who suffer heart attacks. (See Chapter 12.) The National Heart, Lung, and Blood Institute currently is studying 2,000 cardiac patients to determine if treating their depression may improve the quality of their lives and their survival odds.

Stress and the Immune System

The powerful chemicals triggered by stress dampen or suppress the immune system—the network of organs, tissues, and white blood cells that defend against disease. Impaired immunity makes the body more susceptible to many diseases, including infections (from the common cold to tuberculosis) and disorders of the immune system itself.

As psychoneuroimmunology research has shown, traumatic stress, such as losing a loved one through death or divorce, can impair immunity for as long as a year. Even minor hassles take a toll. Under exam stress, students experience a dip in immune function and a higher rate of infections. Ohio State University researchers found a significant drop in the immune cells that normally ward off infection and cancer in medical students during exam periods.[7]

Scientists have identified what may be an important biological link between stress and the common cold: interleukin-6 (IL-6), a chemical pathway used by the immune system. In a 1999 study, researchers at the Children's Hospital of Pittsburgh measured the levels of 55 volunteers before infecting them with an influenza virus. While all developed flu symptoms, the concentration of IL-6, as measured from nasal secretions, was higher in those reporting greater psychological stress before being infected.[8]

The immune response induced by vaccination against pneumococcal pneumonia is lower in people under stress, such as caregivers to relatives with dementia.[9] Studies of university students and staff in the United States and in Spain have implicated stress and a generally negative outlook as increasing susceptibility to the common cold, even in individuals taking vitamin C and zinc to ward off infection.[10]

Stress also interferes with the body's ability to heal itself. By inflicting small cuts in volunteers who are then subjected to controlled stressful situations, researchers have shown a significant delay in healing among those under stress.[11]

Stress hormones also may play a role in the progression of breast cancer. In research on women with metastatic breast cancer, psychiatrist David Spiegel of Stanford University, correlated variations in cortisol secretion with survival rates. The average survival time of women with normal cortisol patterns (high levels in the early morning and progressively lower concentrations during the day) was significantly longer than that of the women whose cortisol remained high all day (a stress indicator).[12]

Aging seems to compound the negative impact of stress on health. Older adults show even greater immunological impairments associated with stress or depression than younger adults and face a greater risk of illness and death.[13]

Certain uplifts, including humor and altruism, may buffer the harmful effects of stress. In studies of college students, watching videotapes of comedians bolstered immune function. Students who provided services to others show a temporary boost in immunity.

Writing about stressful events also can improve the health of people suffering from immune disorders such as chronic asthma or rheumatoid arthritis. In one study, volunteers who wrote about "the most stressful event they had ever undergone" for 20 minutes on three consecutive days showed significant improvements compared with those who spent the same amount of time writing about neutral topics. It is not known why writing about traumatic experiences can relieve immune system disorders, but the researchers theorize that it may help patients make sense of what had happened to them and come to terms with its impact.[14]

Stress and the Digestive System

Do you ever get butterflies in your stomach before giving a speech in class or before a big game? The digestive system is, as one psychologist quips, "an important stop on the tension trail." To avoid problems, pay attention to how you eat: Eating on the run, gulping food, or overeating results in poorly chewed foods, an overworked stomach, and increased abdominal pressure. The combination of poor eating habits and stress can add up to real pain in the stomach.

As noted in Chapter 13, scientists, after identifying the bacterium *H. pylori* as a cause of most peptic ulcers, had downplayed the role of stress. However, more recent studies suggest that stress may indeed be a factor. About 80 percent of people carrying the *H. pylori* bacteria do not get ulcers; about 30 percent of patients who do have ulcers test negative for the bacteria. Researchers now contend that stress does contribute to the development of ulcers, hamper their healing, and increase the likelihood of their recurrence.[15]

Good nutrition can help soothe a stressed-out stomach. Complex carbohydrates are an ideal antistress food because they boost the brain's level of the mood-enhancing chemical serotonin. Good sources include broccoli, leafy greens, potatoes, corn, cabbage, spinach, whole-grain breads and pastas, muffins, crackers, and cereals. Leafy vegetables, whole grains, nuts, and seeds also are rich in other important nutrients, including magnesium and vitamin C.

Some simple strategies can help you avoid stress-related stomachaches. Many people experience dry mouth or sweat more under stress. By drinking plenty of water, you replenish lost fluids and prevent dehydration. Fiber-rich foods counteract common stress-related problems, such as cramps and constipation. Do not skip meals. If you do, you're more likely to feel fatigued and irritable.

Be wary of overeating under stress. Some people eat more because they scarf down meals too quickly. Others reach for snacks to calm their nerves or comfort themselves. Watch out for caffeine. Coffee, tea, and cola drinks can make your strained nerves jangle even more. Also avoid sugary snacks. They'll send your blood sugar levels on a roller coaster ride—up one minute, down the next.

Other Stress Symptoms

Stress can affect any organ system in the body, causing painful symptoms or a flare-up of chronic conditions such as asthma. By interfering with our alertness and ability to concentrate, stress also increases the risk of accidents at home, at work, and on the road.

Headaches are one of the most common stress-related conditions. The most common type, tension headache, is caused by involuntary contractions of the scalp, head, and neck muscles. **Migraine headache** is the result of constriction (narrowing), then dilation (widening) of blood vessels within the brain; chemicals leak through the vessel walls, inflame nearby tissues, and send pain signals to the brain. Surveys of college women show that Type-A behavior can trigger both types of headache.

Stress also is closely linked to skin conditions. If you break out the week before an exam, you know firsthand that skin can be extremely sensitive to stress. Skin conditions worsened by stress include acne, psoriasis, herpes, hives, and eczema. With acne, increased touching of the face, perhaps while cramming for a test, may be partly responsible. Other factors, such as temperature, humidity, and cosmetics and toiletries, may also play a role.

Stress and the Student

You've probably heard that these are the best years of your life, but being a student—full-time or part-time, in your late teens, early twenties, or later in life—can be extremely stressful. You may feel pressure to perform well to qualify for a good job or graduate school. To meet steep tuition payments, you may have to juggle part-time work and coursework. You may feel stressed about choosing a major, getting along with a difficult roommate, passing a particularly hard course, or living up to your parents' and teachers' expectations. If you're an older student, you may have children, housework, and homework to balance. Your days may seem so busy and your life so full that you worry about coming apart at the seams. One thing is for certain: You're not alone. (See Student Snapshot: "Freshman Stress.")

Stress levels among college students have been rising steadily, especially among women. (See the X & Y Files: "Men, Women, and Stress.") According to surveys of students at colleges and universities around the country and the world, stress levels are consistently high and stressors are remarkably similar.[16] Among the most common are:

- Test pressures.
- Financial problems.
- Frustrations, such as delays in reaching goals.
- Problems in friendships and dating relationships.
- Daily hassles.
- Academic failure.

- Pressures as a result of competition, deadlines, and the like.
- Changes, which may be unpleasant, disruptive, or too frequent.
- Losses, whether caused by the breakup of a relationship or the death of a loved one.

Many students bring complex psychological problems with them to campus, including learning disabilities and mood disorders like depression and anxiety. "Students arrive with the underpinnings of problems that are brought out by the stress of campus life," says one counselor. Some have grown up in broken homes and bear the scars of family troubles. Others fall into the same patterns of alcohol abuse that they observed for years in their families or suffer lingering emotional scars from childhood physical or sexual abuse.

The X & Y Files   Men, Women, and Stress

Women, who make up 56 percent of today's college students, also shoulder the majority of the stress load. In a nationwide survey of students in the class of 2004, freshmen women were twice as likely to be anxious as men. More women (36.4 percent) described themselves as "overwhelmed by all I have to do," compared with just 17.9 percent of men. More women than men reported feeling depressed, insecure about their physical and mental health, and worried about paying for college. More men—60.2 percent, compared with 48.6 percent of women—considered themselves above average or in the top 10 percent of people their age in terms of emotional health.

Gender differences in lifestyle may help explain why women feel so stressed. College men, the survey revealed, spend significantly more time doing things that are fun and relaxing: exercising, partying, watching TV, and playing video games. Women, on the other hand, tend to study more, do more volunteer work, and handle more household and child-care chores.

The stress gender gap, which appeared in the mid-1980s, is "one of the ironies of the women's movement," says Alexander Astin of UCLA, founder of the annual American Freshman Survey, which has tracked shifting student attitudes for 35 years. "It's an inevitable consequence of women adding more commitments and responsibilities on top of all the other things they have to cope with." He believes that college women are experiencing an early version of the stress that "supermoms" feel later in life when they pursue a career, care for children, and maintain a household.

Where can stressed-out college women turn for support? The best source, according to University of

California research, is other women. In general, the social support women offer their friends and relatives seems more effective in reducing the blood pressure response to stress than that provided by men.

At all ages, women and men tend to respond to stress differently. While males (human and those of other species) react with the classic "fight-or-flight" response, females under attack try to protect their children and seek help from other females—a strategy dubbed "tend-and-befriend." When exposed to experimental stress (such as a loud, harsh noise), women show more affection for friends and relatives; men show less. When working mothers studied by psychologists had a bad day, they coped by concentrating on their children when they got home. Stressed-out fathers were more likely to withdraw.

The gender difference in stress responses may be the result of hormones and evolution. While both men and women release stress hormones, men also secrete testosterone, which tends to increase hostility and aggression. For prehistoric women, who were usually pregnant, nursing, or caring for small children, neither fight nor flight was a wise strategy. Smaller and weaker than males, women may long ago have reached out to other women to form a social support system that helped ensure their safety and that of their children.

Sources: Sax, Linda, et al. *The American Freshman: National Norms for Fall 2000.* Los Angeles: Higher Education Research Institute, UCLA, 2000. Glynn, Laura, et al. "Women's Social Support More Beneficial than Men's." *Psychosomatic Medicine,* Vol. 61, April 1999. "How Women Handle Stress: Is There a Difference?" *Harvard Mental Health Letter,* Vol. 17, No. 10, April 2001.

HEALTH

© 2000 PhotoDisc

▲ The first year of college can be overwhelming as you learn your way around the campus, become acquainted with new people, and strive to succeed.

For many students, the first year at college is the most stressful. Many have to deal with issues like sexism, racism, and financial difficulties for the first time in their lives. They may experience social discrimination in cafeterias and dorms. Older students may feel out of place taking the same classes as 18-year-olds and worry about going into debt to pay for tuition after years of earning their own money. Students of all ages feel intense pressure to succeed and may worry about not being able to manage their time, get good grades, or decide on a major and a career.

While the self-esteem of college freshmen typically falls, students recover their self-confidence in their second year. They become more positive, introspective, and independent and have a stronger sense of their own intellectual ability. It may well be that as students acclimate to college, they experience less stress and therefore view themselves more positively.

Students say they react to stress in various ways: physiologically (by sweating, stuttering, trembling, or developing physical symptoms); emotionally (by becoming anxious, fearful, angry, guilty, or depressed); behaviorally (by crying, eating, smoking, being irritable or abusive); or

Student Snapshot Freshman Stress

Percentage of Freshmen Who Felt Frequently Overwhelmed

Stress levels among college freshman have reached record levels, with 30.2 percent of first-year students saying that they feel frequently overwhelmed by all they have to do. Many more women than men report high stress. Among the class of 2002, 38.5 percent of women say they felt frequently overwhelmed, compared with 19.2 percent of men.

Source: Sax, Linda, et al. *The American Freshman: National Norms for Fall 2000.* Los Angeles: Higher Education Research Institute, UCLA, 2000.

Student Stress Scale

HEALTH

The Student Stress Scale, an adaptation of Holmes and Rahe's Life Events Scale for college-age adults, provides a rough indication of stress levels and possible health consequences.

In the Student Stress Scale, each event, such as beginning or ending school, is given a score that represents the amount of readjustment a person has to make as a result of the change. In some studies, using similar scales, people with serious illnesses have been found to have high scores.

To determine your stress score, add up the number of points corresponding to the events you have experienced in the past 12 months.

1.	Death of a close family member	100
2.	Death of a close friend	73
3.	Divorce of parents	65
4.	Jail term	63
5.	Major personal injury or illness	63
6.	Marriage	58
7.	Getting fired from a job	50
8.	Failing an important course	47
9.	Change in the health of a family member	45
10.	Pregnancy	45
11.	Sex problems	44
12.	Serious argument with a close friend	40
13.	Change in financial status	39
14.	Change of academic major	39
15.	Trouble with parents	39
16.	New girlfriend or boyfriend	37
17.	Increase in workload at school	37
18.	Outstanding personal achievement	36
19.	First quarter/semester in college	36
20.	Change in living conditions	31
21.	Serious argument with an instructor	30
22.	Getting lower grades than expected	29
23.	Change in sleeping habits	29
24.	Change in social activities	29
25.	Change in eating habits	28
26.	Chronic car trouble	26
27.	Change in number of family get-togethers	26
28.	Too many missed classes	25
29.	Changing colleges	24
30.	Dropping more than one class	23
31.	Minor traffic violations	20
	Total Stress Score	_____

Here's how to interpret your score: If your score is 300 or higher, you're at high risk for developing a health problem. If your score is between 150 and 300, you have a 50–50 chance of experiencing a serious health change within two years. If your score is below 150, you have a 1-in-3 chance of a serious health change.

Making Changes

Coping with Life Changes

If you're going through a lot of change, you can take steps to minimize harmful effects. Here are some suggestions:

- Review the Student Stress Scale often so you're familiar with different life events and the amount of stress they can cause.
- When change occurs, think about its meaning and your feelings about it.
- Try to come up with different ways of adjusting to the change.
- Don't rush into action; take time to make a careful decision.
- Pace yourself. Even if you have a lot to do, stick to a reasonable schedule that allows you some time off to relax.
- Look at each change as a part of life's natural flow, rather than as a disruption in the way things should be.

Source: Mullen, Kathleen, and Gerald Costello. *Health Awareness Through Discovery.*

---

cognitively (by thinking about and analyzing stressful situations and strategies that might be useful in dealing with them).

 Social support makes a difference. Students with a truly supportive network of friends and family available to them report greater satisfaction and less psychological distress. Effective time management, discussed later in this chapter, helps buffer academic stress.[17] Higher levels of positive experiences, such as forming close friendships, also reduce stress and compensate for the despressive effects of negative experiences, such as failing a test.[18]

Campuses are providing more "frontline services" than they have in the past, including career-guidance workshops, telephone hot lines, and special social programs for lonely, homesick freshmen. At a growing number of schools, peer mentors provide companionship and psychological support. These programs may be particularly beneficial for minorities and women, who most often feel excluded in the academic world.[19]

Test Stress

For many students, midterms and final exams are the most stressful times of the year. Studies at various colleges and universities found that the incidence of colds and flu soared during finals. Some students feel the impact of test stress in other ways—headaches, upset stomachs, skin flare-ups, or insomnia.

Test stress affects people in different ways. Sometimes students become so preoccupied with the possibility of failing that they can't concentrate on studying. Others, including many of the best and brightest students, freeze up during tests and can't comprehend multiple-choice questions or write essay answers, even if they know the material.

The students most susceptible to exam stress are those who believe they'll do poorly and who see tests as extremely threatening. Unfortunately, such negative thoughts often become a self-fulfilling prophecy. As they study, these students keep wondering, "What good will studying do? I never do well on tests." As their fear increases, they try harder, pulling all-nighters. Fueled by caffeine, munching on sugary snacks, they become edgy and find it harder and harder to concentrate. By the time of the test, they're nervous wrecks, scarcely able to sit still and focus on the exam.

Can you do anything to reduce test stress and feel more in control? Absolutely. One way is to defuse stress through relaxation. In a study by researchers Janice Kiecolt-Glaser and Ron Glaser of Ohio State University, one group of students was taught relaxation techniques—such as controlled breathing, meditation, progressive relaxation, and guided imagery (visualization)—a month before finals. The more the students used these "stress busters," the higher were their levels of immune cells during the exam period. The extra payoff was that they felt calmer and in better control during their tests.[20] (See Pulse Points: "Top Ten Stress Busters.")

▲ Test stress can affect your immune system, cause digestive problems, and even cause you to freeze during the exam. But you can take control of your stress responses by practicing relaxation techniques, avoiding cramming, and being positive about your performance on the test.

© Ulrike Welsch

STRATEGIES FOR PREVENTION

Defusing Test Stress

✔ *Plan ahead.* A month before finals, map out a study schedule for each course. Set aside a small amount of time every day or every other day to review the course materials.

✔ *Be positive.* Picture yourself taking your final exam. Imagine yourself walking into the exam room feeling confident, opening up the test booklet, and seeing questions for which you know the answers.

✔ *Take regular breaks.* Get up from your desk, breathe deeply, stretch, and visualize a pleasant scene. You'll feel more refreshed than you would if you chugged another cup of coffee.

✔ *Practice.* Some teachers are willing to give practice finals to prepare students for test situations, or you and your friends can test each other.

✔ *Talk to other students.* Chances are that many of them share your fears about test taking and may have discovered some helpful techniques of their own. Sometimes talking to your adviser or a counselor can also help.

✔ *Be satisfied with doing your best.* You can't expect to ace every test; all you can and should expect is your best effort. Once you've completed the exam, allow yourself the sweet pleasure of relief that it's over.

PULSE POINTS

Top Ten Stress Busters

1. **Strive for balance.** Review your commitments and plans, and if necessary, scale down.

2. **Get the facts.** When faced with a change or challenge, seek accurate information, which can bring vague fears down to earth.

3. **Talk with someone you trust.** A friend or a health professional can offer valuable perspective as well as psychological support.

4. **Exercise.** Even when your schedule gets jammed, carve out 20 or 30 minutes several times a week to walk, swim, bicycle, jog, or work out at the gym.

5. **Express yourself in writing.** Keeping a journal is one of the best ways to put your problems into perspective.

6. **Take care of yourself.** Get enough sleep. Eat a balanced diet. Limit your use of sugar, salt, and caffeine, which can compound stress by leading to fatigue and irritability. Watch your alcohol intake. Drinking can cut down on your ability to cope.

7. **Set priorities.** Making a list of things you need to do and rank-ing their importance help direct your energies so you're more efficient and less stressed.

8. **Help others.** One of the most effective ways of dealing with stress is to find people in a worse situation and do something positive for them.

9. **Cultivate hobbies.** Pursuing a personal pleasure can distract you from the stressors in your life and help you relax.

10. **Master a form of relaxation.** Whether you choose meditation, yoga, mindfulness, or another technique, practice it regularly.

Minorities and Stress

Regardless of your race or ethnic background, college may bring culture shock. You may never have encountered such a degree of diversity in one setting. You probably will meet students with different values, unfamiliar customs, entirely new ways of looking at the world—experiences you may find both stimulating and stressful.

Mental health professionals have long assumed that minority students may feel a double burden of stress. Many undergraduates experience emotional difficulties (see Chapter 3), and researchers have theorized that students from a racial or ethnic minority would be especially likely to develop psychological symptoms, such as anger, anxiety, and depression, as a result of increased stress.

Racism has indeed been shown to be a source of stress that can affect health and well-being.[21] In the past, some African American students have described predominately white campuses as hostile, alienating, and socially isolating and have reported greater estrangement from the campus community and heightened estrangement in interactions with faculty and peers.[22] However, the generalization that all minority students are more stressed may not be valid.

Courtesy of U. of Florida-Gainesville

Courtesy of North Carolina Hillel

▲ Although minority students may perceive interpersonal tensions between themselves and nonminority students, they can often find culturally sensitive support services on campus.

A review of the eleven objective studies of ethnic differences among college students conducted in the last decade and a half has found that the number of minority students included was too small to warrant conclusions about their mental health and that the results were not consistent.[23] A more recent study conducted at a racially diverse university in a large metropolitan area in the Northeast evaluated 595 freshmen, including students of both genders and various racial and ethnic backgrounds, including Asians, African Americans, and Latino/Hispanics.[24] Less than 15 percent of these students—whether Asian, African American, Latino/Hispanic, white, or another ethnic minority—reported clinically significant levels of anger, anxiety, and depression, and there was no correlation between these stress-linked symptoms and ethnicity or race.

"Diversity, in and of itself, is unlikely to be related to higher levels of reported psychological symptoms on campus," the researchers concluded, theorizing that minority students "may have developed strengths while growing up within their particular cultures, subcommunities, and families that have often gone unrecognized or unnoted." They called for more research into "the psychosocial dynamics of stress, psychological symptoms, and resilience among racial and ethnic minority," as well as greater emphasis on developing culturally sensitive ways of providing support to those minority students who may need them.[25]

All minority students do share some common stressors. In one study of minority freshmen entering a large, competitive university, Asian, Latino, Filipino, African-American, and Native-American students all felt more sensitive and vulnerable to the college social climate, to interpersonal tensions between themselves and nonminority students and faculty, to experiences of actual or perceived racism, and to racist attitudes and discrimination (discussed later in this chapter, under Societal Stressors). Despite scoring above the national average on the SAT, the minority students in this study did not feel accepted as legitimate students and sensed that others viewed them as unworthy beneficiaries of affirmative action initiatives. While most said that overt racism was rare and relatively easy to deal with, they reported subtle pressures that undermined their academic confidence and their ability to bond with the university. Balancing these stressors, however, was a strong sense of ethnic identity, which helped buffer some stressful effects.

Latino students have identified three major types of stressors in their college experiences: academic (related to exam preparation and faculty interaction), social (related to ethnicity and interpersonal competence), and financial (related to their economic situation). Some Asian students who recently immigrated to the United States report feeling ostracized by students of similar ancestry who are second- or third-generation Americans. While they take pride in being truly bicultural and bilingual, the newcomers feel ambivalent about mainstream American culture. "My parents stress the importance of traditions; my friends tell me to get with it and act like an American," says one Asian-born student who has spent five years in the United States. "I feel trapped between cultures."

Other Personal Stressors

At every stage of life, you will encounter challenges and stressors. Among the most common are those related to anger, conflict, work, and overwork.

???? Why Is Everyone So Angry?

According to the AAA Foundation for Traffic Safety, violent aggressive driving—which some dub "mad driver disease"—has been rising by 7 percent per year.[26] Sideline rage at amateur and professional sporting events has become so widespread that a Pennsylvania midget football game ended in a brawl involving more than 100 coaches, players, parents, and fans.

No one seems immune. Women fly off the handle just as often as men, although they're less likely to get physical. The young and the infamous, including several rappers and musicians sentenced to anger management classes for violent outbursts, may seem more volatile, but ordinary senior citizens have erupted into "line rage" and pushed ahead of others simply because they feel they've "waited long enough" in their lives.

"Everyone everywhere seems to be hotter under the collar these days," observes Sybil Evans, a conflict resolution expert who singles out three primary culprits: time, technology, and tension. "Americans are working longer hours than anyone else in the world. The cell phones and pagers that were supposed to make our lives easier have put us on call 24–7–365. Since we're always running, we're tense and low on patience, and the less patience we have, the less we monitor what we say to people and how we treat them."[27]

The sheer complexity of our lives also has shortened our collective fuse. We rely on computers that crash, drive on roads that gridlock, place calls to machines that put us on endless hold. "It's not any one thing but lots of little things that make people feel they don't have control of their lives," comments consultant Jane Middleton-Moz, author of *Boiling Point: The High Cost of Unhealthy Anger to Individuals and Society.* "A sense of helplessness is what triggers rage. It's why people end up kicking ATM machines."[28]

Getting a Grip

For years therapists encouraged people to "vent" their anger. However, recent research shows that letting anger out only makes it worse. "Catharsis is worse than useless," says psychology professor Brad Bushman of Iowa State University, whose research has shown that letting anger out makes people more aggressive, not less. "Many people think of anger as the psychological equivalent of the steam in a pressure cooker that has to be released or it will explode. That's not true. People who react by hitting, kicking, screaming, and swearing aren't dealing with the underlying cause of their anger. They just feel more angry."[29]

Over time, temper tantrums sabotage physical health as well as psychological equanimity. By churning out stress hormones, chronic anger revs the body into a state of combat readiness, multiplying the risk for stroke and heart attack—even in healthy individuals. In one study by Duke University researchers, young women with "Jerry-Springer type anger," who tended to slam doors, curse, and throw things in fury, had higher cholesterol levels than those who reacted more calmly.

The first step to dealing with anger is figuring out what's really making you mad. Usually the jammed soda machine is the final straw that unleashes bottled-up fury over a more difficult issue, such as a recent breakup or a domineering parent. Also monitor yourself for early signs of exhaustion and overload. While stress alone doesn't cause a blowup, it makes you more vulnerable to overreacting.

"People blame anyone and everything for their anger, but there's never any justification for an outburst," says therapist Doris Helmering of St. Louis, author of *Sense Ability: Expanding Your Sense of Awareness for a Twenty-First Century Life*. "It's not easy, but you can learn to control your anger rather than letting it control you. Like any other feeling, anger lasts only about three seconds. What keeps it going is your own negative thinking." As long as you focus on who or what irritated you—like the oaf who rammed his grocery cart into your heels—you'll stay angry. "Once you come to understand that you're driving your own anger with your thoughts," says Helmering, "you can stop it."[30]

Conflict Resolution

Disagreements are inevitable; disagreeable ways of dealing with them are not. One of the most important skills in any setting—from dormitory floor to staff meeting to corporate boardroom—is resolving conflicts. The key is to focus on the problem, not the individual. Try to put aside unconscious biases, such as assuming a person is difficult to deal with, or preconceived notions about what others really want. Rather than planning what you might say, focus your attention on what others are saying.

▲ How you manage your anger has consequences for your health and personal and professional relationships.

© Michael Newman/PhotoEdit

STRATEGIES FOR CHANGE

How to Deal with an Angry Person

✔ Become an impartial observer. Act as if you were watching someone else's two-year-old have a temper tantrum at the supermarket.

✔ Stay calm. Letting your emotions loose only adds fuel to fury. Talk quietly and slowly; let the person know you understand that he or she is angry.

✔ Refuse to engage. Step back to avoid invading his or her space. Retreat further if need be until the person is back in control.

✔ Find something to agree with. Look for common ground, if only to acknowledge that you're both in a difficult situation.

Professionals recommend the following steps:

▸ **Listen.** To work through a conflict, you need to understand the other person's point of view. This demands careful listening in a quiet, private setting, away from activity and background noise. If conflict erupts in a public place, move the discussion elsewhere.

▸ **Assimilate.** Rather than taking a position and focusing only on defending it, try not to shut yourself off to other possibilities. Keep open the possibility that no one party is completely right or completely wrong. To get a fresh perspective, consider the situation from the "third person." If you were seeing the conflict from the outside, what would you think about the information? Once you've taken in all available information, ask yourself: What do I know now about the overall situation? Has my opinion changed?

▸ **Respond.** Especially if another person is responding in anger, give a calm, well-reasoned response. It will help defuse a highly emotional situation. Try to find a common goal that will benefit you both. Restate the other person's position when both of you are finished speaking so you both know you've been heard and understood.

Job Stress

More so than ever, many people find that they are working more and enjoying it less. Many people, including working parents, spend 55 to 60 hours a week on the job. More people are caught up in an exhausting cycle of overwork, which causes stress, which makes work harder, which leads to more stress. Even the workplace itself can contribute to stress. A noisy, open-office environment can increase levels of stress without workers realizing it.[31]

Yet work in itself is not hazardous to health. Attitudes about work and habits related to how we work are the true threats. In fact, a job—stressful or not, enjoyable or not—can be therapeutic.

Workaholism and Burnout

People who become obsessed by their work and careers can turn into *workaholics,* so caught up in racing toward the top that they forget what they're racing toward and why. In some cases they throw themselves into their work to mask or avoid painful feelings or difficulties in their own lives. One consequence is **burnout,** a state of physical, emotional, and mental exhaustion brought on by constant or repeated emotional pressure. Particularly in the helping professions, such as social work or nursing, men and women who've dedicated themselves to others may realize they have nothing left in themselves to give.

Early signs of burnout include exhaustion, sleep problems or nightmares, increased anxiety or nervousness, muscular tension (headaches, backaches, and the like), increased use of alcohol or medication, digestive problems, such as nausea, vomiting, or diarrhea, loss of interest in sex, frequent body aches or pain, quarrels with family or friends, negative feelings about everything, problems concentrating, job mistakes and accidents, and feelings of depression, hopelessness, and helplessness.

Who Experiences Burnout?

Age is the one variable most consistently associated with burnout: Younger employees between ages 30 and 40 report the highest rates. Both men and women are susceptible to burnout. Unmarried individuals, particularly men, seem more prone to burnout than married workers. Single employees who've never been married have higher burnout rates than those who are divorced.

North American workers are more likely to experience burnout than employees in Western Europe. High burnout also has been reported in Japan, Taiwan, and other Asian countries. Certain occupations, particularly the helping professions, such as social work and nursing, have been linked with a greater risk of burnout. However, burnout also is common in teaching, law enforcement, and medicine.

People who have an external locus of control—that is, who attribute events to chance or forces beyond themselves—have higher burnout rates than those with an internal locus of control, who attribute achievements to their own ability and effort. Workers who have little participation in decision-making and who receive little feedback from their superiors also are more prone to burnout.[32]

Preventing Burnout

Personal satisfaction with your work helps avoid burnout. In a recent study of physicians, researchers found that hard work and fatigue can be countered by job satisfaction. A high sense of accomplishment was associated with an increase in the number of T cells, the white blood cells that protect the body against disease.[33] However, the best way to avoid burnout is learning to cope well with smaller, day-to-day stresses. Then, tiny frustrations won't smolder into a blaze that may be impossible to put out.

Desk Rage

Job stress has intensified into a more intense and dangerous condition that has been dubbed "desk rage." According to a survey of 1,305 men and women, 42 percent of employees have witnessed yelling or verbal abuse; 29 percent yelled at coworkers themselves; 23 percent cried over work-related issues; 10 percent reported physical violence.[34]

Why are workers so upset? Experts blame corporate downsizing, intense competition, longer hours, economic insecurity, and nonstop electronic communication. "Many employees today have a sense of voiceless overload," says Ken Jacobsen, an expert in workplace distress at the University of Northern Iowa, "Each is doing the job of two or two-and-a-half people, and the demands on them may be completely unrealistic. In the past, there was a belief that if you worked harder or longer, you'd be rewarded. That's no longer the case, and it flies in the face of an employee's sense of fairness."[35]

While rage can smolder in any workplace, it is most likely to reach a boiling point when job responsibilities are ambiguous or unpredictable or when many people think they can hold a worker accountable. Frustration and anger also intensify when employees think they can't or shouldn't express negative feelings. The perpetrators of desk rage typically feel they're not listened to, heard or respected. They're often afraid to speak up for fear of being labeled as a squeaky wheel and missing out on a promotion or a raise.

However, those who try to ignore their negative emotions suffer on the job and off. Employees may procrastinate or indulge in "toxic" gossip with other disgruntled colleagues. Many develop physical symptoms, such as insomnia or indigestion, or take up self-destructive habits, like eating or drinking too much. As resentment turns to hostility, workers may fantasize about what they might do to get even with those who've wronged them. Withdrawing from their coworkers, they direct their anger outward—pounding their desks, firing off irate e-mails, flinging a coffee mug (or, in some cases, an entire computer) across the room, getting into shouting matches or name-calling. Verbal aggression can escalate into physical violence. Coworkers or former employees account for abou;g 15 percent of violent incidents in the workplace.

Illness and Disability

Just as the mind can have profound effects on the body, the body can have an enormous impact on our emotions. Whenever we come down with the flu or pull a muscle, we feel under par. When the problem is more serious or persistent—a chronic disease like diabetes, for instance, or a lifelong hearing impairment—the emotional stress of constantly coping with it is even greater.

A common source of stress for college students is a learning disability, which may affect one of every ten Americans. Most learning-disabled have average or above-average intelligence, but they rarely live up to their ability in school. Some have only one area of difficulty, such as reading or math. Others have problems with attention, writing, communicating, reasoning, coordination, social

STRATEGIES FOR PREVENTION

Defusing Desk Rage

Desk rage builds in little steps, so you can take it away in little steps. Here are suggestions on how to do so:

✔ Take better care of yourself. Get enough sleep. Schedule a softball game or work out at the end of the day to release physical tension. Avoid excess caffeine and alcohol.

✔ If you sense a problem, monitor the situation for a week. Write down when you're feeling hungry, tired, overloaded. Try to identify the triggers that might cause you to do something you'll later regret.

✔ Get feedback from friends. An objective person who knows you well can provide a fresh take on a troubling situation.

✔ If your irritation stems from a coworker, approach him or her in a nonthreatening way. You might say, "Could you hear me out for a few minutes?" To lower the hostility level, start by stating something you have in common, such as "We both want this project to work."

✔ If you fly off the handle, learn from the experience. Do immediate damage control by apologizing to coworkers and explaining that you've been under stress. Plan what you might do differently the next time someone sets you off.

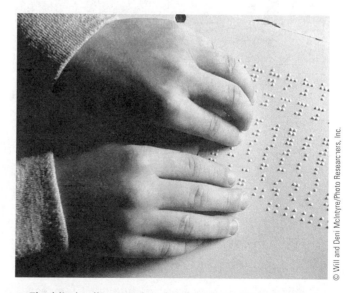

▲ The blind college student has unique challenges and stressors that sighted students do not.

competence, and emotional maturity—all of which may make it difficult, if not impossible, for them to find and keep jobs. Special training and a better understanding of what's wrong can make an enormous difference.

Learning disorders can be hard to recognize in adults, who often become adept at covering up or compensating for their difficulties. However, someone with a learning disability may be

▶ Unable to engage in a focused activity such as reading.
▶ Extremely distractible, forgetful, or absentminded.
▶ Easily frustrated by waiting, delays, or traffic.
▶ Disorganized, unable to manage time efficiently and complete tasks on time.
▶ Hot-tempered, explosive, constantly irritated.
▶ Impulsive, making decisions with little reflection or information.
▶ Easily overwhelmed by ordinary hassles.
▶ Clumsy, with a poor body image and poor sense of direction.
▶ Emotionally immature.
▶ Physically restless.

Individuals with several of these characteristics should undergo diagnostic tests to evaluate their skills and abilities and to determine whether remedial training, available through state offices of vocational rehabilitation, can help.

Societal Stressors

Not all stressors are personal. Centuries ago the poet John Donne observed that no man is an island. Today, on an

AP/Wide World Photos

▲ Protest marches are one way in which college students have often responded to national and international crises, including acts of terrorism.

increasingly crowded and troubled planet, these words seem truer than ever. Problems such as discrimination and terrorism can no longer be viewed only as economic or political issues. Directly or indirectly, they affect the well-being of all who inhabit the Earth—now and in the future. Even more mundane stressors, such as traffic, can lead to outbursts of anger that have come to be known as "road rage."[36] (This common stress-related response is discussed in Chapter 17.)

Discrimination

Discrimination can take many forms—some as subtle as not being included in a conversation or joke, some as blatant as threats scrawled on a wall, some as violent as brutal beatings and other hate crimes. Because it can be hard to deal with individually, discrimination is a particularly sinister form of stress. By banding together, however, those who experience discrimination can take action to protect themselves, challenge the ignorance and hateful assumptions that fuel bigotry, and promote a healthier environment for all.

In the last decade, there have been reports of increased intolerance among young people and greater tolerance of expressions and acts of hate on college campuses. To counteract this trend, many schools have set up programs and classes to educate students about each other's backgrounds and to acknowledge and celebrate the richness diversity brings to campus life. Educators have called on universities to make campuses less alienating and more culturally and emotionally accessible, with programs and policies targeted not only at minority students but also at the university as a whole.

Violence and Terrorism

The deliberate use of physical force to abuse or injure is a leading killer of young people in the United States—and a potential source of stress in all our lives. Chances are that you or someone you know has been the victim of a violent crime, and awareness of our own vulnerability adds to the stress of daily living. After the terrorist attacks on New York and Washington DC, on September 11, 2001, 44 percent of Americans in a national survey conducted several days later reported one or more substantial symptoms of stress. They coped with their increased sense of vulnerability by talking with others, turning to religion, participating in group activities, and making donations.[37]

Stress Survival

Although stress is a very real threat to emotional and physical well-being, its impact depends not just on what happens to you, but on how you handle it. If you tried to predict who would become ill based simply on life-change units or other stressors, you'd be correct only about 15 percent of the time.

The key to coping with stress is realizing that your *perception* and *response* to a stressor are crucial. Changing the way you interpret events or situations—a skill called *reframing*—makes all the difference. An event, such as a move to a new city, is not stressful in itself. A move becomes stressful if you see it as a traumatic upheaval rather than an exciting beginning of a new chapter in your life.

To get a sense of your own stress level, ask yourself the following questions about the preceding week of your life:

- How often have you felt out of control?
- How often have you felt confident that you'd be able to handle personal problems?
- How often have you felt things were generally going your way?
- How often have you felt that things were piling up so high you'd never be able to catch up?

Think through your answers. If the experiences of being out of control or overwhelmed outnumbered those of confidence and control, it's time to develop a stress-management plan and put it into action.

To achieve greater control over the stress in your life, start with some self-analysis: If you're feeling overwhelmed, ask yourself: Are you taking an extra course that's draining your last ounce of energy? Are you staying up late studying every night and missing morning classes? Are you living on black coffee and jelly doughnuts? While you may think that you don't have time to reduce the stress in your life, some simple changes can often ease the pressure you're under and help you achieve your long-term goals.

Relieving Short-Term Stress

Acute stress strikes every day: You forget your wallet. You show up late for work—again. You blow a big test. The computer crashes just as you're about to print out a term paper. Frustrated and anxious, you'd love to start the day all over again. Unfortunately, no one can undo the past. However, you can control how you react in the present. Simple exercises, like the following examples, can stop the stress buildup inside your body and help you regain a sense of calm and control:

- **Breathing.** Deep breathing relaxes the body and quiets the mind. Draw air deeply into your lungs, allowing your chest to fill with air and your belly to rise and fall. You will feel the muscle tension and stress begin to melt away. When you're feeling extremely stressed, try this calming breath: Sit or lie with your back straight and place the tip of your tongue on the roof of your mouth behind your teeth. Exhale completely through the mouth, then inhale through the nose for 4 seconds. Hold the breath for 7 seconds, then exhale audibly through the mouth for 8 seconds. Repeat four times.

- **Refocusing.** Thinking about a situation you can't change or control only increases the stress you feel. Force your mind to focus on other subjects. If you're stuck in a long line, distract yourself. Check out what other people are buying or imagine what they do for a living. In the car, turn on the radio to a music station you like. Imagine that you're in a hot shower and a wave of relaxation is washing your stress down the drain.

- **Serenity breaks.** Build moments of tranquility into your day. For instance, while waiting for your computer to warm up or a file to download, look at a photograph of someone you love or a poster of a tropical island. If none is available, close your eyes and visualize a soothing scene, such as walking in a meadow or along a beach.

- **Stress signals.** Learn to recognize the first signs that your stress load is getting out of hand: Is your back bothering you? Do you have a headache? Do you find yourself speeding or misplacing things? Whenever you spot these early warnings, force yourself to stop and say, "I'm under stress. I need to do something about it."

- **Reality checks.** To put things into proper perspective, ask yourself: Will I remember what's made me so upset a month from now? If you had to rank this problem on a scale of 1 to 10, with worldwide catastrophe as 10, where would it rate?

- **Stress inoculation.** Rehearse everyday situations that you find stressful, such as speaking in class. Think of how you might make the situation less tense, for instance, by breathing deeply before you talk or jotting down notes beforehand. Think of these small "doses" of stress as the psychological equivalent of allergy shots: They immunize you so you feel less stressed when bigger challenges come along.[38]

- **Rx: Laughter.** Humor counters stress by focusing on comic aspects of difficult situations and may, as various studies have shown, lessen harmful effects on the immune system and overall health. However, humor may have different effects on stress in men and women. In a study of 131 undergraduates, humor buffered stress-related physical symptoms in men and women. However, it reduced stress-linked anxiety only in men. The researchers theorized that men may prefer humor as a more appropriate way of expressing emotions such as anxiety, whereas women are more likely to use self-disclosure, that is, to confide in friends.[39]

- **Spiritual coping.** Saying a prayer under stress is one of the oldest and most effective ways of calming yourself. Other forms of spiritual coping, such as putting trust in

Savvy Consumer

Can Stress-Relief Products Help?

You're stressed out, and you see an ad for a product—an oil, candle, cream, herbal tea, pill, or potion—that promises to make all your cares disappear. Should you soak in an aromatic bath, have a massage, try kava, squeeze foam balls? In most cases, you're probably not doing yourself much harm, but you aren't necessarily doing yourself much good either. Keep these considerations in mind:

• Be wary of instant cures. Regardless of the promises on the label, it's unrealistic to expect any magic ingredient or product to make all your problems disappear.

• Focus on stress-reducing behavior, rather than a product. An aromatic candle may not bring instant serenity, but if you light a candle and meditate, you may indeed feel more at peace. A scented pillow may not be a cure for a stress, but if it helps you get a good night's sleep, you'll cope better the next day.

• Experiment with physical ways to work out stress. Exercise is one of the best ways to lower your stress levels. Try walking, running, swimming, cycling, kickboxing—anything physical that helps you release tension.

• Don't make matters worse by smoking (the chemicals in cigarettes increase heart rate, blood pressure, and stress hormone), consuming too much caffeine (it speeds up your system for hours), eating snacks high in sugar (it produces a quick high followed by a sudden slump), or turning to drugs or alcohol (they can only add to your stress when their effects wear off.)

• Remember that stress is a matter of attitude. Remind yourself of some basic words of wisdom: Don't sweat the small stuff—and it's all small stuff.

God and doing for others (for instance, by volunteering at a shelter for battered women) also can provide a different perspective on daily hassles and stresses.

▸ **Sublimation.** This term refers to the redirection of any drives considered unacceptable into socially acceptable channels. Outdoor activity is one of the best ways to reduce stress through sublimation. For instance, if you're furious with a friend who betrayed your trust or frustrated because your boss rejects all of your proposals, you might go for a long run or hike to sublimate your anger.

Dealing with Long-Term Stress

If you're going through a transition or you're coming to terms with a setback or loss, you need time to regain a sense of perspective. Any major change, positive or negative, triggers a mixed array of feelings, and you have to sort these out by thinking through what happened, why, and where it might lead.

Journaling

One of the simplest, yet most effective, ways to work through stress is by putting your feelings into words that only you will read. The more honest and open you are as you write, the better. According to the research of psychologist James Pennebaker of the University of Texas, Austin, college students who wrote in their journals about trau-

matic events felt much better afterward than those who wrote about superficial topics. Recording your experiences and feelings on paper or audiotape may help decrease stress and enhance well-being.[40]

▲ Writing in your journal about feelings and difficulties is a simple and very effective way to help control your stress.

© CORBIS

As noted earlier in this chapter, recent research has shown that writing about stressful events can actually ease the symptoms of chronic illnesses like asthma and arthritis. As psychiatrist David Spiegel, M.D., of Stanford University notes, stress affects both mind and body, and illness may trigger associations to past stressful events that were beyond individual control. Writing about traumatic experience may alter the way people think about the event, giving it order and structure and enhancing their own feelings of control.[41]

A "stress journal" can serve a similar purpose. Focus on intense emotional experiences and "autopsy" them to try to understand why they affected you the way they did. Rereading and thinking about your notes may reveal the underlying reasons for your response.

???? What Can Help Me Relax?

Relaxation is the physical and mental state opposite that of stress. Rather than gearing up for fight or flight, our bodies and minds grow calmer and work more smoothly. We're less likely to become frazzled and more capable of staying in control. The most effective relaxation techniques include progressive relaxation, visualization, meditation, mindfulness, and biofeedback.

Progressive relaxation works by intentionally increasing and then decreasing tension in the muscles. While sitting or lying down in a quiet, comfortable setting, you tense and release various muscles, beginning with those of the hand, for instance, and then proceeding to the arms, shoulders, neck, face, scalp, chest, stomach, buttocks, genitals, and so on, down each leg to the toes. Relaxing the muscles can quiet the mind and restore internal balance.

Visualization, or **guided imagery,** involves creating mental pictures that calm you down and focus your mind. Some people use this technique to promote healing when they are ill (see Chapter 10). Visualization skills require practice and, in some cases, instruction by qualified health professionals.

Meditation has been practiced in many forms over the ages, from the yogic techniques of the Far East to the Quaker silence of more modern times.

Brain scans have shown that meditation activates the sections of the brain in charge of the autonomic nervous system, which governs bodily functions, such as digestion and blood pressure, that we cannot consciously control.[42] Although many studies have documented the benefits of meditation for overall health, it may be particularly helpful for people dealing with stress-related medical conditions such as high blood pressure.

In a study of African Americans with atherosclerosis, or hardening of the arteries, those who meditated showed a marked decrease in the thickness of their artery walls, while the

nonmeditators showed an increase. This benefit is particularly important because African Americans are twice as likely to die from cardiovascular disease as are whites.[43]

Meditation helps a person reach a state of relaxation, but with the goal of achieving inner peace and harmony. There is no one right way to meditate, and many people have discovered how to meditate on their own, without even knowing what it is they are doing. Among college students, meditation has proven especially effective in increasing relaxation. Most forms of meditation have common elements: sitting quietly for 15 to 20 minutes once or twice a day, concentrating on a word or image, and breathing slowly and rhythmically. If you wish to try meditation, it often helps to have someone guide you through your first sessions. Or try tape recording your own voice (with or without favorite music in the background) and playing it back to yourself, freeing yourself to concentrate on the goal of turning the attention within.

Mindfulness is a modern form of an ancient Asian technique that involves maintaining awareness in the present moment. You tune in to each part of your body, scanning from head to toe, noting the slightest sensation. You allow whatever you experience—an itch, an ache, a feeling of warmth—to enter your awareness. Then you open yourself to focus on all the thoughts, sensations, sounds, and feelings that enter your awareness. Mindfulness keeps you in the here-and-now, thinking about what *is* rather than about *what if* or *if only*.

▲ Spending time outdoors is a great way to leave behind daily tensions.

HEALTH

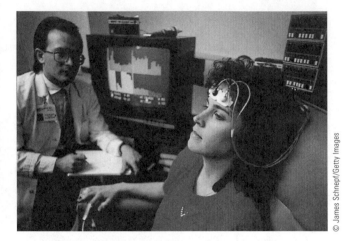

© James Schnepf/Getty Images

▲ Biofeedback training uses electronic monitoring devices to teach conscious control over heart rate, body temperature, and muscle tension. Once the technique is learned, the electronic devices are unnecessary.

Biofeedback, discussed in Chapter 10, is a method of obtaining feedback, or information, about some physiological activity occurring in the body. An electronic monitoring device attached to the body detects a change in an internal function and communicates it back to the person through a tone, light, or meter. By paying attention to this feedback, most people can gain some control over functions previously thought to be beyond conscious control, such as body temperature, heart rate, muscle tension, and brain waves. Biofeedback training consists of three stages:

1. Developing increased awareness of a body state or function.
2. Gaining control over it.
3. Transferring this control to everyday living without use of the electronic instrument.

The goal of biofeedback for stress reduction is a state of tranquility, usually associated with the brain's production of alpha waves (which are slower and more regular than normal waking waves). After several training sessions, most people can produce alpha waves more or less at will.

Time Management

We live in what some sociologists call hyperculture, a society that moves at warp speed. Information bombards us constantly. The rate of change seems to accelerate every year. Our "time-saving" devices—pagers, cell phones, modems, faxes, palm-sized organizers, laptop computers—have simply extended the boundaries of where and how we work.

As a result, more and more people are suffering from "timesickness," a nerve-racking feeling that life has become little more than an endless to-do list. The best antidote is time management, and hundreds of books, seminars, and experts offer training in making the most of the hours in the day. Yet these well-intentioned methods often fail, and sooner or later most of us find ourselves caught in a time trap.

Poor Time Management

Every day you make dozens of decisions, and the choices you make about how to use your time directly affect your stress level. If you have a big test on Monday and a term paper due Tuesday, you may plan to study all weekend. Then, when you're invited to a party Saturday night, you go. Although you set the alarm for 7:00 A.M. on Sunday, you don't pull yourself out of bed until noon. By the time you start studying, it's 4:00 P.M., and anxiety is building inside you.

How can you tell if you've lost control of your time? The following are telltale symptoms of poor time management:

▶ Rushing.
▶ Chronic inability to make choices or decisions.
▶ Fatigue or listlessness.
▶ Constantly missed deadlines.
▶ Not enough time for rest or personal relationships.
▶ A sense of being overwhelmed by demands and details and having to do what you don't want to do most of the time.

One of the hard lessons of being on your own is that your choices and your actions have consequences. Stress is just one of them. But by thinking ahead, being realistic about your workload, and sticking to your plans, you can gain better control over your time and your stress levels.

???? How Can I Better Manage My Time?

Time management involves skills that anyone can learn, but they require commitment and practice to make a difference in your life. It may help to know the techniques that other students have found most useful:

▶ **Schedule your time.** Use a calendar or planner. Beginning the first week of class, mark down deadlines for each assignment, paper, project, and test scheduled that semester. Develop a daily schedule, listing very specifically what you will do the next day, along with the times. Block out times for working out, eating dinner, calling home, and talking with friends as well as for studying.

▲ A calendar or planner is an important tool in time management. You can use it to keep track of assignment due dates, class meetings, and other "to do's."

© CORBIS

margins, which will help you retain more information. Even if you're racing to start a paper, take a few extra minutes to prepare a workable outline. It will be easier to structure your paper when you start writing.

▌ **Focus on the task at hand.** Rather than worrying about how you did on yesterday's test or how you'll ever finish next week's project, focus intently on whatever you're doing at any given moment. If your mind starts to wander, use any distraction—the sound of the phone ringing or a noise from the hall—as a reminder to stay in the moment.

▌ **Turn elephants into hors d'oeuvres.** Cut a huge task into smaller chunks so it seems less enormous. For instance, break down your term paper into a series of steps, such as selecting a topic, identifying sources of research information, taking notes, developing an outline, and so on.

▌ **Keep your workspace in order.** Even if the rest of your room is a shambles, try to keep your desk clear. Piles of papers are distracting, and you can end up wasting lots of time looking for notes you misplaced or an article you have to read by morning. Try to spend the last ten minutes of the day getting your desk in order so you get a fresh start on the new day.

▌ **Develop a game plan.** Allow at least two nights to study for any major exam. Set aside more time for researching and writing papers. Make sure to allow time to type and print out a paper—and to deal with emergencies like a computer breakdown. Set daily and weekly goals for every class. When working on a big project, don't neglect your other courses. Whenever possible, try to work ahead in all your classes.

▌ **Identify time robbers.** For several days keep a log of what you do and how much time you spend doing it. You may discover that disorganization is eating away at your time or that you have a problem getting started. (See the following section on Overcoming Procrastination.)

▌ **Make the most of classes.** Read the assignments before class rather than waiting until just before you have a test. By reading ahead of time, you'll make it easier to understand the lectures. Go to class yourself. Your own notes will be more helpful than a friend's or those from a note-taking service. Read your lecture notes at the end of each day or at least at the end of each week.

▌ **Develop an efficient study style.** Some experts recommend studying for 50 minutes, then breaking for 10 minutes. Small incentives, such as allowing yourself to call or visit a friend during these 10 minutes, can provide the motivation to keep you at the books longer. When you're reading, don't just highlight passages. Instead, write notes or questions to yourself in the

Overcoming Procrastination

Putting off until tomorrow what should be done today is a habit that creates a great deal of stress for many students. It also takes a surprising toll. In studies with students taking a health psychology course, researchers found that although procrastinating provided short-term benefits, including periods of low stress, the tendency to dawdle had long-term costs, including poorer health and lower grades. Early in the semester, the procrastinators reported less stress and fewer health problems than students who scored low on procrastination. However, by the end of the semester, procrastinators reported more health-related symptoms, more stress, and more visits to health-care professionals than nonprocrastinators. They also received significantly lower grades on term papers and exams.[44]

The three most common types of procrastination are: putting off unpleasant things, putting off difficult tasks, and putting off tough decisions. Procrastinators are most likely to delay by wishing they didn't have to do what they must or by telling themselves they "just can't get started," which means they never do.

To get out of the procrastination trap, keep track of the tasks you're most likely to put off, and try to figure out why you don't want to tackle them. Think of alternative ways to get tasks done. If you put off library readings, for instance, is the problem getting to the library or the reading itself? If

HEALTH

it's the trip to the library, arrange to walk over with a friend whose company you enjoy.

Develop daily time-management techniques, such as a to-do list. Rank items according to priorities: A, B, C, and schedule your days to make sure the A's get accomplished. Try not to fixate on half-completed projects. Divide large tasks, such as a term paper, into smaller ones, and reward yourself when you complete a part.

Do what you like least first. Once you have it out of the way, you can concentrate on the tasks you do enjoy. You also should build time into your schedule for interruptions, unforeseen problems, unexpected events, and so on, so you aren't constantly racing around. Establish ground rules for meeting your own needs (including getting enough sleep and making time for friends) before saying yes to any activity. Learn to live according to a three-word motto: Just do it!

???? Is Stress Hazardous to Psychological Health?

The lifetime prevalence of major stressful events is high. In one study of 1,000 adults in four cities in the southeastern United States, 21 percent of the sample reported a traumatic event (such as a robbery, assault, or traumatic death of a loved one) during the previous year, and 69 percent reported at least one such event in their lifetime.[45] Such stressors always take a toll on an individual, and it's normal to feel sad, tense, overwhelmed, angry, or incapable of coping with the ordinary demands of daily living. Usually such feelings and behaviors subside with time. The stressful event fades into the past, and those whose lives it has touched adapt to its lasting impact. But sometimes individuals remain extremely distressed and unable to function as they once did. While the majority of individuals who survive a trauma recover, at least a quarter of such individuals later develop serious psychological symptoms.[46]

Posttraumatic Stress Disorder

In the past, **posttraumatic stress disorder (PTSD)** was viewed as a psychological response to out-of-the-ordinary stressors, such as captivity or combat. However, other experiences can also forever change the way people view themselves and their world. Thousands of individuals experience or witness traumatic events, such as fires or floods. Children, in particular, are likely to develop PTSD symptoms when they live through a traumatic event or witness a loved one or friend being assaulted. Sometimes an entire community, such as the residents of a town hit by a devastating hurricane, develops symptoms.

STRATEGIES FOR PREVENTION

Recognize the Warning Signals of Stress Overload

✔ Experiencing physical symptoms, including chronic fatigue, headaches, indigestion, diarrhea, and sleep problems.

✔ Having frequent illness or worrying about illness.

✔ Self-medicating, including nonprescription drugs.

✔ Having problems concentrating on studies or work.

✔ Feeling irritable, anxious, or apathetic.

✔ Working or studying longer and harder than usual.

✔ Exaggerating, to yourself and others, the importance of what you do.

✔ Becoming accident-prone.

✔ Breaking rules, whether it's a curfew at home or a speed limit on the highway.

✔ Going to extremes, such as drinking too much, overspending, or gambling.

According to recent research, almost half of car accident victims may develop PTSD. Individuals who were seriously injured are especially vulnerable.[47] The main symptoms are re-experiencing the traumatic event, avoiding the site of the accident, refraining from driving in weather and road conditions similar to those on the day of the accident, and feeling a general increase in distress.

 A history of childhood sexual abuse can greatly increase the likelihood of developing PTSD.[48] An episode that repeats the abuse, such as a sexual assault or rape, can trigger an intense reaction as individuals "re-experience" the initial trauma. Childhood abuse—physical, sexual, or emotional—can affect student dropout rates. In one study that followed 210 freshmen (aged 17–21 years) for four years, those suffering PTSD symptoms in the second week of their freshman year were less likely to remain enrolled through their senior years. Half of those who'd been sexually abused and 65 percent of those who'd experienced multiple forms of abuse dropped out.[49]

In PTSD, individuals re-experience their terror and helplessness again and again in their dreams or intrusive thoughts. To avoid this psychic pain, they may try to avoid anything associated with the trauma. Some enter a state of emotional numbness and no longer can respond to people and experiences the way they once did, especially when it comes to showing tenderness or affection. Those who've been mugged or raped may be afraid to venture out by themselves.

The sooner trauma survivors receive psychological help, the better they are likely to fare. Often talking about what happened with an empathic person or someone who's shared the experience as soon as possible—preferably before going to sleep on the day of the event—can help an individual begin to deal with what has occurred. Group sessions, ideally beginning soon after the trauma, allow individuals to share views and experiences. Behavioral, cognitive, and psychodynamic therapy (described in Chapter 3) can help individuals suffering PTSD.

Resilience: Bouncing Back from Adversity

Adversity—whether in the form of a traumatic event or chronic stress—has different effects on individuals. Some people never recover and continue on a downward slide that may ultimately prove fatal. Others return, though at different rates, to their prior level of functioning. In recent years researchers have focused their attention on a particularly intriguing group: those people who not only survive stressful experiences but also thrive, that is, who actually surpass their previous level of functioning.

Resilience can take many forms.[50] A father whose child is kidnapped and killed may become a nationwide advocate for victims' rights. A student whose roommate dies in a car crash after a party may campaign for tougher

▲ Trauma survivors can often find support and comfort from those who have shared the experience.

© AFP/CORBIS

laws against drunk driving. A couple whose premature baby spends weeks in a neonatal intensive care unit may find that their marriage has grown closer and stronger. Even though their experiences were painful, the individuals often look back at them as bringing positive changes into their lives.

Researchers have studied various factors that enable individuals to thrive in the face of adversity. These include:

▸ **An optimistic attitude.** Rather than reacting to a stressor simply as a threat, these men and women view stress as a challenge—one they believe they can and will overcome. Researchers have documented that individuals facing various stressors, including serious illness and bereavement, are more likely to report experiencing growth if they have high levels of hope and optimism.
▸ **Self-efficacy.** A sense of being in control of one's life can boost health, even in times of great stress.
▸ **Stress inoculation.** People who deal well with adversity often have had previous experiences with stress that toughened them in various ways, such as teaching them skills that enhanced their ability to cope and boosting their confidence in their ability to weather a rough patch.
▸ **Secure personal relationships.** Individuals who know they can count on the support of their loved ones are more likely to be resilient.
▸ **Spirituality or religiousness.** Religious coping may be particularly related to growth and resilience. In particular, two types seem most beneficial: spiritually based religious coping (receiving emotional reassurance and guidance from God) and good-deeds coping (living a better, more spiritual life that includes altruistic acts).

Resilience sometimes means developing new skills simply because, in order to get through the stressful experience, people had to learn something they hadn't known how to do before—for instance, wrangling with insurance companies or other bureaucracies. By mastering such skills, they become more fit to deal with an unpredictable world and develop new flexibility in facing the unknown.

Along with new abilities comes the psychological sense of mastery. "I survived this," an individual may say. "I'll be able to deal with other hard things in the future." Such confidence keeps people actively engaged in the effort to cope and is itself a predictor of eventual success. Stress also can make individuals more aware of the fulfilling aspects of life, and they may become more interested in spiritual pursuits. Certain kinds of stressful experiences also have social consequences. If a person experiencing a traumatic event finds that the significant others in his or her life can be counted on, the result can be a strengthening of their relationship.

Researchers are trying to determine ways in which more people can derive positive benefits from stressful experiences. One important step, they believe, is to encourage people to view a traumatic situation as an opportunity for personal growth, rather than a test of whether or not they "have what it takes" to survive.

In a study of the life narratives of midlife adults (aged 35–65 years) and college students (aged 18–24), both groups reported greater psychological well-being when the stories of low points and turning points in their lives contained images of redemption and they were able to find benefits and lessons in their experiences of adversity.[51]

Focusing on finding meaning in their experience—what some call "cognitive coping"—can help individuals move beyond initial emotional responses such as anxiety, distress, and confusion. Over time, some people may develop what may be the ultimate "gift" of a stressful experience: wisdom.

CHAPTER 2

Making This Chapter Work for You

1. Stress can be defined as
   a. a negative emotional state related to fatigue and similar to depression.
   b. the physiological and psychological response to any event or situation that either upsets or excites us.
   c. the end result of the general adaptation syndrome.
   d. a motivational strategy for making life changes.

2. According to the general adaptation syndrome theory, how does the body typically respond to an acute stressor?
   a. The heart rate slows, blood pressure declines, and eye movement increases.
   b. The body enters a physical state called eustress and then moves into the physical state referred to as distress.
   c. If the stressor is viewed as a positive event, there are no physical changes.
   d. The body demonstrates three stages of change: alarm, resistance, and exhaustion.

3. Over time, increased levels of stress hormones have been shown to increase a person's risk for which of the following conditions?

   a. diabetes, high blood pressure, memory loss, and skin disorders
   b. stress fractures, male pattern baldness, and hypothyroidism
   c. hemophilia, AIDS, and hay fever
   d. none of the above

4. Stress levels in college students
   a. may be high due to stressors such as academic pressures, financial concerns, learning disabilities, and relationship problems.
   b. are usually low because students feel empowered, living independently of their parents.
   c. are typically highest in seniors because their self-esteem diminishes during the college years.
   d. are lower in minority students because they are used to stressors such as a hostile social climate and actual or perceived discrimination.

5. Which of the following statements about anger is true?
   a. The healthiest way to deal with anger is to express the rage.
   b. When confronted by an angry person, you can usually defuse the situation quickly by explaining that he or she is acting immaturely and inappropriately.
   c. Venting anger can adversely affect one's physical health over time.
   d. Statistics show that anger-related public behaviors such as aggressive driving and workplace outbursts have been on the decrease.

6. One consequence of job stress is burnout, which can be defined as
   a. injuries caused by computer overuse.
   b. company initiatives to enhance employee's work-life balance.
   c. lack of career advancement.
   d. physical and psychological exhaustion resulting from work pressures.

7. Which of the following situations is representative of a societal stressor?
   a. Peter has been told that his transfer application has been denied because his transcripts were not sent in by the dealine.
   b. Nia and Kwame find an unsigned note pinned to the door of their new home, ordering them to move out or face the consequences.
   c. Kelli's boyfriend drives her car after he had been drinking and has an accident.
   d. Joshua, who is the leading basketball player on his college varsity team, has just been diagnosed with diabetes.

8. If you are stuck in a traffic jam, which of the following actions will help reduce your stress level?
   a. deep slow breathing
   b. honking your horn

c. berating yourself for not taking a different route

d. getting on your cell phone to reschedule appointments

9. A relaxed peaceful state of being can be achieved with which of the following activities?

a. an aerobic exercise class

b. playing a computer game

c. meditating for 15 minutes

d. attending a rap concert

10. A person suffering from posttraumatic stress disorder may experience which of the following symptoms?

a. procrastination

b. constant thirst

c. drowsiness

d. terror-filled dreams

Answers to these questions can be found on page 640.

 What is the difference between short term and long term stress? How does stress affect your health?

Critical Thinking

1. Stress levels among college students have reached record highs. What reasons can you think of to account for this? Consider possible social, cultural, and economic factors that may play a role.

2. Identify three stressful situations in your life and determine whether they are examples of eustress or distress. Describe both the positive and negative aspects of each situation.

3. Can you think of any ways in which your behavior or attitudes might create stress for others? What changes could you make to avoid doing so?

4. What advice might you give an incoming freshman at your school about managing stress in college? What techniques have been most helpful for you in dealing with stress? Suppose that this student is from a different ethnic group than you? What additional suggestions would you have for this student?

SITES & BYTES

Stress Assess
http://wellness.uwsp.edu/Health_Service/services/stress
This three-part outline educational tool was developed by the National Wellness Institute at the University of Wisconsin—Steven's Point. Designed to increase your knowledge about stress, this questionnaire features separate evaluations for stress sources, distress symptoms, and stress-balancing strategies.

Stress4Teens
http://health4teens.org/stress/index.html
This site describes signs of stress as well as strategies to cope with stress, written for adolescents.

How to Survive Unbearable Stress
http://www.teachhealth.com
This comprehensive website is written specifically for college students by Steven Burns, M.D. It features the following topics: signs of how to recognize stress, two stress surveys for adults and college students, information on the pathophysiology of stress, the genetics of stress and stress tolerance, and information on how to best manage and even treat stress.

Please note that links are subject to change. If you find a broken link, use a search engine such as http://www.yahoo.com and search for the website by typing in key words.

InfoTrac Activity "How Women Handle Stress: Is There a Difference?" Harvard Mental Health Letter, April 2001, Vol. 17, No. 10.

(1) Name two reasons for the observed differences in how men cope with stress when compared to women's coping mechanisms.

(2) When exposed to stress, how do men and women deal with family conflict?

(3) How can different hormones result in the observed gender differences in coping with stress?

For additional links, resources, and suggested readings on InfoTrac, visit our Health & Wellness Resource Center at http://health.wadsworth.com.

Key Terms

The terms listed here are used within the chapter on the page indicated. Definitions of the terms are in the Glossary at the end of the book.

adaptive response 40	**guided imagery** 57	**psychoneuroimmunology** 41
allostasis 40	**homeostasis** 40	**stress** 40
biofeedback 58	**meditation** 57	**stressor** 40
burnout 52	**migraine headache** 44	**visualization** 57
distress 40	**mindfulness** 57	
eustress 40	**posttraumatic stress disorder**	
general adaptation syndrome	**(PTSD)** 60	
(GAS) 40	**progressive relaxation** 57	

References

1. Lazarus, R., and R. Launier. "Stress-Related Transactions Between Person and Environment" in *Perspectives in Interactional Psychology*. New York: Plenum, 1978.

2. Gadzella, Bernadette. "Student-Life Stress Inventory: Identification of and Reactions to Stressors." *Psychological Reports,* Vol. 74, No. 2, April 1994.

3. Senior, Kathryn. "Should Stress Carry a Health Warning?" *Lancet,* Vol. 357, No. 9250, January 13, 2001, p. 126.

4. Booth, Roger, et al. "The State of the Science: The Best Evidence for the Involvement of Thoughts and Feelings in Physical Health." *Advances in Mind-Body Medicine,* Vol. 17, No. 1, Winter 2001, p. 2.

5. Davis, Mary, et al. "Body Fat Distribution and Hemodynamic Stress Responses in Premenopausal Obese Women: A Preliminary Study." *Health Psychology* Vol. 18, No. 6, November 1999, p. 625.

6. Epel, Elissa. "Can Stress Shape Your Body? Stress and Cortisol Reactivity Among Women with Central Body Fat Distribution." *Yale University, U.S. Dissertation Abstracts International: Section B: The Sciences & Engineering,* Vol. 60, No. 5-B, December 1999, p. 2403.

7. Glaser, Ronald, and Janice Kiecolt-Glaser. *Handbook of Human Stress and Immunity.* San Diego: Academic Press, 1994.

8. Cohen, Sheldon, et al. "Susceptibility to the Common Cold." *Psychosomatic Medicine,* March 1999.

9. Glaser, Ronald, et al. "Chronic Stress Modulates the Immune Response to a Pneumococcal Pneumonia Vaccine." *Psychosomatic Medicine,* Vol. 62, No. 6, November–December 2000, p. 804.

10. Takkouche, Bahi, et al. "Stress and Susceptibility to the Common Cold." *Epdiemiology,* Vol. 11, April 2001, p. 345.

11. Rubin, Aaron, and Karageanes, Steven. "Stress, Cytokine Changes, and Wound Healing." *Physician and Sportsmedicine,* Vol. 28, No. 5, May 2000, p. 21.

12. Turner-Cobb, Julie, et al. "Social Support and Salivary Cortisol in Women with Metastatic Breast Cancer." *Psychosomatic Medicine,* Vol. 62, No. 3, May–June 2000, p. 337.

13. Kiecolt-Glaser, Janice, and Ronald Glaser. "Stress and Immunity: Age Enhances the Risks." *Current Directions in Psychological Science,* Vol. 10, No. 1, February 2001, p. 18.

14. Smyth, Joshua, et al. "Effects of Writing About Stressful Experiences on Symptom Reduction in Patients with Asthma or Rheumatoid Arthritis: A Randomized Trial." *Journal of the American Medical Association,* Vol. 281, No. 14, April 14, 1999.

15. Senior, "Should Stress Carry a Health Warning?"

16. "Stressed Out on Campus." *Techniques,* Vol. 75, No. 3, March 2000.

17. Misra, Ranjita, and Michelle McKean. "College Students, Academic Stress and Its Relation to Their Anxiety, Time Management and Leisure Satisfaction." *American Journal of Health Studies,* Vol. 16, No. 1, Winter 2000.

18. Dixon, Wayne, and Reid, Jon. "Positive Life Events as a Moderator of Stress-Related Depressive Symptoms." *Journal of Counseling and Development,* Vol. 78, No. 3, Summer, 2000.

19. Murray, Bridget. "Peer Mentoring Gives Rookies 'Inside Advice.'" *American Psychological Monitor,* Vol. 29, No. 12, December 1998.

20. Glaser and Kiecolt-Glaser, *Handbook of Human Stress and Immunity.* Hornig-Rohan, Mary. "Stress, Immune-Mediators, and Immune-Mediated Disease." *Advances: The Journal of Mind-Body Health,* Vol. 11, No. 2, Spring 1995.

21. Harrell, Shelly. "A Multidimensional Conceptualization of Racism-Related Stress: Implications for the Well-Being of People of Color." *American Journal of Orthopsychiatry,* Vol. 70, No. 1, January 2000.

22. Launier, Raymond. "Stress Balance and Emotional Life Complexes in Students in a Historically African American College." *Journal of Psychology,* Vol. 131, No. 2, March 1997.

23. Rosenthal, Beth Spenciner, and Schreiner, Arleen Cedeno. "Prevalence of Psychological Symptoms Among Undergraduate Students in an Ethnically Diverse Urban Public College." *Journal of American College Health,* Vol. 49, No. 1, July 2000.

24. Ibid.

25. Ibid.

26. AAA Foundation for Traffic Safety website. http://www.aaafts.org

27. Evans, Sybil. Personal interview.

28. Middleton-Moz, Jane. Personal interview.

29. Bushman, Brad. Personal interview.

30. Helmering, Doris. Personal interview.

31. Evans, Gary, and Dana Johnson. "Stress and Open-Office Noise." *Journal of Applied Psychology,* Vol. 85, No. 5, October 2000.

32. Maslach, Christina, et al. "Job Burnout." *Annual Review of Psychology,* 2001, p. 397.

33. Bargellinia, Annalisa, et al. "Relation Between Immune Variables and Burnout in a Sample of Physicians." *Occupational and Environmental Medicine,* Vol. 57, July 2000.

34. Maslach, "Job Burnout."

35. Jacobsen, Ken. Personal interview.

36. "Driving-Induced Stress in Urban College Students." *Perceptual and Motor Skills,* Vol. 90, No. 2, April 2000.

37. Schuster, Mark et al. "A National Survey of Stress Reactions after the September 11, 2001, Terrorist Attacks," New England Journal of Medicine, Vol. 345, No. 20, November 15, 2001, p. 1507.

38. Saunders, Teri, et al. "The Effect of Stress Inoculation Training on Anxiety and Performance." *Journal of Occupational Health Psychology,* Vol. 1, No. 2, pp. 170–186.

HEALTH

39. Abel, Millicent. "Interaction of Humor and Gender in Moderating Relationships Between Stress and Outcomes." *Journal of Psychology,* Vol. 132, No. 3, May 1998.

40. Pennebaker, James. "Putting Stress into Words: Health, Linguistic and Therapeutic Implications." *Behavioral Research,* Vol. 31, No. 6, 1993.

41. Spiegel, David. "Healing Words: Emotional Expression and Disease Outcome." *Journal of the American Medical Association,* Vol. 281, No. 14, April 14, 1999.

42. Barbar, Cary. "The Science of Meditation." *Psychology Today,* May–June 2001, p. 54.

43. "Is Meditation Good Medicine?" *Harvard Women's Health Watch,* Vol. 8, No. 5, January 2001, p. 1.

44. "Procrastinators Always Finish Last, Even in Health," *American Psychological Monitor,* Vol. 20, No. 1, January 1998.

45. Calhoun, Lawrence, and Richard Tedeschi. "Beyond Recovery from Trauma: Implications for Clinical Practice and Research." *Journal of Social Issues,* Vol. 54, No. 2, Summer 1998.

46. Spiegel, David, and Jose Maldonado. "Dissociative Disorders" in *American Psychiatric Press Textbook of Psychiatry,* 3rd ed., Robert Hales et al. (eds.). Washington, DC: American Psychiatric Press, 1999.

47. Schnyder, Ulrich, et al. "Incidence and Prediction of Posttraumatic Stress Disorder Symptoms in Severely Injured Accident Victims." *American Journal of Psychiatry,* Vol. 158, No. 4, April 2001, p. 594.

48. Wijma, Klaas, et al. "Prevelance of Post-traumatic Stress Disorder Among Gynecological Patients with a History of Sexual and Physical Abuse." *Journal of Interpersonal Violence,* Vol. 15, No. 9, September 2000, p. 944.

49. Duncan, Renae. "Childhood Maltreatment and College Drop-out Rates: Implications for Child Abuse Researchers." *Journal of Interpersonal Violence,* Vol. 15, No. 9, September 2000, p. 987.

50. Lindstroem, Bengt. "The Meaning of Resilience." *International Journal of Adolescent Medicine & Health,* Vol. 13, No. 1, January–March 2001, p. 7.

51. McAdams, Dan, et al. "When Bad Things Turn Good and Good Things Turn Bad: Sequences of Redemption and Contamination in Life Narrative and Their Relation to Psychosocial Adaptation in Midlife Adults and in Students." *Personality & Social Psychology Bulletin,* Vol. 27, No. 4, April 2001, p. 474.

CHAPTER 9

AMERICAN HISTORY

Studying the sample American history chapter "The Furnace of Civil War" (found at the end of this chapter) you will learn to

- Preview a history chapter
- Make connections to the Civil War
- Mark and annotate important information in a chapter
- Study for a history exam by
  - Using headings to create summaries
  - Making key name and date cards
  - Creating concept maps
  - Creating a time line
  - Taking a practice test from the study guide
  - Predicting test questions
  - Working with a study partner or group
  - Recording and listening to your notes
  - Visualizing the battles and locations of the battles

PREVIEW

Before you begin this American history textbook chapter or any history textbook, you need to begin to think like a historian. A college history course is different from a high school history course. Rather than just memorizing facts, you are asked to think about them and connect them to each other so that you can determine relationships. History is not just one event after another; history is made up of people like you who had loved ones, felt fear, and didn't always know what was the right thing to do. Their actions changed and made the world as it is today. You have to learn to select relevant facts from among all the things that have occurred in the past, and you need to evaluate this information in an unbiased manner.

You will be reading Chapter 21 from an American history textbook. To help you understand the information in this textbook chapter, the following summary of Chapter 20 in the textbook (taken from the instructor's manual) is provided.

Chapter 20 Summary

South Carolina's firing on Fort Sumter aroused the North for war. Lincoln's call for troops to suppress the rebellion drove four upper South states into the Confederacy. Lincoln used an effective combination of political persuasion and force to keep the deeply divided Border States in the Union.

The Confederacy enjoyed initial advantages of upper-class European support, military leadership, and a defensive position on its own soil. The North enjoyed the advantages of lower-class European support, industrial and population resources, and political leadership.

The British upper classes sympathized with the South and abetted Confederate naval efforts. But effective diplomacy and Union military success thwarted those efforts and kept Britain as well as France neutral in the war.

Lincoln's political leadership proved effective in mobilizing the North for war, despite political opposition and resistance to his infringement on civil liberties. The North eventually mobilized its larger troop resources for war and ultimately turned to an unpopular and unfair draft system.

Northern economic and financial strengths enabled it to gain an advantage over the less-industrialized South. The changes in society opened new opportunities for women, who had contributed significantly to the war effort in both the North and South. Since most of the war was waged on Southern soil, the South was left devastated by the war.

Survey the Chapter

Read the title and all headings; look over the graphics and their captions; and read the first and last subsections. As you page through the chapter, list those study aids that the authors have provided to help you read and study this chapter.

_____

_____

_____

_____

_____

The authors have provided the following study aids for you:

The _quotation_ by Abraham Lincoln on the first page.
The _gray blocks of print_ throughout the chapter provided to add human points of interest.
The "_Chronology_" at the end of the chapter. This provides you with a list of important events and their dates.
The "_Varying Viewpoints_" located at the end of the chapter. These help you understand that history is not just facts. Different historians (and different students) can interpret events in different manners.

Make Connections

Have you ever read or heard talk about anything that you have surveyed in this chapter? Have you ever been to a Civil War reenactment? What do you remember? Do you recall information about any of the battles? What do you recall about Abraham Lincoln? If you have not already read the two history articles in Part Three, read them now to gain some background knowledge on this topic. Then write some information here concerning any topic in this chapter.

_____

_____

_____

_____

_____

Discuss the preceding information with a classmate, and think about a question that you would like to have answered as you read this chapter. Write that question here:

_____

_____

Determining a question of your own gives you a reason to read the chapter and helps you connect with the material in the chapter.

Journal Entry

Before you begin the next section, write a journal entry describing what you know about marking and annotating a textbook chapter.

MONITOR

How to Mark and Annotate

Marking and annotating is a method of taking notes in the textbook. It involves more than just underlining or highlighting text. The following suggestions explain how to effectively mark and annotate text.

1. Turn headings into questions and read for the answers. For example, "Bull Run Ends the 'Ninety-Day War'" can be turned into the question: Why did Bull Run end the ninety-day war? Use the answers to your questions to help you determine what to mark and annotate.

2. Read at least one paragraph before marking and annotating; you cannot read for the first time and mark and annotate simultaneously. Read, think about what you have read, and then mark and annotate.

3. Be selective. When you study this chapter, you will reread only what you have marked and annotated in the textbook. You do not want to reread the entire chapter.

4. Double underline stated main ideas of paragraphs. Write implied main ideas in the margin.

5. Single underline all important details.

6. Circle key terms, events, and dates.

7. Number steps or lists of details.

8. Box important transitions to indicate certain organizational patterns.

9. Annotate (write explanatory comments in the margins).
   - Write implied main ideas.
   - Write important ideas to remember.
   - Write important organizational patterns.
   - Write key words.

10. Create some of your own markings; you may use stars or asterisks or wavy lines to emphasize material. The objective is to have some system and to stick with that system.

11. Be consistent. For example, always use a double underline to indicate stated main ideas and a single underline to indicate important details. Do not switch back and forth.

12. *Do not* mark and annotate more than 20 percent of a page. Marking and annotating, like taking notes on paper, should be used to narrow down the amount of material to be studied.

Taking notes in this manner keeps you actively reading and will cut down on the amount of required study time. *Do not use a highlighter* because it does not allow you to annotate.

Determining What to Mark and Annotate

Read the first paragraph of the sample chapter and then write its main idea on the following lines:

Main Idea:_____

_____

The main idea would be "In 1861 Lincoln believed that the war would not last long, and he did not intend to interfere with slavery; but, when the war ended 4 years later, the country was changed and had a great challenge ahead of it." This is not stated in one sentence. You need to double underline parts of the first and second sentences as well as parts of the last sentence. You do not have to underline every word. Be selective; get all of the important ideas. Look at the following paragraph that has been marked and annotated; note the annotation in the margin to help you remember the main idea. Copy this marking and annotation into your textbook chapter. Do not underline complete sentences. You may add your own markings to help you remember additional details, but be sure to include what is already marked and do not add too much.

When <u>President Lincoln</u> <u>issued his call</u> to the states for seventy-five thousand militia-amen on (April 15, 1861), he envisioned them <u>serving</u> for only <u>ninety days</u>. Reaffirming his limited war aims, he declared that he had "<u>no purpose</u>, directly or indirectly, <u>to interfere with slavery</u> in the States where it exists." With a swift flourish of federal force, he hoped to show the folly of secession and rapidly return the rebellious states to the Union. But the war was to be neither brief nor limited. When the guns fell silent four years later, hundreds of thousands of soldiers on both sides lay dead, slavery was ended forever, and the nation faced the challenge of reintegrating the defeated but still recalcitrant South into the Union.

Lincoln thought war would be 90 days

Read the first heading of the sample chapter: "Bull Run Ends the 'Ninety-Day War' "; turn it into a question. You may use the example that was given in the preceding section or make up a different question. Having read the marked first paragraph, you have an idea of why this was called the "ninety-day war." Your question may deal with why it was not over quickly.

_____

_____

Read the first paragraph under this heading. After reading the paragraph, write the main idea on the following lines.

Main Idea:_____

_____

Again, the main idea is not in one sentence: Under public pressure, President Lincoln decided to send an ill-prepared Union army to attack at Bull Run. Also important but not the main idea would be the information about why a success was important to the Union cause. Look at the following marked and annotated paragraph and copy the markings and annotation onto your chapter page.

Bull Run Ends the "Ninety-Day War"

Northern newspapers, at first sharing Lincoln's expectation of a quick victory, raised the cry, "On to Richmond!" In this yeasty atmosphere, a <u>Union army</u> of some thirty thousand men drilled near Washington in the summer of 1861. It was <u>ill prepared for</u> <u>battle</u>, but the press and the public clamored for action. Lincoln eventually concluded

Why Lincoln attacked

① that <u>an attack on</u> a smaller Confederate force at <u>Bull Run</u> (Manassas Junction), some thirty miles (48 kilometers) southwest of Washington, might be worth a try. <u>If suc-</u> ② <u>cessful</u>, it would <u>demonstrate</u> the <u>superiority of Union arms</u>. It might even lead to the <u>capture of the Confederate capital at Richmond</u>, one hundred miles to the south. If ③④ Richmond fell, <u>secession would be thoroughly discredited</u>, and the <u>Union could be</u> <u>restored</u> without damage to the economic and social system of the South.

Read the next paragraph and write the main idea.

Main Idea:_____

_____

This is a sequence paragraph. The main idea is that the Union lost to Stonewall Jackson and his troops at Bull Run. No sentence states this, so you need to write this implied main idea in the margin as an annotation. You also need to single underline and number the major events in the battle sequence and to annotate that it is a sequence paragraph. Mark and annotate your paragraph to resemble the following:

① Raw <u>Yankee recruits swaggered</u> out of Washington <u>toward Bull Run</u> on (July 21, 1861), as if they were headed for a sporting event. Congressmen and spectators trailed along

Union loses to Stonewall Jackson

② with their lunch baskets to witness the fun. At first the battle <u>went well for the Yankees</u>. ③ But "Stonewall" <u>Jackson</u>'s gray-clad <u>warriors stood like a stone wall</u> (here he won his nickname), and Confederate reinforcements arrived unexpectedly. Panic seized the

Sequence of battle

④ green <u>Union troops</u>, <u>many</u> of whom <u>fled</u> in shameful confusion. The <u>Confederates</u>, ⑤ themselves <u>too exhausted or disorganized to pursue</u>, feasted on captured lunches.

Read the final paragraph in this section. Write the main idea.

Main Idea:_____

_____

The main idea is "Bull Run, though not decisive militarily, had psychological and political consequences for both the North and South." Most of the main idea is expressed in the first sentence with the exception of the fact that the North and South both were affected. The important details would be the effects on each side. You would also want to annotate this in the margin because causes and effects are an important part of history and history exams. Compare your markings and annotations with the following paragraph:

The "military picnic" at <u>Bull Run</u>, though <u>not decisive militarily</u>, bore <u>significant psy-</u> <u>chological and political consequences</u>; many of them paradoxical. Victory was worse

Effects on South

than defeat for the (South) because it <u>inflated</u> an already dangerous <u>overconfidence</u>. ① <u>Many</u> of the Southern soldiers promptly <u>deserted</u>, some boastfully to display their tro- ② phies, others feeling that the war was now surely over. Southern <u>enlistments fell off</u> ③ sharply, and <u>preparations for a protracted conflict slackened</u>. Defeat was better than

North

④ victory for the (Union) because it <u>dispelled all illusions of a one-punch war</u> and <u>caused</u>

Effects on North

① ② the <u>Northerners</u> to <u>buckle down</u> to the staggering task at hand. It also set the stage for a war that would be waged not merely for the cause of Union but also, eventually, for the abolitionist ideal of emancipation.

Now return to your question at the beginning of this section: "How did Bull Run end the ninety-day war?" This is not answered in any one sentence in this section, so you need to write your answer in the margin above the heading. Your answer should be that Bull Run ended what Lincoln thought would be a short (90-day) war.

Read the next heading " 'Tardy George' McClellan and the Peninsula Campaign"; turn it into a question.

This heading contains two parts, so two types of questions are possible. First, you might ask "Who is George McClellan, and why is he called 'tardy' ?" You might also ask about the peninsula: "Where is this peninsula, and what was the campaign?" When you read, search for the answers to all questions. Read the first paragraph. Double underline the main idea. The main idea is contained in the first sentence. The remainder of the paragraph describes McClellan and gives reasons why he brightened the Northern hopes. Single underline the points that state why he brightened Northern hopes: "He was a brilliant West Pointer and a serious student of warfare." Annotate your reason for the single underlines; compare your markings and annotation with the following paragraph:

"Tardy George" McClellan and the Peninsula Campaign

Northern hopes brightened later in 1861, when General George B. McClellan was given command of the Army of the Potomac, as the major Union force near Washington was now called. Red-haired and red-mustached, strong and stocky, McClellan was a brilliant, thirty-four-year-old West Pointer. As a serious student of warfare who was dubbed "Young Napoleon," he had seen plenty of fighting, first in the Mexican War and then as an observer of the Crimean War in Russia.   *Description of McClellan*

Read the second paragraph and double underline the main idea. The first sentence is again the main idea, so you should double underline it. The remainder of the paragraph lists examples of McClellan's virtues and defects. Single underline the word or phrase that signals a virtue or defect and annotate this in the margin next to each underlining.

The words *organizer, drillmaster,* and *idolized by his men* should be single underlined with "virtue" or a word with a similar meaning written in the margin close to these words. The words *perfectionist, believed that the enemy outnumbered him,* and *overcautious* should be single underlined with a "defect" or a word with a similar meaning written in the margin near them.

Cocky George McClellan embodied a curious mixture of virtues and defects. He was a superb organizer and drillmaster, and he injected splendid morale into the Army of the Potomac. Hating to sacrifice his troops, he was idolized by his men, who affectionately called him "Little Mac." But he was a perfectionist who seems not to have realized that an army is never ready to the last button and that wars cannot be won without running some risks. He consistently but erroneously believed that the enemy outnumbered him, partly because his intelligence reports from the head of Pinkerton's Detective Agency were unreliable. He was overcautious—Lincoln once accused him of having "the   *good* *bad** slows"—and he addressed the president in an arrogant tone that a less forgiving person would never have tolerated. Privately the general referred to his chief as a "baboon."

Read the third paragraph and double underline the main idea. This paragraph is about two points: (1) McClellan was not moving and (2) Lincoln ordered him to move. These points are found in the first and last sentences. You should double underline part of the first sentence and all of the last sentence. Your underlines and annotations also answer the first question made from the heading.

As <u>McClellan</u> doggedly <u>continued to drill</u> his army <u>without moving</u> it toward Richmond, the derisive Northern watchword became "All Quiet along the Potomac." The song of the hour was "Tardy George" (McClellan). After threatening to "borrow" the army if it was not going to be used, <u>Lincoln finally issued firm orders to advance.</u>

Read the next paragraph, which has no stated main idea. What type of paragraph is it?

_____

What information does it give?

_____

_____

This paragraph chronicles the sequence of the Peninsula Campaign battles. Annotate the organizational pattern in the margin and then single underline and number each of the major events in the text.

A reluctant <u>McClellan</u> at last <u>decided upon a waterborne approach to Richmond</u>, which lies at the western base of a narrow peninsula formed by the James and York Rivers—hence the name given to this historic encounter: the (Peninsula Campaign). McClellan warily <u>inched toward the Confederate capital</u> in the (spring of 1862) with about 100,000 men. After <u>taking a month to capture historic Yorktown</u>, which bristled with imitation wooden cannons, he <u>finally came</u> within sight of the spires of <u>Richmond</u>. At this crucial juncture, <u>Lincoln diverted McClellan's anticipated reinforcements to chase</u> "Stonewall" <u>Jackson</u>, whose lightning feints in the Shenandoah Valley seemed to put Washington, D.C., in jeopardy. Stalled in front of Richmond, <u>McClellan</u> was further <u>frustrated when "Jeb" Stuart's Confederate cavalry rode completely around his army</u> on reconnaissance. Then <u>General Robert E. Lee launched a devastating counterattack</u>— the (Seven Days' Battles—June 26–July 2, 1862). The <u>Confederates slowly drove McClellan back to the sea</u>. The Union forces abandoned the Peninsula Campaign as a costly failure, and <u>Lincoln temporarily abandoned McClellan</u> as commander of the Army of the Potomac—though Lee's army had suffered some twenty thousand casualties to McClellan's ten thousand.

Margin annotations: Sequence of battle ① ② ③ ④ ⑤

Read the next paragraph and double underline the main idea. The main idea is found in the first two sentences. The transition word *yet* indicates the importance of the second sentence. You also need to single underline the irony of this victory for Lee. (An *irony* is an outcome that is the opposite of what one expects.) This irony is repeated throughout the remainder of the paragraph and needs to be underlined only once. The irony is that Lee's victory secured continuing war and the end of slavery. In the margin, annotate the irony.

Lee had <u>achieved a brilliant, if bloody, triumph.</u> Yet the <u>ironies of his accomplishment</u> <u>are striking.</u> If McClellan had succeeded in taking Richmond and ending the war in mid-1862, the Union would probably have been restored with minimal disruption to the "peculiar institution." Slavery would have survived, at least for a time. <u>By his suc-</u> <u>cessful defense of Richmond</u> and defeat of McClellan, <u>Lee had in effect ensured that</u> <u>the war would endure until slavery was uprooted and the Old South thoroughly</u> <u>destroyed.</u> Lincoln himself, who had earlier professed his unwillingness to tamper with slavery where it already existed, now declared that the rebels "cannot experiment for ten years trying to destroy the government and if they fail still come back into the Union unhurt." He began to draft an emancipation proclamation.

Effect of Lee's victory (Irony)

Read the last paragraph and double underline the main idea. The second sentence contains the main idea: "The Northern military plan had six components." Each of the components is numbered, so you need to circle the number and single underline the main points of each component. Use key words in the margin to annotate.

Union strategy now turned toward total war. As finally developed, the <u>Northern mili-</u> <u>tary plan</u> had six components: first slowly <u>suffocate the South by blockading its coasts;</u> second <u>liberate the slaves</u> and hence <u>undermine</u> the very <u>economic foundations</u> of the Old <u>South;</u> third <u>cut the Confederacy in half</u> by <u>seizing control of the Mississippi River</u> backbone; fourth chop the <u>Confederacy to pieces</u> by <u>sending troops through Georgia</u> <u>and the Carolinas;</u> fifth decapitate it by <u>capturing its capital</u> at Richmond; and sixth (this was Ulysses Grant's idea especially), try everywhere to <u>engage</u> the <u>enemy's main</u> <u>strength</u> and to <u>grind it</u> into submission.

North Plan - 6 parts

Now go back to the beginning of the section and answer the questions about McClellan and the Peninsula Campaign. Check that the answers to each of the questions are underlined.

Who is George McClellan, and why is he called "tardy"?
McClellan was the commander of the Army of the Potomac and was called "tardy" because it took an order from Lincoln to get him to move his troops.
Where was the peninsula, and what was the campaign?
The peninsula was at Richmond, which lies at the western base of a narrow peninsula formed by the James and York Rivers. (See the map on page 207 of the history textbook chapter.) The campaign events are numbered in the fourth paragraph.

Turn the next heading, "War at Sea," into a question.

You may have asked which sea; you also need to ask what happened during this war and who won.
Now read each paragraph in the "War at Sea" section. Follow the directions for marking and annotating. When you have completed all seven paragraphs, compare your markings and annotations with the following markings and annotations.

The main idea of the first paragraph is never stated in one sentence. The paragraph is about the impossibility of blockading the entire eastern coast and about how the North concentrated on principal parts. Certain parts of different sentences must be double underlined to obtain a main idea. The annotation indicates that this section contains two important ideas about the war at sea.

The War at Sea

The blockade started leakily; it was not clamped down all at once but was extended by degrees. A watertight patrol of some thirty-five hundred miles of coast was impossible for the hastily improvised Northern navy, which counted converted yachts and ferryboats in its fleet. But blockading was simplified by concentrating on the principal ports and inlets where dock facilities were available for loading bulky bales of cotton.

The second paragraph is about England's recognizing the blockade only because it was England's chief offensive weapon, and England did not want to be held to similar standards in a later war. The reason is single underlined with an annotation in the margin to explain the underlining.

How was the blockade regarded by the naval powers of the world? Ordinarily, they probably would have defied it, for it was never completely effective and was especially sievelike at the outset. But Britain, the greatest maritime nation, recognized it as binding and warned its shippers that they ignored it at their peril. An explanation is easy. Blockade happened to be the chief offensive weapon of Britain, which was still Mistress of the Seas. Britain plainly did not want to tie its hands in a future war by insisting that Lincoln maintain impossibly high blockading standards.

Britain recognized blockade

reason why

The third paragraph has its main idea at the beginning, with an example following it. Single underline part of the example and annotate the organizational pattern in the margin. The last sentence is also double underlined because it relates to the end of the blockade-running, which refers back to the main idea sentence.

Blockade-running soon became riskily profitable, as the growing scarcity of Southern goods drove prices skyward. The most successful blockade runners were swift, gray-painted steamers, scores of which were specially built in Scotland. A leading rendezvous was the West Indian port of Nassau, in the British Bahamas, where at one time thirty-five of the speedy ships rode at anchor. The low-lying craft would take on cargoes of arms brought in by tramp steamers from Britain, leave with fraudulent papers for "Halifax" (Canada), and then return a few days later with a cargo of cotton. The risks were great, but the profits would mount to 700 percent and more for lucky gamblers. Two successful voyages might well pay for capture on a third. The lush days of blockade-running finally passed as Union squadrons gradually pinched off the leading Southern ports, from New Orleans to Charleston.

The fourth paragraph's main idea is again the first sentence, with an example following it. Single underline the example and annotate the organizational pattern in the margin.

The Northern navy enforced the blockade with high-handed practices. Yankee captains, for example, would seize British freighters on the high seas, if laden with war supplies } ex for the tiny port of Nassau and other halfway stations. The justification was that obviously these shipments were "ultimately" destined, by devious routes, for the Confederacy.

The fifth paragraph adds to the idea of the second paragraph. Again, England is recognizing the enforcement of the blockade for its own purposes in a future war, which in fact becomes a reality. Only the first sentence needs to be double underlined as the main idea because the reason for England's acquiescence has been given in the second paragraph.

London, although not happy, acquiesced in this disagreeable doctrine of "ultimate destination" or "continuous voyage." British blockaders might need to take advantage of the same far-fetched interpretation in a future war—as in fact they did in the world war of 1914–1918.

The sixth and seventh paragraphs are about the ironclads. The first sentence of paragraph 6 states the main idea of both paragraphs. The remainder of the paragraphs states the sequence of events in the first battle-testing of the ironclads. Each of the events should be single underlined and numbered. Key words are added as annotations.

The most alarming Confederate threat to the blockade came in 1862. Resourceful ① South Southerners raised and reconditioned a former wooden U.S. warship, the Merrimack, and plated its sides with old iron railroad rails. Renamed the Virginia, this clumsy but powerful monster easily destroyed two wooden ships of the Union navy in the Virginia ② Iron ship battle waters of Chesapeake Bay; it also threatened catastrophe to the entire Yankee blockading fleet. (Actually the homemade ironclad was not a seaworthy craft.)

A tiny Union ironclad, the Monitor, built in about one hundred days, arrived on the scene in the nick of time. For four hours, on March 9, 1862, the little "Yankee North cheesebox on a raft" fought the wheezy Merrimack to a standstill. Britain and France had already built several powerful ironclads, but the first battle-testing of these new ③ North wins craft heralded the doom of wooden warships. A few months after the historic battle, the Confederates destroyed the Merrimack to keep it from the grasp of advancing Union ④ troops.

Return to your questions. To which sea does the heading refer?

Although the paragraphs do not mention the sea by name, you can infer the Atlantic Ocean because it borders the mentioned southern ports and England. You also know that the North ultimately won this war at sea both with its blockading and its Union ironclad, the Monitor.
Next, make up a question for the heading "The Pivotal Point: Antietam."

One important question would be, "Why was Antietam a pivotal point?" Read through the section and mark and annotate. Then compare your section with the marked and annotated section that follows.

The first paragraph is about Lee's victory over Pope at the Second Battle of Bull Run.

The Pivotal Point: Antietam

Lee defeats Pope

Robert E. Lee, having broken the back of McClellan's assault on Richmond, next moved northward. At the Second Battle of Bull Run (August 29–30, 1862), he encountered a Federal force under General John Pope. A handsome, dashing, soldierly figure, Pope boasted that in the western theater of war, from which he had recently come, he had seen only the backs of the enemy. Lee quickly gave him a front view, furiously attacking Pope's troops and inflicting a crushing defeat.

The second and third paragraphs are about Lee's move into Maryland and the fact that Marylanders did not respond. The cause for Lee's move should have a single underline and annotation.

Emboldened by this success, Lee daringly thrust into Maryland. He hoped to strike a blow that would not only encourage foreign intervention but also seduce the still-wavering Border State and its sisters from the Union. The Confederate troops sang lustily:

Thou wilt not cower in the dust,

   Maryland! my Maryland!

Thy gleaming sword shall never rust,

   Maryland! my Maryland!

reason why →

But the Marylanders did not respond to the siren song. The presence among the invaders of so many blanketless, hatless, and shoeless soldiers dampened the state's ardor.

The fourth paragraph states the sequence of events concerning the Battle of Antietam. Annotate this in the margin and number the events.

Antietam MD

① Events finally converged toward a critical battle at Antietam Creek, Maryland. Lincoln, yielding to popular pressure, hastily restored "Little Mac" to active command of the main Northern army. His soldiers tossed their caps skyward and hugged his horse as they hailed his return. Fortune shone upon McClellan when two Union soldiers found a copy of Lee's battle plans wrapped around a packet of three cigars dropped by a careless Confederate officer. With this crucial piece of intelligence in hand, McClellan succeeded in halting Lee at Antietam on September 17, 1862, in one of the bitterest and bloodiest days of the war.

McClellan halts Lee ②

③

Paragraph 5 states the result and the effects on both commanders: Lee retired across the Potomac, and McClellan was again removed from command.

A draw

Lee moves

Antietam was more or less a draw militarily. But Lee, finding his thrust parried, retired across the Potomac. McClellan, from whom much more had been hoped, was removed from his field command for the <u>second and final time</u>. His numerous critics, con-demning him for not having boldly pursued the ever-dangerous Lee, finally got his scalp.

McClellan removed

The remainder of the section explains the reasons for the importance of this battle and why it was a pivotal point in the war. Double underline the first sentence of paragraph 6 and number the two reasons in the sixth and seventh paragraphs: (1) The victory for the North held off any intervention by England and France and (2) the victory enabled Lincoln to have reason to issue the Emancipation Proclamation, turning the Civil War into a fight against slavery. Other phrases can be single underlined to complete the idea of Lincoln's victory and to state the date of the Emancipation Proclamation. Annotate key words in the margin. These reasons also answer the question created from the section heading.

The landmark <u>Battle of Antietam</u> was one of the <u>decisive engagements of world his-tory</u>—probably the most decisive of the Civil War. Jefferson Davis was perhaps never again so near victory as on that fateful summer day. The <u>British and French govern-ments</u> were on the verge of diplomatic mediation, a form of interference sure to be angrily resented by the North. An almost certain rebuff by Washington might well have spurred Paris and London into armed collusion with Richmond. But both capitals <u>cooled off when the Union displayed unexpected power at Antietam</u>, and their chill deepened with the passing months.

decisive battle reasons ①

Bloody Antietam was also the long-awaited "<u>victory</u>" that <u>Lincoln needed for</u> ② <u>launching his Emancipation Proclamation</u>. The abolitionists had long been clamoring for action: Wendell Phillips was denouncing the president as a "first-rate second-rate man." By midsummer of 1862, with the Border States safely in the fold, Lincoln was ready to move. But he believed that to issue such an edict on the heels of a series of military disasters would be folly. It would seem like a confession that the North, unable to conquer the South, was forced to call upon the slaves to murder their masters. Lincoln therefore decided to wait for the outcome of Lee's invasion.

Antietam served as the needed emancipation springboard. The halting of Lee's offensive was just enough of a victory to justify Lincoln's issuing, on September 23, 1862, the preliminary Emancipation Proclamation. This hope-giving document announced that on January 1, 1863, the president would issue a final proclamation.

On the scheduled date, he fully redeemed his promise, and the Civil War became more of a moral crusade as the fate of slavery and the South it had sustained was sealed. The war now became more of what Lincoln called a "remorseless revolutionary struggle." After January 1, 1863, Lincoln said, "The character of the war will be changed. It will be one of subjugation. . . . The [old] South is to be destroyed and replaced by new propositions and ideas."

Read the next heading "A Proclamation Without Emancipation" and turn it into a question.

_____

_____

(If you are not sure about the meanings of the words *proclamation* and *emancipation,* use context clues, word parts, and/or a dictionary to help you.) Two possible questions are, "Why was this a proclamation without emancipation?" and "Why was Lincoln proclaiming the slaves free but not really freeing them?" Go ahead and read the section and mark and annotate. Remember to read for the main ideas and major details and to search for the answers to your questions. Compare your marking and annotating with the sections that follow.

Paragraph 1 has an implied main idea, so it needs to be annotated. It explains exactly which slaves were set free, as well as Lincoln's tone and intent with the proclamation. Use the margin to show the main idea and single underline the effects on slaves.

A Proclamation Without Emancipation

Not all slaves set free

Lincoln's Emancipation Proclamation of 1863 declared "forever free" the slaves in those Confederate states still in rebellion. Bondsmen in the loyal Border States were not affected, nor were those in specific conquered areas in the South—all told, about 800,000. The tone of the document was dull and legalistic (one historian has said that it had all the moral grandeur of a bill of lading). But if Lincoln stopped short of a clarion call for a holy war to achieve freedom, he pointedly concluded his historic document by declaring that the Proclamation was "an act of justice," and calling for "the considerate judgment of mankind and the gracious favor of Almighty God."

The second paragraph continues to explain what the proclamation did not do. (The last sentence of this paragraph is a good context clue for the meanings of *emancipation* and *proclamation.*)

No slaves freed in reality

The presidential pen did not formally strike the shackles from a single slave. Where Lincoln could presumably free the slaves—that is, in the loyal Border States—he refused to do so lest he spur disunion. Where he could not—that is, in the Confederate states—he tried to. In short, where he *could* he would not, and where he *would* he could not. Thus the Emancipation Proclamation was stronger on proclamation than emancipation.

The third paragraph has an implied main idea. The paragraph is about the effects of the Emancipation Proclamation. Annotate the implied main idea, and number and underline the effects.

Yet much unofficial do-it-yourself liberation did take place. Thousands of jubilant slaves, learning of the proclamation, flocked to the invading Union armies, stripping already rundown plantations of their work force. In this sense the Emancipation Proclamation was heralded by the drumbeat of running feet. But many fugitives would have come anyhow, as they had from the war's outset. Lincoln's immediate goal was not only to ① liberate the slaves but also to ② strengthen the moral cause of the Union at home and abroad. This he succeeded in doing. At the same time, Lincoln's proclamation

③
clearly foreshadowed the ultimate doom of slavery. This was legally achieved by action

of the individual states and by their ratification of the Thirteenth Amendment in 1865,

eight months after the Civil War had ended. The Emancipation Proclamation also fun-

④
damentally changed the nature of the war because it effectively removed any chance of

a negotiated settlement. Both sides now knew that the war would be a fight to the finish.

Effects of Emancipation Proclamation

The fourth paragraph has its stated main idea at the beginning followed by examples of
the varied reactions. Annotate the organizational pattern in the margin to remind yourself of
this when you return to study.

Public reactions to the long-awaited proclamation of 1863 were varied. "God bless

Abraham Lincoln," exulted the antislavery editor Horace Greeley in his *New York Tri-*

bune. But many ardent abolitionists complained that Lincoln had not gone far enough.

On the other hand, formidable numbers of Northerners, especially in the "Butternut"

regions of the Old Northwest and the Border States, felt that he had gone too far. A

cynical Democratic rhymester quipped,

North reactions to proclamation varied

ex

Honest old Abe, when the war first began,

Denied abolition was part of his plan;

Honest old Abe has since made a decree,

The war must go on till the slaves are all free.

As both can't be honest, will some one tell how,

If honest Abe then, he is honest Abe now?

The fifth paragraph also begins with a stated main idea of northern opposition with examples to back it. Annotate the organizational pattern in the margin and single underline the
important examples that show opposition.

Opposition mounted in the North against supporting an "abolition war"; ex-president

Pierce and others felt that emancipation should not be "inflicted" on the slaves. Many

Boys in Blue, especially from the Border States, had volunteered to fight for the Union,

not against slavery. Desertions increased sharply. The crucial congressional elections in

the autumn of 1862 went heavily against the administration, particularly in New York,

Pennsylvania, and Ohio. Democrats even carried Lincoln's Illinois, although they did

not secure control of Congress.

ex

Paragraph 6 is about reactions in both the South and Europe. European reactions were
split depending on whether they were from aristocrats (upper class) or the middle class. Annotate with key words in the margin to show the topic, and single underline the reactions.

The Emancipation Proclamation caused an outcry to rise from the South that "Lincoln

the fiend" was trying to stir up the "hellish passions" of a slave insurrection. Aristo-

crats of Europe, noting that the proclamation applied only to rebel slaveholders, were

Reactions in South & Europe

inclined to <u>sympathize with Southern protests</u>. But the <u>Old World working classes</u>, especially in Britain, <u>reacted otherwise</u>. They sensed that the proclamation spelled the ultimate doom of slavery, and many laborers were more determined than ever to oppose intervention. Gradually the diplomatic position of the Union improved.

The final paragraph restates that the North now had a stronger moral cause (stated back in the third paragraph.) The first sentence contains the main idea and the annotation shows its importance.

Most important outcome The <u>North now had much the stronger moral cause</u>. In addition to preserving the Union, it had committed itself to freeing the slaves. The moral position of the South was correspondingly diminished.

Journal Entry

Write a journal entry explaining what you have learned about marking and annotating a textbook chapter.

RECITE

At this point, you have completed reading and marking and annotating one third of the chapter. Review everything you have marked and annotated; then complete Part I of the American History Study Guide Practice Test on pages 197–203. Check your answers in Appendix A.

When you have completed Part I of the practice test, continue to mark and annotate the American history chapter. Write your questions in the margins next to the headings before you read. Read each paragraph and continue to mark and annotate. Have your instructor check your markings and annotations and discuss them with you. Once you have completed reading and marking the section titled "Sherman Scorches Georgia," review your markings and annotations and take Part II of the study guide practice test. Then finish reading and marking the rest of the history chapter.

REVIEW

Review Your Notes

When you have completed reading and marking the chapter, review the questions that you formed from the headings. Answer each of the questions from memory or by rereading only what has been marked or annotated. Do this at least once each week until you have taken a test on the chapter.

Methods of Studying

SUMMARIES

Use your markings and annotations to write a summary of each heading on an index card. For example, the first heading "Bull Run Ends the 'Ninety-Day War' " would be written on the front of an index card; on the back, list the steps in the battle, the winner, the effects, and why the heading is appropriate for this section. Your next card would be titled "Tardy George McClellan and the Peninsula Campaign." Review these summaries instead of your markings and annotations on a weekly schedule.

KEY NAME AND DATE CARDS

Write the names of important people, battles, events, and dates on index cards. Define the importance on the back of each. Include all of the events listed in the "Chronology" at the end of the history textbook chapter.

CONCEPT MAPS

This American history chapter is different to map than the health chapter because it contains no subheadings. You may choose to create a concept map for each heading, you may use the chronology at the end of the chapter and create a concept map for each year, or you may think of another method of creating concept maps for this history chapter. Follow the guidelines for creating concept maps in Chapter 8, but be aware that information presented in history textbooks is not always concepts related but instead may deal with people and events. Thus, the information that you place in your boxes or circles will likely be more in depth than if you were mapping a health or business or psychology textbook chapter. Important information about battles usually includes causes and/or effects as well as what happened during the battle (the sequence of events).

The following concept map has been created from the first heading in the chapter, "Bull Run Ends the 'Ninety-Day War.' " Review this concept map and then create concept maps for the remainder of the chapter.

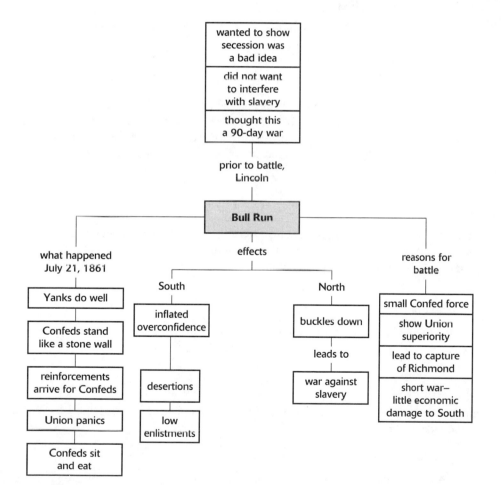

Battle of Bull Run

TIME LINE

Draw a time line of the events listed in the chronology at the end of the history textbook chapter. Write the importance of each event next to its date and title on the time line.

STUDY GUIDE

You should have already completed and checked Parts I and II of the study guide practice test. Review your third section of markings and annotations and complete Part III of the practice test. Then check your answers against those in Appendix A. Pay careful attention to the questions you answered incorrectly in any of the practice test parts; be sure you know the correct answers as well as the reasons for your incorrect responses.

PREDICTED TEST QUESTIONS

Create questions on different levels of thinking for each section of the chapter. Then answer the questions. *Do not* ask only knowledge questions concerning names and dates. Ask for reasons, effects, and outcomes.

GROUP OR PARTNER STUDY

Use your key name and date cards to quiz other students or a partner on key people, events, battles, and dates. Ask a partner your predicted test questions, and then answer his or her questions.

RECORDING AND LISTENING

Record your summaries and key name and date card information on tape and then listen to them.

VISUALIZING

Visualize the battles and the soldiers. Use the photographs in the chapter to help you visualize some of the key characters. Put yourself in their shoes. Try to think as they did. For example, if you had been President Lincoln, would you have trusted Grant, with his reputation, to command the army? Had you been a slave in the South, how would you have felt about the Emancipation Proclamation?

USING MAPS

Review the maps in the chapter; be sure that you can visualize where battles occurred in relation to each other. If you have a difficult time doing this, find a U.S. map and mark the locations of each of the battles.

PREPARE FOR THE TEST

Review the section titled "Preparing for and Taking the Test" in Chapter 7 to help you prepare for the test.

AFTER THE TEST

Complete the test review charts at the end of Chapter 7 to help you determine what you did right and what you did wrong.

Journal Entry

Try marking and annotating a chapter from a textbook in another course you are taking, and then write a journal entry explaining whether it was helpful or not, and why.

AMERICAN HISTORY STUDY GUIDE PRACTICE TEST

Part I

TRUE OR FALSE

Write *T* in the blank if the statement is true, *F* if the statement is false. If it is false, write the correct statement in the space provided.

_____ 1. The first Battle of Bull Run was the turning point of the Civil War because it convinced the South the war would be long and difficult.

_____

_____ 2. The Emancipation Proclamation was more important for its political effects on the North and Europe than for its freeing of large numbers of slaves.

_____

_____ 3. The Battle Antietam was a turning point of the war because it prevented British and French recognition of the Confederacy.

_____

_____ 4. Lincoln's decision to make the war a fight against slavery was universally popular in the North.

_____

MULTIPLE CHOICE

Write the letter of the *best* answer in the blank.

_____ 5. One effect of the first Battle of Bull Run was to
   a. convince the North that victory would not be difficult.
   b. increase the South's already dangerous overconfidence.
   c. demonstrate the superiority of Southern volunteer soldiers over Northern draftees.
   d. cause a wave of new Southern enlistments in the army.

_____ 6. The primary weakness of General George McClellan as a military commander was his
   a. inability to gain the support of his troops.
   b. tendency to rush into battle with inadequate plans and preparations.
   c. lack of confidence in his own abilities.
   d. excessive caution and reluctance to use his troops in battle.

_____ 7. After the unsuccessful Peninsula Campaign, Lincoln and the Union turned to a
   a. new strategy based on "total war" against the Confederacy.
   b. new strategy based on an invasion through the mountains of western Virginia and Tennessee.
   c. pattern of defensive warfare designed to protect Washington, DC.
   d. reliance on the navy rather than the army to win the war.

_____ 8. The Union blockade of Confederate ports was
   a. initially leaky but eventually effective.
   b. threatened by the powerful navies of Britain and France.
   c. immediately effective in capturing Confederate blockade-running ships.
   d. largely ineffective in shutting off the sale of Confederate cotton in Europe.

_____ 9. Antietam was probably the crucial battle of the Civil War because it

     a. ended any possibility of Confederate invasion of the North.
     b. destroyed Lee's army in the East.
     c. fundamentally undermined Confederate morale.
     d. prevented British and French recognition of the Confederacy.

_____ 10. Officially, the Emancipation Proclamation freed only slaves

     a. who had fled their masters and joined the Union army.
     b. in those Confederate states still in rebellion.
     c. in the border states and areas under Union army control.
     d. in Washington, DC.

_____ 11. The political effects of the Emancipation Proclamation were to

     a. bolster public support for the war and the Republican Party.
     b. strengthen the North's moral cause but weaken the Lincoln administration in the border states and parts of the North.
     c. turn the Democratic Party from support of the war toward favoring recognition of the Confederacy.
     d. weaken support for the Union among British and French public opinion.

IDENTIFICATION

Write the correct identification for each description in the blank.

_____ 12. First major battle of the Civil War, in which untrained Northern troops joined civilian picnickers in a flight back to Washington

_____ 13. McClellan's disastrously unsuccessful attempt to capture Richmond quickly by following an invasion route between the York and James Rivers

_____ 14. Battle that was probably the most decisive of the war, despite its being a military draw, because it forestalled European intervention and led to the Emancipation Proclamation

_____ 15. Document that proclaimed a war against slavery and guaranteed a fight to the finish

Part II

TRUE OR FALSE

Write *T* in the blank if the statement is true, and *F* if the statement is false. If it is false, write the correct statement in the space provided.

_____ 1. The use of Black soldiers in the Union army proved militarily ineffective.

_____

_____ 2. Lee's invasion of Pennsylvania in 1863 was intended to encourage the Northern peace movement and promote foreign intervention.

_____

_____ 3. The Northern victories at Vicksburg and Gettysburg effectively spelled doom for the Confederacy.

_____

_____ 4. In the final year of the conflict, Grant and Sherman waged a "total war" that was immensely destructive of Southern lives and property.

_____

MULTIPLE CHOICE

Write the letter of the *best* answer in the blank.

_____ 5. The thousands of Black soldiers in the Union army

    a. added a powerful new weapon to the antislavery dimension of the Union cause.
    b. were prevented from participating in combat.
    c. seldom fought effectively in battle.
    d. saw action in the very first days of the war.

_____ 6. Lee's goal in invading the North in the summer of 1863 was to

    a. capture major Northern cities like Philadelphia and New York.
    b. deflect attention from "Stonewall" Jackson's movements against Washington.
    c. strengthen the Northern peace movement and encourage foreign intervention in the war.
    d. cut off Northern supply lines and damage the Union's economic foundations.

_____ 7. Grant's capture of Vicksburg was especially important because it

    a. quelled Northern peace agitation and cut off the Confederate trade routes along the Mississippi.
    b. ended the threat of a Confederate invasion from Mexico.
    c. blocked a possible French invasion from Mexico.
    d. destroyed Southern naval power.

_____ 8. Sherman's march "from Atlanta to the sea" was especially notable for its

    a. tactical brilliance against Confederate calvary forces.
    b. effective use of public relations to turn Southern sympathies against the Confederacy.
    c. brutal use of "total war" tactics of destruction and pillaging against Southern civilian populations.
    d. impact in inspiring Northern public opinion to turn against slavery.

IDENTIFICATION

Write the correct identification for each description in the blank.

_____ 9. General U. S. Grant's nickname, taken from his military demand to the enemy at Fort Donelson and elsewhere

_____ 10. The crucial Confederate fortress on the Mississippi, whose fall to Grant in 1863 cut the South in two

_____ 11. Pennsylvania battle that ended Lee's last hopes of achieving victory through an invasion of the North

_____ 12. Mississippi site where Black soldiers were massacred after their surrender

_____ 13. Georgia city captured and burned by Sherman just before the election of 1864

Part III

TRUE OR FALSE

Write *T* in the blank if the statement is true, *F* if the statement is false. If it is false, write the correct statement in the space provided.

_____ 1. The Union's greatest military breakthroughs came on the eastern front, and this paved the way for later successes in the West.

_____ 2. The Northern Democrats were deeply divided between those who backed the war and those who favored peace negotiations with the South.

_____

_____ 3. The formation of a temporary "Union party" in 1864 was a device used by Lincoln to gain support of prowar Democrats.

_____

_____ 4. As a popular war leader, Lincoln received overwhelming support within the Republican Party and in the nation as a whole.

_____

_____ 5. The South's last hope was that the victory of a "Peace Democrat" in 1864 would enable it to achieve its political goals.

_____

_____ 6. Most Southerners eventually came to see Lincoln's assassination as a tragedy for them.

_____

_____ 7. The Civil War failed to settle the central issues of slavery, states' rights, and secession that caused the war.

_____

MULTIPLE CHOICE

Write the letter of the *best* answer in the blank.

_____ 8. The "Copperheads" were

    a. Northern Democrats who opposed the Union war effort.
    b. Republicans who opposed the Lincoln administration.
    c. Democrats who backed Lincoln and the war effort.
    d. radical Republicans who advocated a war to destroy slavery and punish the South.

_____ 9. Andrew Johnson, Lincoln's running mate in 1864, was a

    a. Copperhead.
    b. War Democrat.
    c. conservative Republican.
    d. radical Republican.

_____ 10. Lincoln's election victory in 1864 was sealed by Union military successes at

    a. Gettysburg, Antietam, and Vicksburg.
    b. the Wilderness, Lookout Mountain, and Appomattox.
    c. Bull Run, the Peninsula, and Fredericksburg.
    d. Mobile, Atlanta, and the Shenandoah Valley.

_____ 11. As the Democratic Party nominee in 1864, General George McClellan

    a. denounced Lincoln as a traitor and called for an immediate end to the war.
    b. repudiated the Copperhead platform that called for a negotiated settlement with the Confederacy.
    c. indicated that if elected president, he would take personal command of all Union armies.
    d. called for waging a "total war" against the civilian population to the South.

IDENTIFICATION

Write the correct identification for each description in the blank.

_____ 12. Northern Democrats who opposed the Civil War and sympathized with the South

_____ 13. Edward Everett Hale's story of treason and banishment, inspired by the wartime banishing of Copperhead Clement Vallandigham

_____ 14. The 1864 coalition of Republicans and War Democrats that backed Lincoln's reelection

_____ 15. Washington site where Lincoln was assassinated by Booth on April 14, 1865

_____ 16. Virginia state where Lee surrendered to Grant in April 1865

_____ 17. Romantic name given to the Southern fight for independence, indicating nobility despite defeat

MATCHING PEOPLE, PLACES, AND EVENTS

Match the person, place, or event in the right column with the proper description in the left column by writing the letter in the blank.

_____ 18. daring Southern commander killed at the Battle of Chancellorsville

_____ 19. southern officer whose failed charge at Gettysburg marked "the high water mark of the Confederacy"

_____ 20. ruthless Northern general who waged a march through Georgia

_____ 21. fortress whose capture split the Confederacy in two

_____ 22. site where Lee's last major invasion of the North was turned back

_____ 23. gentlemanly top commander of the Confederate army

_____ 24. site of Grant's bloody attacks on Confederates near Richmond in 1864

_____ 25. crucial battle in Maryland that staved off European recognition of the Confederacy

_____ 26. Lincoln's secretary of the treasury who hungered for the presidency in 1864

_____ 27. fanatical actor whose act of violence harmed the South

_____ 28. Union commander who first made his mark with victories in the West

_____ 29. pro-Union War Democrat from the South who ran as Lincoln's "Union party" vice-presidential candidate in 1864

_____ 30. notorious Copperhead, convicted of treason, who ran for governor of Ohio while exiled to Canada

_____ 31. former Union general who repudiated his party's Copperhead platform and polled 45 percent of the popular vote in 1864

_____ 32. site of Union defeat in a very early battle of the war

a. Bull Run

b. George McClellan

c. Robert E. Lee

d. Antietam

e. "Stonewall" Jackson

f. George Pickett

g. Ulysses S. Grant

h. Gettysburg

i. Vicksburg

j. William T. Sherman

k. Clement Vallandigham

l. Salmon P. Chase

m. the Wilderness

n. Andrew Johnson

o. John Wilkes Booth

PUTTING THINGS IN ORDER

Put the following events in correct order by numbering them from 1 to 5.

_____ 33. Within one week, two decisive battles in Mississippi and Pennsylvania almost ensure the Confederacy's eventual defeat.

_____ 34. Defeat in a battle near Washington, D.C. ends Union military complacency.

_____ 35. A militarily indecisive battle in Maryland enables Lincoln to declare that the Civil War has become a war on slavery.

_____ 36. The Civil War ends with the defeated army granted generous terms of surrender.

_____ 37. In both Georgia and Virginia, determined Northern generals wage bloody and destructive "total war" against a weakened but still-resisting South.

MATCHING CAUSE AND EFFECT

Match the historical cause in the right column with the proper effect in the left column by writing the letter in the blank.

_____ 38. enabled Lincoln to issue the Emancipation Proclamation and blocked British and French intervention

_____ 39. split the South in two and opened the war for Sherman's invasion of Georgia

_____ 40. deprived the nation of experienced leadership during Reconstruction

_____ 41. made it difficult for Lincoln to prosecute the war effectively

_____ 42. helped lead to the enlistment of Black fighting men in the Union army

_____ 43. ended the South's effort to win the war by aggressive invasion

_____ 44. guaranteed that the South would fight to the end to save slavery

_____ 45. forced Lee to surrender at Appomattox

_____ 46. led some Southerners to believe they would win an easy victory

_____ 47. ensured Lincoln's reelection and ended the South's last hope of achieving independence by political means

a. political dissent by Copperheads and jealous Republicans

b. series of Union military victories in late 1864

c. assassination of Lincoln

d. Grant's Tennessee and Mississippi River campaigns

e. Battle of Bull Run

f. Battle of Antietam

g. Battle of Gettysburg

h. Grant's final brutal campaign in Virginia

i. Emancipation Proclamation

j. growing Union manpower shortage in 1863

MAP MYSTERY

Using the maps and charts in the history chapter excerpt, answer the following questions.

48. Which two states of the Southeast saw little of the major fighting of the Civil War?

49. In which four states were the slaves *all* freed by state action—without any federal involvement?

50. Which two states practiced slavery until it was finally abolished by the Thirteenth Amendment to the Constitution?

51. On what three rivers were the major Confederate strategic points that Grant successfully assaulted in 1862–1863?

52. What secessionist South Carolina city was *not* in the direct path of Sherman's army in 1864–1865?

21

The Furnace of Civil War

⤬

1861–1865

My paramount object in this struggle is to save the Union, and is not either to save or to destroy slavery.

ABRAHAM LINCOLN, 1862

When President Lincoln issued his call to the states for seventy-five thousand militiamen on April 15, 1861, he envisioned them serving for only ninety days. Reaffirming his limited war aims, he declared that he had "no purpose, directly or indirectly, to interfere with slavery in the States where it exists." With a swift flourish of federal force, he hoped to show the folly of secession and rapidly return the rebellious states to the Union. But the war was to be neither brief nor limited. When the guns fell silent four years later, hundreds of thousands of soldiers on both sides lay dead, slavery was ended forever, and the nation faced the challenge of reintegrating the defeated but still recalcitrant South into the Union.

Bull Run Ends the "Ninety-Day War"

Northern newspapers, at first sharing Lincoln's expectation of a quick victory, raised the cry, "On to Richmond!" In this yeasty atmosphere, a Union army of some thirty thousand men drilled near Washington in the summer of 1861. It was ill prepared for battle, but the press and the public clamored for action. Lincoln eventually concluded that an attack on a smaller Confederate force at Bull Run (Manassas Junction), some thirty miles southwest of Washington, might be worth a try. If successful, it would demonstrate the superiority of Union arms. It might even lead to the capture of the Confederate capital at Richmond, one hundred miles to the south. If Richmond fell, secession would be thoroughly discredited, and the Union could be restored without damage to the economic and social system of the South.

Raw Yankee recruits swaggered out of Washington toward Bull Run on July 21, 1861, as if they were headed for a sporting event. Congressmen and spectators trailed along with their lunch baskets to witness the fun. At first the battle went well for the Yankees. But "Stonewall" Jackson's gray-clad warriors stood like a stone wall (here he won his nickname), and Confederate reinforcements arrived unexpectedly. Panic seized the green Union troops, many of whom fled in shameful confusion. The Confederates, themselves too exhausted or disorganized to pursue, feasted on captured lunches.

The "military picnic" at Bull Run, though not decisive militarily, bore significant psychological and political consequences, many of them paradoxical. Victory was worse than defeat for the South, because it inflated an already dangerous overconfidence. Many of the Southern soldiers promptly deserted, some boastfully to display their trophies, others feeling that the war was now surely over. Southern enlistments fell off sharply, and preparations for a protracted conflict slackened. Defeat was better than victory for the Union, because it dispelled all illusions of a one-punch war and caused the Northerners to buckle down to the staggering task at hand. It also set the stage for a war that would be waged not merely for the cause of Union but also, eventually, for the abolitionist ideal of emancipation.

"Tardy George" McClellan and the Peninsula Campaign

Northern hopes brightened later in 1861, when General George B. McClellan was given command of the Army of the Potomac, as the major Union

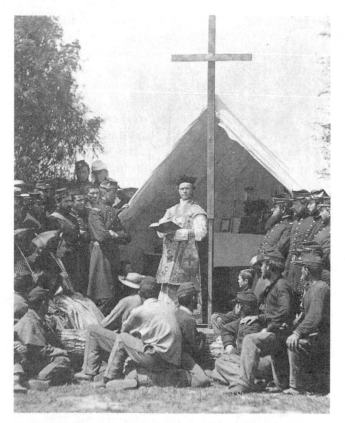

Preparing for Battle   These troops of the 69th New York State Militia, a largely Irish regiment, were photographed attending Sunday morning Mass in May 1861, just weeks before the Battle of Bull Run. Because the regiment was camped near Washington, D.C., women were able to visit.

The Army of the Potomac Marching Up Pennsylvania Avenue, Washington, D.C., 1861   In this painting Union troops parade before the Battle of Bull Run. Colorfully uniformed, they are a regiment of Zouaves, who adopted the name and style of military dress from a legendarily dashing French infantry unit. But bright uniforms were not enough to win battles, and these troops were soon to be routed by the Confederates.

An observer behind the Union lines described the Federal troops' pell-mell retreat from the battlefield at Bull Run:

"We called to them, tried to tell them there was no danger, called them to stop, implored them to stand. We called them cowards, denounced them in the most offensive terms, put out our heavy revolvers, and threatened to shoot them, but all in vain; a cruel, crazy, mad, hopeless panic possessed them, and communicated to everybody about in front and rear. The heat was awful, although now about six; the men were exhausted—their mouths gaped, their lips cracked and blackened with powder of the cartridges they had bitten off in battle, their eyes staring in frenzy; no mortal ever saw such a mass of ghastly wretches."

first in the Mexican War and then as an observer of the Crimean War in Russia.

Cocky George McClellan embodied a curious mixture of virtues and defects. He was a superb organizer and drillmaster, and he injected splendid morale into the Army of the Potomac. Hating to sacrifice his troops, he was idolized by his men, who affectionately called him "Little Mac." But he was a perfectionist who seems not to have realized that an army is never ready to the last button and that wars cannot be won without running some risks. He consistently but erroneously believed that the enemy outnumbered him, partly because his intelligence reports from the head of Pinkerton's Detective Agency were unreliable. He was overcautious—Lincoln once accused him of having "the slows"—and he addressed the president in an arrogant tone that a less forgiving person would never have tolerated. Privately the general referred to his chief as a "baboon."

As McClellan doggedly continued to drill his army without moving it toward Richmond, the derisive Northern watchword became "All Quiet Along the Potomac." The song of the hour was "Tardy George" (McClellan). After threatening to "borrow" the army if it was not going to be used, Lincoln finally issued firm orders to advance.

A reluctant McClellan at last decided upon a waterborne approach to Richmond, which lies at

force near Washington was now called. Red-haired and red-mustached, strong and stocky, McClellan was a brilliant, thirty-four-year-old West Pointer. As a serious student of warfare who was dubbed "Young Napoleon," he had seen plenty of fighting,

Masterly Inactivity, or Six Months on the Potomac, 1862 McClellan and his Confederate foe view each other cautiously while their troops engage in visits, weddings, and sports.

Abraham Lincoln (1809–1865) treated the demands of George McClellan for reinforcements and his excuses for inaction with infinite patience. One exception came when the general complained that his horses were tired. On October 24, 1862, Lincoln wrote,

"I have just read your dispatch about sore-tongued and fatigued horses. Will you pardon me for asking what the horses of your army have done since the battle of Antietam that fatigues anything?"

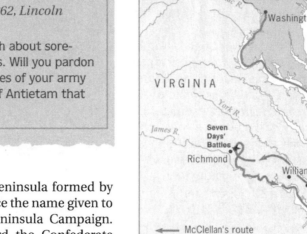

Peninsula Campaign, 1862

the western base of a narrow peninsula formed by the James and York Rivers—hence the name given to this historic encounter: the Peninsula Campaign. McClellan warily inched toward the Confederate capital in the spring of 1862 with about 100,000 men. After taking a month to capture historic York-town, which bristled with imitation wooden cannon, he finally came within sight of the spires of Richmond. At this crucial juncture, Lincoln diverted McClellan's anticipated reinforcements to chase "Stonewall" Jackson, whose lightning feints in the Shenandoah Valley seemed to put Washington, D.C.,

in jeopardy. Stalled in front of Richmond, McClellan was further frustrated when "Jeb" Stuart's Confederate cavalry rode completely around his army on reconnaissance. Then General Robert E. Lee

Civil War Scene (detail)
A Federal brigade repulses a Confederate assault at Williamsburg, Virginia, in 1862, as the Peninsula Campaign presses toward Richmond. General Winfield Scott Hancock commanded the troops. For his success in this action, Hancock earned the nickname "The Superb."

launched a devastating counterattack—the Seven Days' Battles—June 26–July 2, 1862. The Confederates slowly drove McClellan back to the sea. The Union forces abandoned the Peninsula Campaign as a costly failure, and Lincoln temporarily abandoned McClellan as commander of the Army of the Potomac—though Lee's army had suffered some twenty thousand casualties to McClellan's ten thousand.

Lee had achieved a brilliant, if bloody, triumph. Yet the ironies of his accomplishment are striking. If McClellan had succeeded in taking Richmond and ending the war in mid-1862, the Union would probably have been restored with minimal disruption to the "peculiar institution." Slavery would have survived, at least for a time. By his successful defense of Richmond and defeat of McClellan, Lee had in effect ensured that the war would endure until slavery was uprooted and the Old South thoroughly destroyed. Lincoln himself, who had earlier professed his unwillingness to tamper with slavery where it already existed, now declared that the rebels "cannot experiment for ten years trying to destroy the government and if they fail still come back into the Union unhurt." He began to draft an emancipation proclamation.

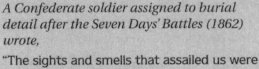

A Confederate soldier assigned to burial detail after the Seven Days' Battles (1862) wrote,

"The sights and smells that assailed us were simply indescribable . . . corpses swollen to twice their original size, some of them actually burst asunder with the pressure of foul gasses. . . . The odors were so nauseating and so deadly that in a short time we all sickened and were lying with our mouths close to the ground, most of us vomiting profusely."

Union strategy now turned toward total war. As finally developed, the Northern military plan had six components: first, slowly suffocate the South by blockading its coasts; second, liberate the slaves and hence undermine the very economic foundations of the Old South; third, cut the Confederacy in half by seizing control of the Mississippi River backbone; fourth, chop the Confederacy to pieces by

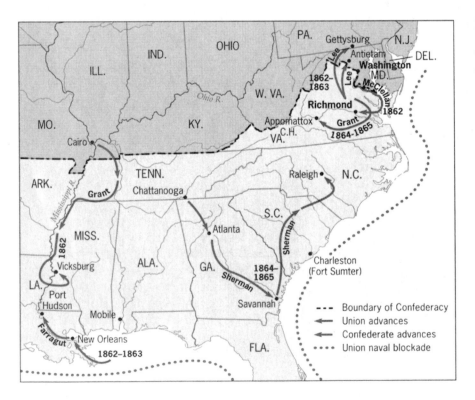

Main Thrusts, 1861–1865
Northern strategists at first believed that the rebellion could be snuffed out quickly by a swift, crushing blow. But the stiffness of Southern resistance to the Union's early probes, and the North's inability to strike with sufficient speed and severity, revealed that the conflict would be a war of attrition, long and bloody.

sending troops through Georgia and the Carolinas; fifth, decapitate it by capturing its capital at Richmond; and sixth (this was Ulysses Grant's idea especially), try everywhere to engage the enemy's main strength and to grind it into submission.

The War at Sea

The blockade started leakily: it was not clamped down all at once but was extended by degrees. A watertight patrol of some thirty-five hundred miles of coast was impossible for the hastily improvised Northern navy, which counted converted yachts and ferryboats in its fleet. But blockading was simplified by concentrating on the principal ports and inlets where dock facilities were available for loading bulky bales of cotton.

How was the blockade regarded by the naval powers of the world? Ordinarily, they probably would have defied it, for it was never completely effective and was especially sievelike at the outset. But Britain, the greatest maritime nation, recognized it as binding and warned its shippers that they ignored it at their peril. An explanation is easy. Blockade happened to be the chief offensive weapon of Britain, which was still Mistress of the Seas. Britain plainly did not want to tie its hands in a future war by insisting that Lincoln maintain impossibly high blockading standards.

Blockade-running soon became riskily profitable, as the growing scarcity of Southern goods drove prices skyward. The most successful blockade runners were swift, gray-painted steamers, scores of which were specially built in Scotland. A leading rendezvous was the West Indies port of Nassau, in the British Bahamas, where at one time thirty-five of the speedy ships rode at anchor. The low-lying craft would take on cargoes of arms brought in by tramp steamers from Britain, leave with fraudulent papers for "Halifax" (Canada), and then return a few days later with a cargo of cotton. The risks were great, but the profits would mount to 700 percent and more for lucky gamblers. Two successful voyages might well pay for capture on a third. The lush days of blockade-running finally passed as Union squadrons gradually pinched off the leading Southern ports, from New Orleans to Charleston.

The Northern navy enforced the blockade with high-handed practices. Yankee captains, for example, would seize British freighters on the high seas, if laden with war supplies for the tiny port of Nassau and other halfway stations. The justification was that obviously these shipments were "ultimately" destined, by devious routes, for the Confederacy.

London, although not happy, acquiesced in this disagreeable doctrine of "ultimate destination" or "continuous voyage." British blockaders might need to take advantage of the same far-fetched interpretation in a future war—as in fact they did in the world war of 1914–1918.

The most alarming Confederate threat to the blockade came in 1862. Resourceful Southerners raised and reconditioned a former wooden U.S. warship, the *Merrimack*, and plated its sides with old iron railroad rails. Renamed the *Virginia*, this clumsy but powerful monster easily destroyed two wooden ships of the Union navy in the Virginia waters of Chesapeake Bay; it also threatened catastrophe to the entire Yankee blockading fleet. (Actually the homemade ironclad was not a seaworthy craft.)

A tiny Union ironclad, the *Monitor*, built in about one hundred days, arrived on the scene in the nick of time. For four hours, on March 9, 1862, the little "Yankee cheesebox on a raft" fought the

When news reached Washington that the Merrimack *had sunk two wooden Yankee warships with ridiculous ease, President Lincoln, much "excited," summoned his advisers. Secretary of the Navy Gideon Welles (1802–1878) recorded,*

"The most frightened man on that gloomy day . . . was the Secretary of War [Stanton]. He was at times almost frantic. . . . The *Merrimack,* he said, would destroy every vessel in the service, could lay every city on the coast under contribution, could take Fortress Monroe. . . . Likely the first movement of the *Merrimack* would be to come up the Potomac and disperse Congress, destroy the Capitol and public buildings."

Battle of the *Merrimack*
and the *Monitor*,
March 9, 1862

wheezy *Merrimack* to a standstill. Britain and France had already built several powerful ironclads, but the first battle-testing of these new craft heralded the doom of wooden warships. A few months after the historic battle, the Confederates destroyed the *Merrimack* to keep it from the grasp of advancing Union troops.

The Pivotal Point: Antietam

Robert E. Lee, having broken the back of McClellan's assault on Richmond, next moved northward. At the Second Battle of Bull Run (August 29–30, 1862), he encountered a Federal force under General John Pope. A handsome, dashing, soldierly figure, Pope boasted that in the western theater of war, from which he had recently come, he had seen only the backs of the enemy. Lee quickly gave him a front view, furiously attacking Pope's troops and inflicting a crushing defeat.

Emboldened by this success, Lee daringly thrust into Maryland. He hoped to strike a blow that would not only encourage foreign intervention but also seduce the still-wavering Border State and its sis-

ters from the Union. The Confederate troops sang lustily:

Thou wilt not cower in the dust,
    Maryland! my Maryland!
Thy gleaming sword shall never rust,
    Maryland! my Maryland!

But the Marylanders did not respond to the siren song. The presence among the invaders of so many blanketless, hatless, and shoeless soldiers dampened the state's ardor.

Events finally converged toward a critical battle at Antietam Creek, Maryland. Lincoln, yielding to popular pressure, hastily restored "Little Mac" to active command of the main Northern army. His soldiers tossed their caps skyward and hugged his horse as they hailed his return. Fortune shone upon McClellan when two Union soldiers found a copy of Lee's battle plans wrapped around a packet of three cigars dropped by a careless Confederate officer. With this crucial piece of intelligence in hand, McClellan succeeded in halting Lee at Antietam on September 17, 1862, in one of the bitterest and bloodiest days of the war.

Antietam was more or less a draw militarily. But Lee, finding his thrust parried, retired across the

The Killing Fields of Antietam
These Confederate corpses testified to the awful slaughter of the battle. The twelve-hour fight at Antietam Creek ranks as the bloodiest single day of the war, with more than ten thousand Confederate casualties and even more on the Union side. "At last the battle ended," one historian wrote, "smoke heavy in the air, the twilight quivering with the anguished cries of thousands of wounded men."

Potomac. McClellan, from whom much more had been hoped, was removed from his field command for the second and final time. His numerous critics, condemning him for not having boldly pursued the ever-dangerous Lee, finally got his scalp.

The landmark Battle of Antietam was one of the decisive engagements of world history—probably the most decisive of the Civil War. Jefferson Davis was perhaps never again so near victory as on that fateful summer day. The British and French governments were on the verge of diplomatic mediation, a form of interference sure to be angrily resented by the North. An almost certain rebuff by Washington might well have spurred Paris and London into armed collusion with Richmond. But both capitals cooled off when the Union displayed unexpected power at Antietam, and their chill deepened with the passing months.

Bloody Antietam was also the long-awaited "victory" that Lincoln needed for launching his Emancipation Proclamation. The abolitionists had long been clamoring for action: Wendell Phillips was denouncing the president as a "first-rate second-rate man." By midsummer of 1862, with the Border States safely in the fold, Lincoln was ready to move. But he believed that to issue such an edict on the heels of a series of military disasters would be folly. It would seem like a confession that the North, unable to conquer the South, was forced to call upon the slaves to murder their masters. Lincoln therefore decided to wait for the outcome of Lee's invasion.

Antietam served as the needed emancipation springboard. The halting of Lee's offensive was just enough of a victory to justify Lincoln's issuing, on September 23, 1862, the preliminary Emancipation Proclamation. This hope-giving document announced that on January 1, 1863, the president would issue a final proclamation.

On the scheduled date, he fully redeemed his promise, and the Civil War became more of a moral crusade as the fate of slavery and the South it had sustained was sealed. The war now became more of what Lincoln called a "remorseless revolutionary struggle." After January 1, 1863, Lincoln said, "The character of the war will be changed. It will be one of subjugation. . . . The [old] South is to be destroyed and replaced by new propositions and ideas."

A Proclamation Without Emancipation

Lincoln's Emancipation Proclamation of 1863 declared "forever free" the slaves in those Confederate states still in rebellion. Bondsmen in the loyal Border States were not affected, nor were those in specific conquered areas in the South—all told, about 800,000. The tone of the document was dull and legalistic (one historian has said that it had all the moral grandeur of a bill of lading). But if Lincoln stopped short of a clarion call for a holy war to achieve freedom, he pointedly concluded his historic document by declaring that the Proclamation was "an act of justice," and calling for "the considerate judgment of mankind and the gracious favor of Almighty God."

The presidential pen did not formally strike the shackles from a single slave. Where Lincoln could presumably free the slaves—that is, in the loyal Border States—he refused to do so, lest he spur disunion. Where he could not—that is, in the Confederate states—he tried to. In short, where he *could* he would not, and where he *would* he could not. Thus the Emancipation Proclamation was stronger on proclamation than emancipation.

Yet much unofficial do-it-yourself liberation did take place. Thousands of jubilant slaves, learning of the proclamation, flocked to the invading Union armies, stripping already rundown plantations of their work force. In this sense the Emancipation Proclamation was heralded by the drumbeat of running feet. But many fugitives would have come anyhow, as they had from the war's outset. Lincoln's immediate goal was not only to liberate the slaves but also to strengthen the moral cause of the Union at home and abroad. This he succeeded in doing. At the same time, Lincoln's proclamation clearly foreshadowed the ultimate doom of slavery. This was legally achieved by action of the individual states and by their ratification of the Thirteenth Amendment in 1865, eight months after the Civil War had ended. (For text, see the Appendix.) The Emancipation Proclamation also fundamentally

Many of the British aristocrats were unfriendly to the North, and the London Spectator *sneered at Lincoln's so-called Emancipation Proclamation:*

"The Government liberates the enemy's slaves as it would the enemy's cattle, simply to weaken them in the coming conflict. . . . The principle asserted is not that a human being cannot justly own another, but that he cannot own him unless he is loyal to the United States."

changed the nature of the war because it effectively removed any chance of a negotiated settlement. Both sides now knew that the war would be a fight to the finish.

Public reactions to the long-awaited proclamation of 1863 were varied. "God bless Abraham Lincoln," exulted the antislavery editor Horace Greeley in his *New York Tribune*. But many ardent abolitionists complained that Lincoln had not gone far enough. On the other hand, formidable numbers of Northerners, especially in the "Butternut" regions of the Old Northwest and the Border States, felt that he

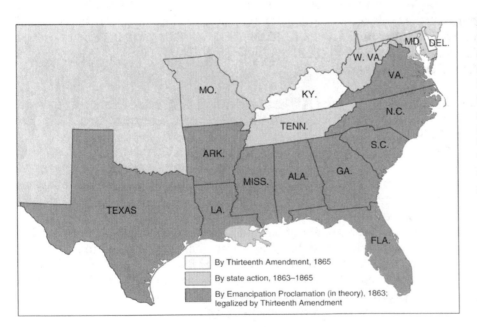

Emancipation in the South President Lincoln believed that emancipation of the slaves, accompanied by compensation to their owners, would be fairest to the South. He formally proposed such an amendment to the Constitution in December 1862. What finally emerged was the Thirteenth Amendment of 1865, which freed all slaves *without* compensation.

Map labels: MD., DEL., W. VA., VA., MO., KY., N.C., TENN., ARK., S.C., MISS., ALA., GA., TEXAS, LA., FLA.

Legend:
By Thirteenth Amendment, 1865
By state action, 1863–1865
By Emancipation Proclamation (in theory), 1863; legalized by Thirteenth Amendment

AMERICAN HISTORY

had gone too far. A cynical Democratic rhymester quipped,

> *Honest old Abe, when the war first began,*
> *Denied abolition was part of his plan;*
> *Honest old Abe has since made a decree,*
> *The war must go on till the slaves are all free.*
> *As both can't be honest, will some one tell how,*
> *If honest Abe then, he is honest Abe now?*

Opposition mounted in the North against supporting an "abolition war"; ex-president Pierce and others felt that emancipation should not be "inflicted" on the slaves. Many Boys in Blue, especially from the Border States, had volunteered to fight for the Union, not against slavery. Desertions increased sharply. The crucial congressional elections in the autumn of 1862 went heavily against the administration, particularly in New York, Pennsylvania, and Ohio. Democrats even carried Lincoln's Illinois, although they did not secure control of Congress.

The Emancipation Proclamation caused an outcry to rise from the South that "Lincoln the fiend" was trying to stir up the "hellish passions" of a slave insurrection. Aristocrats of Europe, noting that the proclamation applied only to rebel slaveholders, were inclined to sympathize with Southern protests. But the Old World working classes, especially in Britain, reacted otherwise. They sensed that the proclamation spelled the ultimate doom of slavery, and many laborers were more determined than ever to oppose intervention. Gradually the diplomatic position of the Union improved.

The North now had much the stronger moral cause. In addition to preserving the Union, it had committed itself to freeing the slaves. The moral position of the South was correspondingly diminished.

Lincoln (1809–1865) defended his policies toward blacks in an open letter to Democrats on August 26, 1863:

"You say you will not fight to free negroes. Some of them seem willing to fight for you; but, no matter. Fight you, then, exclusively to save the Union. I issued the proclamation on purpose to aid you in saving the Union."

Blacks Battle Bondage

As Lincoln moved to emancipate the slaves, he also took steps to enlist blacks in the armed forces. Although some African-Americans had served in the Revolution and the War of 1812, the regular army contained no blacks at the war's outset, and the War Department refused to accept those free Northern blacks who tried to volunteer. (The Union navy, however, enrolled many blacks, mainly as cooks, stewards, and firemen.)

But as manpower ran low and emancipation was proclaimed, black enlistees were accepted, sometimes over ferocious protests from Northern as well as Southern whites. By war's end some 180,000

Recruiting Black Troops in Boston, 1863   Led by the white Boston Brahmin Robert Gould Shaw, the 54th Massachusetts Regiment lost nearly half its men, including Shaw, in a futile attack on South Carolina's Fort Wagner in July 1863. A memorial to the regiment stands today on the Boston Common.

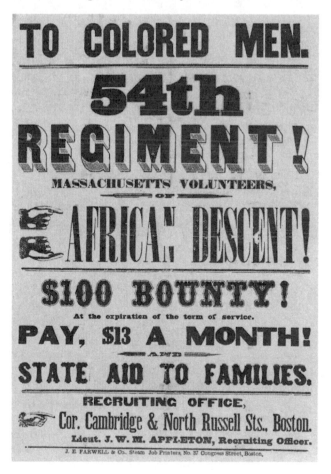

AMERICAN HISTORY

A Bit of War History: Contraband, Recruit, Veteran This painting done in 1865–1866 by Thomas Waterman Wood dramatically commemorates the contributions and the sacrifices of the 180,000 African-Americans who served in the Union Army during the Civil War.

blacks served in the Union armies, most of them from the slave states, but many from the free-soil North. Blacks accounted for about 10 percent of the total enlistments in the Union forces on land and sea and included two Massachusetts regiments raised largely through the efforts of the ex-slave Frederick Douglass.

Black fighting men unquestionably had their hearts in the war against slavery that the Civil War had become after Lincoln proclaimed emancipation. Participating in about five hundred engagements, they received twenty-two Congressional Medals of Honor—the highest military award. Their casualties were extremely heavy; more than thirty-eight thousand died, whether from battle, sickness, or reprisals from vengeful masters. Many, when captured, were put to death as slaves in revolt, for not until 1864 did the South recognize them as prisoners of war. In one notorious case, several black soldiers were massacred after they had formally surrendered at Fort Pillow, Tennessee. Thereafter vengeful black units cried "Remember Fort Pillow" as they swung into battle and vowed to take no prisoners.

For reasons of pride, prejudice, and principle, the Confederacy could not bring itself to enlist slaves until a month before the war ended, and then it was too late. Meanwhile, tens of thousands were forced into labor battalions, the building of fortifications, the supplying of armies, and other war-connected activities. Slaves moreover were "the stomach of the Confederacy," for they kept the farms going while the white men fought.

Ironically, the great mass of Southern slaves did little to help their Northern liberators, white or black. A thousand scattered torches in the hands of

An affidavit by a Union sergeant described the fate of one group of black Union troops captured by the Confederates:

"All the negroes found in blue uniform or with any outward marks of a Union soldier upon him was killed—I saw some taken into the woods and hung—Others I saw stripped of all their clothing and they stood upon the bank of the river with their faces riverwards and then they were shot—Still others were killed by having their brains beaten out by the butt end of the muskets in the hands of the Rebels."

> *In August 1863 Lincoln wrote to Grant that enlisting black soldiers*
>
> "works doubly, weakening the enemy and strengthening us."
>
> *In December 1863 he announced,*
>
> "It is difficult to say they are not as good soldiers as any."
>
> *In August 1864 he said,*
>
> "Abandon all the posts now garrisoned by black men, take 150,000 [black] men from our side and put them in the battlefield or cornfield against us, and we would be compelled to abandon the war in three weeks."

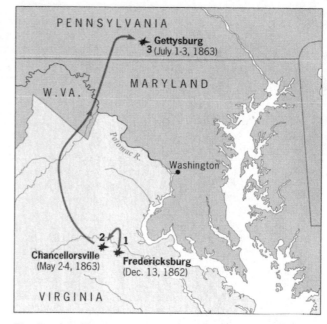

The Road to Gettysburg, December 1862–July 1863

a thousand slaves would have brought the Southern soldiers home, and the war would have ended. Through the "grapevine," the blacks learned of Lincoln's Emancipation Proclamation. The bulk of them, whether because of fear, loyalty, lack of leadership, or strict policing, did not cast off their chains. But tens of thousands revolted "with their feet" when they abandoned their plantations upon the approach or arrival of Union armies, with or without emancipation proclamations. About twenty-five thousand joined Sherman's march through Georgia in 1864, and their presence in such numbers created problems of supply and discipline.

Lee's Last Lunge at Gettysburg

After Antietam, Lincoln replaced McClellan as commander of the Army of the Potomac with General A. E. Burnside, whose ornate side-whiskers came to be known as "burnsides" or "sideburns." Protesting his unfitness for this responsibility, Burnside proved it when he launched a rash frontal attack on Lee's strong position at Fredericksburg, Virginia, on December 13, 1862. A chicken could not have lived in the line of fire, remarked one Confederate officer. More than ten thousand Northern soldiers were killed or wounded in "Burnside's Slaughter Pen."

A new slaughter pen was prepared when General Burnside yielded his command to "Fighting Joe" Hooker, an aggressive officer but a headstrong subordinate. At Chancellorsville, Virginia, May 2–4, 1863, Lee daringly divided his numerically inferior force and sent "Stonewall" Jackson to attack the Union flank. The strategy worked. Hooker, temporarily dazed by a near hit from a cannonball, was badly beaten but not crushed. This victory was probably Lee's most brilliant, but it was dearly bought. Jackson was mistakenly shot by his own men in the gathering dusk and died a few days later. "I have lost my right arm," lamented Lee. Southern folklore relates how Jackson outflanked the angels while galloping into heaven.

Lee now prepared to follow up his stunning victory by invading the North again, this time through Pennsylvania. A decisive blow would add strength to the noisy peace prodders in the North and would also encourage foreign intervention—still a Southern hope. Three days before the battle was joined, Union general George G. Meade—scholarly, unspectacular, abrupt—was aroused from his sleep at 2 A.M. with the unwelcome news that he would replace Hooker.

Quite by accident, Meade took his stand atop a low ridge flanking a shallow valley near quiet little

EXAMINING THE EVIDENCE

Abraham Lincoln's Gettysburg Address

Political speeches are unfortunately all too often composed of claptrap, platitudes, and just plain bunk—and they are frequently written by someone other than the person delivering them. But Abraham Lincoln's address at the dedication of the cemetery at Gettysburg battlefield on November 19, 1863, has long been recognized as a masterpiece of political oratory and as a foundational document of the American political system, as weighty a statement of the national purpose as the Declaration of Independence (which it deliberately echoes in its statement that all men are created equal) or even the Constitution itself. In just two hundred seventy-two simple but eloquent words that Lincoln himself indisputably wrote, he summarized the case for American nationhood. What are his principal arguments? What values did he invoke? What did he think was at stake in the Civil War? (Conspicuously, he makes no direct mention of slavery in this address.) Another speech that Lincoln gave in 1861 offers some clues. He said, "I have often inquired of myself what great principle or idea it was that kept this [nation] together. It was not the mere separation of the colonies from the motherland, but that sentiment in the Declaration of Independence which gave liberty not alone to the people of this country, but hope to the world, for all future time."

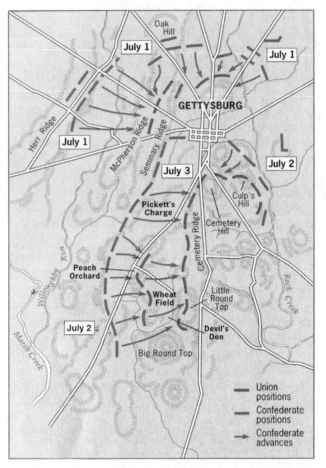

The Battle of Gettysburg, 1863 With the failure of Pickett's charge, the fate of the Confederacy was sealed—though the Civil War dragged on for almost two more bloody years.

Gettysburg, Pennsylvania. There his 92,000 men in blue locked in furious combat with Lee's 76,000 gray-clad warriors. The battle seesawed across the rolling green slopes for three agonizing days, July 1–3, 1863, and the outcome was in doubt until the very end. The failure of General George Pickett's magnificent but futile charge finally broke the back of the Confederate attack—and broke the heart of the Confederate cause.

Pickett's charge has been called the "high tide of the Confederacy." It defined both the northernmost point reached by any significant Southern force and the last real chance for the Confederates to win the war. As the Battle of Gettysburg raged, a Confederate peace delegation was moving under a flag of truce toward the Union lines near Norfolk, Virginia. Jefferson Davis hoped his negotiators would arrive

in Washington from the south just as Lee's triumphant army marched on it from Gettysburg to the north. But the victory at Gettysburg belonged to Lincoln, who refused to allow the Confederate peace mission to pass through Union lines. From now on, the Southern cause was doomed. Yet the men of Dixie fought on for nearly two years longer, through sweat, blood, and weariness of spirit.

Later in that dreary autumn of 1863, with the graves still fresh, Lincoln journeyed to Gettysburg to dedicate the cemetery. He read a two-minute address, following a two-hour speech by the orator of the day. Lincoln's noble remarks were branded by the London *Times* as "ludicrous" and by Democratic editors as "dishwatery" and "silly." The address attracted relatively little attention at the time, but the president was speaking for the ages.

The War in the West

Events in the western theater of the war at last provided Lincoln with an able general who did not have to be shelved after every reverse. Ulysses S. Grant had been a mediocre student at West Point, distinguishing himself only in horsemanship, although he did fairly well at mathematics. After fighting creditably in the Mexican War, he was stationed at isolated frontier posts, where boredom and loneliness drove him to drink. Resigning from the army to avoid a court-martial for drunkenness, he failed at various business ventures, and when war came, he was working in his father's leather store in Illinois for $50 a month.

Grant did not cut much of a figure. The shy and silent shopkeeper was short, stooped, awkward, stubble-bearded, and sloppy in dress. He managed with some difficulty to secure a colonelcy in the volunteers. From then on, his military experience—combined with his boldness, resourcefulness, and tenacity—catapulted him on a meteoric rise.

Grant's first signal success came in the northern Tennessee theater. After heavy fighting, he captured Fort Henry and Fort Donelson on the Tennessee and Cumberland Rivers in February 1862. When the Confederate commander at Fort Donelson asked for terms, Grant bluntly demanded "an unconditional and immediate surrender."

Grant's triumph in Tennessee was crucial. It not only riveted Kentucky more securely to the Union but also opened the gateway to the strategically important region of Tennessee, as well as to Georgia and the heart of Dixie. Grant next attempted to exploit his victory by capturing the junction of the main Confederate north-south and east-west railroads in the Mississippi Valley at Corinth, Mississippi. But a Confederate force foiled his plans in a gory battle at Shiloh, just over the Tennessee border from Corinth, on April 6–7, 1862. Though Grant successfully counterattacked, the impressive Confederate showing at Shiloh confirmed that there would be no quick end to the war in the West.

Lincoln resisted all demands for the removal of "Unconditional Surrender" Grant, insisting, "I can't spare this man; he fights." When talebearers later told Lincoln that Grant drank too much, the president allegedly replied, "Find me the brand, and I'll send a barrel to each of my other generals." There is no evidence that Grant's drinking habits seriously impaired his military performance.

Other Union thrusts in the West were in the making. In the spring of 1862, a flotilla commanded by David G. Farragut joined with a Northern army to strike the South a blow by seizing New Orleans. With Union gunboats both ascending and descending the Mississippi, the eastern part of the Confederacy was left with a jeopardized back door. Through this narrowing entrance, between Vicksburg, Mississippi, and Port Hudson, Louisiana, flowed herds of vitally needed cattle and other provisions from Louisiana and Texas. The fortress of Vicksburg, located on a hairpin turn of the Mississippi, was the South's sentinel protecting the lifeline to the western sources of supply.

General Grant was now given command of the Union forces attacking Vicksburg and in the teeth of grave difficulties displayed rare skill and daring. The siege of Vicksburg was his best-fought campaign of the war. The beleaguered city at length surrendered, on July 4, 1863, with the garrison reduced to eating mules and rats. Five days later came the fall of Port Hudson, the last Southern bastion on the Mississippi. The spinal cord of the Confederacy was now severed, and, in Lincoln's quaint phrase, the Father of Waters at last flowed "unvexed to the sea."

The Union victory at Vicksburg (July 4, 1863) came the day after the Confederate defeat at Gettysburg. The political significance of these back-to-back

General Ulysses S. Grant and General Robert E. Lee
Trained at West Point, Grant (left) proved to be a better general than a president. Oddly, he hated the sight of blood and recoiled from rare beef. Lee (right), a gentlemanly general in an ungentlemanly business, remarked when the Union troops were bloodily repulsed at Fredericksburg, "It is well that war is so terrible, or we should get too fond of it."

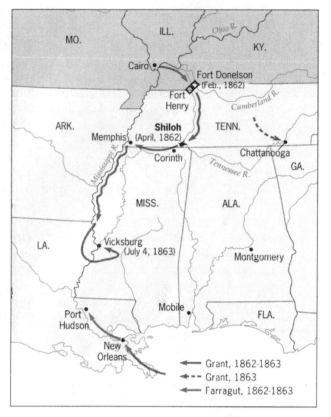

The Mississippi River and Tennessee, 1862–1863

Grant, 1862-1863
Grant, 1863
Farragut, 1862-1863

In the southern tier of Ohio, Indiana, and Illinois, sympathy for the South combined with hostility to the Northeast to stimulate talk of a "Northwest Confederacy" that would itself secede from the Union and make a separate peace with the Confederacy. These sentiments were fueled by economic grievances stemming from the closure of the Mississippi River to trade, and they gained strength after Lincoln's Emancipation Proclamation. Warned one Ohio congressman in January 1863,

"If you of the East, who have found this war against the South, and for the negro, gratifying to your hate or profitable to your purse, will continue it . . . [be prepared for] eternal divorce between the West and the East."

Another Ohio congressman, giving great urgency to the Union effort to reopen the Mississippi River, declared,

"The erection of the states watered by the Mississippi and its tributaries into an independent Republic is the talk of every other western man."

military successes was monumental. Reopening the Mississippi helped to quell the Northern peace agitation in the "Butternut" area of the Ohio River valley. Confederate control of the Mississippi had cut off that region's usual trade routes down the Ohio-Mississippi River system to New Orleans, thus adding economic pain to that border section's already shaky support for the "abolition war." The twin victories also conclusively tipped the diplomatic scales in favor of the North, as Britain stopped delivery of the Laird rams to the Confederates and as France killed a deal for the sale of six naval vessels to the Richmond government. By the end of 1863, all Confederate hopes for foreign help were irretrievably lost.

Sherman Scorches Georgia

General Grant, the victor of Vicksburg, was now transferred to the east Tennessee theater, where Confederates had driven Union forces from the bat-

tlefield at Chickamauga into the city of Chattanooga, to which they then laid siege. Grant won a series of desperate engagements in November 1863 in the vicinity of besieged Chattanooga, including Missionary Ridge and Lookout Mountain ("the Battle Above the Clouds"). Chattanooga was liberated, the state was cleared of Confederates, and the way was thus opened for an invasion of Georgia. Grant was rewarded by being made general in chief.

Georgia's conquest was entrusted to General William Tecumseh Sherman. Red-haired and red-bearded, grim-faced and ruthless, he captured Atlanta in September 1864 and burned the city in November of that year. He then daringly left his supply base, lived off the country for some 250 miles, and weeks later emerged at Savannah on the sea. A rousing Northern song ("Marching Through Georgia") put it,

*"Sherman's dashing Yankee boys will never
    reach the coast!"*
*So the saucy rebels said—and 't was a handsome
    boast.*

But Sherman's hated "Blue Bellies," sixty thousand strong, cut a sixty-mile swath of destruction through Georgia. They burned buildings, leaving only the blackened chimneys ("Sherman's Sentinels"). They tore up railroad rails, heated them red-hot, and twisted them into "iron doughnuts" and "Sherman's hairpins." They bayoneted family portraits and ran off with valuable "souvenirs." "War . . . is all hell," admitted Sherman later, and he proved it by his efforts to "make Georgia howl." One of his major purposes was to destroy supplies destined for the Confederate army and to weaken the morale of the men at the front by waging war on their homes.

Sherman was a pioneer practitioner of "total war." His success in "Shermanizing" the South was attested by increasing numbers of Confederate desertions. Although his methods were brutal, he probably shortened the struggle and hence saved lives. But there can be no doubt that the discipline of his army at times broke down, as roving riffraff (Sherman's "bummers") engaged in an orgy of pillaging. "Sherman the Brute" was universally damned in the South.

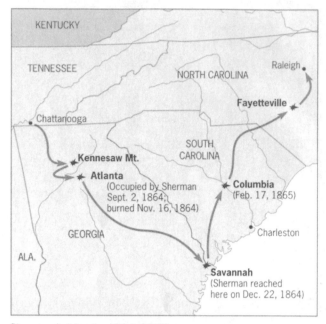

Sherman's March, 1864–1865

After seizing Savannah as a Christmas present for Lincoln, Sherman's army veered north into South Carolina, where the destruction was even more vicious. Many Union soldiers believed that this state, the "hell-hole of secession," had wantonly provoked the war. The capital city, Columbia, burst

A Study in Black and White
Soldiers of the 7th Tennessee Cavalry posed with their slaves—whose bondage the Confederacy fought to perpetuate.

A letter picked up on a dead Confederate in North Carolina and addressed to his "deer sister" concluded that

it was "dam fulishness" trying to "lick shurmin." He had been getting "nuthin but hell & lots uv it" ever since he saw the "dam yanks," and he was "tirde uv it." He would head for home now, but his old horse was "plaid out." If the "dam yankees" had not got there yet, it would be a "dam wunder." They were thicker than "lise on a hen and a dam site ornerier."

into flames, in all probability the handiwork of the Yankee invader. Crunching northward, Sherman's conquering army had rolled deep into North Carolina by the time the war ended.

The Politics of War

Presidential elections come by the calendar and not by the crisis. As fate would have it, the election of 1864 fell most inopportunely in the midst of war.

Political infighting in the North added greatly to Lincoln's cup of woe. Factions within his own party, distrusting his ability or doubting his commitment to abolition, sought to tie his hands or even remove him from office. Conspicuous among his critics was a group led by the overambitious secretary of the Treasury, Salmon Chase. Especially burdensome to Lincoln was the creation of the Congressional Committee on the Conduct of the War, formed in late 1861. It was dominated by "radical" Republicans who resented the expansion of presidential power in wartime and who pressed Lincoln zealously on emancipation.

Most dangerous of all to the Union cause were the Northern Democrats. Deprived of the talent that had departed with the Southern wing of the party, those Democrats remaining in the North were left with the taint of association with the seceders. Tragedy befell the Democrats—and the Union—when their gifted leader, Stephen A. Douglas, died of typhoid fever seven weeks after the war began.

Unshakably devoted to the Union, he probably could have kept much of his following on the path of loyalty.

Lacking a leader, the Democrats divided. A large group of "War Democrats" patriotically supported the Lincoln administration, but tens of thousands of "Peace Democrats" did not. At the extreme were the so-called Copperheads, named for the poisonous snake, which strikes without a warning rattle. Copperheads openly obstructed the war through attacks against the draft, against Lincoln, and especially, after 1863, against emancipation. They denounced the president as the "Illinois Ape" and condemned the "Nigger War." They commanded considerable political strength in the southern parts of Ohio, Indiana, and Illinois.

Notorious among the Copperheads was a sometime congressman from Ohio, Clement L. Vallandigham. This tempestuous character possessed brilliant oratorical gifts and unusual talents for stirring up trouble. A Southern partisan, he publicly demanded an end to the "wicked and cruel" war. The civil courts in Ohio were open, and he should

Democracy Versus Rebellion   The two American combatants exchange blows while Britain and France look on. Note the copperhead snake that threatens to distract the Union. "Copperhead" was the name given to those Northern Democrats who were willing to settle for a negotiated peace with the Confederacy.

have been tried in them for sedition. But he was convicted by a military tribunal in 1863 for treasonable utterances and was then sentenced to prison. Lincoln decided that if Vallandigham liked the Confederates so much, he ought to be banished to their lines. This was done.

Vallandigham was not so easily silenced. Working his way to Canada, he ran for the governorship of Ohio on foreign soil and polled a substantial but insufficient vote. He returned to his own state before the war ended, and although he defied "King Lincoln" and spat upon a military decree, he was not further prosecuted. The strange case of Vallandigham inspired Edward Everett Hale to write his moving but fictional story of Philip Nolan, *The Man Without a Country* (1863), which was immensely popular in the North and which helped stimulate devotion to the Union. Nolan was a young army officer found guilty of participation in the Aaron Burr plot of 1806 (see p. 223). He had cried out in court, "Damn the United States! I wish I may never hear of the United States again!" For this outburst he was condemned to a life of eternal exile on American warships.

The Election of 1864

As the election of 1864 approached, Lincoln's precarious authority depended on his retaining Republican support while spiking the threat from the Peace Democrats and Copperheads.

Fearing defeat, the Republican party executed a clever maneuver. Joining with the War Democrats, it proclaimed itself to be the Union party. Thus the Republican party passed temporarily out of existence.

Lincoln's renomination at first encountered surprisingly strong opposition. Hostile factions whipped up considerable agitation to shelve homely "Old Abe" in favor of his handsome nemesis, Secretary of the Treasury Chase. Lincoln was accused of

lacking force, of being overready to compromise, of not having won the war, and of having shocked many sensitive souls by his ill-timed and earthy jokes. ("Prince of Jesters," one journal called him.) But the "ditch Lincoln" move collapsed, and he was nominated by the Union party without serious dissent.

Lincoln's running mate was ex-tailor Andrew Johnson, a loyal War Democrat from Tennessee who had been a small slaveowner when the conflict began. He was placed on the Union party ticket to "sew up" the election by attracting War Democrats and the voters in the Border States, and, sadly, with no proper regard for the possibility that Lincoln might die in office. Southerners and Copperheads alike condemned both candidates as birds of a feather: two ignorant, third-rate, boorish, backwoods politicians born in log cabins.

Embattled Democrats—regular and Copperhead—nominated the deposed and overcautious war hero, General McClellan. The Copperheads managed to force into the Democratic platform a plank denouncing the prosecution of the war as a failure. But McClellan, who could not otherwise have faced his old comrades-in-arms, repudiated this defeatist declaration.

The campaign was noisy and nasty. The Democrats cried, "Old Abe removed McClellan. We'll now remove Old Abe." They also sang, "Mac Will Win the Union Back." The Union party supporters shouted for "Uncle Abe and Andy" and urged, "Vote as you shot." Their most effective slogan, growing out of a remark by Lincoln, was "Don't swap horses in the middle of the river."

Lincoln's reelection was at first gravely in doubt. The war was going badly, and Lincoln himself gave way to despondency, fearing that political defeat was imminent. The anti-Lincoln Republicans, taking heart, started a new movement to "dump" Lincoln in favor of someone else.

But the atmosphere of gloom was changed electrically, as balloting day neared, by a succession of Northern victories. Admiral Farragut captured

NORTHERN DEMOCRATS   REPUBLICANS

| COPPERHEADS | PEACE DEMOCRATS | WAR DEMOCRATS |

Union Party, 1864
The blue area represents the Union party.

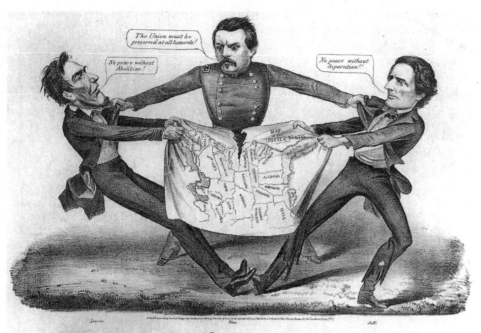

THE TRUE ISSUE OR "THATS WHATS THE MATTER".

McClellan as Mediator, 1865   This 1864 poster shows Presidents Lincoln and Davis trying to tear the country in half, while former General George McClellan, the candidate of the Democratic party, attempts to mediate.

Mobile, Alabama, after defiantly shouting the now famous order, "Damn the torpedoes! Go ahead." General Sherman seized Atlanta. General ("Little Phil") Sheridan laid waste the verdant Shenandoah Valley of Virginia so thoroughly that in his words "a crow could not fly over it without carrying his rations with him."

The president pulled through, but nothing more than necessary was left to chance. At election time many Northern soldiers were furloughed home to support Lincoln at the polls. One Pennsylvania veteran voted forty-nine times—once for himself and once for each absent member of his company. Other Northern soldiers were permitted to cast their ballots at the front.

Lincoln, bolstered by the "bayonet vote," vanquished McClellan by 212 electoral votes to 21, losing only Kentucky, Delaware, and New Jersey. But "Little Mac" ran a closer race than the electoral count indicates. He netted a healthy 45 percent of

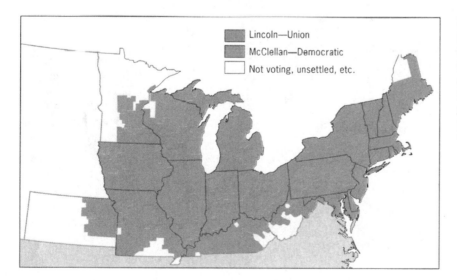

■	Lincoln—Union
■	McClellan—Democratic
□	Not voting, unsettled, etc.

Presidential Election of 1864 (showing popular vote by county) Lincoln also carried California, Oregon, and Nevada, but there was a considerable McClellan vote in each. Note McClellan's strength in the Border States and in the southern tier of Ohio, Indiana, and Illinois—the so-called "Butternut" region.

the popular vote, 1,803,787 to Lincoln's 2,206,938, piling up much support in the Southerner-infiltrated states of the Old Northwest, in New York, and also in his native state of Pennsylvania (see map on p. 470).

One of the most crushing losses suffered by the South was the defeat of the Northern Democrats in 1864. The removal of Lincoln was the last ghost of a hope for a Confederate victory, and the Southern soldiers would wishfully shout, "Hurrah for McClellan!" When Lincoln triumphed, desertions from the sinking Southern ship increased sharply.

Grant Outlasts Lee

After Gettysburg, Grant was brought in from the West over Meade, who was blamed for failing to pursue the defeated but always dangerous Lee. Lincoln needed a general who, employing the superior resources of the North, would have the intestinal stamina to drive ever forward, regardless of casualties. A soldier of bulldog tenacity, Grant was the man for this meat-grinder type of warfare. His overall basic strategy was to assail the enemy's armies simultaneously, so that they could not assist one another and hence could be destroyed piecemeal. His personal motto was "When in doubt, fight." Lin-

coln urged him to "chew and choke, as much as possible."

A grimly determined Grant, with more than 100,000 men, struck toward Richmond. He engaged Lee in a series of furious battles in the Wilderness of Virginia, during May and June of 1864, notably in the leaden hurricane of the "Bloody Angle" and "Hell's Half Acre." In this Wilderness Campaign, Grant suffered about fifty thousand casualties, or nearly as many men as Lee commanded at the start. But Lee lost about as heavily in proportion.

In a ghastly gamble, on June 3, 1864, Grant ordered a frontal assault on the impregnable position of Cold Harbor. The Union soldiers advanced to almost certain death with papers pinned on their backs bearing their names and addresses. In a few minutes, about seven thousand men were killed or wounded.

Public opinion in the North was appalled by this "blood and guts" type of fighting. Critics cried that "Grant the Butcher" had gone insane. But his basic strategy of hammering ahead seemed brutally necessary; he could trade two men for one and still beat the enemy to its knees. "I propose to fight it out on this line," he wrote, "if it takes all summer." It did— and it also took all autumn, all winter, and a part of the spring.

In February 1865 the Confederates, tasting the bitter dregs of defeat, tried desperately to negotiate

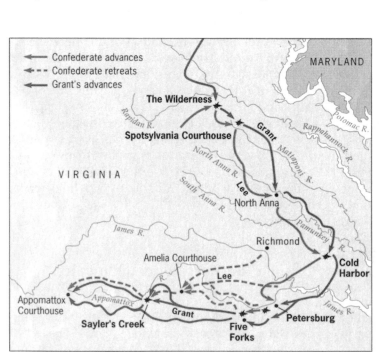

Grant's Virginia Campaign, 1864–1865
The Wilderness Campaign pitted soldier against desperate soldier in some of the most brutal and terrifying fighting of the Civil War. "No one could see the fight fifty feet from him," a Union private recalled of his month spent fighting in Virginia. "The lines were very near each other, and from the dense underbrush and the tops of trees came puffs of smoke, the 'ping' of the bullets and the yell of the enemy. It was a blind and bloody hunt to the death, in bewildering thickets, rather than a battle."

The Burning of Richmond, April 1865   The proud Confederate capital, after holding out against repeated Union assaults, was evacuated and burned in the final days of the war.

for peace between the "two countries." Lincoln himself met with Confederate representatives aboard a Union ship moored at Hampton Roads, Virginia, to discuss peace terms. But Lincoln could accept nothing short of Union and emancipation, and the Southerners could accept nothing short of independence. So the tribulation wore on—amid smoke and agony—to its terrible climax.

The end came with dramatic suddenness. Rapidly advancing Northern troops captured Richmond and cornered Lee at Appomattox Courthouse in Virginia, in April 1865. Grant—stubble-bearded and informally dressed—met with Lee on the ninth, Palm Sunday, and granted generous terms of surrender. Among other concessions, the hungry Confederates were allowed to keep their own horses for spring plowing.

Tattered Southern veterans—"Lee's Ragamuffins" —wept as they took leave of their beloved commander. The elated Union soldiers cheered, but they were silenced by Grant's stern admonition, "The war is over; the rebels are our countrymen again."

Lincoln traveled to conquered Richmond and sat in Jefferson Davis's evacuated office just forty hours after the Confederate president had left it. "Thank God I have lived to see this," he said. With a small escort of sailors, he walked the blasted streets of the city. Freed slaves began to recognize him, and crowds gathered to see and touch "Father Abraham." One black man fell to his knees before the Emancipator, who said to him, "Don't kneel to me. This is not right. You must kneel to God only, and thank Him for the liberty you will enjoy hereafter." Sadly, as many freed slaves were to discover, the hereafter of their full liberty was a long time coming.

The Martyrdom of Lincoln

On the night of April 14, 1865 (Good Friday), only five days after Lee's surrender, Ford's Theater in Washington witnessed its most sensational drama.

New York Mourns Lincoln's Death, 1865 Thousands of New Yorkers lined the black-draped urban canyons of Manhattan to observe Lincoln's funeral procession.

A half-crazed, fanatically pro-Southern actor, John Wilkes Booth, slipped behind Lincoln as he sat in his box and shot him in the head. After lying unconscious all night, the Great Emancipator died the following morning. "Now he belongs to the ages," remarked the once-critical Secretary Stanton—probably the finest words he ever spoke.

Lincoln expired in the arms of victory, at the very pinnacle of his fame. From the standpoint of his reputation, his death could not have been better timed if he had hired the assassin. A large number of his countrymen had not suspected his greatness, and many others had even doubted his ability. But his dramatic death helped to erase the memory of his shortcomings and caused his nobler qualities to stand out in clearer relief.

The full impact of Lincoln's death was not at once apparent to the South. Hundreds of bedraggled ex-Confederate soldiers cheered, as did some Southern civilians and Northern Copperheads, when they learned of the assassination. This reaction was only natural, because Lincoln had kept the war grinding on to the bitter end. If he had only been willing to stop the shooting, the South would have won.

As time wore on, increasing numbers of Southerners perceived that Lincoln's death was a calamity for them. Belatedly they recognized that his kindliness and moderation would have been the most effective shields between them and vindictive treatment by the victors. The assassination unfortunately increased the bitterness in the North, partly because of the fantastic rumor that Jefferson Davis had plotted it.

A few historians have argued that Andrew Johnson, now president-by-bullet, was crucified in Lincoln's stead. The implication is that if the "rail-splitter" had lived, he would have suffered Johnson's fate of being impeached by the embittered members

The powerful London Times, *voice of the upper classes, had generally criticized Lincoln during the war, especially after the Emancipation Proclamation of 1862. He was then condemned as "a sort of moral American Pope" destined to be "Lincoln the Last." When the president was shot, the* Times *reversed itself (April 29, 1865):*

"Abraham Lincoln was as little of a tyrant as any man who ever lived. He could have been a tyrant had he pleased, but he never uttered so much as an ill-natured speech. . . . In all America there was, perhaps, not one man who less deserved to be the victim of the revolution than he who has just fallen."

of his own party who demanded harshness, not forbearance, toward the South.

The crucifixion thesis does not stand up under scrutiny. Lincoln no doubt would have clashed with Congress; in fact, he had already found himself in some hot water. The legislative branch normally struggles to win back the power that has been wrested from it by the executive in time of crisis. But the surefooted and experienced Lincoln could hardly have blundered into the same quicksands that engulfed Johnson. Lincoln was a victorious president, and there is no arguing with victory. In addition to his powers of leadership refined in the war crucible, Lincoln possessed in full measure tact, sweet reasonableness, and an uncommon amount of common sense. Andrew Johnson, hot-tempered and impetuous, lacked all of these priceless qualities.

Ford's Theater, with its tragic murder of Lincoln, set the stage for the wrenching ordeal of Reconstruction.

The Aftermath of the Nightmare

The Civil War took a grisly toll in gore, about as much as all of America's subsequent wars combined. Over 600,000 men died in action or of disease, and in all over a million were killed or seriously

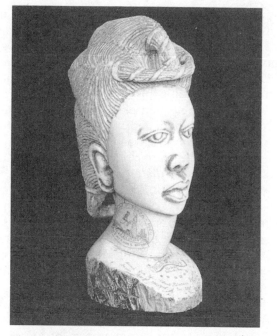

Nora August: The Fruits of Emancipation An unidentified Union soldier carved this ivory bust of the freedwoman Nora August during the Civil War. Note the elaborately braided hair —a direct adaptation of a West African style. The anonymous sculptor etched the following legend into the base of the statue: "Carved from life. Retreat Plantation. Presented to the Nurses of Darien GA in the year of Our Lord 1865. Nora August (slave). Age 23 years. Purchased from the Market, St. Augustine, Florida, April 17th 1860. Now a Free Woman."

AMERICAN HISTORY

Prisoners from the Front, by Winslow Homer, 1866 This celebrated painting reflects the artist's firsthand observations of the war. Homer brilliantly captured the enduring depths of sectional animosity. The Union officer somewhat disdainfully asserts his command of the situation; the beaten and disarmed Confederates exhibit an out-at-the-elbows pride and defiance.

wounded. To its lasting hurt, the nation lost the cream of its young manhood and potential leadership. In addition, tens of thousands of babies went unborn because potential fathers were at the front.

Direct monetary costs of the conflict totaled about $15 billion. But this colossal figure does not include continuing expenses, such as pensions and interest on the national debt. The intangible costs—dislocations, disunities, wasted energies, lowered ethics, blasted lives, bitter memories, and burning hates—cannot be calculated.

The greatest constitutional decision of the century, in a sense, was written in blood and handed down at Appomattox Courthouse, near which Lee surrendered. The extreme states' righters were crushed. The national government, tested in the fiery furnace of war, emerged unbroken. Nullification and secession, those twin nightmares of previous decades, were laid to rest.

Beyond doubt the Civil War—the nightmare of the Republic—was the supreme test of American democracy. It finally answered the question, in the words of Lincoln at Gettysburg, whether a nation dedicated to such principles "can long endure." The preservation of democratic ideals, though not an officially announced war aim, was subconsciously one of the major objectives of the North.

Victory for Union arms also provided inspiration to the champions of democracy and liberalism the world over. The great English Reform Bill of 1867, under which Britain became a true political democracy, was passed two years after the Civil War ended. American democracy had proved itself, and its success was an additional argument used by the disfranchised British masses in securing similar blessings for themselves.

The "Lost Cause" of the South was lost, but few Americans today would argue that the result was not for the best. The shameful cancer of slavery was sliced away by the sword, and African-Americans were at last in a position to claim their rights to life, liberty, and the pursuit of happiness. The nation was again united politically, though for many generations still divided spiritually by the passions of the war. Grave dangers were averted by a Union victory, including the indefinite prolongation of the "peculiar institution," the unleashing of the slave power on weak Caribbean neighbors, and the transformation of the area from Panama to Hudson Bay into an armed camp, with several heavily armed and hostile states constantly snarling and sniping at one another. America still had a long way to go to make the promises of freedom a reality for all its citizens, black and white. But emancipation laid the necessary groundwork, and a united and democratic United States was free to fulfill its destiny as the dominant republic of the hemisphere—and eventually of the world.

Chronology

1861	First Battle of Bull Run		**1863**	Battle of Chancellorsville
				Battle of Gettysburg
1862	Grant takes Fort Henry and Fort Donelson			Fall of Vicksburg
	Battle of Shiloh			Fall of Port Hudson
	McClellan's Peninsula Campaign			
	Seven Days' Battles		**1864**	Sherman's march through Georgia
	Second Battle of Bull Run			Grant's Wilderness Campaign
	Naval battle of the *Merrimack* (the			Battle of Cold Harbor
	Virginia) and the *Monitor*			Lincoln defeats McClellan for presidency
	Battle of Antietam			
	Preliminary Emancipation Proclamation		**1865**	Hampton Roads Conference
	Battle of Fredericksburg			Lee surrenders to Grant at Appomattox
	Northern army seizes New Orleans			Lincoln assassinated
				Thirteenth Amendment ratified
1863	Final Emancipation Proclamation			

VARYING VIEWPOINTS

What Were the Consequences of the Civil War?

With the end of the Civil War in 1865, the United States was permanently altered, despite the reunification of the Union and the Confederacy. Slavery was officially banned, secession was a dead issue, and industrial growth surged forward. For the first time, the United States could securely consider itself as a singular nation rather than a union of states. Though sectional differences remained, there would be no return to the unstable days of precarious balancing between Northern and Southern interests. With the Union's victory, power rested firmly with the North, and it would orchestrate the future development of the country. According to historian Eric Foner, the war redrew the economic and political map of the country.

The constitutional impact of the terms of the Union victory created some of the most far-reaching transformations. The first twelve amendments to the Constitution, ratified before the war, had all served to limit government power. In contrast, the Thirteenth Amendment, which abolished slavery, and the revolutionary Fourteenth Amendment, which conferred citizenship and guaranteed civil rights to all those born in the United States, marked unprecedented expansions of federal power.

Historian James McPherson has noted still other ways in which the Civil War extended the authority of the central government. It expanded federal powers of taxation. It encouraged the government to develop the National Banking System, print currency, and conscript an army. It made the federal courts more influential. And through the Freedmen's Bureau, which aided former slaves in the South, it instituted the first federal social welfare agency. With each of these actions, the nation moved toward a more powerful federal government, invested with the authority to protect civil rights, aid its citizens, and enforce laws in an aggressive manner that superseded state powers.

Some scholars have disputed whether the Civil War marked an absolute watershed in American history. They correctly note that racial inequality scandalously persisted after the Civil War, despite the abolition of slavery and the supposed protections extended by federal civil rights legislation. Others have argued that the industrial growth of the post–Civil War era had its real roots in the Jacksonian era, and thus cannot be ascribed solely to war. Thomas Cochran has even argued that the Civil War may have retarded overall industrialization rather than advancing it. Regional differences between North and South endured, moreover, even down to the present day.

Yet the argument that the Civil War launched a modern America remains convincing. The lives of Americans, white and black, North and South, were transformed by the war experience. Industry entered a period of unprecedented growth, having been stoked by the transportation and military needs of the Union army. The emergence of new, national legal and governmental institutions marked the birth of the modern American state. All considered, it is hard to deny that the end of the Civil War brought one chapter of the nation's history to a close, while opening another.

For further reading, see page A14 of the Appendix. For web resources, go to **http://college.hmco.com**.

CHAPTER 10

BUSINESS: HUMAN RESOURCE MANAGEMENT AND MOTIVATION

Using the chapter excerpt titled "Human Resource Management and Motivation" (found at the end of this chapter) taken from *Contemporary Business,* you will learn to

- Preview the chapter
- Make connections to the material in the chapter
- Outline the important information in the chapter
- Study for a business test by
  - Using learning goals to write summaries
  - Creating vocabulary cards
  - Creating concept maps
  - Taking a practice test from the study guide
  - Predicting test questions
  - Recording and listening to your notes
  - Working with a study partner or group

PREVIEW

You have read the first excerpted textbook chapter as a "physician," and the last chapter as a "historian"; now you must think as a businessperson as you read this next chapter excerpt. Think about how you would manage and motivate your employees if you had your own business. If you have a current job, compare some of the topics like recruitment, evaluation, compensation, and benefits to your own situation. Human resources, the people who work at a company, are the greatest resource of a company. If you were the chief executive officer of a company, how would you treat your employees? What would you do to get the most work out of them and still have them want to work for you? This is the way you should think as you read this business textbook chapter.

Survey the Chapter

Read all headings and subheadings, introductory and summary material, captions and graphics, as well as any questions that are within or at the end of the chapter. Note how the subheadings are arranged. This textbook chapter is similar to the health chapter in that it has subheadings included under main headings. For example, the heading "Employee Separation" on page 268 has the subheadings "Downsizing" and "Outsourcing." Think about the relationships among these sections as you read the subheadings and headings. When you have completed surveying the chapter, list the study aids that the author has supplied to help you learn the material in the chapter.

_____

_____

_____

_____

The author uses many study aids to help you learn and study the material.

1. Read the learning goals listed on the first page of the chapter; these goals help you to know exactly what you will learn and need to know for a test. Refer back to the goals as you read through the chapter, and use them to guide your reading and note-taking. For example, Learning Goal 1 states that you need to describe the importance of human resource management and the responsibilities of human resource managers. When you read about these topics in the chapter, be sure to describe this type of management and list the responsibilities of the managers in your notes.

2. Read the introductory material titled "Ryder System Goes the Extra Mile for Employees—and Their Children" and "Chapter Overview." This material gives you an idea of what the chapter is about and how it applies to the workplace. The author helps you set up hooks that will enable you to remember the material and its importance in the workplace. These hooks will act as pieces of information that you already know about the material in the chapter on which you can "hang" new information.

3. Read the main topic headings found in boldfaced print and all capital letters. Also read the boldfaced subheadings; these use both capital and lowercase letters.

4. Read each of the key vocabulary terms and definitions the authors have placed in the "Business Directory" features found at the bottom of several pages. You will also need to note other important business terms and their definitions. These boldfaced terms are found throughout the text but are not placed in the directory.

5. Look at the photographs and graphics; read all captions.

6. Read the "Summary of Learning Goals" at the end of the chapter. This provides a short summary for each of the goals. Again, it sets up hooks on which you will be hanging new information.

7. Read "Business Terms You Need to Know" at the end of the chapter. These review the vocabulary terms listed in the "Business Directory" features sections found throughout the chapter. Also review the list of vocabulary terms in the section "Other Important Business Terms."

8. Read through the "Review Questions" and "Questions for Critical Thinking" sections at the end of the chapter. Use these questions as a guide for your reading.

9. Read the "Experiential Exercise" section. Complete this exercise by thinking of places you've worked. Compare your answers to the results of the study.

10. Read through "Nothing but Net" and access at least two of the Web sites that are of interest to you.

11. Finally, read "Video Case 9" and the questions at the end. The video case will give you more background information, and the questions will help you begin to think on the application level as you read and take notes on the text.

Make Connections

Before you begin to read and take notes, think about what you already know about the topic of human resources. Some of the headings or subheadings may have made you think of some particular experience you have had or heard about from a friend. If you have not already read the two business articles in Part Three, read them now to gain some background knowledge on this topic. Then write down some information that you know about the topic or something the chapter makes you think about.

_____

_____

_____

_____

_____

Discuss the preceding information with the class or with a partner. Explain why the surveying of this chapter made you think of the preceding information. Listen to others' experiences with the topics. Write two or three questions you would like to have answered as you read. For example, you may want to know some tips on getting hired, or you may want to learn different methods that managers use to evaluate employees, or you may want to discover some methods that managers use to determine salaries and bonuses. Think of a question to which you want an answer and write it on the lines here.

_____

_____

_____

_____

_____

Now that you have surveyed the chapter and made some connections to the reading material, it is time to begin reading and taking notes. The format that you will be using to take notes in this business chapter is outlining.

Journal Entry

Before you begin the next section, write a journal entry describing what you know about outlining notes from a textbook chapter.

MONITOR

This section will teach you how to outline the important points from the business chapter to narrow down the material that you will have to study for the exam. Before you begin, write the name of the chapter and the date in the upper right-hand corner of your loose-leaf paper.

How to Outline

Outlining is a systematic method of taking notes that uses indentations to show the relative importance of ideas and details. For example, all main ideas or topics that you need to understand are positioned farther to the left than the details that you need to memorize at the right. Look at this sample outline:

     I. Topic/Main Heading of Section
       A. Subheading Topic
         1. main ideas of paragraphs under subheadings
           a. details—vocabulary, names, dates, and so on to memorize

Roman numerals (*I, II, III, IV, V, VI, VII, VIII, IX, X*) are used first with the main topics of the chapter. This textbook chapter is set up nicely with main headings in all capital letters and boldfaced print. So as not to become confused as you write your outline, page through the chapter now and place a Roman numeral next to each main topic. "Human Resource Management: A Vital Managerial Function" would be I, "Human Resource Planning" would be II, "Recruitment and Selection" would be III, "Orientation, Training, and Evaluation" would be IV, and so on to X, "What's Ahead."

Capital letters are used next to indicate subheadings within major sections. Go back to III, "Recruitment and Selection," and place the capital letters *A* and *B*, respectively, in front of each subheading under that main heading. Now do the same for Roman numerals *IV, VI, VII, VIII,* and *IX*. (It is not necessary to do this for Roman numerals *I, II, V,* and *X* because there are no subheadings under any of those headings.) Note that under IV, A—"Training Programs"— the author uses sub-subheadings that begin a paragraph. Treat these as main ideas with numbers because they include all types of training programs, and write all details under them as letters.

Here are some other rules to follow:

1. Continue to indent to the right and to use numbers to indicate main ideas of paragraphs and lowercase letters to indicate major details.
2. Read at least one paragraph before writing any notes in your outline.
3. Do not write all notes in complete sentences. Main ideas should be in complete sentences, but details do not need to be.
4. Abbreviate words and use symbols consistently. You will be rereading your outline 2 or 3 weeks after you have written it, so you want to be able to read and understand the abbreviations and symbols.

Determining the Notes for Your Outline

As with the other notetaking methods, you will need to determine the main ideas and important details. Use the headings and subheadings. Also use the "Summary of Learning Goals," "Review Questions," and "Questions for Critical Thinking" as you read. If you recognize the answer to any of the questions, be sure to place the answer in your outline notes.

Outlining the Chapter

Before reading the first section, write the Roman numeral *I* and the title "Human Resource Management: A Vital Organizational Function" on the left side of your paper. As you write the main ideas and details in your outline, try to use your own words. Writing the information in your own words ensures that you understand the information. You do not need to write everything in complete sentences; details can be listed in words or phrases. Before you begin to read, turn the heading "Human Resource Management: A Vital Organizational Function" into a question. Write your question here:

_____

Some questions that you would phrase from this heading would be "Why is human resource management a vital managerial function?" or "What are the functions of human resource management?" or, using the learning goals on the first page of the chapter, "How can one describe the importance of human resource management?" The answers to these questions are found in the main ideas and details of this section. Read the first paragraph, which has two main ideas: one defines a term and the other addresses one of the learning goals. Write the main ideas here:

_____

_____

The first paragraph defines the term *human resource management* and then lists the responsibilities of the managers. Learning Goal 1 requires you to know these responsibilities, so write them as a second main idea.

Now read the second paragraph beginning with "Relationships between . . ." and write the main idea.

_____

_____

The main idea of the second paragraph is "The relationship between employers and employees has changed over the last 100 years." Only a main idea is necessary because the remainder of the paragraph as well as Figure 9.1 of the excerpt gives examples of this change.

The third paragraph, which begins with "Today, flexibility . . . ," and has two main ideas. Write those main ideas here:

_____

_____

_____

In paragraph three, the first sentence contains the first main idea. Then the second half of the paragraph lists a number of challenges faced by human resource managers. Thus, the second main idea would be "Challenges of human resource managers are many." The various challenges would be written as details under the second main idea.

The next paragraph, beginning with "Large organizations . . . ," has one main idea and two details. Write the main idea here:

_____

_____

This paragraph is about two types of human resource managers in large organizations. The two types of managers become the details under the main idea.

Paragraph 5 begins with "Entrepreneurs and . . ." and is a definition paragraph with one main idea and some details. Write the main idea here:

_____

_____

The main idea is the definition of a PEO: A professional employer organizations (PEO) is a company that helps midsized and small firms with human resource services. Be sure to write the acronym (*PEO*) and the words for the acronym because the test may contain either one. The details would include some of the services that a PEO provides and the fact that it works in partnership with employers, negotiates benefits for all clients, and allows the firms to have time for other functions. The Fennville, Michigan, example is not necessary in your notes unless you decide it helps you remember the definition.

Paragraph 6 begins with "One can view . . ." and also contains two main ideas. Write the two main ideas here:

_____

_____

The first sentence of paragraph 6 presents the first main idea. Human resource management can be viewed in two ways. The two ways to view managers are listed as details under this main idea. The second main idea is that "More firms are rewarding those who retain and recruit qualified job candidates." The remainder of the paragraph discusses an example.

The final paragraph again has two main ideas. Write them here:

_____

_____

_____

The paragraph begins with a list of responsibilities (Learning Goal 1) and then numbers the objectives of the human resource managers. Write these as separate numbers in your outline.

Each of the main ideas and details should be placed into an outline. Begin with the Roman numeral *I* and write all main ideas as numbers and all details as lowercase letters indented to the right. (Capital letters are not needed because of the lack of subheadings in this section.) Write your outline now on a sheet of loose-leaf paper and then compare yours with the following outline:

I. Human Resource Management: A Vital Organizational Function
    1. definition of h-r management is function of attracting, developing, and retaining sufficient numbers of qualified employees to perform the activities necessary to accomplish organizational goals.
    2. h-r managers develop programs and activities and create environment for employee satisfaction and efficiency
    3. relationships between employers & employees have changed much in last 100 years
    4. flexibility and complexity characterize relationship between employers & employees
    5. h-r managers have many challenges
        a. changes in labor force makeup, shortage of job candidates, changes in workplace structure, employee desire for balance in work/personal lives
        b. satisfy diverse employees and monitor employee-related laws
    6. large companies have h-r departments with 2 types of managers
        a. generalists—h-r managers who have several tasks
        b. specialists—h-r managers who focus on individual areas
    7. professional employer organizations (PEOs) are companies that help mid-sized & small firms with h-r services
        a. services—hire, train, payroll, benefits, workers' comp, compliance with laws
        b. work in partnership with employers
        c. negotiate benefits for all clients
        d. help firms focus on other functions
    8. 2 ways to view h-r management:
        a. narrow—h-r professional's role
        b. broad—entire organization, supervisors/managers hire, train, motivate; even some employees help
    9. more firms are rewarding those who retain and attract qualified candidates
   10. core responsibilities of h-r managers are
        a. plan for staff needs
        b. recruitment & selection
        c. training & evaluating
        d. compensation & benefits
        e. terminating employees
   11. objectives of h-r managers
        a. provide qualified, well-trained employees
        b. maximize employee effectiveness
        c. satisfy individual needs—$, benefits, opportunities, & job satisfaction

Section II, "Human Resource Planning," contains three paragraphs, with each containing one main idea. Think about a question that you can form from this heading and write it here:

_____

_____

A good question would be "How is planning done for human resources?" Keep your question in mind as you read this section and write the main ideas for each of the paragraphs on the lines below. The first few words of each paragraph are written to help you quickly find the correct one to read.

Paragraph 1 ("Human resource managers . . .")

_____

_____

Paragraph 2 ("Human resource managers also . . .")

_____

_____

Paragraph 3 ("Like Trilogy . . .")

_____

_____

The main idea of the first paragraph is found in the first sentence, with specific details that explain what the managers do. The main idea is human resource managers develop a staff plan based on the company's competitive strategies.

In the second paragraph, the first sentence also contains the main idea. The remainder of the paragraph provides a specific example and no details are needed. The main idea is human resource managers must plan how to get and keep good employees with pay benefits and working conditions.

The main idea of the third paragraph is expressed in the first and second sentences: High-tech businesses must be ambitious in expending their human resources and sometimes acquire other businesses to meet their needs. An example completes the paragraph and section.

Continue your outline with the preceding points on your paper and then compare it with the following outline.

    II. Human Resource Planning
        1. h-r managers/development staff plans based on company's competitive strategies
            a. determine # of employees & types of skills
            b. adjust workforce for expanding markets, reducing costs or adapting technology
            c. make long- & short-term plans
        2. h-r managers must plan how to get and keep good employees with pay, benefits, and working conditions, e.g., Trilogy Software
        3. high-tech businesses must be ambitious in expending their h-r; sometimes acquire other businesses to meet needs

The next major section is titled "Recruitment and Selection." Turn this heading into a question and write it on the lines below:

_____

_____

A good question would be "How are employees recruited and selected?" As you read and find main ideas and important details, keep in mind this question as well as Learning Goal 3: "Discuss the ways firms recruit and select employees and the importance of compliance with employment-related legislation."

The first paragraph has one main idea; combine both sentences to create one main idea and write it here:

_____

_____

The main idea would be "Striving to match applicant skills with organization needs, human resource managers use the seven-step recruitment and selection process." The seven steps in Figure 9.3 of the excerpted chapter become the details and your notes should look similar to these.

    III. Recruitment and Selection
        1. Striving to match applicant skills with organization needs, h-r managers use the 7-step recruitment and selection process
            a. ID job requirements
            b. choose sources of candidates
            c. review apps and resumes
            d. interview
            e. conduct employment test; check references
            f. conduct follow-up interviews
            g. select candidate; negotiate offer

The next section will begin with subheading A, "Finding Qualified Candidates." Indent about one-half inch from the left and place this subheading in your outline. Then find the main ideas for each of the four paragraphs under this subheading.

Paragraph 1 ("Businesses access . . .")

_____

_____

Paragraph 2 ("One of the most . . .")

_____

_____

Paragraph 3 ("Many firms are . . .")

_____

_____

Paragraph 4 ("Cisco Systems . . .")

_____

_____

Be sure to read and answer the questions about TJX in the "Clicks and Mortar" feature. You do not need to take notes on this section; the author has provided this example to provide a hook for the recruiting information.

The first sentence of the first paragraph contains its main idea. You should also include details about each source in your outline. Paragraphs 2, 3, and 4 also have their main idea in the first sentence, and the remainder of each paragraph provide examples.

Complete the notes to your outline and compare it with the following outline.

    A. Finding Qualified Candidates
        1. businesses use both internal (within the co.) and external (outside the co.) sources to find qualified candidates.
            a. internal first; less expensive and boosts morale
            b. external sources require advertising (TV, paper, radio, magazines) employment agencies, college recruiting, internship offices, retiree job banks, job fairs, state and private employment agencies
        2. most effective external source—employee referrals; employees recommend friends & are rewarded with bonuses/prizes.
        3. Internet—quick, inexpensive, efficient recruitment on Web sites & job banks
        4. Cisco uses electronic recruiting; e.g., ads, job search sites, job descriptions, links to employees

The next subheading, "Selecting and Hiring Employees," is level B. Write this in your outline and determine the main ideas of each paragraph.

Paragraph 1 ("In selecting . . .")

_____

_____

Paragraph 2 ("Failure to comply . . .") This is a difficult paragraph with three main ideas.

_____

_____

_____

Paragraph 3 ("Increases in protected . . .")

_____

_____

Paragraph 4 ("Employers must . . .") and Paragraph 5 ("The law prohibits . . ."). These paragraphs share one main idea.

_____

_____

Paragraph 6 ("Recruitment and selection . . .") This paragraph has two main ideas.

_____

_____

Paragraph 7 ("To avoid . . .")

_____

_____

Paragraph 8 ("Following a hiring decision . . .")

_____

_____

The first sentence of the first paragraph presents the main idea. Be sure to include in your notes examples of the federal and state laws.

As stated previously, paragraph 2 has three main ideas. The first is a cause and effect dealing with the failure to comply with equal opportunity legislation. Then the authors discuss the actions of the opponents the laws. Finally, the authors state what companies are doing to find the best employees.

Paragraph 3 is also a cause-and-effect paragraph. It provides two examples, one rule human resource managers must follow when interviewing applicants, and then another way human resource managers can assist in preventing lawsuits. Place both examples under the main idea.

Paragraph 4 and 5 both cover the legal restrictions over hiring practices. Your notes will also include two specific examples, one from each paragraph.

Paragraph 6 contains two main ideas. The author begins the paragraph discussing the topic recruitment and selection and then changes the topic to bad hiring decisions.

Paragraph 7 focuses on preventing a bad hire with the testing of applicants; this is followed with examples.

Paragraph 8 has its main idea in the first sentence; you must also include the vocabulary term "employment at will" with a definition in your notes.

Now place your main ideas and important details into outline form and compare it to the following outline.

B. Selecting and Hiring Employees
1. h-r managers must follow fed. & state laws
   a. Title VII of Civil Rights Act of 64—no discrimination of race, religion, color, sex, or national origin
   b. Am. With Disabilities Act of 1990
   c. Equal Employment Opportunity Commission (EEOC) created by Civil Rights Act to investigate discrimination complaints; helps set up affirmative action program
   d. Civil Rights Act of 1991—increased remedies for victims; include jury trial, punitive damages, damage for emotional distress
2. failure to comply with equal opportunity legislation can lead to fines, penalties, possible bad publicity, poor employee morale
3. opponents to laws launched initiatives to protect employers while other legislation protects employees
4. companies broaden pool of applicants to comply with laws and find best employees
5. lawsuits against employers have increased the importance of h-r managers in hiring
   a. train managers in interviewing
   b. establish systems for fairness
6. other legal restrictions
   a. drug tests—restricted in some states; controversial
   b. polygraph (lie detector) tests—illegal except for fed., state, & county govt., firms working for FBI, CIA, Dept of Defense, pharmaceutical firms, & security guard services
7. recruitment and selection is expensive
8. bad hire is even more expensive because potential lawsuits, unemployment compensation claims, recruiting/training replacement, reduction in productivity, poor morale
9. skills tests help determine applicants' knowledge of mechanical, technical, language & computer skills and prevent bad hires
10. firms protect selves with employment-at-will policies (state start or termination can occur at any time by employer or employee)

Journal Entry

Write a journal entry explaining what you have learned about outlining a textbook chapter.

RECITE

You have completed approximately one third of the chapter on human resource management. At this point, review your outline notes; then take Part I of the Business Study Guide Practice Test found on pages 244–251. After completing Part I, check your answers in Appendix A. Pay careful attention to the incorrect answers and determine why you answered them incorrectly.

Continue Outlining

The next three Roman numerals and headings are labeled "IV. Orientation, Training, and Evaluation"; "V. Compensation"; and "VI. Employee Benefits." Use the blank outline on the next page to help you complete your outline notes on paper. Remember to think about the following points as you read and take notes:

1. learning goals related to the topics or subtopics

2. answers to questions that you have formed from the headings and subheadings

3. main ideas or types of paragraphs

4. important vocabulary, names, and steps

As you fill in the outline, include a main idea for each number and an important detail for each lowercase letter.

IV. Orientation, Training, and Evaluation

    1. This paragraph has two main ideas. The first main idea explains why companies have orientation, training, and evaluation.

    2. The second main idea lists three outcomes the h-r department and employee's department provide.

      a.

      b.

      c.

A. Training Programs

    1. Paragraph 1 ("Employees are . . .") presents one main idea. (Be sure to read the "Business Hits and Misses" feature; you do not need to take notes.)

    2. Paragraph 2 ("A firm should . . ."); you may wish to add the example to the main idea.

    3. Paragraph 3 ("Information technology . . .") has one main idea.

    4. Paragraph 4 ("On-the-Job Training") is a boldfaced subheading; it and the next two subheadings with their text are types of training programs, and the information needs to be placed in this section. Place the main idea of this paragraph here.

      a. variation of on-the-job training

    5. Paragraph 5 ("Classroom and Computer-Based Training") contains one main idea.

      a. one type of program

      b. second type of program

    6. Paragraph 6 ("Today, off-the-job training . . .") has one main idea.

    7. Paragraph 7 ("When a firm decides . . .") discusses one main idea.

    8. Paragraph 8 ("Management Development") includes one main idea with one detail providing the reason for this type of program.

      a.

    9. Paragraph 9 ("Management training . . .") has one main idea—definition with three parts

      a.

      b.

      c.

   10. Paragraph 10 ("General Electric's . . .") contains one main idea, although it is an example and does not need to be included in your notes.

B. Performance Appraisals

    1. Paragraph 1 ("Organizations also help . . .") has one main idea.

      a. definition

        i. 2 reasons for performance appraisal

        ii.

    2. Paragraph 2 ("Some firms . . .") contains one main idea.

      a. definition

    3. Paragraph 3 ("Still, the 360-degree system . . .") includes one main idea.

V. Compensation

    1. Paragraph 1 ("Human resource . . .")

      a.

      b.

2. Paragraph 2 ("The terms . . .")
   a.
   b.
3. Paragraph 3 ("An effective . . .") has two main ideas.
   a.
   b.
   c.
4. Second main idea of paragraph 3.
   a.
   b.
   c.
   d.
   e.
5. Paragraph 4 ("On average . . .") discusses two main ideas.
6. Second main idea of paragraph 4.
7. Paragraph 5 ("Many employers . . .")
   a.
   b.
   c.
   d.
8. Paragraph 6 ("In addition . . .") contains two main ideas.
9. Second main idea of paragraph 6.
10. Paragraph 7 ("Incentive compensation . . .") has two main ideas.
11. Second main idea of paragraph 7.

VI. Employee Benefits
1. Paragraph 1 ("In addition to . . .") describes one main idea.
   a.
   b.
   c.
2. Paragraph 2 ("Benefits represent . . .") has one main idea.
   a.
   b. (add information from Figure 9.5)
3. Paragraph 3 ("A growing number . . .") contains one main idea.
(Be sure to read the section titled "Solving an Ethical Controversy"; you do not need to take notes on this section.)

A. Flexible Benefits
1. Paragraph 1 ("In response to . . .") has one main idea.
   a.
2. Paragraph 2 ("Another way of . . .") presents one main idea.

B. Flexible Work
1. Paragraph 1 ("Another part . . .") has one main idea.
   a. Paragraph 2 ("Flextime is . . ."). This and all other paragraphs under this subheading are types of flexible work plans and are therefore placed under the main idea.
   b. Paragraph 3 ("The compressed . . .").
   c. Paragraph 4 ("A job sharing . . .").
   d. Paragraph 5 ("A home-based work program . . .").
      i. Paragraph 6 ("Because telecommuters . . ."). This is information about home-based work.
      ii. Paragraph 7 ("The trend . . ."). The authors present one more point about home-based work.

At this point, review your outline of sections IV, V, and VI; then take Part II of the business practice test. When you have completed Part II, check your answers in Appendix A. Remember to pay careful attention to your incorrect answers and determine why you answered them incorrectly.

Now outline the last four sections of the business chapter on your own. In all four sections you will use capital letters to indicate subheadings. For example, under "VII. Employee Separation," you will have "A. Downsizing," and "B. Outsourcing." These will be indented in your outline like this:

VII. Employee Separation
    1.
       a.
    2.
       a.
   A. Downsizing

Check with your instructor if you have any problems creating your outline. Remember to relate what you read to the learning goals, to turn headings and subheadings into questions to answer, and to determine main ideas and details as you take the notes in outline form. When you have completed the third section of your outline notes, complete Part III of the business practice test. Then check your answers in Appendix A.

REVIEW

Review Your Notes

Review your outline. Do this by rereading the outline notes and by asking and answering the questions that you have formed from the headings. Then complete Part IV of the business practice test. Check your answers in Appendix A and review the incorrect answers to determine why you answered them incorrectly.

Review your outline at least once each week until you have taken a test on the chapter.

Methods of Studying

SUMMARIES

Write a summary of each learning goal on an index card. Include only the main points for each goal in your own words. For example, the first learning goal asks to describe the importance of human resource management and the responsibilities of human resource managers. You may want to include the definition of human resource management from the text, but be sure to also include the importance and responsibilities, which really constitute a summary of the entire subsection. Use the "Summary of Learning Goals" at the end of the business chapter to help you. Review these summaries instead of your outline on a weekly basis.

VOCABULARY CARDS

The business chapter contains 27 key vocabulary terms. Make vocabulary cards for each of the terms listed in "Business Terms You Need to Know" and "Other Important Business Terms" at the end of the chapter. Write the word on one side of the card and the definition and/or diagram on the other side.

CONCEPT MAPS

The concept map shown in Figure 10.1 was created using the information under "I. Human Resource Management: A Vital Organizational Function." Certain boxes have been left blank; use your outline to fill in those areas with the needed information. Then create concept maps for the remaining sections of the business chapter. See the guidelines for creating concept maps in Chapter 8 under "Methods of Studying."

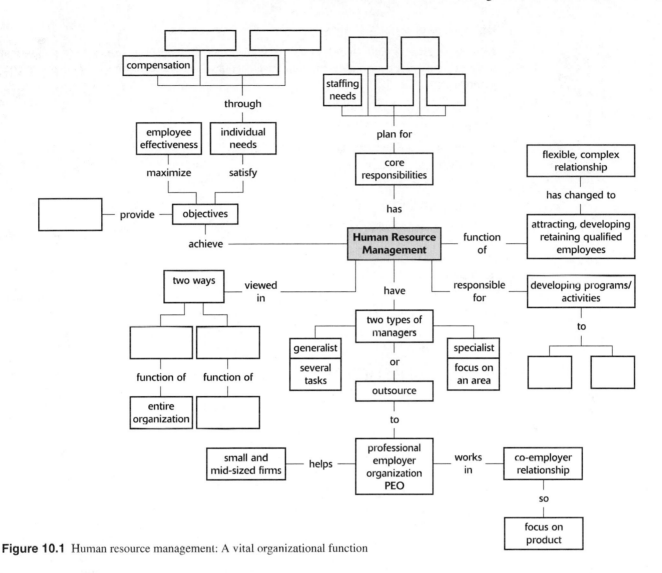

Figure 10.1 Human resource management: A vital organizational function

PRACTICE TESTS

Answer the "Review Questions" and the "Questions for Critical Thinking" and complete the "Experiential Exercise" at the end of the business chapter. Check your answers against your notes and the text. If you are not sure of an answer, check with your instructor.

STUDY GUIDE

If you have not already done so, complete Parts I, II, and III of the business study guide practice test. Then complete Part IV, Self-Review.

PREDICTED TEST QUESTIONS

Using the different levels of thinking, make up your own questions for each heading in the chapter, and then answer each question.

RECORDING AND LISTENING

Record your summaries, vocabulary terms and definitions, and predicted test questions and answers. Listen to them as often as possible.

GROUP OR PARTNER STUDY

Use the vocabulary cards and summaries to quiz other students or a partner on the important learning goals. Ask each other your predicted test questions and review his or her learning goal summaries.

PREPARE FOR THE TEST

Read the section titled "Preparing for and Taking the Test" in Chapter 7 to help you prepare for the test.

AFTER THE TEST

Complete the test review charts at the end of Chapter 7 to help you determine what you did right and what you did wrong.

Journal Entry

Try outlining a chapter from a textbook in another course you are taking, and then write a journal entry explaining whether it was helpful or not, and why.

BUSINESS STUDY GUIDE PRACTICE TEST

Part I

Learning Goal 9.1: Describe the importance of human resource management and the responsibilities of human resource managers.

TRUE OR FALSE

Write *T* in the blank if the statement is true, *F* if the statement is false.

_____ 1. As technology has advanced, the need for human resource management has declined.

_____ 2. Human resource management includes finding, training, motivating, compensating, and appraising enough qualified employees to accomplish organizational objectives.

_____ 3. Managers outside the human resources department rarely have human resource management responsibilities.

_____ 4. Developing an organizational climate that improves employee motivation, satisfaction, and efficiency is a key focus of human resource management.

_____ 5. Whereas large organizations generally have a human resource department to perform human resource management activities, small firms with fewer employees need not worry about human resource management issues.

_____ 6. A growing number of small firms outsource their human resource management activities to professional employer organizations (PEOs).

Learning Goal 9.2: Explain the role of human resource planning in an organization's competitive strategy.

TRUE OR FALSE

Write *T* in the blank if the statement is true, *F* if the statement is false.

_____ 7. Human resource planning is designed to provide the right number of properly skilled employees.

_____ 8. Human resource planning has little to do with motivating workers.

_____ 9. Today there is a shortage of qualified job candidates.

_____ 10. Human resource managers must adjust their firms' workforce to meet the requirements of expanding in new markets, reducing costs, and adapting to new technology.

Learning Goal 9.3: Discuss how firms recruit and select employees, and the importance of compliance with employment-related legislation.

SHORT ANSWER

11. What is the recruitment process? Where do employers look for potential employees?

12. What are the six steps in the typical selection process? At what stage of this process may candidates be rejected?

13. Why do human resource managers need to be aware of employment law?

Part II

Learning Goal 9.4: Describe how firms train and evaluate employees to develop effective workforces.

SHORT ANSWER

1. What sorts of employee training do organizations utilize?

2. What is a performance appraisal? To what uses are these appraisals applied?

Learning Goal 9.5: Identify the various pay systems and benefit programs.

MULTIPLE CHOICE

Write the letter of the *best* answer in the blank.

_____ 3. Payment to workers calculated on a weekly, monthly, or annual basis is known as

      a. wages.
      b. salary.
      c. benefits.
      d. incentive compensation.

_____ 4. Compensation programs such as profit sharing, gain sharing, pay for knowledge, bonuses, and stock options are known as

      a. wages.
      b. salary.
      c. incentive compensation programs.
      d. employee benefit programs.

_____ 5. A satisfactory compensation program should

      a. attract well-qualified applicants.
      b. keep workers satisfied in their jobs.
      c. inspire workers to be productive.
      d. all of the above.

_____ 6. The compensation policy of most employers is based upon

      a. compensation offered by competitors for labor in the same area.
      b. government legislation and the cost of living.
      c. the company's ability to pay and worker productivity.
      d. all of the above.

_____ 7. Benefit programs

      a. include benefits required by law such as social security.
      b. include pension plans, insurances, paid vacation, sick leave, and family leave.
      c. account for 28 percent of a typical employee's earnings.
      d. all of the above.

_____ 8. Companies increasingly adopt flexible benefit plans, often called

      a. compressed workweeks.
      b. work/life trends.
      c. cafeteria benefit plans.
      d. employment at will.

Part III

Learning Goal 9.6: Discuss employee separation and the impact of downsizing and outsourcing.

COMPARE AND CONTRAST

Which of the following applies to downsizing? to outsourcing? Place a check mark in the appropriate column.

	Downsizing	Outsourcing
1. reduces the number of workers in an organization	_____	_____
2. relies on outside specialists to do work formerly done by employees	_____	_____
3. adds flexibility	_____	_____
4. reduces cost	_____	_____
5. streamlines the organization's structure	_____	_____
6. means wider job responsibilities for remaining workers	_____	_____
7. allows a company to focus on activities it does best	_____	_____
8. is a prevailing modern trend	_____	_____

Learning Goal 9.7: Explain the concept of motivation in terms of satisfying employee needs.

SHORT ANSWER

9. Maslow's hierarchy of needs is based on three assumptions. What are they?

   a.

   b.

   c.

10. Maslow identified five needs in his analysis of motivation. List and define each.

    a.

    b.

    c.

    d.

    e.

Learning Goal 9.8: Discuss how human resource managers apply theories of motivation in attracting, developing, and maintaining employees.

TRUE OR FALSE

Write *T* in the blank if the statement is true, *F* if the statement is false.

_____ 11. Learning new skills, rotating jobs with others, and having more authority to plan and execute one's own job are all examples of job enrichment.

_____ 12. Although job enrichment can make for greater job satisfaction, there is no evidence that it leads to greater productivity or organizational success.

_____ 13. Job enlargement merely expands a worker's assignment.

MULTIPLE CHOICE

Write the letter of the *best* answer in the blank.

_____ 14. A manager who thinks that workers are lazy, dislike work, and need constant and close supervision is characterized as

     a. Theory X.
     b. Theory Y.
     c. Theory Z.

_____ 15. Managers who realize that workers want to meet their higher level needs at work are characterized as

     a. Theory X.
     b. Theory Y.
     c. Theory Z.

_____ 16. Theory Z organizations

     a. blend the best of American and Japanese management practices.
     b. rely on worker empowerment and participative management styles.
     c. may not evaluate and promote workers as frequently as more traditional organizations.
     d. all of the above.

_____ 17. The trends of downsizing organizations and empowering work teams favor the use of

     a. Theory X.
     b. Theory Y.
     c. Theory Z.

Learning Goal 9.9: Identify trends that influence the work of human resource managers in the 21st century.

TRUE OR FALSE

Write *T* in the blank if the statement is true, *F* if the statement is false.

_____ 18. Today, firms are more anxious than ever to encourage older workers to leave.

_____ 19. The trend toward two-career households and single-parent households creates challenges employers will have to address.

_____ 20. Modern management must ensure equal opportunity for our increasingly diverse and global workforce.

_____ 21. By 2010, the number of childless households is expected to increase by 50 percent.

_____ 22. The use of contingency and contract workers is expected to diminish significantly as we enter the 21st century.

_____ 23. More workers with disabilities are expected to enter the workforce in coming years.

Part IV

SELF-REVIEW

TRUE OR FALSE

Write *T* in the blank if the statement is true, *F* if the statement is false.

_____ 1. According to Theory X, most people welcome increased responsibility.

_____ 2. Telework is expected to accelerate as firms increasingly use the Internet.

_____ 3. Employment at will means that employers must have a good reason to fire an employee or face a suit.

_____ 4. Theory Y is associated with the idea that people are self-motivated.

_____ 5. Theory Y advocates are more likely to delegate authority than Theory X advocates.

_____ 6. Employment skills tests are often used as a screening device.

_____ 7. Hiring from within contributes to employee morale.

_____ 8. All firms have the right to give a polygraph test to any employee.

_____ 9. The recruitment and selection process includes finding and evaluating job applicants.

_____ 10. Once hired, the first thing an applicant should receive is training.

_____ 11. Employee training should be viewed as an ongoing process throughout a worker's tenure with the company.

_____ 12. Although operating workers require training, few organizations have programs aimed at developing the skills of managers.

_____ 13. Performance appraisals are used to make objective decisions about compensation, promotions, additional training needs, transfers, and terminations.

_____ 14. Job enrichment, by focusing on motivational aspects of a job, often improves employee morale.

_____ 15. Fringe benefits account for less than 10 percent of the typical employee's compensation.

MULTIPLE CHOICE

Write the letter of the *best* answer in the blank.

_____ 16. The mental attitude people have toward their employment is known as

  a. perception.
  b. Theory X.
  c. morale.
  d. maintenance factors.

_____ 17. When a firm decides to enter a foreign market, human resource managers must prepare employees who will work in overseas assignments by

  a. providing training in language skills.
  b. acquainting them with customs they will encounter in the foreign environment.
  c. giving them tools to help them adapt to the everyday living requirements abroad.
  d. all of the above.

_____ 18. According to Maslow,

  a. a fully satisfied need is the best motivator.
  b. needs arise in a hierarchy.
  c. self-actualization needs are the most fundamental and arise first.
  d. all of the above.

_____ 19. Actions taken to avoid danger and the unexpected generally represent responses to

    a. physiological needs.
    b. safety needs.
    c. social needs.
    d. esteem needs.
    e. self-actualization needs

_____ 20. Gaining respect from others or recognition for a job well done helps to satisfy

    a. physiological needs.
    b. safety needs.
    c. social needs.
    d. esteem needs.
    e. self-actualization needs

_____ 21. The desire to have friends, family, and to be accepted are motivated by

    a. physiological needs.
    b. safety needs.
    c. social needs.
    d. esteem needs.
    e. self-actualization needs.

_____ 22. An organization that offers workers challenging and creative work assignments is appealing to employees'

    a. physiological needs.
    b. safety needs.
    c. social needs.
    d. esteem needs.
    e. self-actualization needs.

_____ 23. Stock options

    a. give employees the opportunity to buy stock in the company at a preset price within a certain period of time.
    b. are legally mandated in all modern organizations.
    c. are not considered incentive pay programs.
    d. do all of the above.

_____ 24. When organizations downsize

    a. they hope to reduce costs and improve performance by streamlining the organization's structure.
    b. they always utilize layoffs.
    c. trust and loyalty of remaining employees is automatically enhanced.
    d. it means that they can avoid outsourcing.

_____ 25. Outsourcing

    a. relies on outside specialists to perform functions previously performed by the company's own employees.
    b. adds flexibility while reducing costs.
    c. allows a company to focus on what it does best.
    d. all of the above.

Application Exercises

Anita Martinez operates her own business-services consulting company. She has hired several employees in the past, some of whom have worked out well, but many of whom have stayed only a short time before quitting or being fired for failure to perform as she had hoped. She is currently in need of an additional employee and wonders what she might do to enhance her chances of finding the right candidate for the job. Anita has come to you and asked your help in setting up a procedure for selecting suitable candidates.

ESSAY

26. What suggestions can you make to help her find the right employee?

27. Once Anita has hired a new employee, what steps can she take to help ensure employee satisfaction?

ESSAY

28. What is human resource management? What activities are involved, and how important are they in achieving organizational objectives?

29. What is motivation, and how can motivation theory be applied in the workplace? Your answer should include Maslow's hierarchy of needs, and an analysis of Theory X, Theory Y, and Theory Z. What essential lessons do these theories give us as we try to improve worker motivation?

Human Resource Management and Motivation

Learning Goals

1. Describe the importance of human resource management and the responsibilities of human resource managers.

2. Explain the role of human resource planning in an organization's competitive strategy.

3. Discuss the ways firms recruit and select employees and the importance of compliance with employment-related legislation.

4. Summarize how firms train and evaluate employees to develop effective workforces.

5. Identify the various pay systems and benefit programs.

6. Discuss employee separation and the impact of downsizing and outsourcing.

7. Explain the concept of motivation in terms of satisfying employee needs.

8. Describe how human resource managers apply theories of motivation in attracting, developing, and maintaining employees.

9. Identify trends that influence the work of human resource managers in the 21st century.

From *Contemporary Business*, 10th edition by Boone and Kurtz. Chapter 9. © 2003. Reprinted with permission of Wadsworth, a division of Thomson Learning.

Ryder System Goes the Extra Mile for Employees—and Their Children

You've seen those yellow rental trucks everywhere. Sometimes they're transporting the goods of people moving into a new home or apartment. Small businesses often rent them to ship inventory from one factory or retail store to another. A few years ago, you may even have seen them on television hauling presidential ballots from Miami to Tallahassee. Ryder System is the company that leases trucks and solves transportation problems for individuals and companies worldwide. But you may not know that the company also has 30,000 employees. Like many of today's organizations, Ryder knows the importance of its human resources. "We recognize our employees—our knowledge capital—as our most valuable asset," states the Career Information Center page on the company's Web site. "We're looking for experienced, career-minded individuals who value professionalism, teamwork, innovation, and the highest level of service to clients, both external and internal." To find such talent to help the company grow and maintain its competitive edge, Ryder's human resource professionals search the globe for the best people. You can apply for a job at Ryder anywhere in the world with the click of your computer mouse. In fact, the Web site will even help you build a resume—the company is that serious in its endeavor.

To attract the "best and brightest," as Ryder refers to its employees, the company offers a full range of benefits—everything from competitive salaries and wages to medical and dental benefits, to profit sharing and pension plans. All of these benefits are common among *Fortune* 500 companies, as is subsidized day care. Understanding the needs of working parents, Ryder even opened a day care center right across

the street from its Miami headquarters. But here's a new twist: the company is building an elementary school next door. That way, 300 children of Ryder employees will con-

tinue to go to school near the building where their parents work.

"The school is helping us reinforce the concept that we want to be the employer of choice in south Florida," explains Ryder CEO Anthony Burns. Ryder will spend $5 million of its own money to build the school on property it has already donated for the purpose. The gain? Aside from attracting high-quality employees, Ryder will receive tax breaks and about $4,000 a year per student from the state to cover its costs. Because it's a charter school, Ryder receives public funding, but the company has much greater latitude in establishing a curriculum, setting school rules, and hiring teachers and other employees. The school plans to limit enrollment to 20 students per class, require students to wear uniforms, teach several languages, and be equipped with state-of-the-art computer technology. The school day will run a bit longer than a typi-

cal public school day, and after-school programs will last until 6:30 to accommodate parents' work schedules. The impact of this benefit will be immediate: "with the kids right across the street, I can afford an extra hour at work," says James Green, a claims analyst with two young children.

Ryder isn't the first corporation to build its own school as a way of attracting and keeping employees. American Bankers Insurance Group and Hewlett-Packard, among others, have already done so. But those schools are corporate-sponsored and private. Ryder's will be a chartered public school, which means that it will also be open to students whose parents are not Ryder employees.[1] As you read this chapter, you'll come across a number of organizations that are going the extra distance to help their employees balance work and family responsibilities, which may be one of the greatest changes in the employer–employee relationship over the past 100 years.

CHAPTER OVERVIEW

The importance of people to the success of any organization is stressed in the very definition of *management:* the use of people and other resources to accomplish organizational objectives. Ryder System is just one of the thousands of businesses that have found creative ways to attract the best workers and encourage them to stay with the company.

In this chapter we address the critical issues of human resource management and motivation. We begin with a discussion of the ways organizations attract, develop, and retain employees. Then we describe the concepts behind motivation and the way human resource managers apply them to increase employee satisfaction and organizational effectiveness.

HUMAN RESOURCE MANAGEMENT: A VITAL ORGANIZATIONAL FUNCTION

Most organizations devote considerable attention to **human resource management,** the function of attracting, developing, and retaining enough qualified employees to perform the activities necessary to accomplish organizational objectives. Human resource managers are responsible for developing specific programs and activities as well as creating a work environment that generates employee satisfaction and efficiency.

Relationships between employers and employees changed enormously during the past century. At the beginning of the 20th century, firms hired employees by posting notices at their sites stating that workers were needed and would be hired the following day. Such a notice might list required skills, such as carpentry or welding, or simply list the number of employees the firm required. People looking for work would line up at the employer's shop or factory the next day—a small number in prosperous times and a larger number in leaner times. Someone in authority made hiring decisions after reviewing these candidates, often based on arbitrary criteria; sometimes the first people in line were hired, sometimes the healthiest and strongest were hired. After being hired, the new employees were expected to work under a precise set of rules, such as the humorous list shown in Figure 9.1.

Today, flexibility and complexity characterize the relationship between employers and employees. In Chapter 1, you learned that developing and sustaining a world-class workforce is essential for a firm to compete effectively. Human resource managers face challenges created by profound changes in the makeup of the labor force, a shortage of qualified job candidates, changes in the structure of the workplace, and employees' desires to balance their work and personal lives. These managers must also develop programs and policies that satisfy an increasingly diverse employee population while monitoring a growing number of employment-related laws that influence how they implement their firms' practices.

Large organizations create human resource departments that systematically handle the tasks of attracting, training, and retaining employees. Some human resource managers are *generalists,* because they are responsible for several tasks. Others are *specialists,* because they focus on individual areas of human resource management such as diversity training or employee benefits.

Entrepreneurs and small-business managers usually assume most of the responsibility for human resource management. However, a growing number of small firms are outsourcing the function of human resource management to **professional employer organizations (PEOs).** A PEO is a company that helps small and midsized firms with a wide range of human resource services, including hiring and training employees, administering payroll and benefits programs, handling workers' compensation and unemployment insurance, and maintaining compliance with labor

THEY SAID IT

"You can dream, create, design, and build the most wonderful place in the world, but it requires people to make the dream a reality."

WALT DISNEY (1901–1966)
AMERICAN FILM PRODUCER AND
CREATOR OF DISNEYLAND AND
DISNEY WORLD

BUSINESS

FIGURE 9.1
Rules for Clerks, 1900

1. This store must be opened at sunrise. No mistake. Open at 6:00 A.M. summer and winter. Close about 8:30 or 9 P.M. the year round.

2. Store must be swept and dusted, doors and windows opened, lamps filled and trimmed, chimneys cleaned, counters, base shelves, and showcases dusted, pens made, a pail of water and the coal must be brought in before breakfast, if there is time to do it and attend to all the customers who call.

3. The store is not to be opened on the Sabbath day unless absolutely necessary and then only for a few minutes.

4. Should the store be opened on Sunday the clerks must go in alone and get tobacco for customers in need.

5. Clerks who are in the habit of smoking Spanish cigars, being shaved at the barber's, going to dancing parties and other places of amusement, and being out late at night will assuredly give the employer reason to be overly suspicious of employee integrity and honesty.

6. Clerks are allowed to smoke in the store provided they do not wait on women while smoking a "stogie."

7. Each store clerk must pay not less than $5.00 per year to the church and must attend Sunday school regularly.

8. Men clerks are given one evening a week off for courting and two if they go to the prayer meeting.

9. After the 14 hours in the store, leisure hours should be spent mostly in reading.

laws. PEOs work in partnership with employers in these key decisions. Because the PEO typically negotiates benefits for all its clients, it can shop for better deals. And by handling a firm's human resource activities, a PEO enables a small firm to focus on production, marketing, and finance, as well as on motivating and leading employees. In Fennville, Michigan, West Michigan Flocking & Assembly uses a PEO called ADP TotalSource to provide employee benefits, process payroll, and give advice on human resource issues. West Michigan Flocking, which produces a decorative finish used in automobiles, also wanted to improve workplace safety. ADP's safety manager responded by developing a safety policy, conducting regular inspections, and helping the manufacturer set up a safety committee.[2]

One can view human resource management in two ways. In a narrow sense, it includes the functions performed by human resource professionals. But in a broader sense, it involves the entire organization, even when a staff department assumes those responsibilities or a firm outsources the functions. Supervisors and general managers also participate in hiring, training, evaluating performance, and motivating employees. Since a company's success depends largely on the commitment and talents of its people, a growing number of firms are measuring and rewarding managers' performance in retaining employees and attracting qualified job candidates. Autodesk, American Express, and Hartford Insurance are among the companies at which managers' performance reviews include measures of employee turnover.[3] Similarly, many companies consider workforce diversity to be a source of competitive advantage in serving diverse customer groups and thinking creatively. At these organizations, management goals may also include measures of employee diversity. At Alliant Energy a belief that diversity is a source of competitive advantage has

BUSINESS DIRECTORY

➤ **human resource management** *function of attracting, developing, and retaining sufficient numbers of qualified employees to perform the activities necessary to accomplish organizational goals.*

FIGURE 9.2
Human Resource Management Responsibilities

prompted the company to reward managers for their performance in hiring women and minorities.[4] In addition, some firms ask non-management employees to participate in hiring decisions and evaluating their coworkers' performance.

The core responsibilities of human resource management include planning for staffing needs, recruitment and selection, training and evaluating performance, compensation and benefits, and terminating employees. In accomplishing these five tasks shown in Figure 9.2, human resource managers achieve their objectives of (1) providing qualified, well-trained employees for the organization, (2) maximizing employee effectiveness in the organization, and (3) satisfying individual employee needs through monetary compensation, benefits, opportunities to grow and advance, and job satisfaction.

HUMAN RESOURCE PLANNING

Human resource managers develop staffing plans based on their organization's competitive strategies. They forecast the number of employees their firm will need and determine the types of skills necessary to implement its plans. Human resource managers are responsible for adjusting their company's workforce to meet the requirements of expanding in new markets, reducing costs (which may require laying off employees), or adapting new technology. They formulate both long-term and short-term plans to provide the right number of qualified employees.

Human resource managers also must plan how to attract and keep good employees with the right combination of pay, benefits, and working conditions. At Trilogy Software, this aspect of human resource planning is at the core of the company's strategy. Trilogy develops software that handles information processing related to sales and marketing, an industry in which only fast-moving, highly sophisticated companies can succeed. So, the company has a strategy to continually expand its staff of software developers. Knowing that it is competing for talent with rich software giants like Microsoft and Cisco Systems, Trilogy targets college campuses, recruiting the brightest, most energetic students it can find. As a substitute for work experience, the company sends these young recruits to an intense three-month orientation program called Trilogy University, where they work on Trilogy products as they learn about the software industry and the company culture. The long workdays at Trilogy University, followed by company-sponsored parties, are an early taste of working for the company, which consciously strives to maintain the intense atmosphere of a start-up. When recruiting employees, Trilogy sells that atmosphere as an asset, attracting people who are stimulated by working on challenging projects in a close-knit team of bright and energetic coworkers. It's a strategy that attracts people like Joshua Walsky, who has no complaints about working until late at night: "Trilogy hires people who are smart, talented, interesting, and cool. Those are exactly the sort of people I want to be around."[5]

Like Trilogy, many high-tech businesses set ambitious plans for expanding their human resources, and the market for talent is highly competitive. Some of these companies plan acquisitions of other businesses to meet human resource needs. Kana Communications needed more engineers to meet growth targets for its software firm. So Kana purchased smaller companies, including Net Dialogue and BEI. Similarly, Redback Networks purchased Siara Systems, most of whose employees were engineers. Redback then put its human resource personnel to work meeting with each of those engineers to help them with the transition.[6]

RECRUITMENT AND SELECTION

In recruiting and selecting employees, human resource managers strive to match applicants' skills with those the organization needs. To ensure that potential employees bring the necessary skills or have the capacity to learn them, most firms implement the recruitment and selection process shown in Figure 9.3.

Finding Qualified Candidates

Businesses access both internal and external sources to find qualified candidates for specific jobs. Policies of hiring from within emphasize internal sources, so employers consider their own employees first for job openings. Internal recruiting is less expensive than external methods, and it helps boost employee morale. But if recruiters can find no qualified internal candidates, they must look for people outside the organization. Recruitment from external sources involves advertising in newspapers and trade magazines, placing radio and television ads, and working through employment agencies, college recruiting and internship offices, retiree job banks, job fairs, and state employment agencies. Some firms find creative ways to recruit from external sources, as did TJX in the "Clicks and Mortar" box.

One of the most effective external sources is employee referrals, in which employers ask current employees to recommend applicants, rewarding them with bonuses or prizes for new hires. The demand for employees with high-tech skills is so great that some companies are offering generous rewards to employees who refer qualified candidates. Docent, which provides online learning resources, pays $5,000 to any employee whose referral the company hires. Software firm Adobe Systems also pays $5,000 for referrals, and employees with three referrals get an additional $5,000 toward a vacation. Respond.com awarded an employee a Hawaii trip for two for referring an engineer who joined the company.[7]

Many firms are using the Internet as a recruiting tool. They may post jobs and accept résumés at their own Web sites, as well as list positions at job banks such as Headhunter.net, HotJobs.com, Monster.com, and America's Job Bank (www.ajb.dni.us), sponsored by the U.S. Department of Labor. Internet recruiting is a quick, efficient, inexpensive way to reach a large, global pool of job seekers. According to employers and career counselors, online recruiting is becoming the prevalent method of finding qualified job candidates.

Cisco Systems, which develops and sells Internet connection technology, relies heavily on electronic recruiting to help the company find thousands of new employees every year. To lure job hunters to the recruiting pages of its own Web site, Cisco posts banner ads on a variety of Web sites. The company targets its efforts by placing ads on job search sites like Monster.com, as well as by directing that ads appear on the screens of people with designated Web addresses, such as those of competitors. Other recruiting efforts, from newspaper advertising to booths at public events, also direct interested people to the Cisco Web site. Once there, job hunters find links to job descriptions, which they can search by title, job type, location, and other relevant factors. Links are even provided to Cisco employees who will share information about working there. Job hunters also can provide information about themselves, which helps the company link them to appropriate jobs. With these resources, Cisco receives over two-thirds of candidates' résumés electronically. Once those résumés arrive at Cisco, the company uses software to screen each one for key words that signal the expertise or backgrounds it needs and to match résumés with job openings.[8]

Selecting and Hiring Employees

In selecting and hiring employees, human resource managers must follow the requirements set out by federal and state laws. Chapter 2 describes legislation that

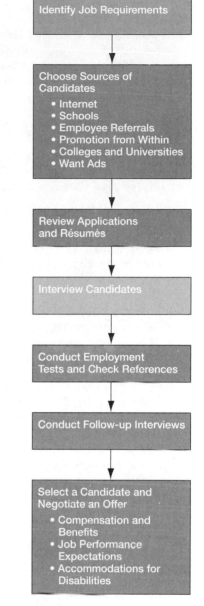

FIGURE 9.3
Steps in the Recruitment and Selection Process

BUSINESS

TJX Takes Recruiting to the Maxx

Background. Everyone loves a booming economy; everyone, that is, except managers who are trying to find qualified people to work for them. With the unemployment rate close to below 4 percent, it's hard for many businesses—including TJX Cos., the parent of off-price retailers T.J. Maxx and Marshalls. "The job market is such that you can't go out and hire good people—you have to make them," explains John D'Amico, a T.J. Maxx store manager.

What Happened? When the U.S. government announced its welfare reform policy in the late 1990s, TJX founder Ben Cammarata went to Washington and pledged to hire 5,000 people from the welfare rolls by the year 2000. The only problem was, where would he find them? One strategy was to hire CIC Enterprises to set up and run a job hot line connected to various agencies that help get welfare recipients ready for the world of work. Through the hot line network, a store manager for a T.J. Maxx or Marshalls in any location could call and request potential candidates for a job opening.

The Response. The results of the hot line have been even better than TJX managers had hoped. For every ten calls made to the hot line, eight calls have resulted in a candidate who has been hired. Traditionally, retailers retain only about 43 percent of the people they hire, but TJX claims that 61 percent of the former welfare recipients hired are still with the company after a year. TJX chairman Ted English notes, "The welfare-to-work associates we're hiring are looking for a little bit more stability and a little bit more of a long-term relationship. It's worked out great for us." So, the company has reduced its recruiting and hiring costs in the long run.

Many of these employees do need special training, since they may come to the job without a high school diploma or be unprepared for the daily requirements of work. To that end, TJX started a pilot program called First Step. The program prepares former welfare recipients for work and follows them for at least a year.

Today and Counting. The job hot line has been so successful that TJX has recently expanded it to include searches for older workers, immigrants, and individuals with developmental disabilities as the nation and the workforce continue to change. Although the First Step program does not solve everyone's problems—a number do drop out—it has helped workers like Vicki Glover, a single mom who dropped out of high school 20 years ago. Glover has already received three promotions and is now on an assistant manager's track. She still has trouble paying all her bills on $8.50 an hour, but she's determined to stick with it. TJX vows to continue its programs, helped in part by the tax credits it receives for hiring these candidates. It's a step in the right direction.

QUESTIONS FOR CRITICAL THINKING

1. Would the Internet be an effective recruiting tool for TJX? Why or why not?
2. In what ways must TJX human resource managers be careful to comply with equal employment opportunity legislation?

Sources: "About TJX," TJX company Web site, **www.tjx.com**, accessed February 19, 2001; Ann Harrington, "How Welfare Worked for T.J. Maxx," *Fortune*, November 13, 2000, pp. 453–456; Chris Reidy, "3. TJX Cos.," The Eleventh Annual Globe 100, *The Boston Globe*, **www.boston.com/globe**, May 18, 1999.

influences employers' hiring practices. Title VII of the Civil Rights Act of 1964 prohibits employers from discriminating against applicants based on their race, religion, color, sex, or national origin. The Americans with Disabilities Act of 1990 prohibits employers from discriminating against disabled applicants. The Civil Rights Act created the Equal Employment Opportunity Commission (EEOC) to investigate discrimination complaints. The EEOC also assists employers in setting up affirmative-action programs to increase job opportunities for women, minorities, disabled people, and other protected groups. The Civil Rights Act of 1991 expanded the remedies available to victims of employment discrimination by including the right to a jury trial, punitive damages, and damages for emotional distress.

Failure to comply with equal employment opportunity legislation can expose an employer to such risks as fines and penalties, bad publicity, and poor employee morale. The EEOC files hundreds of cases each year, with damages paid by businesses in the tens of millions annually. At the same time, opponents to such laws have launched initiatives to restrict affirmative-action standards and protect employers against unnecessary litigation. In one instance, California voters passed a proposition that prohibits the state from granting hiring preferences to minorities. Other proposed federal legislation is aimed at protecting employees from discrimination because of their religious beliefs or sexual orientation. In this environment of change coupled with a tight labor market, many companies are trying to broaden their pool of applicants so that they can comply with legal requirements even as they increase the odds of finding talented people. Xerox, for example, develops relationships with colleges, including those with significant enrollments of African American or Hispanic students. The company also supports organizations ranging from the National Society of Black Engineers to the Institute for Women and Technology.[9]

Increases in protected employees and discrimination lawsuits have elevated the importance of human resource managers in the hiring process. To prevent violations, human resource personnel must train managers involved in interviewing to make them knowledgeable about employment law. For example, the law prohibits asking an applicant any questions relating to marital status, number of children, race, nationality, religion, or age. Interviewers also may not ask questions about applicants' criminal records, mental illness histories, or alcohol-related problems. In addition, human resource managers can help organizations establish systems to promote fair employment practices. Home Depot was sued by women who claimed they were more often unfairly steered toward lower-paying jobs than were males with similar qualifications. As part of the settlement, Home Depot began using software called the Job Preference Program, which automates the process of ranking candidates for jobs and promotions. Not only does the software provide store managers with lists of candidates based on legitimate criteria, it also creates lists of questions and criteria for evaluating the answers. Besides creating more opportunities for its female employees, Home Depot's software has helped its managers make better employment decisions.[10] For more information about employment-litigation issues, visit the Web sites of the Society for Human Resource Management and the EEOC.

Employers must also observe various other legal restrictions governing hiring practices. Some firms try to screen out high-risk employees by requiring drug testing for job applicants, particularly in industries where employees are responsible for public safety, such as airlines and other public transportation. Drug testing is controversial, however, due to concerns about privacy. Also, positive test results may not accurately indicate drug use; traces of legal drugs, such as prescribed medications, may chemically resemble traces of illegal substances. Several states have passed laws restricting drug testing by employers.

The law prohibits the use of polygraph (lie detector) tests in almost all prehiring decisions, as well as in random testing of current employees. The only organizations exempt from this law are federal, state, and county governments; firms that do sensitive work under contract to the Defense Department, Federal Bureau of Investigation, or Central Intelligence Agency; pharmaceuticals firms that handle controlled substances; and security guard services.

Recruitment and selection is an expensive process, because a firm incurs costs for advertising job openings, interviewing applicants, and conducting background checks, employment tests, and medical exams. A bad hiring decision is even more expensive, though. A hiring mistake costs a firm in efforts to train and motivate a less than optimal employee, as well as potential costs of poor decisions by that employee. Other costs resulting from a bad hiring decision may include lawsuits, unemployment compensation claims, recruiting and training a replacement, and reductions in productivity and employee morale.

To avoid the costly results of a bad hiring decision, many employers require applicants to complete employment tests. These tests help verify the skills that candidates list on their application forms or résumés to ensure that they meet the performance expectations of the job. A variety of tests are available to gauge applicants' knowledge of mechanical, technical, language, and computer skills. One example is the Basic Skills Tests published by Wonderlic in Libertyville, Illinois, which measure candidates' basic math and verbal skills. These tests are intended to be a more objective and accurate way to measure qualifications than simply asking candidates about their educational background.[11] Capital One Financial established tests through a process that was more complicated but better tailored to the company's specific needs. Capital One had 1,600 of its current employees take skills tests to create a database the company could use as a basis for comparing new job candidates. The database also helps the company analyze who will be the best performers; it learned that applicants referred by existing employees tend to perform better on the tests. Consequently, Capital One has begun to rely more heavily on referrals as part of its recruitment strategy.[12]

Following a hiring decision, a growing number of firms protect themselves from discrimination lawsuits by including explicit employment-at-will policies in their employee manuals. **Employment at will** means that the employment relationship can be started or terminated at any time by either the employee or the employer for any reason. Many people believe that the law prohibits employers from firing employees, but successful lawsuits must cite specific illegal practices such as discrimination in hiring based on sex, race, age, or disability. Although most state laws recognize the principle of employment at will, court decisions in firing disputes sometimes favor employees when their employers have failed to provide written proof of at-will policies and employees' acceptance of the policies. For further protection, some employers are also publishing policies that call for mandatory arbitration of employment disputes and waivers of the right to jury trials in such disputes.

ORIENTATION, TRAINING, AND EVALUATION

FIGURE 9.4
New Horizons: Communicating the Importance of Training

Once hired, employees need information about what is expected of them and how well they are performing. Companies provide this information through orientation, training, and evaluation. A newly hired employee often completes an orientation program administered jointly by the human resource department and the department in which the employee will work. During orientation, employer representatives inform employees about company policies regarding employee rights and benefits. Many organizations give new hires copies of employee manuals that describe benefits programs and working conditions and expectations. They also provide different types of training to ensure that employees get a good start at the company.

Training Programs

Employees are increasing their requests for training so they can build skills and knowledge that will prepare them for new job opportunities. Training is also a good investment from the employer's perspective. As Figure 9.4 reports, untrained employees take six times longer to perform tasks than trained employees, so it is important to help new employees build their skills quickly. In a relatively new industry, such as Internet retailing, companies need to find creative ways to train their employees, as described in the "Business Hits & Misses" box.

A firm should view employee training as an ongoing process throughout each employee's tenure with the company. At Federal Express Corp., training is part of the company's investment in its people, which helps keep employees committed to the firm. Of FedEx's total expenses, 3 percent goes to training. Although the percentage may sound small, it is six times higher than most companies of similar size. Employees attend FedEx's Leadership

Institute, where they learn about the company's operations and culture. As Larry McMahan, vice president for human resources, puts it, "One reason people like to work here is that they just don't come in with a set of skills that stay stagnant. We believe heavily in individual development."[13]

Information technology (IT) employees tend to place a high value on knowledge. For employees like these, training is essential. At accounting firm BDO Seidman, IT employee training develops their ability to apply technology to the company's specific situation, so it is a good investment. The field technicians who staff the company's offices in various locations receive encouragement to train for the accounting firm's higher-level jobs. BDO's director of field operations received such training when he was a field technician, and he now manages 200 employees.[14]

On-the-Job Training   One popular instructional method is on-the-job training, which prepares employees for job duties by allowing them to perform the tasks under the guidance of experienced employees. A variation of on-the-job training is apprenticeship training, in which an employee learns a job by serving for a time as an assistant to a trained worker. Patio Enclosures, a construction firm, made its employees more productive and more committed to the company by setting up an apprenticeship program. Employees who manufacture and install sunrooms receive a booklet that details skills and training requirements. As employees meet the requirements for each level of skill, they have the booklet stamped—and receive an increase in pay. Patio Enclosures' executive vice president, Jerry Fox, says the apprenticeship program builds commitment to the company: "If an employee knows he's two or three jobs from the next pay level, why would he want to jump to another place?"[15] Apprenticeship programs are much more common in Europe than in the United States. While American apprenticeships usually focus on blue-collar trades, in Europe many new entrants to white-collar professions complete apprenticeships.

Classroom and Computer-Based Training   Off-the-job training involves some form of classroom instruction such as lectures, conferences, audiovisual aids, programmed instruction, and special machines to teach employees everything from basic math and language skills to complex, highly skilled tasks. Some firms are replacing classroom training with computer-based training programs. These programs can save an employer money by reducing travel costs and employee time away from work. In addition, computer-based training offers consistent presentations, since the training content won't vary with the quality of the instructor. Audio and visual capabilities help these systems to simulate the work environment better than some classroom training could, and employees also benefit from greater control over the learning process. They can learn at their own pace and convenience, and they generally do not have to wait for the company to schedule a class before they can begin adding to their knowledge. Despite these advantages, firms also offer traditional classroom training, because it usually provides more opportunities for employees to interact with the instructor and with one another. Some people learn more readily from human interaction, and some have difficulty disciplining themselves to complete a computer-based learning program on their own.[16]

Today, off-the-job training frequently involves use of the Internet. The Web provides a convenient means of delivering text, audio, and video training materials to employees wherever they are located. Online training programs also can offer interactive learning, such as simulations in which employees see the results of their decisions.

When a firm decides to enter a foreign market, human resource managers must prepare employees who will work in overseas assignments by providing training in language skills, cultural practices, and adapting to the everyday living requirements abroad. Employees may begin an international assignment with the

BUSINESS DIRECTORY

➤ **employment at will**   *practice that allows the employment relationship to begin or end at any time at the decision of either the employee or the employer for any legal reason.*

➤ **on-the-job training**   *training method that teaches an employee to complete new tasks by performing them under the guidance of an experienced employee.*

BUSINESS

E-tailers Learn the Value of the Question, "May I Help You?"

You wouldn't automatically think of the Internet as a place for personal assistance from a salesperson. But many e-tailers, stung by customer dissatisfaction with their Internet shopping experiences, have begun to pay closer attention to personal customer service at their Web sites. Datamonitor PLC in London estimates that worldwide, Web sites may lose $3.2 billion in sales because they do not offer personal assistance. According to Forrester Research, two-thirds of all consumers who place goods in an electronic shopping cart during a visit to a site do not complete the sale. That's a lot of business lost, and a growing number of companies are now doing something about it.

A shopper who logs on to www.landsend.com can chat live with a Lands' End operator, asking questions about size, style, and color. "They make you feel incredibly comfortable," says Julia Deputy, who bought a pair of cargo pants for her daughter because the operator's daughter had a pair too. Other e-tailers, such as HometownStores.com, personally "greet" each consumer as he or she enters the site, asking if they can help. Still others are upgrading their sites with Internet-telephone capability so that shoppers who have only one phone line can browse online and talk with a salesperson at the same time.

Staffing for these positions requires human resource managers to look for people who have both technical and people skills. Knowledgeable service representatives may mean the difference between success and failure to some companies. Zany Brainy, an Internet toy retailer, insists that its online customer service staff know as much about the company's merchandise as regular store clerks and trains them to become "certified KIDsultants." In fact, as part of its training program, the company sends the online reps to its bricks-and-mortar stores to familiarize them with the toys. Trainees also take a creativity test to determine whether they can think fast in difficult customer situations. Zany Brainy managers believe that having live reps available to answer questions is vital to the success of their business, which is largely educational toys.

"We're learning a lot in the same way that Zany Brainy stores learned from listening to our customers," says Thomas G. Vellios, Zany Brainy's president.

Not all e-tailers agree with this approach. Instead of training employees in customer service, they are putting more effort into stocking items and improving delivery times. But companies that have spent the time and money to train employees to increase their customer service efforts say they are already seeing a payoff. HometownStores.com, which has a personal greeter service, reports that sales rose 30 percent in the first month of the service's operation. Cameraworld.com says that after it installed a service allowing shoppers to talk with reps by Internet phone, 1 in 4 bought something, compared with only 3 of every 100 of all visitors previously.

Consumers will undoubtedly let Internet retailers know—with their credit cards—whether training for personal service makes the difference between a visit and a purchase. Meanwhile, human resource managers have the same task they've always had: to find the best people for the job, train them for excellence, and keep them.

QUESTIONS FOR CRITICAL THINKING

1. Which type (or combination of types) of training do you think would be most effective for online customer service reps? Why?
2. On what basis might online customer service reps be evaluated?

Sources: Lands' End Web site, **www.landsend.com,** accessed February 19, 2001; "Zany Service," Zany Brainy Web site, **www.zanybrainy.com,** accessed February 19, 2001; Timothy J. Mullaney, "Needed: The Human Touch," *Business Week, E.Biz,* December 13, 1999, pp. EB53–54.

---

professional skills and job qualifications they need, but most benefit from additional cultural and language training to help them make successful transitions.

Management Development   A management development program provides training designed to improve the skills and broaden the knowledge of current and potential executives. This type of training is critical to organizations today, because traditional sources of top talent are not as plentiful as they once were. When companies downsized to become more efficient during the 1980s and 1990s, they often eliminated middle-management jobs that once were a training ground for a company's top executives. Also, the share of the workforce in their mid-20s to mid-30s, who traditionally have been the group developing management skills, is shrinking, and a large share of the workforce is approaching retirement age. Without the luxury of developing executive talent slowly over the years, organizations must instead provide programs that help managers quickly learn how to lead a fast-moving company through turbulent times.[17]

Management training is often conducted off the company premises. The content of management development programs may involve reviews of issues facing the company, as well as benchmarking, or learning the best practices of the best

BUSINESS

companies so they can serve as performance standards to strive for. The teachers may be the company's own executives. At other times, managers may be encouraged to receive counseling from an outside management coach, who helps them improve interpersonal skills. When Twentieth Century Fox's chief information officer Justin Yaros wanted to give more responsibility to Sharon McCracken, Fox's vice president of information technology, he asked McCracken to receive coaching to develop her leadership skills. McCracken's coach has helped her focus on broad business issues and improve her ability to convey a vision to her employees.[18]

General Electric's management development programs are widely considered to be a major reason why that company has been able to succeed in a number of different industries. Every January, the company's top 500 executives travel to Boca Raton, Florida, for meetings at which they set companywide priorities and trade ideas. Beginning in March, GE holds quarterly meetings of its Corporate Executive Council to foster development among the company's highest executives. Each April, GE's chief executive, human resource vice president, and other executives evaluate management needs and performance, and they discuss plans and expectations with managers who are viewed as capable of filling top jobs in the future. Managers receive additional guidance and coaching in follow-up meetings led by the chief executive in May and November. Also, executives of the company's business units recommend managers to attend management training at company headquarters to groom them for promotion to top leadership positions. GE managers also can participate in development programs where they analyze case studies of actual challenges facing GE, reporting their recommendations to the company's top leaders.[19]

Performance Appraisals

Organizations also help employees improve their performance by providing feedback about their past performance. A **performance appraisal** is an evaluation of an employee's job performance by comparing actual results with desired outcomes. Based on this evaluation, managers make objective decisions about compensation, promotions, additional training needs, transfers, or firings. Rating employees' performance and communicating perceptions of their strengths and weaknesses are important elements in improving a firm's productivity and profits. Performance appraisals are not confined to business. Government agencies, not-for-profit organizations, and academic institutions also conduct them.

Some firms conduct peer reviews, in which employees assess the performance of coworkers, while other firms allow employees to review their supervisors and managers. A fairly recent trend in performance appraisal is the **360-degree performance review,** a process that gathers feedback from a review panel of about 8 to 12 people, including coworkers, supervisors, team members, subordinates, and sometimes customers. The idea is to get as much frank feedback from as many perspectives as possible. However, this approach to performance appraisal tends to generate considerable work for both employees and managers—who may each have to review 20 or more people—and volumes of paperwork. Also, since the evaluations are anonymous, staff members with an ax to grind can use the system to even scores.

Still, the 360-degree system is extremely popular. A recent survey of large U.S. firms found that two-thirds are using the multirater system, up from about 40 percent in 1995. At United Parcel Service (UPS), managers receive 360-degree reviews every six months. The managers' peers, employees, and supervisors rate them on such areas of performance as leadership, customer focus, people skills, and knowledge of financial and business issues. To ensure that the feedback is used constructively, UPS's human resource department first provides employees with training in the purpose of the regular surveys and ways to use them. The training includes instruction in how to give constructive feedback. Then, after each evaluation is complete, the human

BUSINESS DIRECTORY

➤ **management development program** *training designed to improve the skills and broaden the knowledge of current and potential executives.*

➤ **performance appraisal** *method of evaluating an employee's job performance by comparing actual results with desired outcomes.*

resource department analyzes the data and prepares a report comparing the manager's self-rating with the ratings of others. Managers are expected to develop goals for themselves, based on the feedback from the 360-degree reviews. UPS trainer Hope Zoeller Stith believes managers appreciate the information they get from the process: "I think people are hungry for this type of feedback. It's vitally important to us that communication is ongoing."[20]

COMPENSATION

Human resource managers work to develop an equitable compensation system spanning wages and salaries plus benefits. Because human resource costs represent a sizable percentage of any firm's total product costs, excessive wage rates may make its goods and services too expensive to compete effectively in the marketplace. Inadequate wages, however, lead to difficulty in attracting qualified people, high turnover rates, poor morale, and inefficient production.

The terms *wages* and *salary* are often used interchangeably, but they refer to different types of pay systems. **Wages** represent compensation based on an hourly pay rate or the amount of output produced. Firms pay wages to production employees, maintenance workers, and sometimes retail salespeople. **Salaries** represent compensation calculated on a weekly, monthly, or annual basis. Office personnel, executives, and professional employees usually receive salaries.

An effective compensation system should attract well-qualified workers, keep them satisfied in their jobs, and inspire them to succeed. Most firms base their compensation policies on five factors:

1. Salaries and wages paid by other companies that compete for the same people
2. Government legislation, including the federal, state, or local minimum wage
3. The cost of living
4. The firm's ability to pay
5. Worker productivity

On average, earnings of U.S. workers, adjusted for inflation, declined slightly in the 1980s and first half of the 1990s. During the second half of the decade, earnings began to rise as companies enjoyed greater productivity gains and faced increased competition for qualified workers.[21] Some of that increase is driven by increases in pay for entry-level jobs. Random House—a major publisher—recently raised the bottom of its pay scale by 20 percent, and some local governments require a minimum wage above the national standard. Several cities—including Chicago, Detroit, and Los Angeles—have required businesses with city contracts to pay a so-called *living wage* of as much as $10 per hour. In spite of worries that requiring higher wages will increase unemployment, evidence so far suggests that in a tight labor market, companies will reduce their profit margins rather than cut jobs or leave town.[22]

Many employers balance rewarding workers with maintaining profits by linking more of their pay to superior employee performance. They try to motivate employees to excel by offering some type of incentive compensation in addition to salaries or wages. Most implement several types of incentive compensation programs:

- Profit sharing, which awards bonuses based on company profits
- Gain sharing, which awards bonuses based on surpassing predetermined performance goals
- Lump-sum bonuses, which award one-time cash payments based on performance
- Pay for knowledge, which distributes wage or salary increases as employees learn new job tasks

In addition, many large companies award part of employees' compensation in the form of stock options, which reward executives for increases in their firms' stock prices by giving them opportunities to buy stock at preset prices within certain time periods. Today, almost one-tenth of the compensation of salaried workers is some form of variable pay.[23]

Incentive compensation based on profitability and stock performance is especially common among corporate executives. Most top U.S. executives receive salaries plus long-term incentives such as stock options. The compensation paid to top management has accelerated a trend in which the pay of highly paid employees is growing much faster than the pay of those at the bottom of the compensation ladder. Earnings vary dramatically according to the skills offered and risks taken by employees. Twenty years ago, the typical college graduate earned 38 percent more, on average, than a high school graduate, and that difference has almost doubled to 71 percent today.[24]

EMPLOYEE BENEFITS

In addition to wages and salaries, firms provide many benefits to employees and their families as part of the compensation they pay. Employee benefits are rewards such as retirement plans, insurance, sick leave, child care and elder care, and tuition reimbursement, provided entirely or in part at the company's expense. Some benefits are required by law. Firms are required to make social security contributions and payments to state employment insurance and workers' compensation programs that protect workers in case of job-related injuries or illnesses. The Family and Medical Leave Act of 1993 requires covered employers to offer up to 12 weeks of unpaid, job-protected leave to eligible employees. Firms voluntarily provide other employee benefits, such as child care and health insurance, to help them attract and retain employees. Sometimes companies try to change the way benefits, such as pension plans, are structured, which creates controversy, as in the case of the cash-balance pension plans discussed in the "Solving an Ethical Controversy" box.

Benefits represent a large component of an employee's total compensation. Although wages and salaries account for 72 percent of the typical employee's earnings, benefits make up the other 28 percent. The share of total compensation provided as benefits has grown over the past few decades, especially in the categories of insurance and legally mandated benefits such as Social Security.[25] Figure 9.5 illustrates the breakdown of employer-paid benefits. Perhaps because the cost of noncash benefits is rising, some employers are scaling back. The Department of Labor found that the share of employees with health insurance, life insurance, and paid vacation time declined during the 1990s. However, most employees still receive these benefits, especially at medium-sized and large companies.[26]

A growing number of companies are meeting employee demands for "family-friendly" benefits that help them care for children, aging parents, or other dependents. Such benefits, from child care facilities to paid time off and flexible work hours, assist employees in juggling responsibilities. Almost nine out of ten large U.S. companies currently offer dependent-care spending accounts to help pay for child care, and almost half offer some form of elder-care program.[27] AFLAC, a 2,600-employee insurance company based in Columbus, Georgia, goes further. It has an on-site child-care center for employees' children and grandchildren and offers up to 12 weeks of fully paid leave to employees who need to care for a sick child, parent, or spouse. Such benefits can pay off in terms of improved productivity, greater employee satisfaction, and a chance to recruit the best employees. AFLAC recently received 12,143 applications to fill 546 jobs at the growing company.[28]

BUSINESS

BUSINESS DIRECTORY

> **employee benefits** *employee rewards such as health insurance and retirement plans that employers give, entirely or in part, at their own expense.*

The Dispute over Cash-Balance Pension Plans

One of the challenges a human resource manager faces is determining the best way to distribute benefits to employees. Recently, about 500 large companies, including IBM and AT&T, have switched from traditional pensions to cash-balance pension structures, and they have come under fire for doing so. Under a traditional plan, benefits are calculated based on the number of years an employee has worked and on the average earnings during the last five to ten years of work, which is when earnings are typically highest. The cash-balance plan, on the other hand, bases benefits on a worker's average annual wages over a lifetime. In many situations, older workers would have accumulated more under the traditional plan than under the cash-balance plan, and younger workers, who enter at higher pay rates, will potentially accrue more under the cash-balance plan. And in many situations, workers have not been given a choice about which plan they prefer to adopt.

Are cash-balance pension plans fair to workers?

PRO

1. Unlike traditional plans, cash-balance pensions are portable—workers can transfer them from one company to another when they change jobs—making them potentially more valuable in today's less-permanent work arrangements.
2. Younger and shorter-term workers, who earn fewer benefits under the traditional plans, will do better with the cash-balance plan.
3. Many companies, such as Kodak, give everyone the option to choose which type of plan they want, so those who choose the cash-balance plan do so fairly.

CON

1. Older workers will lose under the cash-balance plan. "Because of the way cash-balance plans are structured," explains AARP senior economic lobbyist David Certner, "hundreds of thousands of midcareer employees may have been stripped of as much as one-half of their expected benefits."
2. Some companies such as IBM have only made choice available to a limited number of employees and will not disclose what the impact of the conversion will be on individual workers.
3. Once the traditional plan has been converted to a cash-balance plan by a company, many older employees actually stop earning any pension benefits at all for several months or even years, a situation known as "wear away" or "pension plateau."

SUMMARY

Not surprisingly, a series of lawsuits have been filed against companies that have made the conversion, particularly those that have not given their employees a choice in the matter. In addition, members of Congress have filed bills to regulate the new plans, and three government agencies—the IRS, Department of Labor, and Equal Employment Opportunity Commission—have begun to review cash-balance pensions.

Sources: Curt Anderson, "Making It Easier to Save," **ABCNEWS.com** September 12, 2000, accessed February 28, 2001, **http://www.abcnew.go.com/ sections/business/dailynews/retirementplans000912.html**; "AARP's Perkins Criticizes Cash Balance Pension Plan Conversions," AARP news release, June 5, 2000. February 28, 2001, **http://www.aarp.org/press/2000/ nr060500a.html**; Robert Lewis, "Objections from Workers, Feds Brake Cash-Balance Bandwagon," *AARP Bulletin,* November 1999, p. 4; Robert F. Hill and William K. Carr, "Are Cash-Balance Pension Plans Good for Older Workers? No: They Conceal Benefit Cutbacks," *AARP Bulletin,* November 1999, p. 29; James M. Delaplane, Jr., "Are Cash-Balance Pension Plans Good for Older Workers? Yes: Workers of All Ages Benefit from New Plans," *AARP Bulletin,* November 1999, p. 29; Stephanie Armour, "Workers Continue Pension Debate," *USA Today,* November 24, 1999, p. B1.

Flexible Benefits

In response to the increased diversity in the workplace, human resource managers are developing creative ways to tailor their benefit plans to the varying needs of employees. One approach sets up **flexible benefit plans,** also called *cafeteria plans.* Such a benefit system offers employees a range of options from which they can choose, including different types of medical insurance coverage, dental and vision plans, life and disability insurance, and extra vacation days. This way, one working spouse may choose his or her firm's generous medical coverage for the entire family and the other spouse can allocate benefit dollars to purchasing other types of coverage. Some plans also offer memberships in health clubs and child-care benefits. Typically, each employee receives a set allowance (called *flex dollars* or *credits*) to pay for purchases from this menu. Xerox Corp. employees receive an allowance to spend on health insurance; if they spend less than the maximum, they can use the balance for benefits such as disability or dental insurance.[29]

Another way of increasing the flexibility of employee benefits involves time off from work. Instead of establishing set numbers of holidays, vacation days, and sick days, some employers give each employee a bank of *paid time off (PTO).* Employees use days from their PTO accounts without having to explain why they need the time.

Flexible Work

Another part of the trend toward responsiveness to employee needs is the option of flexible work plans. **Flexible work plans** are benefits that allow employees to adjust their working hours and places of work to accommodate their personal lives. Flexible work plan options include flextime, compressed workweeks, job sharing, and home-based work. By implementing these benefit programs, employers have reduced employee turnover and absenteeism and boosted productivity and job satisfaction.

Flextime is a scheduling system that allows employees to set their own work hours within constraints specified by the firm. An employer may require employees to be at work between the core hours of 10 A.M. and 3 P.M., rather than the regular workday hours of 9 A.M. to 5 P.M. Outside the core hours, employees can choose when to start and end their workdays, opting either to arrive at work early, say at 7 A.M., and leave early, or to arrive later and work later. Flextime works well in jobs where employees can work relatively independently but not so well when they must work together in teams, such as in manufacturing, or must provide direct customer services. Flextime is common in European countries; an estimated 40 percent of the Swiss workforce and 25 percent of German workers set flextime schedules. Growing numbers of U.S. firms are offering flextime, and increasing numbers of employees are taking advantage of this benefit.

The **compressed workweek** is a scheduling option that allows employees to work the regular number of weekly hours in fewer than the typical five days. Employees might work four ten-hour days and then have three days off each week. Such arrangements not only reduce the number of hours employees spend commuting each week but can stretch out the company's overall workday, providing more availability to customers in other time zones. At Northern Trust in Chicago, one-fourth of the employees have compressed workweeks, as do two-thirds of the employees at insurer USAA.[30]

A **job sharing** program allows two or more employees to divide the tasks of one job. This plan appeals to a growing number of people who prefer to work part-time rather than full-time, such as older workers, students, working parents, and people who want to devote time to personal interests or leisure. Job sharing requires a high degree of cooperation and communication between the partners, but it can permit a company to benefit from the talents of people who do not want to work full-time. Job sharing enabled Sandra Cavanah and Kathleen Layendecker to participate in the exciting but demanding world of Internet start-ups. They had plenty of management experience and a burning desire to be part of the Internet revolution, but they also wanted time with their children. So the two women presented themselves as a team to Mark Jung, CEO of Snowball.com, an Internet media company. Jung was reluctant to accept their proposal to share a position as vice president, but he agreed to try them as joint directors of affiliate services. Each woman spends three days at work, and during their overlapping time, they brief one another and discuss work-related issues. Within a few months, the two women proved themselves and received a promotion to the job they originally wanted. Cavanah believes the job-sharing arrangement offers

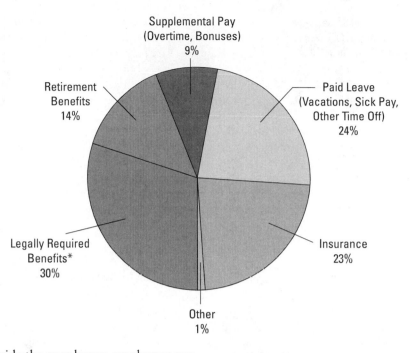

FIGURE 9.5
Types of Employer-Paid Benefits
Note: Percentages do not total 100 due to rounding.
*Social Security, Medicare, unemployment insurance, and workers' compensation

BUSINESS DIRECTORY

➤ **flexible benefit plan**   *benefit system that offers employees a range of options from which they may choose the types of benefits they receive.*

➤ **flexible work plan**   *employment that allows personnel to adjust their working hours and places of work to accommodate their personal lives.*

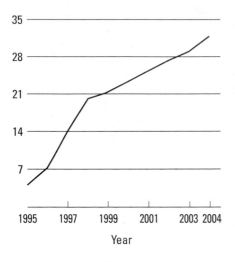

Number of adults using
the internet for business
from home (in millions)

Year

FIGURE 9.6
Workers Using the Internet for
Business from Home

great benefits to workers and company alike: "A job share is intoxicating. You start realizing how much better you are as two, and you want to discuss every issue [with your partner]."[31]

A **home-based work** program allows employees to perform their jobs from home instead of at the workplace. Home-based workers are sometimes called *teleworkers* or *telecommuters,* because many "commute" to work via telephones, e-mail, computers, and fax machines. Working from home has great appeal to disabled workers, elderly people, and parents with small children. Over 16 million teleworkers are currently employed in the United States, and their numbers are growing. About one-fifth of them have supervisors in another state. Although the U.S. is ahead of the European Union in its reliance on telecommuters, three EU countries—Finland, the Netherlands, and Sweden—have a greater share of their workforce engaged in telework, and EU businesses are moving workers home at a faster rate than U.S. businesses.[32]

Because telecommuters work with minimal supervision, they need to be self-disciplined and reliable employees. They also need managers who are comfortable with setting goals and managing from afar. Companies that succeed in their use of telecommuting provide training in how to manage from a remote location by focusing on results and improving communication. At Merrill Lynch, employees and their managers undergo team training that includes opportunities for the employees and managers to discuss their goals and expectations for projects and communications.[33] Under those circumstances, telecommuting can improve productivity. At AT&T, almost three out of ten managers work from home at least one day a week, and many of these teleworking managers work exclusively from home. Since the company began permitting this practice, productivity at AT&T has risen.[34]

The trend toward telework is likely to accelerate because the Internet has provided so many ways to collaborate and share information over great distances. As shown in Figure 9.6, the share of U.S. workers who use the Internet for business from their homes has already surpassed 20 million and is expected to exceed 30 million within two or three years. Often, these workers say they get more done when they are away from workplace distractions.[35]

EMPLOYEE SEPARATION

Either employer or employee can take the initiative to terminate employment. Employees decide to leave firms to start their own businesses, take jobs with other firms, move to another city, or retire. Some firms ask employees who leave voluntarily to participate in **exit interviews** to find out why they decided to leave. These interviews give employers a chance to learn about problems in the workplace, such as unreasonable supervisors or unfair work practices.

Employers sometimes terminate employees due to poor job performance, negative attitudes toward work and coworkers, or misconduct such as dishonesty or sexual harassment. Terminating poor performers is necessary, because they lower productivity and employee morale. Coworkers resent employees who receive the same pay and benefits as themselves without contributing fairly to the company's work. But employers need to document reasons for terminating employees carefully. Complaints of wrongful dismissal are often involved in complaints filed by the EEOC. Besides poor performance, reasons for terminating employees include downsizing and outsourcing.

Downsizing

During the 1980s and 1990s, employers terminated millions of employees, including many middle managers, through downsizing. Downsizing is the process of reducing the number of employees within a firm by eliminating jobs. Many downsizing firms have reduced their workforces by offering early retirement plans, voluntary severance programs, and opportunities for internal reassignment to different jobs. Employers who valued their employees helped them to find jobs with other companies and set up job counseling centers.

Companies downsize for many reasons. The two most common objectives of downsizing are to cut overhead costs and streamline the organizational structure. Some firms report improvements in profits, market share, employee productivity, quality, and customer service after downsizing. Others, however, lose so many valuable, high-performing employees that their ability to compete declines. Chevron downsized some years back and ended up losing some of its most experienced managers. For a while, enough talented people remained, but eventually the company had to begin focusing more on developing management expertise. Now the company conducts annual reviews to spot possible human resource shortages before they occur, and it actively encourages retired employees to serve as consultants.[36]

Eliminating jobs through downsizing often has devastating effects on employee morale. Workers who remain after a downsizing worry about job security and become angry when they have to work harder for the same pay. As their feelings of commitment to their jobs wane, many employees may leave the firm voluntarily to seek employment offering greater job security. This situation has contributed to a shift in values away from loyalty to an employer in favor of concern for individual career success.

Recent employee surveys reveal that workers are now more interested in *career security* than in *job security.* Specifically, the typical employee wants opportunities for training to improve the skills needed for the next job. People are willing to work hard at their current jobs, but they also want to share in the success of their companies by receiving pay-for-performance compensation and stock options. For human resource managers, the new employer–employee relationship requires developing continuous training and learning programs for employees.

Outsourcing

In their continuing efforts to remain competitive against domestic and international rivals, a growing number of firms choose to hold down costs by evolving to a *leaner* organization. A number of functions that were performed previously by company employees may be contracted to other firms whose employees will perform them on a contractual basis in a practice called *outsourcing.* Outsourcing began on a small scale, with firms contracting out services such as maintenance, cleaning, and delivery. Services commonly outsourced today include housekeeping; architectural design; grounds, building, utility, and furniture maintenance; food service; security; and relocation services. Today, outsourcing has expanded to include outside contracting of many tasks once considered fundamental internal functions. Early in the chapter we explain how many small firms outsource the entire human resource function by using the services of PEOs. Large firms also outsource certain human resource tasks such as recruiting, training, and compensation. Some companies outsource such functions as information technology management, production of one or more elements of their product lines, accounting and legal services, and warehousing and delivery services. The "Clicks and Mortar" box discusses one company that helps others retain valuable knowledge that could be lost when employees leave for other jobs, a difficult problem in the fast-moving high-tech sector.

Motorola recently arranged to outsource the production of many of the cellular phones, pagers, and switches bearing its name. The company contracted with Flextronics International, a Singapore firm known for building a variety of electronics at plants in China, Brazil, Hungary, and Mexico. Outsourcing production to flexible factories like those of Flextronics enables Motorola to move quickly in introducing new products without the expense of building and staffing new factories. The

BUSINESS DIRECTORY

➤ **downsizing**   *process of reducing a firm's workforce to reduce costs and improve efficiency.*

Ecora Helps Companies Save a Mountain of Knowledge

Background. Employee turnover is costly for any company. The expenses of recruiting, hiring, and training new employees continue to increase, so it's natural for human resource managers to want to keep employees once they are hired. A major expense in today's information economy is knowledge itself. "Businesses lose millions of dollars when a knowledgeable employee leaves a company," explains Alex Bakman, founder of a growing firm called Ecora. This loss is felt especially hard with information technology (IT) employees who set up and maintain information systems. Often, the employee leaves with his or her knowledge, and the company must scramble to find consultants and others to try to figure out how a network or system operates.

What Happened? Bakman, a self-described "serial entrepreneur," recognized the problem of employee turnover several years ago and founded Ecora, a company designed to help businesses fill their gaps in IT. "What we did is, we basically figured out a way to preserve knowledge about the way IT systems are set up within a company automatically," explains Bakman. Since the people who maintain systems often are not the same people who set them up, Ecora generates reports that help troubleshoot problems. Ecora can deliver its software either via its Web site or through an appliance that functions inside a customer's network. According to Bakman, the service works on 80 percent of the IT systems now in existence.

The Response. Ecora quickly landed more than 350 clients, ranging from small businesses to large ones like Motorola and McGraw-Hill. "The marketplace has really responded," says Bakman. "We are growing fast because we have plenty of interested investors.

We're not a dot.com company with no revenue. [Our software] addresses a real need. This is not 'MyStupidIdea.com.' At the end of the day, every business has got to be a business, selling something that people want."

Today and Counting. Success with a popular product means that Bakman faces a new challenge: finding and hiring his own knowledge workers. "My philosophy on people is very simple," he remarks. "We hire above-average people, we pay above-average wages, we expect above-average results." Bakman notes that being near Boston and having access to the pool of graduates from University of New Hampshire—fifteen minutes from his office—is a plus. "I was actually very pleasantly surprised with the local talent pool," he says. He values his employees and expects a lot of them. Even so, we have to assume that he'll hedge his bets by having his own software in place—just in case there's some turnover.

QUESTIONS FOR CRITICAL THINKING
1. How might Ecora's software help human resource managers carry out some of their core responsibilities?
2. What factors point to Ecora's potential long-term success from a human resources perspective?

Sources: "About Us," Ecora Web site, **www.ecora.com**, accessed February 18, 2001; "Products Briefs: Ecora Gives Plain-English Analyses of Domino Networks," *Group Computing Online*, **www.groupcomputing.com**, November/December 2000; Christine Gillette, "Software Dreams Come True," *Portsmouth Herald Sunday*, October 1, 2000, pp. D1, D7.

idea of an electronics company not building its own products is relatively new, but it is already a widespread practice. Companies like Flextronics build most computer components, and they are expanding their services to include product design, order taking, and repairs.[37] If Motorola outsources production, what is its role as a business? The core challenge left is for Motorola to find out what customers need and tell them how its products can meet those needs.

Outsourcing complements today's focus on business competitiveness and flexibility. It allows a firm to continue performing the functions it does best, while hiring other companies to do tasks that they can handle more competently and cost-effectively than its own people can. Another benefit of outsourcing is the firm's ability to negotiate the best price among competing bidders and the chance to avoid the long-term resource costs associated with in-house operations. Firms that outsource also gain flexibility to change suppliers at the end of contract periods, if they desire. The key to successful outsourcing is a total commitment by both parties to form a partnership from which each derives benefits.

MOTIVATING EMPLOYEES

As illustrated in Figure 9.7, effective human resource management makes important contributions to employee motivation. This ad for Principal Financial Group says, "Do you look forward to going to work? If you had great benefits, you might."

Flexible benefit programs, flexible work schedules, on-site child care, and bonus pay are all designed to motivate people to join a firm and become satisfied and productive employees. When The Coca-Cola Company decided to lay off over 5,000 employees, it tried to boost morale by improving its benefits and working conditions. The company switched to a compressed workweek in which employees work longer on Monday through Thursday in exchange for Friday afternoons off. It also added a new paid holiday, May 8, which is the anniversary of Coca-Cola's introduction in 1886.[38]

In his book *A Great Place to Work,* author Robert Levering examined 20 top U.S. firms to discover what made them outstanding employers. He identified three factors, which he calls "the three *R*s." The first *R* is expanding workers' *responsibility* for their jobs. The second involves sharing the *rewards* that the firm generates as fairly as possible. The third *R* calls for ensuring that employees have *rights,* including some kind of grievance procedure, access to corporate records, and the right to confront those in authority without fearing reprisals.

Building the three *R*s into an organization should contribute to employee morale. **Morale** is the mental attitude of employees toward their employer and jobs. It involves a sense of common purpose among the members of work groups and throughout the organization as a whole. High morale is a sign of a well-managed organization, because workers' attitudes toward their jobs affect the quality of their work. One of the most obvious signs of poor manager–worker relations is poor morale. It lurks behind absenteeism, employee turnover, and strikes. It shows up in falling productivity and rising employee grievances.

In contrast, high employee morale occurs in organizations where employees feel valued and heard and where they are able to contribute what they do best. This climate reinforces a human tendency—that people perform best when they believe they are capable of succeeding.[39] High morale also results from an organization's understanding of human needs and its success at satisfying those needs in ways that reinforce organizational goals. Each person is motivated to take action designed to satisfy needs. A **need** is simply a lack of some useful benefit. It reflects a gap between an individual's actual state and his or her desired state. A **motive** is an inner state that directs a person toward the goal of satisfying a felt need. Once the need—the gap between where a person is now and where he or she wants to be—becomes important enough, it produces tension. The individual is then moved—the root word for motive—to reduce this tension and return to a condition of equilibrium. Figure 9.8 depicts the principle behind this process. A need produces a motivation, which leads to goal-directed behavior, resulting in need satisfaction.

FIGURE 9.7
Principal Financial Group: Recognizing the Importance of Employee Benefits

Maslow's Hierarchy of Needs Theory

The studies of psychologist Abraham H. Maslow have provided an understanding of how employers can motivate employees. Maslow developed a widely accepted list of human needs based on these important assumptions:

- People are wanting animals whose needs depend on what they already possess.

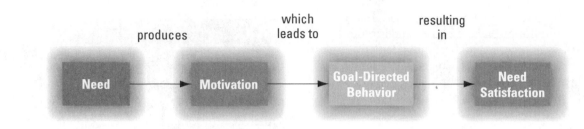

FIGURE 9.8
The Process of Motivation

- A satisfied need is not a motivator; only needs that remain unsatisfied can influence behavior.
- People's needs are arranged in a hierarchy of importance; once they satisfy one need, at least partially, another emerges and demands satisfaction.

In his hierarchy of needs theory, Maslow proposed that all people have basic needs that they must satisfy before they can consider higher-order needs. He identified five types of needs:

1. *Physiological needs.* These most basic human needs include food, shelter, and clothing. In the workplace, employers satisfy these needs by paying salaries and wages and establishing comfortable working environments.
2. *Safety needs.* These needs refer to desires for physical and economic protection. Employers satisfy these needs by providing benefits such as retirement plans, job security, and workplaces that comply with OSHA requirements.
3. *Social (belongingness) needs.* People want to be accepted by family and other individuals and groups. At work, employees want to maintain good relationships with their coworkers and managers and to participate in group activities.
4. *Esteem needs.* People like to receive attention, recognition, and appreciation from others. Employees feel good when they are recognized for good job performance and respected for their contributions.
5. *Self-actualization needs.* These needs drive people to seek fulfillment, realizing their own potential, fully using their talents and capabilities. Employers can satisfy these needs by offering challenging and creative work assignments and opportunities for advancement based on individual merit.

According to Maslow, people must satisfy the lower-order needs in the hierarchy (physiological and safety needs) before they are motivated to satisfy higher-order needs (social, esteem, and self-actualization needs). Table 9.1 elaborates on employers' efforts to motivate employees by satisfying each level of needs.

The diversity of today's workforce challenges employers to satisfy the belongingness needs of people from many different cultures and ethnic backgrounds. The challenge is even greater in organizations where employees telecommute or spend much of their time with clients. At Butler International, a firm providing technical services to business customers, most employees spend their days at client sites, so management consciously seeks ways to reinforce what CEO Ed Kopko calls "a sense of belonging and connectedness to Butler." The firm holds quarterly conference calls with all employees, and employees meet regularly in teams to hear and implement one another's ideas. Butler has also set up its Web site to serve as a "virtual office" for its employees, enabling them to carry out activities employees would normally do in an office setting.[40]

Because most people in industrialized nations can afford to satisfy their lower-order needs, higher-order needs typically play more important roles in motivating employees. Effective managers who understand higher-order needs can design programs to satisfy them. At A. G. Edwards brokerage, management asked its account executives what job title they preferred. They asked to be called "financial consultants," reflecting the service they provide for their clients.[41] Honoring this request was a way for the investment firm to satisfy the consultants' esteem needs. Likewise, a management development program gives an employee the opportunity to grow by

Table 9.1   **Maslow's Hierarchy of Human Needs**

Human Needs	Key Ingredients	Example
1. Physiological needs	Wages and working environment	Granite Rock, an operator of rock, sand, and gravel quarries, pays entry-level employees $15.90 per hour and gives opportunities to move up to a "job owner" or "improvement champion" and earn base pay of $29.50 an hour.
2. Safety needs	Protection from harm, employee benefits	Computer software maker SAS Institute believes that healthy employees make good employees. Two doctors and ten nurses staff its 7,500-square-foot on-site medical center, where employees and their dependents get free consultations, physical exams, emergency care, and many wellness programs.
3. Social (belongingness) needs	Acceptance by other employees	Valassis Communications, which prints coupon inserts for newspapers, sends employees memos introducing new hires. The employees, including the president of the company, then write "welcoming" notes to the new employee. "On your first day on the job, you're so nervous and you feel uncomfortable, and it just really makes a difference and makes you feel comfortable," says one new employee.
4. Esteem needs	Recognition and appreciation from others	Entrepreneur Candace Bryan, chief executive of Kendle, a firm that designs clinical tests for drugs, keeps a photo gallery of her 288 employees posing with their favorite outside activities, from scuba diving to grandparenting. The recognition boosts employee morale and helps to make Bryan an inviting supervisor for prospective employees.
5. Self-actualization needs	Accomplishment, opportunities for advancement, growth, and creativity	Procter and Gamble's promotion-from-within policy gives employees chances to grow. Human resource manager Carol Tuttle has been promoted 7 times in 22 years. She's worked in brand management, advertising, and recruiting and spent 6 years in Venezuela. "It's always challenging, always exciting. I don't think I've ever been bored for 5 minutes," she says.

learning leadership skills. But how do firms satisfy higher-order needs for first-line employees such as factory workers? Some companies are experimenting with ways to add meaning to these workers' jobs through job enlargement and job enrichment.

Motivating Employees through Job Design

In their search for ways to improve employee productivity and morale, a growing number of firms are focusing on the motivation inherent in the job itself. Rather than simplifying the tasks involved in a job, employers are broadening tasks to add meaning and satisfaction to employees' work. Two ways employers are applying motivational theories to restructure jobs are job enlargement and job enrichment.

Job enlargement is a job design change that expands an employee's responsibilities by increasing the number and variety of tasks they entail. Some firms have successfully applied job enlargement by redesigning the production process. A typical approach is to replace assembly lines where each worker repeats the same step on each product with modular work areas in which employees perform several tasks on a single item. Many companies have enlarged administrative assistants' jobs from the traditional tasks of word processing, filing, and answering phones. Those tasks have been largely automated, but especially at companies that have downsized, administrative assistants are taking on a variety of duties related to record keeping and communications. Phyllis Moseley, a senior executive secretary at Dallas-based Central and South West Corp., once spent much of her time with a word processor, but today her duties extend to updating her division's Web site.[42]

Job enrichment is a change in job duties to increase employees' authority in planning their work, deciding how it should be done, and learning new skills that help them grow. Many companies have developed job enrichment programs that empower employees to take responsibility for their work. The concept of worker empowerment is discussed in the next chapter.

Through job enrichment, employers can motivate employees to satisfy higher-level needs. Born Information Services, a consulting firm specializing in

THEY SAID IT

"Every morning in Africa, a gazelle awakens. It knows it must run faster than the lion or it will be killed. Every morning in Africa, a lion awakens. It knows it must run faster than the gazelle or it will starve. It does not matter whether you are a lion or a gazelle. When the sun comes up, you'd better be running."

ANONYMOUS

BUSINESS DIRECTORY

➤ **job enrichment**   *change in job duties to increase employees' authority, responsibility, and skills.*

Table 9.2 Assumptions of Theory X and Theory Y	
Theory X Assumptions	**Theory Y Assumptions**
1. Employees dislike work and will try to avoid it whenever possible.	1. Employees view work as a normal activity as natural as play or rest.
2. Employees must be coerced, controlled, or threatened to achieve organizational goals.	2. Employees will exercise self-direction when they are committed to achieving organizational objectives.
3. Employees try to avoid responsibility and want direction.	3. Employees typically accept and even want to take responsibility for their work.
4. Employees view job security as the most important factor associated with their work.	4. Employees have the intellectual potential to make decisions and find creative solutions to problems.

computer systems, has made interesting work part of its strategy for attracting and keeping talent. When the company was founded a decade ago, big companies relied heavily on mainframe computers, and a business like Born could find a steady stream of clients by writing software for mainframes. However, the work was also routine. Company founder Rick Born concluded, "The really good people want to do new stuff," so he decided to focus on new technologies, beginning with networking and later moving into Internet applications. The company routinely asks employees what new technologies they want to add to their repertoire. The focus on giving employees interesting work has helped Born Information Services exceed its financial goals as well as keep a dedicated staff of talented programmers.[43]

Motivating Employees through Managers' Attitudes

The attitudes that managers display toward employees also influence worker motivation. Managers' traditional view of workers as cogs in the production process—much like lathes, drill presses, and other equipment—led them to believe that money was the best way to motivate employees. Maslow's theory helped managers to understand that employees feel needs beyond those satisfied by monetary rewards.

Psychologist Douglas McGregor, a student of Maslow, studied motivation from the perspective of how managers view employees. After observing managers' interactions with employees, McGregor coined the terms *Theory X* and *Theory Y* as labels for the assumptions that different managers make about worker behavior and how these assumptions affect management styles.[44] Table 9.2 lists these assumptions.

Theory X assumes that employees dislike work and whenever possible try to avoid it. So, managers must coerce or control them or threaten punishment to achieve the organization's goals. Managers who accept this view feel that the average person prefers to receive direction, wishes to avoid responsibility, has relatively little ambition, and can be motivated only by money and job security. Managers who hold these assumptions are likely to keep their subordinates under close and constant observation, holding out the threat of disciplinary action, and demanding that they adhere closely to company policies and procedures.

Theory Y assumes that the typical person likes work and learns, under proper conditions, to accept and seek out responsibilities to fulfill social, esteem, and self-actualization needs. Theory Y managers consider the expenditure of physical and mental effort in work as an ordinary activity, as natural as play or rest. They assume that most people are capable of conceiving creative ways to solve work-related problems but that most organizations do not fully utilize the intelligence that most employees bring to their jobs. Unlike the traditional management philosophy that relies on external control and constant supervision, Theory Y emphasizes self-control and self-direction.

Theory Y requires a different management approach that includes worker participation in decisions that Theory X would reserve for management. If people actually behave in the manner described by Theory X, they may do so because the

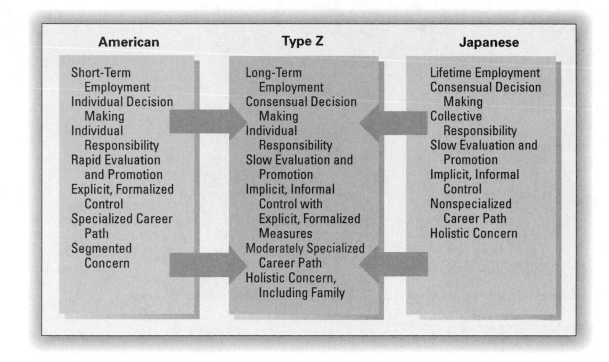

American	Type Z	Japanese
Short-Term Employment	Long-Term Employment	Lifetime Employment
Individual Decision Making	Consensual Decision Making	Consensual Decision Making
Individual Responsibility	Individual Responsibility	Collective Responsibility
Rapid Evaluation and Promotion	Slow Evaluation and Promotion	Slow Evaluation and Promotion
Explicit, Formalized Control	Implicit, Informal Control with Explicit, Formalized Measures	Implicit, Informal Control
Specialized Career Path	Moderately Specialized Career Path	Nonspecialized Career Path
Segmented Concern	Holistic Concern, Including Family	Holistic Concern

FIGURE 9.9
Theory Z Management: A Blend of American and Japanese Methods

organization satisfies only their lower-order needs. If the organization instead designs ways to satisfy their social, esteem, and self-actualization needs as well, employees may be motivated to behave in different ways.

One company that applies Theory Y is Kraft Foods. When Kraft's director of finance for research and development, Kathy McKenna, wanted shorter work hours so that she would have more time for her family, Kraft put her to work on solving the problem—both for herself and other employees. The company appointed her to a task force that studied ways to offer more flexible work arrangements and also encourage women to advance within the organization. McKenna and others on the task force proposed an in-house consulting group: the Financial Resources Group. Qualified employees in finance—men as well as women—could join this group and work part-time on specific projects with specific duties and goals. McKenna, the first to participate, worked four days a week. Others have since joined, and thanks in part to their challenging, visible projects, several have received promotions at Kraft. Ralph Nicoletti, Kraft's vice president of financial planning and analysis, says, "Through the program, we have highly talented people working on important projects—and no one's career is in a holding pattern."[45]

Another perspective on management proposed by UCLA management professor William Ouchi has been labeled Theory Z. Organizations structured on Theory Z concepts attempt to blend the best of American and Japanese management practices. Figure 9.9 shows how the strengths of the two approaches are combined. This approach views worker involvement as the key to increased productivity for the company and improved quality of work life for employees. Many U.S. firms have adopted the participative management style used in Japanese firms by asking workers for suggestions to improve their jobs and then giving them the authority to implement proposed changes.

A growing number of U.S. firms are showing concern for employees and their families. Many employers are adjusting the workplace to satisfy the needs of employees. Internet data company digitalNATION offers them buffets, bowling nights, yachting trips, and outings to play paintball. Says digitalNATION's CEO,

BUSINESS DIRECTORY

➤ **Theory X** *assumption that employees dislike work and will try to avoid it.*

➤ **Theory Y** *assumption that employees enjoy work and seek social, esteem, and self-actualization fulfillment.*

➤ **Theory Z** *assumption that employee involvement is key to productivity and quality of work life.*

A growing number of employers are adjusting the workplace to satisfy the needs of their workforce. If you're working for Kansas City architectural firm Gould Evans Goodman and get tired, you can head for the nap tent. Three separate tents await you. The nap tents are camping tents pitched in a corner of the office and equipped with sleeping bags, pillows, alarm clocks, and soothing music.

Bruce Waldack, "Employees want good salaries, but today, they also want more. They want to like their coworkers and hang out with them." Waldack believes that meeting those needs has helped his company keep most of its employees on board in an industry where employee turnover is the norm.[46] At San Antonio–based Valero Energy, concern for employees extends to the community as well. Valero actively seeks employees who share management's commitment to community involvement. Chief executive Bill Greehey also routinely eats in the employee cafeteria and visits work sites to make himself available to employees. Greehey considers sending a note to employees before surgery a part of letting employees know the company appreciates them. Says Greehey, "[Employees] know when management is sincere."[47]

HUMAN RESOURCE CONCERNS FOR THE 21ST CENTURY

Four kinds of trends—demographic, workforce, economic, and work/life events—are shaping the responsibilities and practices of human resource managers. Managers need to monitor these trends to prepare their organizations for recruiting, training, and retaining workers who are motivated to direct their efforts toward achieving company goals.

Demographic Trends

As discussed in Chapter 1, the percentage of older people in the workforce is growing. This trend poses a number of human resource challenges. One is that a growing share of the workforce will be reaching the age at which employees traditionally retire. Another is that as the population ages, many employees will be juggling the responsibility of caring for aging parents—sometimes along with child-care responsibilities. These challenges require that employers develop more flexibility in creating an environment in which they can attract and keep older workers.

Some companies are responding by structuring jobs to fit the needs and availability of older workers. This accommodation may entail letting workers gradually cut back their hours instead of shifting abruptly from full-time work to retirement. When chemical engineer Jesse B. Krider was approaching retirement at Chevron, the company let him switch to work he found more fulfilling than managing technological operations: he began developing the company's younger executives. Then, when Krider retired as a Chevron employee, the company arranged consulting contracts with him. Explains Chevron vice chairman James N. Sullivan, "He brings 30 to 40 years of detailed technical expertise and experience that we just can't replace right now." At Deloitte Consulting, partners typically retired from their demanding jobs at age 50, when they became eligible for their full pensions. To retain this valuable talent, Deloitte launched its Senior Leaders Program, which gives its top employees the option to redesign their jobs, including the content and hours of their work.

Flexibility at Deloitte kept Daniel G. Gruber with the company. Gruber was worn out from long hours and travel, but instead of leaving, he arranged to work three days a week and says he is doing "the best consulting of [his] life."[48]

Another form of flexibility, discussed earlier, involves flexible benefits. Aging workers rarely need child-care benefits, but they may need time off to help ailing parents. They may also want more health care for themselves or a chance to update their skills for the high-tech economy. Cafeteria plans are attractive in companies with diverse employees, so the use of such plans is likely to accelerate, especially as firms outsource this function.

Flexibility is also necessary in dealing with other aspects of workforce diversity. Because of the rising education level of people with disabilities, more-sophisticated assistive technology, and the influence of the Americans with Disabilities Act, disabled people are entering the workforce in increasing numbers. This trend is just beginning. Of the 15 million Americans of working age who have disabilities, only about one in four is currently employed, but most of the rest would like to have jobs. Among those who are working is Chris Harmon, a customer service representative with Crestar Bank. He cannot use his arms or legs, but voice-activated technology lets him use a computer to resolve customers' problems when they call.

Other technologies that enable disabled workers include software that converts text into synthetic speech, programs that convert the eyes' gazing at points on a computer screen into "typed" commands, and large-type displays on computer screens for workers with visual impairment. Pitney Bowes has introduced an accessible photocopier called the Universal Access Copier System. It features Braille labels, speech recognition software, a large-type graphic-user interface, and buttons that can be operated by mouse, fingers, or pointing stick. The copier is designed to sit low to the ground, so that a user in a wheelchair can operate it. Companies that invest in assistive technology can tap a segment of the workforce that is eager for jobs, as well as keep talented employees who become disabled. When lawyer Joseph Martin began to lose the ability to control his arms and legs because of Lou Gehrig's disease, his employer, Bank of America, outfitted his office with an Eyegaze System by LC Technologies. By directing his gaze to control keys on his computer monitor, Martin uses the system to activate the keys with a laser beam. He uses a voice synthesizer to deliver speeches.[49]

Other sources of diversity involve differences in ethnic and cultural backgrounds. As discussed in Chapters 1 and 2, ethnic minorities are becoming a larger share of all employees. Immigration is an important source of employees in the U.S. Family structures are diverse, too. Increasing numbers of employees will be single people and couples without children. The number of childless couples is expected to grow by almost 50 percent by 2010.

Workforce Trends

The use of contingent workers, already about one-quarter of the workforce, is expected to grow. **Contingent workers** are employees who work part-time, temporarily, or for the length of time involved in fulfilling a specific contract. Hiring contingent workers enables companies to maintain the efficiency of a pared-down workforce while being flexible enough to meet new and changing needs. Traditionally, contingent workers often earned less pay than full-time employees and did not receive benefits or have access to employer-provided pension plans. However, among highly skilled workers, contingent work may be a profitable alternative to traditional employment, as these workers negotiate contracts with generous enough pay to cover self-paid benefits. Figure 9.10 shows a few recent ads for contingent workers. In a survey of workers who consider themselves "free agents," six out of ten respondents said they earn more money as consultants than they did as employees, and over half said their quality of life

BUSINESS DIRECTORY

➤ **contingent worker**   *employee who works part-time, temporarily, or for the length of time involved in fulfilling a specific contract.*

FIGURE 9.10
Current Want-Ads for Contingent Workers

improved after they became consultants. Some people enjoy the variety and flexibility that can accompany contingent work. However, others miss the continuing relationships with coworkers and the predictability of a regular paycheck.[50]

The demand for skilled workers is growing significantly, but employers are concerned about a potential shortage of educated and qualified workers. Adult illiteracy continues to be a problem. Some companies are coping by providing training in basic skills. A growing number of businesses are hiring immigrants, which intensifies the need for expertise in managing a diverse workforce. Human resource professionals are responding with training and advice in this aspect of management.

The wired, globalized marketplace is changing the definition of work hours. Customers and employees are online and on the phone day and night. Although hospital workers and police officers routinely have worked night shifts, night work is becoming part of the lives of new categories of employees. Software engineers are fixing crashed Web sites at midnight, and stockbrokers are tracking stocks on exchanges open halfway around the world. When these workers need toner or light bulbs, they expect to find a store open. An estimated 23 million Americans are currently working nights, evenings, or split or rotating shifts, and their numbers are growing.[51] Not only does this trend pose recruiting challenges, but human resource professionals must find ways to make their own services available to people working when traditional offices are usually closed.

Work teams are expected to be the most important format for high-performance work, with employees from different functions such as marketing, purchasing, service delivery, and human resources collaborating on producing goods and services. Work teams are discussed in detail in the next chapter.

Economic Trends

Changes in the economic environment will create new sets of human resource needs. With a significant portion of economic growth occurring in countries outside the U.S. and Europe, programs and practices of American firms will show a growing influence from conditions and cultures of other countries. Employers will need to recruit global managers and employees with international skills and experience. They also will require human resource plans that address the needs of employees in more than one country. Many will work with benefits providers and professional employer organizations that can help with international operations. For example, Figure 9.11 describes the services of a company that offers insurance and financial benefits in many countries.

With the growing discrepancy between earnings at the top and bottom of America's income distribution, companies will have to consider that some workers will be motivated by relatively basic needs. Job enrichment and similar programs are key trends, but minimum-wage employees may be more concerned about making ends meet. Jen-Cyn, a distributor of galvanized steel, hires workers near its facility in Camden, New Jersey, where wages are low and unemployment is high.

The company helps workers cope with emergencies by making small pay advances when they need help to buy a car or put a security deposit on an apartment. Jen-Cyn also picks up the cost of workers' steel-toed shoes.[52]

Companies will continue to focus on reducing costs, including labor costs. For human resource managers, this trend creates a challenge of finding ways to motivate employees to increase their productivity by making the workplace attractive while reducing employment costs. Employee discontent with executive compensation will grow, and workers will demand an increasing portion of firms' profits. Company shareholders and investors will want stronger voices in determining the employment-related policies that influence a firm's economic performance.

Austin, Texas-based Trilogy Software responds in a creative way to its needs for skilled technical personnel. The firm recruits the best engineers it can hire from college campuses and immediately enrolls them in Trilogy University, a 3-month-long intensive training program where every teacher is a member of the firm's top management. The new-hires learn not only how they can contribute to the company but how they can reshape it. To date, six new companies have been spun off, including an online auto site that sells hundreds of millions of dollars' worth of cars annually. "The same way people look at customers, we look at our jobs," says president Joe Liemandt. "If you don't get the best people into the company, there is no product."

Work/Life Trends

Employer-sponsored benefits and programs for elder care and child care will become increasingly common as employers recognize the need to accommodate aging workers, single parents with children, and two-income families. As a result of improved treatments, some AIDS patients have returned to work. Employers must integrate these workers into their organizations and comply with laws that prohibit discrimination against them.

The physical work environment also has changed. Casual dress policies have become widespread. Even such hallowed institutions of Wall Street as Dean Witter, Goldman Sachs, and J. P. Morgan have permitted their employees to leave their dark suits in the closet—or at least hanging on the office door, in case an important client shows up. HBO and Credit Suisse First Boston each have invited Banana Republic to set up shop in their offices temporarily to help employees define—and find—casual clothing.

Another environmental change is that a growing number of companies are making room for play. Campus Pipeline, which develops Internet software, has an 18-hole indoor golf course installed in its fifth-floor office. At the Los Angeles headquarters of advertising firm TBWA/Chiat/Day, an indoor "Main Street" boasts a basketball court, Tilt-a-Whirl cars, punching bags decorated with executives' faces, and much, much more. Other companies are providing for naps. Technest has furnished a nap room with bunk beds, and Gould Evans Goodman Associates has placed three tents in a quiet corner, along with air mattresses, sleeping bags, and tapes of peaceful music. One company that seems to have all of employees' needs covered is BMC Software. The Houston company stocks its kitchens with free popcorn, fruit, coffee, and soft drinks. A massage therapist works on site, and a pianist plays welcoming music near the entrance each morning. Outside, employees can take a break to enjoy the basketball court, putting green, or beach volleyball court. Also on the premises are a bank, hair stylist, dry cleaner, and other services.[53]

Companies are adding benefits like these to reduce the level of stress that many of today's employees feel, because they are often expected to work ten-hour days or longer. These nonmonetary benefits add convenience to workers' daily lives, and these efforts can make the workplace feel like home. Companies are helping

Does the employee in you agree with what the benefits manager in you is doing?

Your company's most valuable assets aren't made of wire and steel. They're made of body and soul. They're your employees. Which also means you.

At CIGNA, we provide benefit plans that satisfy both the employee and the benefits manager in you. We provide health benefits that deliver medical, dental, pharmacy, vision and behavioral health care through a single, integrated network with integrated administration. We provide disability benefits that are easy to understand, easy to use and easy to administer.

Why do we do this? Because when employee benefits are working better for your employees, you feel a lot better, too.

For more on the health, life and disability benefits that work for you and your employees, visit us at www.cigna.com.

CIGNA
A Business of Caring.

Employee Health, Life and Disability Benefits

FIGURE 9.11
CIGNA: Providing Benefits for a Global Workforce

employees resolve work/life dilemmas by deciding that work *is* life. The big question for the 21st century may become "Why go home?" Some people are already wondering. BMC Software provides many ways to get away from work stress, whether in the gym, on a hammock on the grounds, or in BMC's bright cafeterias. The firm's human resource manager, Roy Wilson, says, "It gives you a balanced life without having to leave." In the 21st century, employees will have to sort out whether their company and colleagues are a valid, partial substitute for community, friends, and family. If a firm no longer needs their talents, will it treat them like valued friends or obsolete resources? Will employees grieve the lost relationships or simply find another company to which they can transfer their affections? Employees' answers to these questions will go a long way toward influencing the meaning of work/life balance in the 21st century.

WHAT'S AHEAD

Treating employees well by enriching the work environment will continue to gain importance as a way to recruit and retain a highly motivated workforce. In addition, managers can tap the full potential of their employees by empowering them to make decisions, leading them to work effectively as teams, and fostering clear, positive communication. The next chapter covers these three means of improving performance. By involving employees more fully through empowerment, teamwork, and communication, companies can benefit from the employees' knowledge while the employees enjoy a more meaningful role in the company.

> ## Summary of Learning Goals

1. Describe the importance of human resource management and the responsibilities of human resource managers.

Organizations devote considerable attention to attracting, training, and retaining employees to help maintain their competitiveness. Human resource managers are responsible for recruiting, selecting, training, compensating, terminating, and motivating employees. They accomplish these tasks by developing specific programs and creating a work environment that generates employee satisfaction and efficiency.

2. Explain the role of human resource planning in an organization's competitive strategy.

A human resource plan is designed to implement a firm's competitive strategies by providing the right number of employees, training them to meet job requirements, and motivating them to be productive and satisfied workers.

3. Discuss the ways firms recruit and select employees and the importance of compliance with employment-related legislation.

Firms use internal and external methods to recruit qualified employees. Internal recruiting, or hiring from within the organization, is less expensive than external methods and can boost employee morale. For needs that the company cannot meet with existing employees, the company may find candidates by encouraging employee referrals, advertising, accepting resumes at its Web site, and using job search Web sites. In selecting from among the resulting candidates, human resource managers must follow legal requirements designed to promote equal employment opportunity. Failure to comply with employment laws can result in legal cases and negative publicity.

4. Summarize how firms train and evaluate employees to develop effective workforces.

Human resource managers use a variety of training techniques, including on-the-job training, computerized training programs, and classroom methods. In addition, management development programs help managers make decisions and improve interpersonal skills. Companies conduct performance appraisals to assess employees' work, as well as their strengths and weaknesses. With 360-degree performance reviews, companies provide feedback from coworkers, supervisors, employees, and sometimes customers.

5. Identify the various pay systems and benefit programs.

Firms compensate employees with wages, salaries, and incentive pay systems such as profit sharing, gain sharing, bonuses, and pay-for-knowledge programs. Benefit programs vary among firms, but most companies offer health care programs, insurance, retirement plans, paid holidays, and sick leave. A growing number of companies are offering flexible work plans such as flextime, compressed workweeks, job sharing, and home-based work.

6. Discuss employee separation and the impact of downsizing and outsourcing.

Either an employer or an employee can decide to terminate employment. Downsizing reduces a company's workforce in an effort to improve the firm's competitive position by reducing labor costs. The company may transfer some responsibilities to contractors, a practice called outsourcing. The goals of outsourcing

are to reduce costs by giving work to more efficient specialists and to allow the company to focus on the activities it does best.

7. Explain the concept of motivation in terms of satisfying employee needs.

All employees feel needs, and these needs differ among employees. Each person is motivated to take actions that satisfy his or her needs. Employers who recognize and understand differences in employee needs can develop programs that satisfy different needs and motivate workers to achieve organizational goals.

8. Describe how human resource managers apply theories of motivation in attracting, developing, and maintaining employees.

Human resource managers develop benefits and other policies and programs to satisfy employees' physiological, safety, social, esteem, and self-actualization needs. Some motivational efforts, such as job enlargement and job enrichment, focus on the job duties themselves. Managers' attitudes toward employees also influence workers' motivation. Managers who display positive attitudes toward employees can motivate them by including them in decision making and problem solving.

9. Identify trends that influence the work of human resource managers in the 21st century.

Demographic, workforce, economic, and work/life trends will influence the tasks of human resource managers. The workforce is aging and becoming more diverse, trends that require great flexibility in terms of human resource management. Organizations are increasing their use of contingent workers, night workers, and teams, and they are addressing skills shortages by providing training. Economic growth outside the U.S. is creating a need for international human resource strategies, and companies are under pressure to meet human resource needs while keeping costs down. Employers of the 21st century also are expected to help employees manage work/life issues.

Business Terms You Need to Know

human resource management 326
employment at will 332
on-the-job training 333
management development program 334
performance appraisal 335
employee benefits 337
flexible benefit plan 338

flexible work plan 339
downsizing 340
job enrichment 345
Theory X 346
Theory Y 346
Theory Z 347
contingent worker 349

Other Important Business Terms

professional employer organization (PEO) 326	flextime 339	morale 343
360-degree performance review 335	compressed workweek 339	need 343
wages 336	job sharing 339	motive 343
salaries 336	home-based work 340	job enlargement 345
	exit interview 340	

➤ Review Questions

1. In what ways have relationships between employers and employees changed during the past century?

2. What are the core responsibilities of human resource management? What are the three main objectives of human resource managers?

3. What methods do companies use to find qualified candidates? How has the Internet influenced this process?

4. In what ways does equal employment opportunity legislation restrict or guide recruitment decisions made by human resource managers?

5. What techniques do firms use to train employees? How has the Internet changed training methods?

6. Identify and define four types of incentive compensation programs. Why are they so popular today?

7. Describe four types of flexible work plans. Name an industry that would be well suited to each type of plan and explain why.

8. Why do companies downsize? What are some of the difficulties they may encounter in doing so?

9. What types of needs on Maslow's hierarchy do firms in industrialized nations try to satisfy? What types of needs must they satisfy in developing nations? Explain the difference.

10. Identify the four trends that are shaping the responsibilities and practices of human resource managers. Why is it important for these managers to monitor these trends?

➤ Questions for Critical Thinking

1. In the United States, CEO compensation is currently 475 times greater than that of the average production worker. Do you think this discrepancy is justified in most cases? Why or why not?

2. Would you accept or keep a job you didn't like because the company offered an attractive benefits package? Why or why not? Do you think you will give the same answer ten years from now? Why or why not?

3. Choose one of the following organizations (or select one of your own) and write a memo describing a plan for outsourcing some of the tasks performed by workers in the company. Give reasons for your choices.

   a. A family resort in Florida

   b. A regional high school

   c. A software development firm

   d. A hospital

   e. An Internet retailer

4. Suppose you are a human resource manager and you have determined that your organization, a health maintenance organization, would benefit from hiring some older workers. Write a memo explaining your reasons for this conclusion. Alternatively, select another company or industry that interests you and make the same determination.

5. Many companies are adding more employer-sponsored benefits aimed at enhancing the quality of their employees' lives. Do you think this trend will continue? Why or why not?

➤ Experiential Exercise

Background: A recent survey of more than 1,200 U.S. workers was conducted by Sibson & Co. in partnership with WorldatWork. The so-called Rewards of Work Study examined worker attitudes toward monetary and nonmonetary rewards to determine their impact on employee performance, retention, and satisfaction.

This exercise focuses on the portion of the study that examined the importance of rewards for performance motivation. Of the five reward categories on which this study is based, a majority of the respondents reported that all five types of rewards are "very important" or "extremely important" to them in motivating their best performance.

Directions: To compare what motivates you to perform your best on the job with the results of this research, complete the following steps:

1. Rank the five reward categories presented in the following table according to how important each is to motivating your best performance.

2. Within each category, rate the reward using numbers 1 through 5, with 1 = most important to 5 = least important.

3. After filling in the table, compare your rankings with the two charts that present the results of the Rewards of Work Study.

4. Be prepared to answer this question: "What have you learned about motivation from this exercise?"

Reward Category	Brief Definition	Your Rank
Direct financial	All the monetary rewards you receive	
Indirect financial	Your benefits	
Work content	The satisfaction that comes from the work you do	
Affiliation	The feeling of belonging to an admirable organization that shares your values	
Career	Your long-term opportunities for development and advancement in the organization	

Results of Rewards of Work Study:

**Overall Results
Importance for Motivation**

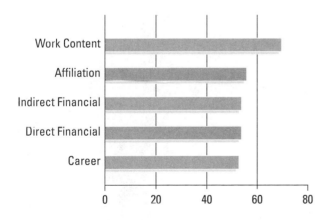

Percent indicating very or extremely important

**Percent of Respondents by Age
Indicating High Importance for
Motivating Performance**

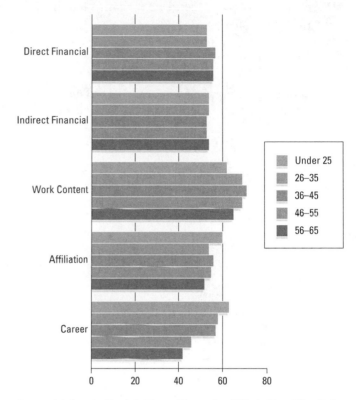

Source: Mulvey, Ledford, LeBlanc, "Rewards of Work: How They Drive Performance, Retention and Satisfaction," *Worldat Work Journal*, Third Quarter 2000, pp. 6–18.

➤ Nothing but Net

1. **Using the Web to find a job.** Many companies advertise open positions on their Web sites. Some will even allow you to submit applications online. Visit the following company Web sites and explore the employment sections. Write a brief summary of the types of positions advertised, the application procedure, and other employment information provided. Based on your visits to the three sites, would you be interested in working for any of these companies? Why or why not?

www.ey.com/global/gcr.nsf/us

www.dell.com/dell/careers/index.html

www.johnsonandjohnson.com/job_posting/
career_ops.html

2. **Employee benefits.** The Bureau of Labor Statistics conducts regular surveys on employee benefits. Visit the Bureau's Web site (**stats.bls.gov.ebshome.htm**) and review the results of the most recent survey. Answer the following:

a. List the benefits offered by the "typical employer."

b. Rank these benefits in terms of importance to you specifically.

c. What percentage of employees enroll in employer health care plans, retirement plans, and flexible spending plans?

d. Are there any differences between the benefits offered by large employers and those offered by small employers?

3. **Outsourcing.** An organization called The Outsourcing Center provides a wide range of information and tools on outsourcing. Visit the Center's Web site and prepare a report on the ten most frequently asked questions concerning outsourcing and the thirteen most common outsourcing mistakes.

www.outsourcing-center.com

Note: Internet Web addresses change frequently. If you do not find the exact sites listed, you may need to access the organization's or company's home page and search from there.

A few years ago, it seemed that every office worker's dream was to go to work in pajamas. Not that they'd actually *go* to work. They'd wake up, get the kids off to school, flick on the coffeemaker, and shuffle off to a corner of the house, where they'd check e-mail messages that had arrived overnight on their home computer. Many employees did try telecommuting, with their companies' sometimes reluctant blessing. But often it didn't work out. People quickly dropped out of the communication loop, had equipment problems, or couldn't establish a work routine—and productivity suffered. Lonely employees drifted back into the office. Companies reeled others in or cut them loose. It seemed as though telecommuting, which was supposed to revolutionize the workforce and the workday, was a flop.

But not at Merrill Lynch, where managers were determined to develop a highly effective workforce and satisfy the needs of employees at the same time. Merrill Lynch concluded that the key to developing a successful group of telecommuters is planning and training. "You can't just give people computers, send them home, and call them telecommuters," explains Camille Manfredonia, a Merrill Lynch vice president in charge of the company's alternative work arrangements group. "There are so many issues. What kind of equipment do you need? How will working from home affect your clients, your manager, your coworkers? How will it affect your career? How do you manage people effectively from a distance?" So Manfredonia and her colleagues set up a rigorous training program for prospective Merrill Lynch telecommuters. First, applicants must submit a detailed proposal for telecommuting; second, they must attend a series of meetings with their own managers and with Manfredonia's group; and third, they spend two weeks simulating a telecommuting situation while still at the office. The program focuses on four principles:

1. Communicate. "Don't expect people to connect with you," says Manfredonia. "You have to stay connected with them."
2. Get organized. "You have to learn to think like a telecommuter," notes Manfredonia. "You have to plan a day ahead, a week ahead."
3. Create new routines and stick with them.
4. Make sure you have the right equipment for the job you plan to do.

Why was developing a strong telecommuting workforce so important to Merrill Lynch? It is part of the company's competitive strategy to satisfy employee needs, create loyalty by doing so, and ultimately increase productivity. When the company started the program, "We didn't care about cutting costs," remarks chief technology officer and senior vice president Howard Sorgen. "Our goal was to promote loyalty and productivity." In addition, Merrill Lynch sought to recruit the best staff from a tight labor market in which there were not enough skilled technical workers. "To become the employer of choice, we had to consider all the things we could be doing above and beyond what we had in place today to give us the edge over the competition," says Sorgen. "One of them was telecommuting." Manfredonia explains further, "We're a technology organization. What do technologists need to be happy [in their work]? . . . You just know that [telecommuting makes] people feel comfortable and productive."

But even though Merrill Lynch developed its telecommuting program methodically and deliberately, there were glitches. For instance, in the beginning the company underestimated the need for technical support for its telecommuters. "If I couldn't get my computer to work, I had to come into the office," recalls Susan Davelman, a systems analyst. So Merrill Lynch organized an information technology support group for its remote workers, available from 7:00 AM to 7:00 PM on weekdays.

Three years after the telecommuting training program was established, an in-house survey showed that employee satisfaction was up 30 percent, particularly among working parents. The magazine *Working Mother* voted Merrill Lynch one of its top 100 places to work, and *Business Week* named the company one of the top family-friendly workplaces. Eileen Keyes, business manager for the alternative work group says that productivity has increased, and turnover among the telecommuting group has decreased. "These people genuinely love their jobs," she says. "There's a lot less stress. Their satisfaction levels are way up." Has the telecommuting program been a successful competitive strategy for Merrill Lynch? Howard Sorgen thinks so. "This is an employee perk to create loyalty to the firm and a happy populace that wants to jump on a grenade for Merrill Lynch," he comments. "It's a tremendous retention tool and a phenomenal recruiting tool."

QUESTIONS

1. How might Merrill Lynch use the telecommuting program to create a more diverse workforce as part of its equal opportunity hiring program?
2. The case discusses ways telecommuters are trained at Merrill Lynch. What steps could the firm take to train in-house managers of those telecommuters?
3. Do you think that telecommuters are motivated by different factors than employees who might be eligible for a telecommuting assignment but choose to continue working at the company?
4. Access Merrill Lynch's Web site at **www.ml.com**. List some ways that the company could use its Web site to assist its telecommuters.

Sources: Company Web site, **www.ml.com,** accessed February 12, 2001; "Merrill Lynch Selects the National Organization on Disability to Receive $50,000 Grant," company press release, November 27, 2000; "Merrill Lynch's Approach to Flexible Workforce Management," *Best Practices*, February 2, 1999, **http://internet8.eapps.com.**

CHAPTER 9

1. "Corporate Information," Ryder System Web site, www.corporate-ir.net/ireye, accessed February 21, 2001; "Ryder Opens the Nation's First Charter School-in-the-Workplace," company press release, August 19, 1999; Susan Adams, "Build It and They Will Come," *Forbes,* April 5, 1999, pp. 66–67.
2. Phaedra Brotherton, "HR Efficiency without the Hassles," *Black Enterprise,* September 2000, pp. 49–50.
3. Stephanie Armour, "Bosses Held Liable for Keeping Workers," *USA Today,* April 12, 2000, p. 1B.
4. Susan DeGrane, "Davis Champions Diversity," *Chicago GSB* (University of Chicago Graduate School of Business), Summer 2000, pp. 12–13.
5. Chuck Salter, "Insanity Inc.," *Fast Company,* January 1999, pp. 101–108.
6. Karen Southwick, "To Survive: Hire Up," *Forbes ASAP,* April 3, 2000, pp. 117–118.
7. Erika Brown, "Have Friends, Will Hire," *Forbes,* October 30, 2000, p. 62.
8. Adrian Slywotzky, "How Digital Is Your Company?" *Fast Company,* February/March 1999, pp. 94–96; John Bryne, "The Search for the Young and Gifted," *Business Week,* October 4, 1999, pp. 108–110+.
9. Hemisphere Inc., "Diversity: The Bottom Line, Part I: Building a Competitive Workforce," *Forbes,* special advertising section, May 31, 1999, pp. 2–6.
10. Cora Daniels, "To Hire a Lumber Expert, Click Here," *Fortune,* April 3, 2000, pp. 267–268, 270.
11. Ellen Paris, "SATs at Work," *Entrepreneur,* March 2000, p. 32.
12. Nicholas Stein, "Winning the War to Keep Top Talent," *Fortune,* May 29, 2000, pp. 132–134+.
13. Byrne, "The Search for the Young and Gifted," p. 116.
14. "While Supplies Last," *HR Magazine,* June 2000, downloaded from the Society for Human Resources Management Web site, www.shrm.org.
15. Christopher Caggiano, "The Appeasement Trap," *Inc.,* September 2000, pp. 39–40+.
16. Charlotte Garvey, "Human, Tech Factors Affect Web Training," *HR News Online,* January 6, 2000, downloaded from the Society for Human Resource Management Web site, www.shrm.org.
17. Robert J. Grossman, "Heirs Unapparent," *HR Magazine,* February 2001, downloaded from the Society for Human Resource Management Web site, www.shrm.org.
18. Rochelle Garner, "Coach Works," *CIO,* February 1, 2000, pp. 114–122.
19. Stein, "Winning the War to Keep Top Talent," p. 134; Ram Charan, "GE's Ten-Step Talent Plan," *Fortune,* April 17, 2000, p. 232.
20. "Travelling beyond 360-Degree Evaluations," *HR Magazine,* September 1999, downloaded from the Society for Human Resource Management Web site, www.shrm.org; Carol Hymowitz, "Do '360' Job Reviews By Colleagues Promote Honesty or Insults?" *The Wall Street Journal,* December 12, 2000, p. B1.
21. Bureau of Labor Statistics, "National Employment Hours, and Earnings," downloaded from the BLS We site, www.bls.gov, November 9, 2000; Dean Foust, "Wooing the Worker," *Business Week,* May 22, 2000, pp. 44–46; R. C. Longworth, "Middle-Wage Earners Lagging," *Chicago Tribune,* September 6, 1999, sec. 1.
22. Steven V. Brull, "What's So Bad about a Living Wage?" *Business Week,* September 4, 2000, pp. 68, 70.
23. Michelle Conlin and Peter Coy, "The Wild New Workforce," *Business Week,* December 6, 1999, pp. 39–42+.
24. U.S. Department of Labor, "Futurework: Trends and Challenges for Work in the 21st Century," Labor Day 1999, downloaded from the Labor Department Web site, www.dol.gov.
25. William J. Wiatrowski, "Tracking Changes in Benefit Costs," *Compensation and Working Conditions* (U.S. Department of Labor), Spring 1999, pp. 32–37.
26. U.S. Department of Labor, "Current Labor Statistics: Compensation & Industrial Relations," *Monthly Labor Review,* July 2000, p. 70.
27. Hewitt Associates, "More Employees Offer Work/Life Benefits to Gain Edge in Tight Labor Market," news release, May 4, 2000, downloaded from the Hewitt Associates Web site, http://was.Hewitt.com.
28. Robert Levering and Milton Moskowitz, "The 100 Best Companies to Work For," *Fortune,* January 10, 2000, pp. 84+.
29. Ron Winslow and Carol Gentry, "Health-Benefits Trend: Give Workers Money, Let Them Buy a Plan," *The Wall Street Journal,* February 8, 2000, pp. A1, A12.
30. Levering and Moskowitz, "The 100 Best Companies to Work For," pp. 98, 110.
31. Patricia Nakache, "One VP, Two Brains," *Fortune,* December 20, 1999, pp. 327–328, 330.
32. International Telework Association & Council, "Telework America (TWA) 2000: Research Results," downloaded from the ITAC Web site, www.telecommute.org, November 7, 2000.
33. Lin Grensing-Pophal, "Training Supervisors to Manage Workers," *HR Magazine,* January 1999, downloaded from the Society for Human Resource Management Web site, ww.shrm.org.
34. Carol Hymowitz, "Remote Managers Find Ways to Narrow the Distance Gap," *The Wall Street Journal,* April 6, 1999, p. B1.
35. Bret Begun, "USA: The Way We'll Live Then," *Newsweek,* January 1, 2000, pp. 34–35; Sue Shellenbarger, "Sailboats and Showers: Home Offices Look Weirder All the Time," *The Wall Street Journal,* March 29, 2000, p. B1.
36. Jennifer Reingold, "Brain Drain," *Business Week,* September 20, 1999, pp. 112–126.
37. Gary McWilliams, "Motorola Becomes Latest Member of Technology-Outsourcing Wave," *The Wall Street Journal,* June 1, 2000, downloaded from the Interactive Edition Web site, http://interactive.wsj.com; Pete Engardio, "The Barons of Outsourcing," *Business Week,* August 28, 2000, pp. 177–178.
38. Del Jones, "Coke Cooks Up Some Perks to Refresh Workers," *USA Today,* May 4, 2000, p. 1B.
39. See, for example, Alexander D. Stajkovic and Fred Luthans, "Social Cognitive Theory and Self-Efficacy: Going beyond Traditional Motivational and Behavioral Approaches," *Organizational Dynamics,* Spring 1998, pp. 62–74.
40. "Motivating and Retaining Employees," *Fortune,* Arthur Andersen Best Practices Awards special advertising section, March 6, 2000.
41. Levering and Moskowitz, "The 100 Best Companies to Work For," p. 92.
42. Charlene Oldham, "Goodbye Secretary, Hello Administrative Professional," *Mobile Register,* May 28, 2000, p. 4F.
43. Donna Fenn, "Redesign Work," *Inc.,* June 1999, pp. 75–76+.
44. Douglas McGregory, "The Human Side of Enterprise (New York: McGraw-Hill, 1960), pp. 33–48.
45. Carol Kleiman, "Flex Hours a Dream for Kraft Finance Workers," *Chicago Tribune,* November 14, 2000, sec. 3, p. 1.
46. Robert McGarvey, "Fun and Games," *Entrepreneur,* April 1999, pp. 82–84.
47. Stein, "Winning the War to Keep Top Talent," p. 133.
48. Reingold, "Brain Drain."
49. Michelle Conlin, "The New Workforce," *Business Week,* March 20, 2000, pp. 64–66, 68; John Williams, "Enabling Technologies," *Business Week,* March 20, 2000, pp. 68, 70.
50. Michelle Conlin, "And Now, the Just-in-Time Employee," *Business Week,* August 28, 2000, pp. 169–170.
51. Laura Bird, "The New 24/7 Work Cycle: Logging Time on the Night Shift," *The Wall Street Journal,* September 20, 2000, downloaded from the Interactive Edition at http://interactive.wsj.com.
52. Emily Barker, "The Company They Keep," *Inc.,* May 2000, pp. 85–86+.
53. Jerry Useem, "Welcome to the New Company," *Fortune,* January 10, 2000, pp. 62–66+; Reshma Memon Yaqub, "The Play's the Thing," *Worth,* pp. 116–123.

CHAPTER 11

PSYCHOLOGY

The main purpose of this last chapter in Part Two of the textbook is to give you an opportunity to decide which notetaking and study methods work best for you. The Psychology Study Guide Practice Test will also assess your skills and help you decide which study/reading methods you find most effective. In this chapter, you will learn to

- Decide which study methods work best for you
- Keep a log of your study time and activities
- Work on your own or with a classmate to prepare for a psychology exam

PREVIEW

Survey the Chapter

List the study aids and materials that you will survey before beginning to take notes on the sample psychology chapter titled "Personality." Be sure to complete the demonstrations in the psychology chapter; these are study aids unique to this chapter.

_____

_____

_____

_____

_____

_____

MAKE CONNECTIONS

List any discussions or writing that you have completed to help you set up hooks and make connections with the topics on personality in this chapter. If you have not read the two psychology articles in Part Three, read them now to gain some background knowledge on this topic.

_____

_____

_____

_____

_____

_____

_____

_____

_____

_____

_____

_____

MONITOR

Place a check mark next to the method of taking notes that you will use as you read the excerpted psychology chapter. You may use a combination of methods. If you choose to use a different method from what is listed, check with your instructor first.

_____ Notetaking with key words

_____ Marking and annotating

_____ Outlining

_____ Other (describe) _____

List your reasons for deciding on this particular method.

_____

_____

_____

_____

_____

Write your notes on loose-leaf paper or directly on the chapter pages. Turn headings and subheadings into questions and read for the answers as well as for main ideas and important details in paragraphs. Have your notes checked by your instructor.

Note: Throughout the chapter, the author uses references to indicate quoted or paraphrased information by placing a name and date or a date only in parentheses. The original sources are listed at the end of the chapter under "References."

RECITE

Once you have finished taking notes on each section of the sample psychology chapter, review your notes and then complete the corresponding part of the *Psychology Study Guide Practice Test* on pages 290–312. For example, when you have completed taking notes on the psychodynamic approach, complete Part I of the practice test; after taking notes on the humanistic approach, complete Part II of the practice test; and so on. Check your answers with those found in Appendix A and analyze your incorrect responses. Part V of the practice test is a review of the entire chapter and may be completed after reviewing all of your notes.

REVIEW

Review Your Notes

How did you review your notes after you had completed them?

_____

_____

_____

_____

_____

How many times did you review the notes, and on the average, how long did it take to review each time?

_____

_____

_____

Did you complete all parts of the psychology practice test? On which part did you do best? worst? Why? Did you analyze your incorrect answers to determine why you answered incorrectly? What did you not understand?

_____

_____

_____

_____

_____

Methods of Studying

What methods of study or reading did you use? Place a check mark next to each of the study methods that you used and estimate the amount of time that you spent completing the activity.

_____   Set up a study/reading schedule   Time spent _____

_____   Made and reviewed summary cards of the four
             approaches   Time spent _____

_____   Made and reviewed vocabulary cards   Time spent _____

_____   Completed review questions   Time spent _____

_____   Created concept maps   Time spent _____

_____   Completed the study guide practice test for this
             chapter   Time spent _____

_____   Checked study guide practice test answers in
             the appendix; analyzed wrong answers   Time spent _____

_____   Wrote predicted test questions and answered
             them   Time spent _____

_____   Completed demonstrations within the sample
             chapter   Time spent _____

_____   Worked with a classmate   Time spent _____

_____   Other   Time spent _____

_____   Other   Time spent _____

PREPARE FOR THE TEST

Review the section titled "Preparing for and Taking the Test" in Chapter 7 to help you prepare for the test. Look at previous test review charts at the end of Chapter 7 to determine how you might change your approach to preparing for and taking the test.

AFTER THE TEST

Complete the test review charts at the end of Chapter 7 for this chapter's practice test to determine what you did right and what you did wrong.

PSYCHOLOGY STUDY GUIDE PRACTICE TEST

Part I—The Psychodynamic Approach

MATCHING I

Match the term in the right column with the definition in the left column by writing the letter in the blank.

_____   1. the energy for all human behavior

_____   2. holds everything you are aware of at a particular moment

_____   3. component of personality that includes the conscience, ideals, and values

_____   4. refers specifically to Freud's original theory, developed about a century ago

_____   5. component of personality that serves as a mediator between the id and reality

_____   6. consistent patterns of thought, feelings, and behavior that originate within the individual

_____   7. consists of the basic drives (for example, eating and sexual activities) and provides the energy for all human behavior

_____   8. approach to the explanation of personality that emphasizes that humans have enormous potential for personal growth

_____   9. holds thoughts, feelings, and desires that are far below the level of conscious awareness and hidden from the outside world

_____   10. approach to the explanation of personality that emphasizes childhood experiences and unconscious motivations and conflicts

_____   11. psychoanalytic technique in which patients are instructed to report anything that occurs to them, no matter how silly or irrelevant it may seem to their conscious judgment

a. id

b. ego

c. libido

d. superego

e. conscious

f. personality

g. unconscious

h. trait approach

i. free association

j. humanistic approach

k. psychoanalytic approach

l. psychodynamic approach

m. social cognitive approach

_____ 12. approach to the explanation of personality that emphasizes social factors (for example, observational learning) and cognitive factors (for example, the way we think about events in our lives)

_____ 13. approach to the explanation of personality that proposes that human personality is a combination of specific, stable personality characteristics (such as shyness or aggressiveness)

MATCHING II

Match the term in the right column with the definition in the left column by writing the letter in the blank.

_____ 14. conscious, remembered story line of a dream

_____ 15. psychosexual stage during which the mouth experiences the most tension

_____ 16. unconscious, underlying aspects of a dream (as interpreted by the analyst)

_____ 17. psychosexual stage during which children's sexual feelings are not obvious

_____ 18. psychosexual stage during which the sex organs experience the most tension

_____ 19. psychosexual stage during which the anal region experiences the most tension

_____ 20. results in an individual being rigidly locked in conflict about a particular erogenous zone

_____ 21. conflict in which a boy's sexual impulses are directed toward his mother, and he views his father as a rival

_____ 22. different parts of the body where the libido becomes centered, which can be stimulated pleasantly to reduce tension

_____ 23. psychosexual stage that occurs during puberty when sexual urges reappear and the genitals once again becomes an erogenous zone

a. fixation

b. oral stage

c. anal stage

d. phallic stage

e. genital stage

f. latency stage

g. latent content

h. manifest content

i. erogenous zone

j. Oedipus complex

MATCHING III

Match the term in the right column with the definition in the left column by writing the letter in the blank.

_____ 24. acting in ways that are characteristic of earlier life stages

_____ 25. describes a person who derives pleasure from being mistreated

_____ 26. pushing back unacceptable thoughts and feelings into the unconscious

_____ 27. attributing your own unacceptable traits and feelings to another person

a. projection

b. repression

c. regression

d. masochistic

e. displacement

f. projective tests

g. reaction formation

_____ 28. deep layer of the unconscious that presumably
stores fragments from our ancestral past

_____ 29. replacing an anxiety-producing feeling with its
exact opposite, often in an exaggerated manner

_____ 30. redirecting an emotion toward someone who is
less dangerous than the real object of that emotion

_____ 31. mental activities designed to reduce the anxiety
that results from conflicts between the id and the
superego

_____ 32. focuses on the development of ideas about the
self in relation to other people—especially
during the first 2 years of life

_____ 33. personality tests in which responses to ambiguous
stimuli presumably reflect a person's needs,
emotions, and other personality characteristics

_____ 34. projective personality test in which a person is
presented with a series of ambiguous scenes
and asked to describe what is happening now,
what happened in the past, and what will occur
in the future

_____ 35. projective personality test during which people
respond to a series of ambiguous inkblots, and
their responses are analyzed according to
characteristics such as recurring themes, number
of responses, the region of the inkblot that
attracts attention, and whether the nature of the
response is common or unusual

h. defense mechanisms

i. collective unconscious

j. Rorschach Inkblot Test

k. object-relations approach

l. Thematic Approach Test
(TAT)

MULTIPLE CHOICE

Write the letter of the *best* answer in the blank.

_____ 36. Which of the following is *not* included in the definition of personality?

    a. consistent patterns
    b. originate within the individual
    c. thoughts, feelings, and behavior
    d. unstable, external characteristics

_____ 37. Which of the following approaches to the explanation of personality is paired
correctly with its major emphasis or assumption?

    a. psychoanalytic—humans have enormous potential for personal growth
    b. social cognitive—emphasizes genetic factors that determine personality
    c. humanistic—emphasizes childhood experiences and unconscious motivations
    d. trait—personality should be described in terms of specific, stable characteristics

_____ 38. Personality theories are important because they

    a. influence our view of human nature.
    b. give different explanations for the origins of psychological disorders.
    c. provide a general framework for explaining why people behave in certain ways.
    d. all of the above.

_____ 39. Dr. Chang wrote an article called "Using Four Dimensions to Compare and
Contrast Theories of Personality." Which of the following was *least* likely to be
one of the dimensions she used in her article?

a. sources of data
b. causes of behavior
c. explanation for people's motivation
d. historical versus contemporary methodology

_____ 40. Which of the following quotations is *most* likely to appear in a book written about the four theoretical approaches to explaining personality by an expert on this topic?

   a. "When all four perspectives are combined, it becomes possible to understand human personality completely."
   b. "We must not make the mistake of assuming that one of these approaches is completely correct and that the rest are, therefore, completely incorrect."
   c. "If the quality of these four approaches is measured in terms of the amount of research data that can support them, then the psychodynamic approach is by far the most successful of the four."
   d. "The beauty of these four perspectives is their mutual exclusivity; that is, each of them deals with such a different aspect of human behavior that there is no overlap among them at all."

_____ 41. Armand is talking to his friend Hans about his weekly counseling session with Dr. Gomez. If Armand mentions the following words—*unconscious, childhood,* and *conflict*—then Dr. Gomez is most likely a psychologist who advocates the _____ approach to the explanation of personality.

   a. trait
   b. humanistic
   c. psychodynamic
   d. social cognitive

_____ 42. The psychodynamic approach emphasizes three central concepts. Which of the following is *not* one of them?

   a. Childhood experiences determine adult personality.
   b. Unconscious conflict underlies most human behavior.
   c. Unconscious mental processes influence everyday life.
   d. Personality develops from an unconscious urge to actualize the potential of human growth.

_____ 43. More recent psychodynamic theorists place _____ emphasis on social roles and _____ emphasis on sexual roles than Freud.

   a. more, less
   b. less, more
   c. equal, less
   d. equal, more

_____ 44. _____ theory has been called "the single most sweeping contribution to the field of personality."

   a. Jung's
   b. Freud's
   c. Horney's
   d. Erikson's

_____ 45. Freud's theory has played an important role in psychology and has also influenced many other aspects of life such as

   a. our everyday vocabulary.
   b. scholars in the humanities.
   c. high school health textbooks.
   d. all of the above.

_____ 46. Dr. Feldsein asked her students to "Give one characteristic of the id" on her last test. Which of the following students received the *highest* score?

   a. Elaine: "The id provides the energy for all our behaviors."
   b. George: "The id develops because of our need to deal effectively with the outside world."
   c. Jerry: "The id guides our moral behavior; without it, we would always be doing bad things."
   d. Cosmo: "The id is the logical, mature part of our personality, which guides our everyday behavior."

_____ 47. When Jerome asked Claire to bring home some file folders from work so that he could organize their income tax records, she said she didn't feel right taking them from work, but that she would go to the office supply store and buy him some folders during her lunch break. From Freud's perspective, Claire has a strong

   a. id.
   b. ego.
   c. superego.
   d. all of the above.

_____ 48. The ego

   a. is completely conscious.
   b. begins to function at birth.
   c. develops because of the need to deal with the outside world.
   d. all of the above.

_____ 49. Information stored in the unconscious

   a. may relate to a particular traumatic childhood event.
   b. cannot influence your behavior if you are not aware of it.
   c. is likely to reach consciousness during normal daily activities.
   d. both *a* and *b*.

_____ 50. The _____ is most likely to help you reach a compromise when you are faced with a difficult moral decision.

   a. id
   b. libido
   c. ego
   d. superego

_____ 51. According to Freud, the superego

   a. is present from birth.
   b. suppresses sexual impulses.
   c. attempts to work against a person's conscience, ideals, and values.
   d. must be controlled by the id in order to keep a person from violating the rules of society.

_____ 52. Ten-year-old Mario spent the whole sermon by daydreaming about the new bike he wanted but couldn't have because his savings account was still $20 short. It was his family's turn to clean up the church after the service and, while he was walking between the pews, he found a $20 bill that must have fallen out of the collection plate. His mind was immediately flooded with confusing and disturbing thoughts telling him to do different things. Freud would say his _____ would tell him to take the money and use it to buy the new bike; his _____ would tell him to give the money to the priest immediately before God could have a chance to punish him; and his _____ would tell him to take the money to his father who might reward him for his honesty by lending him the rest of the money he needed to buy his new bike.

    a. id, ego, superego
    b. superego, ego, id
    c. id, superego, ego
    d. ego, id, superego

_____ 53. According to Freud, the answer to the question about Mario's dilemma is most likely in your _____ and the memory of an extremely traumatic childhood experience is most likely in your _____.

    a. id, ego
    b. id, superego
    c. conscious, unconscious
    d. conscious, id

_____ 54. According to Freud, the _____ and the _____ operate on both a conscious and an unconscious level, whereas the _____ operates only on an unconscious level.

    a. id, ego, superego
    b. ego, id, superego
    c. superego, id, ego
    d. none of the above

_____ 55. Which of the following was *not* one of Freud's methods for studying personality?

    a. dream analysis
    b. free association
    c. object-relations analysis
    d. interpretation of reactions

_____ 56. Manifest content is to _____, as latent content is to _____.

    a. waking, sleeping
    b. dream, nightmare
    c. conscious, unconscious
    d. underlying aspects, story line

_____ 57. According to Freud, all of the following are erogenous zones *except* the

    a. anal region.
    b. brain.
    c. mouth.
    d. genitals.

_____ 58. Which of the following is the *correct* order of Freud's stages of psychosexual development?

    a. oral, anal, latency, genital, phallic
    b. oral, anal, latency, phallic, genital
    c. oral, anal, phallic, latency, genital
    d. oral, anal, genital, latency, phallic

_____ 59. An individual can presumably develop a fixation by being _____ during a particular psychosexual stage.

    a. overindulged
    b. underindulged
    c. either *a* or *b*
    d. neither *a* nor *b*

_____ 60. Linda often dreams about pacifiers and thumbs. Freudian theorists would say that she is most likely in the _____ stage.

    a. anal
    b. latency
    c. oral
    d. phallic

_____ 61. Linda's older brother Jeremy avoids girls completely. Freudian theorists would say that he is most likely in the _____ stage.

    a. oral
    b. latency
    c. phallic
    d. genital

_____ 62. Jeremy's older brother Todd never avoids girls. In fact, he spends most of his time thinking about them, talking to them on the phone, and trying to be with them. Freudian theorists would say that he is most likely in the _____ stage.

    a. anal
    b. latency
    c. phallic
    d. genital

_____ 63. The Oedipus complex presumably helps _____ identify with their _____.

    a. girls, mothers
    b. girls, fathers
    c. boys, mothers
    d. boys, fathers

_____ 64. The ego attempts to reduce anxiety produced by conflicts between the superego and the id by using

    a. fixations.
    b. free association.
    c. erogenous zones.
    d. defense mechanisms.

_____ 65. Defense mechanisms

    a. are abnormal coping processes.
    b. produce only negative outcomes.
    c. illustrate Freud's pessimism about human nature.
    d. are used by the superego in order to control the desires of the id.

_____ 66. Jeff is an unfaithful husband who often accuses his faithful wife of cheating on him. Freud would use the defense mechanism of _____ to explain Jeff's false accusations.

    a. projection
    b. repression
    c. displacement
    d. reaction formation

_____ 67. Phil's boss yells terrible things at him whenever things go wrong in the office. Although Phil hates it when this happens, he is too frightened of his boss to tell him to stop doing it. Unfortunately, whenever this happens, Phil goes home after work and screams at his wife and kids all evening. Freud would say that Phil is using _____ as a defense mechanism in this situation.

a. repression
b. reaction formation
c. displacement
d. projection

_____ 68. Whenever they receive bad news, Joan bursts into tears and locks herself in her room and Jack becomes enraged and starts throwing things. Apparently their predominant defense mechanism is

a. regression.
b. displacement
c. repression.
d. projection.

_____ 69. Gwen has always been sexually attracted to girls, but hid her feelings from other people because of her religion's strict ban on homosexuality. As her urges became stronger when she entered college—and her anxiety about them increased—she tried to counter them by being sexually active with as many men as she could. This unfortunate situation would be explained as an example of _____ by a psychodynamic theorist.

a. regression
b. displacement
c. reaction formation
d. projection

_____ 70. According to Freud, girls' superegos never develop fully because

a. they lack a large, obvious genital organ.
b. their Oedipus complexes are stronger than those experienced by boys.
c. they identify less strongly with their mothers than boys identify with their fathers.
d. both *a* and *c*.

_____ 71. Dr. Mead is an anthropologist who has just written a book in which she argues that human beings from different cultures are much more similar than they are different. The evidence that she has collected to support her thesis consists of a variety of remarkably similar symbols that she has collected from very different cultures; she argues that all cultures share similar memories of an ancestral past. Which of the following psychologists would you be *most* likely to find quoted frequently in her book?

a. Sigmund Freud
b. Anna Freud
c. Karen Horney
d. Carl Jung

_____ 72. Which of the following statements will you be *most* likely to hear if you attend a lecture presented by a psychologist who supports Karen Horney's theory of personality?

a. "Young children feel relatively helpless and threatened."
b. "As normal people develop, they move steadily from introversion to extraversion."
c. "Women begin to feel inferior as soon as they discover they don't possess a penis."
d. "Children learn to move around, under, or between people in order to cope with anxiety."

_____ 73. The self in relationship to other people is the main focus of _____ psychodynamic approach.

    a. Jung's
    b. Horney's
    c. Erikson's
    d. the object-relations

_____ 74. Which of the following combinations is incorrect?

    a. Freud—penis envy
    b. Jung—erogenous zones
    c. Chodorow—interdependence
    d. Horney—affection, hostility, and withdrawal

_____ 75. Ross and Rachel are dating, but their relationship seems doomed because Ross can't seem to commit himself to the relationship, and Rachel can't seem to function unless she is with Ross because she depends on him to make all her decisions. Which of the following psychodynamic theorists would be *most* successful in explaining why Ross and Rachel are like this?

    a. Jung
    b. Horney
    c. Chodorow
    d. Freud

_____ 76. Which of the following is *true* about projective tests?

    a. They have become more popular in recent years.
    b. They involve requesting people to describe their attitudes and beliefs.
    c. They involve the presentation and interpretation of ambiguous stimuli.
    d. The most common projective test is the Minnesota Multiphasic Personality Inventory.

_____ 77. When Dr. Tinta administers the Rorschach Inkblot Test to her clients, she pays very close attention to the _____ of their responses.

    a. themes
    b. number
    c. commonness or unusualness
    d. all of the above

_____ 78. The Rorschach test is

    a. composed of a series of ambiguous scenes.
    b. supported by strong reliability and validity coefficients.
    c. particularly valuable for assessing the personality of Hispanics.
    d. favored by psychologists who support the psychodynamic theory of personality.

_____ 79. As Dr. Bild administered the TAT to Christine, he asked her to

    a. free associate to specific stimulus words.
    b. interrelate all the components of an inkblot.
    c. answer questions about her typical daily activities.
    d. make up a story that tells what is happening in a picture.

_____ 80. The TAT

    a. is insensitive to current motivational and emotional conditions.
    b. is an example of the type of self-report test preferred by behaviorists.
    c. was designed to reveal the unconscious aspects of a person's personality.
    d. can be administered, scored, and interpreted with little or no formal training.

_____ 81. According to psychodynamic theorists, an advantage of projective tests is that

    a. their purpose is obvious to test takers.
    b. they are more standardized than objective tests.
    c. test takers clearly understand the tasks involved.
    d. test takers can relax their defense mechanisms when taking them.

_____ 82. Freud's theory has been criticized because

    a. it is too easy to test.
    b. it is biased against men.
    c. it is too optimistic about human nature.
    d. when it is tested, the studies are often inadequate.

_____ 83. Which of the following statements does _not_ reflect valid praise of Freud's theory?

    a. His concept of the unconscious is valuable to many modern psychologists.
    b. He proposed that women derive pleasure from being mistreated (that is, they are masochistic).
    c. He contributed many useful concepts to psychology (for example, anxiety and defense mechanisms).
    d. He encouraged psychology to explore human emotions and motivation rather than focusing on only thoughts and intellectual reactions.

_____ 84. Which of the following statements is true?

    a. Horney agreed with Freud's theory of penis envy.
    b. Psychological research has produced strong evidence for the existence of penis envy in girls.
    c. The ego gains more and more control over our thought processes as we fall deeper and deeper asleep.
    d. Jung's belief in the collective unconscious was based on the similarity of cultural and religious symbols and themes in many different cultures.

_____ 85. Which of the following statements is false?

    a. The ego begins to function at about the age of 6 months.
    b. A masochistic person derives pleasure from hurting other people.
    c. College students are more likely to hear about Freud from their humanistic professors than their psychology professors.
    d. According to Freud, personality and behavior are created by the constant conflict and interplay among the id, the ego, and the superego.

Part II—The Humanistic Approach

MATCHING

Match the term in the right column with the definition in the left column by writing the letter in the blank.

_____ 1. nonjudgmental and genuine love, given without any strings attached

    a. self-actualization

_____ 2. natural tendency of humans to move forward and fulfill their true potential

    b. conditional positive regard

_____ 3. experienced when parents withhold their love and approval if a child fails to conform to their standards

    c. Maslow's hierarchy of needs

    d. unconditional positive regard

_____ 4. hierarchical arrangement of human needs in which each lower need must be satisfied before the next level of need can be addressed

MULTIPLE CHOICE

Write the letter of the *best* answer in the blank.

_____ 5. The humanistic approach to personality

   a. is very optimistic about human goals.
   b. argues that people have enormous potential for personal growth.
   c. proposes that each person has subjective experiences that are unique.
   d. all of the above.

_____ 6. You are glancing through the table of contents of a book written by Carl Rogers. Which of the following chapter titles are you *most* likely to see?

   a. "Human Kindness: A Mask for Evil Intentions"
   b. "The Role of the Unconscious in Self-Actualization"
   c. "The Contributions of Animal Research to Humanistic Psychology"
   d. "Discovering How Your 'Real World' Differs from Everyone Else's"

_____ 7. Humanistic psychology is often referred to as "Third Force" psychology. The best explanation for this label is that this perspective

   a. emphasized that humans cannot be controlled by either positive or negative forces.
   b. was originally proposed as an alternative to psychoanalytic and behavioristic psychology.
   c. was based on the three basic needs that force all humans to behave (that is, hunger, sexuality, and sleep).
   d. forced psychology to investigate all three major dimensions of personality (past, present, and future).

_____ 8. Rogers viewed _____ as the key to personality.

   a. heredity
   b. the unconscious
   c. reinforcement and punishment
   d. none of the above

_____ 9. Rogers's theory of personality

   a. is based on a set of developmental stages.
   b. places emphasis on behavior rather than mental processes.
   c. proposes that people constantly strive toward self-actualization.
   d. assumes that all people interpret external stimuli in the same way.

_____ 10. The active tendency toward self-_____ provides the underlying basis for the person-centered approach to the explanation of personality.

   a. development
   b. entitlement
   c. manifestation
   d. projection

_____ 11. Which of the following is the *correct* order (from lowest to highest) of Maslow's hierarchy of needs?

   a. physiological, safety, esteem, belongingness and love, self-actualization
   b. belongingness and love, esteem, physiological, self-actualization, safety
   c. self-actualization, esteem, belongingness and love, safety, physiological
   d. physiological, safety, belongingness and love, esteem, self-actualization

_____ 12. If Georgia finds herself constantly pretending to be someone who she is not in order to make people like her, humanistic theorists would say it is likely that she experienced a high degree of _____ regard from her parents while she was growing up.

   a. conditional positive
   b. conditional negative
   c. unconditional positive
   d. unconditional negative

_____ 13. If Luciana is a self-actualized person according to Maslow's theory, then she is *most* likely to possess which of the following characteristics?

   a. a desire to focus more on problems and their solutions than on herself
   b. a very flexible set of personal values that is dependent upon her current situation
   c. the tendency to be cautious and conservative in her thoughts, emotions, and actions
   d. the willingness to conform in order to fit in well with any type of person or group she is with at the time

_____ 14. Humanistic psychology has been criticized because it

   a. is too selfish.
   b. is too pessimistic.
   c. relies too heavily on objective experience.
   d. places too much emphasis on the past and not enough on the present or the future.

_____ 15. Which of the following is *not* considered to be a strength of the humanistic approach?

   a. its integrated view of humans
   b. its emphasis on different realities
   c. its emphasis on human uniqueness
   d. its focus on how an individual's past determines her or his future

_____ 16. Dr. Ward is a psychodynamic theorist, and Dr. D'Amario is a humanistic theorist. If they discussed their theories over a cup of coffee, they would probably discover that they disagree most completely in the area of

   a. data sources.
   b. cause of behavior.
   c. explanation for motivation.
   d. comprehensiveness.

Part III—The Trait Approach

MATCHING

Match the term in the right column with the definition in the left column by writing the letter in the blank.

_____ 1. characteristic seen only in certain situations

_____ 2. person's evaluation of his or her life satisfaction

_____ 3. trait that dominates and shapes a person's behavior

_____ 4. consistent tendency to have certain kinds of beliefs, desires, and behaviors

_____ 5. describes people who actively look for new adventures, new experiences, and risky situations

_____ 6. general characteristic, found to some degree in every person, that shapes much of our behavior

a. trait
b. heritability
c. central trait
d. cardinal trait
e. secondary trait
f. sensation seeking
g. subjective well-being
h. person-situation debate

_____ 7. objective personality test that asks a large number of true-false questions in order to assess personality traits

_____ 8. estimate of how much of the variation in some characteristic can be traced to differences in heredity, as opposed to differences in environment

_____ 9. proposes that the most important cluster of traits include extraversion, agreeableness, conscientiousness, emotional stability, and openness to experience

_____ 10. controversy in which the "person" position indicates that each person possesses stable, internal traits that cause him or her to act consistently in a variety of situations and the "situation" position assumes that an individual's behavior depends upon the specific characteristics of each situation

i. five-factor model (the Big Five traits)

j. Minnesota Multiphasic Personality Inventory (MMPI)

MULTIPLE CHOICE

Write the letter of the *best* answer in the blank.

_____ 11. Of the four personality approaches described in this chapter, the trait approach places the most emphasis on

    a. the self.
    b. individual differences.
    c. unconscious mental processes.
    d. the role of the environment in personality development.

_____ 12. Trait theorists examine whether traits remain stable across

    a. time
    b. situations.
    c. both *a* and *b*.
    d. neither *a* nor *b*.

_____ 13. Gordon Allport's conversation with Sigmund Freud caused him to focus on _____ factors in his explanation of personality.

    a. unconscious
    b. conscious
    c. genetic
    d. environmental

_____ 14. Cardinal traits

    a. are found to some degree in all people.
    b. dominate and shape a person's behavior.
    c. are quite common in most normal people.
    d. all of the above.

_____ 15. Sam is a college student who spends most of his time thinking about rock climbing, reading climbing magazines and books, practicing on the climbing wall he has built in his room, and planning trips to exotic places where he can climb new and more dangerously exciting routes. Allport would call Sam's single-minded preoccupation with rock climbing a _____ trait.

    a. central
    b. secondary
    c. primary
    d. cardinal

_____ 16. Honesty, extraversion, and cheerfulness are examples of _____ traits.

    a. central
    b. cardinal
    c. secondary
    d. peripheral

_____ 17. When Allport said "The same fire that melts the butter hardens the egg," he meant that

    a. no two people respond identically to the same environmental situation.
    b. central traits play a more influential role in human behavior than secondary or cardinal traits.
    c. external situations are more important than internal traits when attempting to predict human differences.
    d. when you make an omelet, it is crucially important to melt the butter before you place the egg in the pan.

_____ 18. Which of the following is *true* in regard to the five-factor model?

    a. It contradicts the trait approach to personality.
    b. It has been assessed with the NEO Personality Inventory.
    c. It has not been supported with the results of cross-cultural research.
    d. It can capture virtually all the rich and diverse aspects of human personality.

_____ 19. Your professor showed a video titled *The Person-Situation Debate*. Which of the following psychologists was *most* likely to have defended the "situation" position most aggressively in this video?

    a. Jung
    b. Allport
    c. Skinner
    d. Maslow

_____ 20. Mischel says we overestimate the consistency of personality characteristics across situations because

    a. we prefer consistency over inconsistency.
    b. we usually see a person in only a limited number of situations.
    c. our natural tendency is to overestimate the probability of all events.
    d. we want to believe that "good" people act good and that "bad" people act bad.

_____ 21. Researchers who have investigated the factors that relate to consistency have discovered that people show more consistency from one situation to the next if

    a. the situation is unfamiliar.
    b. they are observed for a long, rather than a brief, period.
    c. they receive specific instructions about how they should act.
    d. all of the above.

_____ 22. Although he supported the situation side of the person-situation debate for decades, Mischel has recently conceded that people do show remarkable consistency in their personalities if the _____ features of a situation in which they are acting can be specified.

    a. geographical
    b. temporal
    c. financial
    d. psychological

_____ 23. What can we safely conclude about the person-situation debate?

    a. The "person" position is correct.
    b. The "situation" position is correct.

c. Psychologists interested in personality have decided that this debate is non-productive, and they no longer consider it to be a worthwhile topic for research.

d. If we want to predict how people will behave, we need to have some understanding of both their inner traits and the characteristics of the external situation in which they are behaving.

_____ 24. Heritability

a. can be used to study the biological basis of individual differences.
b. typically ranges between 75 and 95 percent for different personality traits.
c. estimates how much variation in a personality characteristic is due to the environment.
d. all of the above.

_____ 25. Research has shown that complex characteristics such as _____ have a strong genetic basis.

a. the tendency to enter certain occupations
b. a person's evaluation of his or her life satisfaction
c. the tendency to look for new adventure, new experiences, and risky situations
d. both *b* and *c*

_____ 26. Recent scientific research on the genetic basis of personality

a. has produced results that favor the "situation" position of the person-satisfaction debate.
b. has determined that environment is more important than heredity in the determination of human personality.
c. indicates that biological factors appear to account for a substantial portion of individual differences in personality traits.
d. has produced results indicating that even highly idiosyncratic behaviors (for example, giggling) are determined primarily by biological factors.

_____ 27. Sam (from question 15) would most likely score high on a test that measures

a. sensation seeking.
b. extraversion.
c. subjective well-being.
d. conditional positive regard.

_____ 28. The Minnesota Multiphasic Personality Inventory (MMPI)

a. is a projective personality test.
b. is often used in psychological research to assess personality traits.
c. contains a series of ambiguous stimuli that test takers must interpret.
d. all of the above.

_____ 29. A question is included in the MMPI if

a. it sounds like it would predict the presence of a particular mental disorder.
b. it has been demonstrated to be a valid question on the TAT and Rorschach.
c. a majority of psychologists and psychiatrists agree that it should be included.
d. a group of people diagnosed with a particular psychological disorder answer it differently than a group of normal people.

_____ 30. The depression, psychopathic, paranoia, and lie scales are all part of the

a. TAT.
b. MMPI-2.
c. Sensation-Seeking Test.
d. Rorschach Inkblot Test

_____ 31. The fact that self-report tests (for example, the MMPI-2) are easy to administer and can be scored objectively in a standardized manner is

    a. a disadvantage because they can be used inappropriately.
    b. an advantage because their results do not depend upon the training or personal interpretations of the examiner.
    c. both *a* and *b.*
    d. neither *a* nor *b.*

_____ 32. One of the true-false items Elena encountered when she took the MMPI-2 was "I never gossip." This item is most likely to be part of the test's _____ scale.

    a. depression
    b. paranoia
    c. psychopathic deviant
    d. lie

_____ 33. The following students were asked to "Compare and contrast the trait approach and the humanistic approaches to the explanation of personality" on their last psychology test. Which statement received full credit for the portion of his answer that *contrasted* these two approaches (that is, explained how they differ from each other)?

    a. Gordon: "The humanistic approach is very optimistic in its explanation for human motivation, and the trait approach is very pessimistic."
    b. Walter: "The trait approach is very comprehensive in its ability to explain human personality, and the humanistic approach tends to lack comprehensiveness."
    c. Carl: "Humanistic and trait theorists obtain their data in radically different ways. Humanistic psychologists perform carefully controlled laboratory research and trait theorists rely more on naturalistic observations."
    d. Abraham: "Trait theorists are beginning to investigate the biological causes of personality differences, whereas humanistic theorists often emphasize environmental factors (for example, conditional positive regard) in their explanations of why people differ from each other in meaningful ways."

_____ 34. The trait approach has been criticized because it

    a. is not an integrated theory.
    b. relies too heavily on the influence of unconscious forces.
    c. concentrates on explaining why people display traits to varying degrees.
    d. overestimates the role of situations in the explanation of individual differences.

_____ 35. Research has demonstrated that people are predictable only in certain circumstances and only when we know the details about the situation. These findings tend to _____ trait theory.

    a. strengthen
    b. weaken
    c. validate
    d. both *a* and *c*

Part IV—The Social Cognitive Approach

MATCHING

Match the term in the right column with the definition in the left column by writing the letter in the blank.

_____ 1. groups of three individuals   a. triads

_____ 2. belief in one's ability to organize and perform the actions required to reach desired goals   b. self-efficacy

                                                          c. reciprocal influences

_____ 3. occurs when new behaviors are learned by watching and imitating the behavior of others

_____ 4. maintain that you must assert yourself and appreciate how different you are from other people

_____ 5. maintain that you must fit in with other people and live in interdependent relationships with them

_____ 6. principle that states there are three factors that strengthen individual differences—personal/cognitive, behavior, and environmental—and that they all influence each other

d. observational learning

e. individualist cultures (independent cultures)

f. collectivist cultures (interdependent cultures)

MULTIPLE CHOICE

Write the letter of the *best* answer in the blank.

_____ 7. The social cognitive approach has its roots in

  a. Skinner's behaviorism.
  b. object-relations theory.
  c. early psychoanalytic theory.
  d. both *b* and *c.*

_____ 8. If Skinner had written a book on personality, which of the following chapter titles would be *least* likely to appear in its table of contents?

  a. "Genetic Effects on Individual Differences"
  b. "How Reinforcement Shapes our Personalities"
  c. "Personality: The Result of Enduring Personal Traits"
  d. "The Effects of Environmental Stimuli on Our Personalities"

_____ 9. Bandura and Skinner would *not* agree that

  a. the human mind makes an important contribution to personality.
  b. people learn more by observational learning than by trial-and-error.
  c. social factors and thoughts contribute to the explanation of human personality.
  d. all of the above.

_____ 10. Which of the following factors does *not* influence the other three, according to Bandura's principle of reciprocal influence?

  a. behavior
  b. unconscious
  c. environment
  d. personal/cognitive

_____ 11. If you were a strong believer in Bandura's principle of reciprocal influence, then you would most likely explain that Jerome is plagued by feelings of incompetence and inferiority because he

  a. assumes he will perform poorly on tasks he is required to perform in new situations.
  b. avoids new situations in which he may have to perform tasks he feels he may not perform well.
  c. "freezes up" and performs poorly when he finds himself required to perform a task in a new situation.
  d. all of the above.

_____ 12. According to Bandura, the most important personal/cognitive characteristic of personality is based on a person's

a. heritability and genetic makeup.
b. self-efficacy, thoughts, and expectations.
c. possible self, dreams, and unconscious wishes.
d. behavioral competence and ability to perform well.

_____ 13. Joe and Tim have just received their final grade reports and are in the process of registering for next semester's classes. Although Joe received a lower grade in Algebra I (a C), he is enthusiastic about enrolling in Algebra I, whereas Tim (who received a B+ in Algebra I) is very hesitant about enrolling in Algebra I because he is afraid he will not do well. It would be more difficult for _____ to explain this puzzling situation than for _____.

a. Skinner, Bandura
b. Kelly, Mischel
c. Bandura, Skinner
d. Bandura, Mischel

_____ 14. Julio has a strong sense of self-efficacy. His friends would describe him as

a. persistent.
b. lacking in confidence.
c. depressed and anxious.
d. a below-average student.

_____ 15. Low self-efficacy often leads to

a. high self-esteem.
b. higher aspirations.
c. depression.
d. superior metacognitive skills.

_____ 16. When Julio (from question 14) is initially unsuccessful at a task, he

a. gives up.
b. tries a new approach.
c. works harder.
d. both *b* and *c*.

_____ 17. You are a job-hunting college senior living in a country that possesses a collectivist culture. You have written rough drafts of your cover letter and resume and have asked your favorite teacher to critique them. Which of the following statements is your advisor likely to suggest you *omit* from the final drafts of these documents?

a. I have often worked as a member of productive teams.
b. I have learned how to deal successfully with a wide variety of people.
c. My extremely strong mathematical skills make me uniquely qualified for this job.
d. The interpersonal skills I developed in my classes will help me fit well into your company.

_____ 18. When her sociology teacher asked her class to write an essay about how they are different from their friends, Allie wrote the following: "I don't think I'm very different from my friends. We all just try to get along together well and do things that are good for our group." Allie is *most* likely a student at the University of

a. Chicago.
b. London.
c. Beijing.
d. Toronto.

_____ 19. Dr. Popiolek is a psychology professor at the University of Michigan who spent a semester as a visiting professor teaching Introductory Psychology at the University of Hong Kong. He found his Chinese students to be very positive about many of the theories and concepts he covered in the class, but when he taught theories of personality, he discovered that they reacted rather negatively toward _____ concept of _____.

   a. Allport's, traits
   b. Jung's, symbols
   c. Maslow's, self-actualization
   d. Bandura's, observational learning

_____ 20. You are a recruiter for a company that has sent you to a college campus to interview graduating seniors for a job. Your favorite interview question is: "Tell me three things about yourself that you believe make you a better candidate for this job than anyone else I will interview on your campus." You will be _least_ likely to hire a(n) _____ student to fill this position if you base your hiring decision on the quality of her or his answer to this question.

   a. Japanese male
   b. Japanese female
   c. American male
   d. American female

_____ 21. The psychoanalytic approach is to _____, as the social cognitive approach is to _____.

   a. less comprehensive, more comprehensive
   b. data collected from normal people, data collected from people in therapy
   c. optimistic explanation for motivation, pessimistic explanation for motivation
   d. internal factors cause behavior, both internal and external factors cause behavior

_____ 22. The social cognitive approach is testable because it

   a. allows data to be collected.
   b. produces testable hypotheses.
   c. is specific rather than general.
   d. all of the above.

_____ 23. Which of the following statements is false?

   a. The social cognitive approach emphasizes conscious rather than unconscious thought processes.
   b. Albert Bandura emphasizes that the human mind makes an important contribution to personality.
   c. Social cognitive theory has been criticized because it is not a comprehensive and integrated theory.
   d. A major disadvantage of the social cognitive theory is that it does not fit in successfully with the research on other aspects of human experience.

Part V—End-of-Chapter Quiz

MULTIPLE CHOICE

Write the letter of the _best_ answer in the blank.

_____ 1. Dr. Taylor asked Sheila to make a poster advertising the convocation he would be presenting next week. He asked her to make the title of his presentation "Consistent Patterns of Thought, Feelings, and Behavior That Originate Within the Individual." Sheila ran out of room on the poster, so instead of using Dr. Taylor's title, she shortened it considerably. Which of the following shortened titles would have pleased Dr. Taylor most?

a. "The Self"
b. "Character"
c. "Personality"
d. "Individuality"

_____ 2. You are listening to your history professor give a lecture on famous thinkers of the 20th century. As he talks about Sigmund Freud, which of the following sentences are you *least* likely to hear him say?

a. "Even Freud's wife regarded his theory to be pornographic."
b. "His theory disagreed with Wundt's, which was the dominant theory of scientific psychology."
c. "His emphasis on the conscious aspects of behavior placed him in conflict with other major theorists."
d. "Even though he was not appreciated during his lifetime, his theory still continues to be a dominant force in psychology and other academic disciplines."

_____ 3. Virginia is an extremely modest person and has never allowed another adult human being to see her without her clothes on. The night before her wedding, she dreamed that a terrible tornado carried off her entire apartment building and left her standing terrified and unprotected in the place where her living room used to be. According to Freud, the manifest content of her dream is _____, and the latent content might be _____.

a. the wedding, her apartment building
b. her apartment building, the wedding
c. her fear of her new husband seeing her naked, the tornado
d. the tornado, her fear of her new husband seeing her naked

_____ 4. Sherry got pregnant and had Lawrence when she was only 13 years old. Deep down inside, she resents Lawrence because he looks like his father (who left town as soon as he heard she was pregnant) and because he reminds her of her carefree childhood that his conception ended so abruptly. Whenever these resentful feelings become too strong, Sherry has a sudden, uncontrollable urge to buy Lawrence all the toys and clothes her credit card will allow. Freud would say that this urge to lavish Lawrence with expensive gifts is a result of

a. projection.
b. regression.
c. repression.
d. reaction formation.

_____ 5. You are reading a book titled *Freud and His Theoretical Descendants,* written by a noted historian of psychology. Which of the following sentences are you *most* likely to encounter?

a. "Karen Horney carried on the legacy of Sigmund Freud by strongly advocating his principle of penis envy."
b. "Carl Jung would have remained faithful to Sigmund Freud if Freud had not decided to place so much emphasis on the role of archetypes and the collective unconscious."
c. "Erik Erikson and Sigmund Freud parted company when Erikson's writings began to imply that human beings stay very much the same during their entire lives, rather than going through a series of stages."
d. "Nancy Chodorow would have argued that Freud should have paid more attention to mothers, because this is an important factor in whether children develop too much or too little independence from others."

_____ 6. Janice asked her father if she could help him fix dinner. He was delighted by her offer and gave her the duty of cutting the six potatoes into cubes for the stew he was making. He got a phone call just as Janice was beginning her job, and he returned 15 minutes later to find her in tears after she put the potato cubes from all six potatoes down the garbage disposal because none of them were as "perfect" as the one he had cut for her as an example. Freud would say that Janice is most likely fixated in the _____ stage of psychosexual development.

a. oral
b. anal
c. phallic
d. latency

_____ 7. The TAT and the Rorschach Inkblot Test share many similarities. Which of the following is *not* one of them?

a. They are projective tests.
b. Both tests require a person to interpret a series of ambiguous scenes.
c. Their results are often interpreted from a psychodynamic perspective.
d. Both tests were designed to help test takers reveal important personal information they might be unwilling or unable to reveal in other circumstances.

_____ 8. Marguerite's parents praise her when she lives up to their very high academic expectations, but ignore her athletic and musical accomplishments. According to Rogers, Marguerite is experiencing _____ positive regard.

a. conditional
b. unconditional
c. preconditional
d. postconditional

_____ 9. The results of the research conducted on the effects of different parenting styles (authoritarian, authoritative, and permissive) has

a. been used as evidence to support Rogers's theory.
b. demonstrated that Rogers's concept of unconditional positive regard is correct.
c. revealed that unconditional positive regard, without clear-cut standards, does not produce self-actualization.
d. demonstrated that authoritarian and permissive parents produce the happiest and most well-adjusted children.

_____ 10. Fernando was a soldier in Operation Desert Storm, during which he was wounded and saw two of his buddies killed. During this period, Maslow would say that Fernando was operating at the _____ level of needs.

a. safety
b. esteem
c. belongingness
d. self-actualization

_____ 11. An important characteristic of the humanistic approach is its emphasis on

a. observable behaviors.
b. our enormous potential for personal growth.
c. unseen forces that motivate our daily behavior.
d. the interaction between behaviors and environments.

_____ 12. The humanistic approach has been criticized because of its

a. overly objective approach.
b. pessimistic approach to human nature.
c. lack of support from traditional research techniques.
d. reliance on the results of research performed with animals.

_____ 13. Your coworker Cheryl always seems to be happy and optimistic at work. Psychologists who agree with Walter Mischel's criticism of trait theory would say that

a. measurements of optimism are not very reliable.

b. you don't appreciate that her optimism is a result of reaction formation

c. a person's level of optimism does not contribute significantly to the Big Five personality traits.

d. your impression is biased because you have seen her in only a limited number of situations (that is, at work).

_____ 14. Dr. Owens told his class to read the section of the text on the trait approach so they could discuss it from a knowledgeable perspective. On the basis of the following four statements made during the discussion, which of Dr. Oweris's students possesses the most accurate knowledge of the material from this section?

a. Seymour: "Sensation seeking appears to be a trait that is influenced more by nurture than nature."

b. Zooey: "The major strength of trait theory is its ability to explain why people's personalities are so different from one another."

c. Franny: "There is considerable empirical support for the hypothesis that many personality traits have a strong genetic component."

d. Holden: "The person-situation debate centers around the fact that when identical twins are placed in different situations, their personalities are more similar to their adopted parents than to their biological parents."

_____ 15. Each year the students and faculty of the Wossamotta University Psychology Department divide themselves into four groups, according to their theoretical approaches to the understanding of human personality, and hold a basketball tournament to decide which perspective is best. This year the trait team had shirts printed for the tournament. What was printed on their shirts?

a. Triads

b. Big Five

c. Optimists

d. Libidos

_____ 16. Charlie considers himself to be an honest person, but he is experiencing a difficult moral dilemma at this very moment. He is not prepared for the test he is taking, he is sitting next to the person who usually gets the highest grade in the class, and this person's answer sheet is in full view. To cheat or not to cheat; that is the question! The fact that Charlie may be having second thoughts about his honesty at this time is evidence of the existence of a _____ from Allport's perspective on personality.

a. central trait

b. hierarchy of needs

c. defense mechanism

d. triad

_____ 17. Which of the following statements about the theory and research regarding the trait approach is true?

a. Trait theorists tend to agree with the person position of the person-situation debate.

b. The Big Five traits include introversion, honesty, self-efficacy, masochism, and psychoticism.

c. People show remarkable consistency in personality characteristics (for example, punctuality) in different situations.

d. Recent biological research has proven that we inherit specific personality traits, rather than just the biological structures that are coded in our DNA.

_____ 18. The most reasonable conclusion we can currently draw from the person-situation debate is that

    a. personality is influenced more by the environment than by our traits.
    b. personality is influenced more by our traits than by the environment.
    c. both traits and environment are important; we are unsure which is the stronger determinant of behavior.
    d. this debate has outlived its usefulness because more accurate methods to measure the genetic determinants of behavior are being currently introduced.

_____ 19. Which of the following approaches to the investigation of personality emphasizes that we need to examine *both* internal personality characteristics *and* external environmental factors in order to understand personality?

    a. trait
    b. humanistic
    c. psychodynamic
    d. social cognitive

_____ 20. According to the social cognitive approach, people's personalities are determined primarily by

    a. sexual desires and unconscious conflicts.
    b. noble motives, such as the desire for self-actualization.
    c. stable internal characteristics, which often have strong genetic causes.
    d. an interaction of our environments, our behaviors, and personal/cognitive factors.

_____ 21. _____ is most likely to have said, "We evaluate our skills and then use that information to regulate our future behaviors."

    a. Freud
    b. Allport
    c. Bandura
    d. Maslow

_____ 22. Felicity's new therapist encourages her to relax during their sessions and tell him about anything that comes into her mind (her dreams, funny or odd things she has said, and puzzling things she has done). If her therapist has a picture of a famous personality theorist on his office wall, it is *most* likely a portrait of

    a. Carl Rogers.
    b. Gordon Allport.
    c. Albert Bandura.
    d. Sigmund Freud.

_____ 23. People who live in collectivist cultures

    a. are reluctant to talk about themselves.
    b. tend to overrate their personal characteristics.
    c. place a great deal of value on self-actualization.
    d. both *a* and *c*.

_____ 24. Imagine that one of your assignments in this class is to assess the validity of the four approaches to personality on the basis of how well they are supported by the results of scientific research. After spending an afternoon in the library locating this type of information, you are *most* likely to conclude that the _____ approach is the most strongly supported by this type of evidence.

    a. psychodynamic
    b. trait
    c. humanistic
    d. social cognitive

CHAPTER 13

Abigail and Brittany Hensel are conjoined twins, produced by a single fertilized egg that somehow failed to divide completely into a pair of separate but identical twins. Together, they have a single pair of legs and a single pair of arms, but two separate heads, as you can see in the photo above. The two girls have the same genetic makeup, and they have shared virtually the same environment. However, their parents have encouraged them to pursue different interests. Abigail enjoys playing with animals, and Brittany likes to draw. Abigail likes blue leggings, but Brittany prefers pink. Sometimes they work together on projects, but other times they work independently. For example, at school they never copy each other's answers on tests.

Their parents report that the daughters have had different temperaments since infancy. Abigail is somewhat more impulsive, and she is usually the leader. Brittany is more reflective, and she is more interested in academics. Brittany wants to be a pilot, but Abigail is planning to become a dentist. (As their dad muses, it will be busy in the cockpit, while one daughter is flying and the other is working on someone's teeth.) However, sometimes the sisters seem to share the same thoughts. While watching television one day, Abigail asked her sister, "Are you thinking what I'm thinking?" Brittany replied "Yup," and they immediately ran off to the bedroom to read the same book (Miller & Doman, 1996).

From *Psychology,* 3rd edition by Matlin, Chapter 13. © 1999. Reprinted with permission of Wadsworth, a division of Thomson Learning.

PSYCHOLOGY

PERSONALITY

The situation of Abigail and Brittany makes us ponder some intriguing questions. How do we define a person? On the practical level, how should the twins' classmates interpret the school rule that only two children can play simultaneously at the Play-Doh table? If Abigail and Brittany are there, can a third child join them? On the theoretical level, how can two people with nearly identical nature and nurture develop such different personalities?

As the story of Abigail and Brittany illustrates, personality is an inherently complicated topic—one that a variety of theorists have attempted to explain. In this chapter, we'll define **personality** as consistent patterns of thought, feelings, and behavior that originate within the individual (Burger, 1993). Notice, then, that we will focus on stable internal characteristics that help to explain our individual differences.

In this chapter, we will consider how four different theories explain personality processes:

1. The **psychodynamic approach,** which originated with Sigmund Freud, emphasizes childhood experiences and unconscious motivations and conflicts.

2. The **humanistic approach** argues that humans have enormous potential for personal growth.

3. The **trait approach** proposes that human personality is a combination of specific stable, internal personality characteristics—such as shyness or aggressiveness.

4. The **social cognitive approach** emphasizes social factors such as observational learning, and cognitive factors such as the way we think about the events in our lives.

Students in my introductory psychology class often wonder why psychologists feel compelled to examine personality theories. A theory is important, however, because it provides a general framework for understanding how personality operates, for explaining why people behave in certain ways, and for predicting how they will act in the future. In addition, each of the four approaches that we will discuss identifies critical questions that psychologists must address. Research therefore advances in a more orderly and systematic fashion (Mendelsohn, 1993; Monte, 1995).

In addition, the personality approach we adopt can influence our view of human nature (Rychlak, 1981). Suppose that a person firmly supports the psychodynamic view, which argues that humans are irrational, and they are governed by unconscious wishes. This individual would approach the judicial system differently than would someone who prefers the social cognitive view, which suggests that people commit crimes because they have observed antisocial models. Also, psychodynamic theorists would probably conclude that wars and other forms of interpersonal violence are inevitable. Firm supporters of the humanistic and social cognitive theories would disagree.

Finally, the various theories of personality provide different explanations for the origin of psychological disorders. The theories also take different approaches in treating these disorders.

In this chapter, we'll compare the four central theoretical approaches on the following dimensions:

1. What is the source of the data? Are the data obtained from an expert therapist, from an objective test, or from self-reports? Are the observations gathered from people in therapy or from a more general population?

2. What is the cause of behavior? Is the cause internal or external to the person?

3. What is the explanation for people's motivation? Is it optimistic, pessimistic, or neutral?

4. How comprehensive is the approach? Does it attempt to explain almost all behavior, or does it focus on isolated characteristics?

Let's discuss two precautions before we begin. First, these four perspectives do not need to be mutually exclusive. To some extent, the approaches focus on different aspects of human personality, so they do not conflict. We should not assume that one approach must be correct, and all others must be wrong. Instead, most psychologists favor one approach but admire some aspects of at least one other approach (Mischel, 1993).

A second precaution is that human personality is inherently complex, and so it cannot be captured adequately even by four different perspectives. In fact, each approach provides just a partial view of individuals. Theorists from each of the four perspectives have gathered information about personality for several decades. Still, we need additional decades—and perhaps even new perspectives—to describe human personality adequately.

THE PSYCHODYNAMIC APPROACH

We'll begin by describing the psychodynamic approach, which was the first theory that attempted to explain personality. The psychodynamic approach emphasizes three central ideas: (1) childhood experiences determine adult personality; (2) unconscious mental processes influence everyday behavior; and (3) unconscious conflict underlies most human behavior. Sigmund Freud was the founder of an earlier version of this theory, called the psychoanalytic approach. This narrower term, the **psychoanalytic approach,** refers specifically to Freud's original theory, developed about a century ago. Whereas Freud emphasized sexual forces, more recent psychodynamic theorists have emphasized social roles (Hale, 1995). Let's begin with Freud's psychoanalytic approach before we consider several of the more recent psychodynamic theories.

Sigmund Freud was born in 1856 and grew up in a Jewish family in Vienna, Austria. He was trained in medicine, with specific interests in neurology and psychological problems. We should emphasize that Freud's theories were controversial during an era known for its straitlaced attitudes toward sexuality. Another source of controversy was that Freud focused on the unconscious. In contrast, most theorists favored the views of Wilhelm Wundt. As we mentioned in Chapter 1, Wundt emphasized conscious experiences.

Freud's (1900/1953) groundbreaking book, *The Interpretation of Dreams,* was not well received. It sold only 351 copies in the first six years after publication (Gay, 1988). However, Freud's approach became more influential several decades later. In fact, his theory has been called "the single most sweeping contribution to the field of personality" (Phares, 1988, p. 75).

Many current psychologists have abandoned Freud; we will examine some of their criticisms later. However, his ideas still influence many areas of popular culture (Eisenman, 1994). Phrases such as "Freudian slip" and "unconscious" are part of our daily vocabulary. High school health textbooks present terms such as "reaction formation" and "repression" as if they were documented facts, rather than theoretical speculations.

In fact, at the college level, you'll typically hear more references to psychoanalytic concepts from humanities professors than from psychology professors (Kihlstrom, 1994; Lippmann, 1996; Welsh, 1994). Scholars in the humanities believe that a Freudian perspective can provide insights about a character's emotions and inner conflicts. However, some scholars may overinterpret the material. For example, Acocella

(1995) describes an essay written by a humanities professor who wanted to demonstrate that the American novelist Willa Cather had been a lesbian. Cather describes a boat named *Berengaria,* and the essayist—in the Freudian tradition—tried to decode the symbol by rearranging the letters into phrases that presumably reveal "lesbian energies," such as *raring engine,* and *barrage* of *anger.* Willa Cather may indeed have been a lesbian, but the essayist should have known that Cather had just sailed back from Europe on an ocean liner called *Berengaria.* Critical thinkers in the humanities—as well as psychology—must consider alternative explanations. In this case, the correct explanation for *Berengaria* did not rely on any symbolism.

Let's begin our overview of the psychodynamic approach by considering Freud's basic theories on the structure of personality. We'll then discuss his methods, the stages of psychosexual development, Freud's views on defense mechanisms, and his representation of women. We'll end by considering some other psychodynamic theories, some personality tests designed to reveal hidden motives, and an evaluation of the psychodynamic approach.

Structure of Personality

Freud envisioned three basic components to personality: the id, the ego, and the superego (Freud, 1933/1964). He proposed that humans are born with an **id,** which is immature and illogical. The id consists of the basic drives—such as eating and sexual activities—and it provides the energy (or **libido**) for all human behavior. Freud also maintained that the id lacks moral judgment; it cannot distinguish between good and evil. The id is unconscious, a "hidden self" that can influence our everyday actions (Elliott, 1994).

The **ego,** in contrast, supposedly develops because the individual needs some factor that will mediate between the id and reality. For example, Freud argues that the ego helps young children delay their impulses until the situation is appropriate.

So far, we have an irrational id, governed by pleasure, and a cooler, calmer ego. Freud's third personality component is the **superego,** which includes a person's conscience, ideals, and values. Parents and society convey these principles. Because the society in Freud's era often discouraged sexual expression, Freud argued that the superego suppresses the sexual impulses.

In Freud's theory, then, the ego acts as a supervisor. The ego must negotiate a compromise between the id's drives and the superego's rules about moral behavior. In Freudian theory, personality is created through the constant conflict and interaction among the id, the ego, and the superego (Domjan, 1993).

Let's see how the id, ego, and superego are related to a person's awareness. Freud compared the human mind to an iceberg. As in Figure 13.1, only a small part of the iceberg rises above the surface of the water. This portion represents the **conscious,** which includes everything you are aware of at a particular moment. As Chapter 5 described, our conscious experiences include our awareness of the outside world and of our perceptions, thoughts, and feelings. As Figure 13.1 shows, only the ego and the superego are included in the conscious. (Note, however, that parts of both the ego and the superego lie below the conscious.) The id is entirely unconscious.

Freud was especially interested in the **unconscious,** which holds thoughts, feelings, and desires that are far below the level of a person's awareness, hidden from the outside world. Freud argued that your unconscious may hold denied wishes or a particularly traumatic childhood memory, for example (Cloninger, 1996). Freud proposed that traumatic memories can influence your behavior, even though you may not be consciously aware of them.

Freud's Methods

In traditional psychoanalysis, the individual is seen several times a week, and analysis may continue for many years. Freud used three major psychoanalytic techniques. One

FIGURE 13.1

Freud's model of the conscious and the unconscious, similar to an iceberg. As you can see, the ego and the superego can be in the conscious or the unconscious, but the id is entirely unconscious.

© Thomson Wadsworth

technique, **free association,** requires patients to report anything that occurs to them; normal critical analysis should be suspended (Macmillan, 1992). The thoughts may be silly, irrational, and unrelated to the present time. For example, a woman in therapy may suddenly recall an image of a perfume bottle. Perhaps this image brings forth a childhood recollection, such as a fight with a brother near her mother's bureau. Freud argued that free association was one tool that allowed access to the unconscious.

A second Freudian method was dream analysis. Freud believed that the unconscious reveals itself though symbols in our dreams. Freud argued that the ego censors our thoughts when we are awake. However, the ego relaxes its control when we sleep, so that the unconscious is more obvious in our dreams (McGrath, 1992). People supposedly try to disguise their own wishes from themselves by constructing symbols. For example, an individual may report a dream about riding on a bull in an amusement-park carousel. This conscious, remembered story line of a dream is called its **manifest content.** The analyst may interpret the bull as a symbol of the person's father. These underlying, unconscious aspects of the dream (as interpreted by the analyst) are called the **latent content.** Try Demonstration 13.1 to see whether you can decode the latent content of a fairy tale.

In the third Freudian technique, the therapist interprets the patient's reactions. For instance, a modern-day analyst was helping a 2-year-old girl who was concerned about broken crayons (Chehrazi, 1986). This analyst interpreted the broken crayons as a symbol of the girl's wish for a penis.

Critical Thinking Exercise 13.1

Write down your answers to the following questions about Freud's psychoanalytic methods.

a. In Chapter 1, we noted that one requirement of critical thinking is to determine whether conclusions are supported by the evidence that has been presented. What evidence is presented that the dream about the carousel bull really does represent the dreamer's father?

b. One of the guidelines for critical thinking, is to consider other possible interpretations of an explanation. What other interpretations can you supply for the little girl's preoccupation with broken crayons?

DEMONSTRATION 13.1   Decoding a Fairy Tale

Psychoanalyst Bruno Bettelheim argues that children's fairy tales are filled with hidden messages, and children can translate the manifest content into the appropriate latent content at an unconscious level. Read the following summary of part of the fairy tale "Sleeping Beauty" and search for the latent-content items; place the corresponding number next to the relevant passage in the summary. To make the task more challenging, I listed four items irrelevant to the story.

Sleeping Beauty

A 15-year-old princess climbs a circular staircase, unlocks the door, and enters the forbidden little room. Inside, an old woman sits spinning cloth. Seeing the cylinder-shaped spindle, the young princess asks the old woman about the object that jumps in such an unusual fashion. She touches the spindle, her finger bleeds, and she falls into a deep sleep. After sleeping for 100 years, she is awakened by a kiss from the handsome prince. They are later married.

Possible Latent-Content Items

1. a brutal father figure
2. a penis
3. bowel movements
4. female genitals
5. sucking (oral needs)
6. menstruation
7. attachment to mother
8. sexual intercourse

Also, what is the implied message of this fairy tale? Check the end of the chapter (Page 448) for the answers to this demonstration.

Sources: Based on Bettelheim, 1977; McAdams, 1990.

Stages of Psychosexual Development

Freud's analysis of his patients persuaded him that psychological disorders have their origin in childhood. As a result, he argued that many aspects of adult personality can be explained by examining important early events. Freud argues that the libido is centered at different body parts—or **erogenous zones**—as the individual matures. The first erogenous zone is the mouth, followed at later ages by the anus, and finally the genitals. Pleasant stimulation presumably reduces the tension that the person experiences.

Freud also proposed that children experience conflicts between urges in these erogenous zones and the rules of society. For example, society demands that toddlers be toilet trained. Suppose that a conflict in a particular erogenous zone is not successfully resolved, because the individual is either overindulged or underindulged. Freud argued that this individual may experience a **fixation,** in which he or she is rigidly locked in conflict about that erogenous zone. Table 13.1 lists the five stages of psychosexual development. Let's explore them further.

During the **oral stage,** the mouth presumably experiences the most tension. The id tries to reduce this tension by encouraging the child to suck on nipples, thumbs, and pacifiers. Freud argued that a fixation during the later part of the oral period—after the child has teeth—produces an adult who is "bitingly" aggressive (Burger, 1993).

In the **anal stage,** the erogenous zone shifts to the anal region. Freud proposed that toddlers experience satisfaction when their anal region is stimulated, for instance by retaining or eliminating feces. Parents begin toilet training at this stage, insisting that the child must eliminate feces in the toilet. Conflict arises between the child's id and the new restrictions imposed by society. According to Freud's theory, a child may become fixated at the anal stage if this conflict is not successfully resolved. An individual may become "anal retentive," too orderly and overly concerned about being punctual. On the other hand, a person can become "anal expulsive," or messy and perpetually late.

During the **phallic stage,** the erogenous zone shifts to the sex organs, and the child presumably finds pleasure in masturbation. Freud proposed that boys in the phallic stage experience an Oedipus complex (pronounced "*Ed*-ih-pus). In the ancient Greek tragedy *Oedipus Rex,* King Oedipus unknowingly kills his father and marries his mother. Similarly, in psychoanalytic theory, an **Oedipus complex** is a

Freud argued that humans first experience tension in the mouth area, during the oral stage.

TABLE 13.1   Freud's Five Stages of Psychosexual Development

AGE	STAGE	DESCRIPTION
0–18 months	Oral stage	Stimulation of the mouth produces pleasure; the baby enjoys sucking, chewing, biting.
18–36 months	Anal stage	Stimulation of the anal region produces pleasure; the toddler experiences conflict over toilet training.
3–6 years	Phallic stage	Self-stimulation of the genitals produces pleasure; the child struggles with negative feelings about the same-gender parent.
6–puberty	Latency	Sexual feelings are repressed; the child avoids members of the other gender.
Puberty onward	Genital stage	Adolescent or adult has mature sexual feelings and experiences pleasure from sexual relationships with others.

conflict in which a boy's sexual impulses are directed toward his mother, and he views his father as a rival. The young boy is afraid that his father may punish him for these desires by castrating him, or cutting off his penis. A boy who develops normally will reduce this castration anxiety by identifying with his father, internalizing his father's values, and developing a strong superego.

Freud maintained that a girl in the phallic stage notices that she lacks a penis, so she experiences penis envy. She decides that her mother was responsible for castrating her and therefore develops hostile feelings for her mother. Meanwhile, her love for her father grows.

During the **latency stage,** children's sexual feelings are not obvious. Children are presumably ashamed and disgusted about sexual issues, and so they tend to avoid members of the other gender. Children are likely to show gender segregation. However, we have no evidence that any of these childhood behaviors are sexually motivated (Macmillan, 1992).

Freud's final stage of psychosexual development is the **genital stage;** during puberty, sexual urges reappear. Genital pleasure during the genital stage now arises from sexual relationships with others.

Defense Mechanisms

So far, we have examined Freud's ideas about the structure of personality, his methods for exploring personality, and his proposed stages of psychosexual development. Another central concept in Freud's psychoanalytical approach is called defense mechanisms. We emphasized earlier that the conflict among the id, the ego, and the superego is central in Freudian theory. Freud proposed that the id may express a particular desire; the superego responds that this desire is socially inappropriate. Then the ego tries to resolve this conflict. Often, it resolves the conflict by using **defense mechanisms,** which are mental activities designed to reduce the anxiety resulting from this conflict (Bond, 1995). Defense mechanisms are often harmless or even helpful, but rigid and severe defense mechanisms can cause psychological problems. Table 13.2 lists five selected defense mechanisms, which Sigmund Freud developed in collaboration with his daughter, Anna.

Notice that Freud's pessimism about people's motivations is often revealed in the defense mechanisms. For example, why are you helpful toward your neighbors? According to Freud, you really feel aggressive toward them (Wallach & Wallach, 1983). You shovel snow from their sidewalk every winter morning because of a reaction formation, designed to reduce the anxiety about your hatred.

Repression, the first defense mechanism listed in Table 13.2, is currently very controversial. Some therapists and theorists believe that people can temporarily forget about an especially traumatic event. More specifically, they argue that traumatized individuals may *repress* these memories (Horowitz, 1994). In contrast, cognitive psychology researchers are more likely to argue that the memories are not really repressed, and some people may even create false memories for events that did not really occur (Bower, 1990; Holmes, 1994). Each position in this controversy is probably at least partially correct (Schacter, 1996; Schooler, 1994).

Freudian Theory and Women

Before we consider other psychodynamic theorists, let's evaluate Freud's theory with respect to gender. During the last three decades, people who support the equality of women and men have argued that Freudian theory reveals gender biases (e.g., Greenspan, 1993; Lerman, 1986; Slipp, 1993). Freud's writing often refers to female inferiority, which he traces primarily to women's lack of a penis. Freud argued that when young girls notice that they are missing a penis, they "feel themselves heavily handicapped . . . and envy the boy's possession of it" (Freud, 1925/1976, p. 327).

TABLE 13.2 Some Representative Defense Mechanisms Proposed by Freud

DEFENSE MECHANISM*	DEFINITION	EXAMPLE
Repression	Pushing back unacceptable thoughts and feelings into the unconscious.	A rape victim cannot recall the details of the attack.
Regression	Acting in ways characteristic of earlier life stages.	A young adult, anxious on a trip to his parents' home, sits in the corner reading comic books, as he often did in grade school.
Reaction formation	Replacing an anxiety-producing feeling with its exact opposite, typically going overboard.	A man who is anxious about his attraction to gay men begins dating women several times a week.
Displacement	Redirecting an emotion (e.g., anger) toward someone who is less dangerous than the "real" object of that emotion.	A husband, angry at the way his boss treats him, screams at his wife.
Projection	Attributing your own unacceptable thoughts and feelings to another person.	An employee at a store, tempted to steal some merchandise, suspects that another employee is stealing.

Sources: Holmes, 1984b; Monte, 1995; Plutchik, 1995.

*These five defense mechanisms are listed with the New Terms at the end of this chapter.

Freud also argued that boys strongly identify with their fathers after resolving their Oedipal conflicts; girls cannot identify as strongly with their mothers because their struggle is milder. As a consequence, girls' superegos never develop fully (Freud, 1925/1976).

We should note that psychological research has not produced evidence for penis envy in females (Fisher & Greenberg, 1977; Lerman, 1986; Slipp, 1993). In fact, most young girls are unconcerned about genital differences. Some are even relieved that they lack this anatomical structure. Consider, for instance, the little girl who took a bath with a young male cousin and observed the genital differences in silence. Later, she said softly to her mother, "Isn't it a blessing he doesn't have it on his face?" (Tavris & Offir, 1977, p. 155). Most important, men and women do not differ significantly in their moral development. In judging Freud, though, many psychodynamic theorists urge us to remember that he was writing in an era when women were considered inferior, so his ideas may partially reflect his own culture and historical context (Kurzweil, 1995).

Other Psychodynamic Theories

Sigmund Freud has influenced our thinking about personality both directly through his own writing and indirectly through the ideas of his followers. We will discuss two of these theorists—Carl Jung and Karen Horney— as well as the more recent object relations theory. In general, you can see that these psychodynamic theorists emphasize social roles, whereas Freud emphasized sexual factors.

Jung's Theory The Swiss analyst Carl Jung (pronounced "Yoong") supported Freud's notion of the unconscious (Jung, 1917/1953). In addition, he proposed an even deeper layer. Jung's **collective unconscious** presumably stores fragments from our ancestral past. Jung's theory proposes, then, that all humans share the same collective unconscious. The concept of a collective unconscious has been greeted more enthusiastically by artists and anthropologists than by psychologists (Robertson, 1995).

Horney's Theory   Karen Horney (pronounced "*Horn*-eye") challenged Freud's theory of penis envy and proposed that women are more likely to envy men's status in society than their genitals (Horney, 1926/1967; Mitchell & Black, 1995). Horney proposed that young children feel relatively helpless and threatened. Children develop several strategies to cope with the anxiety generated by this helplessness (Enns, 1989; Horney, 1945). Specifically, they can show affection or hostility toward others, or they can withdraw from relationships. Horney proposed that normal people balance the three strategies. However, psychological disorders develop when one strategy dominates personality.

Object-Relations Approach   We have summarized the ideas of two theorists who were strongly influenced by Freud. A more recent development is the **object-relations approach,** which focuses on the development of ideas about the self in relation to other people—especially during the first two years of life. This approach minimizes Freud's notion of drives and emphasizes the developing relationship between the self and objects—that is, significant people in the child's life (Klein, 1948; Monte, 1995; "Psychodynamic Therapy: Part II," 1991).

A prominent object-relations theorist is Nancy Chodorow (1978, 1989, 1994), who argues that Freud did not pay enough attention to mothers in his theory. Chodorow argues that boys and girls both identify with their mother initially. Infant girls grow up with a feeling of similarity to their mother, which develops into interdependence, or a connection with others in general. Infant boys, in contrast, must learn that they are different from their mothers in order to develop a male identity. As a consequence, the two genders face different potential problems in their relationships. Specifically, females may not develop sufficient independence, and males may not develop close attachments (Gilligan, 1982).

Psychodynamic Theory and Projective Tests

Another outgrowth of psychodynamic theory is the development of personality tests. Theorists have also devised a variety of personality tests. In this section, we'll consider **projective tests,** in which responses to ambiguous stimuli presumably reflect a person's needs, emotions, and other personality characteristics (Hood & Johnson, 1991). In other words, people supposedly *project* their personality onto the test stimuli. Let's consider two projective tests: the Rorschach Inkblot Test and the Thematic Apperception Test. Be sure that you try Demonstration 13.2 before you read further.

The Rorschach Inkblot Test   Hermann Rorschach (1884–1922) developed an interest in inkblots as an adolescent. The test named after him remains extremely

---

DEMONSTRATION 13.2 Responding to an Inkblot

Look at the inkblot to the right, which is similar to those on the Rorschach Inkblot Test. Try to describe what the picture looks like and what it could be. Write down your answer. (You do not need to use complete sentences.)

When you have finished your description, go back over it and explain how you arrived at each part of that description. It is important to keep in mind, however, that this is not a true Rorschach Test, and that these tests cannot be interpreted adequately without expert training. Furthermore, as the text that follows will explain, many critics question its value.

popular, despite its many critics (Butcher & Rouse, 1996; Dawes, 1994). In the **Rorschach Inkblot Test,** people respond to a series of ambiguous inkblots, and the responses are analyzed according to characteristics such as recurring themes, number of responses, the region of the inkblot that attracts attention, and whether the nature of the response is common or unusual (Groth-Marnat, 1990). The Rorschach is designed to be administered by rigorously trained professionals (Exner, 1993).

Consider how one woman responded to a card from the Rorschach Test, a black-and-white design similar to the colored inkblot you saw in Demonstration 13.2. Ms. T. reported that she saw "two elephants, two itty-bitty elephants . . . fighting over a roach—cockroach—in the middle . . . [The elephants] both got their—their snozzoolas—[half laughs] or their trunks or whatever you call them wrapped around the cockroach" (Allison et al., 1988, p. 203).

The therapist's interpretation of this response proposed that Ms. T.'s defense mechanisms had attempted to shrink a huge attacking creature into something small and playful. The interpretation also noted that she focused on the elephants' penislike trunks, yet she blocked momentarily on the specific name. As you can see, the Rorschach provides psychodynamically inclined professionals with a test rich with symbolic possibilities.

Some researchers argue that the Rorschach has moderate reliability (consistency) and validity—the ability to accurately measure psychological disturbances (Exner, 1993, 1996; Parker et al., 1988). However, others complain that the scoring is arbitrary and that people's scores are not correlated with their psychiatric diagnoses. These critics also point out that these negative findings have not been sufficiently publicized (Dawes, 1994; Wood et al., 1996a, 1996b). An additional problem is that the Rorschach has not been adequately tested with people of color (Velásquez & Callahan, 1992).

The Thematic Apperception Test The second most popular projective test is the TAT (Butcher & Rouse, 1996). The **TAT (Thematic Apperception Test)** consists of a series of ambiguous scenes; the test taker describes what is happening now, what happened in the past, and what will occur in the future. The TAT was first published by Christina Morgan and Henry Murray in 1935. The TAT is used to test achievement motivation. It has also been used to assess power motivation, and the test has been used to assess personality in psychiatric and in business settings (Butcher & Rouse, 1996; McClelland, 1993).

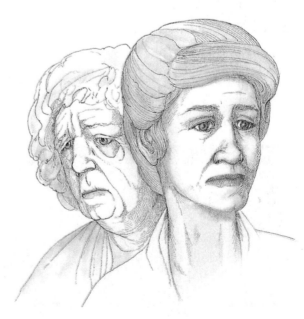

FIGURE 13.2

An item similar to those that appear on the Thematic Apperception Test.

© Thomson Wadsworth

PSYCHOLOGY

Critical Thinking Exercise 13.2

Write down your answers to the following questions about projective tests.

a. A group of psychologists wants to test the validity of the Rorschach Inkblot Test. They give the test to 100 people who have requested treatment for a variety of psychological disorders. The psychologists score the Rorschach responses according to the established methods for detecting depression on the Rorschach. Next, these same psychologists diagnose these people on the basis of self-reported psychological symptoms. The psychologists discover that, of the 50 people diagnosed with depression, 40 also have high depression scores on the Rorschach. Of the 50 people diagnosed with other disorders, only 5 have high depression scores on the Rorschach. Why would you mistrust this validity study?

b. A student is taking the TAT in the hopes of being admitted to a special college program. The first card shows a violin, and he thinks he will receive a high score on this test if he finds a common thread interwoven through all the scenes. He painstakingly forces every story to revolve around violins and music. Why would this student's attempt to second-guess the purpose of this test lower the validity of the measure?

Figure 13.2 shows a picture similar to those on the TAT. In responding to a picture like this, one woman wrote the following:

> This is a woman who has been quite troubled by memories of a mother she was resentful toward. She has feelings of sorrow for the way she treated her mother; her memories of her mother plague her. These feelings seem to be increasing as she grows older and sees her children treating her in the same way she treated her mother. (Aiken, 1989, p. 364)

The TAT was designed to bring forth unconscious tendencies that a person may be unwilling or unable to reveal, such as difficulties with one's parents. The test takers presumably project their personality traits onto one or more of the characters in the scene. The people administering and scoring the test must be professionally trained, as you can imagine. Furthermore, the results are often interpreted within a psychodynamic framework. For instance, when a person omits reference to a gun shown in a TAT picture, the examiner may conclude that he or she tends to repress aggressive impulses (Phares, 1988).

Research on the TAT shows that the reliability and validity measures are rather low when personality traits are assessed (Groth-Marnat, 1990; Kaplan & Saccuzo, 1993; Spangler, 1992). Furthermore, like the Rorschach, the TAT has primarily been tested with European American populations (Velásquez & Callahan, 1992).

Evaluation of Projective Tests   One major advantage of projective tests is that their purpose is disguised: Test takers are seldom aware how their responses will be interpreted (Anastasi, 1988). In contrast, people taking an objective self-report test often choose the most socially acceptable answer, even if another option is more truthful. For instance, a suicidal person may answer "No" to the question "Sometimes I think I may kill myself." However, he or she may spontaneously mention death on a projective test.

A second, related advantage proposed by psychodynamic psychologists is that test takers can presumably relax their defense mechanisms (such as repression) when taking a projective test. This relaxation supposedly allows the release of unconscious material (Groth-Marnat, 1990).

A significant disadvantage of projective tests is that they are not as standardized as objective tests. Several alternative scoring systems may be used, and the accuracy also depends on the examiner's professional training.

Most important, the reliability and the validity of projective tests may not be high, even when the examiners are well trained (Wolfe, 1998). A test is not useful when people receive inconsistent scores and when the test does not measure the characteristic it is supposed to measure!

TABLE 13.3 A Summary of the Psychodynamic Approach

	PSYCHODYNAMIC APPROACH
Source of Data	Obtained from expert analyst from people in therapy.
Cause of Behavior	Internal conflict, unconscious forces, childhood experiences.
Explanation for Motivation	Pessimistic explanation.
Comprehensiveness of Theory	Very comprehensive.

Evaluation of the Psychodynamic Approach

We have outlined Freud's theory and also briefly noted the contributions of three more recent theories. Let's now evaluate the psychodynamic approach, as represented by the prototype theorist, Sigmund Freud. Table 13.3 summarizes four important characteristics of psychodynamic theory.

What can we conclude about Freud's psychodynamic approach, roughly a century after it was formulated? By current standards, this theory has several major problems:

1. *It is difficult to test.* Psychodynamic theory emphasizes the unconscious. However, the unconscious rarely expresses itself directly, so this concept is difficult to measure. Also, consider the following problem: Suppose that an analyst suspects that a man is pessimistic. Any pessimistic feelings expressed during therapy will be taken as evidence of pessimism. However, any *optimistic* feelings will also be considered evidence of pessimism, because these feelings could be a reaction formation against the original pessimism. We cannot test a theory if it predicts both a particular characteristic and its opposite.

2. *When the theory is tested, the studies are often inadequate.* The psychodynamic approach has often been criticized for improper methodology (e.g., Dawes, 1994; Ewen, 1993). For instance, the observers may be biased, interpreting ambiguous observations so that they are consistent with a particular part of the theory. Critical Thinking Exercise 13.1 noted that the little girl's concern about broken crayons may have a more obvious explanation than penis envy. Also, Freud's theory was based on a nonrepresentative sample from a different era. We cannot generalize from a small sample of troubled, wealthy Viennese people—studied about a century ago—to a variety of cultures in the current era. Some psychodynamic theorists have conducted more rigorous research (e.g., Shulman, 1990; Silverman & Weinberger, 1985). However, other theorists argue that we still have no clear-cut evidence of basic Freudian concepts such as repression (e.g., Holmes, 1994).

3. *Freud's theory is biased against women.* As we noted earlier, Freud maintained that women have inferior moral judgment, a gender bias that is not supported by the research. He also proposed that women are **masochistic** (pronounced "mass-uh-*kiss*-tick"), which means that they would derive pleasure from being mistreated. This view does a disservice to women, and it encourages people to think—incorrectly—that women enjoy being battered or raped (Caplan & Caplan, 1994).

4. *It is too pessimistic about human nature.* Freudian theory proposes that our helpfulness can be traced to a reaction formation against our aggressive feelings.

We do not help simply because we want to be moral or good (Wallach & Wallach, 1983). Also, the theory proposes that we act ethically because we fear punishment from our superegos. However, even very young children are helpful toward others—before their superegos could be well developed. As Wallach and Wallach point out, humans *are* basically concerned about others. Freud's explanation is unnecessarily indirect and negative.

We have described several problems with Freud's psychodynamic theory. Still, we need to remember that we cannot blame Freud for being unable to predict how our society would behave a century after he developed his theories. Here are some of the theory's strengths:

1. *It examines motivation and emotion.* We need to praise Freud for encouraging psychology to explore human motivations and emotions, rather than focusing only on thoughts and intellectual reactions. Freud's concept of the unconscious is clearly valuable to many current cognitive psychologists (e.g., Jacoby et al., 1992; Loftus & Klinger, 1992).

2. *Freud's theory is impressively comprehensive.* Sigmund Freud's approach is the most fully developed and comprehensive approach we'll consider in this chapter. He tried to explain an impressive range of human behaviors, addressing developmental patterns as well as psychological disorders. We have to admire Freud's brilliance and persistence in developing such an all-encompassing theory that was so strikingly different from the trends of his own culture.

SECTION SUMMARY: *THE PSYCHODYNAMIC APPROACH*

1. The psychodynamic approach emphasizes childhood experiences and unconscious motivations and conflicts; one kind of psychodynamic approach, Freud's psychoanalytic theory, was radically controversial when it was first proposed, but it eventually had a strong impact on psychology, popular culture, and the humanities.

2. Freud proposed three components of personality: the id, ego, and superego; the ego and the superego are partly represented in the conscious, whereas the id is completely unconscious.

3. Freud's methods include free association, dream analysis, and action interpretation.

4. Freud argued that the erogenous zone shifts throughout development, during the oral, anal, phallic, latency, and genital stages.

5. The psychoanalytic defense mechanisms include repression, regression, reaction formation, displacement, and projection.

6. Freud's theory emphasizes penis envy and less complete ethical development in women; these claims are not supported by the research.

7. Other psychodynamic theories have been proposed by Erikson, Jung (collective unconscious), Horney (challenging penis envy; strategies of interacting with other people), and the object-relations approach (the self in relation to other people).

8. Two projective tests that are compatible with the psychodynamic approach are the Rorschach Inkblot Test and the Thematic Apperception Test (TAT), but these tests are not high in reliability or validity.

9. Criticisms of psychodynamic theory include the difficulty of testing it, inadequate research, its bias against women, and its extreme pessimism. Positive features include its emphasis on emotions and some useful theoretical concepts, as well as its comprehensive scope.

THE HUMANISTIC APPROACH

In contrast to the pessimism of the psychodynamic perspective, the humanistic approach optimistically argues that people have enormous potential for personal growth. The humanistic approach gained prominence in the early 1960s when Carl Rogers (1961) and Abraham Maslow (1962) published important books. Many psychologists were dissatisfied with the two dominant theories of that era. On the one hand, the psychodynamic approach proposed that human kindness and caring often arise from evil impulses. On the other hand, the behaviorist approach—which we discussed in Chapter 6—focused on animal research. How could experiments with rats and pigeons inform us about higher human goals, such as the search for truth and beauty? (We should note that the social cognitive approach had not yet been proposed, and the humanistic theorists did not consider the trait approach to be a full-fledged personality theory.)

Rogers, Maslow, and others developed the humanistic approach as an alternative to the psychodynamic and behaviorist approaches. Let's examine the ideas of these two most prominent humanistic theorists, and then we'll evaluate the humanistic approach.

Rogers's Person-Centered Approach

Carl Rogers (1902–1987) was born in Illinois and began his professional career working with troubled children, though he later extended his therapy to adults. Rogers's approach requires the therapist to try to see the world from each client's personal perspective, rather than from the therapist's own framework. Rogers emphasized that each of us interprets the same set of stimuli differently, so there are as many different "real worlds" as there are people on this planet (Rogers, 1980).

Self-Actualization   Carl Rogers used the term **self-actualization** to capture the natural, underlying tendency of humans to move forward and fulfill their true potential (Rogers, 1963, 1980; Thorne, 1992). He marveled that this actualizing tendency could persist, even in the most hostile environments. For example, Rogers often interacted with people in the back wards of large psychiatric hospitals. The lives of these clients had been terribly warped, yet Rogers believed that these people were still striving toward growth. Rogers emphasized that this active self-development tendency provided the underlying basis of the person-centered approach.

Personality Development   Carl Rogers proposed that even young children need to be highly regarded by other people. Children also need positive *self-regard*—to be esteemed by oneself as well as others. From his work with clients who had psychological disorders, Rogers found that self-actualizing tendencies were frequently stifled by restricting self-concepts. Specifically, these clients had often acted in ways that distorted their "true selves" in order to win positive regard from others.

Rogers proposed that most children experience **conditional positive regard;** parents withhold their love and approval if children fail to conform to their elders' standards. For instance, parents might award positive regard to their son only in certain conditions—for example, only if he makes the football team. However, they may withhold positive regard if he fails to achieve in athletics or if he succeeds in other areas, such as music or the debate club.

In contrast, Rogers believed that everyone should be given **unconditional positive regard,** which is a nonjudgmental and genuine love, without any strings attached (Ewen, 1993; Rogers, 1959). The research partly supports Rogers's ideas. Authoritarian parents, who demand unquestioning obedience, do tend to produce unhappy, ineffective offspring. However, permissive parents, who allow children to make all their own decisions, often produce immature offspring with little self-control. Unconditional positive regard does not necessarily encourage self-actualization. The most successful parenting style is authoritative, with both love and clear-cut standards.

Maslow's Hierarchy of Needs

Abraham Maslow (1908–1970) was born in Brooklyn, New York. As a young psychologist, he was initially attracted to behaviorism. However, when his first child was born, Maslow realized that behaviorism could not account for the miracle and mystery of human infancy (Cloninger, 1996).

Maslow is probably best known for his theoretical exploration of self-actualization, the important tendency to realize our own potential. Maslow proposed that our human motives are arranged in a hierarchy, with the most basic needs at the bottom. At the top are the more highly developed needs (esteem needs and—finally—self-actualization).

Figure 13.3 shows **Maslow's hierarchy of needs,** in which each lower need must be satisfied before the next level of need can be addressed. For instance, people whose homes have just been destroyed by a flood will primarily be concerned with physiological and safety needs, rather than the more lofty goal of self-actualization. Let's examine the five levels in Maslow's hierarchy, beginning with the most basic level.

1. *Physiological needs:* We need food, water, sleep, and sex. Notice that these needs are also those that motivate lower animals.

2. *Safety needs:* These needs include security, protection, and the avoidance of pain.

3. *Belongingness and love needs:* These needs focus on affiliation with other people, affection, and feeling loved; sexual relationships as an expression of affection can also be included in this category.

4. *Esteem needs:* We also need to respect ourselves and to win the esteem of other people. Otherwise we feel discouraged and inferior, according to Maslow, so we will not strive for the highest level of hierarchy.

5. *Self-actualization needs:* A person who has satisfied all the lower needs can seek self-actualization, attempting to reach her or his full potential.

Maslow became particularly intrigued with this highest level, self-actualization, and he devised a list of characteristics of self actualized people. Demonstration 13.3 encourages you to think about some attributes of self-actualizers, based on Maslow's theory.

Later, Maslow began to identify other prominent people as self-actualizers. These were healthy, well-adjusted people who had used their full potential. The list included social worker Jane Addams, presidents Thomas Jefferson and Abraham Lincoln, first lady and social activist Eleanor Roosevelt, and physicist Albert Einstein.

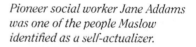

Pioneer social worker Jane Addams was one of the people Maslow identified as a self-actualizer.

Self-actualization

Esteem needs

Belongingness and love needs

Safety needs

Physiological needs

FIGURE 13.3

Maslow's hierarchy of needs.

DEMONSTRATION 13.3 Qualities of a Self-Actualized Person

Think about someone you know who seems to be a self-actualized person, who has lived up to his or her potential. (Ideally, this is someone you know personally, so you are familiar with this person's qualities.) Now read each of the characteristics listed below and decide whether they apply to the person you know. Place an X in front of each one that does describe this person.

_____ An acceptance of himself or herself

_____ An acceptance of other people

_____ Involvement in some cause outside of himself or herself

_____ Very spontaneous in both actions and emotions

_____ Great need for privacy

_____ Focused on problems and solutions rather than himself or herself

_____ Resists pressures to conform

_____ Superior creativity

_____ Fresh appreciation of other people, rather than stereotyped reactions

_____ Strongly developed set of values

How many of these characteristics apply to your target person? If any did *not* apply, do you think that this person would be even more self-actualized if she or he possessed these qualities?

In addition, you might try evaluating several famous people on these dimensions. How would you rate Mother Theresa, various politicians, and some major entertainers?

Source: Based on Maslow, 1968, 1971.

Critical Thinking Exercise 13.3

Write down your answers to the following questions about the theories of Rogers and Maslow.

a. Several humanistic theorists want to test Rogers's notions about self-actualization and other theoretical concepts. How would research be more complicated because of Rogers's notion that we all interpret the world differently?

b. Maslow himself created a list of qualities of self-actualized people, many of which you saw in Demonstration 13.3. As a critical thinker, how would you evaluate this process for generating criteria?

Evaluation of the Humanistic Approach

Table 13.4 summarizes four important characteristics of the humanistic approach, contrasting it with the psychodynamic approach. As presented in the table, you can see that the data in the humanistic approach are gathered from people in therapy, in the case of Rogers; Maslow provided self-reports from nonclinical populations, and he also analyzed the writing of important historical figures (DeCarvalho, 1991). Behavior is motivated by self-concepts and the tendency to self-actualize. Compared with the psychodynamic approach, humanistic psychology proposes a blissfully optimistic view of human nature. Finally, the theory is reasonably comprehensive, though not as far-reaching as the psychodynamic approach.

The humanistic approach can be criticized for several reasons:

1. *It relies on subjective experience.* The humanistic approach emphasizes that reality lies in a person's own interpretation of the world. Some people have only a limited ability to express themselves, so their self-reports probably do not reflect their experiences (Phares, 1988). We are therefore left with somewhat limited data.

2. *The studies are often inadequate.* Both Rogers and Maslow examined a selected sample of people, who were more intelligent and verbal than average. Humanistic principles may not apply to other groups. Also, as Maslow (1971) admits and Critical Thinking Exercise 13.3 pointed out, the work on self-actualizing people isn't really *research*. His list is arbitrary, and the people he selected did not completely meet his criteria. For instance, Abraham Lincoln had periods of severe depression,

TABLE 13.4 A Comparison of the Humanistic Approach With the Psychodynamic Approach

	PSYCHODYNAMIC APPROACH	HUMANISTIC APPROACH
Source of Data	Obtained from expert analysis from people in therapy.	Obtained from self-reports from the general population and people in therapy.
Cause of Behavior	Internal conflict, unconscious forces, childhood experiences.	Self-concepts, self-actualizing tendencies.
Explanation for Motivation	Pessimistic explanation.	Optimistic explanation.
Comprehensiveness of Theory	Very comprehensive.	Fairly comprehensive.

and Eleanor Roosevelt's family relationships were not ideal. Much of the so-called support is too subjective, and little empirical research has been conducted on humanistic personality theory (Ewen, 1993).

3. *Humanistic theory is too selfish.* Altruism is not included in Maslow's hierarchy, and it is not central in many discussions of self-actualization. The theories emphasize personal goals, often ignoring our responsibilities toward others (Wallach & Wallach, 1983, 1990). Our globe is plagued with hundreds of problems. Should issues such as homelessness, social justice, and world peace be placed on the back burner while we all concentrate on self-actualization?

4. *It is too optimistic.* If you glance at today's newspaper, you will probably find little evidence that people are inherently good, striving toward self-actualization. Reported incidents of suicide, murder, battering, child abuse, and rape have all increased in recent decades, suggesting that the humanistic theory of personality is not realistic.

Despite these criticisms, humanistic psychology must be praised for its substantial strengths:

1. *Humanistic theory emphasizes the present and future.* The psychodynamic perspective makes us "captives of the past" (Phares, 1988, p. 217). In contrast, the humanistic perspective focuses on the present and the future. These differing outlooks have implications for therapy. Psychodynamic therapists encourage clients to develop insight about earlier life events. In contrast, humanistic therapists encourage clients to change the way they live their lives in the future.

2. *It describes individual differences in perspective.* The humanistic approach deserves credit for pointing out that we each have different interpretations of reality. This point emphasizes human uniqueness and helps us understand how two individuals may have completely different viewpoints about the same issue.

3. *Humanistic theory provides an integrated view of humans.* As you'll soon see, trait theory and the social cognitive approach each offer glimpses of some component parts of personality. In contrast, humanistic theory emphasizes that each of us is a whole person, rather than a collection of isolated characteristics.

SECTION SUMMARY: *THE HUMANISTIC APPROACH*

1. The humanistic approach emphasizes the potential for personal growth.

2. Carl Rogers's person-centered approach points out that each of us perceives a different reality and that we strive toward self-actualization; everyone should receive unconditional positive regard.

3. Abraham Maslow's hierarchy proposes that our needs must be fulfilled in a specified order, from physiological, safety, and love to the higher needs of esteem and

self-actualization; Maslow also specified a list of characteristics descriptive of self-actualized people.

4. The humanistic approach can be criticized for relying on subjective experience, as well as the inadequacy of the research, its emphasis on selfishness, and its excessive optimism. Its strengths include its focus on the present and future—rather than the past, its emphasis on different realities, and its integrated view of humans.

THE TRAIT APPROACH

Of the four personality approaches described in this chapter, the trait approach most strongly emphasizes our theme of individual differences. As we discussed in the introduction to this chapter, the trait approach proposes that personality is a combination of specific stable, internal personality characteristics called traits. Thus, a **trait** is a consistent tendency to have certain kinds of beliefs, desires, and behaviors (Wakefield, 1989).

Trait theorists often examine whether a trait remains stable across time. For example, if a person is outgoing at age 5, will he or she also be outgoing at age 55? You may recognize this issue as the stability-change question. Trait theorists also examine whether a trait remains stable across situations. For example, if a person is outgoing at work, will he or she also be outgoing in social situations?

In this section, we'll first examine the theory of Gordon Allport, a psychologist who was prominent in developing the trait approach. Then we'll discuss the influential five-factor model of personality, followed by the controversial person-situation debate. We'll also consider some of the biological research on personality, as well as the MMPI, the major current test of personality. We'll conclude this section by evaluating the trait approach.

Allport's Trait Theory

For this young woman, an intense interest in infants and children constitutes a cardinal trait.

Gordon Allport (1897–1967) began his undergraduate years at Harvard University with C's and D's in his courses. It's hard to imagine how someone who began so unpromisingly and ended so prominently could have formulated a theory that focused on stability, rather than change. A lucky meeting with Sigmund Freud helps to explain the transformation. After arriving at Freud's office, Allport began the conversation by mentioning a 4-year-old boy he had met on the train who seemed to have been extremely concerned about getting dirty. At the end of the story, Freud gently asked Allport, "And was that little boy you?" (Allport, 1967, p. 8). At that point, Allport realized that the psychodynamic approach overemphasized hidden symbols and motivations. He resolved to focus, instead, on conscious motives and on personal traits.

Eventually, Allport (1937, 1961) decided to bring order to the study of personality by proposing three levels of traits:

1. A **cardinal trait** is one that dominates and shapes a person's behavior. For my daughter Beth, for example, a focused interest in infants and children shaped her life. At the age of 21 months, she showered affection and tiny gifts on her newborn sister. She studied early childhood education in college and started a

Head-Start type program for preschoolers in Nicaragua. She's now teaching kindergarten in the Boston public schools. Perhaps you know someone who is obsessed with becoming wealthy, or another person whose life focus is religion. Allport proposed, however, that these cardinal traits are rare. Most of us lack a single overarching theme in our lives.

2. A **central trait** is a general characteristic, found to some degree in every person, that shapes much of our behavior. Some central traits could be honesty, cheerfulness, and shyness.

3. A **secondary trait** is a characteristic seen only in certain situations. These must be included to provide a complete picture of human complexity. Some typical secondary traits might be "uncomfortable in large crowds" and "likes to drive sports cars."

Allport argued that a person's unique pattern of traits determined his or her behavior. No two people are completely identical; as a result, no two people respond completely identically to the same environmental situation. As Allport said: "The same fire that melts the butter hardens the egg" (Allport, 1937, p. 102).

The Five-Factor Model

How many basic trait dimensions do we need to capture all the rich complexity of our personalities? Some researchers suggest as few as 2, whereas others propose as many as 16 basic traits (Mischel, 1993). The most widely accepted solution to the search for trait clusters is called the five-factor model (McCrae & Costa, 1997; L. R. Goldberg, 1993; Halverson et al., 1994). The **five-factor model,** also called the **Big Five traits,** proposes that the most important clusters of traits include extraversion, agreeableness, conscientiousness, emotional stability, and openness to experience.

Numerous studies have tested the five-factor model. For example, Havill and her coauthors (1994) discovered that U.S. mothers described their children using terms from the five clusters. In other words, the model seems appropriate for laypeople, as well as professional psychologists. Researchers have also found evidence of this five-factor model in cross-cultural studies with people in Canada, Finland, Poland, and Germany (Paunonen et al., 1992), and in Portugal, Israel, China, Korea, and Japan (Costa & McCrae, 1992a; McCrae & Costa, 1997). Therefore, the model is not limited to North American populations or to languages resembling English.

Costa and McCrae (1992b, 1995) have also developed a self-report test, called the NEO Personality Inventory, which is based on the five-factor model. Demonstration 13.4 is an informal version of this test. The reliability and validity measures on the NEO Personality Inventory are reasonably high (Goldsmith et al., 1994; McCrae & John, 1992).

As you can imagine, not all psychologists agree with the five-factor model (e.g., Block, 1995). In fairness, however, the model never claimed that these five dimensions capture all aspects of personality.

The Person-Situation Debate

A major ongoing controversy in studies examining the trait approach is called the person-situation debate. Like many other controversies in psychology, the **person-situation debate** features two extreme positions:

1. *Person:* Each person possesses stable, internal traits that cause him or her to act consistently in a variety of situations.

DEMONSTRATION 13.4 The Five-Factor Model

This demonstration allows you to assess yourself informally on each of the Big Five traits. Use the basic 7-point rating scale shown below, each time supplying a number in the blank space to indicate where you belong on a given scale (e.g., sociable-retiring). After you have rated yourself on the three scales that comprise each dimension, calculate an average (e.g., for extraversion). Which end of each dimension seems most characteristic of your personality? Please keep in mind, however, that any informal demonstration such as this is not intended to provide an accurate assessment.

1	2	3	4	5	6	7

1. Extraversion   (Average rating =   )

_____ Sociable   Retiring
_____ Enthusiastic   Unenthusiastic
_____ Affectionate   Reserved

2. Agreeableness   (Average rating =   )

_____ Sympathetic   Unsympathetic
_____ Trusting   Suspicious
_____ Helpful   Uncooperative

3. Conscientiousness   (Average rating =   )

_____ Well organized   Disorganized
_____ Careful   Careless
_____ Responsible   Irresponsible

4. Emotional Stability   (Average rating =   )

_____ Calm   Worrying
_____ Secure   Insecure
_____ Self-satisfied   Self-pitying

5. Openness to Experience   (Average rating =   )

_____ Imaginative   Down-to-earth
_____ Preference for variety   Preference for routine
_____ Independent   Conformity

Note: The "emotional stability" scale is sometimes called the "neuroticism" (instability) scale.

Source: Based on McCrae & Costa, 1986; McCrae & John, 1992.

---

2. *Situation:* Each person does not possess stable internal traits. Instead, his or her behavior depends on the specific characteristics of each situation.

Psychologists who support trait theory typically favor the "person" position. In contrast, behaviorists in the tradition of B. F. Skinner believe that environmental stimuli are far more important, and thus they tend to agree with the "situation" position. To predict someone's response, they say, all we need to do is specify the external stimuli in a situation; we don't need to discuss any internal characteristics. Psychologists who favor the situation position might even suggest that we eliminate the personality chapter of introductory textbooks: Personality doesn't exist, and only situations count. Let's examine this controversy.

Mischel's Position   For many decades, personality psychologists had supported the person position, especially because it matches our common sense. Of course people are consistent! Julie is consistently unconcerned about other people, whereas Pete is always compassionate. A strong challenge to this position was presented by Walter Mischel (pronounced "Mih-*shell*"), who came from a behaviorist tradition.

Mischel (1968) examined dozens of earlier studies. He discovered that various behaviors that supposedly reflect the same internal trait are only weakly correlated with each other. For example, students' tendency to arrive on time for one event is correlated only +.19 with their tendency to arrive on time for another event (Dudycha, 1936). This very weak correlation does not support the person position.

But why do we persist in believing that personality characteristics are consistent across situations? Mischel (1968) argued that our perception is biased. For example, we usually see a person in only a limited set of situations. Think of someone from your high school whom you believe had a consistently friendly personality. You never saw this person on a college interview—where he or she may have acted timid and withdrawn. Mischel (1979) argued that each of us does show some slight personality consistency from one situation to another, but the people who know us tend to exaggerate that consistency.

Factors Related to Consistency   One intriguing finding is that people show more consistency if we measure their average behavior across several events, rather than just one single event (Epstein, 1983; Epstein & O'Brien, 1985; Rogers, 1995). This makes sense. You might be late to class one day, but early four other days. Your *average* punctuality for classes is probably correlated with your *average* punctuality for other events.

Furthermore, traits are more easily expressed in some situations than others (Buss, 1989; Kenrick & Funder, 1988; Wiggins & Pincus, 1992). For instance, some situations constrain our behavior, so the traits cannot be easily expressed. At a funeral, the friendly people will not act much different from the unfriendly people. However, at a picnic, individual differences will be strong. Cross-situational consistency will be higher if the situation is familiar, if people receive no instructions about how they should act, and if they are observed for a long time, rather than a brief period.

Conclusions About the Person-Situation Debate   Behavior is probably not as consistent across situations as our intuitions suggest; systematic biases encourage us to believe in traits too strongly. However, some consistency really does exist (Funder, 1993; 1995). Furthermore, the consistency can be reasonably high—in some situations, for some people, some traits, and some methods of measuring those traits. Obviously, our theme of complexity fits the data on the person-situation debate!

Walter Mischel began the debate in 1968, and about 30 years later, he suggested a new way to view the debate. Specifically, Mischel and his coauthor Yuichi Shoda (1995) reexamined some data from several studies and noticed that people really are fairly consistent in their personality if we carefully examine the external features of the situations they encounter.

For example, Mischel and Shoda examined the personality trait of "verbal aggression" in children. One child seemed to be fairly low in verbal aggression on some occasions, for example, but very high on this same trait on other occasions. On the surface, the child's personality appears to be inconsistent. When Mischel and Shoda reexamined the data, however, they found that this child was consistently low in aggression when a peer approached, but consistently very high in aggression when an adult gave a warning. Other children showed different profiles. Most important, if we can specify the external features of the situation (e.g., "peer approaching" or "adult warning"), then people *can* show remarkable consistency in their personalities.

We cannot answer which factor is more important in several debates. For example, both nature and nurture are important—not just one of them. Similarly, we cannot answer which factor is a better predictor of behavior—person or situation. Again, both are important. To predict how a person will behave, we need some measure of his or her internal traits, but we must also understand the specific characteristics of the external situation.

Critical Thinking Exercise 13.4

Write down your answers to the following questions about the five-factor model and about the person-situation debate.

a. Compare the kind of self-report test you took in Demonstration 13.4 (based on the five-factor model) with the Rorschach Test (the projective test on which Demonstration 13.2 is based). What are the advantages of each kind of test?

b. The primacy effect, which proposes that we tend to maintain our first impression of someone even if he or she acts very differently on later occasions. Why would the primacy effect encourage us to believe that personality characteristics are more consistent than they really are?

The Biological Basis of Individual Differences

The trait theory argues that we can understand personality by examining the characteristics that people bring to the situation. For many psychologists, the next logical step is to examine the biological bases of those characteristics (Zuckerman, 1994a). The most active biological research focuses on the genetic basis of personality. Genetic researchers have conducted twin studies on personality, as well as in other areas such as cognitive abilities and psychological disorders.

The popular press has widely publicized the research on identical twins who have been reared apart (e.g., Begley, 1996; C. Bouchard et al., 1990; Lykken et al., 1992). After all, it's fascinating to read about a pair of twins reared in separate homes who behave identically at the beach; both enter the water backwards and avoid water levels above their knees. Some critics suggest that the high degree of similarities between the twin pairs is partly due to a nonrandom sample (T. Adler, 1991b). Furthermore, we must remember from the discussion of decision making in Chapter 8 that many unusual-looking outcomes can occur by chance alone.

The research on twins reared together and apart typically reports a measure called **heritability,** which is an estimate of how much of the variation in a characteristic can be traced to differences in heredity, as opposed to differences in environment. For example, research on each of the personality characteristics in the five-factor model shows that the heritability is typically in the range of 25% to 55% (Hartup & van Lieshout, 1995; Viken et al., 1994; Zuckerman, 1995).

Psychologists have begun to examine the biological basis of some characteristics. For example, **subjective well-being,** is a person's evaluation of his or her life satisfaction. Research on the genetic basis of subjective well-being suggests that heritability is about 50% (Lykken & Tellegen, 1996). Keep in mind, however, that environmental factors are still responsible for about half of the variation in these characteristics. In other words, people whose parents are dissatisfied with their lives are not doomed to become miserable themselves. Instead, they can seek a more positive environment.

Consider a trait called sensation seeking. People who are high in **sensation seeking** actively look for adventure, new experiences, and risky situations (Zuckerman, 1993, 1994b). In general, the heritability for sensation seeking is estimated to be 58%, which is relatively high for personality traits. The research comparing high sensation seekers with low sensation seekers shows that the two groups differ in a variety of brain chemicals, including neurotransmitters, endorphins, and hormones (Zuckerman, 1994b, 1995). Recent studies have also focused on DNA analysis, identifying a genetic basis for the novelty-seeking component of sensation seeking (Benjamin et al., 1996; Ebstein et al., 1996). This is the first step toward understanding the specific genetic maps of personality.

In summary, then, biological factors seem to account for a substantial portion of individual differences in personality traits. Keep in mind, however, that other variables—primarily environmental factors—account for at least half of these individual differences.

The Minnesota Multiphasic Personality Inventory

The most widely used personality test in psychology is the **Minnesota Multiphasic Personality Inventory (MMPI),** an objective personality test that asks a large number of true-false questions in order to assess personality traits. The MMPI has also been extremely popular in research, with more than 4,000 reports on this instrument published between 1974 and 1994 (Butcher & Rouse, 1996).

To design the MMPI, Starke Hathaway and J. C. McKinley administered a wide range of questions to more than 800 psychiatric patients, who represented the major clinical subgroups such as depression and schizophrenia. They also administered the questions to more than 1,500 unhospitalized people, such as students and hospital visitors.

An item was selected for a particular scale of the MMPI only if the two groups—the group with psychological disorders and the normal group—showed significantly different response patterns. For example, people with a particular psychological disorder were much more likely than people in the control group to say "true" to the item "Someone has been trying to poison me." In each case, the *content* of the item is irrelevant; the critical point is whether the item discriminates between the normal group and the group with a psychological disorder.

In 1989, a revised form of the MMPI was published (Butcher et al., 1989). This new MMPI-2 is based on a larger, more ethnically diverse sample of test takers. The revised version also eliminated gender-biased language, outdated items, and items that assumed the test taker was Christian (Graham, 1990; Hood & Johnson, 1991).

The items on the new MMPI-2 are grouped into 15 clinical scales and 5 validity scales, making a total of 567 questions. Table 13.5 shows some examples of the scales, the characteristics they are designed to assess, and some hypothetical test items. Notice, for example, that the "lie scale" helps assess one aspect of validity. Anyone who says "yes" to the item "I smile at everyone I meet" cannot be telling the truth!

The reliability of the MMPI-2 is considered to be reasonably high for a personality test. The test-retest reliability measures generally range between .75 and .85 (Graham, 1990; Kaplan & Saccuzzo, 1993). Numerous studies have been conducted to establish the validity of the MMPI-2. For example, when married couples took the MMPI-2, each person's answers were highly correlated with his or her spouse's evaluation of the person on these same items (Butcher et al., 1990).

A reasonable amount of research on the MMPI has been conducted with Hispanic and Black individuals, but Asians and Native Americans have not been extensively studied (Greene, 1987; Valásquez & Callahan, 1992). Psychologists are encouraging researchers to conduct additional studies, keeping in mind the variety of different cultures within each ethnic group (Dana, 1988; LaFromboise et al., 1997; Puente, 1990).

A major advantage of the MMPI-2 and other self-report tests is that they can be easily administered, even in large groups. The test can be computer scored; it does not require a trained examiner (Hood & Johnson, 1991). A disadvantage is the length of the test. After answering the first 500 questions on the MMPI, would you really answer the remaining 67 questions honestly and carefully? As you will see in the next chapter, the MMPI is considered to be a valuable tool when clinical psychologists need to diagnose a psychological disorder.

PSYCHOLOGY

TABLE 13.5 Some Examples of Scales From the Minnesota Multiphasic Personality Inventory

NAME OF SCALE	KIND OF SCALE	DESCRIPTION	HYPOTHETICAL TEST ITEM (answer indicating the disorder is in parentheses)
Depression Scale	Clinical	Derived from patients who show extreme pessimism and feelings of hopelessness.	"I usually feel that life is interesting and worthwhile." *(False)*
Psychopathic Deviate Scale	Clinical	Derived from patients who show extreme disregard for social customs and who show aggressiveness.	"My activities and interests are often criticized by others." *(True)*
Paranoia Scale	Clinical	Derived from patients who show abnormal suspiciousness or delusions.	"There are evil people trying to influence my mind." *(True)*
Lie Scale	Validity	Measures overly good self-image.	"I smile at everyone I meet." *(True)*

Source: Minnesota Multiphasic Personality Inventory-2. Copyright © by the Regents of the University of Minnesota 1942, 1943, (renewed 1970), 1989. Reproduced by permission of the publisher.

Evaluation of the Trait Approach

Table 13.6 summarizes four important characteristics of the trait approach, contrasting it with the other two approaches discussed so far. As you can see, the trait approach is very different from the psychodynamic approach. Although it is similar to the humanistic approach in the way the data are gathered, the two approaches differ considerably on the other three characteristics. The trait approach can be criticized for several reasons:

1. *It is not an integrated theory.* In fact, the trait approach is really a research technique, rather than a theory. The approach produces a wealth of information about people's characteristics, but no comprehensive view of humanity. It

TABLE 13.6 A Comparison of the Trait Approach With the Psychodynamic and Humanistic Approaches

	PSYCHODYNAMIC APPROACH	HUMANISTIC APPROACH	TRAIT APPROACH
Source of Data	Obtained from expert analyst from people in therapy.	Obtained from self-reports from the general population and people in therapy.	Obtained from observation of behavior and questionnaire responses from the general population as well as people in therapy.
Cause of Behavior	Internal conflict, unconscious forces, childhood experiences.	Self-concepts, self-actualizing tendencies.	Stable, internal characteristics; some emphasize genetic basis
Explanation for Motivation	Pessimistic explanation.	Optimistic explanation.	Neutral explanation.
Comprehensiveness of Theory	Very comprehensive.	Fairly comprehensive.	Not very comprehensive.

does not examine unconscious forces, and it generally does not attempt to explain *why* people have certain traits to varying degrees. (The prominent exception here is the new biologically based research, which does attempt to uncover causality.)

2. *The trait approach underestimates the role of situations.* Taken to its extreme, trait theory predicts that people act consistently, even in different situations. As we saw in the research, however, people are not very predictable. A person may be aggressive in one circumstance and unaggressive in another. People are predictable only in certain circumstances and only when we know the details about the situation.

We cannot be too critical, however, because the trait approach never aspired to be comprehensive and integrated. It has been a valuable tool, with strengths including the following:

1. *The theory has generated information about traits.* A major emphasis of this approach is to look for trait consistency, independent of the situation. To its credit, the trait approach provides abundant information about internal characteristics, such as the stability of traits.

2. *The trait approach has helped develop personality measurement.* Trait theorists have clearly contributed to the measurement of personality. In this section, we emphasized the NEO Personality Inventory and the MMPI. In addition, personality researchers have developed hundreds of other tests to assess more specific personality traits.

SECTION SUMMARY: *THE TRAIT APPROACH*

1. Allport proposed three levels of personality traits: cardinal, central, and secondary; he suggested that the combination of these traits determines a person's behavior.

2. The five-factor model is the most widely accepted categorization of trait dimensions; these traits are extraversion, agreeableness, conscientiousness, emotional stability, and openness to experience.

3. The resolution to the person-situation debate seems to be that people have traits that are somewhat consistent across situations, though our cognitive biases enhance this apparent consistency.

4. Cross-situational consistency is higher in unconstrained situations, when instructions have not been given, and when the observation period is long; consistency is also higher for some people, some traits, and some methods. Finally, Mischel and Shoda

(1995) have suggested that personality is likely to be consistent once we know the specific psychological features of the situation.

5. Research suggests that heritability is reasonably high for personality characteristics in the five-factor model, for subjective well-being, and for sensation seeking; research on brain chemicals and genetics has been especially active for the personality trait of sensation seeking.

6. The trait approach is not an integrated theory—though it never aspired to be one—and the extreme form of the trait approach underestimates the importance of situations; however, it has inspired much research about traits and many useful personality tests, such as the NEO Personality Inventory and the MMPI.

THE SOCIAL COGNITIVE APPROACH

We began this chapter by exploring the psychodynamic approach, which argues that people are ruled by their sexual organs and by forces of unconscious conflict. Then we considered the humanistic approach, which proposes that people are ruled by more noble motives, such as the striving for self-actualization. Our third topic was the trait approach, which maintains that people are ruled by stable, internal characteristics that may have a genetic basis.

In contrast especially to the psychodynamic approach, the social cognitive approach makes humans seem much less passionate and much more levelheaded. In fact, some personality theorists have pointed out that you can read dozens of books about the social cognitive approach without ever learning that humans have genitals! The social cognitive approach focuses on the way people observe, evaluate, regulate, and think. This approach is consistent with the view of cognitive psychology. Humans actively process information—for example, when you read this paragraph in your textbook. The social cognitive approach to personality also emphasizes that humans actively process information about their own behavior, their social world, and their personal characteristics (Hattie, 1992; Magnusson & Törestad, 1993).

We'll begin by investigating the origins of this social cognitive approach, and then we'll review the basic concepts of observational learning. Our next topic is reciprocal influences—the concept that environmental factors, personal factors, and behaviors all interact to form an individual's personality. Next we'll consider self-efficacy, or people's sense that they are competent and effective. Then the "In Depth" feature focuses on cross-cultural views on the self. We'll conclude with an evaluation of the social cognitive approach.

Origins of the Social Cognitive Approach

The social cognitive approach traces its origins to behaviorism. Behaviorism emphasizes observable behavior, instead of unobservable mental processes. Operant conditioning explains how reinforcement and punishment influence behavior. For example, you do your physics homework, and you are reinforced by good grades on exams, so you continue to do homework in the future.

In B. F. Skinner's behaviorist theory, we do not need to talk about internal characteristics when we discuss people's personal traits. For instance, we can explain the behavior of a friendly person in terms of past and present reinforcement and punishment—that is, external factors—and genetic factors. Skinner (1974) argued that we achieve nothing by discussing personality characteristics such as an "extraversion trait."

Albert Bandura is one of the major theorists who found Skinner's approach inadequate (Grusec, 1992). Bandura (1986) argues that people learn much more by observational learning than by operant conditioning. Bandura also emphasizes that people think about and interpret events. Unlike Skinner, Bandura argues that the human mind makes an important contribution to personality. Bandura (1986) called his approach social cognitive theory, because it emphasizes the contribution of social factors (e.g., observational learning) and thought (e.g., beliefs about competence) in explaining personality and behavior.

Observational Learning

Observational learning, a major component in the social cognitive approach, was discussed in Chapter 6, together with classical conditioning and operant conditioning. In **observational learning,** we learn new behaviors by watching and imitating the behavior of others (Bandura, 1986, 1989). However, other complex cognitive factors also play crucial rules in the development of personality.

Reciprocal Influences

My daughter Sally is outgoing and adventurous. At age 16, she went by herself to Mexico to perfect her Spanish, and she lived with a Mexican family. Sally made dozens of friends, including members of a local band. On her last evening there, her Mexican family and friends arranged a surprise farewell party, and the band played backup while she sang solo on her favorite Latin American song, "Doce Rosas." I pictured myself at 16 and marvel at the difference in our personalities. I was not so outgoing, and I could never have gone alone to a foreign country. Also, the option of singing solo in Spanish would have been only slightly less horrifying than walking barefoot on hot coals.

Bandura (1986) has proposed an explanation for the way initial individual differences become even stronger through reciprocal influences. According to the principle of **reciprocal influences,** three factors—personal/cognitive, behavior, and environmental—all influence one another (Figure 13.4). As a consequence, initial tendencies can become even stronger.

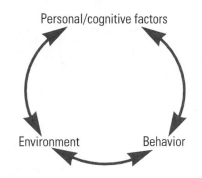

FIGURE 13.4
The principle of reciprocal influences.

As an example of reciprocal influences, consider a young woman who is outgoing and friendly and expects that she will be successful in interpersonal interactions (personal/cognitive). She will therefore be likely to introduce herself to strangers and react positively to them (behavior). Furthermore, someone who is outgoing and friendly is likely to seek out social situations, rather than sitting in her room (environment). The environment, in turn, promotes even more friendly behavior, more self-confidence, and an even greater expectation for success in interpersonal interactions. In contrast, a shy, withdrawn person will dread interpersonal interactions, avoid strangers, and stay away from social situations. This behavior and lack of exposure to new environments will encourage the person to become even more withdrawn and to expect future interactions to be unsuccessful.

Skinner's theory proposes that the environment shapes human behavior. In contrast, Bandura argues that the process is more complex; behavior can be a *cause,* as well as an *effect* (Cloninger, 1996). In fact, personality, behavior, and environment shape one another in a reciprocal fashion. This more complex approach is necessary to explain the impressive complexity of humans.

Self-Efficacy

Let's examine the personal/cognitive part of Bandura's theory, because this component is most central to personality. Bandura (1986, 1997) believes that the most important personal/cognitive factor is self-efficacy. **Self-efficacy** is a person's belief in his or her ability to organize and perform the actions required to reach desired goals (Bandura, 1997). According to Bandura (1992b), your thoughts and expectations about success are more important than your actual behavior. For example, if you are trying to decide whether to try a new dance step in public, the relevant factor is whether you *think* you are a good dancer, not whether you *are* a good dancer!

Research confirms that people with a strong sense of self-efficacy do indeed manage their lives more successfully. In general, these people tend to be more persistent in school, intensifying their efforts when a task is difficult. They also have higher aspirations, as well as more flexible problem-solving strategies. They also have better metacognitive skills; they think about their thinking processes and regulate how they approach tasks (Bandura, 1997; Zimmerman, 1995). People who are confident about their abilities typically approach new challenges with optimism, and they set high goals for themselves (Bandura & Jourden, 1991). In contrast, people with low self-efficacy may set inappropriate goals, often leading to depression (Bandura, 1997).

When people with high self-efficacy are initially unsuccessful, they try a new approach and work harder. Bandura (1997) points out that the American poet and novelist Gertrude Stein submitted poems to a variety of editors for about 20 years before one was eventually accepted. How could reinforcement theory explain that persistence? Also, Vincent van Gogh sold only one painting during his lifetime. Still, both of these individuals persisted. In contrast, a person with low self-efficacy would give up when faced with such overwhelming rejection.

Bandura (1986, 1997) points out that self-efficacy is possible because humans can analyze their varied experiences and think about their own thought processes. In earlier chapters, we discussed metacognition (thinking about thinking). You can also think about your many other psychological attributes. Consider how often you have evaluated attributes such as your helpfulness, athletic ability, and friendliness. In fact, when you were reading the description of self-efficacy, you probably evaluated your own self-efficacy. We humans evaluate our skills and then use that information to regulate our future behavior (Bandura, 1991). The thoughts we have about ourselves are the focus of the "In Depth" feature that follows—an examination of our views of the self.

IN DEPTH

Cross-Cultural Views of the Self

In the past, virtually all of the theories and data in psychology have come from Western, northern-hemisphere populations, such as the United States, Canada, and Europe. However, about 70% of the people in the world live in other regions—Asia, Latin America, and Africa (Kitayama & Markus, 1995; Triandis, 1996). For many years, psychologists assumed that the basic principles of psychology—gathered on European American samples—could be accurately applied to other cultural groups. Now researchers have begun to study people living in other cultures. They sometimes conclude that these "basic principles" cannot be very basic if they do not apply to other cultures.

Now, we introduce the concepts of individualistic and collectivist cultures. Let's review these terms, examining them in more depth, and then we'll see how people from these two kinds of cultural approaches have different views of personality and the self. First, however, try Demonstration 13.5, which assesses individualistic and collectivist values. See whether your pattern of answers is consistent with the culture to which you belong, keeping in mind that individual differences can be substantial for people from either of these two cultural backgrounds (Markus et al., 1996).

Individualistic Versus Collectivist Cultures

North American cultures and many Western European cultures emphasize an individualistic viewpoint. These **individualistic cultures** (also called **independent cultures**) maintain that you must assert yourself and appreciate how you are different from other people. In contrast, people in Asia, Africa, Latin America, and many southern European cultures—such as Italy and Greece—have a different perspective. These **collectivist cultures** (also called **interdependent cultures**) maintain that you must fit in with other people and live in interdependent relationships with them.

DEMONSTRATION 13.5   Assessing Values Related to Individualism and Collectivism

For each of the following items, write *true* if you think the statement is correct and *false* if not. Check Page 448 at the end of the chapter to see how to score your answers.

_____ 1. Without competition, it is not possible to have a good society.

_____ 2. I enjoy being unique and different from others.

_____ 3. I would do what would please my family, even if I detested that activity.

_____ 4. When another person does better than I do, I get tense and aroused.

_____ 5. It is important to me to maintain harmony within my group.

_____ 6. I rely on myself most of the time; I rarely rely on others.

_____ 7. I like sharing little things with my neighbors.

_____ 8. It is important to me that I respect the decisions made by my groups.

_____ 9. It is important that I do my job better than others.

_____ 10. I often do "my own thing."

_____ 11. I usually sacrifice my self-interest for the benefit of my group.

_____ 12. It is important to consult close friends and get their ideas before making a decision.

Source: Based on Singelis et al., 1995.

People in individualistic cultures base their identity on the characteristics that make them unique. In contrast, people in collectivist cultures base their identity on their interconnectedness with others. Later, in Chapter 12, we saw that people in individualistic cultures base their subjective well-being on their own personal happiness. In contrast, people in collectivist cultures base their subjective well-being on their sense of harmony with other people.

People in the two kinds of cultures also seem to view the self differently. For example, Hazel Markus and her colleagues (1996) discuss a study in which interviewers asked Japanese respondents, "How would you describe yourself to yourself?" The respondents struggled with this question, and their answers seemed vague and indirect. In contrast, U.S. respondents answered the same question easily and directly. For example, one American responded, "How long an answer would you like? I could talk all day about myself, you know, it's my favorite topic" (p. 885). Markus and her coauthors comment that this individualistic response would be considered extremely rude and inappropriate in Japanese culture. Let's look more closely at two components of cross-cultural views of personality: self-actualization and self-evaluation.

Self-Actualization in Individualistic and Collectivist Cultures

In the personality theories we have explored so far, the isolated individual is most important. Consider humanistic psychology, for example. Self-actualization is a central concept in Carl Rogers's theory, and it is the highest motivational level in Abraham Maslow's approach. Through self-actualization, a person achieves his or her individual potential; no larger group needs to be considered.

Is self-actualization equally important in other cultures? Harry Triandis and his colleagues (1990) showed that this characteristic may not always be desirable. These researchers conducted their research in both the United States and Hong Kong. In each location, they studied 40 **triads,** or groups of three individuals. Each triad was given one word at a time, and the three individuals were instructed to discuss this word and decide whether this characteristic was either important or unimportant in their culture. If 85% of the triads in one culture agreed—within one minute—that the characteristic was indeed important, then this characteristic was considered to be valuable in that culture. For example, all 40 of the Hong Kong triads decided within an average of three seconds that persistence is indeed important in their culture. According to the operational definition, therefore, persistence qualifies as a valuable characteristic. However, in the United States, persistence did not meet the criterion. How did self-actualization fare? In the United States, 39 of the 40 triads decided with an average of four seconds that self-actualization is important in the culture. In contrast, self-actualization did not meet the criterion in Hong Kong. These data suggest that the notion of self-actualization may be a highly valued personality characteristic in U.S. culture, but this humanistic concept would not rate at the top of a hierarchy in Hong Kong. Perhaps future personality theorists can determine whether this difference is maintained in other individualistic and collectivist societies. However, this "basic" principle of Maslow's hierarchy may not be equally useful in all cultures.

The Self-Serving Bias in Individualistic and Collectivist Cultures

We have pointed out that people in individualistic cultures focus on the self and on being superior to others in one's group. In contrast, people in collectivist cultures are encouraged to fit in, *not* to stand out. The research has consistently shown that people in North America tend to be self-serving when they evaluate themselves. That is, they give themselves high ratings on a variety of scales (e.g., Markus & Kitayama, 1991b; Matlin & Stang, 1978). Will people in collectivist cultures do the same, or will they avoid this tendency in order to fit in and maintain a sense of harmony with their group?

Hazel Markus and Shinobu Kitayama (1991b) compared U.S. college students studying in the United States and Japanese college students studying in Japan. They asked a series of questions based on a standard format: "What proportion of students have higher intellectual ability than yourself?" The questionnaire asked questions about abilities (intellectual ability, memory, and athletic ability), independence

Critical Thinking Exercise 13.5

Write down your answers to the following questions about cross-cultural research on personality.

a. Analyze the questions in Demonstration 13.5 with respect to social desirability. Which responses would a person from an individualistic society provide in order to look good? How about a person from a collectivist society? Would the social desirability factor tend to increase or decrease the size of the difference between the two cultural groups?

b. In the study by Triandis and his colleagues (1990), the U.S. triads agreed, within the one-minute time limit, that self-actualization is a valuable characteristic; the Hong Kong students did not meet this criterion. Why would that finding be difficult to interpret if we didn't also learn that the Hong Kong students agreed, within the same time limit, that persistence is a valuable characteristic, but the U.S. students did not meet this criterion?

(IN DEPTH continued)

(independent; hold more strongly to their own view), and interdependence (more sympathetic; more warmhearted).

Table 13.7 shows the results for the men and women in the two cultures. The table lists the percentage of people whom the participant judged to be superior to himself or herself in each of the three domains. (A student who believes that he or she is just average on an attribute would therefore supply a rating of 50%.) Notice that the U.S. men are self-serving on all three characteristics. For example, they estimate that only 36% of the students on their campus have greater abilities than themselves. They have a self-serving bias because they believe relatively few students are better than themselves on this attribute. Notice that the U.S. women are self-serving with respect to both independence and interdependence—but not abilities. The Japanese men are relatively modest about their attributes, with just a hint of a self-serving bias for interdependence. Finally, the Japanese women show no evidence of a self-serving bias; in fact, they may even be *too* modest. They do not claim to have unique skills that make them stand out from their peer group.

Earlier in the chapter, we saw that the five-factor model applies reasonably well when people in other cultures rate their personality traits. However, we have seen in this "In Depth" feature that individualistic and collectivist cultures have different perspectives on the self. People in collectivist societies are reluctant to talk about themselves, they do not value self-actualization, and they do not tend to overrate their personal characteristics.

TABLE 13.7 Judgments About the Percentage of People Who Are Superior to the Self in Each Specified Domain (averaged across all participants in each group)[*]

Domain	UNITED STATES		JAPAN	
	Men	Women	Men	Women
Abilities	36%	47%	49%	58%
Independence	33%	34%	46%	54%
Interdependence	30%	26%	40%	49%

Source: Markus & Kitayama (1991b).

[*]High numbers indicate modesty, and low numbers indicate a self-serving bias.

TABLE 13.8 Contrasting the Four Approaches to Personality

	PSYCHODYNAMIC APPROACH	HUMANISTIC APPROACH	TRAIT APPROACH	SOCIAL COGNITIVE APPROACH
Source of Data	Obtained from expert analyst from people in therapy.	Obtained from self-reports from the general population and people in therapy.	Obtained from observation of behavior and questionnaire responses from the general population as well as people in therapy.	Obtained from experiments, observation of behavior, and questionnaire responses from the general population.
Cause of Behavior	Internal conflict, unconscious forces, childhood experiences.	Self-concepts, self-actualizing tendencies.	Stable, internal characteristics; some emphasize genetic basis.	Reciprocal influence of personal/cognitive, behavior, and environment.
Explanation for Motivation	Pessimistic explanation.	Optimistic explanation.	Neutral explanation.	Neutral explanation.
Comprehensiveness of Theory	Very comprehensive.	Fairly comprehensive.	Not very comprehensive.	Not very comprehensive.

Evaluation of the Social Cognitive Approach

Table 13.8 summarizes four important characteristics of the social cognitive approach, contrasting it with the other three approaches discussed in this chapter. As you can see, it differs most from the psychodynamic approach. The social cognitive approach can be criticized for two major reasons:

1. *It is not comprehensive.* At present, the social cognitive approach is relatively narrow in scope. It does emphasize the importance of our thoughts about our own competence and how these thoughts organize our behavior. Still, the social cognitive approach underemphasizes emotions and sexual urges. Also, it has not examined in detail how personality develops from childhood to adulthood.

2. *It is not an integrated theory.* At present, the social cognitive approach consists of a collection of isolated ideas. We have observational learning, reciprocal influences, and self-efficacy from Bandura. Markus and others have examined notions of the self, and additional researchers are actively pursuing other components. However, a loose collection of ideas does not constitute a satisfying, cohesive theory.

The problems with the social cognitive approach certainly will not doom it to failure. Researchers are likely to tackle these two problems in the near future, and they may find some satisfying solutions. Furthermore, here are some of the strengths of the social cognitive approach:

1. *The theory is testable.* A major advantage of the social cognitive approach is that its proposals can be studied empirically, partly because the theories are specific, rather than general. In contrast, you'll recall that the psychodynamic approach is frequently too general to be tested.

2. *The social cognitive approach is compatible with other disciplines in psychology.* For example, this approach fits in successfully with the wealth of knowledge that psychologists have gathered on human cognitive processes. The

same brain that collects information to make a decision or produce a sentence also manages to form a judgment about self-efficacy. Of the four approaches to personality considered in this chapter, the social cognitive approach is most compatible with other ongoing research on humans.

SECTION SUMMARY: *THE SOCIAL COGNITIVE APPROACH*

1. The origins of the social cognitive approach can be traced to behaviorism.

2. Observational learning explains how we acquire some personality characteristics.

3. The concept of reciprocal influences points out that personal/cognitive factors, behavior, and environment all influence one another.

4. People high in self-efficacy are persistent and have high aspirations; people low in self-efficacy may be at risk for depression.

5. The research on cross-cultural views of the self shows that people in collectivist societies—in comparison to people in individualistic societies—are reluctant to talk about themselves, they do not value self-actualization, and they do not tend to overrate their personal characteristics.

6. The social cognitive approach is neither comprehensive nor integrated; however, its strengths are that it is testable and that it is compatible with research in other psychological disciplines.

REVIEW QUESTIONS

1. Imagine that a high school student you know has asked you to describe the chapter you have most recently read in your psychology textbook. Define the word *personality* and summarize each of the four approaches.

2. Try to reproduce the information in Table 13.8 from memory. Label the columns with the names of the four approaches (psychodynamic, humanistic, trait, and social cognitive). Label the rows with the four dimensions we considered (source of the data, cause of behavior, explanation for motivation, and outlook on humans). Then compare your table with Table 13.8.

3. Describe Freud's stages of normal human development. Now compare the following theorists with respect to their explanations about the origins of abnormal behavior: Freud, Horney, Rogers, a trait theorist who favors the biological approach, Skinner, and Bandura.

4. Imagine that you are a talk show host. The two invited guests today—miraculously—are Sigmund Freud and Carl Rogers. How might each respond to your questions: (a) Are wars inevitable? (b) Why do people sometimes perform heroic, altruistic acts? (c) What should people strive for in life?

5. What is self-actualization, in the views of Carl Rogers and Abraham Maslow? How does the research from the social cognitive perspective raise questions about this characteristic?

6. What is the person-situation debate? Think about a particularly noticeable trait of a close friend. Does this trait seem to persist across situations? Why might you tend to believe that this trait is more stable than it might really be? How would

Walter Mischel's most recent theory explain how the trait may depend upon the specific situation?

7. This chapter discussed several personality tests: the Rorschach, the TAT, the NEO Personality Inventory, and the MMPI. Which situations would be most appropriate for using each test? Where relevant, what are the advantages and disadvantages of each test?

8. Why does the cross-cultural research suggest that theorists must be careful about overgeneralizing their ideas to other cultures? We noted that part of the humanistic approach does not seem congruent with the values of collectivist cultures. How would psychodynamic theory, other aspects of humanistic theory, and social cognitive theory be likely to fare if they were tested cross-culturally?

9. How do the four approaches compare with respect to the emphasis on internal forces versus external stimuli? Also compare behaviorism on this dimension.

10. Which of the four approaches to personality do you find most appealing? If you had to design your own comprehensive theory, what features of the other three approaches would you incorporate? Can you list any aspects of personality that have not been addressed by any of these approaches?

NEW TERMS

personality
psychodynamic approach
humanistic approach
trait approach
social cognitive approach
psychoanalytic approach
id
libido
ego
superego
conscious
unconscious
free association
manifest content
latent content
erogenous zones
fixation
oral stage
anal stage
phallic stage
Oedipus complex
latency stage
genital stage
defense mechanisms
repression
regression
reaction formation
displacement
projection
collective unconscious

object-relations approach
projective tests
Rorschach Inkblot Test
Thematic Apperception Test (TAT)
masochistic
self-actualization
conditional positive regard
unconditional positive regard
Maslow's hierarchy of needs
trait
cardinal trait
central trait
secondary trait
five-factor model
Big Five traits
person-situation debate
heritability
subjective well-being
sensation seeking
Minnesota Multiphasic Personality
    Inventory (MMPI)
observational learning
reciprocal influences
self-efficacy
individualistic cultures
independent cultures
collectivist cultures
interdependent cultures
triad

PSYCHOLOGY

REFERENCES

Acocela, J. (1995, November 27). Cather and the academy. *New Yorker,* pp. 56–71.

Adler, T. (1991b, January). Seeing double? Controversial twins study is widely reported, debated. *APA Monitor,* pp. 1,8.

Allison, J., Blatt, S. J., & Zimet, C. M. (1988). *The interpretation of psychological tests.* Washington, DC: Hemisphere.

Allport, G. W. (1937). *Personality: A psychological interpretation.* New York: Holt.

Allport, G. W. (1961). *Pattern and growth in personality.* New York: Holt.

Allport, G. W. (1967). Gordon W. Allport. In E.G. Boting & G. Lindzey (Eds.), *A history of psychology in autobiography* (Vol. 5). New York: Appleton-Century-Crofts.

Anatasi, A. (1988). *Psychological testing* (6th ed.). New York: Macmillan.

Bandura, A. (1986). *Social foundations of thought and action: A social cognitive theory.* Englewood Cliffs, NJ: Prentice Hall.

Bandura, A. (1989). Social cognitive theory. *Annals of Child Development, 6,* 1–60.

Bandura, A. (1991). Social cognitive theory of self-regulation. *Organizational Behavior and Human Decision Processes, 50,* 248–287.

Bandura, A. (1992b). Self-efficacy: Thought control of action. In R. Schwarzer (Ed.) *Self-efficacy: Thought control of action* (pp. 3–38). Washington, DC: Hemisphere.

Bandura, A. (1997). *Self-efficacy: The exercise of control.* New York: Freeman.

Bandura, A., & Jourden, F. J. (1991). Self-regulatory mechanisms governing the impact of social comparison on complex decision making. *Journal of Personality and Social Psychology, 60,* 941–951.

Benjamin, J., et al. (1996). Population and familial association between the D4 domanine receptor gene and measures of novelty seeking. *Nature Genetics. 12,* 81–84.

Block, J. (1995). A contrarian view of the five-factor approach to personality description. *Psychological Bulletin, 117,* 187–215.

Bond, R., & Smith, P. B. (1996). Culture and conformity: A meta-analysis of studies using Asch's (1952b, 1956) line judgment task. *Psychological Bulletin, 119,* 111–137.

Bouchard, C., et al. (1990). The response to long-term overfeeding in identical twins. *New England Journal of Medicine, 322,* 1477–1487.

Bower, G. H. (1990). Awareness, the unconscious, and repression: An experimental psychologist's perspective. In J. L. Singer (Ed.), *Repression and dissociation* (pp. 209–230). Chicago: University of Chicago.

Burger, J. M. (1993). *Personality* (3rd ed.). Pacific Grove, CA: Brooks/Cole.

Buss, A. H. (1989). Personality as traits. *American Psychologist, 44,* 1378–1388.

Butcher, J. M., et al. (1989). *Minnesota Multiphasic Personality Inventory (MMPI-2). Manual for administration and scoring.* Minneapolis: University of Minnesota Press.

Butcher, J. M., et al. (1990). *Development and use of the MMPI-2 content scales.* Minneapolis: University of Minnesota Press.

Butcher, J. M., & Touse, S. B. (1996). Personality: Individual differences and clinical assessment. *Annual Review of Psychology, 47,* 87–111.

Caplan, P. J. & Caplan, J. B. (1994). *Thinking critically about research on sex and gender.* New York: HarperCollins.

Chehrazi S. (1986). Female psychology. *Journal of American Psychoanalytic Association, 43,* 111–162.

Chodorow, M. J. (1978). *The reproduction of mothering.* Berkeley: University of California Press.

PSYCHOLOGY

Chodorow, M. J. (1989). *Feminism and psychoanalytic theory.* New Haven, CT: Yale University Press.

Chodorow, M. J. (1994). *Femininities, masculinities, sexualities: Freud and beyond.* Lexington: University Press of Kentucky.

Cloninger, S. C. (1996). *Theories of personality: Understanding persons* (2nd ed.). Upper Saddle River, NJ: Prentice Hall.

Costa, P. T., Jr., & McCrae, R. R. (1992a). Four ways five factors are basic. *Personality and Individual Differences, 13,* 653–665.

Costa, P. T., Jr., & McCrae, R. R. (1992b). Normal personality assessment in clinical practice: The NEO Personality Inventory. *Psychological Assessment, 4,* 5–13.

Costa, P. T., Jr., & R. R. (1995). Solid ground in the wetlands of personality: A reply to Block. *Psychological Bulletin, 117,* 216–220.

Dana, R. H. (1988). Culturally diverse groups and MMPI interpretation. *Professional Psychology: Research and Practice, 19,* 490–495.

Dawes, R.. M. (1994). *House of cards: Psychology and psychotherapy built on myth.* New York: Free Press.

DeCarvalho, R.J. (1991). *The founders of humanistic psychology.* New York: Praeger.

Domjan, M., & Purdy, J. E. (1995). Animal research in psychology: More than meets the eye of the general psychology student. *American Psychologist, 50,* 496–503.

Ebstein, R. P., et al. (1996). Dopamine D4 receptor (D4DR) exon III polymorphism associated with the human personality trait of novelty seeking. Nature Genetics, 12, 78–80.

Eisenman, R. (1994). Studies in personality, social, and clinical psychology: Nonobvious findings. Lanham, MD: University Press.

Elliott, A. (1994). *Psychoanalytic theory: An introduction.* Oxford, England: Blackwell.

Enns, C. Z. (1989). Toward teaching inclusive personality theories. *Teaching of Psychology, 16,* 111–117.

Epstein, S., & O'Brien, E. J. (1983). Aggregation and beyond: Some basic issues on the prediction of behavior. *Journal of Personality, 51,* 360–392.

Epstein, S., & O'Brien, E. J. (1985). The person-situation debate in historical and current perspective. *Psychological Bulletin, 98,* 513–537.

Ewen, R. B. (1993). *An introduction to theories of personality* (4th ed.). Hillsdale, NJ: Erlbaum.

Exner, J. E., Jr. (1993). *The Rorschach: A comprehensive system: Vol. 1. Basic foundations* (3rd ed.). New York: Wiley.

Exner, J. E., Jr., (1996). A comment on "The comprehensive system for the Rorschach": A critical examination. *Psychological Science, 7,* 11–13.

Fisher, S., & Greenberg, R. P. (1977). *The scientific credibility of Freud's theories and therapy.* New York: Basic Books.

Freud, S. (1925/1976). Some physical consequences of the anatomical distinction between the sexes. In J. Strachey (Ed. Trans.), *The complete psychological works: Standard edition* (Vol. 19). New York: Norton.

Freud, S. (1933/1964). New introductory lectures on psychoanalysis. In J. Strachey (Ed.), *The standard edition of the complete psychological works of Sigmund Freud* (Vol. 23). London: Hogarth.

Funder, D. C. (1993). Judgments as data for personality and developmental psychology: Error versus accuracy. In D. C. Funder, R. D. Parke, C. Tomlinson-Keasey, & K. Widaman (Eds.), *Studying lives through time: Personality and development* (pp.121–146). Washington, DC: American Psychological Association.

Funder, D. C. (1995). On the accuracy of personality judgment: A realistic approach. Psychological Review, 102, 652–670.

PSYCHOLOGY

Gilligan, C. (1982). *In a different voice.* Cambridge, MA: Harvard University Press.

Goldberg, L. R. (1993). The structure of phenotypic personality traits. *American Psychologist, 48,* 26–34.

Goldsmith, H. H., Loosoya, S. H., & Bradshaw, S. H. (1994). Genetics of personality: A twin study of the five-factor model and parent-offspring analyses. In C.H. Halverson, Jr., G. A. Kohnstamm, & R. P. Martin (Eds.), *The developing structure of temperament and personality from infancy to adulthood* (pp.241–265). Hillsdale, NJ: Erlbaum.

Graham, J. R. (1990). *MMPI-2: Assessing personality and psychopathology.* New York: Oxford University Press.

Greene, R. L. (1987). Ethnicity and MJPI performance: A review. *Journal of Consulting and Clinical Psychology, 55,* 497–512.

Greenspan, M. (1993). *A new approach to women and therapy* (2nd ed.). Bradenton, FL: Human Services Institute.

Groth-Marnat, G. (1990). *Handbook of psychological assessment* (2nd ed.). New York: Wiley.

Grusec, J. E. (1992). Social learning theory and developmental psychology: The legacies of Robert Sears and Albert Bandura. *Developmental Psychology, 28,* 776–786.

Hale, N. G. Jr. (1995). *The rise and crisis of psychoanalysis in the United States: Freud and the Americans, 1917–1985.* New York: Oxford University Press.

Halverson, C. F. Jr., Kohnstamm, G. A., & Martin, R. P. (Eds.). (1994). *The developing structure of temperament and personality from infancy to adulthood.* Hillsdale, NJ: Erlbaum.

Hartup, W. W., & van Lieshout, C. F. M. (1995). Personality development in social context. *Annual Review of Psychology, 46,* 655–687.

Hattie, J. (1992). *Self-concept.* Hillsdale, NJ: Erlbaum.

Havill, B. L., Allen, K., Halverson, C. F., & Kohnstamm, G. A. (1994). Parents' use of Big Five categories in their natural language descriptions of children. In C.F. Halverson, Jr., G. A. Kohnstamm, & R. P. Martin (Eds.), *The developing structure of temperament and personality from infancy to adulthood* (pp. 371–386). Hillsdale NJ: Erlbaum.

Holmes, D. S. (1994, June). Is there evidence for repression? Doubtful. *Harvard Mental Health Letter,* pp. 4–6.

Hood, A. B., & Johnson, R. W. (1991). *Assessment in counseling: A guide to the use of psychological assessment procedures.* Alexandria, VA: American Association for Counseling and Development.

Horney, K. (1926/1967). The flight from womanhood. In H. Kelman (Ed.), *Feminine psychology* (pp. 54–70). New York: Norton.

Horney, K. (1945). *Our inner conflicts.* New York: Norton.

Horowitz, L., et al. (1994, July). Does repression exist? Yes. Harvard Mental Health Letter, pp.4–6.

Jacoby, L. L., Lindsay, D. S., & Toth, J. P. (1992). Unconscious influences revealed: Attention, awareness, and control. *American Psychologist, 47,* 802–809.

Jung, C. G. (1917/1953). On the psychology of the unconscious. In H. Read, M. Fordham, & G. Adler (Eds.), *Collected works of C.G. Jung* (Vol. 7). Princeton, NJ: Princeton University Press.

Kaplan, R. M., & Saccuzzo, D. P. (1993). *Psychological testing: Principles, applications, and issues* (3rd ed.). Pacific Grove, CA: Brooks/Cole.

Kihlstrom, J. F. (1994). Persons transcendent, persons embedded [Review of the book *Fifty years of personality psychology*]. *Contemporary Psychology, 39,* 705–706.

Kitayama, S., & Markus, J. R. (1995). Culture and self: Implications for internationalizing psychology. In N. R. Goldberge & J. B. Veroff (Eds.), *The culture and psychology reader* (pp. 366–383). New York: New York University Press.

Klein, M. (1948). *Contributions to psychoanalysis, 1921–1945.* London: Hogarth.

Kurzweil, E. (1995). *Freudians and feminists*. Boulder, CO: Westview Press.

LaFromboise, T. D., Choney, S. B., James, A., & Running Wolf, P. R. (1997). American Indian women and psychology. In H. Landrine (Ed.), *Bringing cultural diversity to feminist psychology: Theory, research, and practice* (pp. 197–239). Washington, DC: American Psychological Association.

Lerman, H. (1986). From Freud to feminist personality theory: Getting here from there. *Psychology of Women Quarterly, 10,* 1–18.

Lippmann, P. (1996). Freud, the ambitious writer of fiction: A view from the English department [Review of the book *Freud's wishful dream book*]. *Contemporary Psychology, 41,* 555–556.

Loftus, E. F., & Klinger, M. R. (1992). Is the unconscious smart or dumb? *American Psychologist, 47,* 19–31.

Lykken, D. T., McGue, M., Tellegan, A., & Bouchard, T. J., Jr. (1992). Emergenesis: Genetic traits that may not run in families. *American Psychologist, 47,* 1565–1577.

Lykken, D. T., & Tellegen, A. (1996). Happiness is a stochastic phenomenon. *Psychological Science, 7,* 186–189.

Macmillan, M. (1992). The sources of Freud's methods for gathering and evaluating clinical data. In T. Gelfand & J. Kerr (Eds.), *Freud and the history of psychoanalysis* (pp. 99–151). Hillsdale, NJ: Analytic Press.

Magunsson, D., & Torestad, B. (1993). A holistic view of personality: A model revisited. *Annual Review of Psychology, 44,* 427–452.

Markus, H. R., & Kitayama, S. (1991b). Cultural variation in the self-concept. In J. Strauss & G. R. Goethals (Eds.), *The self: Interdisciplinary approaches* (pp. 18–48). New York: Springer-Verlag.

Markus, J. R., Kitayama, S., & Heiman, R. J. (1996). Culture and "basic" psychological principles. In E. T. Higgins & A. W. Kruglanski (Eds.), *Social psychology: Handbook of basic principles* (pp. 857–913). New York: Guilford Press.

Maslow, A. H. (1962). *Toward a psychology of being.* Princeton, NJ: Van Nostrand.

Maslow, A. H. (1971). *The farther reaches of human nature.* New York: Viking.

Matlin, M. W., & Stang, D. J. (1978). *The Pollyanna Principle: Selectivity in language, memory, and thought.* Cambridge, MA: Schendman.

McClelland, D. C. (1993). Motives and health. In G. G. Brannigan & M. R. Merrens (Eds.), *The undaunted psychologist: Adventures in research* (pp. 128–141). Philadelphia: Temple University Press.

McCrae, R. R., & Costa, P. T., Jr. (1997). Personality trait structure as a human universal. *American Psychologist, 52,* 509–516.

McCrai, R. R., & John, O. P. (1992). An introduction to the five-factor model and its applications. *Journal of Personality, 60,* 175–215.

McGrath, W. J. (1992). Freud and the force of history. In T. Gelfand & J. Kerr (Eds.), *Freud and the history of psychoanalysis* (pp. 79–97). Hillsdale, NJ: Analytic Press.

Mendelson, M. (1990). It's time to put theories of personality in their place, or, Allport and Stagner got it right, why can't we? In K. H. Craik, R. Hogan, & R. N. Wolfe (Eds.), *Fifty years of personality psychology* (pp. 103–115). New York: Plenum.

Mischel, W. (1968). Personality and assessment. New York: Wiley.

Mischel, W. (1979). On the interface of cognition and personality: Beyond the person situation debate. *American Psychologist, 34,* 740–754.

Mischel, W. (1993). *Introduction to personality* (5th ed.). Fort Worth, TX: Harcourt Brace Jovanovich.

Mischel, W., & Shoda, Y. (1995). A cognitive-affective system theory of personality: Reconceptualizing situations, dispositions, dynamics, and invariance in personality structure. *Psychological Review, 102,* 246–268.

PSYCHOLOGY

Mitchell, S. A., & Black, M. H. (1995). *Freud and beyond: A history of modern psychoanalytic thought.* New York: Basic Books.

Monte, C. F. (1995). *Beneath the mask: An introduction to theories of personality.* Fort Worth, TX: Harcourt Brace.

Parker, K. C. H., Hanson, R. K., & Hunsley, J. (1988). MMPI, Rorschach, and WAIS: A meta-analytic comparison of reliability, stability, and validity. *Psychological Bulletin, 103,* 367–373.

Paunonen, S. V., Jackson, D. N., Trzebinski, J., & Forsterling, F. (1992). Personality structure across cultures: A multi-method evaluation. *Journal of Personality and Social Psychology, 62,* 447–456.

Phares, E. J. (1988). *Introduction to personality* (2nd ed.). Glenview, IL: Scott, Foresman.

Puente, A. E. (1990). Psychological assessment of minority group members. In G. Goldstein & M. Herson (Eds.), *Handbook of psychological assessment* (2nd ed., pp. 505–520). New York: Pergamon.

Robertson, R. (1995). Jungian archetypes: *Jung, Godel, and the history of archetypes. York Beach,* ME: Nicholas-Hays.

Rogers, C. R. (1961). *On becoming a person: A therapist's view of psychotherapy.* Boston: Houghton Mifflin.

Rogers, C. R. (1963). Actualizing tendency in relation to "motives" and to consciousness. In M. R. Jones (Ed.), *Nebraska symposium on motivation* (pp. 1–24). Lincoln: University of Nebraska Press.

Rogers, C. R. (1980). *A way of being.* Boston: Houghton Mifflin.

Rogers, T. B. (1995). *The psychological testing enterprises: An introduction.* Pacific Grove, CA: Brooks/Cole.

Richly, J. F. (1981). *Instructor's manual to Introduction to Personality and Psychotherapy* (2nd ed.). Boston: Houghton Mifflin.

Schoolar, J. W. (1994). Seeking the core: The issues and evidence surrounding recovered accounts of sexual trauma. *Consciousness and Cognition, 3,* 452–469.

Schuster, D. L. (1996). *Searching for memory: The brain, the mind, and the past.* New York: Basic Books.

Shulman, D. G. (1990). The investigation of psychoanalytic theory by means of the experimental method. *International Journal of Psycho-Analysis, 71,* 487–498.

Silverman, L. H., & Weinberger, J. (1985). Mommy and I are one: Implication for psychotherapy. *American Psychologist, 12,* 1296–1308.

Slipp, S. (1993). *The Freudian mystique: Freud, women, and feminism.* New York: New York University Press.

Tarvis, C., & Offir, C. (1977). *The longest war: Sex differences in perspective.* New York: Harcourt Brace Jovanovich.

Thorne, B. (1992). *Carl Rogers.* Thousand Oaks, CA: Sage.

Triandis, H. C. (1996). The psychological measurement of cultural syndromes. *American Psychologist, 51,* 407–415.

Triandis, H. C., Bontempo, R., Leung, K., & Hui, C. K. (1990). A method for determining cultural, demographic, and personal constructs. *Journal of Cross-Cultural Psychology, 21,* 302–318.

Velasquez, R. J., & Callahan, W. J. (1992). Psychological testing of Hispanic Americans in clinical settings: Overview and issues. In K. F. Geisinger (Ed.), *Psychological testing of Hispanics* (pp. 253–265). Washington, DC: American Psychological Association.

Viken, R. J., Rose, R. J., Kaprio, J., & Koskenvuo, M. (1994). A developmental genetic analysis of adult personality: Extraversion and neuroticism from 18–59 years of age. *Journal of Personality and Social Psychology, 66,* 722–730.

Wakefield, J. C. (1989). Level of explanation in personality theory. In D. M. Buss & N. Cantor (Eds.), *Personality psychology: Recent trends and emerging directions* (pp. 333–346). New York: Springer-Verlag.

Welsh, A. (1994). *Freud's wishful dream book*. Princeton, NJ: Princeton University Press.

Wiggins, J. S., & Pincus, A. L. (1992). Personality: Structure and assessment. *Annual Review of Psychology, 43,* 473–504.

Wolfe, R. N. (1998). *Personality research: Can it be a self-correcting discipline?* Paper presented at the annual meeting of the Eastern Psychological Association, Boston.

Wood J. M., Nezworski, M. T., & Stejskal, W. J. (1996a). The comprehensive system for the Rorschach: A critical examination. *Psychological Science, 7,* 3–10.

Wood, J. M., Nezworski, M. T., & Stejskal, W. J. (1996b). Thinking critically about the comprehensive system for the Rorschach: A reply to Exner. *Psychological Science, 7,* 14–17.

Zimmerman, B. J. (1995). Self-efficacy and educational development. In A. Bandura (Ed.), *Self-efficacy in changing societies* (pp. 202–231). New York: Cambridge University Press.

Zuckerman, M. (1993). Out of sensory deprivation and into sensation seeking: A personal and scientific journey. In G. G. Brannigan & M. R. Merrems (Eds.), *The undaunted psychologist: Adventures in research* (pp. 44–57). Philadelphia: Temple University Press.

Zuckerman, M. (1994a). Impulsive unsocialized sensation seeking: The biological foundations of a basic dimension of personality. In J. E. Bates & T. D. Wachs (Eds.), *Temperament: Individual differences at the interface of biology and behavior* (pp. 219–255). Washington, DC: American psychological Association.

Zuckerman, M. (1994b). *Behavioral expressions and biosocial bases of sensation seeking.* New York: Cambridge University Press.

Zuckerman, M. (1995). Good and bad humors: Biochemical bases of personality and its disorder. *Psychological Science, 6,* 325–332.

Answers to Demonstrations

Demonstration 13.1

Climbing the staircase and unlocking the door symbolizes sexual intercourse (No. 8); the small forbidden room represents the female genitals (No. 4); the spindle is a symbol for a penis (No. 2); and pricking the finger indicates menstruation (No. 6). As far as I know, the other four items on the list are not symbolized in this fairy tale! Incidentally, Bettelheim tells us about the implied message for anxious little girls hearing this story: "Don't worry and don't try to hurry things—when the time is ripe, the impossible problem will be solved, as if all by itself" (p. 233) (We can only speculate whether females who wait for a kiss from a handsome prince are likely to thrive in the current era.)

PERIODICAL RESEARCH

arts One and Two provided practice reading and studying content-area textbooks. Part Three, on the other hand, contains selections from journals and magazines devoted to the same four disciplines: health, American History, business, and psychology. Each of the selections is followed by a set of questions to be used at your instructor's discretion. The reading you do in this part will be similar to the reading required to complete assignments in college-level courses: Typically, you will read other materials in addition to your textbook.

Returning to the analogy of learning to drive discussed in the introductions of Parts One and Two of this book, Part Three allows you to practice skills that you will not use regularly but still need to know. For example, when you hit a patch of ice while driving, it's important to know to turn into the direction of the spin if you lose control of the vehicle. You won't use this skill as often as other driving skills, but it's still necessary to learn it. As you progress to upper-level college courses, you will use the skills covered in this part of the book more often, and the writing exercises will provide you with some practice.

As stated, the goal of Part Three is to introduce you to a different type of reading material and to give you practice applying the skills learned in Part One. The questions that follow each selection require higher levels of thinking and give you practice using reading skills that you would need to do research in a particular content area. For example, you may be assigned to research and argue a particular side in the Civil War. Your research would include not only finding an article or chapter but also determining if that article was the best for your purpose and what sections would be best to use in your writing. You would need to determine what is fact and what is opinion and whether the opinions are backed with enough evidence to prove a point.

Part Three begins with instruction on how to read journal articles. First, you need to know your purpose for reading. Instructors may ask you to write a summary and/or a reaction to any of the articles, or they may assign the questions that follow the articles. *How* you read will depend on *why* you are reading. For example, if you were asked to write a summary, you would need to take notes or mark and annotate the main ideas as you read. If you were assigned a particular question that asks your opinion on a certain issue, you would need to take notes on specific sections of the article to help defend your opinion.

Continue to practice metacognition and use different parts of PQ3R to help you select and narrow portions of the reading to fit your purpose. Understand your purpose for reading and read appropriately.

READING AND TAKING NOTES FROM PERIODICALS

You read a journal article to learn new information. At times, you will want to read the entire article and at other times you will skim the article for the information that you need and then read more closely and take notes on those parts that are most important to you.

To skim an article, follow the steps for previewing found at the beginning of this textbook. Use the headings to help you narrow down what to read more closely. After you have found the section of the article that you want to take time to read, skim through the first sentences of the paragraphs to help you get an idea of exactly what you can use. When you have narrowed down what to read in depth, begin to take notes.

Taking notes is similar to writing a summary except that you need to take notes only on your thesis (main idea of your paper). Follow these steps for taking notes:

1. Record the bibliographic information at the top of an index card. Include the same information that you do for the summary (author; title of article; name of journal; date; and pages on which the article can be found). If the article is from an electronic source, you will need to also record the online database or the electronic address as well as the date accessed. When you write notes referring to specific information in the article on an index card, record the exact page on which you found the information. For instance, if you are reading a three-page article, and you take notes from information on the second page, you would record that page number next to the notes.

2. Skim through the article to determine what information you want to include in your paper. For example, if you were writing a research paper showing the effects of advertising on children's spending, the article "Food Fight!" would be perfect. You would want to include information on how much money children spend and why.

3. Reread important information that you may want to include in your paper, and write it in your own words. Use quotation marks around any words or group of words that you write verbatim (word for word) from the article. Be sure to include the sources of any studies.

4. Keep all cards together so that when you write your paper, you'll have all the textual and bibliographic information at your fingertips.

SAMPLE NOTES FOR A RESEARCH CARD

Following are sample notes from "Food Fight!" You can find this article in Chapter 2 under "Writing a Summary of an Article."

Chaplin, Heather. "Food Fight!" *American Demographics*, June 1999, pp. 64–65.

6- to 11-year-olds spent $25 billion of own money and influenced $187 billion spending in 1998. p. 64

Reasons—growing affluence, bigger allowances, dual-income families, greater freedom, kids "trying to find their place in the world." p. 65

Top 5 items bought by kids with their own money, 8–17—food/drink, clothes, audio/visual, shoes, toys p. 65

A NOTE ON PLAGIARISM

Plagiarism means to pass off as one's own work what one has read or heard from another source. If you were to incorporate any of the preceding notes into a research paper, you would need to provide a *citation* (a note informing the reader of the original source) in your paper to identify the source of the information. Many readers know that when they use a *direct quote* (the exact words of an author), they must include a citation. Even when you use information from another source in your own words (paraphrase or summarize), you must also provide a citation. If you are required to write a summary, only direct quotes need to be cited because you are providing the source information for the reader at the beginning of the summary. Any other writing in which you include information from an article in your own words would require a citation within your paragraph.

For example, you are writing that paper on the influence of advertising on children. Your paper would look like the following:

> Companies that produce products for young consumers are aware that a great deal of money is available for spending. In 1998, six-to-eleven-year-olds spent $25 billion of their own money and influenced adults to spend another $187 billion. (Chaplin 64)

The preceding citation is written in the MLA (Modern Language Association) system, a system commonly used to document sources in the humanities. Typically, the author's last name along with the page number of the source would be listed. No abbreviation (*p.* or *pp.*) is used to identify page numbers.

Another system is the APA (American Psychological Association). This style is recommended for the social sciences. Using APA style, the two pieces of information used to cite a source are usually the last name of the author and the year of publication. When the author's name is not available, then a shortened title is used. Only direct quotations require the page number (using the abbreviations *p.* or *pp.*) to also be listed in the citation. For instance, if the prior paper were written using the APA system, the citation would look like this:

> (Chaplin, 1999)

If there were a direct quote, the citation would look like this:

> (Chaplin, 1999, p. 64)

Other systems exist for various disciplines, so check with your instructor to determine which style you should use in your paper. An English style handbook is recommended to give you more detail on citations and references in papers.

HEALTH ARTICLES

Alternative and Complementary Modalities for Managing Stress and Anxiety

Lynn Keegan, RN, PhD, HNC

Lynn Keegan is director of Holistic Nursing Consultants in Temple, Tex, and Port Angeles, Wash, and editor of Holistic Nursing Update. She has written 9 books and numerous journal publications and serves on the boards of several nursing organizations.

Stress is endemic in our society. More than two thirds of office visits to physicians are for stress-related illnesses, such as heart disease, anxiety disorders, high blood pressure, coronary artery disease, cancer, respiratory disorders, accidental injuries, cirrhosis of the liver, and attempted suicide, all of which are leading causes of death in the United States. In addition to causing illness, stress can aggravate other conditions such as multiple sclerosis, diabetes, herpes, mental illness, alcoholism, drug abuse, and family discord and violence. Stress is not always adverse, however; managed correctly, the problems caused by stress can be minimized. Realistically, stress is a normal aspect of life that must be endured at some level. Additionally, a stress response can be helpful in many ways, motivating persons to work or study or increasing their alertness while taking a test or giving a talk. The problem occurs when stress exceeds a productive level and interferes with the ability to think, remember, and focus on tasks. Stress that is ineffectively managed and remains too high for too long can contribute to multiple illnesses.

Americans are using alternative and complementary therapies, often for stress-related complaints. The results of a nationwide survey of 1539 adults published in the New England Journal of Medicine indicated that 1 in 3 Americans uses therapies considered unconventional.[1] This study was the landmark investigation that opened the floodgates to exploring and understanding these new therapies and how they work. The most frequently used therapies mentioned in the survey were relaxation techniques, chiropractic, massage therapy, imagery, spiritual healing, lifestyle diets, herbal medicine, mega-vitamin therapy, self-help groups, energy healing, biofeedback, hypnosis, homeopathy, acupuncture, folk remedies, exercise, and prayer. A 1997 follow-up national survey by the same team found that use of at least 1 of 16 alternative therapies during the preceding year increased from 33.8% in 1990 to 42.1% in 1997. Overall, use of alternative therapies increased by 25%, total visits to alternative medicine practitioners increased by 47%, and expenditures for alternative goods and services increased by 45% (exclusive of inflation). Results from the follow-up study also indicated that ailing persons most often seek nonmainstream treatments for chronic conditions, such as back problems, anxiety, depression, and headaches. In 1990, an estimated 3 in 10 Americans used at least one alternative therapy; in 1997, the rate was 4 in 10 Americans. Of additional interest, the increased use does not appear to be linked to any particular sociodemographic group.[2] Another researcher found that compared with nonusers, the majority of users of alternative medicine were more educated and reported poorer health status. They used the alternative therapies not so much as a result of being dissatisfied with conventional medicine, but largely because they found that these healthcare alternatives were more congruent with their own values, beliefs, and philosophical orientations toward health and life.[3] Indeed, many acute care nurses are becoming aware of ways to incorporate complementary modalities to combat the effects of stress.

Q: What exactly is stress and what causes it?

The term stress refers to a heightened physical or mental state produced by a change in the internal or external environment. In humans, physical stress is caused by injuries or illnesses and psychological stress by real, perceived, or anticipated threats. Whether stress arises from a cause perceived by sense organs that relay the danger to the brain or from mental actions such as worry or fear, the course of events can be the same.

Q: What is the relationship between stress and the body's hormonal system?

When an event such as hospitalization for a patient or environmental work conditions for a staff member is perceived as threatening by the higher cortical centers, signals are sent to the motor cortex and hypothalamus. Several hormones are released from the pituitary and adrenal glands, resulting in a number of physiological manifestations that can produce further harm to already compromised systems.

Q: What are some of the symptoms or manifestations of stress?

Stress shows itself in 3 general areas: physical, social, and psychological. Physical signs of stress include

- fatigue and exhaustion,
- headaches or migraines,
- neck and back pains or stiffness,
- gastrointestinal problems (nausea, diarrhea, constipation, or colitis),
- chest pains or palpitations,
- vulnerability to colds and flu (weakened immune system), and
- sleep disturbances.

Social manifestations of stress include family conflicts, job tensions, and change in sexual energy. Psychological signs of stress are 3-fold (Table 1). Any patient or staff member with subjective or objective signs of stress is a candidate for one or more stress-reduction therapies.

Q: How do you define alternative and complementary therapies?

An alternative therapy is one that is used instead of a conventional or mainstream therapy. For example, acupuncture is an alternative therapy. A complementary therapy may be an alternative therapy, but becomes complementary when used in conjunction with conventional ther-

Table 1 Psychological manifestations of stress

Emotional symptoms	Intellectual symptoms	Behavioral symptoms
Depression	Forgetfulness	Mood swings
Anxiety or frustration	Slower thinking	Absenteeism
Decreased job satisfaction	Day dreaming	Difficulty completing tasks
Apathy or boredom	Decreased concentration	Possible substance abuse

© Thomson Wadsworth

apy. It helps to potentiate the effect of the conventional therapy. For example, massage, which can stand alone as an alternative therapy, can also be used in conjunction with conventional regimens for a variety of problems.

Q: What are some of the specific alternative and complementary therapies that you find helpful to counteract stress?

Many different therapies that everyone can enjoy are available. See Table 2 for a brief description of the most widely used, evidence-based therapies; for more information, see *Holistic Nursing: A Handbook for Practice.*[4]

Q: What is the research that validates use of these therapies?

All of these modalities have research results to back them up. That is why the therapies in Table 2 are so popular. Let's take a look at a couple of them individually.

Table 2 Brief description of stress-buster complementary therapies

Therapy	Description
Aquatherapy	Use of some form of water to augment healing. Water may be used internally or externally in the form of ice, liquid, or vapor. You can partake of water at a spa during rehabilitation and for general health maintenance and prevention. Warm baths or hot-tub therapy can reduce stress.
Aromatherapy	Use of essential oils to stimulate bodily responses via the sense of smell. These essential oils are commonly used in aromatherapy: citrus, lavender, peppermint, and rosemary.
Energy therapies	Practitioners and recipients adhere to the belief that the human body is surrounded by an energy field. Through the noninvasive manipulation of this field, energy is shifted and altered to produce a positive change.
Humor	Humor has been recognized since antiquity for its healing power. It is important to note that different people respond in different ways to humor so it is important to personalize this therapy.
Imagery	Imagery is a nonverbal, noninvasive intervention that can be implemented by patients alone or with guidance. Imagery uses the internal experiences of memories, dreams, fantasies, and visions to serve as the bridge for connecting body, mind, and spirit. Guided imagery plus relaxation is being used with increasing frequency to help people improve their performance and control their responses to stressful situations.
Massage	Massage is one of numerous physical touch interventions designed to reduce stress, alleviate anxiety, promote circulation, and generally stimulate a state of well-being.
Music	Music is nonverbal communication and has been used in rituals of celebration, funerals, and ordinary transitions of daily life. It involves passive relaxation combined with listening to soothing, relaxing music for the purpose of changing behavior, physiological responses, and emotions; it affects physiological responses through mind modulation.
Relaxation	Relaxation is a generic term for a variety of techniques designed specifically to reduce both physiological and psychological stress. Progressive muscle relaxation involves a series of clenching and relaxing steps designed to relax both the body and mind.

Aquatherapy

Low back pain is one of the most common chronic conditions. In a study[5] with a random sample of 50 patients with low-back pain who received spa therapy and 52 who received standard ambulatory care, the findings for the 2 groups were significantly different. Compared with the patients who did not have spa therapy, patients who had the therapy had a significant improvement in spin mobility and in functional scores and a reduction in the daily duration of pain. Assessment of the long-term effects 9 months after therapy showed continued reduction in pain and drug consumption and improvement in spine mobility among the patients who had spa therapy.[5]

Another study[6] consisted of 25 randomly selected patients in a hospital setting who had pain from fibromyalgia. Twelve patients had hydrogalvanic baths, and 13 had Jacobson relaxation training. Different dimensions of pain were measured at the beginning and the end of therapy. Patients receiving bath therapy had a significantly greater decrease in pain intensity from breakfast to lunch than did patients who received the Jacobson relaxation therapy.[6] Numerous other studies are detailed in the book *Healing Waters.*[7]

Aromatherapy

In a study[8] of 122 patients in an intensive care unit, 3 therapies were compared for their effects on increasing the quality of sensory input that patients receive and reducing patients' levels of stress and anxiety. The key findings were that patients who had aromatherapy reported significantly greater improvement in their mood and perceived levels of anxiety. They also felt less anxious and more positive immediately after the therapy, although this effect was not sustained or cumulative.[8] When pilot studies on aromatherapy that combined use of essential oils of rose and lavender with touching were done at Columbia Presbyterian Medical Center, the heart variation monitor showed parasympathetic peaks as a subject's feet were stroked with diluted essential oil. Sometimes just thinking about an aroma or an odor can be as powerful as smelling the actual aroma or odor itself.[9]

Aromas have measurable effects on person's feelings. Torii et al[10] report on the psychologically stimulating effect of jasmine. Manley[11] reports on both the psychologically stimulating effect of lemon, lemon-grass, peppermint, and basil and the relaxing effects of bergamot, chamomile, and sandalwood. Other aromas found to be relaxing are rose and lavender.[12] Sweet orange essential oil was effective in both induction of anesthesia and recovery time from anesthesia in children.[13]

These 2 therapies, along with several others, are explored fully in the AACN Protocols for Practice. If you are unfamiliar with these and other complementary therapies, take the opportunity to explore them personally. When you are comfortable with using them yourself, it is easier to introduce them to others.

Critical care nursing is more than just meeting the physiological needs of patients. Helping patients and staff members alike to cope with the multiple stressors in the acute care environment is an integral part of nursing. Learning to recognize the manifestations of stress is the first step; the next step is adding knowledge and skills about the emerging alternative and complementary therapies in order to cope and prevent the adverse effects of stress.

References

1. Eisenberg DM, Kessler RC, Foster C, Nortack FE, Calkins DR, Delbanco TL. Unconventional medicine in the United States: prevalence, costs, and patterns of use. *N Engl J Med,* 1993;328(suppl 4):S246-S252.
2. Eisenberg DM, Davis RB, Ettner, SL, et al. Trends in alternative medicine use in the United States, 1990–1997: results of a follow-up national survey, *JAMA,* 1998;280:1569–1575.
3. Astin JA. Why patients use alternative medicine: results of a national study, *JAMA,* 1998;279:1548–1553.
4. Dossey B, Keegan L, Guzzetta C. *Holistic Nursing: A Handbook for Practice,* 3rd ed. Gaithersburg, MD: Aspen Publishers; 2000.

5. Guillemin F, Constant F, Collin JF, Boulange M. Short- and long-term effect of spa therapy in chronic low back pain. *Br J Rheumatol.* 1994;33:148–151.
6. Gunther V, Mur E, Kinigadner U, Miller C. Fibromyalgia: the effects of relaxation and hydro-galvanic bath therapy on the subjective pain experience. *Clin Rheumatol.* 1994;13:573–578.
7. Keegan L, Keegan G. *Healing Waters: The Miraculous Health Benefits of Earth's Most Essential Resource.* New York, NY: Berkeley/Putnam Publishers; 1998.
8. Dunn C, Sleep J, Collett D. Sensing an improvement: an experimental study to evaluate the use of aromatherapy; massage and periods of rest in an intensive care unit, *J Adv Nurs,* 1995;21:34–40.
9. Betts T. The fragrant breeze: the role of aromatherapy in treating epilepsy, *Aromather Q.* Winter 1996;51:25–27.
10. Torii S, Fukuda H, Kanemoto H, et al. Contingent negative variation and the psychological effects of odor. In: Van Toller S, Dodd GH, eds *Perfumery: The Psychology and Biology of Fragrance,* London: Chapman & Hall, London; 1988:107–120.
11. Manley CH. Psychophysiological effect of odor. *Crit Rev Food Sci Nutr.* 1993;33:57–62.
12. Yamaguchi H. Effect of odor on heart rate. In: Koryo M, ed. *The Psychophysiological Effect of Odor.* Tokyo; Indo; 1990;168.
13. Mehta S, Stone DN, Whitehead HF. Use of essential oils to promote induction of anaesthesia in children. *Anaesthesia,* 1998;53:720–721.

Reading and Writing Activities for "Alternate and Complementary Modalities for Managing Stress and Anxiety"

1. Write a summary of the article.

2. Try one of the alternative therapies mentioned in this article. Use it at least three times and report on the effects it had on your stress level. Keep notes as you use the therapy. How long does it take you to feel less stressed? How well does it work? Would you recommend it to others? Why or why not?

3. Compare the definition of *stress* in this article to the definition in the textbook chapter excerpt "Personal Stress Management." How are they alike? How are they different?

4. Write a journal entry on the article. Did the article make you think of anything? Can the information be of use to you? If so, how? Did you visualize anything while you were reading the article? If so, what?

5. On index cards, take notes from the article to support a paper with the following title: "How Well Do Alternative Therapies Solve the Stress Problem?" Be sure to cite all research projects.

10 Simple Ways to Manage *Stress*

Stress is one problem we have in common. Much of it is self-inflicted.
David B. Posen, MD Oakville, Ontario

Contents

1. Decrease or Discontinue Caffeine
2. Regular Exercise

Source: Review of Ophthalmology, Aug2000, Vol. 7 Issue 8, p39, 3p

From "10 Simple Ways to Manage Stress," *Review of Opthalmology,* Aug. 2000, Vol. 7, Issue 8, p. 39, 3p. Reprinted with permission.

3. Relaxation/Mediation

4. Sleep

5. Time-outs and Leisure

6. Realistic Expectations

7. Reframing

8. Belief Systems

9. Ventilation/Support System

10. Humor

STRESS IS THE MOST COMMON cause of ill health in our society, probably underlying up to 70 percent of all visits to family physicians. It is also the one problem that every doctor shares with every patient. That makes it an issue we can relate to and one in which we can use ourselves as a reference point.

Stress can be classified as external or internal. External *stress* factors can include staff members complaining or resigning, the headaches of managed care or financial pressure from declining reimbursements. However, most of the *stress* we feel actually is internal or self-generated. Since we create it, we can do something about it.

The simple truth about *stress:* To master *stress,* you must change. You have to figure out what you are doing that is contributing to your problem and change it. Here are 10 practical strategies that I have found helpful over the years for both myself and my patients. Some are simple and can be implemented quickly; others are a bit more involved.

1. Decrease or Discontinue Caffeine

It's hard to beat this simple intervention. Most of us do not perceive caffeine (coffee, tea, chocolate and cola) as a drug, a strong stimulant that actually generates a *stress* reaction in the body.

The best way to observe the effect of caffeine is to get it out of your system long enough to see if there is a difference in how you feel. Three weeks is adequate. I estimate 75–80 percent of those who try it notice a benefit. They feel more relaxed, less jittery or nervous, sleep better and have more energy (a paradox, since you are removing a stimulant). They have less heartburn and fewer muscle aches. You, too, may feel dramatically better.

One warning, however: Wean yourself gradually, or you'll get migraine-type withdrawal headaches. I suggest decreasing by one drink per day until you are down to zero; then abstain for three weeks.

2. Regular Exercise

As a way of draining off *stress* energy, nothing beats aerobic exercise. To understand why, let's review what *stress* is. People often think of *stress* as pressure at work, a demanding boss, a sick child or rush-hour traffic. All these may be triggers, but *stress* is actually the body's reaction to factors such as these. *Stress* is the fight-or-flight response in the body, mediated by adrenaline and other *stress* hormones, and comprising such physiologic changes as increased heart rate and blood pressure, faster breathing, muscle tension, dilated pupils, dry mouth and increased blood sugar.

In other words, *stress* is the state of increased arousal necessary for an organism to defend itself at a time of danger. Exercise is the most logical way to dissipate this excess energy. It is Mint our bodies are trying to do when we pace around or tap our legs and fingers. It is much better to channel it into a more complete form of exercise like a brisk walk, a run, a bike ride, or a game of squash.

During times of high *stress,* we could benefit from an immediate physical outlet, but this often is not possible. However, regular exercise can drain off ongoing *stress* and keep things under control. I recommend physical activity every day or two. At the very best, try to exercise three times per week for a minimum of 30 minutes each time. Aerobic activities like walking, jogging, swimming, bicycling, racquet sports, aerobics classes and dancing are suitable.

3. Relaxation Mediation

Another way to reduce bodily *stress* is through certain relaxation techniques. Just as we are all capable of mounting and sustaining a *stress* reaction, we have also inherited the ability to put our bodies into a state of deep relaxation. In this state, all the physiologic events in the *stress* reaction are reversed: Pulse slows, blood pressure falls, breathing slows and muscles relax.

While the *stress* reaction is automatic, however, the relaxation response needs to be brought forth by intention. Fortunately, there are many ways of doing this. Sitting by a lake or fireplace, gently petting the family cat, and other restful activities can generate this state. There also are specific skills that can be learned that are efficient and beneficial.

A state of deep relaxation achieved through meditation or self-hypnosis is actually more physiologically restful than sleep. These techniques are best learned through formal training courses, though books and relaxation tapes may be used when courses are not convenient. I can attest to the benefits of regular meditation from personal experience.

On days when exercise is not possible, relaxation techniques are an excellent way to bring down the body's *stress* level. Whereas exercise dissipates *stress* energy, relaxation techniques neutralize it, producing a calming effect. As little as 20 minutes once or twice per day confers significant benefit.

4. Sleep

Mundane though it sounds, sleep is an important way of reducing *stress.* The chronically stressed almost all suffer from fatigue (in some cases resulting from *stress*-induced insomnia), and people who are tired do not cope well with stressful situations.

These dynamics can create a vicious cycle. When you get more sleep, you feel better and are more resilient and adaptable in dealing with day-to-day events. Most people know what their usual sleep requirement is (the range is five to 10 hours per night; the average being seven to eight), but a surprisingly large percentage of the population is chronically sleep deprived.

Try going to bed 30–60 minutes earlier and monitor the results after a few days or a week. If you're still tired, go to bed 30 minutes earlier than this. Eventually, you'll find what works for you. The three criteria of success are waking refreshed, good daytime energy and waking naturally before the alarm goes off in the morning.

5. Time-outs and Leisure

Many otherwise rational physicians think nothing of working from dawn to dusk without taking intermissions, and then wonder why they become distressed. The two major issues are pacing and a balance of work and leisure.

Pacing is about awareness and vigilance: knowing when to extend yourself and when to ease up. It is also about acting on the information your body gives you. A key is taking periodic time-outs. Too many doctors go far too long without breaks. For busy physicians, it's not always convenient to take time-outs when nature tells us to, but we can all become better at this.

A mid-morning break, lunch, a midafternoon break and supper divide the day into roughly two-hour segments. These time-outs can include power naps, meditation, daydreaming, a social interlude, a short walk, a refreshment break, a change to low-concentration tasks or listening to music. Despite all our labor-saving devices, leisure is still an elusive commodity for most people. Statistics show that the average American works an extra four hours per week compared with 20 years ago. That translates into an extra month of work each year.

Leisure time and levels of distress are inversely proportional—the less leisure, the more *stress.* Think of your life (excluding sleep time) in four compartments: work, family, community and self. Then assess what percentage of your time and energy in an average week goes into each part. There is no "normal" range, but I'd be concerned if work is over 60 percent and/or self is less than 10 percent. We all require time to meet our own needs (self-care, self-nurturing, etc.), and when that is neglected, trouble usually follows.

Self-directed activities can include exercise or recreation, relaxation, socializing, entertainment and hobbies.

6. Realistic Expectations

People often become upset about something, not because it is innately stressful, but because it does not concur with what they expected. If, for example, slow-moving traffic happens at rush hour, you may not like it, but it will not surprise you. However, if it occurs on a Sunday afternoon, especially if it makes you late for something, you are more likely to be stressed by it.

When expectations are realistic, life feels more predictable and more manageable. There is an increased feeling of control, because you can prepare yourself (physically and psychologically).

You can *stress* yourself with unrealistic personal expectations, too. I remember a patient berating himself and feeling guilty because he did not love his stepdaughter as much as his own biologic children. Blended families are common, and I suspect many people struggle with this issue of love and loyalty. I asked this man where he got the idea that he would love his second wife's children as if they were his own. I suggested that his expectation was probably unrealistic, especially early in the new marriage. He felt relieved by this idea and stopped putting pressure on himself to feel something he did not feel.

7. Reframing

This is one of the most powerful and creative *stress* reducers I know of. Reframing is a technique used to change the way you look at things in order to feel better about them. The key is to recognize that there are many ways to interpret the same situation. Is the glass half empty or half full? There are many ways of seeing the same thing, so you might as well pick the one you like.

A busy ophthalmologist can reframe his interpretation of a loaded schedule. Instead of feeling pressured by the heavy workload, feel exhilarated by the opportunity to help so many patients. In an instance when a staff member is resigning, look upon it as an opportunity to bring another talented person into the practice. Reframing does not change the external reality but simply helps you to view things less stressfully. You are not denying or ignoring a problem, but simply seeing the more positive side.

8. Belief Systems

A lot of *stress* results from our beliefs. We have literally thousands of premises and assumptions about all kinds of things that we hold to be the truth: "You can't fight City Hall." "The customer is always right." "Men shouldn't show their emotions." Most of our beliefs are held unconsciously, so we are unaware of them. This gives them more power over us and allows them to run our lives.

Beliefs cause *stress* in two ways. The first is the behavior that results from them. For example, if you believe that work should come before pleasure, you are likely to work harder and have less leisure time than you would otherwise. If you believe that people should meet the needs of others before they meet their own, you are likely to neglect yourself to some extent. These beliefs are expressions of people's philosophy or value system, but all lead to increased effort and decreased relaxation—a formula for *stress.*

There is no objective truth. These are really just opinions, but they lead to stressful behavior. Uncovering the unconscious assumptions behind your actions can help you to change.

Beliefs also cause *stress* when they are in conflict with those of other people. One of my patients had a fight with his son, because the child wore the same clothes several days in a row. I asked why it bothered him, and he replied, "Because you should change your clothes every day." I asked him where this idea originated: "Well, my mother taught me that." I told him that this was not "the truth," but merely his opinion based on the way he was raised. Once he recognized his belief was not "true," his anger diminished.

9. Ventilation/Support System

There's an old saying: "A problem shared is a problem halved." We all have patients who come into the office upset, talking incessantly about a problem and feeling better when they are finished. They have told their story, cried or made some admission and the act of doing so in the presence of a trusted and empathetic listener has been therapeutic.

People who keep things to themselves carry a considerable and unnecessary burden. We can do much for ourselves by developing a support system (a few trusted relatives, colleagues or friends to talk to when we are upset or worried).

Another form of ventilation is writing, for example, in a private journal at home. Former tennis star Guillermo Vilas once said: "When my life is going well, I live it. When it's not going well, I write it." If you are angry, write a letter to the person with whom you are angry. These letters are not for sending; they should be destroyed—unread—once they are written. The value is in expressing the feelings and getting them out.

10. Humor

Laughter relieves tension. In fact, we often laugh hardest when we have been feeling most tense. Humor is an individual thing—what is funny to one person may be hurtful to another. It's wonderful when you can poke fun at yourself. Be careful when making jokes about staff members or patients. If you think of something funny to say at the office, say it if you feel it will ease tension and not be offensive. When it is done sensitively, laughter is a great gift to the people around you. In this busy world, the best gift we can give ourselves is *stress management.*

This article was adapted from "*Stress Management* for Patients and Physicians," which appeared in The Canadian Journal of Continuing Medical Education, April 1995. The full text also appears on Internet Mental Health, *www.mentalhealth.com.*

Dr. Posen also suggests:
Staying Afloat When the Water Gets Rough. Posen D. Toronto: Key Porter, Toronto: 1998
Why Zebras Don't Get Ulcers. Sapolsky, Freeman, 1998.
Time Shifting. Rechtschaffen, Doubleday, 1996.
The Wellness Book. Benson and Stuart, Birch Hill Press, 1992.
Always Change a Losing Game. Posen, Key Porter, Toronto, 1994.

Dr. Posen formerly practiced family medicine but today devotes his time exclusively to stress management, lifestyle counseling and psychotherapy. He has given seminars for major corporations Dr. Posen as a weekly column on the web at www.canoe.ca/HealthStress/home.html.

Reading and Writing Activities for "10 Simple Ways to Manage *Stress*"

1. Write a summary of the article.

2. Review the source (journal title) of this article and explain why the article was written for a particular audience. Compare the ideas for stress reduction to those in the prior article written for nurses.

3. Compare the stress reduction techniques in this article to the techniques presented in the textbook chapter written for students, "Personal Stress Management."

4. Create a stress management program for yourself.

5. Compare the definition of *stress* in this journal article to the definitions found in the textbook chapter "Personal Stress Management" and in the prior article. List the similarities and differences, and explain the differences.

AMERICAN HISTORY ARTICLES

Women in Battle in the Civil War

by Richard Hall

Research in recent years has found strong and growing evidence of the presence of women on Civil War battlefields in numbers far beyond what had been previously believed. Articles in a women's military journal and two recently published books have begun to report the new discoveries (Larson 1990; Larson 1992; Hall 1993; Middleton 1993). However, the research is ongoing and new case histories are turning up regularly.

Although it has long been believed that over a hundred women may have participated in Civil War combat, some contemporary observers believe that the true number may have been much higher (Livermore 1887, 119–120). Whatever the number, it is important to discover and tell about as many of these women as possible, for their stories deserve a place in women's history in American history.

Women Disguised as Men

For every documented case of a woman who served in combat, evidence suggests that there could have been two, three, or even four others who were killed in combat and buried without their gender being discovered, or who survived the war with their male disguises intact.

In 1934, some human bones were dug up in a garden on the former Shiloh battlefield, evidencing a hasty burial. The graves had not been registered. The remains were identified by their military paraphernalia as those of Civil War soldiers. One was found to be a female soldier (Brooke 1978, 29).

A former Civil War soldier known as "Otto Schaffer," a hermit farmer in Butler County, Kansas, was discovered to be a woman only at death.[1] Many similar examples are known. "Albert Cashier" served a full three-year term of enlistment with the 95th Illinois Infantry regiment and saw extensive combat (Davis 1988, 108–112). Her true identity as Jennie Hodgers was not discovered until 1911 when she was struck by an automobile and injured. Hodgers, as a child, had disguised herself as a boy and stowed away on a ship from Ireland to America.[2]

Considering the fact that three million soldiers fought in the war, the discovery that hundreds or even thousands of women served in combat is not significant in terms of percentages. But in social and human terms, and especially given the social values of the mid-1860s, even this number takes on significance.

Women of the Civil War era were severely restricted in their ability to travel widely on their own and to experience the freedom that men had in the human adventure, unless they didn't mind being considered "immoral" or "loose" women. They were supposed to relish hearth and home, not exploration and adventure. The "proper" role for women during the war was to work in one of the soldiers' aid societies that were formed, to roll bandages and supply clothing and personal hygiene kits to the soldiers. Another acceptable activity was service in the commission formed to work for improvements in hospital care and medical practices (Young 1959, 66–81).

In a sense, the Civil War proved to be a great equalizer for certain bold and adventurous women who seized the opportunity to expand their horizons. Some did so in standard female garb; others disguised themselves as men. Adding ferment to the social change were several women born or raised in other countries, who brought with them to America a streak of independence and some experience in shattering norms.

When the Union and Confederate armies clashed in the first major campaign of the Civil War at Bull Run Creek, Manassas, Virginia, on July 21, 1861, a few women were present on both sides. Among them was Kady Brownell, wife of a Rhode Island mechanic, who enlisted in the 1st Rhode Island Infantry regiment. Her father was Angus McKensie, a Scottish soldier in the British army (Middleton 1993, 26–27).

Brownell trained with the regiment, proved to be proficient with arms, and accompanied her husband on the march. On the Bull Run battlefield, probably uniquely among all the women who served in the war, she was color-bearer, carrying the flag in advance of her unit of sharpshooters. She came under direct fire and was forced to flee with the other soldiers at the end of the day when Confederate forces broke through the Union lines. Later she also performed courageously at the battle of New Bern, North Carolina (Moore 1866, 54–64; Brocket 1867, 773–774).

Two of the more famous women who fought in Civil War combat disguised as men also were at the scene, one on each side. For the North, "Frank Thompson" (Sarah Emma Edmonds) was with the 2nd Michigan Infantry regiment that arrived late on the battlefield and helped cover the Union retreat. Thompson was serving as a male nurse in the old stone church near Centreville, Virginia, and was forced to flee when the Confederates overran their position.

Sarah Edmonds had been born in New Brunswick, Canada, in December 1841, the youngest child of a Scotch-Irish couple that had emigrated from the British Isles early in the 19th century. Her father had wanted strong sons to farm the land, and she had tried to please him, but ultimately had fled the oppressive home environment and adopted male disguise as a means of obtaining her freedom and independence.

By selling bibles and religious tracts, Edmonds worked her way into financially rewarding employment in the United States. At the outbreak of the Civil War, she was living in Flint, Michigan, where she enlisted in the Flint Union Greys, which became Company F of the 2nd Michigan Infantry. She served for two years as a combat soldier, nurse, and spy (Edmonds 1865; Dannett 1960; Talmadge & Gilmore 1970).

For the South, "Harry T. Buford" (Loreta Janeta Velazquez) was serving as a courier for General Bernard Bee on the Bull Run battlefield, and participated in the battle from a position near the center of the Confederate line. She then fought at the battle of Balls Bluff and would go on to fight at Shiloh before becoming disenchanted with combat warfare and deciding instead to use her talents as a detective and spy for the Confederacy.

Velazquez was born in Havana, Cuba, of wealthy parents and raised by an aunt in New Orleans. While still a teenager, she had eloped and married a soldier and served with him at obscure military outposts. Early in the war her husband was killed in a training accident, and she adopted male disguise to fight as a soldier. She was able to pay for her own supplies and equipment, and sought combat commissions from individual commanders (Worthington 1876; Jones 1995, 290–298).

Historical evidence has now been found that at least nine women participated in the battle of Shiloh in Tennessee the following spring. They served as soldiers, nurses, "daughters of the regiment," and sometimes in more than one role.

Belle Reynolds, wife of a lieutenant in the 17th Illinois Infantry, was in the Federal camp that was overrun by Confederate forces on April 6, 1862. She and a female companion pitched in to help care for the wounded soldiers and, after the battle, [she] was awarded the commission of major by the Governor of Illinois for her efforts. After the war, she continued her medical training and practiced medicine both in Chicago and Santa Barbara, California (Moore 1866, 254–277; Middleton 1993, 128–129).

Other women on the Union side were Modenia Weston and Lucy Kaiser, who served as battlefield nurses, and Mrs. Jerusha Small, whose husband was with the 12th Iowa Infantry regiment (Young 1959, 167–170). Three women also were accompanying Confederate regiments on the Shiloh battlefield. Bettie Taylor Phillips served with her husband in the 4th Kentucky Infantry regiment, and Betsy Sullivan (known as "Mother Sullivan") soldiered alongside her husband in the 1st Tennessee Infantry regiment (Andrews 1920, 112–115, 120–126).

Loreta Janeta Velazquez described in her memoirs standing on the battlement at Fort Donelson, before Shiloh, with sleet and freezing rain pelting her in the face and wondering whether it was all worthwhile as the fort fell to a Federal siege. At Shiloh she fought with her former battalion of Arkansas soldiers and was dismayed when, on the second day, the tide turned against the South (Worthington 1876, 164–172, 200–218).

From these experiences, she concluded that Confederate leadership was not what it should be and she became depressed. Ultimately she decided that her best way of contributing to the Confederate cause would be to exploit her skills at disguise and subterfuge as a spy and to give up the soldier's life. She served as a double agent, penetrating the operations of the Northern spy master La Fayette C. Baker (Hall 1993, 140–150). The claims made by Velazquez in her memoirs have been controversial.[3] However, recent research has begun to turn up confirmation of key parts of her story (Hall 1993, 207–211).

Another remarkable story is that of Amy Clarke, who was present at Shiloh on the Confederate side with her husband when he was killed in action. She continued in service, but was later wounded and captured and her gender discovered. Union officials released her back into Confederate lines, in a dress that they insisted she wear (Simkins & Patton 1936, 80; Hall 1993, 99–100).

Undaunted, Clarke resumed fighting in Braxton Bragg's command, and was observed by a Texas cavalry soldier in August of 1963 wearing lieutenant's bars (Darst 1971, 37–38). An important clue to her identity and connections was discovered by Stuart Sprague, who found a newspaper story in the *Cairo City Gazette* of December 25, 1862, about an "Anna Clark," a prisoner of war about to be exchanged. She had been serving as "Richard Anderson" in the 11th Tennessee Infantry. The story exactly fits that of Amy Clarke, including reference to her husband being killed at Shiloh and describing the wounds she had received (Hall 1993, 99). This new information should lead to more complete disclosure of her story.

"Daughters of the Regiment"

In addition to women disguised as male soldiers and those who served as nurses, another category of women variously known as vivandieres or "daughters of the regiment" often became what a contemporary writer termed "half-soldier heroines." That is, they served in whatever capacity was necessary under combat conditions, including occasional fighting as soldiers. Their all-purpose service included marching with the soldiers, providing food and drink during battle (hence vivandiere), doing laundry, and caring for the wounded.

Some vivandieres became famous for their battlefield exploits. Anna Etheridge was daughter of the regiment for the 2nd and 5th Michigan regiments and was constantly caring for the wounded on the battlefield, exposed to enemy fire (Moore 1866, 513–518; Brocker 1867, 747–753). Marie Tebe (known as "French Mary") served as a vivandiere in the 115th Pennsylvania Infantry and was said to have been under fire thirteen times (Rauscher 1892; Faust 1986, 744–745). Both women were awarded the Kearny Cross for gallantry, presented by division commander Brig. Gen. David B. Birney (Birney 1867, 381–382).

Bridget Deavers (known by the men as "Biddy") accompanied the 1st Michigan Cavalry and saw extensive combat in Virginia during the 1864–1865 campaigns. Charlotte McKay, a prominent Civil War nurse, knew Bridget and recorded in her diary on March 28, 1865, "[She] has probably seen more of hardship than any other woman during the war" (McKay 1876, 124–125). Bridget repeatedly displayed coolness and bravery under fire, and acquired considerable skill as a medical practitioner on the battlefield (Moore 1866, 109–112, 533–535; Brocket 1867, 771–773).

An Unfolding Story

In addition to the present author and Professor Sprague, two others intensively investigating the role of women in the Civil War are C. Kay Larson and Lee Middleton. The combined effort is turning up significant new information. Larson has concluded from her research that "the roles women played were more numerous and more martial than many of us have been previously led to believe" (Larson 1992, 56). Middleton has documented well over 100 women and plans a new edition of her book with even more biographical sketches (Middleton 1993).

The full story of women in the Civil War is still unfolding, and the vigorous research currently under way promises to produce many exciting new discoveries.

Notes

[1] Prof. Stuart Sprague, Morehead State University, Kentucky, found information about "Otto Schaffer" in Record Group 94 at the National Archives.

[2] Personal history and summary of regimental activities were found in the pension files of "Albert Cashier" in the National Archives.

[3] Simkins and Patton (p. 81) report that "The only person impressed with the valor and worth of Loreta Janeta Velazquez was that woman herself . . . the stories of her adventures have an air of the tawdry and the unreal." Faust (p. 779) states that Velazquez "chronicles an unbelievable series of adventures with more characteristics of fiction than of fact."

References

Andrews, Matthew P. *Women of the South in War Times.* Baltimore: Norman, Remington, 1920.

[Birney]. *Life of David Bell Birney, Major-General United States Volunteers.* Philadelphia: King & Baird, 1867.

Brocket, L. P., and Mary C. Vaughan, *Women's Work in the Civil War: A Record of Heroism, Patriotism and Patience.* Philadelphia: Zeigler McCurdy, 1867.

Brooks, Fed. "Shiloh Mystery Woman." *Civil War Times Illustrated,* August 1978: 29.

Dannett, Sylvia G. I., *She Rode With the Generals: The True and Incredible Story of Sarah Emma Seelye, Alias Franklin Thompson.* New York: Thomas Nelson and Sons, 1960.

Darst, Maury. "Robert Hodges, Jr., Confederate Soldier." *East Texas Historical Journal* 9 (1971): 37–38.

Davis, Rodney O. "Private Albert Cashier as Regarded by His/Her Comrades." *Journal of the Illinois Historical Society,* Summer 1988: 108–112.

Edmonds, S. Emma E. *Nurse and Spy in the Union Army.* Hartford, Conn.: W. S. Williams, 1865.

Faust, Patricia L., ed. *Historical Times Illustrated Encyclopedia of the Civil War.* New York: Harper and Row, 1986.

Hall, Richard. *Patriots in Disguise: Women Warriors of the Civil War.* New York: Paragon House, 1993.

Jones, Katharine M. *Heroines of Dixie: Confederate Women Tell Their Story of the War.* New York: Bobbs-Merrill, 1955.

Larson, C. Kay. "Bonny Yank and Ginny Reb." *MINERVA: Quarterly Report of Women and the Military* VIII-I (Spring 1990): 33–48.

———. "Bonny Yank and Ginny Reb Revisited." *MINERVA: Quarterly Report on Women and the Military* X-2 (Summer 1992): 35–61.

Livermore, Mary A., *My Story of the War: A Woman's Narrative.* Hartford, Conn.: A. D. Worthington, 1887.

McKay, C. E. *Stories of Hospital and Camp.* Philadelphia: Claxton, Remsen, and Haffelfinger, 1876.

Massey, Mary Elizabeth. *Bonnet Brigades.* New York: Alfred A. Knopf, 1966.

Middleton, Lee. *Hearts of Fire: Soldier Women of the Civil War.* Torch, Ohio, 1993.

Moore, Frank, *Women of the War: Their Heroism and Self-Sacrifice.* Hartford, Conn.: S. S. Scranton, 1866.

Rauscher, Frank. *Music on the March,* 1862–65, *With the Army of the Potomac.* Philadelphia: William F. Fell, 1892.

Simkins, Francis Butler, and James Welch Patton. *The Women of the Confederacy.* Richmond, Va.: Garrett and Massie, 1936.

Talmadge, Marian, and Iris Gilmore. *Emma Edmonds: Nurse and Spy.* New York: Putnam, 1970.

Worthington, C. J., ed. *The Woman in Battle* [Memoirs of Loreta Janeta Velazquez]. Hartford, Conn.: T. Belknap, 1876.

Young, Agatha. *The Women and the Crisis: Women of the North in the Civil War.* New York: McDowell, Oblensky, 1959.

Reading and Writing Activities for "Women in Battle in the Civil War"

1. Write a summary of the article.

2. In a paragraph or two, discuss why a great deal of information is still unknown about women and their role in the Civil War.

3. Compare the experiences of women in the Civil War with those of women today in the armed forces.

4. You are writing a research paper on women in Civil War battles. On index cards, take notes compiling information you could use in your paper.

5. Write a journal entry on your reactions to this article. How do you feel about women fighting in wars? How did you react to the article? Of what did it make you think?

Lincoln's Last Hours

Geoffrey J. Flattmann, M.D., J. Patrick O'Leary, M.D., F.A.C.S.

From the Department of Surgery, Louisiana State University School of Medicine, New Orleans, Louisiana

ABRAHAM LINCOLN, THE 16th President of the United States, was shot on Good Friday, April 14, 1865. It had been a joyous time in Washington, D.C., because just 5 days earlier, on Palm Sunday, General Robert E. Lee had surrendered to General Ulysses S. Grant at Appomattox. No one was more joyous than Lincoln, whose heart was tormented by the bloody, brutal war. The 6 foot 4 inch-tall man had lost 35 pounds while in office, and by war's end, "lines of care had cut into his sad, bearded face. His eyes mirrored his soul's agony."[n1] But on this day, he was joyous, remarking to his wife, "I have never felt so happy in my life."[n2] Little did Lincoln know of the conspiracy that was mounting against him.

The conspirators included Lewis Paine, a confederate war veteran, George Atzerodt, a German-born carriage maker, David Herold, a Washington drug clerk, and John Surrat, a confederate courier whose mother owned a boarding house where the group frequently met. Their leader was John Wilkes Booth, a 26-year-old actor and Southern sympathizer. By his command, Paine, guided through the streets of Washington by Herold, was to kill Secretary of State William Seward at his home. Similarly, Atzerodt was to kill Vice-President Andrew Johnson. Booth was to kill Lincoln, all occurring simultaneously on the evening on April 14. It was Booth's decision that the decapitation of the Union Government would give Lee the courage to reconvene his Southern army and march on Washington.

That night, the Lincolns invited General and Mrs. Grant to attend with them Tom Taylor's popular comedy, "Our American Cousin," which was playing at Ford's Theater. The Grants declined the invitation in order to visit their daughter in New Jersey. Instead, the Lincolns attended with Major Henry Reed Rathbone and his fiancee and step-sister, Miss Clara Harris. The Presidential party arrived late after the play had started. They were promptly escorted to the Presidential box, located immediately stage left and elevated 12 feet.

After sipping whiskey at the adjoining Taltavull's Star Saloon, Booth entered the theater and proceeded to gain access to the dress circle adjacent to the Presidential box. The President's guard, John F. Parker, had left his post outside of the box so that he could obtain a better view of the play. With this, Booth entered the corridor behind the box, barred the door, ascertained the President's position within the box via a peep hole that he had drilled earlier, and approached the President from the right. At the end of Act III, Scene II, Booth fired one

© Thomson Wadsworth

shot into the back of ***Lincoln's*** head. He used a single-shot, muzzle-loaded .44 caliber Derringer pistol,(n3) a gun popular at the time among gamblers and adventurers due to its ease of concealment. He threw the pistol to the floor, drew his 7-inch hunting knife, and stabbed Major Rathbone, who was attempting to prevent his escape. Booth vaulted over the balustrade toward the stage 12 feet below. Ironically, the toe of his left boot struck a portrait of George Washington, and the spur of his right boot caught in the American flag, two of the items that had adorned the box. Booth landed awkwardly on the stage, fracturing his left distal fibula.(n4) He recovered to his feet, and as he hobbled off the stage, he waved his knife and shouted "Sic Semper Tyrannis," or "Thus Always to Tyrants."(n5)

Ford's Theater was in a state of mayhem. Captain Oliver Gatch, an eyewitness to the events and a veteran of many Civil War encounters noted, "the crowd went mad, a wilder night I never saw, not in battle, even."(n4) In the box, Mary Lincoln clutched the slumping President, and a bleeding Major Rathbone unbarred the door.

The first person to enter the Presidential box was Dr. Charles A. Leale, a 23-year-old Army surgeon who was in charge of the Wounded Commissioned Officer's Ward at the United States Army General Hospital in Armory Square, Washington, D.C.(n6) As he entered the box, he was approached by Mary Lincoln who asked, "Oh, doctor, is he dead? Can he recover? Will you take charge of him?"(n7) Leale instituted what today would be considered a primary survey. Placing a hand on ***Lincoln's*** right wrist, he perceived no radial pulse. He immediately removed the President from his chair and placed him on the floor. In doing so he noted a small amount of blood on the President's left shoulder. Recalling the flashing dagger in Booth's hand and having never actually heard the pistol shot, Leale at first believed the President had been stabbed,(n7) possibly suffering an injury to the subclavian vessels. He asked William Kent, a government employee who had followed him into the box, to cut away ***Lincoln's*** shirt and coat. This incidentally led to the discovery of the murder weapon. In his haste to follow Leale's order, Kent inadvertently dropped his night key while removing a knife from his pocket. Later that night, he realized that his key was missing and returned to the theater to find it. While on his hands and knees in the dark Presidential box searching for his key, he stumbled upon the Derringer pistol that Booth had discarded.(n4)

With the President's shirt cut away, Leale noted no signs of a thoracic stab wound. After lifting the President's eyelids, he suspected a brain injury. Running his fingers through the President's hair, Leale discovered a single entrance wound to the left posterior aspect of the skull. Later autopsy showed that the bullet entered 1 inch left of the midline, at a level that violated the left transverse sinus.(n8) He removed a small piece of clotted blood from the wound orifice, which "relieved the pressure on the brain."(n7) Noting the President to be pulseless and breathless, Leale inserted two fingers into the President's mouth to push down the tongue and open the larynx. He positioned assistants at each of ***Lincoln's*** arms and then manipulated the arms and the diaphragm in a manner that "caused air to be drawn in and forced out of his lungs."(n7) Leale then used his right index finger to apply sliding intermittent pressure under the left subcostal margin, a crude form of closed chest cardiac massage that was believed to stimulate the apex of the heart. Feeling that more must be done, Leale then began mouth-to-mouth artificial respiration. With these maneuvers, there was a return of pulse and respiration. Leale rose and stated, "his wound is mortal; it is impossible for him to recover."(n7)

By this time, Leale had the help of Dr. Charles Sabin Taft, another Army surgeon who had been boosted into the box by people on the stage below. The surgeons believed that Lincoln should be removed from the theater, where danger might still lurk. It was suggested that the President be taken back to the White House, but Leale did not believe that Lincoln could survive the seven-block carriage ride over cobblestone roads. The surgeons removed the President from the theater, and it was their first inclination to take Lincoln to the adjoining Taltavull's Star Saloon. It was the proprietor of the bar who discouraged the idea, protesting, "It shouldn't be said that President of the United States died in a saloon."(n4)

Instead, the President was taken across the street to a three-story brick house located at 453 10th Street. The house belonged to William Pederson, a Washington merchant tailor. The first two rooms on the first floor were locked, so the President was taken to the back bedroom. The room had been rented to William Clark, who was away for the weekend. It was impeccably well kept but small, measuring only 17 1/2 feet long and 9 1/2 feet wide. To accommodate the President's great height, it was necessary to place him on a diagonal in the short bed, with his head elevated on two pillows. Then, the all-night vigil began.

Mary Lincoln remained in the front parlor, and the room was cleared of all but the medical men. A secondary survey was instituted. The President was stripped of his clothes and his body was examined from his head to his feet. He was noted to be "smoothly muscled, well proportioned, lean, and strong."(n1) The President's body was heated with hot water bottles and blankets, and the wound opening was again cleared of clot, as "symptoms indicated renewed brain compression."(n7) A small button of bone was pushed forward, permitting oozing of blood. Leale then sent for higher authorities, including Surgeon General Joseph K. Barnes, Assistant Surgeon General Charles H. Crane, every member of the President's cabinet, Dr. Robert King Stone (*Lincoln's* family physician), and the Reverend Dr. Phineas D. Gurley, the Lincoln's pastor. Despite Leale's objections, Dr. Taft insisted on instilling a small amount of brandy and water into *Lincoln's* mouth. Leale believed that this would "produce strangulation,"(n7) but yielded to Taft, the more senior surgeon. Indeed, the introduction of the brandy into the President's throat caused "laryngeal obstruction and unpleasant symptoms,"(n7) which took Leale some time to overcome.

Once Surgeon General Barnes and Dr. Stone arrived, the wound was probed with a finger. It was noted that as long as the wound freely oozed blood and cerebral matter, the President's breathing and pulse remained strong. "Whenever the clot was allowed to form over the opening to the wound, the President's breathing became greatly embarrassed,"(n7) and his pulse became feeble. At 2 AM, a silver probe was introduced into the wound by Surgeon General Barnes. At about 2 inches from the wound orifice, the probe struck an obstruction, thought to be a plug of bone. Passing this, the probe was found to be too short to trace the entire track of the bullet. The surgeons sent for a longer Nelaton probe, which was inserted approximately 7 inches, when it was felt to have met the pistol ball that was lying superior to the left orbital plate.(n9) Dr. Taft described the President in the following manner:

"Eyes entirely closed, the left pupil much contracted, the right widely dilated; total insensibility to light in both. The left upper eyelid was swollen and dark from effused blood; discoloration from effusion began in the internal canthus of the right eye, which became rapidly discolored and swollen with great protrusion of the eye."(n9)

It has been estimated that more than 90 visitors were in and out of the tiny room that night, including medical personnel, high-ranking military officials, every member of the President's cabinet except for William Seward (who had been brutally attacked by Lewis Paine), family, friends, and even actors from the play. No visitor was more important than Secretary of War Edwin M. Stanton. Stanton immediately set up headquarters in a room adjacent to the President's and with brutal efficiency, single-handedly ran the government. He telegraphed General Grant back to Washington, warned the military and police to be on utmost alert, asked the Chief Justice to swear in Vice-President Johnson, began not only the investigation of the crime but also the manhunt for the conspirators, and quelled rumors that ran rampant through the streets of Washington. He was, in fact, for that night, acting President of the United States, carrying out his duties just feet from his fallen chief.(n4)

The President's vital signs did not vary until 5:30 AM, when the wound no longer oozed. Then his pulse became feeble and irregular, and his breathing became prolonged, labored, and sonorous. Although the house was full, *Lincoln's* groans echoed through it in a haunting fashion. During the minutes preceding the President's death, Dr. Barnes sat to *Lincoln's* left and monitored the carotid pulse. Dr. Crane controlled the head, and Dr. Stone sat on the foot of the bed. Dr. Leale sat at the President's right, holding his hand firmly in order to "let him in his blindness know, if possible, that he was in touch with humanity and had a friend."(n7) The protracted struggle ended at 22 minutes past 7 on the morning of April 15, 1865, when Dr. Barnes, no longer perceiving a carotid pulse announced, "He is gone."(n4) A 5-minute period of silence was followed by a short prayer led by Reverend Gurley. Then, Edwin Stanton, once described as the most imposing figure of the 19th century, rose, sobbed, and uttered the infamous phrase, "Now he belongs to the ages."(n4) The Great Emancipator was dead.

The most historically accurate depiction of the event is a pen-and-ink sketch by Hermann Faber, a hospital steward who was serving in the Surgeon General's office. At the General's request, he sketched the scene from memory after *Lincoln's* body had been removed.(*n10*) Ironically, and the first of many ironies from this tragic tale, Dr. Leale is not depicted in the sketch.

The second irony concerns the bed and room in which Lincoln died. Due to its proximity to Ford's Theater, the room was frequently rented out to actors of the day. During the theater season of 1864–1865, the room was rented on separate occasions to John Matthews and Charles Warwick, actors and close associates of Booth. Booth not only made use of the room in the months preceding the assassination, he also napped on the very bed in which Lincoln later died.(*n4*)

Third, Major Rathbone was severely wounded by Booth's knife but was not given immediate surgical evaluation because of the attention devoted to the President. It was his fiancee who applied a tourniquet, which, in the opinion of Dr. G. W. Pope, the surgeon who later evaluated him, prevented exsanguination. Unfortunately, on Christmas day, 1883, Major Rathbone murdered the very woman who had saved his life 18 years earlier.(*n11*)

Fourth, the Lincolns originally had invited General and Mrs. Ulysses S. Grant to attend the play with them. The Grants declined the invitation in order to visit their daughter in Burlington. In reality, Mrs. Grant intensely disliked Mrs. Lincoln and forbade their attendance that night. Furthermore, General Grant had a very competent and well-respected bodyguard, much the opposite of *Lincoln's,* who had left his post that night. It is conjectured that had Grant and his guard been present that night, Booth would not have gained access to the Presidential box, and the assassination would have been avoided. It is ironic that a spat between the two wives may have altered the course of American history.

Finally, Booth regarded Lincoln as a tyrant and an enemy of the South. In fact, Lincoln was the strongest voice in the Union Government that preached leniency and forgiveness for the Confederacy. He made these views publicly known during his second inaugural address on March 4, 1865. The conspirators were not only present to hear the address, they were within a pistol shot. It was at this time that they were making a dry run of the assassination attempt to see how close they could get to the President.(*n5*) We, as physicians and surgeons, should always remember words from that address. These words not only illustrate *Lincoln's* attitude, but also typify his great virtue and wisdom:

"With malice toward none; with charity for all; with firmness in the right, as God gives us to see the right, let us strive on to finish the work we are in . . ."(*n12*)

References

(*n1.*) Hayman, L. *The Death of Lincoln: A Picture History of the Assassination.* New York: Scholastic, Inc., 1968, p. 17.

(*n2.*) Freedman, R. A. *Lincoln: A Photobiography.* New York: Clarion Books, 1987, p 120.

(*n3.*) Lattimer, JK. *Kennedy and Lincoln: Medical and Ballistic Comparisons of Their Assassinations.* New York: Harcourt Brace Jovanovich, 1980, p 49.

(*n4.*) Reck, W., Emerson, A. *Lincoln: His **Last** 24 **Hours.*** Jefferson, NC: McFarland & Company, Inc., Publishers, 1987, pp 107–59.

(*n5.*) Kunhardt, PB, Jr., Kunhardt PB III, Kunhardt PW. *Lincoln: An Illustrated Biography.* New York: Alfred A. Knopf, 1992, pp 353–44.

(*n6.*) Jackson, ER. ***Lincoln's last*** *physician: Lesson from history for today. J Florida Med Assoc* 1993;80:616–8.

(*n7.*) Leale, CA. ***Lincoln's last hours.*** *Harper's Weekly,* February 13, 1909, pp 7–14.

(*n8.*) Gilmore, HR. *Medical aspects of the assassination of Abraham Lincoln. Proc R Soc Med* 1953;47:103–8.

(*n9.*) Taft, CS. ***Last hours*** *of Abraham Lincoln. The Medical and Surgical Reporter (Philadelphia),* 1865;12(28):452–4.

(*n10.*) Caelleigh, AS. *Death of Abraham Lincoln: Cover note. Acad Med* 1996;71:111.

(*n11.*) Bishop, Jim. *The Day Lincoln Was Shot.* New York: Harper & Brothers, 1955, p 300.

(*n12.*) Sandburg, C. *Abraham Lincoln: The Prairie Years and the War Years.* Pleasantville, New York: Harcourt Brace Jovanovich, Inc., 1970, p 544.

Reading and Writing Activities for "Lincoln's Last Hours"

1. Write a summary of the article.

2. In a paragraph, explain how Booth was able to shoot the president.

3. Write three questions that you have about the assassination after reading the article. Search for and list two sources that might answer your questions.

4. Compare the information in this journal article to that in the American history textbook chapter "The Furnace of Civil War." List three points that are the same and three that are different.

5. Write a journal entry describing your reactions to this article. Of what did it make you think? What did you visualize as you read?

BUSINESS ARTICLES

Beyond the Suggestion Box

by Michael Barrier

Smart Small Businesses Find Ways to Keep Their Employees' Good Ideas Flowing

You've seen it hanging on the wall in many a store's back room and in many a small factory or warehouse: the box labeled "suggestions." You know—the empty one covered with dust. When, if ever, the boss checks it, you hear muttering about how "those people on the floor just don't care."

At too many companies, the suggestion box is a visible symptom of a toxic company culture. The box may be empty, for example, because of an unwritten rule that all the bright ideas have to come down from the top. Employees may avoid making suggestions because they know they won't be taken seriously—or, worse, their ideas may even get them in trouble.

"In a company where you see somebody berated for thinking, the ideas are still there. They just never see the light of day," says Martin Baird, president of Robinson and Associates, a seven-employee Phoenix marketing firm. "It's a matter of whether the culture allows them to come out and be used."

There has probably never been a time when it made sense for a company to ignore its employees as a source of good ideas, but with the quickening competitive pressures in today's economy, it makes less sense than ever. The question is: What kind of system will bring those good ideas to the surface and keep them coming? Is a formal structure of any kind really the answer?

It's true that in an open company culture, where managers value and encourage employee participation, the idea of relying on a system to generate ideas can sound a little strange because suggestions already flow so freely in that type of environment.

For example, Sensis Corp., a 130-employee electronics manufacturer in DeWitt, N.Y., doesn't rely on a formal system for stimulating ideas, says CEO Jud Gostin; neither does it offer awards for good ideas, although occasionally, "when people do really extraordinary things, we send them a letter and write them a check."

And yet, Gostin says, the ideas keep coming because "we try to communicate to employees what's going on." When employees are kept informed about a company's plans and prospects, he says, "it's encouraging to see how they come up with ideas"—suggesting, for instance, how a product tailored to one customer's needs can be modified to meet another's specifications.

Such employee involvement has helped Sensis, a defense contractor, weather the slow-down in federal military spending; and that success led to the company's being designated a 1995 Blue Chip Enterprise in the annual competition sponsored by Connecticut Mutual Life Insurance Co., the U.S. Chamber of Commerce, and *Nation's Business.*

Another Blue Chip company, Rheaco, of Grand Prairie, Texas, found that a change to self-directed work teams unleashed a torrent of ideas at the business, which supplies parts to aero-space firms in the Dallas area. President Rhea Wallace Jr. says employee suggestions led to a cut in the "machine time" required to manufacture a brake shoe for the C-130 transport aircraft—a part the company had been making for 25 years—from 3 1/2 hours to less than an hour.

For other companies with a healthy culture, an idea-generating system can serve as in-surance when, for whatever reason, the flow of suggestions turns sluggish.

Kacey Fine Furniture, a Denver-based retailer, had been sharing a great deal of infor-mation with its 170 employees for more than two years "with an unbelievable amount of ex-citement and success," says Leslie Fishbein, the firm's president, but last year it began looking for a more formal system because "we weren't really generating ideas from the bottom up."

For companies suffering from a toxic culture, a strong idea-generating system can be a way to turn the culture around if management is sincere about relaxing its grip.

You can encourage employee participation, Jud Gostin says, "either because you believe in it or because you've been told it's a good thing to do, [even though] you don't really believe in it. If it's the latter, it's just like bringing up kids—they know what you're really thinking." And if employees detect insincerity, they won't respond.

During the past few years, around 1,000 companies and other organizations seeking outside help on generating ideas have turned to Boardroom, Inc., a newsletter publisher in Greenwich, Conn. Boardroom offers seminars on what it calls "I-Power," a system for encouraging—indeed, requiring—employees to produce ideas. In I-Power, and in companies that have been successful in stimulating suggestions on their own, there's a discernible pattern for successful idea-generating efforts.

If the tenets of I-Power and those independent efforts were reduced to a few guidelines, they'd read something like this:

USE MEETINGS TO LIGHT A FIRE

It's at meetings, if they're conducted properly, that ideas can ignite productive thinking in one person after another.

Says Stephen Taglianetti, president and chief operating officer of Alga Plastics, a 50-employee manufacturer in Cranston, R.I.: "We would begin to design something without tak-ing into account whether we could actually produce it." Alga now holds meetings on Monday mornings to discuss such new projects, he says, "and we bring production people from all parts of the plant in with our engineers. The ideas that come out are just terrific."

The essence of I-Power is this: Participants are required to come to weekly meetings with at least two ideas in hand. Ken Glickman, who runs the I-Power seminars for Boardroom, emphasized to those attending a recent New York City seminar that "I-Power is not a brain-storming session. We want people to do their thinking in advance."

That may sound a little intimidating, but Marty Baird says such a meeting "is not an en-ergy drainer; it kind of puts energy back."

There are, of course, dangers in meetings, too—mainly that negative thinking will take over. Not all ideas are good, but if bad ideas are knocked down too quickly and vigorously, the flow of good ideas can be blocked, too.

"The worst thing I ever saw in a meeting was when somebody laughed at an idea," Baird says. "As soon as somebody laughs, you've driven a stake through the hearts of probably 70 per-cent of the people in the room. We're all afraid of being laughed at, especially by our bosses."

As a preventive measure, Glickman advises, "start with your most positive people. Then let the negative people be negative, and just ignore the negativity."

UNDERSTAND THE IMPORTANCE OF FOLLOW-THROUGH

"If you don't have a system for processing ideas" as well as generating them, Glickman warns, "you're worse off than when you started."

At Alga Plastics—also a Blue Chip company—the participants in the Monday-morning meetings decide which ideas will be acted upon. A customer-service representative takes minutes, Steve Taglianetti says, "and she follows up with a memo to everyone involved on what the issues were and what we have agreed to follow up on. Everyone knows exactly where we're going."

Many times, he says, the person who has an idea is asked to take the lead in implementing it, "and we make available whatever resources they may need."

But follow-through often can be, and should be, as simple as telling someone whose idea is approved, "Go do it." The boss should not then look over that person's shoulder to make sure the idea is carried out; employees' ideas should not be the pretext for imposing greater control.

If such is the case, the ideas will dry up, fast.

Responding to ideas quickly—approving them, rejecting them, asking for more information—is much more important than keeping track of how, or even whether, every approved idea is implemented, Glickman says.

In the first two months that Kacey Fine Furniture adopted an I-Power program, Leslie Fishbein says, "we had more than 2,000 ideas. There was absolutely no way" to keep track of all those that were approved.

But it doesn't matter if some good ideas fall through the cracks, she suggests, "because if they're good, they'll come up again."

BE CAUTIOUS ABOUT OFFERING LARGE MONETARY AWARDS

Such awards can breed competitiveness and secretiveness, Glickman warns; and when such obstacles are overcome, there may be a complementary problem of deciding who really authored an idea.

Sometimes, too, it's difficult to measure the impact of an idea and give an award in proportion to its value to the company.

I-Power calls for making very small awards, but making them quickly, so that there's a direct connection between the idea and the award.

Marty Baird's firm puts things like Phoenix Suns tickets in a grab-bag for people who contribute particularly outstanding ideas, "but it really doesn't come down to the dollar amount," he says. "It's more a matter of being recognized and having fun." Leslie Fishbein says she's leery of offering too much money because "I don't want someone to be looking for just the big idea."

But not everyone agrees that such dangers are very important. Alga Plastics, for example, gives awards of as much as $150, Taglianetti says, and, beyond that, "if they come up with actual production savings, we give them a percentage of the savings."

If awards create competition among employees, he says, "that's a result of poor communication from management, probably, of just what the aim of the program is."

DON'T SQUELCH SMALL IDEAS BECAUSE THEY'RE SMALL

By doing that, you may discourage someone from offering another idea that could mean big savings—a big idea, or a small idea that may in fact be critical to the success of a big idea.

It's important that you not classify ideas," Taglianetti says. "If an idea is worthy, you act upon it, no matter how large or small it is."

PERMIT AND EVEN ENCOURAGE ANONYMOUS IDEAS

In a small business, it's easy for the president or owner to think that because there is constant interaction, there's a free exchange of ideas. But, as Marty Baird says, "you still run into the same barriers you have in a larger corporation. People look at me and say, 'You're the president. I'd better not tell you about this; you might not like it.' We all have a certain fear of reprisal."

Baird suggests circulating a list that recognizes ideas that were submitted anonymously as well as those that were signed.

ASK VENDORS FOR IDEAS, TOO

Suppliers know ways to save you money, Glickman says, "but they won't tell you unless you ask the right questions, and you're persistent. It will take them time to trust you."

When he approached Alga's vendors for help, Taglianetti says, "most offered help; some have already sent people in to look at our operation and offer any insight that they could."

One of the greatest benefits of a successful idea-generating program may be that it can give owners and managers a more realistic—and probably more pleasing—picture of the people who work for them. "It's been fascinating to me," Fishbein says, "that the quality of the ideas [submitted by employees] has had nothing to do with education or, frankly, with position in the company."

Now that the flow of ideas "has become part of our culture," Alga's Taglianetti says, "I find that I get ideas when I least expect them, from the least expected places."

Two machinists, for example, stayed all night one Friday to finish an emergency order, and, as a gesture of appreciation, Taglianetti later took them to lunch. "The ideas were just flowing," he says, and one of the machinists proposed to him that the company itself make a part that it now buys and that wears out frequently. Moreover, the machinist said, Alga could sell that part itself, nationwide.

"We're reviewing that right now," Taglianetti says—with the machinist leading the exploration of his own idea.

Ken Glickman suggests that, at bottom success in bringing employees' ideas to light is a matter of managers' humbling themselves before human nature: "The greatest source of motivation is giving people some input into what they do every day. Someone is about three times more likely to do something when it's their idea than when you tell them to do it."

Reading and Writing Activities for "Beyond the Suggestion Box"

1. Write a summary of the article.

2. Summarize five of the steps that I-Power follows to generate ideas.

3. In a paragraph, report why the I-Power system works.

4. In a journal, react to this article. What do you think about the I-Power system? Did the system make you think of anything? If so, what?

5. You are the manager of a small video store in a local mall. Write several paragraphs describing how you could use the I-Power system.

Comparative Competitive Aspects of Japanese Use of Human Resources Vis-A-Vis United States and Canada

Norihiro Takeuchi

Executive Vice President and Director, Bridgestone/Firestone, Inc., Akron, Ohio.

Human resources management, as I see it, is an art which endeavors to balance the needs of a company and those of its employees. Some people may disagree that it is characterized as an art, but I choose to call it an art because much more must be developed before it can be called a science. In any event, as a practice of art, some companies do it better or worse than others, and so my remarks must be limited to concepts.

Since human resource management allegedly attempts to balance the needs of a company with those of its employees, its concepts and practices must reflect real-life situations which dictate the contents of various needs. In a short speech such as this, I assume that real-life situations in the United States, Canada and Japan are generally understood by the audience. Needless to say, I do not have to describe what human resource management in North America is like, and I have neither the time, nor the expertise to tell you about the generalities of Japanese human resource management. However, I believe there is a strong similarity between the two systems as to what constitutes the basis of good human resource management, such as mutual trust, mutual respect, fairness and consistency of policies, honesty and good communication.

Many Japanese companies studied American theories and practices, and adopted a number of them. But differences exist, and I would like to call your attention to some of those differences and examine briefly what those differences mean in terms of the value system and objectives of the company. First, there are differences in the employee hiring process. In Japan, at least with larger employers, new hires are recruited from the most recent class of graduates (or those expected to graduate during the next several months) from high schools, colleges or universities. This is a once-a-year event, and is applicable to both production workers and staff. New hires at any other time during the year are very rare. Therefore, an employer is required to develop a great deal of manpower for planning well in advance of the actual hiring date. This once-a-year hiring practice is possible, in part, because new hires are not offered specific jobs, but rather an association with an employer.

Second, this new hire practice is related to the thought that employees are trained in response to the needs of the company in the course of employment. This results in an extensive in-house training program. Most companies provide and require group training, on-the-job training and periodic off-the-job training. If someone leaves the company, temporary help is occasionally brought in, but more often, other people will pick up the workload. Usually when employees resign, they are encouraged to notify their employer well in advance of their resignation date.

Third, new hires are assigned by management to specific jobs after the required training. Employee desires are considered, but are not necessarily the controlling factors. Most employees are expected to be reassigned to other jobs periodically (in many cases at four to five years intervals), and this kind of job reassignment is normally accepted by employees. One example that demonstrates this is an employee's response to the question, "What is your occupation?" The answer in most cases is, "I work at ABC Company." Lateral transfers are a frequent phenomena. This cross-trains employees and breaks down complacency. Lateral transfers also help to prevent a specific manager from developing a "private army." Employees are given annual, sometimes more frequent, performance assessments. This is basically the same as the North American practice except that, first, the scope of the assessment includes not only performance in terms of output, but also attitudes, ability, growth in skills and process for generating output. Second, the assessment is conducted not only by immediate supervisors, but also by the human resources department who take a very active role in the process. Participation by the human resources department is an attempt to introduce greater objectivity and company-wide consistency in the assessment process.

Employees are promoted based on their individual capability and years of service. Available positions become fewer as the employees rise higher in the company, so everyone cannot be promoted unless the business is expanding. Selection among the candidates is inevitable. It is very rare that an open position at the management level is filled by someone from outside the company.

Salary administration is basically the function of the human resources department. Conceptually, salary is paid to a "person" and not to a specific job holder. Therefore, although pay increases (which are usually given once a year at the same time to all eligible employees) differ from one employee to another, the range of difference (which reflects performance assessment) is rather limited. This practice is increasingly becoming a source of difficulty in Japanese companies, and means of rewarding for better performance are being explored. However, in the absence of more objective measures of performance, a majority of employees seem to accept the narrower range of pay disparity.

Employees generally expect, and are expected by the company, to stay with the company at which they started until normal retirement age. Employers attempt to train and develop employees on the assumption (although not a legal commitment) that they will stay until retirement. Job hoppers are often viewed by prospective employers as drop-outs from respectable organizations. It is a common practice for an employer to pay separation allowances if an employee resigns, but the amount progressively increases as the years of service increase, reaching the largest amount at normal retirement age. Some companies are beginning to modify this practice, but the trend still prevails. A workplace in Japan is still more of a Gemeinschaft rather than a Gesellschaft.

Finally, labor/management relations are very unique in Japan. In most cases (except in the merchant marine industry), labor unions are organized by employees working for a particular company. Usually, members include not only production workers but also supervisors, foremen and most of the white collar employees below the management level. Employers tend to treat all employees, whether union members or not, the same way. Many one-time members of the union progress into management positions over time. Unlike the North American practice, seniority of union members does not play a significant role, and job bidding is a very rare phenomenon.

Labor/management relations is a big subject in itself, and I would rather not pursue it any further today, except for a brief comment on the philosophical aspect of a labor/management relations in Japan. Broadly stated, there has been very little confrontation between labor and management in modern Japan, except during the times of hyperinflation in the 1940s and 1950s. Labor unions were something like "gifts" from the Occupation Forces immediately after World War II. Unions do exist in Japan, but the concept of "getting the most out of labor with the least compensation" or "getting the most out of management with the least amount of effort" has not yet materialized.

Obviously, all of these features are undergoing some changes as the general environment and people's desires or values change, but it is a slow process. I feel comfortable with the set of human resources practices which I have just described. However, it has been recognized in recent years that something more is desirable. One of the examples arising out of this recognition are Total Quality Control ("TQC") activities. TQC is not meant to be a part of human resource management, but is much broader in scope. However, its basic concept lies in defining corporate objectives clearly and attempting to deploy the actual and potential talents and creativity of all of employees through communicating these objectives. TQC activities overlap many areas of human resource management. At the same time, TQC aims at reinforcing scientific and disciplined business operations, eventually resulting in better customer satisfaction and better business performance. The success of this approach may be doubtful if viewed in the context of traditional labor/management relations in North America. If management's mission toward labor is to let it work as directed and to expect nothing more, this concern would be valid. But, if management views labor as its partner in success, I do not see any reason why TQC would not work. As a matter of fact, it already seems to be working at a number of workplaces in North America. I do not have prescriptions for the kind of labor contracts which would permit successful TQC activities, but I do believe that a workable relationship can be developed if management wants it. I cannot offer a categorical opinion about whether the Japanese practices I have described today are applicable, or even desirable, to the North American environment. As I stated at the outset, human resource management is closely integrated with a country's culture, history and business conditions. In North America, as anywhere else, an employer has to deal with people who have their own value systems, expectations and needs. Some of you might suspect that Japan's industrial success over the past decade has something to do with its human resource management, and I feel there may be some validity to that, particularly in the field of manufacturing.

Increasingly, in today's manufacturing arena, few things can be accomplished by a single person, thus team work is recognized as necessary. As business becomes larger, "cross functional" communication and collaboration, which is so critical in business, tend to suffer. As an industry matures, it tends to lose its ability to overcome organizational problems by business expansion. Developing a stronger sense of employee affiliation with an employer will help generate greater willingness of the employees to voluntarily contribute to the success of the employer. I do not believe it wise nor proper to force employees to follow a set of values they do not accept, but I suspect that a number of practices are not necessarily tied directly to such a value system, but often are simply a result of historical developments. Once logic and needs are explained, people understand and accept new practices. Particularly, if certain practices, such as TQC, are culturally neutral by nature, or inherently reasonable, there should be no significant difficulty in adopting them. There will always be some resistance to new practices, but more often the resistance originates from such undesirable elements as "turf protection," "not invented here" or an egotistical desire to expand. I believe the only answer is that solutions must be found through close and objective analysis of a particular situation. This is a big challenge to employers, since employees are not only resources which contribute to the needs of the employers, but also human beings with their own emotions. It all comes back to the basics of human resource management; a desirable employer-employee relationship is attained and improved by integrity, trust, fairness and communication.

Reading and Writing Activities for "Comparative Competitive Aspects of Japanese Use of Human Resources Vis-à-Vis United States and Canada"

1. Write a summary of the article.
2. Choose one difference between Japanese and American work practices, summarize that difference in your own words, and provide a personal example of the American practice from your work experience.
3. You are writing an argumentative paper for a business class. The paper requires you to argue for the use of Japanese work practices. On index cards, take notes that can be used in a paper.
4. As a manager of a large company, explain why you would choose to use Japanese work practices. How would you explain the advantages of these practices to a potential employee? Use information from the article in your report.
5. Write one paragraph explaining the pros of Japanese work practices and one paragraph explaining the cons of Japanese work practices.

PSYCHOLOGY ARTICLES

Self-Esteem and Self-Efficacy of College Students with Disabilities

by Teri R. Blake, Middle Tennessee State University and
James O. Rust, Middle Tennessee State University

The present study investigated the relationship between self-esteem and self-efficacy among college students with physical and learning disabilities. Participants included forty-four undergraduate students and four graduate students registered with a university's office for students with disabilities. Collective Self-esteem, Membership Self-esteem, Private Self-esteem, and Public Self-esteem were positively and significantly correlated with General and Social Self-efficacy. Scores were found to be similar to scores from the normative samples. Thus although self-esteem and self-efficacy were significantly related to each other, they were largely unrelated to disability status.

Psychologists have written extensively about the self for over 100 years (e.g., James, 1890). Markus (1977) added to our understanding of the self by developing the notion of self

Source: College Student Journal, Jun2002, Vol. 36 Issue 2, p214, 8p
Reprinted with permission.

© Thomson Wadsworth

schema, the organized views of self, which we all have. Coopersmith (1967) and Bandura (1986) contributed by identifying self-esteem, the evaluative component of self, and self-efficacy, our perceived abilities.

For self-esteem and self-efficacy to be valid and useful, they ought to apply to all groups including those with disabilities, and they ought to be reliably measurable (Kerr & Bodman, 1994). Luhtanen and Crocker (1992) developed a reliable test for measuring self-esteem. Sherer, Maddux, Mercandante, Prentice-Dunn, Jacobs, and Rogers (1982) created a reliable scale to assess self-efficacy.

Although experiencing a disability has been shown to have an important impact on the sense of self (Toombs, 1994), Wright (1983) found that there are no general personality differences between people with disabilities compared to their peers. Likewise Kelly, Sedlacek, and Scales (1994) concluded that college students with physical and learning disabilities did not perceive themselves differently from students from the general population. However, Kelly et al. (1994) found that students from the general population rated their peers with disabilities as being lower in extraversion and in emotional stability compared to other peers. Also, Saracoglu, Minden, and Wilchesky (1989) surveyed college students with learning disabilities to determine perceptions of their college experience. The authors concluded that college students with learning disabilities exhibited poor self-esteem as well as poor emotional adjustment. Penn and Dudley (1980) questioned college students with physical disabilities to determine perceptions of their college experience. The researchers concluded that these students ranked self-confidence as one of the major obstacles confronted while attending college. Thus there is disagreement among studies regarding the sense of self of college students with disabilities. The present study attempted to further investigate the relationship between measures of self (self-esteem and self-efficacy) and disability status of college students with disabilities.

It was hypothesized that self-esteem and self-efficacy scores would be correlated. Additionally, it was hypothesized that these scores would be lower for students with disabilities compared to the normative sample. Further, it was hypothesized that self-esteem would be correlated with reported academic achievement in high school and college among students with disabilities.

Methods

PARTICIPANTS

Forty-four undergraduate students and four graduate students with disabilities enrolled at Middle Tennessee State University (MTSU) served as participants in this study. All of the participants were registered with the Disabled Student Services Office and had provided documentation of their disabilities to the director. Twenty-three females and 25 males participated. The numbers of students for each matriculation classification were as follows: freshman (8); sophomore (13); junior (10); senior (13); and graduate (4). Students' disabilities varied among 19 categories. The largest categories were visual impairment and cerebral palsy with eight students in each. The students reported their high school and college grade point averages.

MATERIALS

The Collective Self-esteem Scale (Luhtaven & Crocker, 1992) and the Self-efficacy scale (Sherer, et al. 1982) were used in this study. The self-esteem scale includes 16 items to determine Membership Self-esteem, Private Self-esteem, Public Self-esteem, and Identity Self-esteem. Responses are made on a seven-point Likert-type scale ranging from strongly disagree to strongly agree. A high score indicates high levels of self-esteem. A score as high as 112 is possible. The lowest possible score is 16. In the research conducted by Luhtanen and Crocker (1992), Cronbach's Alpha coefficients were found to be substantial ranging from 0.83 to 0.88 for all scales.

The Self-efficacy Scale constructed by Sherer, et al. (1982) consists of 23 items; seven of the items are fillers and are not scored. Answers are listed on a five-point scale ranging from strongly agree to strongly disagree. These scores are presented so that a high score indicates higher levels of self-efficacy. A score as high as 115 is possible, and the lowest possible score is 23. Sherer, et al. determined construct validity by correlating the Self-efficacy Scale with several other personality measures such as the Ego Strength Scale, the Interpersonal Competency Scale, and the Rosenberg Scale-Esteem Scale. Cronbach Alpha reliability coefficients of 0.86 and 0.71 were obtained for the general self-efficacy and social self-efficacy factors in the 1982 study.

The present study included gender, matriculation classification (e.g., freshman, senior, etc.), reported high school and college grade point averages, reported socioeconomic status, the students' ratings of the visibility of the disability (visible and not visible), the first author's ratings of the visibility of the disability (visible and not visible), the first author's rating of the global severity of the disability, the students' ratings of the severity of the disability, and reported age of onset of the disability. Socioeconomic status was measured using Mercer's and Lewis's (1979) System of Multicultural Pluralistic Assessment occupation rating system. Severity of the disability and visibility of the disability were measured by asking the participants to indicate their perceptions by circling one of the following: 1 = Not at All; 2 = Just a Little; 3 = Moderate; 4 = Severe; 5 = Very Severe. The first author rated the visibility of the disabilities by coding unseen (invisible) disabilities as 1 and visible disabilities as 2. The following disabilities were coded as invisible: learning disability, attention deficit/hyperactivity disorder, any type of health impairment such as asthma, heart condition, epilepsy or diabetes. Psychological disorders such as an anxiety disorder or a substance-related disorder also were coded as invisible. All remaining disabilities including hearing impairment, visual impairment, physical impairment (e.g., paraplegia, quadriplegia, cerebral palsy, etc.) were coded as visible.

PROCEDURE

Questionnaires, along with a cover letter, were left at the MTSU Disabled Student Services Office. They were given to students registered with that office. Participation was voluntary and confidentiality was maintained. Of the 80 questionnaires that were left in the Disabled Student Services Office to be distributed, 50 were completed. Two of the questionnaires were not used because of incomplete data.

Results

Means and standard deviations of raw scores for the Collective Self-esteem and Self-Efficacy scales are presented in Table 1. These scores were compared to means and standard deviations taken from a normative sample using one-sample t tests (see Table 1). It was predicted that college students with disabilities would score lower on the Collective Self-esteem and the General and Social Self-efficacy scales compared to the normative samples. These hypotheses were not supported using one-sample t tests. In fact, students with disabilities scored higher than the normative sample on the Membership Self-esteem scale, $t(46) = 2.59$, $p < 0.01$ and the Social Self-efficacy scale, $t(46) = 3.46$, $p < 0.01$ (see Table 1).

A significant correlation (see Table 2) was found between the Collective Self-esteem and General Self-efficacy scales, $r = 0.47$, $p < 0.01$. Collective Self-esteem, Membership Self-esteem, and Private Self-esteem were significantly correlated with General and Social Self-efficacy (range of r from 0.34 to 0.60). Public Self-esteem was significantly correlated with General Self-efficacy but not significantly related to Social Self-efficacy. Identity Self-esteem was not significantly correlated with the General or Social Self-efficacy.

Demographics including gender, classification (e.g., freshman, senior) high school and college grade point averages, socioeconomic status, age of onset of the disability, visibility of the disability (e.g., learning disability, cerebral palsy, paraplegic, etc.), and the severity measures were analyzed using Pearson correlations to determine their relationships with self-efficacy and self-esteem (see Table 3). Social Self-efficacy was positively correlated with the visibility of the disability as well as of the severity of the disability as rated by the first author, ($r = 0.30$ and $r = 0.33$ respectfully, $p < 0.05$). Additionally, there was a significant negative

Table 1 Means and Standard Deviations for collective Self-esteem and Its Four Subscales and General and Social Self-efficacy

Legend for Chart:

A – Current Study: M SD
B – Current Study: SD
C – Normative: M SD
D – Normative: SD

	A C	B D
Collective *Self*-esteem	89.71 87.41	12.98 11.68
Membership *Self*-esteem	24.25 22.78	3.93 3.38
Private *Self*-esteem	23.54 23.09	4.12 3.13
Public *Self*-esteem	22.15 21.62	4.02 3.71
Identity *Self*-esteem	19.77 19.65	5.44 4.99
General *Self-efficacy*	66.17 64.31	9.07 8.58
Social *Self-efficacy*	23.04 21.20	3.68 3.63

Table 2 Correlation Summary on General Self-efficacy and Social-efficacy with Collective Self-esteem and Its Four Subscales

Legend for Chart:

A – Scale and Subscales
B – General Self-efficacy
C   Social Self-efficacy

A	B	C
Collective Self-esteem	.47[b]	.60[b]
Membership Self-esteem	.48[b]	.52[b]
Private Self-esteem	.34[a]	.60[b]
Public Self-esteem	.51[b]	.23

bp < .01. a p < .05.

Table 3 Pearson Correlational Analyses for Demographics With Collective Self-esteem and Its Four Subscales and General and Social Self-efficacy

Legend for Chart:

A – GSE
B – SSE
C – MSest.
D – PRest.
E – PUest.
F – IDest.
G – COest.

| | A | B | C | D |
		E	F	G
Gender				
	.14	.11	.08	.21
		.15	.11	.09
Matriculation				
Classification				
	.24	.25	.14	.12
		.19	.13	.19
High School GPA				
	.10	.24	.15	.30[a]
		.19	.01	.20
College GPA				
	.22	.14	.22	.28
		.09	.09	.22
Credit Hours				
	.21	.25	.20	.18
		.24	.13	.25

correlation between Social Self-efficacy and age of onset (N = 0.35, p < 0.05). Reported high school GPA was significantly correlated in the Private Self-esteem, r = 0.30, p < 0.05. No other correlations were significant.

It was hypothesized that self-esteem and self-efficacy would be significantly correlated to reported academic achievement. A stepwise regression analysis was used to determine which combination of variables predicted reported college grade point average. The first variable to enter into the equation for predicting college GPA was matriculation classification status (e.g., freshman to graduate student). The second variable that significantly entered into the equation was socioeconomic status. No other predictors significantly entered into the equation.

Discussion

Self-esteem and self-efficacy were examined among college students with physical and learning disabilities. Although self-esteem and self-efficacy have been investigated for many years, there is little published research dealing with these constructs among college students with disabilities. In the present sample, self-esteem and self-efficacy measures were either the same as or higher than the normative sample. These data are contrary to expectations and to the find-

Table 3 (Continued)

Occupation (Mom)
| | .29 | .03 | .09 | .08 |
| | | .29 | .01 | .10 |

Occupation (Dad)
| | .21 | .06 | .14 | .07 |
| | | .12 | .04 | .01 |

Visibility of Disability (First author's ratings)
| | .11 | .30[a] | .24 | .10 |
| | | .05 | .27 | .23 |

Severity (first author's ratings)
| | .08 | .33[a] | .26 | .14 |
| | | .03 | .23 | .23 |

Age of Onset
| | .19 | .35[a] | .07 | .09 |
| | | .21 | .03 | .06 |

Visibility of Disability (Students' ratings)
| | .17 | .13 | .27 | .05 |
| | | .01 | .10 | .13 |

Severity (student's ratings)
| | .13 | .01 | .19 | .02 |
| | | .15 | .16 | .06 |

Note: GSE = General Self-efficacy; SSE = Social Self-efficacy; MSest. = Membership Self-esteem; PRest. = Private Self-esteem; PUest. = Public Self-esteem; IDest. = Identity Self esteem; COest. = Collective Self-esteem.
a p < .05

ings of Penn and Dudley (1980) and Saracoglu, Minder, and Wilchesky (1989). However, these findings provide support for the view that students with disabilities are part of a typical distribution (Kerr & Bodman, 1994). These data support the view that valid constructs such as self-esteem and self-efficacy ought to apply to students with disabilities as well as to students from the general population.

Collective Self-esteem, Membership Self-esteem, Private Self-esteem, and Public Self-esteem were positively and significantly correlated with General and Social Self-efficacy. Saracoglu et al. (1989) also found a positive correlation between self-esteem and self-efficacy among college students with learning disabilities. The present study expanded on Saracoglu et al.'s work by including college students with physical disabilities in the sample.

The present researchers also examined demographics such as gender, matriculation classification, reported high school and college grade point averages, reported socioeconomic status and ratings of the visibility as well as severity of the disability. High school GPA was positively and significantly correlated with Private Self-esteem. Other correlations with high school GPA were not significant. This finding provides only marginal support for Calsyn and Kenny's (1977) finding that academic achievement relates to self-esteem.

In the present study, the first author's ratings of visibility and severity of the disability were positively and significantly correlated with Social Self-efficacy. As disabilities become more visible and more severe (at least as rated by the first author) participants rated themselves as having higher Social Self-efficacy. One explanation for this may be that persons with visible and relatively severe disabilities are unable to hide their disabilities. Therefore, they must be more open about their disabilities. Roessler and Bolton (1978) make the point that how persons with disabilities perceive themselves influences how other persons are going to perceive them. If persons with disabilities have negative perceptions of themselves, this may hinder social interactions. Persons with unseen disabilities can conceal their disabilities and never come to terms with them. This may affect their Social Self-efficacy. When threatening social situations arise, persons with unseen disabilities may feel that their participation may reveal their disability, and therefore they may be less likely to participate. If they are less likely to participate, then their social self-efficacy may never develop. Dunn (1994) discusses that individuals will search for positive meanings and illusions following a disability. Dunn argues that following the disability, persons may look for a silver lining, by thinking that the disability has added to their lives. Dunn helps explain the positive and significant correlation between the visibility and severity of the students' disabilities and Social Self-efficacy. The students may have searched for positive meaning following the onset of the obvious disability and accepted the disability as part of themselves. On the other hand, students with unseen disabilities may be less likely to search for positive meaning because they feel they can hide the disability.

Reported age of onset of the disabilities was negatively correlated with Social Self-efficacy. The older a participant was at the onset of the disability, the lower his/her Social Self-efficacy. One explanation for this finding may be attributed to a person's acceptance of his/her disability. A person whose disability occurred at birth was likely to be more accepting of his/her disabling condition than a person whose disability occurred later. Whether a disability occurred at birth or later, the disability is seen as a physical and psychosocial shock (Roessler & Bolton, 1978). Persons born with a disability have never experienced life without it, and thus they may report higher Social Self-efficacy compared to peers with a recently acquired disability.

The present study found that measures of Membership Self-esteem and Social Self-efficacy among college students with disabilities were significantly higher than the normative sample. No significant differences were found on the other subscales. The positive relationship between disability status and Membership Self-esteem and Social Self-efficacy are at odds with findings reported by Saracoglu et al.'s (1989). Nothing in Saracoglu et al.'s study alludes to a social support system specifically designed for students with disabilities. Such a support system is available to the participants in the present study. Middle Tennessee State University has its own fraternity/sorority for students with disabilities. The students and the director of Disabled Student Services meet at the beginning of each semester and elect officers, just as any other fraternity/sorority. Almost all of the students with disabilities who live on campus are involved in the social organization. Getting involved with others that face similar challenges may enhance one's feeling of belonging, thus enhancing one's Membership Self-esteem and Social Self-efficacy.

Another explanation for the finding that students with disabilities scored higher than the normative sample on the Social Self-efficacy scale could be that college students with disabilities have had to over-come many obstacles in their lifetime in order to be enrolled at college. Attending college for any person is an accomplishment. Persons with physical and learning disabilities face many more challenges and obstacles than the average person (Penn & Dudley, 1980). Therefore, college students with disabilities who attend college may feel that they have beaten the odds, and therefore, their Social Self-efficacy may be higher.

A limitation of this study was the absence of a control group. The participants with disabilities scores on the self-esteem and self-efficacy scales could have been compared to a more current group of students without disabilities as opposed to the normative samples. It was also unfortunate that only 48 students chose to participate. The wide range of disabilities also can be construed as a limitation. Future researchers may wish to do in-depth interviews of college students with disabilities to further investigate self-esteem and self-efficacy (Kerr & Bodman, 1994).

Even these limitations do not detract from the central findings presented here. Self-esteem and self-efficacy were related for this sample. Also college students with disabilities showed the typical ranges of self-esteem and self-efficacy as students from the normative samples.

Reading and Writing Activities for "Self-Esteem and Self-Efficacy of College Students with Disabilities"

1. Write a summary of the article.

2. On index cards, take notes from the article to support a paper with the following title: "How Do College Students with Disabilities Feel about Themselves?"

3. In a paragraph, explain how this article is different from the other articles in this section of the textbook.

4. Outline the results of this study.

5. Describe the materials used to determine the self-esteem and the self-efficacy of the college students.

Is Freud Finished?

by John Elson. Reported by Janice M. Horowitz

He is rightly regarded as the father of modern psychiatry—as revolutionary a thinker as Darwin, as daring an explorer of the interior world as Columbus was of the exterior. Sigmund Freud not only developed the most profound theory to explain the workings of the human mind, but he also devised much of the terminology—from Oedipus complex to penis envy—that has become part of the language. The discipline he founded, psychoanalysis, became the world's most famous technique for helping the troubled come to grips with the demons haunting their minds.

But with the advent of new drug therapies, Freudian analysis has become almost irrelevant to the treatment of severe depression and schizophrenia. Granted, even the most pharmacology-minded of experts agree that the drugs work best in conjunction with some form of therapy. Yet psychiatrist Samuel Perry of Cornell University Medical College estimates that less than 1% of depression sufferers in the U.S. are being treated with traditional psychoanalysis—that is, a long-term series of regular sessions with a psychiatrist. Though this technique is still considered suitable for treating neurotics who have trouble coping with everyday stress, not even the most fanatic Freudians believe psychoanalysis alone can cope with severe cases of schizophrenia or severe depression.

Relatively little of Freud's voluminous work is devoted to the empirical study of clinical depression. His writings discuss only four patients who were known for certain to have suffered from major depression, and he published only one paper on the subject—"Mourning and Melancholia" (1917)—which contrasted ordinary grief and acute depression. He wrote somewhat more extensively about schizophrenia, which he called "paraphrenia." But he was always doubtful that psychoanalysis would be of much help in treating it. The schizophrenic's lack of interest in the external world, Freud wrote, made him inaccessible to transference. That is the key psychological process by which a patient redirects unconscious feelings retained from childhood toward an analyst. It was Freud's later disciples, rather than the master himself, who popularized the use of psychoanalysis to treat depression and even schizophrenia.

Feminists complain that Freud's view of women, as mercurial creatures with a deficient sense of moral standards, was downright misogynistic. Even some orthodox Freudians concede that his emphasis on sexuality as the root cause of all neuroses was too narrow. Nonetheless, Freud's ideas still have impact. Says Arnold Cooper, past president of the American Psychoanalytic Association: "You and everybody you know is a Freudian, and they probably don't even know it. We have all drunk in basic Freudian tenets." Freud was a pioneer in mapping the unconscious mind and theorizing how it could be reached and interpreted. He was the

"Is Freud Finished?" ©1992 *Time* Inc. Reprinted by permission *Time,* July 6, 1992, p. 80.

first to speculate that traumatic events of childhood could influence the way adults see the world. And he was the first also to postulate that patients in psychoanalysis, rather than the doctor, could direct therapy and contribute to their own cure.

"Freud took two pieces of Vermont folk wisdom and turned them into a science," says psychiatry professor Thomas Gutheil of Harvard medical school. "The first was, 'There's a whole lot more to folks than meets the eye.' This became known as the theory of the unconscious. The second was, 'Keep your mouth shut and you might learn something.' He changed the position of the doctor from that of an authoritarian giving orders to a more receptive role. Freud said, 'Let the patient talk and tell the story.' "

In that sense, all forms of talk therapy can be considered a Freudian legacy. Even the sex obsession of today's society can be read as evidence that contemporary culture indirectly reflects Freud's deepest concerns. Perhaps W. H. Auden got it right after all in his poetic tribute to the Viennese master, written a few months after Freud's death in 1939:

If often he was wrong and at times absurd,
To us he is no more a person now
But a whole climate of opinion
Under whom we conduct our differing lives.

Reading and Writing Activities for "Is Freud Finished?"

1. Write a summary of the article.

2. Answer the title question: Is Freud finished? Justify your answer.

3. Restate Freud's theory of psychoanalysis. Use information from this article and the sample psychology chapter "Personality."

4. Explain why the two pieces of Vermont folk wisdom quoted near the end of the article are appropriate sayings to summarize the work of Freud.

APPENDIX A

ANSWERS TO PRACTICE TESTS

ANSWERS TO THE HEALTH STUDY GUIDE PRACTICE TEST

Part I

Multiple Choice

1. c	4. d
2. a	5. b
3. b	6. d

True or False

7. T	11. F
8. F	12. T
9. T	13. T
10. F	

Short Answer

14. Homeostasis—a stable and consistent state the body strives for

    Allostasis—the body's ability to adapt to a constantly changing environment

    Adaptive response—the way the body attempts to restore homeostasis

15. Psychoneuroimmunology—the field that studies the interconnections of stress and the endocrine system. Looks at the fight-or-flight response and how stress produces stress hormones that may be harmful to our health.

16. Hostile Type A behavior is most closely related to heart disease. Individuals who are always mistrustful, angry, and suspicious are twice as likely to suffer blockages of their coronary arteries.

Part II

Multiple Choice

1. a
2. b
3. c

True or False

4. F
5. T

Part III

Multiple Choice

1. c

True or False

2. F

Short Answer

3. Journaling—putting your feelings into words that only you will read. Recording experiences on paper or audiotape may help decrease stress and enhance well-being.
4. Progressive relaxation—while sitting or lying, tense and release various muscles.

    Visualization or guided imagery—create mental pictures to calm yourself.

    Meditation—sit quietly 15 to 20 minutes once or twice a day, concentrate on a word or image, and breathe slowly.

    Mindfulness—tune in to each part of your body and allow whatever you experience to enter your awareness.

    Biofeedback—develop an awareness of a body state or function with the help of an electronic monitoring device; gain control over it; and transfer control to everyday life without the monitor.

ANSWERS TO THE AMERICAN HISTORY STUDY GUIDE PRACTICE TEST

Part I

True or False

1. F. The Battle of Bull Run made the *North* expect a longer war.
2. T
3. T
4. F. The turn to a war against slavery cost Lincoln popularity.

Multiple Choice

   5. b   9. d

   6. d 10. b

   7. a 11. b

   8. a

Identification

  12. First Battle of Bull Run

  13. Peninsula campaign

  14. Battle of Antietam

  15. Emancipation Proclamation

Part II

True or False

   1. F. Black soldiers were militarily effective.

   2. T.

   3. T.

   4. T.

Multiple Choice

   5. a

   6. c

   7. a

   8. c

Identification

   9. "Unconditional Surrender"

  10. Vicksburg

  11. Gettysburg

  12. Fort Pillow

  13. Atlanta

Part III

True or False

   1. F. The Union first succeeded in the West.

   2. T.

   3. T.

   4. F. Lincoln was opposed by some Republicans and many others in the North.

   5. T.

   6. T.

   7. F. The war settled all those issues.

Multiple Choice

    8. a

    9. b

  10. d

  11. b

Identification

  12. Copperheads

  13. *The Man Without a Country*

  14. Union Party

  15. Ford's Theater

  16. Appomattox Court House

  17. "The Lost Cause"

Matching People, Places, and Events

18. o	23. b	28. m
19. n	24. k	29. i
20. f	25. e	30. g
21. h	26. d	31. l
22. a	27. c	32. j

Putting Things in Order

  33. 3

  34. 1

  35. 2

  36. 5

  37. 4

Matching Cause and Effect

38. d	43. a
39. j	44. f
40. c	45. h
41. b	46. g
42. i	47. e

Map Mastery

  48. Alabama and Florida

  49. Missouri, Tennessee, West Virginia, Maryland

  50. Kentucky, Delaware

  51. Tennessee, Cumberland, Mississippi

  52. Charleston

ANSWERS TO THE BUSINESS STUDY GUIDE
PRACTICE TEST

Part I

LEARNING GOAL 9.1

True or False

1. F   4. T
2. T   5. F
3. F   6. T

LEARNING GOAL 9.2

True or False

7. T
8. F
9. T
10. T

LEARNING GOAL 9.3

Short Answer

11. The recruitment process is the search for applicants. Firms can look at current employees in an effort to enhance morale by hiring from within or they may conduct an outside search for candidates. Outside sources include colleges, advertisements in newspapers and professional journals, public employment agencies, unsolicited applications, and recommendations from current employees.

12. The steps in the selection process are

    a. Identify job requirements.

    b. Recruit applicants using one or more sources.

    c. Review applications and resumes.

    d. Interview candidates.

    e. Conduct employment tests and check references.

    f. Conduct follow-up interviews.

    g. Select a candidate and negotiate an offer.

    An applicant may be rejected at any step in the process.

13. Human resource managers must be familiar with employment law. Inattention to labor law can lead to lawsuits from unhappy employees and to bad publicity that hurts the firm's image.

Part II

LEARNING GOAL 9.4

Short Answer

1. First, a new hire must be oriented—that is acquainted with the organization. Next, initial training will take place. This may involve on-the-job training, apprenticeship programs, classroom training, and, management development programs. Training should be regarded as an ongoing activity that continues as long as the employee is with the firm.

2. A performance appraisal defines acceptable employee performance levels, evaluates the employee's actual performance, then compares actual and desired performance levels. The findings can be used to aid in decisions about training, compensation, promotion, transfers, and terminations.

LEARNING GOAL 9.5

Multiple Choice

3.	b	6.	d
4.	c	7.	d
5.	d	8.	c

Part III

LEARNING GOAL 9.6

Compare and Contrast

1. downsizing and outsourcing
2. outsourcing
3. outsourcing
4. downsizing and outsourcing
5. downsizing and outsourcing
6. downsizing
7. outsourcing
8. downsizing and outsourcing

LEARNING GOAL 9.7

Short Answer

9. Maslow's three assumptions are
   a. People are wanting animals whose needs depend on what they already possess.
   b. A satisfied need is not a motivator; only those needs that have not been satisfied can influence behavior.
   c. People's needs are arranged in a hierarchy of importance; once they satisfy one need, at least partially, another emerges and demands satisfaction.

10. The five needs in Maslow's hierarchy are

    a. Physiological needs: the need for food, water, shelter, and other necessities of life

    b. Safety needs: protection from harm, employee benefits and job security

    c. Social needs: acceptance, affection, affiliation with work groups, family, friends, coworkers, and supervisors

    d. Esteem needs: recognition, approval of others, status, increased responsibilities

    e. Self-actualization needs: accomplishment, opportunities for advancement, growth, and creativity

LEARNING GOAL 9.8

True or False

    11. T
    12. F
    13. F

Multiple Choice

    14. a
    15. b
    16. d
    17. b

LEARNING GOAL 9.9

True or False

18. F	21. T
19. T	22. F
20. T	23. T

Part IV

SELF-REVIEW

True or False

1. F	6. T	11. T
2. T	7. T	12. F
3. F	8. F	13. T
4. T	9. T	14. T
5. T	10. F	15. F

Multiple Choice

16. c	19. b	22. e	25. d
17. d	20. d	23. a	
18. b	21. c	24. a	

Application Exercises

Essay

26. Anita should probably first be clear about the job description she wants the new employee to fulfill. Then she can begin a search for candidates by contacting colleges and universities, public and private employment agencies, asking current employees for possible leads, or perhaps by advertising in newspapers or professional journals. Once she has a pool of candidates, she should get an application form from each, and perhaps do a preemployment skills test. Those candidates who perform well on the test should be called in for an interview. Once she has selected the top two or three candidates, she should contact previous employers or other references and do a background check. Before she makes an offer, it may be wise to have the applicant take a medical examination, perhaps including a test for substance abuse. At each step of the process she must be careful to obey the laws regarding equal opportunity. She may reject applicants at any step in the process, and hopefully by following this careful process will find the right person for the job.

27. Anita should do a complete orientation for the new worker, introducing the worker to key personnel and giving a tour of the facility. If she has an employee manual that describes the organization's mission and benefit programs, this should be part of the orientation. Anita also needs to think about what training methods she will use to be sure the new worker is prepared to do the job initially, and so that the worker can advance to new tasks in the future. Anita should consider several other factors. First, pay: what can she afford to pay, and what are competitors for this skilled labor paying in her area? If possible, she should enrich the job so that a talented employee will be challenged, and find the opportunity to meet higher order needs in the workplace. Anita might also consider offering employees a flexible work schedule or work plan. Finally, she needs to consider how she will tailor benefits to meet the differing needs of her workers.

Essay

28. Human resource management is a complex set of activities designed to acquire, train, develop, compensate, motivate, and appraise a sufficient quantity of qualified employees to perform the activities needed by the organization. It also involves developing an organizational climate conducive to maximum efficiency of workers and to high worker satisfaction and morale. People are the key resource of any organization, and represent a significant cost factor. The right people, trained in the right way, compensated and motivated in a way that produces worker satisfaction, are all essential steps in making any organization a success.

29. Human motivation is based on needs. Where people lack something useful, they are motivated to do something about it. Maslow identified a hierarchy of needs that managers can use in understanding human motivation. The first and most fundamental level of needs is physiological needs, those needs that must be met if the person is to survive. Included at this level are food, shelter, water, and so on. One way to meet these needs in the workplace is to provide adequate pay. The next level in Maslow's hierarchy is safety needs. Organizations can help meet these needs by offering good benefit programs, job security, and a safe work environment. The third level of needs identified by Maslow is social needs. Organizations need to be attentive to providing a climate that is conducive to both effective work and personal satisfaction. Next, Maslow identified esteem needs. These are the needs people have for respect, recognition, and responsibility. Finally, Maslow identified self-actualization needs, those needs met by challenge, by being creative, and by accomplishing something important. These needs can be met by devising enriched jobs that challenge workers, and they require constructing job descriptions that will take advantage of higher level need gratification. Theory X is the belief that people are lazy and need to be coerced or threatened if they are to do a good job. This theory has largely been replaced by

Theory Y, which assumes that workers like work, will accept responsibility under the right circumstances, and seek to meet their higher level needs on the job. Theory Z builds on Theory Y, emphasizing employee participation as the key to increased productivity and improved quality of work life.

The essential lesson we can learn from these theories is that good pay is not enough. Workers must have their lower level needs met to an acceptable degree as a basis for motivation, so good pay and benefits, and safe and pleasant working conditions are extremely important. But we must go further: managers should realize that most people want to meet their higher level needs on the job, and that Theory Y and Theory Z management assumptions should be adopted whenever possible. The most important lesson in motivating employees is that jobs must be constructed so that workers have an opportunity to meet their higher level needs at work. Challenge, creativity, and other job-enriching activities are the key to motivation in the future.

ANSWERS TO THE PSYCHOLOGY STUDY GUIDE PRACTICE TEST

Part I—The Psychodynamic Approach

Matching I

1. c
2. e
3. d
4. k
5. b
6. f
7. a
8. j
9. g
10. l
11. i
12. m
13. h

Matching II

14. h
15. b
16. g
17. f
18. d
19. c
20. a
21. j
22. i
23. e

Matching III

24. c
25. d
26. b
27. a
28. i
29. g
30. e
31. h
32. k
33. f
34. l
35. j

Multiple Choice

36. d	61. b
37. d	62. d
38. d	63. d
39. d	64. d
40. b	65. c
41. c	66. a
42. d	67. c
43. a	68. a
44. b	69. c
45. d	70. d
46. a	71. d
47. c	72. a
48. c	73. d
49. a	74. b
50. c	75. c
51. b	76. c
52. c	77. d
53. c	78. d
54. d	79. d
55. c	80. c
56. c	81. d
57. b	82. d
58. c	83. b
59. c	84. d
60. c	85. b

Part II—The Humanistic Approach

Matching

1. d
2. a
3. b
4. c

Multiple Choice

5. d	13. a
6. d	14. a
7. b	15. d
8. d	16. c
9. c	
10. a	
11. a	
12. a	

Part III—The Trait Approach

Matching

1. e	6. c
2. g	7. j
3. d	8. b
4. a	9. i
5. f	10. h

Multiple Choice

11. b	21. b	31. c
12. c	22. d	32. d
13. b	23. d	33. d
14. b	24. a	34. a
15. d	25. d	35. b
16. a	26. c	
17. a	27. a	
18. b	28. b	
19. c	29. d	
20. b	30. b	

Part IV—The Social Cognitive Approach

Matching

1. a
2. b
3. d
4. e
5. f
6. c

Multiple Choice

7. a
8. c
9. d
10. b
11. d
12. b
13. a
14. a
15. c
16. d
17. c
18. c
19. c
20. b
21. d
22. d
23. d

Part V—End-of-Chapter Quiz

Multiple Choice

1. c
2. c
3. d
4. d
5. d
6. b
7. b
8. a
9. c
10. a
11. b
12. c
13. d
14. c
15. b
16. a
17. a
18. c
19. d
20. d
21. c
22. d
23. a
24. d

APPENDIX B

READING ESSAYS ABOUT LITERARY WORKS

You will be required to perform a different type of reading in English and literature courses. This type of reading requires more interpretation on your part. You are not reading to gain information but to analyze what the writer has written. Some of the skills you have used in textbook reading are the same; for example, it is helpful to survey the material; to review any questions provided; to determine the main ideas, important details, and organizational patterns of the paragraphs; to determine the main idea of the entire essay (the thesis); and then to recite and review the material. Some of the skills are different, however; for example, you need to think about the author's purpose and intended audience and evaluate the organization and content as well as the author's tone and point of view.

The manner or expression with which the author addresses a subject is his or her *tone*. Some examples of tone include the following: anger, bitterness, irony, happiness, humor, sarcasm, professionalism, and insult. Read the following two sentences written about the same subject but with different tones:

> The playful kitten somersaulted down the steps and into the garden where she began leaping after a butterfly.
>
> The striped feline closely inspected the aquarium before cautiously dipping a paw into the water.

The first sentence has a playful tone, whereas the second sounds more professional. *Mood* is the feeling or expression that the writing draws from you, the reader. All of the emotions that can be expressed by the author through tone can also be found in mood. In fact, much of the time, the tone the author takes is the same as the mood he or she wants you to feel as you read. However, this is not always true, particularly if you have had some personal experience with the topic. For example, reading the first essay, "Native Son," about a Black man who overcame his hardships as a result of reading, may create a feeling of pride, or it may cause you to feel anger. Your personal experiences will help determine your reactions and mood to the reading. *Point of view* is the opinion that an author wants you to understand. Sometimes different points of view will be presented on the same topic. Your job as a reader is to determine the point of view of the author and determine the facts that support it.

Following the next section, you will find three articles traditionally used in first-year English courses. The first essay, "Native Son," is used as an example in the "Critical Reading" section that follows. Use that information to help you critically read and analyze that selection as well as the other two selections "Of Headless Mice . . . and Men" and "Ebola River Preston." Once you have read the essays, answer the questions at the end of each for class discussion.

CRITICAL READING

When reading essays, follow these steps:

1. Survey the essay.

   a. Read the title.

   b. Read any information provided about the author or the piece of writing. This will give you an idea of the author's purpose and intended audience. For example, in "Native Son," the paragraph preceding the essay tells the reader that the piece is taken from an autobiography of the author, who is describing the influence books had on him while in prison. The title of the book, from which the article is selected, gives you an idea of the author's purpose for writing. He is disgusted and angry with what young Black men must endure in America, and his purpose is to relate these feelings to the reader. He also wants to relate the impact that a Black writer had upon him and how he was able to change his life through reading. His audience is most likely all of America, Black and White. He wants to show White Americans what young Black men must endure and he wants to show Black Americans, particularly young Black men, that they determine their own fate.

   c. Read subheadings if they are used.

   d. Read the first and last paragraphs of the essay.

   e. Read any questions provided at the end of the essay.

2. Read the article.

   a. Locate the main idea or thesis statement of the essay. This may be stated in the essay or it may be implied. Because the thesis guides the organization and development of the written ideas, it is important to find in order to understand the piece. For example, in "Native Son," the author's thesis is implied. It is never directly stated that reading changed this author's life. It made him realize that others with the same feelings existed and that words and ideas in books have a power to transform a life.

   b. Identify the organizational pattern of the essay. Essays may follow any of the patterns mentioned in Chapter 3 of this textbook (example or list, comparison or contrast, cause or effect, definition, time order, and classification). Additionally, an author may use one of the following organizational patterns:

      i. Argument/Persuasion—the author states an assertion, or proposition, and then offers proof to support the assertion and convince the readers of its truth or validity.

      ii. Narration—the author recreates an experience for a purpose. That purpose may be to explain, to persuade, to entertain, to illustrate a point, or to report information.
      "Native Son" is obviously a narrative; this is stated under "Personal Response" toward the end of the essay. The purpose of this narrative is to illustrate the point made in the thesis.

      iii. Description—the author appeals to the senses (sight, smell, sound, taste, and touch) while depicting some person, place, or thing. The purpose may be to simply convey information with an objective description, or to make some point with a subjective description.

   c. Determine how each paragraph in the reading relates to the thesis. As in textbook informational material, not every paragraph in an essay will have its own main idea, and sometimes a paragraph may have two or three main ideas.

   d. As you read each paragraph, evaluate the essay. Consider whether the author achieves what he or she set out to accomplish. Is the thesis thoroughly explained, developed, or argued? If the text is expository, does the author present enough examples or lists, comparisons or contrasts, causes or effects, definitions, steps, or categories? If the essay is persuasion, does the author have enough proof to convince the reader, and are the proofs logical? If the author uses description, does he or she use enough detail? Finally, if narration is used, does the writer recreate an experience that reinforces the thesis? Other questions for evaluation include how effective the introduction and conclusion are, how organized the piece is, and how effective the author's choice of language is.

The first paragraph of "Native Son" cites the negative mental conditions experienced by the author while in prison and the methods he used to overcome those conditions. This is an effective introduction because it allows the reader to understand the mental strain of a prisoner. As the author moves into the next paragraph and the remainder of the essay, he shows how this hardship was overcome and how his life was changed by reading books—the thesis of the essay.

3. Review the essay by answering the questions at the end of the work. You may have to reread parts of the essay to do this. Summarize your answers to the questions in a sentence or two to be used for class discussion. Consider the opinions you have formed, how you want to present these in a class discussion, and what parts of the essay you have to support your answers and opinions.

The first question at the conclusion of "Native Son" asks you to consider the degree to which reading books might be a solution to American crime and violence. In your answer you might cite some of the specific books read by Nathan McCall, the author, and the impact these books made on him. You might also state that many other prisoners had access to the same books and were not affected by them.

As you read the following three essays think about the steps to critical reading, but also allow yourself to *enjoy* the reading. Reading critically requires work, but is always more enjoyable if you appreciate and relate to what you are reading.

Native Son

Nathan McCall

Nathan McCall was imprisoned for armed robbery at the age of twenty but after prison he earned a college degree and became a journalist. He now writes for the Washington Post. *His autobiography,* Makes Me Wanna Holler: A Young Black Man in America *(1994), describes his youth, his time in prison, and his pivotal discovery of books. In this excerpt from* Makes Me Wanna Holler, *McCall describes the influence on him of reading Richard Wright's* Native Son *while serving his prison term.*

There were moments in that jail when the confinement and heat nearly drove me mad. At those times, I desperately needed to take my thoughts beyond the concrete and steel. When I felt restless tension rising, I'd try anything to calm it. I'd slap-box with other inmates until I got exhausted, or play chess until my mind shut down. When all else failed, I'd pace the cell block perimeter like a caged lion. Sometimes, other inmates fighting the temptation to give in to madness joined me, and we'd pace together, round and round, and talk for hours about anything that got our minds off our misery.

I eventually found a better way to relieve the boredom. I noticed that some inmates broke the monotony by volunteering for certain jobs in the jail. Some mopped the halls, and others worked in the dispensary or the kitchen. When the inmate librarian was released from jail, I asked for and was given his job. I began distributing books on the sixth floor as part of a service provided by the Norfolk Public Library. A couple of times a week, I pushed a cart to each cellblock and let inmates choose books and place orders for literature not on the cart. I enjoyed the library work. It gave me a chance to get out into the halls and walk around, and to stick my face to the screens on the floor windows and inhale fresh air.

Beyond the short stories I'd read in high school, I hadn't done much reading. Naturally, while working for the library, I leafed through more books than I normally would have. One day, shortly after starting the job, I picked up a book featuring a black man's picture on the cover. It was titled *Native Son,* and the author was Richard Wright. I leafed through a few pages in the front of the book, and couldn't put it down. The story was about a confused, angry young black man named Bigger Thomas, whose racial fears lead him to accidentally suffocate a white woman. In doing so, he delivers himself into the hands of the very people he despises and fears.

I identified strongly with Bigger and the book's narrative. He was twenty, the same age as me. He felt the things I felt, and, like me, he wound up in prison. The book's portrait of Bigger captured all those conflicting feelings—restless anger, hopelessness, a tough facade among blacks and a deep-seated fear of whites—that I'd sensed in myself but was unable to express. Often, during my teenage years, I'd felt like Bigger—headed down a road toward a destruction I couldn't ward off, beaten by forces so large and amorphous that I had no idea how to fight back. I was surprised that somebody had written a book that so closely reflected my experiences and feelings.

I read that book every day, and continued reading by the dim light of the hall lamps at night, while everyone slept. On that early morning when I finished reading *Native Son,* which ends with Bigger waiting to go to the electric chair, I broke down and sobbed like a baby. There is one passage that so closely described how I felt that it stunned me. It is a passage where a lawyer is talking to Bigger, who has given up hope and is waiting to die:

> You're trying to believe in yourself. And every time you try to find a way to live, your own mind stands in the way. You know why that is? It's because others have said you were bad and they made you live in bad conditions. When a man hears that over and over and looks about him and sees that life is bad, he begins to doubt his own mind. His feelings drag him forward and his mind, full of what others say about him, tells him to go back. The job in getting people to fight and have faith is in making them believe in what life has made them feel, making them feel that their feelings are as good as others'.

After reading that, I sat up in my bunk, buried my face in my hands, and wept uncontrollably. I cried so much that I felt relieved. It was like I had been carrying those feelings and holding in my pain for years, keeping it pushed into the back of my mind somewhere.

I was unaccustomed to dealing with such deep feelings. Occasionally, I'd opened up to Liz, but not a lot. I was messed up inside, empty and afraid, just like Bigger. *Native Son* confirmed for me that my fears *weren't* imagined and that there were rational reasons why I'd been hurting inside.

I developed through my encounter with Richard Wright a fascination with the power of words. It blew my mind to think that somebody could take words that described exactly how I felt and put them together in a story like that. Most of the books I'd been given in school were about white folks' experiences and feelings. I spent all that time learning about damned white folks, like my reality didn't exist and wasn't valid to the rest of the world. In school, the only time we'd really focused on the lives of black people was during Black History Week, which they set aside for us to learn the same old tired stories about Booker T. Washington and a few other noteworthy, dead black folks I couldn't relate to. But in *Native Son* I found a book written about a plain, everyday brother like myself. That turned me on in a big way and inspired me to look for more books like that.

Before long, I was reading every chance I got, trying to more fully understand why my life and the lives of friends had been so contained and predictable, and why prison—literally—

had become a rite of passage for so many of us. I found books that took me places I'd never dreamed I could travel to and exposed me to a range of realities that seemed as vast as the universe itself.

Once, after reading a book of poems by Gwendolyn Brooks, I wrote to her, not really expecting to receive a reply. She wrote me back and sent me an inspirational paperback of hers titled *Aloneness*. I was thrilled that a well-known black writer like her had taken the time to respond to me.

I was most attracted to black classics, such as Malcolm X's autobiography. Malcolm's tale helped me understand the devastating effects of self-hatred and introduced me to a universal principle: that if you change your self-perception, you can change your behavior. I concluded that if Malcolm X, who had also gone to prison, could pull his life out of the toilet, then maybe I could, too.

Up to that point, I'd often wanted to think of myself as a bad nigger, and as a result, I'd tried to act like one. After reading about Malcolm X, I worked to get rid of that notion and replaced it with a positive image of what I wanted to become. I walked around silently repeating to myself, "You are an intelligent-thinking human being; you are an intelligent-thinking human being . . . ," hoping that it would sink in and help me begin to change the way I viewed myself.

Malcolm X made his conversion through Islam. I'd seen Muslims selling newspapers and bean pies on the streets, but I didn't know anything about their religion. I was drawn to Christianity, mostly because it was familiar. I hadn't spent much time in church. It seemed that all they did in churches I'd been to was learn how to justify suffering at the hands of white folks. But now there were Christian ministers active at the jail, and I became interested. They came around about once a week and talked to inmates through the bars, prayed with them and read Scripture. I started talking to them about God and about life in general.

It wasn't hard to accept the possibility that there was a higher force watching over me. When I looked back at my life, I concluded that there had been far too many close calls— times when I could have offed somebody or gotten killed myself—for me to believe I had survived solely on luck. I wondered, *Why didn't that bullet strike Plaz in the heart when I shot him? Why didn't I pull the trigger on that McDonald's manager when he tried to get away? And why wasn't I on the corner the night my stick partners were shot?* Unable to come up with rational answers to those questions, I reasoned that God must have been pulling for me.

My interest in spiritual things also came from a need to reach out at my most powerless point and tap into a higher power, something beyond me and, at the same time, within me. I longed for a sense of wholeness that I had never known but senses I was entitled to. I set out to learn more about my spiritual self, and I began exploring the Bible with other inmates who held Bible studies some nights in the cellblock.

At some point, I also got a library copy of the book—*As a Man Thinketh*—that Reverend Ellis had given me in college. I immediately understood what he had been trying to get across: that thinking should be an *active* process that, when cultivated, can change a person's behavior, circumstances, and, ultimately, his fate.

When I first started reading, studying, and reflecting on the information I got from books, I had no idea where it all might lead. Really, it didn't matter. I was hungry for change and so excited by the sense of awakening I glimpsed on the horizon that the only thing that mattered was that I had made a start. I often recited the Scripture that Reverend Ellis had given me to read before I was sentenced: "Everything works together for the good of those that love God, for those who are called according to his purpose." *If that's true,* I thought, *maybe I can get something positive out of this time in prison*. It sure didn't seem like it. But it made me feel better just thinking it might be possible.

Personal Response

Comment on your response to McCall's personal narrative.

Questions for Class or Small-Group Discussion

1. Nathan McCall clearly attributes the turning point of his life to reading *Native Son*. Considering the problem of crime and violence in America, to what degree do you think reading books might be a solution?

2. Why do you think McCall was so moved by *Native Son?* What did it offer him that had been missing in his life? What did Christianity do for him?

3. McCall believes that low self-esteem or self-hatred was largely responsible for his criminal behavior and that once he began to think positively about himself, he was able to turn around his life. Discuss the implications of that statement: Don't many behavior problems stem from low self-esteem, regardless of race, class, or gender?

4. McCall believes that thinking positively helps people overcome any difficulty. Do you agree or disagree with that philosophy? Give examples to support your position.

Of Headless Mice . . . and Men

Charles Krauthammer

Charles Krauthammer is a contributing editor to the New Republic *and writes a weekly syndicated column for the* Washington Post. *A political scientist, psychiatrist, journalist, and speech writer, Krauthammer won a Pulitzer Prize in 1981 for his commentary on politics and society. He has published a book,* Cutting Edges: Making Sense of the Eighties *(1985). Krauthammer also contributes to* Time *magazine, where the following opinion piece was published in the "Essay" column of the January 19, 1998 issue.*

Last year Dolly the cloned sheep was received with wonder, titters, and some vague apprehension. Last week the announcement by a Chicago physicist that he is assembling a team to produce the first human clone occasioned yet another wave of Brave New World anxiety. But the scariest news of all—and largely overlooked—comes from two obscure labs, at the University of Texas and at the University of Bath. During the past four years, one group created headless mice; the other, headless tadpoles.

For sheer Frankenstein wattage, the purposeful creation of these animal monsters has no equal. Take the mice. Researchers found the gene that tells the embryo to produce the head. They deleted it. They did this in a thousand mice embryos, four of which were born. I use the term loosely. Having no way to breathe, the mice died instantly.

Why then create them? The Texas researchers want to learn how genes determine embryo development. But you don't have to be a genius to see the true utility of manufacturing headless creatures: for their organs—fully formed, perfectly useful, ripe for plundering.

Why should you be panicked? Because humans are next. "It would almost certainly be possible to produce humans without a forebrain," Princeton biologist Lee Silver told the London *Sunday Times*. "These human bodies without any semblance of consciousness would not be considered persons, and thus it would be perfectly legal to keep them 'alive' as a future source of organs."

"Alive." Never have a pair of quotation marks loomed so ominously. Take the mouse–frog technology, apply it to humans, combine it with cloning, and you become a god: With a single cell taken from, say, your finger, you produce a headless replica of yourself, a mutant twin, arguably lifeless, that becomes your own personal, precisely tissue-matched organ farm.

"Of Headless Mice . . . and Men," by Charles Krauthammer. *Time Magazine.* January 19, 1998.

There are, of course, technical hurdles along the way. Suppressing the equivalent "head" gene in man. Incubating tiny infant organs to grow into larger ones that adults could use. And creating artificial wombs (as per Aldous Huxley), given that it might be difficult to recruit sane women to carry headless fetuses to their birth/death.

It won't be long, however, before these technical barriers are breached. The ethical barriers are already cracking. Lewis Wolpert, professor of biology at University College, London, finds producing headless humans "personally distasteful" but, given the shortage of organs, does not think distaste is sufficient reason not to go ahead with something that would save lives. And Professor Silver not only sees "nothing wrong, philosophically or rationally," with producing headless humans for organs harvesting; he wants to convince a skeptical public that it is perfectly O.K.

When prominent scientists are prepared to acquiesce in—or indeed encourage—the deliberate creation of deformed and dying quasi-human life, you know we are facing a bioethical abyss. Human beings are ends, not means. There is no grosser corruption of biotechnology than creating a human mutant and disemboweling it at our pleasure for spare parts.

The prospect of headless human clones should put the whole debate about "normal" cloning in a new light. Normal cloning is less a treatment for infertility than a treatment for vanity. It is a way to produce an exact genetic replica of yourself that will walk the earth years after you're gone.

But there is a problem with a clone. It is not really you. It is but a twin, a perfect John Doe Jr., but still a junior. With its own independent consciousness, it is, alas, just a facsimile of you.

The headless clone solves the facsimile problem. It is a gateway to the ultimate vanity: immortality. If you create a real clone, you cannot transfer your consciousness into it to truly live on. But if you create a headless clone of just your body, you have created a ready source of replacement parts to keep you—your consciousness—going indefinitely.

Which is why one form of cloning will inevitably lead to the other. Cloning is the technology of narcissism, and nothing satisfies narcissism like immortality. Headlessness will be cloning's crowning achievement.

The time to put a stop to this is now. Dolly moved President Clinton to create a commission that recommended a temporary ban on human cloning. But with physicist Richard Seed threatening to clone humans, and with headless animals already here, we are past the time for toothless commissions and meaningless bans.

Clinton banned federal funding of human-cloning research, of which there is none anyway. He then proposed a five-year ban on cloning. This is not enough. Congress should ban human cloning now. Totally. And regarding one particular form, it should be draconian: The deliberate creation of headless humans must be made a crime, indeed, a capital crime. If we flinch in the face of this high-tech barbarity, we'll deserve to live in the hell it heralds.

Personal Response

Explain your response to Krauthammer's vision of the future of mankind if the law does not prohibit cloning of headless animals, including humans.

Questions for Class or Small-Group Discussion

1. Krauthammer begins by describing examples of the successful cloning of headless mice and tadpoles that died as soon as they were born. "Why then create them?" he asks. How does he answer that question?

2. Paragraph 4 begins with the question, "Why should you be panicked?" Summarize Krauthammer's answer to that question. Are you persuaded that you should panic?

3. Do you agree with Krauthammer that "cloning is the technology of narcissism" (paragraph 12)?

4. Comment on Krauthammer's concluding paragraphs. To what extent do you agree with him?

5. Explain these references: Brave New World (paragraph 1); Frankenstein (paragraph 2); Aldous Huxley (paragraph 6). What does *draconian* mean (paragraph 14)?

Richard Preston

Richard Preston is a journalist who frequently contributes to The New Yorker. *In 1987 he published a book about astronomy,* First Light, *which won the American Institute of Physics Award. His next book,* American Steel, *examined the Nucor Corporation's plan to build a revolutionary steel mill. In 1994 he published* The Hot Zone *documenting the outbreak and spread of the deadly Ebola virus.*

Ebola River

In this passage from The Hot Zone, *Preston details the initial appearance of the Ebola virus in Sudan. Although written in the third person and focusing on objective observation, Preston's use of factual detail creates a chilling drama.*

On July 6, 1976, five hundred miles northwest of Mount Elgon, in southern Sudan, near the fingered edge of the central-African rain forest, a man who is known to Ebola hunters as Yu. G. went into shock and died with blood running from the orifices of his body. He is referred to only by his initials. Mr. Yu. G. was the first identified case, the index case, in an outbreak of an unknown virus.

Mr. Yu. G. was a storekeeper in a cotton factory in the town of Nzara. The population of Nzara had grown in recent years—the town had experienced, in its own way, the human population explosion that is occurring throughout the equatorial regions of the earth. The people of that area in southern Sudan are the Zande, a large tribe. The country of the Zande is savanna mixed with riverine forest, beautiful country, where acacia trees cluster along the banks of seasonal rivers. African doves perch in the trees and call their drawn-out calls. The land between the rivers is a sea of elephant grass, which can grow ten feet high. As you head south, toward Zaire, the land rises and forms hills, and the forest begins to spread away from the river and thickens into a closed canopy, and you enter the rain forest. The land around the town of Nzara held rich plantations of teak and fruit trees and cotton. People were poor, but they worked hard and raised large families and kept to their tribal traditions.

Mr. Yu. G. was a salaried man. He worked at a desk in a room piled with cotton cloth at the back of the factory. Bats roosted in the ceiling of the room near his desk. If the bats were infected with Ebola, no one has been able to prove it. The virus may have entered the cotton factory by some unknown route—perhaps in insects trapped in the cotton fibers, for example, or in rats that lived in the factory. Or, possibly, the virus had nothing to do with the cotton factory, and Mr. Yu. G. was infected somewhere else. He did not go to a hospital, and died on a cot in his family compound. His family gave him a traditional Zande funeral and left his body under a mound of stones in a clearing of elephant grass. His grave has been visited more than once by doctors from Europe and America, who want to see it and reflect on its meaning, and pay their respects to the index case of what later became known as Ebola Sudan.

He is remembered today as a "quiet, unremarkable man." No photograph was taken of him during his lifetime, and no one seems to remember what he looked like. He wasn't well known, even in his hometown. They say that his brother was tall and slender, so perhaps he was, too. He passed through the gates of life unnoticed by anyone except his family and a few of his co-workers. He might have made no difference except for the fact that he was a host.

His illness began to copy itself. A few days after he died, two other salaried men who worked at desks near him in the same room broke with bleeding, went into shock, and died with massive hemorrhages from the natural openings of the body. One of the dead men was a popular fellow known as P. G. Unlike the quiet Mr. Yu. G., he had a wide circle of friends, including several mistresses. He spread the agent far and wide in the town. The agent jumped easily from person to person, apparently through touching and sexual contact. It was a fast spreader, and it could live easily in people. It passed through as many as sixteen generations of infection as it jumped from person to person in Sudan. It also killed many of its hosts. While this is not necessarily in the best interest of the virus, if the virus is highly contagious, and can jump fast enough from host to host, then it does not matter, really, what happens to the previous host, because the virus can amplify itself for quite a while, at least until it kills off much of the population of hosts. Most of the fatal cases of Ebola Sudan can be traced back through chains of infection to the quiet Mr. Yu. G. A hot strain radiated out of him and nearly devastated the human population of southern Sudan. The strain burned through the town of Nzara and reached eastward to the town of Maridi, where there was a hospital.

It hit the hospital like a bomb. It savaged patients and snaked like chain lightning out from the hospital through patients' families. Apparently the medical staff had been giving patients injections with dirty needles. The virus jumped quickly through the hospital via the needles, and then it hit the medical staff. A characteristic of a lethal, contagious, and incurable virus is that it quickly gets into the medical people. In some cases, the medical system may intensify the outbreak, like a lens that focuses sunlight on a heap of tinder.

The virus transformed the hospital at Maridi into a morgue. As it jumped from bed to bed, killing patients left and right, doctors began to notice signs of mental derangement, psychosis, depersonalization, zombie-like behavior. Some of the dying stripped off their clothes and ran out of the hospital, naked and bleeding, and wandered through the streets of the town, seeking their homes, not seeming to know what had happened or how they had gotten into this condition. There is no doubt that Ebola damages the brain and causes psychotic dementia. It is not easy, however, to separate brain damage from the effects of fear. If you were trapped in a hospital where people were dissolving in their beds, you might try to escape, and if you were a bleeder and frightened, you might take off your clothes, and people might think you had gone mad.

The Sudan strain was more than twice as lethal as Marburg virus—its case-fatality rate was 50 percent. That is, fully half of the people who came down with it ended up dying, and quickly. This was the same kind of fatality rate as was seen with the black plague during the Middle Ages. If the Ebola Sudan virus had managed to spread out of central Africa, it might have entered Khartoum in a few weeks, penetrated Cairo a few weeks after that, and from there it would have hopped to Athens, New York, Paris, London, Singapore—it would have gone everywhere on the planet. Yet that never happened, and the crisis in Sudan passed away unnoticed by the world at large. What happened in Sudan could be compared to the secret detonation of an atomic bomb. If the human race came close to a major biological accident, we never knew it.

For reasons that are not clear, the outbreak subsided, and the virus vanished. The hospital at Maridi had been the epicenter of the emergence. As the virus ravaged the hospital, the surviving medical staff panicked and ran off into the bush. It was probably the wisest thing to do and the best thing that could have happened, because it stopped the use of dirty needles and emptied the hospital, which helped break the chain of infection.

There was another possible reason why the Ebola Sudan virus vanished. It was exceedingly hot. It killed people so fast that they didn't have much time to infect other people before they died. Furthermore, the virus was not airborne. It was not quite contagious enough to start a full-scale disaster. It traveled in blood, and the bleeding victim did not touch very many other people before dying, and so the virus did not have many chances to jump to a new host. Had people been coughing the virus into the air . . . it would have been a different story. In any case, the Ebola Sudan virus destroyed a few hundred people in central Africa the way a fire consumes a pile of straw—until the blaze burns out at the center and ends in a heap of ash—rather than smoldering around the planet, as AIDS has done, like a fire in a coal mine, impossible to put out. The Ebola virus, in its Sudan incarnation, retreated to the heart of the bush, where undoubtedly it lives to this day, cycling and cycling in some unknown host, able to shift its shape, able to mutate and become a new thing, with the potential to enter the human species in a new form.

Understanding Meaning

1. What is known about Mr. Yu. G.? What made him important to science?
2. What effect does the Ebola virus have on people? How does it kill?
3. How does the virus spread from one person to another?
4. Why did this outbreak kill only a few hundred people and not spread across the world like AIDS?
5. *Critical Thinking:* What implications do Ebola and similar viruses have in a world where jet travel would make it easy for a single patient to spread the disease to people thousands of miles from the outbreak?

Evaluating Strategy

1. How does Preston organize the chain of events? What chronological pattern does he use?
2. How does Preston assemble scientific facts to create a dramatic story? Can an objective narrative have an emotional impact on readers? Can facts truly "speak for themselves"?
3. In paragraph seven, Preston places his readers into the events by using second person, "If you were trapped in a hospital . . ." What impact does this have? Is this an effective strategy?

Appreciating Language

1. How would you characterize Preston's level of diction? Does the lack of medical terminology weaken the narrative's scientific value? What does it say about the intended audience?
2. Underline those phrases that dramatize the events. How effective are they?
3. What words does Preston use to describe the virus? How does he emphasize its lethality?

Writing Suggestions

1. Write a short essay *analyzing* what threats the Ebola and related viruses could pose in the future. What should happen if the virus broke out in a city like New York or Las Vegas?
2. Write a brief factual but dramatic narrative about an event you experienced or witnessed. Select details that create strong impressions, but avoid exaggerating or distorting facts.
3. *Collaborative Writing:* Working with at least three other students, draft a short persuasive letter to the White House, arguing that the military should be equipped to rapidly respond to biomedical disasters. Use Preston's account to support your thesis.

SELECTED ANSWERS TO THE PART I EXERCISES

EXERCISE 1: USING CONTEXT CLUES

1. detail clue; *hierarchy* = an order that proceeds from lowest to highest
3. detail clue; *self-actualization needs* = needs to realize one's full potential
5. example clue; *constraints* = certain limitations
7. detail/example clue; *telecommuter* = employee who works at home
9. definition clue (with examples); *employee benefits* = rewards an organization gives, entirely, or in part, at its own expense
11. detail clue; *subjective* = cannot be proven because it is individual
13. contrast clue; *futile* = unsuccessful; not good
15. restatement clue; *burnout* = a state of physical, emotional, and mental exhaustion brought on by constant or repeated emotional pressure
17. detail clue; *outsourcing* = relying on contracted employees to perform functions previously performed by company employees
19. restatement clue; *stressors* = things that upset or excite us

EXERCISE 2: USING WORD PART CLUES

1. *psychosexual* = mind and sexual
3. *compressed* = pushed together (into fewer work days)
5. *distrusting* = opposite of trusting; not trusting
7. *posttraumatic* = after trauma

EXERCISE 3: USING CONTEXT AND WORD PART CLUES

1. contrast context clue; *acquiesced* = gave in
3. word part clue and detail context clue; *converged* = came together

5. word part clue and detail context clue; *specialist* = one who focuses on individual areas of resource management

7. word part clue; *nonbiological* = not relating to life or body tissue

9. word part clue and definition context clue; *unconditional positive regard* = total, genuine love without any strings attached

EXERCISE 4: USING MEANINGFUL EXAMPLES TO REMEMBER DEFINITIONS

Student examples will vary.

1. Definition: *ego* = part of personality that deals with what is real; serves as mediator

3. Definition: *central trait* = general characteristic found in most people

5. Definition: *trait* = consistent tendency to act, think, feel a certain way

7. Definition: *flexible benefit plans* = benefit plans that allow employees to pick and choose benefits; cafeteria plans (this alternate term must be included)

9. Definition: *contingent workers* = part-time workers

EXERCISE 5: VISUAL AIDS TO IMPROVE MEMORY

Diagrams will vary; be sure to include all important concepts and definitions.

1. Maslow's hierarchy: often a triangle is used to show needs, with the most basic level on the bottom of the triangle.

3. Reciprocal influences: a circle can be used to show how each of the influences acts to influence the other.

EXERCISE 6: FINDING STATED MAIN IDEAS I

1. Sentence 3 (The physical resemblance . . .)

3. Sentence 1 (Some employees . . .)

5. Sentence 2 (Stress is just that . . .) Students may use the first part of this sentence, the last part, or both parts for the main idea.

7. Sentence 2 (But exchanging . . .)

9. Sentence 1 (The healing power . . .)

11. Sentence 1 (Sherman the soldier . . .)

13. Sentence 2 (If you come . . .)

15. Sentence 1 (Whenever soldiers . . .)

17. Sentence 1 (People who . . .)

19. Sentence 1 (Because of . . .)

EXERCISE 7: FINDING MAIN IDEAS II

1. Sentence 2 (As finally . . .)
3. Sentence 1 (Good nutrition . . .)
5. Sentence 1 (Other Union thrusts . . .)
7. Sentence 1 (One can view . . .)
9. Last sentence (Thus . . .)
11. Sentence 2 (Casual dress policies . . .)

EXERCISE 8: DETERMINING IMPLIED MAIN IDEAS I

1. Topic: Maslow's hierarchy

    Main Idea: Maslow's hierarchy has five steps that show the importance of people's needs and motivation.
3. Topic: Stress

    Main Idea: Many different causes can lead to long- or short-term stress.
5. Topic: feelings of the populace toward the Civil War

    Main Idea: Feelings toward the Civil War changed from glorious to struggling.
7. Topic: McClellan's failing

    Main Idea: As commander of all Union forces, McClellan continued to be overcautious and delayed a Richmond attack.
9. Topic: Atlanta's importance

    Main Idea: Atlanta, because of it's importance, was captured by Sherman.

EXERCISE 9: DETERMINING IMPLIED MAIN IDEAS II

1. Topic: Vallandigham

    Main Idea: Vallandigham, who publicly voiced his disagreement with the war, was convicted of treasonable words and sent to live in the South.
3. Topic: Outsourcing

    Main Idea: Outsourcing, which began small and has expanded, is used by firms to remain competitive and hold down costs.
5. Topic: *Merrimack*

    Main Idea: The *Merrimack,* a Southern-built ironclad, posed a threat to Yankee blockading.

Note: The first sentence alone cannot be the main idea sentence because it fails to mention the *Merrimack.*

7. Topic: Twins behavior

    Main Idea: Research has been done on identical twins who are reared apart and who act identically in certain situations, but this may be due to chance. OR Different opinions exist on the interpretations of research with twins.
9. Topic: Theory on male-female relationship problems

    Main Idea: Theorist Nancy Chodorow theorizes that Freud's lack of attention to mothers caused him to miss the male-female relationship problems stemming from boys' and girls' identities with their mothers.

EXERCISE 10: DETERMINING MIXED STATED AND IMPLIED MAIN IDEAS

1. Topic: Student life

    Main Idea: Second part of sentence 1 (but being a student . . .)

3. Topic: George McClellan

    Main Idea: First sentence (Cocky George McClellan)

5. Topic: Changes made by employers

    Main Idea: Employers must make changes in their workplaces as the employees and their needs change.

7. Topic: Grant's attack on Cold Harbor

    Main Idea: Grant's attack on Cold Harbor cost a great number of lives for the Union.

9. Topic: Reciprocal influence or personal/cognitive, behavioral, and environmental influences

    Main Idea: Three factors—personal/cognitive, behavioral, and environmental—all influence one another.

EXERCISE 11: DETERMINING ORGANIZATIONAL PATTERNS AND IMPORTANT DETAILS I

1. Main Idea: Cold Harbor was an important battle for both Grant and Lee to win.
   Organizational Pattern: Cause and effect
   Important Details: Reasons for Cold Harbor's importance

   - Cold Harbor was only 8 miles from Richmond.
   - This was close to the Confederate capital.
   - Grant could destroy the Northern Virginia army and link up with the Union.

3. Main Idea: Sentence 1. (Besides helping . . .) OR Black soldiers helped their communities after the Civil War.
   Organizational Pattern: Example
   Important Details: An example of Blacks helping the community

   - The Third Colored Arkansas Volunteers built a home for orphaned children.

5. Main Idea: A letter of recommendation is defined.
   Organizational Pattern: Definition
   Important Details: Information about a letter of recommendation

   - This is a letter from a reference.
   - It tells employers why an applicant is a good worker and what skills he or she has.
   - Copies can be given to employers.

7. Main Idea: Stress is defined.
   Organizational Pattern: Definition
   Important Details: Information about the term *stress*

   - It's the physical and chemical response of the body to demands on it.
   - Demands may be good or bad.
   - Whether good or bad, the body's mechanical reaction is the same.
   - Difference in reaction can be in intensity and/or length.

9. Main Idea: Sentence 3: You have to "fail" a number of times to succeed.
   Organizational Pattern: Cause and effect
   Important Details: Reasons why one usually fails before succeeding

- It's unrealistic to think one will succeed immediately. (Not many people hit the bull's eye the first time.)
- Failing helps one discover what does not work.
- Working in steps helps lead to success.

EXERCISE 12: DETERMINING ORGANIZATIONAL PATTERNS AND IMPORTANT DETAILS II

1. Main Idea: Sentence 1 (The campaign was . . .)
    Organizational Pattern: Example or list
    Supporting Details: Examples of Democratic and Union party cries for and against candidates

    - There were Democratic cries to remove Abe and to have Mac win the Union back.
    - Union cries were to support Abe and not change presidents in the middle of a war.

3. Main Idea: Sentence 1 (Let's examine . . .)
    Organizational Pattern: Classification
    Supporting Details: Five levels in Maslow's hierarchy of needs

    - Physiological needs include food, water, sleep, and sex.
    - Safety needs consist of security, protection, and avoidance of pain.
    - Belongingness and love needs include affiliation with others, affection, and feeling loved.
    - Esteem needs are respect for ourselves and from others.
    - Self-actualization needs consist of attempting to reach one's full potential.

5. Main Idea: People exhibit different signs and effects of stress
    Organizational Pattern: Example or list Supporting Details:

    - Signs of stress include physical symptoms (upset stomach, headache, sleep disorder, fatigue) and emotional symptoms (sadness, loss of energy) and physiological symptoms (depression, anxiety, and panic attacks).
    - Effects of stress include self-destructive behaviors (drinking, drug use, and reckless driving).

7. Main Idea: The Union lost the Battle of Bull Run to "Stonewall" Jackson.
    Organizational Pattern: Time order
    Supporting Details:

    - The Yankees march from Washington while spectators trail along.
    - Yankees do well.
    - Confederates stand like a stone wall and reinforcements arrive.
    - Union troops panic and run.
    - Confederates stay and feast on captured lunch.

9. Main Idea: Wages and salary are contrasted.
    Organizational Pattern: Contrast (Students may choose classification as the organizational pattern for this paragraph, but comparison is a better choice when the paragraph contains two topics and/or two categories.)
    Supporting Details:

    - Wages are compensation based on an hourly rate and output or amount of output produced; for example, production employees, maintenance workers, and sometimes retail salespeople earn wages).
    - Salary represents compensation based on a weekly, monthly, or annual basis; for example, office personnel, executives, and professional employees earn salaries.

EXERCISE 13: READING AND INTERPRETING GRAPHICS

A. History map of the Peninsula Campaign

1. Topic: McClellan's Peninsula Campaign
2. Main Idea: McClellan followed a route around this peninsula in his campaign.
3. Which river did McClellan come to on his way to Richmond? (York River)
4. Which river did McClellan use to depart from Richmond? (James River)

C. Psychology Figure 13.1

1. Topic: The conscious and the unconscious
2. Main Idea: Freud's model of the conscious and unconscious is compared to an iceberg.
3. Which part of the personality is mostly in the conscious? (Ego)
4. Why does this model show the id as completely submerged? (The id, according to Freud, is completely in the unconscious. People are not consciously aware of the id's desires.)

E. Psychology Table 13.2

1. Topic: Freudian defense mechanisms
2. Main Idea: A definition and example are given for five defense mechanisms
3. Which defense mechanism explains why a student who has been cheating would accuse other students in the class of the same act? (Projection)
4. Create your own example of displacement. (Any answer that describes an individual redirecting an emotion to someone who did not provoke the emotion is acceptable.)
5. What words accompanying this figure alert you to the fact that the information on this chart is important to know for a test? ("These five defense mechanisms are listed with the New Terms at the end of this chapter.")

EXERCISE 14: INTERPRETING FIGURATIVE LANGUAGE

1. *high-handed* = arbitrary, overbearing
3. *slaughter pen* = a place where more killing would occur
5. *Christmas present* = completing something that would be favorable to Lincoln around Christmas time
7. *written in blood* = caused by many deaths
9. *bulldog tenacity* = holding fast with shrewdness and strength

EXERCISE 15: MAKING INFERENCES

1. Main Idea of Both Paragraphs: The Battle of Bull Run was fought with the thought that it would be an easy victory and possibly end the war.

   In 1861, what did Lincoln see as the main cause of the Civil War? (c. secession)

   Why did the author title this section "Bull Run Ends the 'Ninety-Day War' "? (Lincoln thought this would be a short war [90 days], but this battle proved otherwise.)

   Why was Bull Run chosen as the battle site? (d. all of the above)

3. Main Idea: Lee moves north and quickly defeats General Pope at the Second Battle of Bull Run.

   What do the authors mean by writing that Lee had "broken the back of McClellan's assault"?

   (Lee defeated a major section of the assault; he defeated the most needed part.)

   Where had General Pope fought prior to the Second Battle of Bull Run?

   (He had fought west of Richmond.)

   Explain what General Pope meant when he boasted that he had seen only the backs of the enemy.

   (Pope was boasting that most of the men he fought were running from his army.)

5. Main Idea: Sentence 2 (Yet the ironies . . .)

   What did Lee's victory ensure? (d. both *a* and *b*)

   Why is Lee's victory considered an irony (an irony is an outcome or result that is the opposite of what is expected). (Although he won for the South, his victory lengthened the war and made slavery a major issue in it. Slavery would have survived had the North won.)

7. Main Idea: Sentence 1 (Bloody Antietam . . .)

   Why was Lincoln waiting for a victory before declaring the Emancipation Proclamation? (If the North was losing, it would look like Lincoln was freeing the slaves only to have them fight in the war on the North's side.)

   What is an abolitionist? (The abolitionist was someone who wanted to abolish slavery.)

   What did Phillips mean by stating that Lincoln was a "first-rate second-rate man"? (A second-rate man is mediocre. The speaker was saying that Lincoln was best at being mediocre.)

9. Main Idea: Dreams reveal the unconscious with the use of symbols that analysts interpret.

   According to Freud, symbols are constructed in dreams for the following reason: (c. People do not want to know the latent content.)

   True or False: The latent content of a dream includes those aspects that people recall as soon as they awake from a dream. (False, the latent content includes the underlying unconscious aspects, usually interpreted by an analyst.)

   You have a dream about selling flowers at the beach. What is the latent content? (d. none of the above)

11. Main Idea: The Emancipation Proclamation had many effects.

    The Emancipation Proclamation resulted in which of the following? (d. all of the above)

    "The drumbeat of running feet" refers to which of the following? (c. slaves leaving plantations)

    To where did many of the Southern slaves go? (c. Northern armies)

13. Main Idea: Although Grant's victory in Tennessee was helpful, his loss at Shiloh confirmed that the war would go on in the West.

    Why was the Tennessee victory important? (a. The North had greater control of Kentucky; b. A gateway to the Mississippi was opened; and c. The North had better access to Georgia.)

    Who was the victor at Shiloh? (b. The South.)

    True or False: Grant was able to take the junction of the main Confederate north-south and east-west railroad in the Mississippi Valley. (False, Grant was stopped short at Shiloh.)

15. Main Idea: Sentence 1 (Research confirms . . .)

According to the theory of self-efficacy, which factor is most important in doing well on a test? (c. believing one will do well on the test)

Which of the following will a person with self-efficacy do? (a. set an attainable goal; b. determine what needs to be done to accomplish a goal; c. believe one can complete all the steps to reach a goal; and d. think about what needs to be done during each step of the process to reach the goal)

Which of the following characteristics do people with a strong self-efficacy have? (a. persistence; and b. optimism)

EXERCISE 16: DISTINGUISHING FACTS FROM OPINIONS

1. O	7. F
3. F	9. F
5. O	11. O

EXERCISE 17: IDENTIFYING FACTS THAT SUPPORT OPINIONS

1. Fact = all sentences
3. Fact = sentence 3 (According to the research . . .)
   Opinion = sentence 1 (One of the)
             sentence 2 (The more honest . . .)
             last sentence (Recording your experiences . . .)
5. Fact = sentence 3 (A leading . . .)
          sentence 4 (The low-lying . . .)
          second half of the sentence 5 (but the profits . . .)
          sentence 6 (Two successful . . .)
   Opinion = first part of the sentence 1 (riskily profitable)
             first part of the sentence 2 (most successful)
             first part of the sentence 5 (risks were great)
             last sentence (The lush . . .)
7. Fact = sentence 3 (Lincoln was . . .)
          sentence 4 (Prince . . .)
          last sentence (But the . . .)
   Opinion = sentence 1 (Lincoln's renomination . . .)
             sentence 2 (Hostile . . .)
9. Fact = last sentence (Cross-situational consistency . . .)
   Opinion = all sentences except the last

EXERCISE 18: READING AND ANSWERING TEST QUESTIONS

1. e. all of the above

   Sentence 2 (The two . . .)

3. c. id, superego, ego

   The id is described in the first paragraph, the ego in the second paragraph, and the superego in the third paragraph.

5. a. It is more likely to rely on behavioral observations.

   First section of the chart (Obtained from observation of behavior . . .)

7. d. all of the above

   Last sentence supports *a;* sentence 2 (In general . . .) supports *b;* and sentence 5 (People who are . . .) supports *c.*

9. Theory X

   Sentence 2 (Thus, managers . . .) and the last sentence (Managers who hold . . .)

INDEX

CREDITS

Health Textbook Chapter

152–179: From *An Invitation to Health,* 10th edition by Hales. © 2003. Reprinted with permission of Wadsworth, a division of Thomson Learning.
152, 153: © Stephen Simpson/Getty Images
154: (l) © Royalty-Free/CORBIS; (r) © PhotoDisc/Getty Images
160: © PhotoDisc/Getty Images
162: © Ulrike Welsch
163: (l) Institute of Hispanic/Latino Cultures, "la Casitas," University of Florida-Gainesville; (r) North Carolina Hillel
165: © Michael Newman/PhotoEdit
167: © Will and Deni McIntyre/Photo Researchers, Inc.
168: © AP/Wide World Photos
170: © Royalty-Free/CORBIS
171: © Richard T. Nowitz/Photo Researchers, Inc.
172: © James Schnepf Photography, Inc.
173: © Royalty-Free/CORBIS
175: © AFP/Getty Images

History Textbook Chapter

204–229: Thomas Bailey, David M. Kennedy, Lizabeth Cohen, *The American Spirit,* 12th edition, Chapter 21. Copyright © 2002. Used by permission.
205: (t) Prints & Photographs Division, Library of Congress; (b)West Point Museum Collection, United States Military Academy
206: Frank Leslie's Illustrated Newspaper
207: Division of Armed Forces, Smithsonian Institution

210: Prints & Photographs Division, Library of Congress
211: U.S. Army Military History Institute
213: Massachusetts Historical Society
214: (l) The Metropolitan Museum of Art; (m) The Metropolitan Museum of Art; (r) The Metropolitan Museum of Art
216: John Hay Papers, Manuscript Division, Library of Congress
218: (l) The Granger Collection, New York.; (r) U.S. National Archives and Records Administration
220: Michael Latil
221: Culver Pictures
223: The New York Historical Society
225: Prints & Photographs Division, Library of Congress
226: The Granger Collection, New York.
227: (t) The Sea Island Company; (b) Metropolitan Museum of Art. Gift of Mrs. Frank B. Porter

Business Textbook Chapter

252–286: From *Contemporary Business,* 10th edition by Boone and Kurtz. Chapter 9. © 2003. Reprinted with permission of Wadsworth, a division of Thomson Learning
253: © 2002 Brian Smith
260: New Horizons Computer Learning Centers
271: Principal Financial Group
276: © Robert Wright
279: © Phillippe Diederich
280: CIGNA

Psychology Textbook Chapter

313–351: From *Psychology,* 3rd edition by Matlin. Chapter 13. © 1999. Reprinted with permission of Wadsworth, a division of Thomson Learning.
313: Photo © Steve Wewerka
318: Photo courtesy Margaret Matlin
327: Jane Addams Memorial Collection, (JAMC neg. 55) Special Collections, University of Illinois at Chicago
330: Photo courtesy Arnold H. Matlin
336: Minnesota Multiphasic Personality Inventory-2. Copyright © by the Regents of the University of Minnesota 1942, 1943, (renewed 1970), 1989. Reproduced by permission of the publisher.

Articles

DOULAS

WHY EVERY PREGNANT WOMAN DESERVES ONE

SUSAN ROSS

DEDICATION

I wish to dedicate this book to my two sons, Lachlan and Angus. My pregnancies, labours and births were empowering experiences and mothering continues to be richly rewarding. I also have a very gorgeous grandson, Blake.

A very big thank you to all the wonderful doulas out there. The commitment that you make to support women cannot be underestimated. There is no financial reward large enough to compensate for all the 'doula giving', spiritually, emotionally and physically. It is no wonder women have a strong attachment to their very special doula, recognising the power of this extraordinary relationship.

To all the pregnant women who are buying this book, you do deserve the best care and trusting in a doula is your first step to ensuring an amazing pregnancy and birth.

ACKNOWLEDGEMENT

Thank you to all the contributors to this book. Your ideas, stories, photographs and willingness to participate, often at short notice, is much appreciated. Thanks to Rebecca Fraser from New Beginnings Photography, for her sensitive photography and her wonderful work as a doula; Erika Elliott for her beautiful photographs and doularing; and the wonderful couples who allowed their photographs to be shared — I know they will inspire all who read this book.

CONTENTS

Susan Ross has been a midwife for more than 30 years, working in both the public and private sector, and community health. Susan has worked in city and country hospitals, interstate and overseas, and has witnessed many changes to birthing practises. Susan is a childbirth educator, HypnoBirthing® practitioner, trainer, author of the book *Birth Right* and a hypnotherapist. She is the founder and director of Birth Right, providing information, education, counselling and support to pregnant women and their partners. Birth Right is the leading doula training school in Australia, and the only one run by a midwife with more than 30 years experience. Susan is the mother of two sons and has one grandson. She is passionate about supporting birthing women, making sure they understand their options and choices. www.birthright.com.au

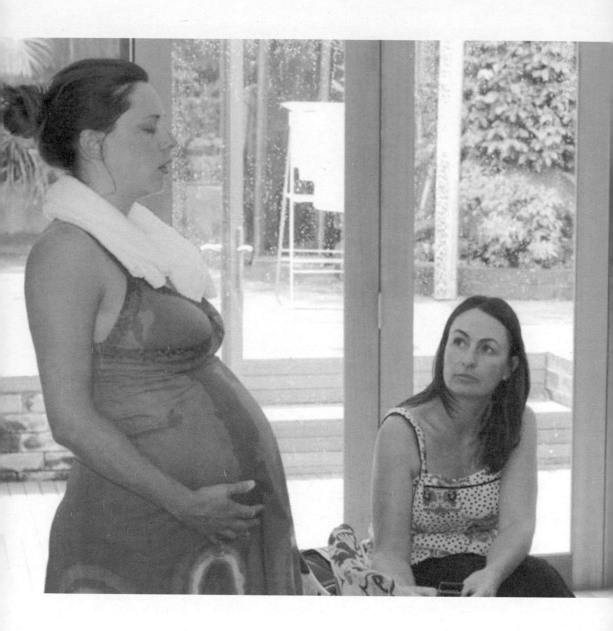

INTRODUCTION

Every pregnant woman deserves a doula

Imagine birthing your baby exactly the way you would like — quietly and peacefully in a dimly lit room in absolute control of your labour and birth, feeling safe and well supported, without interruption, so you could do and be what you needed to, to ensure your baby would emerge gently and calmly from the womb, down the birth path and into the world. What a wonderful start in life you would be giving your baby!

If we want to create a non-violent world, we must begin with how we connect to our babies in utero, how we birth our babies and how we treat each other from the beginning of life, because this is where our deepest patterns of behaviour are set. From these roots grow fear and hatred or love and trust.

The World Health Organization (WHO) advises that for a normal birth there should be a valid reason to interfere with the natural process.

Birth is both a miracle and an experience shared by every one of us. It is our gateway into the human family and forms our first impressions about being here. Pregnancy and birth can certainly be a physical challenge, but what are the possible psychological implications for mother and baby?

Perinatal psychology is the study of the psychological impact of the pregnancy and birthing experience, from conception and gestation to birth and bonding, for the baby and the mother. Psychiatrist Dr Thomas Verny says that a child's personality is moulded during the nine months in utero, probably more than at any subsequent time in his life. So prenatal communication and prenatal bonding have to start at conception. Among his many publications, including his book, *The Secret Life of the Unborn Child* (1981), Dr Verny gives an extraordinary picture of the unborn baby's world:

The womb is the child's first world. At sixteen weeks the unborn child shies away from light. At twenty weeks there is a response to speech patterns. At twenty-five weeks the baby can kick in time to music. And at six months the unborn child can understand the subtle shifts of its mother's emotions.

It is essential information for pregnant parents to know, and that talking, singing, playing games and communicating with your unborn baby throughout pregnancy is not only normal, but very important for their development.

The Secret Life of the Unborn Child presents for the first time the challenging results of two decades of painstaking international research into the earliest stages of life. Dr Verny's evidence of intelligent life in the womb is overwhelming. This knowledge gives both mothers and fathers an opportunity to get to know and help their unborn child. Now they can contribute actively — both before and during birth — to giving their child happiness and security for the rest of their life.

The idea that infants are conscious and learning in utero and encoding these lessons is, however, far from mainstream. And many schools of psychology, psychiatry and medicine virtually ignore the possibility that prenatal and perinatal experiences may contribute to later mental health problems.

Some Western governments, such as those in the USA and Australia, are experiencing crises in their health systems, which are predicted to get worse, placing huge demands on their health budgets. Those in charge of health dollars therefore need to take a long, hard look at the implications of how birth is managed. Birth is not a medical event, it is a normal event. Until that message is properly understood and medicalising birth is brought to an end, the public will demand more and more services. It will become a vicious cycle. If we get birth right and provide good education and proper support for our pregnant women, who are surely the most important people in the community, the ultimate drain on the health budget will be reduced.

Attitudes need to change. Women are becoming more and more fearful about birth. We can't afford to wait another generation for those women who are embracing birth in a positive way to pass on their beautiful stories to their sons and daughters. The media desperately need to be educated and start focusing on amazing positive birth stories, promoting the health benefits for mother, baby and the community, rather than on the fear that pervades every story that is run about birth. Women are bombarded from so many different sources with the fear of birth that it can be hard work to convince them otherwise.

Recently, I met with a couple who were about 16 weeks pregnant with their first baby. Anna and Rick were very excited about being pregnant and simultaneously very, very scared. Both were intelligent and questioning. Both had been brought up in loving families but had been fed a lot of fear around birth. For most of Anna's life she had heard other women in her extended family discussing the horror of pain and suffering in childbirth. Anna and Rick had booked into a major public teaching hospital in Sydney, believing that this was the best place as they would have access to operating theatres, anaesthetists and lots of doctors to cover all bases if 'something went wrong'. They lived five minutes from a good local community hospital but believed it would not be safe to book in there in case there was an emergency.

While they were both convinced, without a doubt, that birth was indeed a medical event, Anna had found my website on the Internet and had read about how positive birth can be, if you have the right support and education. She did want a normal birth. She did understand that this was probably best for baby, but she could not believe that this would be possible. I assured them that birth was simple and that it was important how we birthed our babies. When they asked about the role of the doula, I told them that I would support them emotionally throughout the pregnancy, answer all their questions and concerns, and guide them to make the best decisions for them and their baby. I said that I would support Rick, in particular, so that Anna could relax and enjoy pregnancy, labour and birth, without having the responsibility of making decisions alone and he could enjoy becoming a Dad. I told them that I would provide good education so that they could understand the process and how simple birth was. About two hours later they left with big smiles on their faces. Anna's comment was 'I actually feel positive and am almost looking forward to this experience. I didn't think that was possible.' Rick agreed.

We had email and phone contact and several meetings throughout her pregnancy. We got to know each other well. They also attended HypnoBirthing® classes (these will be discussed in more detail in Chapter 2), which they both embraced with great enthusiasm because they came to understand the simplicity of birth. They both commented about how empowered they felt.

I watched with great joy their complete turnaround from our first meeting to their daughter's amazing birth.

Anna: 'There is no way that I could have had the confidence to birth my baby the way I wanted without having a doula. She was my rock, she was my sounding board, she was my advocate and most of all she was my nurturer. There was support on so many levels.'

Rick: 'I was hesitant at first, took longer to be convinced of the need for a doula, but cannot now imagine doing it on our own. The support, understanding, liaison with staff was amazing. I know it would have been a very different experience, and much more medical, had we not had a doula. I don't know how anyone does birth without one.'

This couple connected with their baby in utero and included the baby in all their conversations and decision making. Throughout the birth, Anna was working with her baby and together they birthed beautifully. What a wonderful start in life she has given her child. This baby will grow up as a happy, healthy and positive person.

There is startling new scientific evidence to support the bond between biology and psychology. According to Dr Bruce Lipton, a Stamford cellular biologist, parents select for their babies gene programs based on their perceived beliefs about their environment, and that it is environment, **not** genes, that controls cells in the developing baby, a discovery which has the potential to rewrite the entire story of life. His study also shows that it is the environment that switches the genes on and off, that the genes are not capable of switching themselves on and off.

What is more, the blood in the placenta contains a lot more than just nutrients: it contains a lot of chemicals that organise the body's structure and function — hormones, for example. The informational molecules in the mother's blood are also accessible to the developing baby. The previous belief that the child unfolds according to a prescheduled genetic code is a false assumption. Rather, the child is dynamically adapting to the environment, but the environment perceived by the mother.

The baby's experience during life in utero and during birth is encoded in memory to be later expressed, as an adult, at the intellectual or emotional level, in his perceptions, attitudes, behaviours and sense of self.

Research shows the developing baby before, during and after birth to be a conscious, exquisitely sensitive and learning being involved in a dynamic interchange with its environment. This creates lifelong patterns of optimism and trust, or fear and distrust.

As Dr Thomas Verny discusses on the DVD *Psychology of Birth*, for a long time we have observed how people act and have then made certain conclusions based on those behaviours. We have not understood what happens on a biological level. One of the main principles of pre- and perinatal psychology is that there is no separation of the mind and the body and therefore whatever happens between two people involved in a conversation, on a psychological level, is immediately translated into changes in biology.

Prebirth parenting, therefore, is so important for Mum, Dad and baby. It also makes accepting the responsibility for parenting once baby has been born much easier, and it is also fun to get to know your baby from the inside. I also believe it contributes enormously to having an enjoyable birthing experience. Those women who establish an amazing connection with their baby in utero can use this relationship to work with their baby during labour and birth, talking to their baby, encouraging their baby to move further down the birth path and telling their baby how much they are looking forward to meeting her.

Findings by authors such as Dr Thomas Verny (1981) and Dr Michael Lazarev (1991) suggest that babies in utero react to vibrations, stroking, tapping, squeezing, conversations, voices, loud noises, television, mobile phones and music. And babies who are exposed to soft music and singing during their time in utero are calmer, happier and better adjusted to life outside. Babies particularly love the sound of their parents' voices. At 34 weeks, Linda attended a very loud rock concert, but had to leave as her baby started kicking furiously. A baby will react if its parents are arguing, letting them know it does not like the sound of their voices. Your baby is already a part of your family and responds best to a happy environment.

Talk to your baby; tell your baby what you are doing and where you are going.
Play with your baby, physically patting, squeezing, rubbing and swaying.
Sing to your baby, gently and softly.
Listen to relaxation and visualisation CDs with your baby.
Play soothing music. Expose your baby to different sounds from piano, harp, flute and nature so that your baby develops a broader awareness.

Imagine yourself in the baby's environment, listening to conversations, experiencing her surroundings, absorbing the emotions and moods of those around you. How welcome do you feel, how loved do you feel and what kinds of messages are you receiving from things that are said about you?

This tiny human being is busy laying down memories. Here is your opportunity to make those memories happy, healthy and loving, because nothing gives a child a more solid foundation.

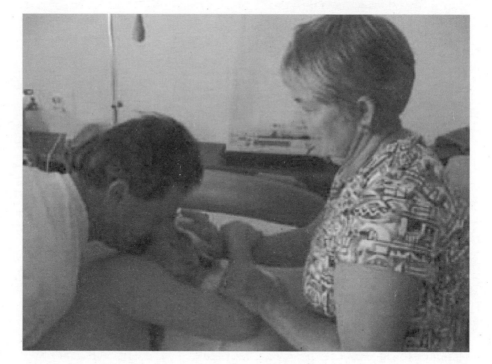

CHAPTER 1

Why choose a doula?

Choosing a doula is one of the most important decisions you will make during pregnancy. This decision should ideally be made early on, so you have the opportunity to really get to know your doula and work with her, taking advantage of all her knowledge and wisdom.

Doula is a Greek word, meaning 'to serve'. A popular interpretation is 'mothering the mother' — although my Greek builder assures me that if he called his 'wife' a doula she would certainly react violently! He says the word means 'slave' and he would never dare use it in reference to his wife!

Doulas are not medically trained and do not provide medical advice; they provide much, much more. They are women supporting women. They are trained to look after you emotionally and physically during pregnancy, labour, birthing and postnatally. Your doula will provide information about choices — how to shop around and choose the caregivers, birth place and prenatal education that is best for you. She will support and guide you during pregnancy. She will be a familiar face that you can turn to and rely on, without judgement. During labour and birthing she will stay with you, wherever you are, at home or in hospital, nurturing you and protecting you. A doula will be your advocate, should you need one. She will most likely provide your only true 'continuity of care', because *this* care is very different from what you receive from other caregivers, such as an obstetrician or a midwife.

A LITTLE HISTORY

Women helping women give birth is an ancient practice. According to anthropological data reviewed for 128 non-industrialised hunting–gathering and agricultural societies, all but one offered women continual support during pregnancy, labour and birthing.

When childbirth moved from home to hospital, this all-important support virtually disappeared.

In many countries, more women are now giving birth in hospital than at home, and continuous support during labour has become the exception rather than the norm. This raises concern about the resultant dehumanisation of women's birth experiences. Modern obstetric care frequently subjects women to institutional routines, which may have adverse effects on labour progressing normally. The type of support you receive from a doula will enhance normal labour, as well as your feelings of control and competence, thus reducing the need for obstetric intervention. A review of studies by

Hodnett et al. (2007), including 16 trials from 11 countries, involving over 13 000 women in a wide range of settings and circumstances, stated:

> *Women who received continuous labour support were more likely to give birth spontaneously, i.e. give birth with neither caesarean nor vacuum nor forceps. In addition, women were less likely to use pain medications, were more likely to be satisfied, and had slightly shorter labours. In general, labour support appeared to be more effective when it was provided by women who were not part of the hospital staff.*

Doulas are very popular and have been around for some decades in the USA and Europe. Studies by Klaus et al. (1986), Campbell et al. (2006) and Hodnett et al. (2007) show the enormous difference a doula can make to labour and birth. Doulas have emerged over the years as a response to the cry of many women for more support and continuity of care.

Anthropologist Dana Raphael first used the term 'doula' in her book, *The Tender Gift: Breastfeeding* (1973), to refer to experienced mothers who assisted new mothers in breastfeeding and newborn care.

WHAT THE RESEARCH SHOWS

In their book, Mothering the Mother: How a Doula Can Help You Have a Shorter, Easier, and Healthier Birth (1993), Marshall Klaus, John Kennell and Phyllis Klaus summarise the scientific studies that have been carried out on the advantages of doula-assisted births. The evidence cited is drawn from six randomised, controlled studies. Two studies were carried out in Guatemala (Central America), the first with 136 women, and the second with 465 women.

One study took place in Houston (Texas) in the USA with 416 women. A further study involving 192 women was carried out in Johannesburg, South Africa. The fifth and sixth studies were done in Helsinki (Finland) and Canada. All participants were primiparas (a medical term used to describe women who are giving birth to their first child). All participants were in good overall health and had had uneventful pregnancies. They were invited to participate when they were admitted to hospital in labour. The Guatemalan doulas were trained in a three-week course. In the South African study the women were untrained laywomen. The doulas were asked to stay with the labouring women constantly. They were instructed to use touch and verbal communication, focusing on three primary factors: comfort, reassurance and praise. All of the doulas in the studies had experienced regular labours and vaginal births.

In all of the above studies, the doulas used soothing words, touch and encouragement. They explained the procedures as they occurred and translated medical terms into layperson's terms. The results of these studies were as follows:

» reduced the overall caesarean rate by 50%
» reduced the length of labour by 25%
» reduced oxytocin use by 40%
» reduced the use of pain medication by 30%
» reduced forceps deliveries by 40%
» reduced requests for epidural pain medication by 60%
» reduced incidences of maternal fever
» reduced the number of days newborns spent in NICU (neo-natal infant care unit)
» reduced the amount of septic workups performed on newborns

» resulted in higher rates of breastfeeding
» resulted in more positive maternal assessments of maternal confidence
» resulted in more positive maternal assessments of maternal and newborn health
» resulted in decreased rates of post-partum depression.

Klaus, Kennell and Klaus (2002) speculate that the mere presence of a doula has a beneficial effect on the emotional state of the mother, resulting in a decrease in catecholamines (adrenaline). This relaxed state allows uterine contractions to be more effective and reduces the occurrence of compromised uterine blood flow.

You might be asking, at this point, why not just have your partner, your mother, your sister or your best friend at the birth of your baby?

Should we really expect partners to take on this role? What a huge ask! They are about to become a dad; they should be able to relax, feel supported and enjoy the birthing experience. I don't believe that attendance at a prenatal class and reading — maybe — a book or two qualifies fathers in any way to provide support. A partner should not have to feel that pressure. In expecting dads to be the main support, our society may have created a very difficult expectation of them. I encourage all couples to have ongoing discussion, throughout pregnancy, about what role Dad would like to play. Ongoing, because it may well change as he gains more education in and understanding of the process!

It is not so long ago that men were not 'allowed' to be present at the birth of their baby. When I was working in a hospital in the early 1970s, men who wanted to be present were required to present written permission from their wife's doctor, which they had to give to the midwife on arrival at the labour ward. If they did not have written permission, the rule was: No Letter; No Admission. They were sent to the 'Father's Room', which was a smoke-filled room, with lots of very nervous men pacing up and down and swapping 'wife' stories! We have certainly come a long way in a relatively short time — but have we really? The majority of men are not asked what their feelings are about being at the birth, or how they feel about taking on the important role of advocate and support.

During the 1980s and 1990s, when there was a global shortage of midwives, it emerged as not a bad thing to have Dad at the birth. Women could be left alone for longer periods because her partner was present. And so it became the norm. Like so many processes in the health system, once something has been accepted, it stays — forever, and without question. Women also began to assume that their partner would be at the birth, and so it became an unwritten law that no self-respecting male would dare question it. They agreed to be at the birth, they went, and many of them were terrified. They had no knowledge, no understanding, no benchmarks for what was normal, and for a number of years sat in the corner of the labour room in a state of panic, without any avenue for expressing their feelings. As one woman remarked, 'I want the doula there for reassurance and to comfort me, and I want my partner there for emotional support'.

Partners and others, including mothers, aunts and best friends, are not only too emotionally attached to you, but do not have the knowledge of birthing to be able to provide appropriate support. Very often, these well-meaning friends or relatives are offering advice based on their own personal experience of birth. A doula, on the other hand, has sound knowledge of the hospital system and the people who work in it, and good negotiating skills.

It is not uncommon for a couple, especially the dad, to be concerned that a doula will take over the birth and therefore erode his role. A doula is very aware that the couple will carry the memory of this experience throughout their lives. She is there to make sure they have the birthing experience they

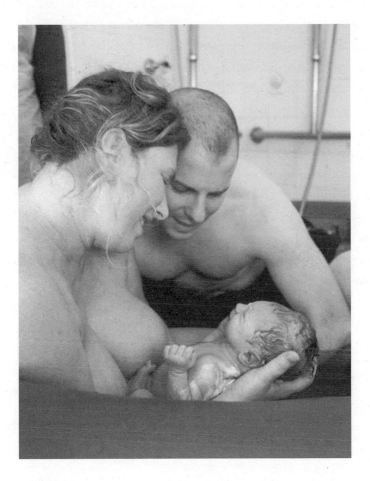

want. On the birthing day, her presence allows the father to play the role that is most comfortable for him. The doula gives a level of support to the woman that is different from the support given by her partner. These two kinds of support complement each other.

The World Health Organization (1985) recommends that the caesarean section rate should not be higher than 15%. Rates lower than 15% have been reported for Holland, Sweden, Austria and Norway. However, Laws, Li and Sullivan (2010) in a publication published by the Australian Institute of Health and Welfare show that in 2008 Australia had a very high medical intervention rate of 31.1%. Other research reported by Sufang et al. (2007) in the Bulletin of the World Health Organization indicates increasing caesarean section rates in countries such as France, Germany, Italy, North America and the United Kingdom, with similar trends in low-income countries such as Brazil, China and India, especially for births in private hospitals.

We know that by engaging the services of a doula these horrific statistics can be reduced. Every pregnant woman deserves a doula — a person who provides compassionate, experienced and unbiased support throughout pregnancy, labour and birthing. With this support, couples can enjoy the unique experience of a natural birth, which lays the foundation for strong attachment as the new family grows.

T hank goodness for our wonderful doula! Without her, I am sure our experience of Lily's birth would have been far less satisfactory than it eventually was.

I had a normal, healthy pregnancy and was excited and happy to be expecting my first baby. At 35 weeks or so, Lily was found to be lying breech. We tried everything under the sun to get her to turn head down, but none of it worked. It looked as though it was going to be difficult to create the kind of natural birth we wanted. Luckily there were voices other than those of a mainstream hospital. Our doula encouraged me to read and think for myself about what I wanted, and to ask for it. In full knowledge of the realities and risks, I decided to attempt a vaginal breech delivery instead of accepting the elective caesarean recommended by the hospital.

My labour was long and irregular, with lots of stops and starts, and Lily was slightly distressed right from the beginning. It was nothing like what I had imagined! Our doula valiantly came and went from the hospital as we needed her, encouraged me, held my hand, massaged me, gave Andrew much needed breaks, talked things through and helped us to make decisions about the labour. Most importantly, she helped me to understand that I had choices and to act on them for the sake and safety of my baby and myself — particularly once it became obvious that we needed an emergency caesarean.

Although I was frightened, and dependent on the hospital staff, I never truly felt like I had lost control of the labour, of my baby's wellbeing, of my story, my body and my self. And for that reason, when I look back at Lily's birth, I feel entirely satisfied with our decisions and the outcomes.

Thank you to our doula for helping us to deliver our beautiful, bright, healthy baby girl, and for facilitating a difficult birth in such a practical, empowered and spiritually satisfying way.

KATE AND ANDREW

WHAT SKILLS A DOULA OFFERS

It is very important to know what services, support and advice a doula can provide for you. A doula understands and trusts birth. She will not provide medical advice, but you can rely on her to:

» be an amazing listener
» trust in you and your ability to birth
» empower you to negotiate the best care for you and your baby
» find out what you want and respect your choices
» acknowledge the power of birth
» understand that birth is not a medical event
» understand the importance of good prenatal education
» respect the birthing environment and 'your space' during labour and birthing
» know the importance of birthing in a quiet, dimly lit room, with no unnecessary interruptions
» provide continuous support, reassurance and encouragement during labour and birthing, whether at home or in hospital
» provide invaluable support and reassurance for your partner
» respect your birthright to labour and birth your baby in your own time and in your own way.

The wisdom and understanding that doulas bring to the birthing environment provide a protective bubble for you, allowing you to feel safe to enter into 'the zone' of birthing your baby without fear. This, in turn, allows your partner to relax and enjoy becoming a dad.

Robyn had been in pre-labour for over a week. She had a 'birth show' a week before, and was in and out of labour, mainly at night, for the remainder of that week. Very frustrating! There were a number of nights when she phoned me, her doula, saying that the surges were now regular and she felt like this was it! As the dawn arrived, the surges would slow, she would get some sleep and have a relatively normal day. I could sense that Derek, her partner, was getting tired as well. I gave them lots of reassurance over the phone, which was what they needed. There were a couple of nights when I suggested that I come over but they wanted to wait and see.

Exactly one week later, it was decided that they should go into the birth centre, as her membranes had released about 36 hours previously, and there was a small amount of meconium (baby's first poo). Some surges were evident, but were not regular. Following an assessment at the birth centre, Robyn was transferred to the delivery suite, due to the presence of meconium. It was suggested that she should have Syntocinon (synthetic oxytocin) to regulate the contractions. Syntocinon can be very rugged on the birthing body and so many of these births lead to an epidural and the beginning of a cascade of medical intervention. This was certainly not on Robyn's birth agenda. Robyn understood that Syntocinon could lead to other medical interventions and, while she was disappointed, she accepted that this was the best course of action, given that she had been pre-labouring for a week and her membranes had released 36 hours ago, and there were not many surges and quite a lot of meconium.

This is a challenging time for a woman. Robyn was amazing. She continued to use her HypnoBirthing® breathing, remaining incredibly calm and relaxed. The Syntocinon drip was started, which also involved continuous foetal monitoring. Having a drip in and being attached to a monitor can be enough of a distraction for a woman to lose focus. Various midwives were continually fidgeting with the two monitor belts around her belly (which can be very irritating). Even with so-called 'mobile' monitoring, it is difficult to maintain a good connection and therefore, from a medical point of view, to get an accurate picture about how the baby is managing with the Syntocinon. Many babies don't like Syntocinon.

Robyn was able to separate her mind from this medical distraction and truly go into her birthing body and focus on her HypnoBirthing® breathing. She was able to walk outside on the balcony, be on all fours on the mat and generally walk around. She felt comfortable being upright. Unfortunately, the staff were not happy about the trace as they did not know the baby's condition. They suggested that Robyn have a foetal scalp electrode inserted via a vaginal examination; this is a small device which is clipped onto the top of baby's head and gives a more accurate reading of the baby's heart rate. It also very often breaks the skin on the baby's head. Robyn and Derek refused this intervention, after some discussion among the three of us. We all felt that baby was absolutely fine, especially Robyn.

I suggested a compromise: that Robyn lie flat on the bed in the one position for approximately 20 minutes so the staff could obtain an accurate picture of her baby. All agreed. Robyn decided that, if she was going to have to lie very still for that amount of time, she would listen to her HypnoBirthing® relaxation CD. Derek made himself comfortable in a chair, I found a comfortable chair, and the next thing we were aware of was that the CD had finished, 30 minutes had passed, and we were all feeling very, very relaxed. We had drifted off to the beautiful relaxation. The energy in the room was very calm and serene. The staff were happy that baby was OK and that they had a 'good trace'.

I went out to make a cup of tea, came back into the room and Robyn was on the toilet, gently breathing her baby down. After about 15 minutes, she moved to an all-fours position on the mat and, 30 minutes later, very gently nudged her baby out and into the world, being very conscious to nudge slowly, to avoid tearing.

We had arrived at hospital at 10 am and her baby was born at 5.30 pm.

What a privilege to be present at this beautiful birth — to witness a woman who chose, in her mind, not to get caught up in the drama of medical intervention or to contemplate what that might lead to, but to remain true in her belief that she would welcome her baby into the world in a gentle, calm and relaxed way.

CHAPTER 2

About pregnancy and choices

It is such a huge privilege to be pregnant. Getting to know your baby and being in tune with him during the many months of growth and development is very important. You are growing a new human being in the world's most perfect environment. Your baby is growing physically, mentally, emotionally and psychically.

So it does matter how we birth our babies!

What our babies experience in utero shapes who they are.

What a woman experiences during pregnancy, labour and birthing changes her completely.

Birthing is a very primal experience in a woman's life, holding the power to transform her forever, especially if that experience is gentle and peaceful. This makes for a smooth transition to mothering and makes families much stronger.

Reading this book will help you become a savvy consumer and not be bullied into believing and trusting those who offer no choice but the medical route. Every decision that you make from conception onwards will influence the outcome of your birthing. If, as parents, you come to understand this, you will be able to reclaim what you didn't even know had been lost.

Which is the road you will travel?

Let's start at the beginning.

UNDERSTAND YOUR CHOICES

The most important thing every pregnant woman needs to know is that she has choices. She has choices about where she is going to birth and who will be her caregiver. However, the range of choices is dependent upon where she lives. Women who live in major cities are blessed with a number of choices, but problems often arise as soon as a woman has her pregnancy test confirmed by her local doctor. I believe that GPs need to be educated in the range of choices that are available for women during pregnancy, labour and the birthing of their baby and need to inform women of these choices.

Roslyn was excited about her positive pregnancy result from her doctor. She immediately asked about her closest birth centre and how she could book in. Her GP replied that birth centres were unsafe, and that she had her own baby in a delivery suite with an obstetrician, and had an epidural immediately upon arrival so she did not have to go through all the pain. She said, 'You can't get that service in a birth centre', and sent Roslyn away with the names of two obstetricians.

A GP is a health professional who is obliged to give unbiased and accurate information to a client. (I refuse to refer to a pregnant woman as a 'patient' as she is not sick!) If a GP is unaware of all the birthing choices available, then they should refer their clients to someone who does understand or, at the very least, make some suggestions about how they can research the options. To offer just your own personal experience (as in the above story) is not only unprofessional but an abrogation of duty of care.

In a consultation with a client about their options, I always start with some basic fact finding, as follows:

» Where do you live? Sometimes women wish to go to their local maternity hospital. However, if the hospital they prefer is not local, this can be a problem, as the department of health will not generally allow bookings from outside a geographical area health service unless the relevant hospital (very often a major public hospital) is overbooked. No matter where you live, you should have choices about where you birth.

» What is your ideal birthing experience? What are you wanting or hoping for?

» What do you know about birthing? This brings up all the stories a woman has heard from family, friends, work colleagues, the media, books, magazines — the list goes on and on. This is an opportunity for demystification of some of the horror stories, for, sadly, a lot of them are negative. It is important to explore the woman's attitudes to birthing.

» Have you visited any hospitals (both delivery suites and birth centres) in your area?

» Do you understand the difference between public hospital and private hospital care? In a private hospital, generally there is only one model of care available, and that is delivered by a private obstetrician. Public hospitals (especially the major ones), on the other hand, offer a number of different midwifery models of care. Explaining to women how to explore these options is very important.

» Have you considered a homebirth? If the answer is yes, it is advisable to meet with at least two homebirth midwives.

It is important that the client receives advice on what needs to be done at their particular stage of pregnancy. If a woman is very early in her pregnancy, say around 12 weeks, then she needs to know about tests that are available, prenatal classes — when and where and how to book, exercise, nutrition and, of course, doula support.

All the decisions that need to be made, often when the woman is just coming to terms emotionally and physically with being pregnant, can be overwhelming unless she has appropriate information and support.

CHOOSE THE RIGHT CAREGIVER FOR YOU

Women often feel pressured into booking in 'somewhere' immediately their pregnancy is confirmed. I know many women who have organised a private obstetrician on the recommendation of a friend or family member, often on the basis that he or she is 'lovely', or that their rooms look very expensive, or, as one woman told me, 'I chose him because all my friends said he was great at suturing'. (Will this woman end up with an episiotomy and being sutured? Most probably. Obviously some fears about birthing here!)

It is difficult facing this decision very early on in your pregnancy. You may be feeling very tired and have little or no knowledge of what you need now, let alone what you may need much later in your pregnancy.

I met with Laura and John three years ago. They had booked a private hospital and a private obstetrician. She was 38 weeks pregnant and, during a routine visit with her obstetrician, he suddenly announced that the baby's head was nowhere near engaged, it was very high and this was not a good sign. He said that, if it wasn't engaged at this stage, then it would never be. He then suggested that he book a caesarean section for the next week so that she didn't have to suffer needlessly going through labour, to no avail. Laura was horrified. She thought he had understood that she wanted a normal birth, no drugs and no intervention. She went home, very upset, and did some research on the Internet, where she learned about doulas. Until this point, she had never heard of a doula.

When we met, Laura was full of fear about what he had said, about the danger she was putting her baby in if she tried to labour for hours, only to end up with an emergency caesarean section. Both parents were very angry. We had a discussion about what she wanted, which was a normal birth with no intervention. She did not realise how very high the medical intervention rates were at this particular private hospital.

Once I had confirmed her wishes, I set about debriefing them both and reassuring them that it was perfectly normal at 38 weeks for a baby's head not to be engaged, and that, if she trusted her body and her baby, she could have the birth she wanted. We discussed how to negotiate with the doctor at the next visit and how to remain in control of the conversation. They could immediately see the benefits of having a doula and left, feeling much more positive and empowered.

Laura birthed two weeks later, laboured beautifully at home and when we arrived at the hospital she was fully dilated. The obstetrician arrived at the last minute, surprised that Laura had not needed drugs! I felt that baby's head had engaged during labour. Laura birthed on a mat on the floor (a first for this obstetrician, who normally liked 'his women' to be on a bed). She felt hugely empowered by this experience: 'If we had not had a doula present who trusted birth and who was such a positive support for both of us, we know this would have been a very different experience.'

WHAT CARE IS AVAILABLE?

No matter which country you live in, it is essential to shop around and find out which types of care are available.

FRANCE

France takes very good care of pregnant women and new mother's. There is no problem with uninsured women, they receive good prenatal care and have nurses who do home visits and help in the first week. Most women give birth in a hospital, with a gynaecologist. Home and natural births are not common in France. Even so, homebirths are becoming more sought after. A homebirth is reimbursed by social security, but not at the rate of 100 per cent as in a hospital or clinic birth.

NETHERLANDS

Maternity care in the Netherlands is different from most other countries, not only because of the relatively high percentage of homebirths, but also because of the autonomy of the midwife, as medical professional, and the structure of the Dutch health care system with a clear boundary between primary and secondary care. Women with health problems are expected to see a general practitioner (GP), who will refer them to a medical specialist, if needed. In maternity care the primary care provider is a midwife, although some GPs still provide part of the care during pregnancy and birth. Most primary care midwives work in group practices and are jointly responsible for their clients. A healthy woman with an uncomplicated pregnancy has no need to see another care provider other than her midwife, and she can freely choose where to give birth — at home, in hospital or at a birth centre, where she will be attended by her own midwife (Wiegers homebirth et al. 1998; DeVries 2001).

NEW ZEALAND

Not too far away and New Zealand's maternity care system offers a wide variety of care options, and it is up to you to decide which type of care best suits you and your baby. You will choose a lead maternity carer, or

LMC, who is the health professional responsible for providing or jointly providing all of your care during the antenatal period, birth and the postnatal period. Your LMC may be a midwife, a general practitioner (GP) or an obstetrician. Alternatively, your LMC may comprise a group of professionals who work together to provide your care.

Independent midwives as LMCs

Independent midwives are qualified to care for women who are expected to have a normal pregnancy and birth. They may refer women to a public or private obstetrician if complications occur.

USA

In America most women have all their care from an OBGYN (obstetrician/gynaecologist). It is almost the 'norm' to have some type of medical intervention during birth. I attended a doula conference in St Louis a few years ago and met some wonderful, like-minded people…or so I thought! Two of them had clinic spaces in New York and invited me, at the end of the conference, to visit. It was wonderful to see their spaces where they ran prenatal classes, supporting normal birth and offered their doula service. I was really curious about why the medical intervention rate was so high, especially in New York, when doulas appeared to be very popular. As one doula explained, 'I see my role as keeping the epidural at bay for longer. For those women who don't have a doula then the epidural would be given very early in labour.' I wanted to know why, then, did New York women choose to have a doula, and what they saw as her role? The doula did not even blink when proudly telling me that it was a social status! Not only can a woman brag about who her OBGYN is but also their doula!

I realised we were on very different paths. Their definition of normal birth and empowering women was entirely different to mine.

Birthing and doulas in the UK

The National Health Service (NHS) in the UK was set up in 1948 to provide quality health care free for everyone. Most women in the UK give birth in an NHS hospital maternity unit, looked after by midwives, with doctors available should they be needed.

Pregnant women have the option of choosing:

» Homebirth. The homebirth rate in 2008 was 2.8 per cent and has remained static over the last few years. Interestingly it is higher in Wales at 3.7 per cent.
» Birth in a local facility, which may be in a hospital or a freestanding unit, under the care of a midwife. This type of setting may be called a birth or birthing centre, a midwife-led unit (MLU), or a community maternity unit (CMU).
» Birth in a hospital, supported by a maternity team including midwives, anaesthetists and obstetricians.

Doulas are very popular in the UK. In 2004, Doula UK, an association of doulas in the UK, conducted a survey of their members. It showed the benefits of having a doula, with a reduction in caesarean sections from 22 per cent in the NHS to 10 per cent of births when supported by a doula. Another interesting result was only 15 per cent of women who were supported by a doula had an epidural, compared to a 33 per cent national average.

The results of a survey of 735 births supported by a doula in the UK in 2008 (Goedkoop 2009) showed that of all the births doulas supported, 45 per cent were completely drug and intervention free; that is, no induction, medicated pain relief, augmentation or instrumental deliveries (forceps/ventouse). There was a low rate of caesarean birth (15 per cent) compared to 24.3 per cent in the most recently available NHS statistics. The survey was extended to post-natal doulas, which showed 88 per cent of mums were still breastfeeding at six weeks and that 67 per cent were still breastfeeding at six months.

The survey concluded:

the role of the doula as a constant and informed support for both labour and in the early post-natal days gets ever more convincing in the current clinical setting. The shortage of midwives, alongside a greater acknowledgement that there is a need to recapture birth as an event associated with normality rather than an obstetric condition, leaves a gap in the support and philosophical context of what care should be available to the woman with a healthy pregnancy.

Models of care in Australia

The main models of care available to women in Australia are:

» Private hospital: model of care — private obstetrician
» Public hospital: models of care — private obstetrician, GP shared care, and any number of different midwifery models discussed below.

Midwifery group practice. Many large teaching hospitals provide this type of service. Essentially, a woman is cared for by two or three midwives throughout her pregnancy, labour, birth and postnatally. The advantages are the continuity of care and actually knowing the midwife when you are birthing. Ask about the continuity model of care, because research by Tracy and Hartz (2006) shows that women and babies have much better outcomes with this type of care.

Midwives clinics. These are offered in major teaching hospitals and some regional hospitals. This model means a woman is cared for during her pregnancy by the same midwife. When it comes time to birth, she will be in a delivery suite and cared for by whichever midwife is on duty at the time.

GP shared care. This model is offered by GPs trained in shared care and is generally very disjointed: some visits to your GP and some to the hospital, where you may be seen by a doctor or a midwife, and often a different person each visit. This model of care means you would birth in the delivery suite and would be cared for by whichever midwife was on duty.

Birth centre care. This type of care is offered mainly by large public hospitals. Not all hospitals have a birth centre, however, so make sure you ask. Here, you will get to meet most of the midwives who work in the birth centre during your pregnancy visits, so that when you are birthing you will feel familiar with the environment and the people and will hopefully have met the midwife assisting you.

Before we move on, let me explain the difference between a delivery suite and a birth centre. A delivery suite is the traditional labour ward.

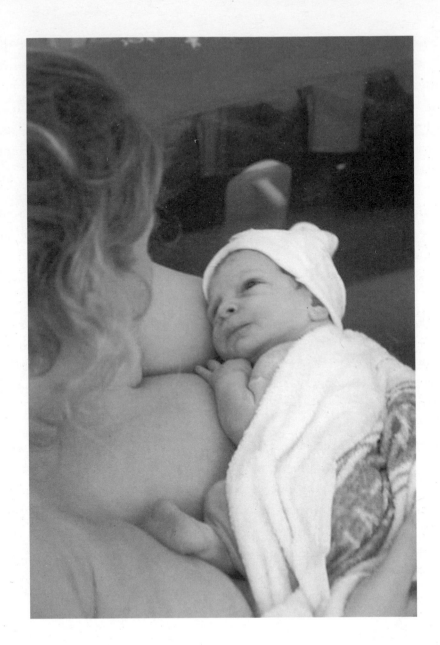

The environment is clinical with obvious signs of medical equipment. Private hospitals only have delivery suites; major public hospitals usually have both.

A birth centre is a more home-like environment, similar to a hotel room — not 5 star, as these centres are provided only by the public hospital system, but certainly a homely room, with a normal double bed and ensuite, usually with a wonderful deep bath. Generally, only birth centres that can accommodate waterbirths, as the baths have been specifically designed for women to labour and give birth in them.

Homebirth through a public hospital birth centre. This model of care is still in the developmental stage and is not available to many women. St George Hospital in Sydney and Belmont Hospital in Newcastle are the only two in New South Wales that offer this service. South Australia has two hospitals that offer this service, Women's and Children's Hospital in Adelaide and the Northern Women's Community Midwifery Program in Elizabeth. The Northern Territory provides this service through the Base Hospital in both Alice Springs and Darwin. This model of care is not available in the other states and the ACT.

The government is trying to convert 'homebirth with an independent midwife' into this option. However, there are fairly strict guidelines as to which women are eligible to participate in this program. Yes, you can birth at home with a midwife who is employed by the birth centre at the above public hospitals, but it does mean that you are still expected to follow all the same hospital policies and protocols. This is a different option from homebirth with an independent midwife.

Homebirth care. With this option you have a primary midwife, and sometimes a backup midwife. She would generally make prenatal visits to your home, be there for your labour and birth, and follow up with postnatal care in your home. A recent Netherlands study (2009), which followed over 500 000 women who had planned homebirths with midwives, showed that homebirth **is** safe. The conclusion was that 'planning a homebirth does not increase risks among low-risk women'.

The homebirth rate declined worldwide over the 20th century. In 1938 the homebirth rate in the USA was 50 per cent; by 2003 it was only 0.57 per cent (MacDorman, Menacker & Declercq 2010). In the UK, the Office for National Statistics (2010) reported that the rate decreased from 80 per cent in the 1920s to 2.9 per cent in 2008. And in Australia less than 2 per cent of women take up this option — probably because they don't know about it (Laws et al.). The only Western country that has maintained a high homebirth rate is The Netherlands, with a rate of around 30 per cent (DeVries 2005).

Women should be presented with all of the above options, including homebirth with an independent midwife (homebirth midwife). The World Health Organization recommends that a woman should give birth in a place she feels is safe and that, for a low-risk pregnant woman, this can be at home, at a small maternity clinic or birth centre, or in a larger hospital.

Freebirthing. Sometimes referred to as 'unassisted birth', freebirthing means a woman birthing, at home, on her own without any medical or other assistance. There are many websites supporting freebirthing. The theory behind freebirthing is that if a woman is left to birth in her own way, without any 'authority' to rely on, she will birth naturally as she is physiologically meant to. She will not be relying on any medical personnel to validate her actions or tell her how she should be birthing, so therefore this woman will absolutely trust in her birthing body, going deep within to the innate primal birthing knowledge that is deep within every woman.

» Don't feel pressured into making a decision until you have done your homework.
» Don't believe that if you have private health insurance you only have *one* option.
» Book an appointment or tour and have a good look at what facilities are available.
» Take a list of questions with you and know what answers you should be getting.
» Meet with a homebirth midwife.
» Try to visualise what it would be like labouring and birthing in the particular environment.
» Think about what your baby would like. Where would your baby like to be born?

CHOOSE THE RIGHT DOULA FOR YOU

Once you have chosen the model of care and the place to birth, the next big decision is to choose a doula.

A doula is not going to look after you medically. She is not going to check your blood pressure, or offer you blood tests or ultrasounds. A doula is going to get to know you, what your fears are, and what you really want for you and your baby. She is going to answer all those questions that some women find difficult to ask their caregiver, or that their caregiver does not have time to discuss. A doula has time — she is not bound by hospital policy and protocols — and she has the knowledge to discuss all your concerns objectively, without judgement, and can refer you to a range of reputable research, so that you can make your own informed decision. She is someone to bounce ideas off, a shoulder to cry on, someone to laugh with and, most of all, she offers a continuum of care.

Very importantly, a doula has time for your partner. She recognises that he has different issues, and acknowledges and respects the importance to him of becoming a dad. For many men, this is the only avenue they have for expressing their concerns.

When should you meet with a doula?

This is best done as early in your pregnancy as possible, preferably after 12 weeks. But remember, it is never too late to make this decision. The journey through pregnancy exposes you to a whole new world of learning with which you may need some assistance. In some states of the USA, hospitals employ doulas, but women do not have an opportunity to meet their doula until they arrive at hospital in labour. Although this is not ideal, it certainly offers those women who would otherwise have no support during labour much needed comfort.

Linda and Jeremy met with me when she was 35 weeks pregnant. She had been referred by her chiropractor. Linda thought it would be a

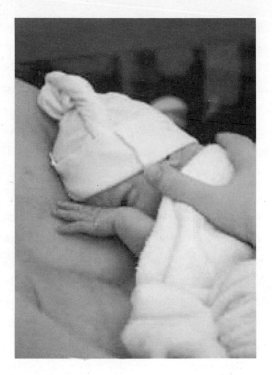

good idea to think about a doula, while Jeremy just did not understand why they would need one, but was happy to support Linda in what she wanted. Linda was seeing a private obstetrician and was booked into a small private hospital, which she chose because her sister and two friends had said that the hospital had good facilities. She did not like her doctor, even from their first meeting. She felt pressured to pay up-front and sign on the dotted line, and all her questions during that visit were dismissed. She made excuses for the doctor, thinking maybe she was rushed or tired, and decided to meet with her again.

As time went on, she felt it was too late to change as she had already paid a large amount of money to the doctor, which she doubted she would get back. She still felt no connection at all with her. Her questions were constantly dismissed and she felt trapped. At 35 weeks she was feeling disillusioned with the doctor and the hospital and told me she didn't want the doctor at her birth as she had no confidence in her. She was angry, which led to fearfulness around how her birth would be.

Jeremy felt that he could support Linda and be her advocate. While this was commendable, a dad can be easily bullied by staff when his partner is in labour into convincing her that intervention is the best and safest way to go. There can also be other agendas on which these decisions are based, especially in the private system.

A doula is the best advocate for a woman in this situation. The mere presence of a doula can prevent such suggestions even being made — she knows about birthing, she supports normal birth, she trusts and believes in the birthing woman, and so, indirectly, is providing some accountability. With all due respect to dads, this is not a role they can, or should have to, play — they are far too emotionally attached to their partner and baby to be an objective advocate, and they don't have an understanding of how the system and its participants operate. A doula does. She can be the difference between having a beautiful normal birthing experience and unnecessary intervention.

Linda and Jeremy could see the benefits of having a doula in their situation while recognising that I did not have continuity of care for them and how important that could be. It is often not until after the birth that a couple really understands and appreciates the role of the doula.

How do you choose the right doula for you?

Choosing the right doula is another very important decision. Try to meet with at least two or three doulas until you find the one you feel most comfortable with.

QUESTIONS TO ASK THE DOULA

- » Where did you do your doula training?
- » How long have you been a doula?
- » What is your philosophy around birth?
- » How many births have you attended?
- » What hospitals/birth centres have you attended?
- » Have you supported at a homebirth?
- » Have you ever been in a situation where you needed to negotiate with hospital staff on behalf of a woman? Do you believe you have good negotiating skills?
- » Do you work with a backup doula?
- » How far away do you live?
- » What does your service include?
- » What is the cost of your service?

When listening to the answers to these questions, you should consider the following points.

The standard of doula training is varied. There are businesses offering only online training. However, this is such a hands-on business that I would suggest you avoid anyone who has completed their training online. Thereare good doula training facilities which take their responsibility very seriously and offer comprehensive training and ongoing education and support for their trainee doulas. Some couples only want to choose an experienced doula and there are obvious benefits in going down this path, but it is also about who you connect with. If the doula you connect with and feel positive about has not had much experience, but has good backup support from her training organisation, then this would be someone to consider.

A doula's philosophy on birth should be to support you in what you want. However, if it is early in your pregnancy and you have a lot of fear and anxiety around birthing, you may not necessarily know what you want, or it may change as you journey through your pregnancy, the books you read and by attending classes. A doula understands and respects normal birth and trusts in a woman's ability to birth. However, she should also encourage you to learn and should provide advice on education.

Don't be afraid to ask about the doula's experience with different types of births — from water births and homebirths to medical interventions.

It is wise for a doula to have a backup, in the rare event that she is unable to attend your birth. This does not happen very often and would usually be due to an emergency. You should meet the other doula during one of your visits.

What does the service include?

Always check what the service includes. Generally, it incorporates access to the doula via phone or email, at least two to four meetings, being on call for your labour and at home with you during your labour, attending at the hospital for the birth (if that is where you are birthing) and at least one postnatal visit for a birth debrief. Many doulas have other useful skills, including massage, acupuncture, chiropractic, reiki, kinesiology, homeopathic and aromatherapy, to name only a few. Women with such careers are often enticed into being doulas because they realise the benefits they can offer birthing women. The service always includes looking after your partner, providing reassurance and normalising the experience, allowing him to do and be what he feels comfortable with on the day of birth.

However in the USA, in some lower socioeconomic areas, doulas are employed by the hospital and for those women who arrive, in labour, with absolutely no support, a hospital doula will be offered. It is not ideally what a doula should be providing but is absolutely better than no support at all.

What is the cost of a doula?

The cost for this service varies, so it is wise to check this with the doulas you visit. Newly trained doulas sometimes offer their services free of charge. If you require your doula to be on call, available when you need her, alert and fresh for between three and five weeks, this can add considerably to the cost.

Paying for a doula is the best gift your family or friends could possibly give you and much more sensible than getting 20 pairs of pink booties. It is guaranteed to give the baby the best start in life. So, if the cost seems overwhelming, suggest this to your family or friends.

Seventy-year-old Ken bought a gift certificate for a doula for his 40-year-old daughter who was having her first baby and was terrified (according to Ken). He did the research and was well educated in what doulas offered by the time he made the purchase. His pregnant daughter and her partner had never heard of doulas, but went on to develop a wonderful relationship with their doula, Rebecca, who provided amazing emotional support for both of them throughout the pregnancy and birth.

PRENATAL EDUCATION

You may have a degree or two from university, you may be the CEO of a company, you may be the best real estate salesperson of the year, you may be a wonderful naturopath who is in tune with her body, you may be a doctor, a painter or a teacher — but, whatever your qualifications, you need education. This will be a brand new field, no matter what your background, and it will be so exciting learning about your pregnancy journey, labour, birthing and, very importantly, about what new babies need.

You can't get this information from a book or a DVD, and certainly not from YouTube! The sceptics will say, 'Birth is natural, it is what women are meant to be doing, how hard can it be?', or 'I have lots of siblings who have had children and I'll learn from them'. You will get some information from all of the above sources. But will it be the right information for you? Will it be objective? The answer is no. This is your pregnancy, your birth and your baby. You will develop your own ideas about what you want over 40 weeks and these may be very different from those of your family, or from what you have read in books or magazines. You need to source classes that have current information presented in an objective way and offer you all the choices, with all their advantages and disadvantages. They should also be lots of fun.

Where can you get a good education?

Don't be pressured to book into hospital classes just because it is convenient and the hospital suggests you do, because if you don't book in immediately you conceive, you won't get in! Having taught hospital classes for many years, I know they leave a lot to be desired. The educators who conduct the classes are bound to abide by not only hospital policies and protocols, but also guidelines from various other health professionals within the system. Over the years, I have taught prenatal classes in major public hospitals, small country hospitals, private hospitals, community centres and privately, offering individual sessions for couples and a variety of education mediums. It is wonderful to be able to provide independent education for couples without the constraints of hospital policies and preferences, to be able to show women that this is about them and their baby and it is they who get to choose how they birth. I want women to leave our classes feeling positive and empowered. I want them to believe, totally, in their absolute ability to birth with grace and ease.

Remember: Women don't need to be taught *how* to birth. They just need to be taught *about* birth.

Why?

Often couples will say that they were advised by various people not to do prenatal classes because they are scary and don't tell you anything that you can't get out of a book. So don't book into those classes because they will not teach you about birth!

Knowledge is power. You are about to embark on an extraordinary journey and a major life change. With any other life change or new beginning, most people do some research and learn about what lies ahead. With this life change, the trick in finding the right education for you is to know what to ask and what answers you should get. There are also many advantages in being in a small group of like-minded people.

What type of class?

There are so many classes on offer that it has become very confusing for most couples. Some are just advertised as prenatal (or antenatal) classes, childbirth education, preparation for birth, or birth and parenting classes. If you are enquiring about any of the above, ask specifically about what is covered in the classes, because they all have very general titles.

Active Birth classes have become very popular over the last couple of decades. As Janet Balaskas wrote in her book, *Active Birth* (1992, p. 1):

Active birth is nothing new, it is simply a convenient way of describing normal labour and birth and the way that a woman behaves when she is following her own instincts and the physiological logic of her body. It is a way of saying that she herself is in control of her body while giving birth, rather than the passive recipient of an actively managed birth on the part of her attendants.

She is encouraging women to follow their natural instincts, which include moving around, using different positions such as pelvic rocking and squatting, and showering and bathing. If a woman feels safe and well supported by her doula and partner, she will naturally follow her instincts. I have observed many women in labour doing the most beautiful rhythmic belly dancing, sometimes for many hours, totally oblivious to what they were

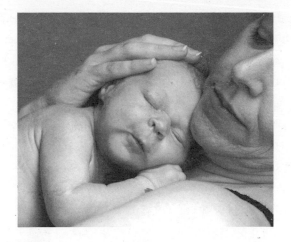

doing. They were not women experienced in belly dancing, but women who trusted birth and allowed their bodies to take over and follow the rhythmic dance of birthing. It is amazing to watch women who trust and feel safe confidently doing their own thing during labour.

HypnoBirthing® classes are equally magical and I highly recommend them. Unfortunately, similar sounding classes are advertised, which makes it confusing when shopping around. These will have titles like hypnosis for birth, relaxation for birth, meditation for birth, hypnotic suggestions for birth, calmness for birth, hypnotherapy for birth — the list goes on. Make sure you ask about the experience of the educator, and if there are any testimonials you could read before booking in. The HypnoBirthing® program was designed by hypnotherapist Maree Mongan and is taught in over 20 countries.

A HypnoBirthing® woman learns to embrace her body's innate knowledge of birthing, to relax into her birthing process, working with her body and her baby. She trusts birth. She wants this experience to unfold normally and without interruption. By doing this, she eliminates fatigue and shortens her labour, resulting in a rewarding and beautiful birthing experience for her, her partner and her baby. These babies are born awake, alert and very calm.

This program teaches the basic physiology of birth and explains the effect that fear has on birthing. You will learn simple techniques for easily bringing yourself into a state of deep relaxation. This will allow your birthing muscles to fully relax, so you can look forward to your labour and birthing with love and joy, rather than fear and anxiety.

After attending our first day of the HypnoBirthing® course, both Geoff and I are so thankful that we are doing this. I felt this overwhelming sense of being exactly where we needed to be and the relief was almost palpable. Watching the DVDs of HypnoBirthers® was an eye-opener; I didn't know birth could be like that. It was incredibly empowering and quite emotional to watch. I now feel much more connection with my baby. Geoff has never done yoga or anything like that before, but he got an enormous amount out of it as well. I don't feel as panicky as I was about labour and birth. I can see that there are accessible tools and techniques to achieve a happy birth, which I am now looking forward to.

EMMA

Certainly, all the HypnoBirthing® births that I have been privileged to support were beautiful, calm and peaceful. Watching these babies emerge from the birth path, often in water, with eyes wide open, fully alert, but quiet and relaxed, is truly amazing. I watch in awe, thinking what a great start in life these little ones are having.

There is so much focus on the pain of childbirth, but with HypnoBirthing® many of the women describe it as a tightening or pressure sensation and, of course, some describe it as an amazing orgasmic experience.

» Is this an independent class? Look for independent classes as they are likely to offer more objective information than hospital classes.

» What is your background? Many educators are midwives, some are doulas, some have other skills. It is very important to find an educator who has had some experience with birthing and working in hospitals. The number of people teaching prenatal classes who have never been to a birth or been inside a maternity unit is astounding. Getting information about the system, how it works and how to navigate your way around it is crucial.

» What is an average class size? Smaller is better. Many hospital classes have 10–12 couples, which does not allow adequate time for asking questions and exploring issues.

» What is the philosophy of the class? How is the information presented? Look for an educator who presents in a fun and positive way and is open to exploring all angles — not just from a personal point of view.

» Do you offer a range of classes? If the answer is yes, this will show that they will make sure you are exposed to different options.

» Can my birthing team attend these classes? Make sure you are allowed to take your birthing team to your classes. It is particularly important for new doulas to attend with you. This will ensure that you are all on the same page.

TESTING IN PREGNANCY

You have options and choices with *all* testing during pregnancy. Many women think they are obliged to have all the tests. These should be presented to you with a full explanation of the advantages and disadvantages for you and your baby. The conversation should go something like this: 'What we offer is an ultrasound, blood test, streptococcus B screen, gestational diabetes, cardiotocography (CTG), etc. If you accept these, they will be done at your next visit. Please let us know your decision then.' Of course, you are going to listen to their advice, suggestions, and pros and cons, but you also need to do your own research and perhaps discuss this with your doula who should be able to provide some balance so that you can make a more informed decision on behalf of your baby. Hospitals will generally want you to have all the screening and testing on offer as this covers them from a legal perspective. Remember, you are not sick, you do not have a disease; you are having a baby — a normal event, not a medical event.

So talk to your baby. I know women who have a wonderful connection with their baby while in utero and are very much in tune with how their baby is feeling and if there are any problems. We know that babies don't like ultrasound, they don't like being poked and prodded by the ultrasonographer to make them wake up and they turn away from the needle when an amniocentesis is being performed. Always ask yourself this question: 'If I have this test, what am I going to do with the information?' Sometimes the information just opens up a can of worms. Many women tell me they wish they had not had the test at all.

Miriam, who had the nuchal translucency test for Down syndrome because she thought it was a routine test and that she didn't have any option, found that her result of a 1 in 800 chance of having a baby with this condition did little to alleviate her fears. In fact, it just created a whole lot of fear that she did not want. She spent the remainder of her pregnancy worrying about what she would do if she was the 1 in 800 — someone had to be.

Other women find they are pleased with this statistic, dismiss the possibility and don't think about it again.

Those women who feel very positive about their pregnancy and have a strong connection with their baby are often the same women who say 'no thanks' to the so-called routine testing.

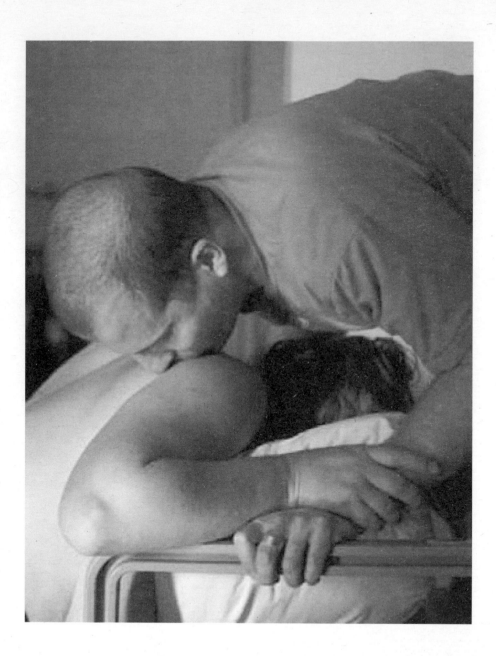

CHAPTER 3

Fear — and how it relates to birthing

Currently, in spite of evidence to the contrary, an amazing number of people who work in maternity services, and even women themselves, continue to accept the myth that pain and suffering are a normal part of birthing. It is even advertised, especially in private hospitals, that the best a woman can do is depend upon her obstetrician, anaesthetist and midwife to help her get through the birth experience. A lot of women want to know that the epidural is close at hand, and many private hospitals conduct epidural education evenings, promoting the joys and benefits of this extraordinary intervention.

P enny was 14 weeks pregnant and had booked into a private hospital in Sydney. She was instructed by the hospital to attend an 'epidural talk'.

'I was so naive and just went along because I was told to. The anaesthetist talked about the joys of having an epidural. One of the benefits, as he saw it, was that it would allow me to read my magazines whilst in labour. Unlike most other couples in the room, this felt very odd to me, as I was hoping for a normal birth, preferably in water. I chose not to sign the consent form for an epidural at this time and felt he was mocking me, saying he would see me on the big day! As I was walking out, I felt for the first time that this — having a baby — was really important stuff and I needed to find out much, much more. I found some great independent classes which talked positively about birth and gave both my partner and me lots of resources, and we decided to look at other options of care.'

The most common cause of complications during labour is FEAR. In fact, we live in a fear-based society.

Birth is a normal event; it is not a medical event. But women accept that a hospital is a normal place to have a baby. Most of us would go to hospital only if we were extremely sick or dying — and even then many of us would think twice. Wouldn't it be wonderful if one day we had a forward-thinking government which recognised the impact that birthing in a hospital environment has on families and set up separate centres for those women who do not want to choose a homebirth.

WHERE DOES ALL THIS FEAR COME FROM?

We are conditioned from the time we are born through both positive and negative messages, in the form of suggestions, from parents, siblings, teachers, relatives, friends and the media. Suggestions are at the root of our behaviour, our self-esteem, our motivation and our overall success or failure. Continued reinforcement of a thought or action tends to make the thought or action more readily acceptable, and it becomes easier for additional suggestions of the same nature to be accepted and acted upon. For example, a child frightened once by a savage dog may become frightened of all dogs, even when there is no reason for fear.

For women who have grown up hearing negative birthing stories in their family, which are then reinforced by discussion about complications and medical procedures, along with advice from friends, they will lean in that direction and shut out all possibility of peaceful birthing.

Once a pregnant woman becomes aware that birth is simple and surrounds herself with support people (such as a doula) who reinforce this idea, she is more readily able to accept that she can birth according to her own natural birthing instincts.

The mind–body connection

What is the mind and where is it? Behavioural scientists have been debating this question for many years. It is now acknowledged and well documented that thoughts and feelings affect the functioning of all systems within our body. But many in Western medicine still advocate total separation between mind and body. Thoughts and feelings are considered to have no relationship to physical wellbeing. When something goes wrong with the body, our culture still promotes that medical drugs or surgery will fix the problem.

I have witnessed many examples of the mind–body connection in birthing situations.

I was supporting a couple who were having their first baby. Fran made it reasonably clear in our meetings during her pregnancy that she and Justin had different views about many topics. Culturally, there were differences, but she said he would be a good financial provider.

Justin phoned one evening about 10 pm to ask if I could come immediately as Fran was in the bath and her contractions were coming every two minutes. When I arrived, she was indeed in good labour and experiencing a lot of pressure. She felt that the baby was very close. With lots of encouragement and reassurance, I got Fran out of the bath and asked Justin to have the car and her suitcases ready. Fran announced that she did not want to go to hospital with her husband and that she wanted to come with me. At that point he was busy shaving! We got in my car, with Fran doubled over on the back seat. Justin was to follow. He arrived at the birth centre 30 minutes after we did. Fran had just settled into a deep bath. She was fully dilated. Justin began to fuss very loudly — he wanted to put music on, telling her this was what she had wanted. At this point, she wanted to be quiet. Still, he put the music on. He made phone calls, he asked her questions, he brought bags up from the car and then he started inviting various family members to come to the hospital.

Two hours later, nothing had changed for Fran. I was curious as to why. We had been there long enough for her to settle in and I was pretty sure she felt safe. The midwife insisted on her getting out of the bath and trying the birth stool. Even midwives in birth centres need to follow time frames! She said she had no urge to bear down or push. Justin was in and out of the room, constantly changing the music to find something that she liked. She did not want any music — he did not hear this. The midwife was very close to her face while Fran was on the birth stool, trying to convince her to push. At one point, we were alone in the room and I asked Fran if there was anything worrying her. She looked me right in the eye and said, 'I don't want Justin to be in the room when I give birth and I don't want the midwife to be in my face. I just want you to be the one who stays close.' I had a discussion with Justin and the midwife. He was almost relieved.

Once I told Fran that Justin would respect her wishes and not be in the room and that the midwife would give her some space, I was able to tell her she could now have her baby. Twenty minutes later she had a beautiful little girl in her arms. Whatever was going on in their relationship, and clearly there was a lot, this was something she needed to do just with me, a doula whom she trusted.

I am constantly in awe of the power of the mind over the body during labour and birthing. Fran had been fully dilated for almost four hours, and had held on for that long, until she felt safe.

Unfortunately, many situations like this lead to medical intervention, to rescue mother and baby. All Fran needed was someone to understand that it was fear that was holding her back. Luckily, it was a simple solution.

Here are two other fascinating stories about the mind–body connection.

Connie had her first baby in the bath in a birth centre. She had a beautiful, peaceful birthing experience and wanted a repeat performance for this second birth.

She had been experiencing some contractions throughout the evening and about 11.30 pm phoned the birth centre to let them know she would probably be in soon. The call was transferred to the delivery suite and the midwife informed Connie that, unfortunately, the midwife from the birth centre had gone home sick and there was no replacement. She told Connie to come in to the delivery suite. Connie asked what time the next midwife shift started at the birth centre as she was planning a water birth and did not want to have her baby in the delivery suite. She was told 7 am the next morning. Connie respectfully declined to go to the delivery suite and told the midwife she would wait until the morning. This conversation took place while she was contracting very regularly.

Connie got off the phone, decided to go to bed and made up her mind to have her baby the next day. She slept well and at precisely 7 am woke up experiencing strong contractions. We all arrived at the birth centre at 8 am and she had her baby at 8.30 am in the bath. Wow! There shouldn't ever be any doubt about the power of the mind over the body.

Jenny was also having her second baby in a private hospital with a private obstetrician. She had a lot of medical intervention with her first labour and this time had chosen to attend HypnoBirthing® classes and have a doula. Her obstetrician had not heard about this method and reassured her that the epidural service was excellent at the hospital.

It was late afternoon with dappled sunshine dancing on the water, and Jenny was in the bath. Alan sat on the edge of the bath and I on a chair. It was very, very quiet, like being on another planet. The only indication that she was having a surge was when she turned on her side, breathing deeply but ever so quietly. Alan asked me if I thought she was really in labour. He was waiting for the same screaming that had happened the first time. I reassured him that she was doing beautifully and was indeed in labour. The very young and inexperienced midwife who wanted to constantly do observations very quickly picked up on the peaceful energy in the room, and so became less intrusive as the labour progressed. About 6.30 pm the obstetrician powered into the room, very loudly announcing that it didn't look like labour was progressing very well but she was happy to give her a little more time as she needed to go home and sort out her children's homework and give them dinner. Who cared?

After she left, Alan was very worried as he knew that Jenny did not want intervention. I checked with Jenny how she was feeling; she told me there was a lot of pressure around her anus, but she was also a little concerned that the obstetrician did not think she was progressing. I had to undo the negative and uninformed seed that had been sown, reassuring both of them. Jenny settled into her beautiful rhythm once again. Within the last half hour she had got out of the bath a couple of times to sit on the toilet (always a good sign that baby is close). She needed to go to the toilet a third time. This time I did not leave the room, but left the door ajar. She quietly said that the baby's head was just there and could I get her the birth stool please. (HypnoBirthing® women are ever so polite.) She slid from the toilet on to the birth stool just as the midwife came into the room. Jenny was deep in the zone of her birthing and thankfully was oblivious to the shock the midwife displayed — she was very worried that she did not have all her equipment laid out and that the doctor was not present. Baby was born with the next surge and Jenny and Alan carefully received him and Alan placed him in her arms. So quiet, so peaceful, such an alert baby!

Doors flung open and the obstetrician arrived. 'What happened?' she asked. 'You were nowhere near ready to have this baby when I left an hour ago.' The doctor and midwife busied themselves getting the hospital bed set up for 'delivery' of the placenta. Lights went on, plastic sheets went on, the bed was pumped up to the right height for the convenience of the doctor. Jenny was still on the birth stool in the darkness of the bathroom with her baby in her arms. There was a bowl between her legs. While all the activity was taking place, I quickly whispered in Jenny's ear, 'Now would be a good time to birth your placenta', and out it came, gently plopping into the bowl. She was so thrilled with her birthing experience, so overwhelmed with how much she enjoyed it and so delighted that she had avoided any medical intervention. The obstetrician expressed disbelief, saying she had never seen such a quiet birth. She contacted me a few weeks later and invited me to meet with her to explain about HypnoBirthing®.

Understanding that, when the mind is free of fear and stress that cause the body to respond with pain, nature is free to process birth in the same well-designed manner that it does for all other normal physiological functions of the body.

All mammals, including humans, share the same basic needs when they give birth. In the wild, a labouring female mammal cannot give birth while there is a predator around. Thanks to a release of adrenaline, which is associated with fear, she can fight or flee. She will give birth when the danger has passed and she feels safe, and her adrenaline level has dropped.

Throughout history, women have tended to give birth close to their mother, or close to a trusted, experienced mother figure with whom they felt safe. This is what midwifery was all about. A midwife was originally the mother figure. In an ideal world, our mother is the one person who we should be able to feel safe with, the one person who does not judge us. If only this ideal midwife had persisted through to the present time. Unfortunately, the midwife has been transformed into an anonymous member of an institution, part of a medical team, and bound to follow the institution's policies and protocols. The focus of a doula, on the other hand, is on what the birthing woman wants, and on being her advocate and making sure she has the experience that she desires.

When men were first encouraged to attend the birth of their children in the late 1960s, their fear was certainly transmitted to their labouring partner. Fear is highly contagious.

Author Michel Odent, known as the 'French Obstetrician', is recognised for the introduction of birthing pools and home-like birthing rooms, and the author of many books, discusses how most women today have babies without relying on the release of their natural hormones. Many who give birth vaginally are having drugs, which block the release of a woman's natural hormones. When a woman is given an intravenous drip of synthetic oxytocin, this then inhibits the release of this hormone, naturally from the pituitary gland. This drug does not reach the brain and it will not have the effect of a 'hormone of love'. This is why it is so important to educate women about the effects of synthetic oxytocin (Syntocinon) because many delivery suites give routine syntocinon for the third stage (birth of the placenta). This means the release of the love hormone will be blocked just after the birth of her baby, right when she really needs it.

Remember that women who are fearful secrete the hormones that delay or inhibit birth. Those who are not fearful are more likely to secrete in abundance the hormones that make labour and birth easy and enjoyable — even orgasmic!

There is concern for our society now that there have been several generations of women giving birth without releasing the flow of these 'love hormones'.

PAIN — A FOUR-LETTER WORD!

What are women most fearful of?

PAIN!

Even before a woman conceives, she has usually heard about how painful labour and birth are from someone, either a family member or a well-meaning friend. She grows up with this firmly imprinted belief, so it is understandable that it can be quite challenging to change this mindset.

As early as 1942, Dr Grantly Dick-Read coined the phrase, 'fear–tension–pain syndrome'. He says in his book, *Childbirth without Fear* (2005):

The fear of pain actually produces true pain through the medium of pathological tension. This is known as the fear–tension–pain syndrome and once it is established a vicious circle demonstrating a crescendo

of events will be observed, for the true pain, fear is justified, and
with mounting fear, resistance is strengthened. The most important
contributory cause of pain in otherwise normal labour is fear.

His book, which has been reprinted many times over the years, is a fascinating insight into normal birth. It was written at a time when endorphins were not known, modern midwifery did not exist, doulas did not exist as they do today and women had already learned to fear labour. He is possibly the world's first childbirth activist.

Many childbirth education programs focus on pain, teaching methods that attempt to take the focus away from pain so that women will not be so aware of it. These distraction techniques often make women exhausted very quickly, as they stamp their feet, squeeze their stress balls and vocalise — loudly. The theory behind this is that, if women can identify the degree of pain — its severity and its frequency — they will be better able to determine where they are in labour and what coping techniques they will use to continue. Throughout my many years as a midwife, I learned to associate certain behaviours in labour with the degree of cervical dilation. I was trained to listen for the screaming and shouting as a sign of transition. In many hospitals, this criterion has not changed. Many regard pain as an unavoidable, but useful, friend that can be tolerated, worked with and learned from. There are even those who revere pain in birthing, seeing it as a vehicle through which to achieve the empowerment of womanhood. It has been suggested that we learn to honour pain, as other societies do, for the strength it builds in our character. These programs feel that, because pain has to serve some purpose, it must be rationalised and accommodated in some way. For most women, these are not convincing arguments:

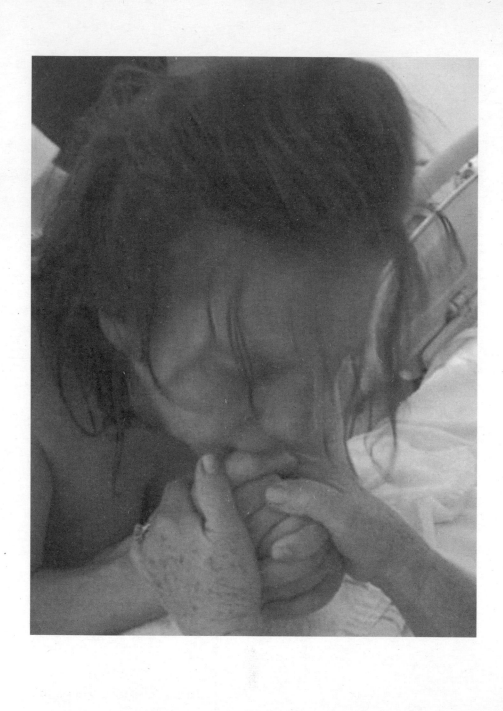

accepting the belief that it is necessary creates the very situation they want to avoid.

There is no physiological reason for pain in birthing. However, hospitals often provide a cocktail of drugs into which the birthing woman can escape. These drugs are offered, not as a last resort during labour, but as a menu, often presented during childbirth education classes so that selections and decisions can be made early on. It is often presented in a way that has women believing that the drugs won't cross the placenta. No one tells them that the placenta has no barrier. They go into their labour believing that their birthing bodies are inadequate, but that they can be 'delivered' by drugs and technology, even when these interventions take them further away from normal and gentle birth for their babies.

What causes pain?

FEAR!

To understand what causes pain in labour, we need to look at how the uterus functions when a woman is fearful and has unresolved anxieties. The uterus has to be the most extraordinary design of all organs in the body. For the purpose of looking at fear, we will focus on the muscle layers, which are designed to work in perfect harmony.

There are three layers of muscle in the uterus. There is the outer layer, which consists of longitudinal muscles, aligned up and down with your baby. The middle layer is composed of fibres running in all directions and matted closely together to support the large blood vessels. And then there are the circular muscle fibres, which run horizontally and surround your baby. These are thickest in the bottom half of the uterus, just above the opening of the uterus, the cervix. In order for this outlet to open and allow your baby to easily move down, through and out of the uterus and into the birth path, these lower, thicker muscles have to relax and thin. As the stronger longitudinal fibres, concentrated at the top of the uterus, tighten and draw up the relaxed circular muscles at the neck of the uterus, they cause the edges of the cervix to progressively thin and open. It is a wavelike motion, with the long muscles shortening and flexing to nudge baby down. When a birthing woman is in a state of relaxation, these muscles work in harmony. The surge of the vertical muscles draws up, flexes and pushes down. The circular muscles relax and draw back to allow this to happen. The cervix thins and opens and birth occurs with grace and ease.

So what happens when a woman is fearful? When a woman goes into labour with unresolved fear and anxiety, her body is already on the defensive, and catecholamines (stress hormones) are released, sending her body into the 'fight, flight or freeze' response. Given that 'fight' and 'flight' are generally not options in labour, her body chooses the third option, the 'freeze' response. The uterus is not part of the defence mechanism of the body and therefore blood is directed away from it to the parts of the body involved in defence, namely the limbs. This causes the big blood vessels going to the uterus to tense and constrict, which restricts the blood and oxygen flow. With limited oxygen and blood, which is vital to the function of the muscles in the uterus, the lower circular fibres at the neck of the uterus tighten and constrict, instead of relaxing and opening. The vertical muscles continue to attempt to draw the circular muscles up and back, but the lower muscles are resistant, so the cervix remains taut and closed.

When these two muscle layers work against each other, it causes pain. Baby's head is forced against a very taut muscle, labour is long and the oxygen supply to the baby is compromised, and it is this that can result in a diagnosis from hospital staff of 'failure to progress', which inevitably results in medical intervention. But women in this situation don't need intervention; they need to feel safe and well supported. They need to be given time to re-establish trust in their ability to birth naturally.

WHAT HAPPENS WHEN THE MIND IS FREE OF FEAR?

We have seen what happens when the mind is swelling with fear and stress and how it can interrupt the body's ability to birth naturally. When the mind is free of fear, through positive thoughts, relaxation and focused breathing, the opposite occurs. The mind and body work best when both are in harmony. Recognising your fears, and being able to release those fears, is essential to a calm, peaceful birth for you and your baby.

Friends and family tend to hold me up as an example of someone with a low pain threshold. However, after a very long and difficult labour culminating in an epidural for my first birth, I was very unsure as to whether I had it in me to achieve the drug-free labour and water birth I really longed to have for my second child. I contacted Susan very late in the pregnancy after months of dithering and angst, and it was the best thing I could possibly have done.

It is difficult to explain the power of having someone so strong, centred and experienced lending balance and calm during the extremes of labour — supporting your decisions, suggesting techniques to help, and reminding you of your own strength and capability. Susan met with me several times before the birth and we worked through my lack of confidence and my fear, resulting from my difficult first birth. She was reassuring and empathetic but also very straightforward and no-nonsense.

After another long pre-labour at home, during which my husband and I spoke regularly to Susan, we met her at the birth centre. I was very discouraged to realise that we had come in prematurely and that I was not particularly dilated. Susan was soothing and encouraging. Her help in getting past this initial blow to my confidence was very important. My husband was similarly traumatised by the first birth and just as in need of encouragement.

Susan noticed that being in the bath relaxed me and helped the labour progress. After about seven hours at the birth centre, with lots of encouragement and gentle reminders to breathe and focus and relax from Susan, Rosalie emerged strong, calm and alert, and breastfed immediately. Her alertness seemed truly miraculous, in sharp contrast to the relative limpness of my first baby after pethidine and an epidural.

Attaining your own goals for an ideal birth for you and your child, with the maximum considered control over your own labour, is indescribably gratifying. For me, this natural water birth was a huge achievement that will remain an important factor in my self-regard all my life. But I really don't think I would have had the focus to endure without Susan's help. I am eternally grateful to her.

Phyllis Klaus, author and psychologist, says: 'When a woman is not continuously supported and does not feel safe then she goes into a frightened state and with this fear the stress hormones come in and tighten everything up, which the brain perceives as pain.'

A doula is experienced in recognising this situation and has the skills to be able to buy some time, so that she can work with the labouring woman, making changes and eliminating any stress that may be preventing her from relaxing. Allowing the body to work at its own pace by using relaxation and visualisation can speed up the release of endorphins and facilitate a shorter labour.

TIPS FOR DEALING WITH FEAR

» Identify any feelings or experiences that are painful and may interfere with your gentle birthing.

» Think about what you feel confident about and what you need to work on.

» Write down a list of your own fears, have your partner write down his fears and then compare notes. You may be surprised to discover what each of you is thinking.

» Enrol in either a HypnoBirthing® course or an appropriate relaxation/meditation class and any other education course that has a positive focus.

» Find a doula you trust and with whom you feel comfortable to discuss your fears. The more you can explore any thoughts that may have a negative impact on your pregnancy and birthing, the better.

» Listen to positive affirmations of calm and gentle birthing — daily.

» Visualise a beautiful birthing and meeting your baby.

» Don't listen to the horror stories, don't watch the horror stories and, most importantly, don't believe the horror stories.

Remember, this is your pregnancy, your birth and your baby and you are the best director of events.

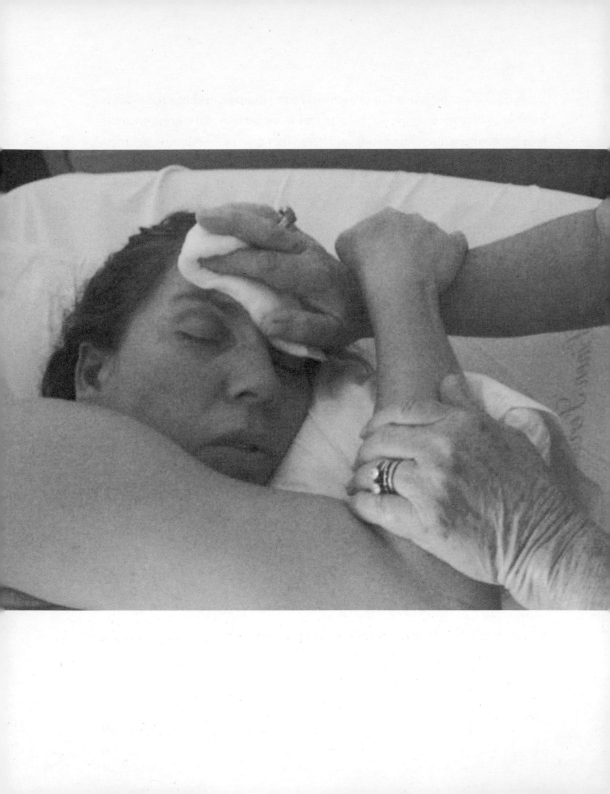

CHAPTER 4

Hormones —
let them flow!

Mother Nature provides an exquisite cocktail of hormones during birthing which takes you outside your usual mental state, so that you can be transformed on every level as you journey through labour and birthing to motherhood. Women who feel safe and well supported and experience this miraculous unfolding sometimes describe birth as 'ecstasy', 'being taken to another planet', 'going to a beautiful place in my mind' and even 'orgasmic'. This is possible for all women who trust birth, believe in themselves and have the right support.

HORMONAL SYSTEMS ACTIVE DURING LABOUR AND BIRTH

The four major hormonal systems active during labour and birth are:

1. **Oxytocin — the 'hormone of love'.** This is released during love making, male and female orgasm, birth and breastfeeding, engendering feelings of love. It is a crucial hormone involved in reproduction, sperm ejection and, importantly, the 'foetal ejection reflex at birth' (a phrase coined by Michel Odent, describing the powerful contractions at the end of an undisturbed labour, which births the baby quickly and easily). Oxytocin is also involved in the placental ejection reflex and the milk ejection (let-down) reflex in breastfeeding. Large amounts are secreted during pregnancy, enhancing nutrient absorption, reducing stress and conserving energy, and oxytocin causes the rhythmic uterine contractions of labour. The baby also produces increasing amounts of this hormone during labour, so in the time immediately following birth both mother and baby are bathed in hormones. Ongoing production of oxytocin is enhanced by skin-to-skin contact, gazing into each other's eyes and the first attempts at suckling.

2. **Beta-endorphin — a naturally occurring opiate.** Beta-endorphin has similar properties to morphine and heroin. High levels are present during sex, pregnancy, birth and breastfeeding. It is also a stress hormone, released under conditions of pain, when it acts as a painkiller and, like other stress hormones, suppresses the immune system. Like addictive opiates, beta-endorphin induces feelings of pleasure,

euphoria and dependency. The levels are high during pregnancy and increase during labour, allowing a woman to enter the altered state of consciousness that we see in peaceful, undisturbed births.

3. **Catecholamines — fight or flight hormones.** These are secreted from the adrenal gland above the kidney in response to stresses such as anxiety, fright, hunger or cold, and also excitement. High levels of catecholamines in labour inhibit oxytocin production, thereby slowing or even stopping labour. They also reduce blood flow to the uterus and the baby. This is useful for animals in the wild when faced with a predator during labour, activating their fight or flight response and diverting blood to their limbs so they can flee to safety. In humans, the release of high levels of catecholamines during labour is associated with long labour and stress to the baby. In an undisturbed labour, when birth is imminent, these hormones act differently. There is a sudden increase in the levels of catecholamines, especially noradrenaline, which activates the foetal ejection reflex. The mother experiences a sudden rush of energy and becomes very alert, birthing her baby quickly and easily. These high levels at birth assure baby's alertness. Baby having immediate contact with mother will cause the levels to drop.

4. **Prolactin — known as the mothering hormone as it is the main hormone involved in breastfeeding.** Levels of prolactin increase during pregnancy, although milk production is inhibited hormonally until the placenta is birthed. Levels decrease during labour, then rise and peak with birth. Prolactin is the hormone of surrender or submission, ensuring that the mother puts her baby's needs first.

HOW THE BIRTHING ENVIRONMENT AFFECTS THE RELEASE OF HORMONES

To allow the release of this complex cocktail of hormones three important environmental factors need to be in place. First, a woman needs to feel safe in her environment. It needs to be a home-like place (if in a hospital) to which she is able to take her favourite items from home and set up the room in the way she chooses. Second, she needs to feel well supported. Having a doula who knows her on a personal level and what her wishes are for her birth is a real advantage. A doula can relay any particular birth preferences to her caregivers so that she is not disturbed in any way. Many women also need to know that their partner is being looked after and that he is not worried unduly about her and baby. Third, the environment needs to be set up by the doula to create a setting conducive to peaceful birthing. The room needs to be dimly lit, quiet and private.

Remember, having a baby has many similarities with making a baby: the same hormones, the same sounds, the same parts of the body, and the same need to feel safe and private. Think about the environment in which you will be giving birth. Would you make love in this environment?

WHAT OTHER FACTORS INTERFERE WITH BIRTH?

Apart from an unsettled environment, the two main contributors to difficult births are stress and what is said, and how it is said, to women during labour and birthing.

Stress

When stress hormones are released they block the release of oxytocin. Stress has many triggers during labour and birthing. Being transferred from home to hospital can cause stress — it is a new environment, with new faces and a different energy — and this is why labour often stops when women arrive at the hospital. Feeling scared can induce stress — some women, often those who are ill prepared, find the power of labour very confronting and feel frightened by what their body is doing. Being watched or monitored is another trigger. Women don't need to be constantly observed during labour. They don't need someone sitting with a clipboard and watch in hand, timing contractions and asking questions about their labour. If a doula has been at home with the woman during her labour, she can answer all those questions and give the midwife a clear picture of what has been happening, so that the paperwork can be attended to and checklists ticked — all without disturbing the labouring woman!

My golden rule for all people present at a birth is 'When in doubt, say nought'! Women are very sensitive to what is said, not only during pregnancy but also during labour and birth. If a woman needs to be told something, the words should be positive and encouraging and should come from the people she trusts most, namely her doula and her partner. If a caregiver needs to ask a question, perhaps because she has concerns about the woman and her labour, this should be asked first of the doula and the woman's partner. If the labouring woman needs to be involved in a decision, then her doula and partner are the best people to present the options to her.

All of these factors, especially being in an unfamiliar place in the presence of an 'observer', cause stress and disturb birth in mammals.

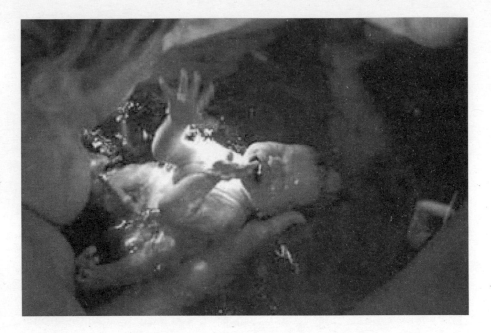

When I was training to be a midwife in a large public teaching hospital in Sydney, I found I was not enjoying my training. I didn't know why until halfway through when a couple presented to the labour ward (now called the delivery suite) and the woman appeared to be in strong labour. She was a petite woman with a very large partner to whom she was clinging. The midwife in charge of the labour ward, a pint-sized dragon who terrified all who came in contact with her, was furious that this dad had presumed that he could enter the hallowed space reserved for 'women only'. It was 1972 and dads were slowly being allowed to 'attend' the birth of their baby, *but* they needed written permission from their wife's obstetrician to be present. As this midwife glared and frothed at the mouth, the partner quickly reached into his pocket and presented the crumpled permission letter to her. Throughout this exchange, the woman was clinging onto her partner, roaring with the power of her contractions.

I was a mere student, hovering and waiting for my instructions as to what to do with this couple. I was equally terrified by the midwife's manner and felt sure she may well explode with anger! She eyeballed the dad, unfolded the letter and ripped it up without taking her eyes off him. 'You now no longer have permission to be in my labour ward,' said the dragon, and sent him scurrying to the smoke-filled father's room (yes, there were smoking rooms in hospitals in 1972! Hard to believe today). I was horrified. The woman was horrified and very, very upset. The dad was totally intimidated. The woman's labour stopped. They tried a medical induction, but there were no more contractions. She was wheeled off for an emergency caesarean section due to 'failure to progress'.

It wasn't until this happened that I realised there was something drastically wrong with the system. Surely we should not be treating women in this way. It was the system I didn't like, not midwifery.

Following my training, I moved to a very small country hospital in western New South Wales. It was there that I fell in love with midwifery. These country women showed me that you didn't need to interfere with labour and birth; labouring women just wanted a room, privacy and to feel safe. They showed me how simple birth could be. It took me a long time to understand the power of keeping my hands off birth, to learn to trust the women and their birthing bodies. This was where I did my true learning about birth.

The words spoken

The words that are spoken to a woman during pregnancy and particularly during labour and birth can also interfere with the free flow of hormones. Joanne, at 37 weeks, met a new midwife at her midwives' clinic appointment. She told the midwife that she had done HypnoBirthing® classes and was practising her breathing and relaxation and that this is what she would be using during labour and birth. Joanne was excited to be sharing this vital piece of information. The midwife responded, 'That will be interesting as I've never seen it work — you just wait and see!' The arrogance in those words is almost beyond belief. Joanne's doula had to reassure her that she was on the right track and was indeed moving towards a beautiful birth.

Doulas spend a lot of their time undoing the fallout from the harsh and damaging words that are spoken by some health professionals. This is the best day of a woman's life; it is her baby's birth day and a time for celebration, not a time for distress.

Sally, resting quietly in the bath during her very peaceful labour, was shocked when there was a shift change and the new midwife came in, sat on the edge of the bath and announced that she needed to know exactly where Sally was at in her labour, so on a scale of 1–10 could she please rank her pain level! This occurred when her doula was out of the room having a very quick toilet break. Thankfully, the doula was able to help Sally disregard this comment and encourage her to continue in her relaxed state. The doula was then able to show Sally's birth plan to the midwife and explain what Sally wanted.

Simon said during a prenatal class that he and his partner were looking forward to having a water birth. They were booked into a private hospital and had a private obstetrician. This particular hospital had a caesarean section rate of 54 per cent (WHO recommends no more than 15 per cent) and an epidural rate of 89 per cent! During their tour of the hospital and inspection of the room, Simon had commented that they loved the big bath, and the obstetrician had told them that a water birth was a 'great thing'. He failed to tell them, however, that the hospital did not 'allow' water births, they did not have a water birth policy and that he had never attended a water birth. Surely the responsible path for the obstetrician would have been to steer this couple in the direction of a birth centre where there were midwives specialising in water births. With an epidural rate that high, there was not much room in that hospital for normal births, let alone in the water! This couple was shocked to hear that they could not have a water birth. After checking the facts during the week, they came back to class in a state of disbelief. They felt cheated.

Simon's partner was already 36 weeks pregnant and it was too late to change carogivers, so they employed a doula who helped them re-think their birth plan and focus on having a normal birth. At least they had time to prepare. If Simon's partner had gone into hospital in labour imagining a beautiful water birth, only to be told on the day that this was not possible, this would certainly have released lots of catecholamines — those stress hormones — which you really don't want during labour.

Following is an amazing story of trust and belief. Alicia and I met when I was introducing the screening of the documentary, The Business of Being Born. I hope her story encourages you to ask questions and to continue seeking until you find the right caregiver and support for you. Always listen to what is inside you, what is in your mind, and surround yourself with people who share that belief. It is so easy during pregnancy to be 'persuaded' to take a different route from what you were hoping for. Women can be presented with very compelling arguments to do so, none more convincing than 'this is the safest way for your baby'.

Thank you again so much for reassuring me two years ago that I could achieve a VBAC [vaginal birth after caesarean]. I'm positive that without your encouraging words I never would have fought for what was rightfully mine! I'd like to share my birth story with you.

Learning to trust ... Sage's birth story began in June 2005 when I had my first ectopic pregnancy. I was distraught to have lost my first baby, and even more so when only three months later I lost my second baby to a corneal ectopic pregnancy, which ruptured and damaged the top left-hand side of my uterus.

When I fell pregnant with Jedd I was absolutely overjoyed that he was in the right place! However, this joy was short lived and I was shattered to be told by my obstetrician that both my baby and I could die if I went ahead with a natural birth — that a caesarean was my only option. Because of the ectopic pregnancies, I had already lost faith in my body's ability to function 'normally', so I accepted the caesarean.

Jedd was born safely into the world in May 2007, but I constantly questioned the necessity for his unnatural birth. Sure, he was healthy and alive — that's all a mother can ask for, right? No. there was something missing — something very important.

I then stumbled across the film, *Business of Being Born,* and my hopes and dreams of having a natural water birth came flooding back. I began doing some long overdue research into the realities of having a normal birth post corneal ectopic, and was surprised to find that there was no medical research indicating that it was unsafe. Why, then, did my obstetrician encourage me to have a caesarean for Jedd?

I had heard about VBACs, and when we discovered that I was pregnant I decided that I would try again for the natural birth that I longed for. Knowing full well that my best chance of having a successful VBAC was to stay at home, I began searching for a midwife. Once I met Betty I knew that I had found the midwife for me, and we began meeting regularly for checkups. It was so lovely to be able to stay at home for her visits — I could plan the visits around Jedd's nap times, and he could get to know her a bit better as well. The thought of taking a young toddler into a hospital for antenatal visits made my blood pressure rise!

At about 36 weeks, I decided to hire Michelle to be my doula — and what an awesome decision that turned out to be! Michelle felt like a guardian over my birth space in the last few weeks of pregnancy, and through the long hours of birth dancing. She had so much time for me — something I will always cherish.

Despite preparing myself for a 42–43 week pregnancy, I secretly hoped that my baby would make her debut soon. I had three acupuncture sessions over a week and by the end of the last treatment my instincts told me that I would be meeting my baby very shortly.

The birth ... Grant and I were enjoying some quiet time together on Friday night when I first realised that I was having surges. It was about 9 pm. I thought that it would be wise to head to bed, so at 10 pm I dragged Grant and myself to bed so we could get some sleep before things heated up. I slept for two hours with a heat pack strapped to my back. Grant heated it for me again at midnight and I slept for another two hours. At 2 am I could no longer sleep through the surges and decided to get out of bed and begin preparing to meet my baby.

I sat, I stood, I swayed, I walked and I waddled for the next few hours. As the surges came, I envisioned them as waves. I would watch the waves roll into the shore, stand in the cold sea water momentarily and then feel the water recede from my feet as the wave rolled back out to sea. This visualisation calmed me immensely, and made the surges easier to breathe through as I could pinpoint the moment when the cold water would reach my feet and make me quickly catch my breath.

Michelle arrived in the midst of my breathing and settled herself in the lounge. As Michelle continued to assure me that I was progressing beautifully, I found her presence calming and soothing. She and Grant tag-teamed with my neighbour in babysitting Jedd, and they continually kept Betty, my midwife, and Mum up to date throughout the birth. They did such a great job that I was oblivious to most of what was happening around me as I was able to focus on bringing my daughter earthside. Grant's encouragement through the whole birth was incredible, continually offering me food and drinks to keep up my energy.

As my lower back began to ache, and the surges became stronger, longer and closer together, Grant began to fill the birth pool for me. Once I lowered my body into the warm water I felt instant relief and was able to relax into the surges once again. Michelle gave me a pillow to rest on and to lean over on the edge of the birth pool, which helped me balance comfortably.

Tiredness began to take its toll, so Michelle suggested that I rest in bed for a while. Off I trundled and, surprisingly, I was able to get about an hour of sleep, waking periodically to rock my body gently through the surges, then napping again until the next one arrived. When I woke up I had a shower to refresh and re-energise myself and the surges returned, but now with more regularity and much more intensity.

I began to baby dance my way around the lounge room once again, staying upright and rocking my body with the surges. I moved regularly between the birth pool and the lounge, swinging and swaying all the while. Soon after, I began to feel the urge to push. By early afternoon Betty arrived and confirmed that I was 8 cm dilated. Bells of excitement rang silently as I glowed in the achievement of my progress so far. We were almost there! Well, we thought I was almost there … turned out I still had quite a few hours of work ahead of me.

As the urge to push became stronger, I listened to my body and went with the flow. After pushing for an hour with no result, Betty checked bub and found that she was posterior. No wonder all this pushing was taking so long!

I didn't feel disturbed or upset about bub being posterior. I knew that I still had the ability to birth her naturally, but there were definitely moments of sheer exhaustion when I felt ready to give up and let someone else take over. However, my pride, determination and sheer stubbornness, and the knowledge that I was so close to meeting my baby, drove me to push even harder. The surges continued coming regularly, and Sage's heart rate remained constant and steady. I stayed active in between surges, but found myself bearing down on all fours against the lounge when the urge to push came.

After four hours of pushing, Betty suggested that lying down would help bub to manoeuvre her way through my pelvis, given her posterior position. It worked! As she began to crown, I reached down and felt her soft head covered in hair and was inspired immediately — I knew I could do this!

One and a half hours later, I finally birthed Sage. Grant reached down and received his daughter and lifted her onto my chest. Love instantly swept over me as I held my baby. The pride in achieving the 'impossible' empowered me. Sage opened her eyes and gazed up at me with such intensity. I introduced myself to her as her Mummy, and within 20 minutes Sage instinctively found her way to the breast and attached perfectly.

Trust restored ... I now realise that THIS is what birth is all about. Women trusting their bodies to do what they're designed to do. Babies being born when they're ready, and being allowed to bond with their mother straightaway rather than being whisked off to cold sterile rooms to be poked and prodded. I feel sad that Jedd missed out on so much — but I thank him every day for enlightening me that his sister might be born the way that nature had intended. Sage is so alert and so content. I attribute her peaceful nature to her peaceful birth.

Thank you to all those who encouraged me to fight for the birth that all babies deserve. Thanks to Betty, my midwife, for believing that I had the ability to do what other 'health professionals' claimed to be impossible. Thanks to Michelle, my doula, for guarding my space and helping me keep positive in the last few weeks of pregnancy. And most of all, thanks to my husband, Grant, for his tireless and unconditional love, trust and patience. Without his support and encouragement, a homebirth would never have been possible.

If only we could get the message across to everyone involved in birthing — midwives, partners, doulas, family, obstetricians, anaesthetists — about the power of language, and what a difference the right words make.

I recently supported a woman who was attending a private obstetrician and was booked into a small private hospital. Debbie had had her first baby at this hospital and had not been happy with their care. She told me that a midwife had told her to 'shut up' during labour because she was making too much noise! The midwife also insisted on continuous monitoring. This, of course, meant that she had to be in bed, which she found very uncomfortable. She also had a number of vaginal examinations which, for her, were very painful. She did not want any of this for her second birth.

Despite this experience, Debbie booked the same private obstetrician and the same private hospital for her second birth, the one difference being that she engaged an experienced doula for this birth.

Debbie's labour began around 3 am and she arrived at hospital at about 5.30 am. I arrived about 6 am to find her having a CTG (which records the baby's heartbeat and the mother's contractions). Debbie had requested to get off the bed, as it was too uncomfortable, and was sitting on a fit ball. She was still uncomfortable. Given that baby was fine and this was an unnecessary intervention that Debbie did not want, we were able to persuade the midwife to detach the CTG so that she could get up and move around, which is what Debbie wanted to do. This very young, newly graduated midwife suggested a vaginal examination as she did not think Debbie was in labour and perhaps might like to go home. Debbie's birth plan had a very clear request for NO vaginal examinations unless medically necessary or at her request. It was also devastating for her to be told she was not in labour and should seriously think about going home. This was Debbie's second labour, she felt she was in labour and definitely did not want to go home. Following this discussion, her labour slowed considerably. The power of words!

Debbie continued to labour slowly throughout the day. We walked around the block a few times; she tried a bath, a shower, leaning over a bean bag. The hospital midwife again told Debbie that there was not much progress and she should consider going home. This was her assessment following some brief appearances during the day to take Debbie's blood pressure and listen to baby's heart rate — not from a vaginal examination. Debbie's labour slowed even further. Her contractions became erratic and she described them as being 'very mild'. Debbie was upset because she felt she was in good labour when she arrived early in the morning.

For labour and birthing to flow smoothly, quietly and peacefully, which allows that wonderful cocktail of hormones to release, women need to be in an environment that is dimly lit, with no unnecessary interruptions, and to feel safe and well supported.

Debbie's obstetrician, whom she liked and trusted, was on holiday. She did not like the relieving obstetrician and had already had a few altercations with him during both her pregnancies. In fact, he had booked her in for a caesarean section due to a low-lying placenta (noted at the 20-week ultrasound). This is very common, and women should be reassured that most placentas move in time. When Debbie's obstetrician returned from holiday, she cancelled the caesarean. Debbie had been very distressed about this.

It was now mid-afternoon and Debbie's contractions were still mild and erratic. The relieving obstetrician sent a phone message via the midwife that he wanted Debbie to have a canula (drip) and intravenous antibiotics for streptococcus B in place by the time he arrived. He was revoking a specific order on her antenatal card from her own obstetrician which read 'no antibiotics in labour'. She had been streptococcus B positive with her first pregnancy, but negative with this pregnancy, and they had both agreed, after lengthy discussion, that

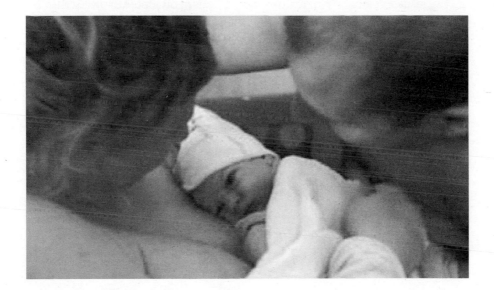

there was no need for antibiotics in this labour. Debbie was very upset and wanted to discuss this with me and her partner. The midwife came back, having spoken to the relieving obstetrician again, and her tone had changed. She announced that he was very, very angry with Debbie and demanded that the antibiotics be commenced. Debbie was now in tears, and her labour had stopped. It took a long time and a lot of reassurance and persuasion from her support team for labour to get going again. A message was sent to the obstetrician, stating that Debbie and her partner did not want antibiotics.

At 8 pm Debbie decided, after much discussion with her partner and me, that she would have a vaginal examination. She was very tired and still had the 'obstetrician's anger' in her head. She was 6 cm dilated, with a bag of forewaters presenting. The midwife asked Debbie if she would like her to break the waters, explaining that it might 'speed up the labour'. Debbie decided this would be a good idea. Following this examination, Debbie got off the bed and, as she stood, leaning over the bed, began to have strong contractions one after another. One hour later she had her baby in her arms. This was a very intense time for Debbie, and for her baby, as she went from 6 cm to a baby in one hour! She also had a large perineal tear, due to the intensity of the contractions, and a feeling of no control.

Debbie had a beautiful baby boy, weighing 2.9 kg. The obstetrician did not make it to the hospital. Debbie birthed and received her own baby with the help of the midwife.

Debbie found the whole experience intense, frustrating, and not what she had hoped for. She wanted to labour in water, with no intervention, and to birth calmly.

This story shows that, if you have not been happy with your first birthing experience, you need to make some changes. First, you need to change your caregiver. In this case, the two obstetricians, who were partners, clearly did not respect each other's expertise, so it would have been better for Debbie to seek out a continuity model of care for her second pregnancy. Second, you need to change the place where you are going to birth. Use the knowledge gained from your first birth to understand what you don't want and shop around until you find the right place for you and the right person to support you in what you do want — someone who understands *normal* birthing and respects birthing women. This is what Celia did.

Preparing for the birth of my first child, I researched my options and decided that I would like a natural birth for my baby. I booked into a birth centre that had a team midwifery program and was allocated a midwife I liked and trusted. My husband was completely supportive of my choices and I was actually looking forward to going through labour with him by my side. I considered finding a doula, but thought, 'We're a great team; we'll be fine!'

As it turned out, I had a long and intense pre-labour in which I became more and more anxious. While we were given lots of advice and support by the birth centre, my husband and I felt quite alone and uncertain of what was to happen, and disappointed that things weren't progressing more smoothly. I was finally admitted to hospital for an induction. I requested an epidural, but although it took the pain of the contractions away, I still felt uncomfortable, immobile, sad and frustrated. Even though the care I received at every stage was good, even great, I felt quite powerless and very much in the hands of the hospital and its practices. I was intensely relieved and happy when I gave birth to a beautiful, healthy baby boy some hours later, but I felt that after a wonderful pregnancy the labour had been a horrible one. When I became pregnant again a few years later I wanted to arm myself as much as possible against things going awry. One of the first things I did was to research doulas and engaged Susan to help us during the labour and birth. One of the reasons I chose Susan was because of her depth of experience. I wanted someone beside us who could help us when we were blurry with fatigue and pain: I now knew what a vulnerable time labour could be. We met a number of times over the next few months, and I knew that I absolutely trusted Susan to help us on the day. I felt tremendously reassured by her strength of character and intelligence.

I was not wrong.

My contractions started at night and only became very intense as morning approached, when we rang Susan. She was a calm and reassuring presence both over the phone and when she arrived at our house, and later when we went into the birth centre. I was so glad that she was there with us. I felt like she gave my husband and me the space to have a calm and peaceful labour. It was as if she cleared the way for us to go through the experience uninterrupted.

This labour was not uneventful. After a few hours of good progression, things slowed right down. Susan encouraged me into different positions: she guessed that the baby was in a posterior position, but wisely did not mention this to me in case I became discouraged. Things eventually got going again and shortly afterwards I gave birth to a beautiful baby girl. It was an unforgettable moment.

I was in the bath and reached down for the baby and delivered her myself, pulling her up onto my chest.

I can't imagine that we could have had such a wonderful experience of labour without Susan at our side, encouraging, supporting and protecting us. As our doula, she cleared the space for us to have a quiet, calm and peaceful birth. It is one of the most treasured moments of my life.

CELIA

Tahnee, a doula, says:

There is no moment more human, more intense or more beautiful than the moment of birth. Just being present at such a miraculous time is a privilege beyond all others. No doctor, obstetrician, doula or anyone else can ever tell a woman how her birth will unfold. No matter how educated they are. That story can only be told by the birthing woman and her child. It's their story to tell and theirs alone. Give a woman the power to make choices and she will always choose the right path.

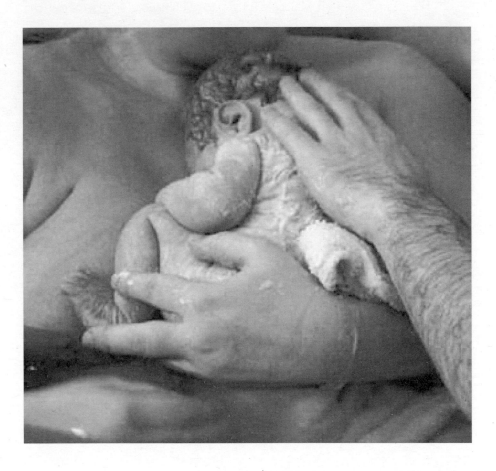

CHAPTER 5

The role of the doula in your labour and birth

Birth is the most powerful experience in a woman's life — miraculous, full of love and extraordinary insight. You need to go into labour feeling confident in the knowledge you have gained and the support you have chosen. I remember during my first pregnancy having an extraordinary sense of curiosity about what labour and birthing would feel like. I very much wanted to have that experience. I wanted to be in awe of what my body could do; I wanted that challenge. The challenge of both of my births did not disappoint; in fact, both went far beyond anything I could have scripted. Birthing took me to another place — a very pure and beautiful place — where I connected with my baby and my body and felt my womanly power take over my whole being. My sons are now young men, but I will never forget their amazing start in life and what this also taught me.

Birthing and becoming a mother changed me emotionally, psychologically and spiritually. And I have observed this extraordinary growth in other women, too, as they begin to understand who they really are. Watching them flourish through pregnancy and birth and becoming a mother has been such a privilege.

Since giving birth to my first child I can now comprehend the power and love that is created in becoming a mother. The birth of Isaac was the most exhilarating, primal and powerful experience in my life as a woman. I invested time in preparing for a natural birth, but it was the unwavering love, care and support from my doula, Melanie, that ensured my birth plan and dreams were realised. As much as I tried with every ounce of my soul to stay in tune with my body and flow with the process, there were moments when I would let my mind run wild and question whether or not I could have a natural birth. During those times Melanie was so gentle, yet strong, in helping me know that I was capable, that I could trust the process, and in providing constant encouragement. I know that she did not leave my side for a single moment of the birth. Melanie was the reason I didn't fear the pain of the contractions or lose my focus, and she helped me believe that surrender would bring my baby to birth. I thank her for showing me the way to make informed decisions about the birth of my baby.

LOUISE

Having doula support gives couples the confidence to stay at home for a good part of the woman's labour and avoid early transfer to hospital. This has many advantages. A woman who feels well supported by her doula in her own home is much more likely to relax into birthing, which in turn will cause the cervix to thin and open more easily and more quickly. A dad is also going to feel more confident about staying at home with the support of a doula. Even the best educated dad will find labour confronting, particularly the first time. He will never have seen this before and, with absolute respect, a dad in this situation is not going to know the best time to head for the hospital. In my experience, most men want to get their partner to hospital as soon as possible! As Luke said, 'Hayley and I did not have a doula for our first birth. The difference for me, second time around, was that, having Erika as our doula, I felt safe and confident. I also felt respected. Erika listened to my views and took them seriously. I also felt that I did not have to use my 'macho brain' to come up with suggestions. I was guided by Erika about what to do and say. We were all on the same page. During normal living, Hayley and I complement each other and rely on each other's thinking. During labour Hayley lost this capacity and it was very reassuring to have Erika's clarity!'

The problem with arriving at the hospital too early in labour is that the labouring woman will be immediately plugged into the policies, procedures and time frames of the hospital. Often, she will be experiencing anxiety and fear about going from home to hospital, and will be thinking about which room she will get, which midwife, what will happen, how far dilated she is, and so on. If labour hasn't really established, then these added stresses can cause it to slow or even shut down. Then the hospital may feel compelled to intervene, in an attempt to 'rescue' mother and baby. In this situation a doula is able to negotiate her return to her own home. If baby is OK and Mum is

OK, then a good response is 'We are happy to wait, thank you'.

During the early stages of labour, a woman who has engaged the services of a doula can phone her, or even organise a home visit for reassurance, so that she doesn't need to go to the hospital too early.

Julia, who was 41 weeks pregnant and had experienced several days of pre-labour said: 'Having Jan, our doula, who lived 10 minutes away, was a blessing. I felt I could ring her as often as I needed to — and I did — during those days of not being sure what was happening. She came over and sat with me on three separate occasions during that time. She did a visualisation and relaxation with me at each visit. After she left I felt totally relaxed and reassured. I could not have got through those few days of pre-labour without her support. When labour did start, it was short and intense and Jan's strong belief in me just shone through. I felt totally safe as she gently guided me through the scripts that we had learned in the HypnoBirthing® classes.'

'Transferring to the hospital was awful as I felt like my baby was about to be born in the car. Jan's quiet, calm presence was amazing as she reassured both Rob and me that we would make it to the hospital in time. Our beautiful baby was born in the water 40 minutes after our arrival. Jan never left our side. She rang ahead and asked the midwife to fill the bath so it was ready for us, as Jan knew I wanted a water birth. She was able to stay with me while Rob quickly parked the car and brought the bags in. I was so grateful to have her with me as I would have hated to be left alone while Rob sorted the car. Even though that was probably only a few minutes, it seemed like forever. Rob says if it had not been for Jan he would have had me in the hospital about four days before the birth! He took his lead from Jan, and the more relaxed she was, the more reassured he felt. Neither of us could imagine having done this without a doula. No matter how many more babies we have, we agree that we will employ a doula, hopefully Jan, for each pregnancy.'

'Thank you. Your calming presence ensured a gentle birth for me and my baby, and I can't thank you enough.'

THE BIRTH PLAN

Are birth plans important? Most definitely! Many books and websites provide templates, with designed questions, and you just need to tick the boxes. Every labour and birth is different. So every birth plan is unique. They need to be intelligent and succinct, with language that health professionals respect.

Think about what you particularly want, think about how you want it and what your facility can provide. This is your space, no matter where you are birthing, that you are hiring for the duration of your labour and birth. You have chosen this facility, maybe, because they provide 'other' services that you may also be interested in using. A birth plan can open up dialogue with your potential caregivers and allow insight into their philosophy and willingness to be flexible and supportive.

A birth plan should not be worded as a risk-averse document. The 'I don't want this' and 'I don't want that' is fear based. The term 'birth plan' is not a true representation of what women are trying to convey, because birthing doesn't generally go to plan. Stephanie, at 36 weeks, proudly showed me her birth plan. I was to support her birth, along with her sister and partner. We each had a plan of about three to four pages, including numbered lists.

Stephanie had put a lot of thought and effort into these plans and so, with this in mind, I gently tried to persuade her to soften her approach and to reword them in a more general way. Her sister had the title of Environment Control Manager for Labour — this apparently included controlling the temperature in the birthing suite (not an option in a public hospital), lighting, candles, blinds — up or down depending on what stage she was at — and even controlling the 'tone' of the voices of those who would be present. Stephanie was a strategist in her professional life and, while we all laughed and joked about her lists, it was difficult for her to change. Of course, as labour is renowned for its unpredictability, we arrived at the hospital with baby's head crowning. Stephanie managed to waddle from the car onto a mat on the floor of the birth centre and immediately birthed her baby. She was both shocked and devastated that not only were the lists and plans not given a chance to be implemented, but they, along with all her bags, were still in the car, which her sister quickly parked after dropping us at the front door. Baby was born while the sister was parking the car.

Very many birth plans are written out of anxiety or lack of trust in the people who will be in attendance. This is why it is important for them to be worded in a way that shows respect for the facility you have chosen, respect for you, the birthing woman, and respect for your baby. They cannot be standardised. For example, many couples want particular religious or cultural rituals during the labour and birth, which should be noted and respected. It is not fair on your partner to rely on him to remember all your wishes. Birth plans are very useful for both doulas and partners as a prompt, if necessary, about what you want.

Letter form is generally a softer way of making your preferences known. The majority of women in labour will be looked after by a midwife whom they don't know. Even when birthing at a birth centre, you may only have met the midwife once or twice during your pregnancy. On the day is not the time to have a discussion about what is important for you and your baby. I suggest making some notes during your pregnancy and what your preferences are will become clearer following completion of your prenatal classes. Your doula will help you to word this very important document. There is no point in writing a lot about your desire to be free to move around and have access to water, as that is a given in most facilities. If your facility has a 'routine practice' that you want to avoid, this should be noted on your birth plan. For example, some hospitals routinely give an injection of Vitamin K to babies within the first hour of birth. However, you may prefer your baby to have it orally in three doses, one at birth, one on day 4 and one at four weeks. Or you may prefer that your baby not have Vitamin K at all. It is wise to research the information available on this vitamin, which will also be discussed in your prenatal classes, and your doula can provide additional information/research, so that you and your partner can make a decision, on behalf of your baby, before you give birth and state this on your birth plan. The fewer decisions you need to discuss and make on the day, the better. A woman needs to go into labour feeling fully prepared and not be distracted by unnecessary questions that could have been answered previously.

So find out what the rules and regulations are in your particular place of birth and then discuss with your doula how to work with them so that you can have the birthing experience you want.

Below I have shared a couple of birth plans as examples only. The power of your words can have a big impact on the midwife who will read your birth plan when you arrive at the hospital in labour. It will be much easier for her if she knows exactly your feelings.

Examples of birth plans

Dear Midwife

I will be using HypnoBirthing® to guide me through the birth process. I will be accompanied by my husband, Rick, and our doula, Susan. Provided it is safe for the baby and me, we would be most grateful if you could observe the following preferences:

» *Because I am HypnoBirthing®, I do not want to be disturbed. Should there be any issue you wish to discuss, then please do so with Susan and Rick.*

» *Please avoid references to pain, and please do not offer me pain relief medication directly.*

» *I would prefer not to have vaginal examinations.*

» *I would appreciate being able to birth without directed pushing, and with no-one's hands touching the baby at any stage except mine and Rick's.*

» *I would like my husband to receive the baby, and I would like to allow the baby to find the breast in his own time.*

» *I would prefer a physiological third stage of labour, no Syntocinon and no cord traction.*

» *I would prefer to wait until the umbilical cord has stopped pulsing, before it is cut, and I would like my husband Rick to cut the cord.*

» *We would like to take the placenta home.*

» *I would prefer the baby to have Vitamin K drops (oral).*

We appreciate your cooperation.

Anna and Rick

Anna and Rick had exactly the birth they wanted, with all of the above being taken into account.

I'm going to labour beautifully. My baby and I will work together to bring him into the world safely and peacefully. He will come out when he's ready.

Assuming it is safe for me and my baby I would like:

- » *a completely natural birth*
- » *no drugs for pain relief*
- » *to labour without time pressure*
- » *intermittent foetal monitoring only*
- » *minimal internal examinations and no tracking of dilation*
- » *not to get on the bed*
- » *to tear naturally rather than have an episiotomy*
- » *a physiological 3rd stage*
- » *the cord to stop pulsating before it is cut by Jason*
- » *my baby put on my chest as soon as he is born*
- » *private time to discuss with Jason and our doula if medical intervention is proposed as necessary for the safety of me and my baby.*

Lynette

This couple had a private obstetrician and was booked into a private hospital. The 'rules' were different and Lana was very aware that their 'routine practice' was continuous foetal monitoring, on arrival, for about 20 minutes, which means lying flat on your back on the bed. This is obviously a very uncomfortable position for a labouring woman and an unnecessary intervention in a normal birth. Lana had strong feelings about this, which is why she needed to make it known on her birth plan. Her doula was able to negotiate on her behalf to avoid this.

A doula will make sure that the midwife is actually given the birth plan to read and understands exactly what the couple would like. If there is a shift change and a new midwife takes over during the labour, then the doula would also make sure that she understood the birth plan.

'As long as it is safe for me and my baby' is the bottom line in all births, and these or similar words are a nice way of introducing your wishes. It is about working with the staff, the facility, and all its rules and regulations in a respectful way for all.

Those women who trust birth and have a doula at their side don't feel the need to elaborate on all the 'what ifs?' This is covered in the words: 'as long as it is safe for me and my baby'. A doula will always reassure a couple that in the rare event that medical intervention is required she will make sure that they have time to discuss options and the parts of the birth plan that are practical and possible to maintain, given the circumstances.

Health-care professionals are duty bound to abide by many rules and regulations and to follow hospital policies and protocols, and therefore the major part of their focus must be on the procedures and inevitable time frames surrounding birthing. A doula is accountable only to the birthing woman/couple. She is free to be their advocate and will work in their best interests, always, as long as it is safe for mother and baby.

It is fun to start making a list early in your pregnancy of what you might like for you and your baby during your labour and birth and to watch over the weeks as you change, move and grow your plan as you gain new knowledge about labour and birthing.

THE BIRTHING ENVIRONMENT

Hopefully every couple has had the opportunity to view their place of birth prior to arriving in labour. This is an essential part of shopping around and ideally should be done very early in pregnancy to help make the best decision for you and your baby. Having an image in your mind when you are at home in labour about where you are going and what it looks like can relieve some of the anxiety.

Most birth centres tend to look more home-like, as they have an ensuite and often a deep bath suitable for water births. Delivery suites certainly look more clinical, with medical equipment being much more obvious. Think about what you might like to take in to soften the environment and make it more like home.

For you to be able to release that magical cocktail of hormones discussed in Chapter 4, you need to feel safe, warm, comfortable and well supported. To achieve this you need to be in a room with soft or minimal lighting, and a quiet and peaceful energy. Dr Michel Odent, the obstetrician who introduced the concepts of birthing pools and home-like birthing rooms, and the author of many books on this subject, says in *The Scientification of Love* (1999, p. 30) the most active parts of the labouring woman's brain are the ancient parts, such as the hypothalamus and pituitary glands. Inhibitions during labour originate in the highly developed part of the brain, the neocortex:

During the birth process there is a period when the mother behaves as if she were 'on another planet', cutting herself off from our everyday world and going on a sort of inner trip. This change in her level of consciousness can be interpreted as a reduction in the activity of the brain of the intellect, that is, the neocortex.

Odent also says (p. 31) that being observed is a type of neocortical stimulation and privacy reduces neocortical control.

Doulas who understand this physiology of birthing know that any neocortical stimulation in general, and any stimulation of the intellect in particular, can have a huge impact on the progress of labour.

What can stimulate the neocortex? Language — in particular, rational language. Imagine a woman who is labouring beautifully on her 'own planet' having to answer questions about her address or phone number. Bright lights also stimulate the neocortex.

Releasing any hormones from the adrenaline family can also stimulate the neocortex. This is why it is so important for a woman to feel safe and secure. This feeling of safety needs to be present for that changed level of consciousness to occur. Throughout the ages and in many cultures women have historically made sure that they felt safe by having a woman present — either their own mother or a mother substitute. Today, more and more women are learning that this is the role of the doula, mothering the mother, who has the added bonus of being well trained and knowledgeable about the hospital system. A woman who has the support of a doula feels secure, rather than observed and judged.

Now that we have set the scene, let's look at labour and birth and what happens.

LABOUR AND BIRTH

Birth is simple. Trusting in your amazing birthing body, believing absolutely in your ability to birth and looking forward to this amazing experience are what will empower you to have a peaceful birth. Think about meeting and welcoming your baby into this world. You have grown him for around 40 weeks, nurtured him, loved him, talked to him and developed a deep connection with him on the inside. Now it is time to meet on the outside.

But before you can do this, you need to pass through labour.

Time frames for labour

This is the bane of everyone — especially the labouring woman. It is understandable why hospitals have time frames for labour, mainly to do with bed capacity and litigation. Most hospitals actively discourage women from being in hospital too early in labour as they take up valuable beds for far too long. Once a woman has been admitted she is immediately plugged in to the hospital time frames. These are essentially that the first stage of labour should be around 8–14 hours, the second stage about 2 hours and the third stage 5–10 minutes.

So why are women today being subjected to this arbitrary and unnaturally short timeline when our ancestors were not?

Emily, concerned about these time frames, told her obstetrician that she would be accompanied by her doula. The obstetrician shrugged, 'That's OK, if you really think it's worth the money, but just make sure your doula remembers who is in charge'. Her doula reminded Emily that Emily was the only one in charge of her birthing. Emily said that was a turning point in her pregnancy. She felt hugely empowered.

HypnoBirthing® women are different. From my observations, these women generally have quite short first stages and longer second stages of labour.

To avoid feeling the pressure of such time constraints, it is advisable to try and avoid vaginal examinations while in labour. Unfortunately, some facilities and most private hospitals have a policy stating that a vaginal examination should be carried out on admission to determine where a woman is at in labour. When a woman who has been labouring for a long time at home arrives at the hospital and the ensuing vaginal examination reveals that the cervix is 'only' 2 cm dilated, generally an intervention will be recommended. While vaginal examinations have their place, doing one as 'routine' has no place.

Sometimes knowing the 'exact measurement' of dilation can affect the outcome of the labour. Some women become very disappointed and disempowered when they hear this news, and it can be a challenge for the doula to reassure them and get them back on track with their labour. If a woman does not know the exact measurement and just trusts her birthing body, then she can more easily proceed to birthing her baby in a relaxed state.

Emma's doula, Laura, knew that on arrival at hospital, the hospital would insist on a vaginal examination and continuous monitoring (which means being in bed, lying on the back) for at least 15–20 minutes. Emma did not want either of these. She had been at home, labouring beautifully for about four hours. She was HypnoBirthing® and therefore appeared very relaxed and calm. Emma was relying on Laura to keep the intervention at bay. When they arrived in the delivery suite room, the midwife was very busy, ushered them in and said she would return in about 10 minutes. Laura ran the bath, which Emma was looking forward to, and by the time the midwife came back, Emma was far too relaxed for anyone to get her out of the bath. She had a wonderful water birth about two hours later. The midwife was able to monitor the baby's heart rate intermittently while Emma relaxed in the bath, which was all that was required. The bath can provide a physical protection for a labouring woman against unwarranted and unwanted interventions.

Everyone wants labour to move forward at a reasonable rate so that neither Mum nor baby gets too tired, but the bottom line should be that if Mum and baby are OK, she should be left to labour and birth in her and her baby's own time.

Be aware also that not only do hospitals have time frames around labour but individual obstetricians also have their own timetables.

A midwife working in a private hospital relayed a disturbing tale of an obstetrician making it very clear to her that he had tickets for the opera that night and needed room to 'deliver' before 6 pm as he had to meet his wife. He told the labouring woman at 4 pm that he would give her another hour and if she hadn't progressed sufficiently by then, he would recommend a caesarean. This woman had been in labour for about 12 hours and was now 7 cm dilated, which I would consider very normal. Obviously, with this 'pressure', the woman's labour slowed and consequently she had a caesarean section at 5.15 pm. It was presented to her that both she and baby were very tired, and that as there had been no progress over the last hour the obstetrician could save both mother and baby from this situation by performing a quick caesarean. If this woman had had a doula, the doula would have been able to successfully negotiate more time as it appears there was no legitimate reason for the caesarean. A doula also ensures unspoken accountability by other caregivers.

This is such a common story and should not be happening to women in hospitals today.

Tina had experienced a few days of pre-labour and had decided to go to hospital once she felt labour had established. The midwife told her she was not in labour and needed to go home. Tina requested a vaginal examination — she was 2 cm dilated, so she decided, after discussion with her doula, to go home. It was 5 pm. Her doula, Jo, reassured her that she was in labour and doing a beautiful job. They each went their separate ways, Jo advising Tina to go home and continue doing what she had been doing all day, resting, eating and drinking lots of liquid.

The phone call to Jo came at 11 pm. Tina wanted to meet at the hospital, so Jo ran the bath on arrival at the hospital and Tina relaxed in the deep, warm water. She was HypnoBirthing®. Her slow, deep breathing was keeping her very calm and peaceful. She looked beautiful as she lay in the bath. Tina had some pressure around her bottom (often a good sign that baby is close), but no real sensation to breathe her baby down. Given the hospital time frame for the second stage of labour (generally around two hours), Jo did not want to make a big announcement about this shift. Also, as mentioned above, HypnoBirthing® women tend to have longer second stages, which many hospitals find distressing.

When the midwife reappeared, she told Tina she would never get her baby out if she just nudged it, that she needed to push really hard to birth her baby. Jo took the midwife aside and pointed out what Tina had written on her birth plan, which was no directed pushing and no negative comments. Jo asked the midwife if she was concerned at all about Mum's or baby's condition. No, came the reply. Tina, overhearing this, piped up, 'Then we are happy to wait, thank you, and do it in our own time'. Baby did emerge four hours later, very calm, relaxed and alert — because both labour and birth had been gentle.

I believe we need to throw the time-frame rules out the window and embrace the concept of letting mother and baby birth at their own pace. Because such women are in tune with both their baby and their body and work with their baby to breathe and nudge him or her down the birth path slowly and gently, there is no need for directed pushing, or to push longer or harder, or for 'you can do it', 'hold your breath for much longer' or 'keep it coming', until you have a woman with haemorrhoids or a swollen perineum, and a baby who has been forced down the birth path. It is so unnatural. I have observed women, in the past, who have ruptured blood vessels in their eyes from being bullied into forced pushing. Women know how to birth their babies. Baby will come, when baby is ready.

Stages of labour

There is much written about the three stages of labour — what happens, how long it takes for the cervix to reach 10-cm dilation, how much pushing is needed, how exhausted you will be. I want you to think, instead, about the day you birth being a very special one. It is your baby's birth day. Finally, after 40 or so weeks of growing this new person, you are going to meet her, hold her, gaze into her eyes and fall in love, on the outside. THIS is really something to look forward to. It is a very exciting day.

The doula's role in this special day is to create an environment where the labouring and birthing process is respected and allowed to unfold in its own time and space. A doula is the protector of normal birth. A very important part of her role is therefore to act as advocate and negotiator on behalf of you, your partner and your baby, to ensure that this happens. So a doula is also a keeper of the peace.

The advantage of getting to know your doula very well during pregnancy is that you will have developed trust in her and will feel confident allowing her to negotiate on your behalf on suggestions made by other caregivers. Even though you may have clearly stated your wishes on issues such as medical intervention while you are in labour on your birth plan, it can be difficult to make a decision on something that is contrary to what has been said in your birth plan when you are labouring. We know that when a woman is in labour the primitive brain is the most active part of the brain, and when a woman is in tune with her birthing body and totally cut off from everyday happenings, she does not have recourse to the part of the brain that controls decision making. So the doula will privately discuss with the appropriate person the options presented and then put these suggestions in context for you and your partner in positive language, so that you can both make an informed decision on the path you would like to take. This is why research shows that having a doula present during labour and birth reduces the need for medical intervention (Kennell et al. 1991). The bottom line is always, of course, that mother and baby must be safe.

One other thing that is writ large in women's minds prior to labour is that four-letter word, PAIN! However, I have found that women who are relaxed and feel safe and supported during labour do not describe this experience as painful. There is no pathological reason for pain during labour. Pain is an indication that something is wrong.

Many HypnoBirthing® women imagine their uterus to be a beautiful big balloon, in their favourite colour, and during a surge they breathe deeply and slowly, as if blowing up a balloon. I have seen the magic of this working. The energy that surrounds a woman who is practising this is a sight to behold: so calm, so quiet, and so in tune with her birthing body and her baby. Such women would not describe the sensation as painful. The dictionary definition of pain is 'an unpleasant feeling caused by injury or disease of the body'; labour and birth are most definitely NOT in this category.

If you go into labour believing all the horror stories you have heard, and fearful that this will be the most excruciating pain in your entire life, then it will be. But if you have done your homework, shopped around for an appropriate caregiver and place to birth where you feel safe, received good education about labour and birth, and have a doula by your side, then it will be your most rewarding experience.

First stage of labour

What do you do? Stay at home as long as possible! There is no doubt that having a doula gives you the confidence to stay in the comfort of your own home during the early phases of labour. Even the most well-intentioned dad will insist on taking you to hospital, usually far too early. This is understandable. He has not seen this before and it is therefore confronting. No matter how many classes you have been to and books you have read together, when labour starts your partner will want to get you to the place where HE feels safe, i.e. the hospital.

Megan phoned her doula when she had a 'show' but no surges. She just wanted to check that all was OK. Megan was both nervous and excited. Her doula, Sarah, acknowledged her feelings and reassured Megan that all was normal and suggested she go about her usual day. The next morning Megan had more show and some irregular surges. She phoned Sarah. Following some phone support Megan felt confident to relax and wait. That night Megan phoned Sarah to let her know the surges were regular but she would like her to come over. Megan's partner, Rob, was still asleep — no point in everyone being sleep deprived! Megan says she relaxed as soon as Sarah arrived: 'I felt reassured and almost immediately my surges increased, became regular, and I felt myself going within my birthing body. We stayed at home for about six hours.

'Rob slept intermittently and was grateful that Sarah was there as he had had a really long day at work and was exhausted. We both recognised that for him to be energised at the birth, he needed to get some sleep. We decided to go into the birth centre just as the sun was rising. It was a beautiful morning. Sarah followed in her car. When we arrived at the birth centre Sarah brought the bags in while Rob parked the car. Once he was back Sarah went and parked her car. I was never left alone. By this stage I felt a lot of pressure, deep in my bottom, like a fullness. Sarah ran the bath as she knew I was hoping for a water birth. It was beautiful to just immerse myself in the deep, warm water. I knew I did not have to answer any questions or worry about anything other than birthing my baby. I was so excited about meeting my baby; I could feel him wriggling down, deep inside. I stroked my belly, talked to him and told him to hurry up as I wanted to see what he looked like. I felt like I was in a bubble. Nothing else mattered. Having our doula, Sarah, allowed me to be like this. To feel safe and well protected.

'I was unaware of her setting up the room the way she knew we had planned — turning the main lights off and just using some lamps we had brought, and getting my drinks organised. It had been suggested in class that we bring in a particular sports drink for energy. She mixed up the drink and made sure I drank after every surge. All I remember was the straw in my mouth and Sarah quietly telling me to drink. It felt good and necessary as I was quite hot in the bath. She made Rob a coffee and toast and constantly reassured him. Rob was able to set up the video and other cameras while Sarah was supporting me. I remember being surprised at how much needed to be attended to when we arrived at hospital and wondering how anyone did this without a doula. Sarah was also in charge of making sure the midwife read our birth plan before she filed it in our notes. It was such a relief for both of us not to have any of this responsibility. I could just do what I needed to do and

Rob felt totally relaxed and confident because we had Sarah with us constantly. She never left our side.

'Once Rob had the cameras set up, he was able to be close to me. Sarah did the drinks, Rob did the cold compresses on my forehead, together with quiet words of encouragement. I knew baby was coming; I could feel his head in my vagina. I didn't want any vaginal examinations and luckily the birth-centre midwife was so busy when we arrived that these were never offered. Sarah suggested that I could pop my fingers in to check as I needed to be convinced that this was what I was feeling. This was so empowering! Being able to actually touch my baby and feel the hardness of his little skull, I wanted more than ever to hold him in my arms. The midwife came in and really sat back, once she had checked the baby's heart rate and my blood pressure. She could see that we were a well-orchestrated team.

'I nudged my baby out as Sarah gently reminded me about allowing my perineum to stretch slowly. The sense of relief once baby's head was born is indescribable. The midwife had a mirror at the bottom of the bath and there was enough light on the mirror for me to see the little head — eyes wide open, amazingly alert. It seemed ages before the next surge and suddenly the rest of the body emerged, floating out into the warmth of the water. Sarah prompted Rob and me to pick our baby up and into our loving arms. We had a daughter! A very calm and alert little girl. 'Grace', because I birthed with grace and ease.

'Sarah was my rock. I felt she knew me on such an emotional level. I had told her stuff that I would never have told a midwife or an obstetrician. She knew about my innermost anxieties, which potentially could have got in the way of labour. I don't think they did, simply because we had talked them through at so many of our meetings. About an hour later I had another huge surge and realised it was the placenta. I could feel it sitting in my vagina but it wasn't coming out. Sarah suggested we empty the bath as I was also getting a bit cold. She put the birth stool in the empty bath, wrapped me in a warm blanket, and together with a bit of gravity out popped the placenta. Rob and I were fascinated and surprised by its size. We stayed in the birth centre for about four hours.

'Sarah made sure we were comfortable, understood what our options were about early discharge or going to the postnatal ward, made us both a cuppa, and left us to cuddle and fall in love with our baby. Her job was done. We are so very grateful for her wisdom and support. I am in no doubt that her presence guaranteed I had the birth experience I had planned.'

The cervix needs to dilate to 10 cm before you can birth your baby. This occurs during stage one and does take time. How long? As long as necessary. There is no doubt that if you are relaxed, feel safe in your environment and are looking forward to this experience, the time will be shorter — and enjoyable.

What is said to the labouring woman during this stage of dilation is, once again, very important. For example, think about the commonly used word 'contraction'. Alternative words for contraction given by the *Macquarie Thesaurus* are 'constriction' and 'spasm'. Can you imagine a woman looking forward to this experience? No. Because these words conjure up images of unbearable pain in the minds of those who choose to listen to all the horror stories surrounding birth. These words and all their negative connotations are firmly imprinted in your subconscious. So choose a word that you would

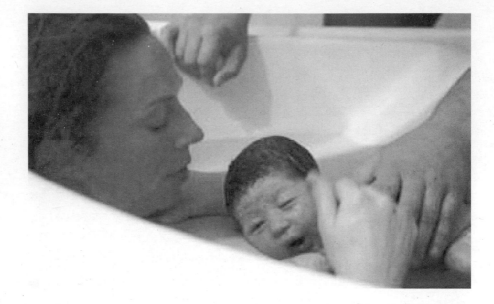

like to associate with your working muscle (the uterus) during labour. Some women focus on 'surges' or 'waves', perhaps a feeling of 'pressure'. These words are softer and invoke relaxation.

When it is time to go to hospital, ideally allow plenty of time to get there. You need to take into account not only the travelling time but also the last-minute things to pack, maybe a change of clothes, packing the car and you getting comfortable in the car. This is all attended to in between surges, so it can be time consuming. Arriving at the hospital involves unpacking the car, getting you from the car into the birthing room (in between surges) and then setting up the room so that it is a comfortable home-like environment. If you are fortunate enough to have the option of a water birth, the big bath needs to be filled, which can take at least 15 minutes. Your partner needs to find the best car park, as you don't know how long you will be there. The midwife needs to do some standard observations — your blood pressure and temperature, as well as listening to the baby's heart rate.

As discussed earlier in this chapter, most private hospitals and some other facilities as well insist on doing a vaginal examination when you are first admitted to hospital, and many hospitals do 'routine' vaginal examinations every four hours! The examination involves measuring the effacement (thinning of the cervix) and dilation of the cervix, which most women find 'uncomfortable'. In fact, the majority of women find vaginal examinations at any time very invasive, but particularly during labour.

One of the principal reasons that the vaginal examination is routinely undertaken is so that the midwife can phone the obstetrician, who is generally not present, to advise them of the cervical dilatation — mainly, so they can organise their day! However, this is very curious as the dilation measurement really does not give an accurate picture of what is happening in labour. If dilation is shown as 2 cm, in as little as one hour's time the woman may still be 2 cm or she may be 10 cm dilated.

As also mentioned earlier, knowing the amount of dilation puts a lot of pressure on the woman 'to perform', and may cause the hospital to suggest 'rescue methods' to 'speed up' labour. This says a lot about the hospital and its time frames, and a lot about not trusting labour to unfold at its own pace.

Cathy was determined that she did not want any vaginal examinations during labour. She felt very strongly about this, but understood that there were some situations where it was necessary. On arrival at hospital the midwife asked her to get on the bed so she could determine what stage she was in. A birthing woman is the best judge of where her labour is at. Cathy looked anxiously at her doula, Margie. Thankfully, the midwife left the room to attend to another woman and Margie quickly suggested that Cathy have a shower, while she filled the bath. When the midwife returned Margie told her that Cathy was in the shower and she would let her know when she was free. Despite the fact that the midwife was very busy, she kept coming into the room to see if Cathy was ready for the vaginal examination.

Cathy was now in the bath and Margie became aware that she was doing some gentle breathing down into her vagina with some of her surges. Cathy asked Margie if she should have the examination as the midwife seemed very anxious. Margie suggested that Cathy could feel for herself, by popping her fingers into her vagina, while she was in the bath. Cathy did this but was alarmed because she couldn't feel anything. She started to become anxious. Margie asked her what she could feel. 'Only something hard' was the reply. Margie smiled and pointed out that this was her baby's head! Cathy felt again and was overwhelmed with joy to realise that it was indeed her baby's head. When the midwife returned Cathy proudly announced that she could feel her baby's head and had started to feel him descend. She didn't need an examination by the midwife.

Some women do want to know the amount of dilation. A doula would always encourage the woman to think about how this information would change what they were already doing. She would also encourage the woman to trust her body and let birth unfold naturally, rather than getting caught up in vaginal examinations which could have a negative impact on her birthing.

There are times, however, when a vaginal examination is necessary:

» if a woman has very high blood pressure
» if a woman is an insulin-dependent diabetic
» if a woman has had a lot of pre (or practise) labour over several days and is very tired
» if a woman has been in labour for a very long time and is showing signs of exhaustion and dehydration
» if the baby's heart rate is showing signs of dipping (an indication that baby is not all that happy)
» if meconium (baby's first poo) is obvious in the waters
» if a woman is requesting drugs — a vaginal examination should always be done in this instance, as this is often an indication that she is very close to birthing her baby.

At 39 weeks my bags were packed, my birth plan was in hand and we were ready. However, during my weekly check-up the doctors found high bile readings in my blood. This meant that my baby had to be birthed because there was a chance of him being stillborn. We started to panic. We were not allowed to leave hospital after finding out the results of the test, as they wanted to start an induction. They explained what would happen during the induction and also the possible cascade of interventions. It was not looking good and we were not prepared for this, but all we were thinking about was having a healthy baby. I was sad that it was looking like I had to let go of a natural water birth at this stage. The induction began at 4 pm and I was wheeled into my room.

Beck, our doula, was great. She made us feel comfortable about what was happening and reassured us every step of the way. I was not progressing from the first dose of gel and not much was happening, so Beck went home, telling us to call if there were any changes. Tony and I settled in for the night. We ordered dinner and waited.

At midnight the midwife came in and gave me the second dose of gel and left. By 1 am I was doubled over with pain that was so intense. I wondered if induction should feel like this. There was absolutely no break in between the surges so I figured that this was part of being induced. Here we go!

At that stage I did not even think about hypno breathing. My body and mind went into shock. I stumbled through the night, confused and in pain and wanting relief. Tony called Beck in the morning in a panic as I was asking for an epidural. That's the point when Tony thought we were in trouble. On the phone Beck told us to get the hypno breathing going — she was on her way.

Tony reminded me about the breathing, so I started to breathe deeply and slowly. By the time Beck arrived I was in the zone, so we headed down to the birthing centre. We could not believe it; we were going to have a natural water birth because I was able to get my surges on track and everything was settling down into a rhythm. We ran a bath and I got in feeling great about my progress, even enjoying the surges as they came and went by focusing on my breathing. Shortly after settling into the bath, a midwife told us we needed to be in the delivery suite as I needed to have continuous monitoring due to the induction. I thought, 'Here's that intervention word again!'

Beck and Tony spoke to the doctors and bought us some valuable time so that I could advance into labour, which was great. I knew that my baby was doing well. As my labour advanced the doctors left us alone on the condition that they break my waters at midday. By this stage I was 7 cm dilated and in a meditative state. As my surges got stronger, my breathing got deeper.

As I was getting closer to meeting my baby, the midwives brought in a blow-up pool. Beck had made sure that we could still have parts of the birth we wanted. I had my baby in the pool that afternoon and it was wonderful seeing him floating calmly in the water, looking heavenly and relaxed. Our baby was born healthy and happy. The midwives, Beck and Tony worked so well together. It was the perfect combination. There were no rules placed on us, but instead there were guidelines that everyone followed at all times, respecting and nurturing our birth rights. Tony says that near the end he looked up and saw a group of women circled around me, waiting and watching this miracle unfold. It was perfect.

Birthing took all the energy, focus and determination I never thought I had. It was a real marathon. I felt so proud of everyone involved, especially my baby. We tell him his story all the time and he absolutely loves it. We will be doing hypno breathing and visualising for our next birth. And, of course, we will again want our wonderful doula, Beck. We were very lucky to have her.

AMBER AND TONY

The negotiating skills of Amber and Tony's doula should not be underestimated. Many conversations were carried out behind the scenes so that Amber and Tony would not be disturbed — tactful and respectful discussions about adhering to Amber's wishes, while acknowledging the hospital's protocols around monitoring. There is no doubt in my mind that, without a doula, this birth would have headed down the path of cascading medical interventions and quite likely would have ended in a caesarean section.

- » Listen to your body and follow your body's lead.
- » Connect with your baby. Touch and talk to your baby during birthing.
- » Rely on your doula to deal with staff.
- » Rely on your doula to set up the environment the way you want.
- » Drink lots and lots — your body is working hard and it is important to stay well hydrated, particularly if you are in an air-conditioned environment.
- » Eat what you feel like eating — yes, it is OK to eat during labour. A relaxed woman often gets quite hungry and eats normally.
- » Release and relax. If you have been practising relaxation, meditation and HypnoBirthing®, then continue to listen to this CD.
- » Relax in a deep, warm bath or under the shower.
- » Rely on your doula to protect your space.
- » Move with your baby and your body, finding positions that work best for you.
- » Have a massage.
- » Surrender.
- » Use hot/cold packs.
- » Play music other than your relaxation music.
- » Trust and marvel in your beautiful birthing body.
- » Release and let go.

Second stage of labour

This is defined as the time from full dilation (10 cm) to birth. As mentioned above, most hospitals like this stage to fall within a two-hour time frame. But HypnoBirthing® women tend to have longer second stages as they breathe their baby down the birth path slowly and gently.

Some women do get an overwhelming sensation to bear down. Other women describe this as a feeling of fullness deep in their vagina, or a lot of pressure. And others don't experience any sensation at all. All of these different experiences are quite normal — just wait and let baby come when baby is ready.

The sensation of breathing your baby down the birth path can feel very satisfying — working with your birthing body and baby, going with the flow of labour, getting closer and closer to meeting your baby on the outside. It is not necessary for anyone to interfere with this progression. Your doula will keep the space calm and peaceful, quietly encouraging you when necessary. She will make sure the lighting is dim, that your requested music is playing softly and that the mood is set for birthing your baby just the way you want. She will also be a guide for Dad, who is often the first to catch a glimpse of baby's head as baby performs her one step down, two steps back routine, with each surge bringing baby nearer and nearer to emerging. It is extraordinary, and oh so beautiful. Enjoy these feelings. Talk to your baby, work with your baby, feel how much you are looking forward to having her in your arms.

You may wish to use 'props' as these can increase your comfort during labour — bean bags, yoga-type mats, birth stools, birth balls (fit balls), a bed for resting/sleeping, pillows, bath/shower and of course the toilet. I never underestimate the benefit of the toilet during labour. I have observed so many women naturally gravitating to sit, in private, on the toilet. Not for doing the obvious, although that may occur, but because it is a safe, comfortable, semi-squatting position that women can stay in for a number of hours. Like the bath, it also provides physical protection — who would disturb a woman on the toilet?

Slowly and gently easing your baby down the birth path is so important. As discussed earlier, there should be no directed pushing, with a midwife or obstetrician instructing you to 'push longer, harder, stronger, hold your breath and keep it coming'! Such instructions will totally dissolve your belief in your ability to do this by yourself, by following your body's lead. It will probably take longer to do it slowly and gently, but tuning in to your body and easing baby down will certainly be much calmer for baby, provide much greater protection for your perineum and result in a much more satisfying birth experience. Many women find that reaching down and touching baby's emerging head provides an even greater sense of connection. I think the main emotion once baby's head is out is one of total relief. Birthing your baby's head requires the most energy. That little head just sits there, baby taking a rest, before the next surge which will birth his shoulders and the rest of his body. The magic of a water birth is watching that little head under water, eyes open, totally calm and very alert. With the next surge baby will be born and Mum, and only Mum, should be the one to scoop him up into her arms. The beauty of watching a Mum, Dad and baby meet for the very first time is overwhelming. So many emotions.

Talk to your baby and welcome him into the world as he likes nothing more than to hear his parents' voices. Bonding is the basis for emotional attachment, beginning in utero, between baby and Mum and baby and Dad.

There is a desire for both connections immediately at birth. This is done by skin-to-skin contact, audiovisual communication, nurturing, breastfeeding, holding, caressing and massaging. Baby is looking for a human face. Bringing your baby up close to your face and talking to him will turn on his infant brain and within minutes your baby will be functioning on a level of response.

Baby knows Mum from the inside; meeting Mum on the outside is a different experience. How they come into contact sets the pattern for how it will happen again and again.

Your doula will make sure that this time is protected so that you and your partner can welcome your baby into Mum's arms. She will make sure that nature's blueprint for this special time is respected. Michel Odent (1998) stresses 'the importance of not interrupting, even with words, and advises that the new mother should feel unobserved and uninhibited in the first encounter with her baby'. When a newborn baby has skin-to-skin contact with the mother's left breast (which is where new mothers in all cultures instinctively cradle their babies), and therefore in contact with her heart rhythm, according to Joseph Chilton Pearce (1992), 'A cascade of supportive confirmative information activates every sense, instinct and intelligence needed for the radical change of environment, thus intelligent learning begins at birth (p. 114)'.

Weighing, measuring and recording the head circumference of baby should be delayed for as long as possible. In fact, you can choose to have this attended to just before leaving hospital, or not at all. It is another box that needs to be filled out for hospital records. In reality, most parents are curious about their baby's weight, but this does not have to be done immediately following the birth. The important bonding between mother and baby should not be interrupted.

Sometimes, of course, things do not go according to plan, and sometimes the doula is called on a bit too late.

Lara was having her second baby. I was present for her first birth, and she was unsure whether she needed doula support for this labour. We had a conversation at around 37 weeks because she realised there were some anxieties 'hanging around' and she felt the need for support. It was a busy Friday morning when I got the call. It was Justin, her partner, asking me to come to their house. Lara had been in labour for about three hours. The trip took a bit longer than usual due to traffic. By the time I arrived Lara appeared to be in good labour, with surges coming regularly, lasting longer and feeling stronger. All good. We stayed at home for about an hour, and then Lara decided it was time to go to hospital, following a discussion about the time of morning and the state of school and work traffic.

They had two cars, and as Justin started to load the car up with bags, he realised there was not enough room for Lara on the back seat, due to a toddler seat and baby capsule in both cars! Justin suggested we all go in my car! My 'empty' sign had been flashing for about five days. (Getting petrol is a task I always leave to the very last minute.) My car was also particularly dirty, another task I had been thinking about. Now was not the time to be concerned, although I did hope we would have enough petrol to get to the hospital. We took off in my car with Justin driving and Lara in the back seat with her head resting in my lap. Justin was a bit worried that we had no petrol, but I reassured him (with fingers crossed). Lara was pushing at this stage, while I was reminding her about breathing through those surges. She was vocal.

It was now about 10.30 am and we got every red light. There were too many people around to run the lights. As we stopped at each red light, Justin, a fairly laid-back person at the best of times, casually leaned over and started taking photos of Lara. It was such a comical situation that both Justin and I got the giggles. I then noticed many people paying a lot of attention to my car. My logo, website details and phone numbers are plastered all over the car, so I watched with some amusement as I could see passers-by slowing and making a connection as to what was happening in the car.

Finally we arrived at the hospital with Justin yelling at everyone to get out of the way. We just left the car in the driveway with the keys in it, and got into the lift as Lara said the baby was coming. We were breathing together, and I was giving lots of reassurance. I realised, as the lift doors closed, that there were about four others in the lift. One very elderly lady in a wheelchair probably got the biggest shock as a very strong contraction caused Lara to grab onto the handles of the wheelchair, and we all watched as the wheelchair shook with the power of her contraction. No-one spoke. It seemed like a very long lift ride. Lara crawled out of the lift, into the birthing room, onto the mat, and finally released and relaxed and birthed her baby.

We know that a woman brings her past into labour from the subconscious imprint of how she was birthed, stories she has been told, books she has read and friendly advice she has been given. For women who have attended HypnoBirthing® classes and practised the recommended techniques, it is less likely they will have any fear going into labour. But sometimes, even for those women, a long-held fear may emerge during labour. Doulas are very

skilled at recognising that fear may be a cause of labour slowing. As has been said previously, a birthing woman is unable to articulate her thoughts clearly. The advantage in a doula getting to know a woman during her pregnancy is that she will be able to gently explore any possible issues that may occur during labour. She can help the woman get back on track by getting her to express her fear, reassuring her, reading a fear-release script or visualisation to her, allowing her to release and relax. Feeling absolutely safe with a doula creates the freedom to allow a woman to explore and trust in her own ability.

Third stage of labour

The third stage, the birthing of the placenta, is often overlooked as it is regarded as not that important. Busy hospitals and obstetricians view it as something that just needs to happen quickly. After all, baby has been born and is healthy and everyone is happy. But both mother and baby are undergoing a huge transition. For baby this involves major physiological changes in adapting to a new and different environment. For Mum it means transformation from pregnant woman to non-pregnant woman within minutes, and many women comment on how different they suddenly feel without their pregnant belly. Your doula will make sure all of the feelings and instinctive behaviours that accompany birth are respected.

If you are birthing in a birth centre or having a homebirth, the midwives are more than happy to support you in having a normal third stage of labour.

This amazing organ, the placenta, is what has fed your baby for 40 weeks. It is fascinating to have a good look at it with your midwife. She will show you the sac where baby grew, the membranous covering and the richness of the blood vessels that transported all those goodies to your growing baby.

Your doula would have discussed the birthing of the placenta with you during your pregnancy visits, so that you would have had time to research and think about what happens and decide what you would like to do. She would also have made sure that you included this on your birth plan.

Unfortunately, in many hospitals, an injection of Syntocinon is routinely given to the woman as her baby is being born. Syntocinon is synthetic oxytocin, which is also released naturally from the pituitary gland. This procedure was introduced with two benefits in mind: to help control bleeding, the implication being that all women bleed heavily, and to speed up the third stage of labour.

The powerful release of natural oxytocin occurs when mother and baby meet, gaze into each other's eyes and baby nuzzles close to the breast, especially if he suckles. (Many babies just want to have a lick, smell and nuzzle before they actually attach to the breast.) This releases the oxytocin from the pituitary gland in the brain, which then causes the placenta to separate from the wall of the uterus and Mum will have an urge to breathe down into her vagina and birth the placenta. Many women describe a sensation of 'fullness' in their vagina and an urge to give a gentle nudge. Changing position from lying to kneeling or standing can assist the birth.

The problem with giving Syntocinon is that the cord will be clamped and cut very quickly, with pressure being applied to the cord, which can involve a lot of 'tugging'. Most women find this painful. At the very least it is important that the clamping and cutting of the cord be delayed until after it stops pulsating. When the cord is prematurely cut, it abruptly cuts off the flow of blood to the baby, depriving him of that source of oxygen and many nutrients. Allowing the baby to take his first breaths with the continued benefit of oxygen from the placenta eases the task of taking air into his lungs once he is outside the womb. It is therefore an easier and more comfortable introduction to breathing.

Another option is to have a lotus birth, where the placenta remains attached to the baby until the cord separates naturally, which may take several days. For many women this is an important bond; they want it to run its natural course, allowing baby to separate from this inner connection in his own time. There is no risk of infection, as there has been no injury. Some women use sea salt to preserve the placenta and prevent odour. They may have a bowl or a placenta bag to carry around with baby. A lotus birth honours the attachment a baby has to his mother, respecting the 'original nourishment', the placenta.

So, what happens to the placenta at the end of the birthing process? You can leave it for the hospital to dispose of, or you can take it home and plant it in a pot or garden with a beautiful shrub or tree. It is wonderful fertiliser. And it's fun to take a photo of your child, each birthday, next to the growing tree. Some couples like to take the placenta home and put it in the deep freeze

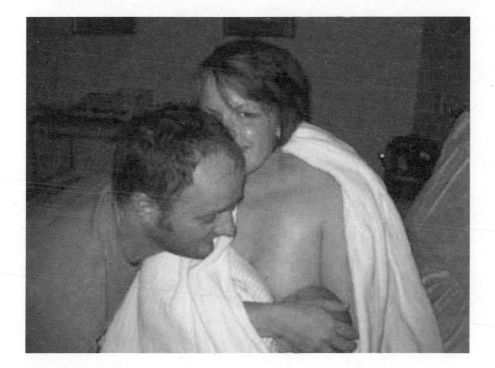

until they decide what they would like to do. No hospital should prevent you from keeping the placenta. It is yours. The placenta can also be cooked, ground finely and inserted in capsules, as below.

- » Boil placenta in water for 40 minutes.
- » Cool and slice.
- » Place in a cool oven (approx. 80°C) for 4 hours.
- » Grind (e.g. in a coffee grinder).
- » Purchase empty capsules from a health food shop and fill with grounds.

There is a longstanding belief that eating the placenta is beneficial. For example, it is believed by some to reduce the incidence of postnatal depression. While there is no scientific evidence to support this, many women report feeling fantastic after having consumed the placenta by cooking or dried and taken in capsule form.

In many cultures the placenta has a special place in rituals following birth. There is the Hawaiian tradition, mentioned above, of planting it with a tree, which then grows alongside the child. In Malaysia it is common practice for the hospital to give the placenta to Malay parents for them to bury. Maori have a word for the ancestral home/land, *turangawaewae*, which is where the placenta (*whenua*) is buried. It is becoming increasingly common for New Zealanders of all ethnic origins to bury the placenta and plant a tree over it.

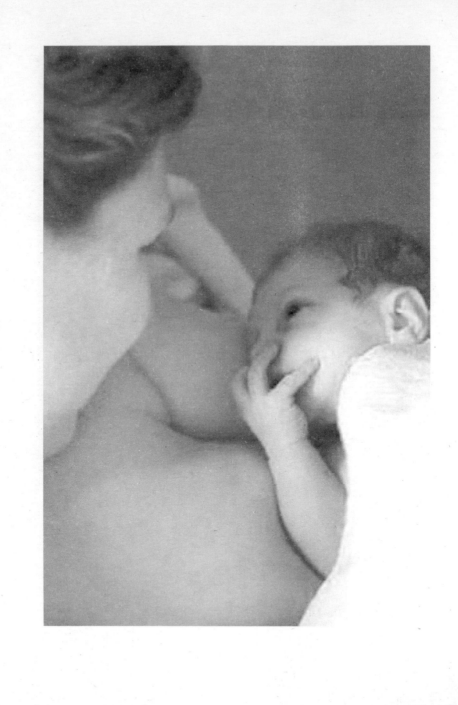

CHAPTER 6

Breastfeeding

And the bonding continues. You have scooped your baby into your loving arms, gazed into her eyes and introduced yourself. Saying hello to your baby, with the softest and gentlest of voices, is important. Birth is overwhelming, often confronting and certainly surreal. Sometimes new mums and dads are simply stunned at the moment of birth and lost for words. Your doula will make sure that you have space to marvel at your precious baby and to talk to, touch and stroke her. This moment should be honoured. There should be no rush to breastfeed. Trust that your baby will let you know when she is ready. If you have skin-to-skin contact and no one else has touched your baby, she will, in her own time, initiate the step–crawl reflex. I am always in awe watching a baby crawling and manoeuvring her way up Mum's body, head bobbing, and eventually latching, perfectly, onto the breast. If the people around you are respectful enough to allow this to take place, without interference, then you will not have any breastfeeding problems. There is plenty of literature explaining, in great detail, the many breastfeeding 'issues' that women can have. Not in this book! I know that if you have educated yourself well in pregnancy, birthing and breastfeeding, have had a wonderful pregnancy, have felt safe with your caregivers, have had a supportive doula, and have experienced a beautiful, peaceful birth, there will be no breastfeeding problems. But I do have some useful tips to share with you.

» Don't worry if your newborn is very sleepy for the first 24 hours. This is normal.

» Keep baby close to you, allowing her to have plenty of time to smell and touch you and to slowly adapt to her strange new world. Imagine if you were this baby, emerging from the world's most perfect environment, and then were suddenly put in a plastic cot, on a plastic mattress, wrapped in sheets and left alone. Your baby needs to be with you.

» Expect that the initial attachment will feel strong as babies have an amazing vice-like grip! Following the initial attachment, that strong sensation should subside and feel comfortable. If not, your postnatal doula or midwife can give you some advice about breaking the suction and detaching baby quickly. Then wait for baby's mouth to be wide and re-attach.

» Don't let baby munch on your nipple. She needs to have a good part of the areola in her mouth.

» Let baby feed when she wants, as long as your nipples are not too tender. Rest and feed. Relax and go with the flow of your baby's needs. Ideally, you and baby should be in bed together.

» Expect that it will take a little while to feel comfortable and easy with breastfeeding. It is a good idea to check with your postnatal doula or midwife to make sure baby is attaching correctly.

» Make sure you have good support – someone to clean, cook and feed you nourishing food.

» Relax and enjoy this very special time.

Your breasts produce colostrum during pregnancy and through the early days of breastfeeding. This special milk is yellow to orange in colour and thick and sticky. It is low in fat and high in carbohydrates, protein and antibodies to help keep your baby healthy. This is the perfect food for your baby and it is very easy to digest. It is low in volume but high in concentrated nutrition. Colostrum has a laxative effect, helping baby pass his early stools, which aids in the excretion of excess bilirubin (a breakdown product of red blood cells) and helps prevent jaundice.

Milk comes in anywhere from two to four days following birth. Your breasts will feel full and heavy. Babies wake up and want to feed very frequently over the first 24–48 hours as your milk comes in properly. It is normal for them to appear quite unsettled as their little gut becomes accustomed to feeling full.

MOTHERING THE MOTHER

Your birth doula may also be qualified as a postnatal doula, so she can be invaluable during this immediate postnatal period, supporting you in your own home. Specialised postnatal doula training equips doulas with knowledge about newborn development, both physical and emotional, breastfeeding, bonding and attachment, understanding a new family's needs and helping you to settle in at home. This will allow you to feel nurtured and supported, and relax and focus on nothing else but falling in love with your baby. Your postnatal doula may come in on a daily basis or even stay overnight. This service should be flexible and based on your needs. The doula will answer all your questions, guide and support you, and make sure you have some good quality sleep and lots of nourishing food.

So many women today don't have immediate family nearby or their family has other commitments and is not available to provide support. The knowledgeable, professional support of a postnatal doula in such instances is indispensable. She will share her wisdom about newborn care, nappies, bathing, massaging and a whole lot more. She will understand and support the transition of breastfeeding, from colostrum to milk, making sure you have plenty of rest and that baby is attached correctly so that your nipples are not damaged.

It can take at least a couple of weeks to feel relaxed about breastfeeding as you and your baby get to know each other.

Remember that a healthy baby, left to make her own way to the breast, following a normal birth, without intervention, will attach herself correctly.

YOUR MATERNAL INSTINCTS

Don't ever underestimate the power you have within. Trust your instincts about what is best for your baby. In our highly technological information age it is easy to be convinced that you know nothing and need to find out what is best for your baby on the Internet, or in a book or from various health professionals.

A new mother knows what is best for her baby. No-one knows your baby better than you do. You have grown this baby for 40 weeks, you have birthed this baby, you have bonded with and breastfed this baby. Rely on your intuition. Your postnatal doula will provide the space and encouragement for you to be in touch with your instinctual maternal knowledge.

Of course there will be information about your newborn that you will need to learn about. The trick is being able to sift through a lot of information and work out what will be useful for you and your baby. Joining a new parent support group can be fantastic, as long as it is a supportive group. Look around for those that have interesting guest speakers. This is also a wonderful opportunity to make new lifetime friends, another new Mum who truly understands what it means to have a new addition to their family.

Be wary of those books that instruct you about routines and time frames. A newborn baby should not be 'controlled'. The implication is often that if you don't have your baby in a 'routine' then you must be a failure. Remember, your baby can't tell the time, or read the book! Observe your baby, listen to your baby, be in tune with your baby and you will find that providing for her needs will engender a loving and trusting baby and child. Her needs will change as she grows and develops and, as parents, we have to be sufficiently flexible to understand these growing needs to adapt to and provide for them appropriately.

BONDING

Bonding is the basis of emotional connection, between mother and baby and father and baby. It forms in utero. At birth, a baby is looking for a face, preferably their Mum or Dad's face and close up. This turns on their brain and their awareness of this new environment they find themselves in. Meeting Mum and Dad on the outside is very important. How a baby comes into contact at the moment of birth sets the pattern for how it happens again and again. Bonding occurs through audiovisual contact, skin-to-skin contact, nurturing (holding, massaging, touching) and breastfeeding. If these things happen spontaneously, you will witness healthy growth in your baby and extraordinary growth in yourself, as a woman and mother.

Your baby's needs are fairly simple in the first few weeks. She needs to be as close to Mum or Dad as possible, to be breastfed often, to have her nappy changed often, and most of all she needs lots of cuddles and to listen to you talking to her. A newborn is not demanding, or attention-seeking or naughty. She is a small person in a very strange new world trying to adapt. This settling in and bonding process should be slow and steady, supportive and nurturing.

I discovered feelings I didn't know I had or even existed. The deep well of feelings, of love, of attachment, of overwhelming protection opening up inside me was simply astounding. This was such a different love from any other I had experienced.

   We followed a tradition that happens in many cultures. We stayed around the house for 30 days, keeping the baby in dim light for the first couple of weeks so we could slowly integrate him into his new environment. He has grown to be very trusting of new things we introduce, and I am sure that is because we started slowly and surely. Having our fabulous postnatal doula, who came every day for two weeks, gave us the support, confidence and reassurance that we were giving our baby a wonderful start in life. I thank her from the bottom of my heart.

SUSIE

BIRTH DEBRIEF

Your doula will visit you at home approximately a week after the birth to do a thorough birth debrief. This is very important, even if you have had a

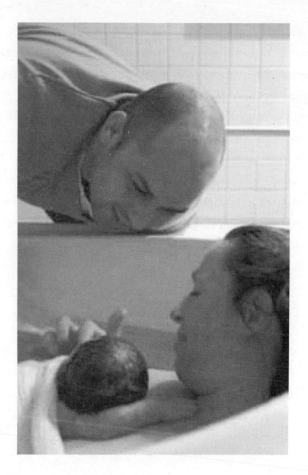

perfect birthing experience! Your doula will talk you through the events of your labour, from the beginning of labour to birth and coming home. She will clarify time frames and put these into context for you. She will confirm conversations that you may have overheard, explain their meaning and remind you of the names of midwives attending the birth.

If there was any intervention that you were unhappy with, this is a great opportunity to discuss it in detail. Your doula will help you to express your feelings around this event and to understand the medical reasons associated with the intervention. She will guide you through what you would do differently next time, changes in caregiver and place of birth, and preparation for labour. She will spend time talking to Dad about how he felt throughout the labour and birth. Labour and birth can be confronting for men. They don't have the same connection with pregnancy and birth that women do — of experiencing a growing, wriggling baby inside and visualising the birth during pregnancy. While women are very much 'in the moment' of birthing, men are, naturally, distanced from it. They have plenty of time to worry about their partner and baby, mostly because they don't know what 'normal' looks like.

I don't know what I would have done without our doula. Megan spent a lot of time under the shower during her labour. Once a surge had finished, she was asking for drinks, wanting the music changed etc., but at the same time not wanting me to leave her side. Our doula was able to do the running around. That allowed me to be totally with Megan, who clung on tight to me, needing me to be physically close. Megan also had other needs, which our doula was able to pre-empt most of the time and satisfy. This allowed us to have the very private birth, together, that we both wanted. Without a doula, I would have been running around, not knowing what to do!

ADAM

We laboured alone in our house until about 3 am — this was an extraordinary, scary, beautiful and momentous time. I then called our doula. Susan drove over to our place and, shortly afterwards, we went independently to the birth centre. Sarah continued to labour there until 11 am when Eva was born in the bath.

Things went well. We were in control. This is probably key to why Susan is such a great doula — she was present without being a presence. In the lead-up to the birth, she made an enormous difference. She encouraged us to ask good questions, she was clear without being prescriptive and she possessed great integrity around the pregnancy and birthing process. Her knowledge of hospital and midwifery structures was superlative.

NIGEL

For me, Nigel's statement 'she was present without being a presence' sums up the role of a doula. Sometimes men are concerned that having a doula might usurp their role or interrupt the privacy and intimacy that couples hope to have during the birth of their baby. A doula supports whatever role a couple chooses on the day. She allows them the space to be close or remote. She supports, encourages and nurtures them, provides them with information, presents them with choices and guides them on a journey of discovery of who they really are and what the best choices are for them and their baby.

Conceiving, growing a baby, labouring and birthing is a major life event. It changes you as a person. Your new-found personal growth will be extraordinary.

CHAPTER 7

Helpful support during pregnancy

During pregnancy, it is vital that your body function at its best, not only for your own health but also to provide the best possible nurturing environment for your developing baby. The following practices are particularly helpful in ensuring that your body is in peak condition during pregnancy, and that you are prepared emotionally, mentally and physically for your labour and birth.

CHIROPRACTIC

Chiropractic is a clinical science based on the law of biology which states that born into all living things is the ability to be healthy. Chiropractic draws on the physiological fact that the nervous system — brain, spinal cord, peripheral nerves and special sense organs — controls and coordinates all other systems, organs and structures in the body, and relates the person to their environment. Removing interference in this master control system allows the body to heal itself and provides optimum conditions for life and health.

When interference occurs in the signals travelling over nerves, parts of the body will not get the appropriate nerve messages and will not be able to function at 100 per cent of their innate ability. In other words, some parts of the body will not work properly. Chiropractors call this state the 'vertebral subluxation complex', or simply 'subluxation'. It therefore makes sense to ensure that your body has the best possible nerve supply so that your developing baby will receive the best possible nutrition and blood supply during pregnancy.

A chiropractor specialises in locating subluxations and reducing or removing them. Chiropractors are the only health professionals who undergo five years of university study and training to gain expertise in correcting subluxations. The procedure specifically designed to correct vertebral subluxations in the spine is called chiropractic adjustment. Chiropractic is safe, gentle and drug free. Ideal for the pregnant woman, it can be performed throughout your entire pregnancy but preferably prior to conception to ensure the optimum health of your nervous system.

Eva had had chiropractic care for years, as part of her healthy lifestyle. When she became pregnant, she naturally continued with her adjustments. She has had two calm water births and was back doing gentle exercise six days after the birth of both babies.

Sally began chiropractic adjustments at 18 weeks gestation due to severe symphysis pubis pain. She was unable to walk comfortably or do any exercise. Sally had a toddler to care for and was finding this very challenging. After six weeks of chiropractic care she was able to move more freely and resume exercise and her sleep had improved. By her third trimester Sally was mostly pain free and looking forward to the birth of her baby. She continued with chiropractic to ensure that she had a well-aligned spine and optimal functioning nervous system for birth and beyond.

JULIE, CHIROPRACTOR AND MIDWIFE

Hormones released during pregnancy, specifically progesterone, oestrogen and relaxin, cause laxity of ligaments and alterations in connective tissue, which increases joint mobility. These hormonal and biomechanical changes alter your normal structure and function

Approximately 60–70 per cent of pregnant women experience back pain during pregnancy (Diakow et al. 1991), due often to the increased weight of the growing uterus which shifts the centre of gravity, putting stress on areas unaccustomed to the added weight. This can lead to back and sacroiliac pain and headaches as the body tries to compensate for the imbalance by holding the shoulders back and carrying the head forward (lumbar lordosis, or increased curve in the lower back region).

Michelle, with her second pregnancy, was experiencing severe low back pain at 28 weeks gestation when she commenced chiropractic care. Within four weeks her back pain had been resolved. Her first birth had been a caesarean section for breech presentation. Michelle had assumed she would need to have another caesarean but was feeling great and interested in the options we discussed. She engaged a doula and started focusing on a normal birth. She felt empowered by her wonderful normal birth.

Adjustment of the pelvis, specifically the sacroiliac region, to remove any restrictions, can provide easier passage through the birth path and allow baby to settle into an optimal position in preparation for birth. Labour time and degree of discomfort in labour appear to be reduced in women who undergo regular chiropractic care. As Julie, a midwife and chiropractor says, 'Chiropractors don't fix things, they simply act as the conduit to the body's amazing ability to heal itself'.

Amanda had read that chiropractic care had many benefits for pregnancy, labour and birth. She had a history of back pain and wanted to have her spine checked, to make sure she was in the best possible shape for birth. On examination, Amanda's spine was subluxated. She had regular chiropractic adjustments until the day before birth. Amanda had a six-hour beautiful normal birth. She said that the two most important decisions she made was to have chiropractic care and a doula.

ACUPUNCTURE

Ngaio, acupuncturist and Chinese herbalist, says:

Many women have benefited from using Chinese herbal medicine and acupuncture during pregnancy. Acupuncture is a wonderful healing modality, and is a safe and effective alternative to taking western pharmaceutical drugs during pregnancy. Acupuncture can reduce some of the most commonly experienced symptoms such as morning sickness, fear and anxiety, insomnia, sinus congestion, headaches, back pain and sciatica, emotional and physical exhaustion, preparation for labour, induction of labour, facilitation of labour and breastfeeding issues, including mastitis.

For breech presentation, usually only one acupuncture treatment is necessary, together with daily moxibustion therapy, which your acupuncturist will show you how to use at home. Success rates for turning a breech baby are around 70–75 per cent (Cardini & Weixin 1998).

Weekly labour-preparation treatments from around 36 weeks help facilitate a more efficient labour. These are not labour-induction treatments. They prepare your body by helping to balance the pelvis, and encourage your baby into an ideal position by clearing energetic blockages and ripening the cervix. This is the time also to learn acupressure techniques for daily use at home. Acupressure goes a long way towards preparing you for labour, and when labour commences these points/techniques will be like old friends helping you through.

Acupuncture for induction of an overdue baby works best when your body is ripe, ready to go, and baby is in a favourable position. It works best for those women who have done the preparatory acupuncture from 36 weeks. Don't leave it until the last minute to arrive on your acupuncturist's doorstep. It may take up to 36 hours to go into labour after one of these treatments, assuming your body is ready.

Acupuncture can also be used to treat mastitis. Go to your acupuncturist as soon as the first symptom is noticed, usually a red patch. You can avoid taking antibiotics if you catch it early and start acupuncture treatment straightaway.

» Monica and her partner had been trying to conceive their second child. She had miscarried three months prior to seeing an acupuncturist. The acupuncturist treated her hormonal imbalance with acupuncture and strengthening herbs. Next time Monica saw the acupuncturist she was 36 weeks pregnant and proclaiming 'It worked!' She had returned to the acupuncturist to begin weekly labour-preparation treatments. Baby was posterior at 39 weeks, so Monica had regular acupuncture and daily moxibustion, which she did at home. She had a beautiful HypnoBirthing® water birth and is very thankful for how acupuncture helped her.

PRENATAL YOGA

Many different types of yoga are available. Shop around and find a yoga teacher who is trained and experienced in prenatal yoga. If you have never done yoga before, it is very important that you discuss with the yoga teacher what best would suit your level of fitness and pregnancy.

Benefits of prenatal yoga include:

» suppleness and elasticity, creating flexibility in the body and mind
» daily stress relief, which will sweeten your baby's environment
» increased muscular strength
» ability to harness the power of your pelvic floor muscles
» toning and assisting your body to perform its natural functions in harmony
» ability to quieten the mind and find deep stillness
» familiarity with birthing positions and the sound of your own breath, deepening the bond between you and your baby
» emotional and physical sustenance for both you and your baby.

Melanie, pregnancy massage specialist, prenatal yoga teacher and doula says:

There are many layers to pregnancy and birth. Taking time to open your body emotionally and physically with massage, yoga and meditation can be the perfect setting to explore feelings about how you were birthed, family birth stories, and your own pregnancy and imminent birth Many women miss out on the full-power of a nourishing birth experience because they simply do not have the knowledge that birth can be amazing, transforming and heart opening. Women have been robbed of their birthing rights. By tailoring massage, yoga and meditation to your own unique story, you can deepen your connection with your femininity, self-power, self-esteem and expression. These are the tools you use when you choose to birth consciously, connecting with your inner woman and transforming your understanding of what it means to give birth in your own way. It is a courageous woman who chooses to change the unconscious patterns in her life and to make a positive and powerful impact on the imprint she leaves on her, her partner's and her newborn's psyches.

PREGNANCY MASSAGE

Most pregnant women realise very quickly the high demands pregnancy places on their bodies and how essential it is to be nurtured at this time. Having regular massage by a trained prenatal massage therapist will help you to create a deeper bond with your baby. Deep relaxation will help you to open your mind and begin to sense and feel what your body is communicating to you. This time can be used to notice changes in your body from week to week and to visualise and connect with your baby in a quiet place.

Massage during pregnancy not only relieves the tensions and discomfort caused by the extra weight and the shift in the body's centre of gravity, it also reduces swelling, calms the nervous system, reduces fatigue and enhances energy.

Massage:

» relieves pain in the muscles and joints that are needed to support extra weight
» increases flexibility, making it easier for your body to adjust to additional weight
» eases constipation, wind and heartburn, as general relaxation stimulates intestinal movement
» reduces excess fluid by gently pushing fluid into circulation where it can be eliminated
» relieves headaches caused by tension, constipation, or build-up of metabolic waste products
» can slow the progress of varicose veins as enhanced circulation lowers the pressure on bulging veins.

Massage is a wonderful way to relax, increase your energy and relieve discomfort during pregnancy. The caring touch of massage can help you experience your changing body in a positive, accepting way. Massage also provides very special nurturing for the busy pregnant woman — some precious time out — and creates awareness of the body, so that you can recognise tension as it builds during the day and consciously release it.

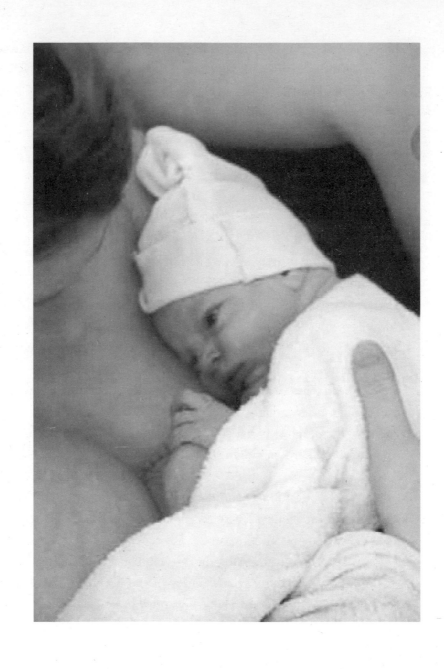

Pregnancy massage therapist, yoga teacher and doula, Melanie, met Sam when she attended her yoga classes. Melanie said, 'Sam had a strong practice, and as her pregnancy progressed we talked more and more. She began having prenatal massages and also asked me to be her doula. During our massage sessions, Sam talked about her pregnancy, different birth options, feelings about her partner and how their relationship was transitioning. We developed a trust and honesty with each other that grew and solidified during her last trimester. Sam and her partner both attended HypnoBirthing®, which they found very reassuring.

'Sam had about a week of pre-labour. What I love most about this is that Sam took all of it in her stride. She continued to go about her usual daily routine, and calmly accepted her body changing and her body's preparation for birth. I attribute this to her deep understanding of her body from her yoga practice, her self-care with prenatal massage and her education from HypnoBirthing®.

'Sam's partner rang about four days after her due date. They had been labouring at home but now wanted to meet me at the private hospital, where she was booked. When I arrived I immediately went to Sam's side and held her hand. She didn't let go until she had her baby in her arms. Sam's partner helped with hydration and making the room comfortable. She was focused on her deep breathing. She would burrow her head into the crook of her arm while holding my hand and breathing. She did this religiously for the next eight hours. Time flew by.

'Sam's focus was absolute. I have yet to witness such intensely focused attention to breath as I did that evening I was doula to Sam. After trialling four different birth positions, Sam finally found the right birthing position for her, on all-fours holding onto a bar. Sam birthed her beautiful baby boy 10 hours after walking into the hospital.

'Despite hospital clock pressure, medical model of care and being categorised in a high-risk group simply for being over the age of 35, with no account given to her good health, Sam demonstrated absolute faith and commitment in her decision to birth. She held to the power of backing herself, she put in place support mechanisms that worked for her, and she completely and unwaveringly trusted in her body and her baby.

NATUROPATHY

'The most important time in your child's life is four months before you conceive' is the sign women see when they arrive for an appointment with Jane, a natural therapist. She says, 'I strongly believe that if you prepare your body before conception you can create the environment that leads to healthy, intelligent and emotionally secure children'. Four months is the time it takes for sperm to be produced and for the egg to mature. This is an ideal time to vastly improve your health and the health of your child.

A client of Jane's was diagnosed with polycystic ovarian syndrome and her chances of conceiving naturally were very slim. A four-month pre-conception program resulted in an easy conception and birth of a beautiful baby boy. Four years later she gave birth to twin girls.

Janette Roberts, co-author of *The Natural Way to Better Babies*, writes: 'If couples spent as much time and money preparing themselves for conceiving a healthy child as they did preparing for their wedding day — we would have a nation of healthy, robust children!'

If you are reading this and already pregnant, don't despair! It's never too late to make healthy changes. Physical, mental and emotional balance during your pregnancy can lead to an easier labour and enhance bonding with your baby, as well as ensuring a very healthy start to your child's life.

The most important point to remember is: pregnancy is not an illness. It's a natural amazing cycle of growth and change that can be symptom free. I have seen many women who have had a fantastic pregnancy with very few, if any, 'side effects', as they are often referred to.

Many women seek natural therapies for the unpleasant symptoms of pregnancy, for example, morning sickness, heartburn, reflux, constipation, asthma, high blood pressure, palpitations, varicose veins, haemorrhoids, cramps, restless legs, urinary tract infections, thrush, herpes, streptococcus B, stretch marks, acne, cravings, blood sugar imbalances, gestational diabetes — just to name a few!

Natural therapies can certainly provide symptomatic relief for all of these, but importantly, the philosophy behind natural therapies is to treat each person as an individual in restoring balance to the body so it can heal itself. Most importantly, natural therapies can restore balance to your body before you conceive, giving you the best possible chance of avoiding the above, or other, 'complications'.

Many tests and procedures offered during pregnancy may be unnecessary or avoidable. The use of natural therapies can reduce the need for unnecessary antibiotics and other medical interventions.

Jane recalls a client coming to see her because she had gestational diabetes during her first pregnancy and was on insulin injections. She was 26 weeks pregnant with her second child and her blood sugars had started to go up. Her doctor had told her she would be starting insulin injections the following week if the levels didn't reduce. After some dietary advice and the use of nutritional and herbal supplements, she needed one dose of insulin per day as opposed to the three doses she had had during her previous pregnancy. If she had started the supplements earlier in the pregnancy, this may have been avoided altogether.

Why would you see a naturopath during pregnancy?

» To ensure a full-term pregnancy. Naturopaths give advice about nutrition, with an emphasis on the changing energy requirements for your growing baby at each stage of development.

» To ensure a short, straightforward labour. Herbal labour tonics and flower essences are used to support labour and natural birth of the placenta, to prevent tearing and to assist postnatal healing.

» To ensure successful breastfeeding and bonding. Adequate nutrition and birthing without intervention support production of the natural hormones that are important for breastfeeding and bonding. Supplementation can also prevent cracked nipples and mastitis.

» To ensure a healthy, happy child. A baby who has received the best nutrition from his mother and has enjoyed a calm, relaxed pregnancy, labour and birth will have the very best start to life.

We started our pre-conception planning at the beginning of 2009. We had been receiving naturopathy advice for three years prior to conceiving our first child and were both fit and healthy, but we wanted to ensure that we gave our new little person the best possible start to life from conception. We were guided by Jane in ways we could improve our external environment and embarked on a course of pre-conception vitamins for our internal environment. We conceived after only three cycles.

I experienced the most magical pregnancy. I did not have nausea, tiredness, food aversions or cravings. I was able to continue running five days a week until 30 weeks. I continued to work full-time until 38 weeks. Our beautiful 4.1 kg spirited daughter was born at home at 39 weeks. She is divine, fiery and delightful. I can confidently say that the reason I felt so strong and well throughout our daughter's conception, pregnancy and birth is because of the combination of pre-conception herbs, acupuncture, energetic healing, positive affirmations and meditation. My easy, quick conception, blissful pregnancy and our beautiful daughter are evidence of the talents of our wonderful healer, Jane. Thank you.

KERYN

Jane followed her own advice and, as a result, birthed her beautiful son, Thomas, in a birth pool at home, in a calm, natural and completely safe way. Breastfeeding continued until he was two years old.

THE MIND–BODY CONNECTION

Trust in the power of the mind-body connection. Many people think of their mind and body as separate from each other. From early on in life we receive constant messages that teach us that thoughts and feelings are irrelevant when it comes to how our body functions. Many women search for information and education during pregnancy that will help them to be 'in control'. We are not meant to be consciously 'in control' of our birthing.

We are not 'in control' of how our heart beats, our breathing rate, how our kidneys function, or have any control of the development of our baby in utero. It is our subconscious mind that controls all of these bodily functions. What is important, is for you to be happy and healthy in both mind and body so that your body can do its job of birthing beautifully.

We have looked at fear and how this can affect labour and birthing. When a woman is fearful, she will tighten her body and have a lot of physical tension. This tension is what causes pain. It can then become a cycle of increased fear leading to increased pain.

Thoughts and feelings powerfully affect your pregnancy, labour and birthing, creating physical responses within your body.

Birth is simple. Do not listen to anyone who tells you otherwise! They are no doubt reporting their own experience or that of a friend's. Surround yourself with the right support, nurturing and education. Go within and connect with your baby. It is such a wonderful experience to get to know your baby from the inside and by the time he is ready to be born you will be so looking forward to connecting on the outside.

This is the most important job we do as women, growing, birthing and mothering our babies. It will change you on so many levels, empowering you in every aspect of your life. I know that choosing the right doula for you will help you to achieve your ultimate birth.

BIBLIOGRAPHY

Balaskas, J., *Active Birth: The New Approach to Giving Birth Naturally* (rev. edn), The Harvard Common Press, Boston MA, 1992.

Campbell D.A., Lake, M.F., Falk, M. and Backstrand J.R., 'A randomized controlled trial of continuous support in labour by a lay doula', *Journal of Obstetrics, Gynecologic and Neonatal Nursing*, vol. 35, issue 4, July 2006, pp. 456–64.

Cardini, F. MD and Weixin, H. MD, 'Moxibustion for correction of breech presentation: a randomized controlled trial', *JAMA: Journal of the American Medical Association*, vol. 280, no. 18, 1998, pp. 1580–84.

de Jonge, A., van der Goes, B.Y., Ravelli, A.C.J., Amelink-Verburg, M.P., Mol, B.W., Nijhuis, J.G., Bennebroek Gravenhorst, J. and Buitendijk, S.E., 'Perinatal mortality and morbidity in a nationwide cohort of 529 688 low-risk planned home and hospital births', *BJOG: An International Journal of Obstetrics & Gynaecology*, vol. 116, issue 9, August 2009, pp. 1177–84.

DeVries, R., *A Pleasing Birth: Midwives and Maternity Care in the Netherlands*, Temple University Press, Philadelphia PA, 2005.

DeVries, R., 'Midwifery in The Netherlands: vestige or vanguard?', *Medical Anthropology, vol. 20*, 2001, pp. 277–311.

Diakow, P.R.P., Gadsby, T.A., Gadsby, J.B., Glediie, J.G., Leprech, D.J. and Scales, A.M., 'Back pain during pregnancy and labour', *Journal of Manipulative and Physiological Therapeutics*, vol. 14, no. 2, February 1991, pp. 116–18.

Dick-Read, G., *Childbirth Without Fear: The Principles and Practice of Natural Childbirth*, Pinter & Martin, London, 2005.

Goedkoop, V., 'Side by side — a survey of doula care in the UK in 2008', MIDIRS Midwifery Digest, vol. 19, no. 2, June 2009, pp. 217–18.

Hodnett, E.D., Gates, S., Hofmeyr, G.J. and Sakala, C., 'Continuous support for women during childbirth', Cochrane Database of Systematic Reviews 2007, Issue 2.

Klaus, M.H., Kennell, J.H. and Klaus, P.H., *Mothering the Mother: How a Doula Can Help You Have a Shorter, Easier, and Healthier Birth*, Perseus, Cambridge MA, 1993.

Klaus, M.H., Kennell, J.H. and Klaus, P.H., *The Doula Book: How a Trained Labor Companion Can Help You Have a Shorter, Easier, and Healthier Birth*, Perseus, Cambridge MA, 2002.

Klaus, M.H., Kennell, J.H., Robertson, S.S. and Sosa, R., 'Effects of social support during parturition on maternal and infant morbidity', *British Medical Journal (Clinical Research Edition)*, vol. 293, issue 6547, 6 September 1986, pp. 585–87.

Kennell, J.H., Klaus, M.H., McGrath, S.K., Robertson, S. and Hinkley, C., 'Continuous emotional support during labor in a US hospital: a randomized controlled trial', *JAMA: Journal of the American Medical Association*, vol. 265, 1991, pp. 2197–201.

Laws, P., Li, Z. and Sullivan, E.A., *Australia's Mothers and Babies 2008*, Perinatal Statistics Series no. 24, cat. no. PER 50, Australian Institute of Health and Welfare, Canberra, 2010.

Lazarev, M. MD, *Sonatal*, Infinite Potential, Inc., Bloomsbury NJ, 1991.

Lipton, B.H. PhD, *The Biology of Belief: Unleashing the Power of Consciousness, Matter & Miracles*, Mountain of Love Productions, 2005.

MacDorman, M., Menacker, F. and Declercq, E., 'Trends and characteristics of home and other out-of-hospital births in the United States, 1990–2006', *National Vital Statistics Reports*, vol. 58, no. 11, 2010, pp. 1–14, 16.

Naish, F. and Roberts, J., *The Natural Way to Better Babies*, Random House Australia, North Sydney, 2011.

Odent, M., 'Don't manage the third stage of labour!', *Practising Midwife*, vol. 1, no. 9, 1998, pp. 31–33.

Odent, M., *The Scientification of Love*, Free Association Books Ltd, London, 1999.

Office for National Statistics, *Birth Statistics: Review of the National Statistician on Births and Patterns of Family Building in England and Wales, 2008*, Series FM1, No. 37, February 2010, www.statistics.gov.uk/downloads/theme_population/FM1-37/FM1_37_2008.pdf, accessed 27 May 2011.

Pearce, J.C., *Evolution's End: Claiming the Potential of Our Intelligence*, Harper, San Francisco CA, 1992.

Raphael, D., *The Tender Gift: Breastfeeding*, Prentice Hall, 1973.

Scott, K.D., Berkowitz, G., Klaus, M.A. 'Comparison of intermittent and continuous support during labour: A meta analysis', *American Journal of Obstetrics and Gynecology*, 180, 1999, pp. 1054 59.

Sufang, G., Padmadas, S.S., Fengmin, Z., Brown, J.J. and Stones, R.W., 'Delivery settings and caesarean section rates in China', *Bulletin of the World Health Organization*, vol. 85, no. 10, 2007, pp. 755–62.

Tracy, S.K. and Hartz, D., *The Quality Review of Ryde Midwifery Group Practice, September 2004 to October 2005*, Final Report, Northern Sydney and Central Coast Health, NSW, 2006.

Verny, T. MD, with Kelly, J., *The Secret Life of the Unborn Child: How You Can Prepare Your Unborn Baby for a Happy, Healthy Life*, Dell Publishing, New York, 1981.

Verny, T., *Psychology of Birth*, produced 2001, distributed by STAR Foundation.

Wiegers, T.A, Zee, J., van der Keirse, M.J.N.C., 'Maternity care in The Netherlands: The changing homebirth rate', *Birth, vol. 25*, 1998, pp. 190–97.

World Health Organization, 'Appropriate technology for birth', *Lancet*, vol. 2, 1985, pp. 436–37.

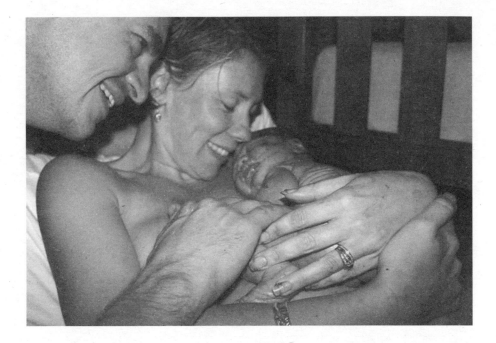